S0-AMP-858

RR ETHICS

**Ready Reference**

# ETHICS

## Volume I

**Abelard, Peter – Freedom and Liberty**

**A Magill Book**
*from the* **Editors of Salem Press**

*Consulting Editor*

**John K. Roth**
**Claremont McKenna College**

Salem Press, Inc.
Pasadena, California    Englewood Cliffs, New Jersey

∞ The paper used in these volumes conforms to the American National Statndard for Permanence of Paper for Printed Library Materials, Z39.48-1984.

**Library of Congress Cataloging-in-Publication Data**

Ethics / consulting editor, John K. Roth
p. cm. — (Ready reference)
"A Magill Book"
Includes bibliographical references and index.
ISBN 0-89356-395-1 (set : alk. paper). — ISBN 0-89356-396-x (v. 1 : alk. paper).
1. Ethics—Encyclopedias. I. Roth, John K. II. Title: Ready reference, ethics. III. Series
BJ63.E54 1994
170' .3—dc20 94-3995
CIP

First Printing

PRINTED IN THE UNITED STATES OF AMERICAN

# Publisher's Note

**Ethics in Perspective.** Ethics, in one form or another, has been a central issue for humankind ever since people began to live together in small communities. People have always wondered whether they were being held accountable for their actions by a higher power or powers. If they believed that such powers existed, they needed to know what their relationships with those powers were and what they were required to do or not to do. If they did not, they needed to believe that their lives had meaning, which ultimately led them to wonder how they should act and what they should do. In addition, people have always needed to know what other people expected of them and what the limits of their freedom of action were.

Early societies wrestled with many of the basic ethical issues that still confront modern societies, but they did not have to deal with nearly as many difficult ethical problems as do modern societies. As humanity's knowledge and technological ability have increased, the number of ethical issues that humanity must face has also increased. Along with the development of computer technology, for example, have come knotty problems regarding the right to privacy, the use of robots rather than human workers, and appropriate attitudes of humans toward artificially created intelligent beings. Along with the development of medical techniques that have made it possible to extend life have come complex bioethical issues such as the question of whether to preserve the biological life of human beings when it seems probable that they will be unable to live fruitful and rewarding lives. At this point, there is not even a consensus regarding how life and death are to be defined. Since genetics has become better understood, questions that early humans never had to face have arisen: Should women of advanced age be allowed to bear children by artificial means? Should society attempt to create superior animals or humans by means of genetic engineering?

Concern regarding ethics has increased dramatically, beginning in the late twentieth century. Inequities regarding the worldwide distribution of food, money, and other resources have become more glaring as the world's population has increased. The industrialized nations have continued to acquire goods and power, and the nonindustrialized nations have continued to suffer from poverty and famine. This situation has caused some people to attempt to determine how much responsibility those who have the means to prosper should take for promoting the welfare of those who do not even have the means to survive. Throughout much of the world, traditional attitudes toward religion have changed, and societies have suffered as more people have rejected the traditional ethical and moral codes of the religions into which they were born and have found no other codes with which to replace them. Many politicians and religious leaders have demonstrated, with disconcerting frequency, that their personal codes of ethics will not bear scrutiny. These developments have led many people to emphasize the importance of ethics. Governments and businesses have adopted codes of ethics in an attempt to improve their images, and many colleges and universities have added ethics classes and programs to their curricula.

Although ethics has become a subject of grave concern to many people, the student with an interest in ethics but no specialized knowledge has had, until now, to study many separate, specialized studies of recent issues of ethical interest in order to gain a general knowledge of applied ethics. Until now there has been no single comprehensive work that has examined the various areas of applied ethics as well as the more traditional ethical areas of religion and philosophy. It is to fill this gap in the literature of ethics that the editors of Salem Press have created *Ethics* in the READY REFERENCE series.

**Scope and Approach.** Magill's *Ethics* is the first set in the new READY REFERENCE series of sets to be published by Salem Press. This three-volume work, which contains 819 alphabetically arranged articles ranging in length from 250 to 3,000 words and covering a wide variety of ethics-related topics, takes an entirely new approach to its subject.

Unlike traditional encyclopedias of ethics, which focus primarily on philosophical and religious ethics, the READY REFERENCE *Ethics* set includes many articles that deal with applied ethics. Although the set's coverage of traditional philosophical and religious ethical subjects is extensive, it is also the only ethics reference set available that covers such areas of ethical inquiry as animal rights ("Animal Consciousness," "Endangered Species"), bioethics ("Genetic Engineering," "Surrogate Motherhood"), environmental ethics ("Nature, Rights of," "Pollution"), political and judicial ethics ("Espionage," "Capital Punishment"), the ethics of science and computing ("Experimentation, Ethics of," "Virtual Reality"), civil and human rights ("Children's Rights," "Civil Disobedience"), military ethics ("Neutron Bomb," "War and Peace"), the ethics of sex and gender ("Gay Rights," "Sexism"), and the ethics of the arts and censorship ("Art and Public Policy," "Book Banning"). Many types of entries are included, among them personages, important events, books, organizations, concepts, and aspects of human behavior.

In the areas of religious and philosophical ethics, too many reference works have focused on the Judeo-Christian tradition of the West at the expense of traditions such as those of Islam, Buddhism, and Hinduism. In an attempt to balance the coverage of *Ethics*, the editors of Salem press have made every attempt to include important topics taken from the religions and cultures of India, East Asia, and other non-Western areas of the globe. In transliteration, diacritical marks have been used for terms in Sanskrit and other Indic languages, a slightly modified version of the transliteration system of the *Inter-*

*national Journal of Middle Eastern Studies* has been used for Arabic and Persian terms, and the familiar Wade-Giles system has been used for Chinese terms. Finally, the editors of the set have used the neutral abbreviation B.C.E. (before the common era) for ancient dates rather than the more conventional B.C. (before Christ), in order to avoid a Western, Christian bias in their use of terms.

**Contents and Format.** In the Magill tradition of making reference works easy to use, the text of each of the alphabetized (by word, not by letter) entries is headed by ready-reference listings that provide such information as dates and places of birth and death for important personages; dates of important events; an entry that provides the "type of ethics" to which the topic relates; an "associated with" entry that may list, for example, important people with whom a concept has been linked; and an entry that explains the "significance" of the topic to the field of ethics. In addition, each entry contains cross-references in the form of a "see also" line that guides the reader to related entries contained in the set. All 1,000-word and 3,000-word entries include bibliographies that list five to ten works, and the bibliographies of the 3,000-word articles are annotated. The set also includes some 200 graphic elements such as photographs, tables, maps, pie charts, and time lines.

The third volume of READY REFERENCE *Ethics* contains a list of ethics organizations; a time line that provides an overview of the history of ethics; a select, categorized bibliography that the reader will find useful in further study of ethical issues; a personages index that lists figures who are discussed in the set; and a comprehensive subject index that makes the set particularly easy and convenient to use. In addition, each volume contains an alphabetized list of all entries in the set (in the front, following the Contents page) and another list of entries that is organized by categories of ethics (in the back).

**Acknowledgments.** The contributors to this work, who are listed in volume 1, represent a wide variety of academic and cultural approaches to ethics. These authors have succeeded in providing clear and objective information in areas that are often extremely conceptual, controversial, and difficult to negotiate. John K. Roth, who served as consultant for this work, deserves special mention for his exhaustive knowledge, his careful and invaluable advice, his superb writing, and his unflagging commitment to a project that often made great demands on his time. His efforts and the efforts of all those who contributed to this project are greatly appreciated.

# List of Contributors


Norman Abeles
*Michigan State University*

Steven C. Abell
*Marquette University*

Joseph K. Adjaye
*University of Pittsburgh*

Richard Adler
*University of Michigan, Dearborn*

Olusoji A. Akomolafe
*Le Moyne-Owen College*

Thomas M. Alexander
*Southern Illinois University at Carbondale*

James August Anderson
*Bellarmine College*

Stanley Archer
*Texas A&M University*

Anne Freire Ashbaugh
*Colgate University*

Bryan C. Auday
*Gordon College*

James V. Bachman
*Valparaiso University*

James A. Baer
*Northern Virginia Community College*

Bruce E. Bailey
*Stephen F. Austin State University*

Daniel G. Baker
*Ocean County College*

Robert Baker
*Union College*

Russell J. Barber
*California State University, San Bernardino*

Evelyn M. Barker
*University of Maryland, Baltimore County*

Stephen F. Barker
*Johns Hopkins University*

Dan Barnett
*California State University, Chico*
*Butte College*

Charles A. Bartocci
*Dabney S. Lancaster Community College*

Rose Ann Bast
*Mount Mary College*

Erving E. Beauregard
*University of Dayton*

Jeff Bell
*University of Southwestern Louisiana*

Richard P. Benton
*Trinity College*

S. Carol Berg
*College of St. Benedict*

Cynthia A. Bily
*Adrian College*

Amy Bloom
*Harris Corporation*
*University of Central Florida*

George P. Blum
*University of the Pacific*

Warren J. Blumenfeld
*Independent Scholar*

Paul R. Boehlke
*Dr. Martin Luther College*

Dallas L. Browne
*Southern Illinois University at Edwardsville*

Anthony R. Brunello
*Eckerd College*

Malcolm B. Campbell
*Bowling Green State University*

Edmund J. Campion
*University of Tennessee, Knoxville*

Michael R. Candelaria
*California State University, Bakersfield*

Byron D. Cannon
*University of Utah*

Paul J. Chara, Jr.
*Loras College*

Weihang Chen
*Hampshire College*

Sandra L. Christensen
*Eastern Washington University*

Ron Christenson
*Gustavus Adolphus College*

Bonnidell Clouse
*Indiana State University*

Robert Clouse
*Indiana State University*

George Connell
*Concordia College*

Arlene R. Courtney
*Western Oregon State College*

D. Kirk Davidson
*Mount Saint Mary's College*

Edwin R. Davis
*Independent Scholar*

Robert C. Davis
*Pikeville College*

Scott A. Davison
*University of Notre Dame*

James M. Dawsey
*Auburn University*

Richard A. Dello Buono
*Rosary College*

Margaret B. Denning
*Slippery Rock University of Pennsylvania*

James D'Entremont
*Boston Coalition for Freedom of Expression*

Fritz Detwiler
*Adrian College*

Ileana Dominguez-Urban
*Southern Illinois University at Carbondale School of Law*

Theodore William Dreier
*Portland State University*

Jennifer Eastman
*Independent Scholar*

Craig M. Eckert
*Eastern Illinois University*

Robert P. Ellis
*Worcester State College*

Anne-Marie Ferngren
*Covenant College*

Gary B. Ferngren
*Oregon State University*

John W. Fiero
*University of Southwestern Louisiana*

David Marc Fischer
*Independent Scholar*

Cheri Vail Fisk
*Oregon State University*

Michael J. Fontenot
*Southern University, Baton Rouge*

Barbara Forrest
*Southeastern Louisiana University*

Catherine Francis
*Independent Scholar*

Donald R. Franceschetti
*Memphis State University*

Carol Franks
*Portland State University*

Norris Frederick
*Queens College*

Gregory Freeland
*California Lutheran University*

C. George Fry
*Lutheran College of Health Professions*

Patricia H. Fulbright
*Portland Community College*

David M. Gallagher
*Catholic University of America*

Paul Gallagher
*Assumption College*

Eric H. Gampel
*California State University, Chico*

Zev Garber
*Los Angeles Valley College*
Thomas Gaskill
*Southern Illinois University at Carbondale*
R. Douglas Geivett
*Biola University*
Mitchel Gerber
*Southeast Missouri State University*
Sanford Golin
*University of Pittsburgh*
Robert F. Gorman
*Southwest Texas State University*
Roy Neil Graves
*University of Tennessee, Martin*
Lloyd J. Graybar
*Eastern Kentucky University*
Noreen A. Grice
*Boston Museum of Science*
Peter J. Haas
*Vanderbilt University*
Don A. Habibi
*University of North Carolina*
Jacqueline Haessly
*Peacemaking Associates*
*Cardinal Stritch College*
Robert Halliday
*Utica College of Syracuse University*
Craig L. Hanson
*Muskingum College*
Robin G. Hanson
*Muskingum College*
Claude Hargrove
*Fayetteville State University*
Keith Harper
*Mississippi College*
Fred R. van Hartesveldt
*Fort Valley State College*
Sterling Harwood
*California State University, San Jose*
Margaret Hawthorne
*Independent Scholar*
Robert M. Hawthrone, Jr.
*Independent Scholar*
James L. Hayward
*Andrews University*
Ruth B. Heizer
*Georgetown College*
Mary A. Hendrickson
*Wilson College*
Howard M. Hensel
*U.S. Air Force, Air War College*
Stephen R. C. Hicks
*Rockford College*
Rita C. Hinton
*Mississippi State University*

Carl W. Hoagstrom
*Ohio Northern University*
William L. Howard
*Chicago State University*
John L. Howland
*Bowdoin College*
Vanessa B. Howle
*Grand Valley State University*
Diane W. Husic
*East Stroudsburg University of Pennsylvania*
Charles C. Jackson
*Northern Kentucky University*
Robert Jacobs
*Central Washington University*
Dale Jacquette
*Pennsylvania State University*
Mary Johnson
*University of South Florida*
*Hillsborough Community College*
Joe Frank Jones, III
*Barton College*
Marcella Joy
*Independent Scholar*
Richard C. Kagan
*Hamline University*
Charles L. Kammer, III
*The College of Wooster*
Laura Duhan Kaplan
*University of North Carolina, Charlotte*
T. E. Katen
*Community College of Philadelphia*
Terry J. Knapp
*University of Nevada, Las Vegas*
Nathan R. Kollar
*St. John Fisher College*
Abraham D. Kriegel
*Memphis State University*
Robert B. Kruschwitz
*Georgetown College*
Rosalind Ekman Ladd
*Wheaton College*
Ralph L. Langenheim, Jr.
*University of Illinois at Urbana-Champaign*
Ron Large
*Gonzaga University*
Michael M. Laskier
*Sephardic Educational Center*
*University of Chicago*
William F. Lawhead
*University of Mississippi*
Richard M. Leeson
*Fort Hays State University*
Stephen D. Livesay
*Liberty University*

Ronald W. Long
*West Virginia Institute of Technology*
Adele Lubell
*Independent Scholar*
David W. Lutz
*University of Notre Dame*
Nancy E. Macdonald
*University of South Carolina, Sumter*
Erin McKenna
*Pacific Lutheran University*
Voula Tsouna McKirahan
*Independent Scholar*
Marguerite McKnight
*Slippery Rock University of Pennsylvania*
Paul Madden
*Hardin-Simmons University*
Paul D. Mageli
*Independent Scholar*
Philip Magnier
*Independent Scholar*
Cynthia Keppley Mahmood
*University of Maine*
Khalid N. Mahmood
*Maine Science and Technology Commission*
Krishna Mallick
*Bentley College*
Bill Manikas
*Gaston College*
Jonathan Hugh Mann
*B.E.S.T., Business Ethics Strategies*
Coleman C. Markham
*Barton College*
Jill S. Marts
*Independent Scholar*
Thomas D. Matijasic
*Prestonsburg Community College*
David M. May
*Midwestern Baptist Theological Seminary*
S. M. Mayo
*Charleston Southern University*
Linda Mealey
*College of St. Benedict*
Gregory F. Mellema
*Calvin College*
Michael W. Messmer
*Virginia Commonwealth University*
Laurence Miller
*Western Washington University*
Roman J. Miller
*Eastern Mennonite College*
Randall L. Milstein
*Oregon State University*
Eli C. Minkoff
*Bates College*

## List of Contributors

Brian K. Morley
*The Master's College*

Rodney C. Mowbray
*University of Wisconsin, La Crosse*

Mark William Muesse
*Rhodes College*

Turhon A. Murad
*California State University, Chico*

Tod Charles Murphy
*Independent Scholar*

D. Gosselin Nakeeb
*Pace University*

Peimin Ni
*Grand Valley State University*

Steve A. Nida
*Franklin University*

Joseph L. Nogee
*University of Houston*

Norma Corigliano Noonan
*Independent Scholar*

Kathleen O'Brien
*Independent Scholar*

Daniel W. O'Bryan
*Sierra Nevada College*

Patrick M. O'Neil
*Broome Community College*

Lisa Paddock
*Independent Scholar*

W. Jackson Parham, Jr.
*Hillsdale College*

Paul Plenge Parker
*Elmhurst College*

Judith A. Parsons
*Sul Ross State University*

Garrett E. Paul
*Gustavus Adolphus College*

Thomas R. Peake
*King College*

William A. Pelz
*DePaul University*

Mark Stephen Pestana
*Grand Valley State University*

Nis Petersen
*Jersey City State College*

James M. Petrik
*Ohio University*

Kathleen D. Purdy
*Basic Business Strategies*

Howard B. Radest
*Independent Scholar*

Habibeh Rahim
*Hofstra University*

Lillian M. Range
*University of Southern Mississippi*

Paul Redditt
*Georgetown College*

Thomas Renna
*Saginaw Valley State University*

Paul August Rentz
*South Dakota State University*

Gregory P. Rich
*Fayetteville State University*

John E. Richardson
*Pepperdine University*

John L. Rittenhouse
*Eastern Mennonite College*

Carl Rollyson
*Baruch College, City University of New York*

John K. Roth
*Claremont McKenna College*

Frank Louis Rusciano
*Rider College*

Sunil K. Sahu
*DePauw University*

Hilel B. Salomon
*University of South Carolina*

Steven M. Sanders
*Bridgewater State College*

John Santelli
*Fairleigh Dickinson University*

John Santore
*Pratt Institute*

Daniel C. Scavone
*University of Southern Indiana*

John H. Serembus
*Widener University*

John M. Shaw
*Education Systems*

Martha Sherwood-Pike
*University of Oregon*

Sanford S. Singer
*University of Dayton*

Andrew C. Skinner
*Brigham Young University*

Jane A. Slezak
*Fulton-Montgomery Community College*

Genevieve Slomski
*Independent Scholar*

James Smallwood
*Oklahoma State University*

Christopher E. Smith
*University of Akron*

Roger Smith
*Linfield College*

Ira Smolensky
*Monmouth College*

Marjorie Smolensky
*Carl Sandburg College*

A. J. Sobczak
*Independent Scholar*

J. Michael Spector
*Armstrong Laboratory*

Richard A. Spinello
*Boston College*

C. Fitzhugh Spragins
*Arkansas College*

Charles E. Sutphen
*Blackburn College*

Roy Arthur Swanson
*University of Wisconsin, Milwaukee*

Leland C. Swenson
*Loyola Marymount University*

Glenn L. Swygart
*Tennessee Temple University*

Larry N. Sypolt
*West Virginia University*

Robert D. Talbott
*University of Northern Iowa*

Harold D. Tallant
*Georgetown College*

Stephen C. Taylor
*Delaware State University*

David R. Teske
*Russell C. Davis Planetarium*

Nicholas C. Thomas
*Auburn University, Montgomery*

Leslie V. Tischauser
*Prairie State College*

Evelyn Toft
*Fort Hays State University*

Mary S. Tyler
*University of Maine*

I. Peter Ukpokodu
*University of Kansas*

Mary Moore Vandendorpe
*Lewis University*

Harry van der Linden
*Butler University*

Diane C. Van Noord
*Western Michigan University*

Gary E. Varner
*Texas A&M University*

Mary E. Virginia
*Independent Scholar*

Paul R. Waibel
*Liberty University*

Randolph Meade Walker
*Le Moyne-Owen College*

William T. Walker
*Philadelphia College of Pharmacy and Science*

Donald V. Weatherman
*Arkansas College*

## Ethics


Marcia J. Weiss
*Point Park College*

Robert Whealey
*Ohio University*

Richard Whitworth
*Ball State University*

Joel Wilcox
*Providence College*

Clifford Williams
*Trinity College, Deerfield*

Robert A. Willingham
*Independent Scholar*

Michael Witkoski
*Independent Scholar*

Shawn Woodyard
*Independent Scholar*

Kerrie Workman
*Hamline University*

Keith E. Yandell
*University of Wisconsin, Madison*

Regina Howard Yaroch
*Independent Scholar*

Clifton K. Yearley
*State University of New York at Buffalo*

Mara Kelly Zukowski
*Iona College*

# CONTENTS

# ALPHABETICAL LIST OF ENTRIES

## Volume I

## Volume II

# Volume III

## Abelard, Peter

**Abelard, Peter** (c. 1079, Le Pallet, Brittany—Apr. 21, 1142, Chalon-sur-Saône, Burgundy): Theologian and philosopher

**TYPE OF ETHICS:** Medieval history

**ACHIEVEMENTS:** Author of numerous works on theology, philosophy, logic, ethics, and biblical exegesis

**SIGNIFICANCE:** Abelard was one of the early schoolmen who advanced the study of dialectics (logic) and applied it to theology and moral philosophy; his now famous theory of intention was considered too radical at the time

In his autobiographical *Historia calamitatum* (c. 1132; *The Story of My Misfortunes*, 1922), Abelard describes his rise to fame as a philosopher and theologian. His love affair with Héloïse—attested in their correspondence—compelled him to leave the cathedral school of Paris and become a monk at St. Denis. Later, Abelard became the leader of a hermitage, the Paraclete, which he gave to Héloïse and her nuns. He remained a wandering maverick because of his dialectics and his sharp criticism of monasticism. His *Sic et non* (c. 1123) used the new methods of the schools, which consisted of posing problems and resolving them by means of logic and close textual analysis. Older methods of teaching and writing consisted of the presentation of texts and commentaries on those texts. Because his writings were twice condemned by the Church, his influence is now difficult to gauge. As an ethical thinker, Abelard viewed himself as a monastic reformer who sought to restore the eremitical spirit to religious practice. Unlike his contemporaries, he believed that some monks should use the new dialectical methods to intensify the monastic life. As an admirer of the ancient pagan philosophers, he tried to reconcile natural law ethics with Christian morality and doctrine. Abelard defined sin as consenting to an evil will (concupiscence) rather than as performing evil actions. He believed that actions were, in themselves, morally neutral.

**See also** Christian ethics.

## Abolition

**TYPE OF ETHICS:** Race and ethnicity

**DATE:** 1831-1865

**ASSOCIATED WITH:** William Lloyd Garrison, Frederick Douglass, Lydia Maria Child, Lewis Tappan, and Theodore Weld

**DEFINITION:** Refers to the movement to abolish slavery based upon moral, rather than practical, considerations

**SIGNIFICANCE:** The abolition movement attempted to apply the concepts of Christian brotherhood and democratic egalitarianism to race relations; it helped to end slavery in the United States

The most prolonged struggle within the United States has been in the area of race relations. Although the nation was founded upon the principle that "all men are created equal," American citizens continued to hold large numbers of African Americans in bondage until 1865. Those who participated in the abolitionist movement called Americans to a higher ethical standard. They demanded that both slaveholder and nonslaveholder take responsibility for the institution of slavery and take immediate measures to liberate their fellow countrymen.

**History.** Antislavery sentiment predates the American Revolution. By the mid-eighteenth century, American Quakers such as John Woolman and Benjamin Lay were denouncing slavery as un-Christian. The rationalism of the Enlightenment, with its stress upon natural law, added ammunition to the arsenal of critics of slavery.

The egalitarian rhetoric of the Revolutionary era illustrated the irony of slaveholders fighting for liberty. As a result, most Northern states abolished slavery by 1784. New York and New Jersey did so afterward. Southern whites felt that they could not afford to abolish slavery, yet they too felt the need to justify the institution on ethical grounds. They concentrated on humanizing the institution and argued that it was a "necessary evil."

Antislavery feeling receded after 1793 because of fear of slave revolts, the increasing profitability of slavery following the invention of the cotton gin, and new scientific theories that reinforced racism. The leading antislavery organization in the early nineteenth century was the American Colonization Society (ACS). The ACS attempted to resettle free blacks in Africa and encouraged voluntary emancipation without challenging the right to own human property. The colonization plan allowed liberal slaveholders and moderate members of the clergy to rationalize their guilt over slavery.

In 1825, a great Protestant religious revival swept the northeastern region of the country. Ministers such as Charles Grandison Finney preached a new perfectionist theology that sought to counter the growing worldliness of Americans. This revival sparked a host of humanitarian crusades designed to protect the rights of the disadvantaged and to cleanse American institutions of contamination.

By the early 1830's, many evangelical reformers began to view slavery and racism as sinful because racism violated the Christian ethic of equality. Known as immediate abolitionists, they demanded the immediate and unqualified liberation of slaves and an end to racial discrimination. With the formation of the American Anti-Slavery Society in 1833, abolitionist speakers toured the Northern states attempting to rally support for their cause. Abolitionists were frequently attacked by angry mobs, and their literature was destroyed in Southern post offices.

The abolition movement failed to end racism in the North. It did, however, spark anti-Southern feelings, which led to increased controversy within the national government. This conflict led directly to the Civil War. During the war, abolitionists pressured the federal government to transform the conflict from a war to preserve the Union into a war to end slavery. Abolition advocates were disappointed by the Emancipation Proclamation because it was based upon military necessity rather than moral principle, but they accomplished their central purpose with the passage of the Thirteenth Amendment, which ended slavery in the United States.

**Garrisonian Ethics.** One major faction within the abolition movement was led by editor William Lloyd Garrison. In a real sense, the publication of the first issue of the *Liberator* on January 1, 1831, established Garrison as the foremost abolitionist in the country. Garrison's harsh attacks upon slaveholders and colonizationists caused a national sensation even though the circulation of his newspaper never exceeded three thousand.

Like all abolitionists, Garrison demanded that everyone recognize a personal responsibility to improve society. The three major tenets of his ethical philosophy were human liberation, moral suasion, and no compromise with evil.

Because of his devotion to human liberation, Garrison actively campaigned on behalf of legal equality for African Americans, temperance, and equality for women. His strong stand in behalf of women's rights helped to cause a major split in the abolition movement in 1840.

Garrison rejected force and violence in human affairs. He sought the moral reformation of slave owners, not their destruction. He never advocated slave revolts, and he wanted the Northern states to allow the South to secede during the crisis of 1860-1861.

Garrison sincerely believed in all that he advocated, and he would not compromise his principles. He rejected any solution to the issue of slavery that involved a program that would delay emancipation. He also demanded that his followers reject participation in the American political system because the Constitution was a proslavery document. The American political system was based on compromise, making it inherently corrupt. Other abolitionists, such as Gerrit Smith and James Birney, attempted to use the political system as a way to gain publicity for the cause of abolition.

**African-American Abolitionism.** In a sense, there were two abolition movements. The white movement was based on a moral abstraction. African Americans were forced to confront the everyday realities of racism in nineteenth century America.

Frederick Douglass emerged as the major spokesman for African Americans during the antebellum period. Douglass self-consciously attempted to use his life as an example to repudiate racist stereotypes. Because of his eloquence, Douglass gained an international reputation as a public speaker, and in doing so, he proved the humanity of African Americans.

Like Garrison, Douglass strongly supported temperance and women's rights. He was, however, willing to use any means to achieve the liberation of slaves, including violence and political action. He approved of John Brown's idea of using the southern Appalachians as an armed sanctuary for runaways. He also supported the Free Soil and Republican parties even though neither advocated the emancipation of Southern slaves. He justified his positions as part of a larger struggle to advance the cause of racial equality in America.

*African Americans celebrate the abolition of slavery in the District of Columbia, on April 19, 1866.* (Library of Congress)

For Douglass, as for other African Americans involved in the cause of abolition, equality was the only acceptable ethical standard for a free society. —*Thomas D. Metijasic*

**See also** Discrimination; Egalitarianism; Emancipation Proclamation; Noninterference with violence; Racial prejudice; Racism; Slavery; *Uncle Tom's Cabin.*

**BIBLIOGRAPHY**

Barnes, Gilbert Hobbs. *The Antislavery Impulse: 1830-1844.* New York: Harcourt, Brace & World, 1964.

Duberman, Martin, ed. *The Antislavery Vanguard: New Essays on the Abolitionists.* Princeton, N.J.: Princeton University Press, 1965.

Huggins, Nathan Irvin. *Slave and Citizen: The Life of Frederick Douglass.* Boston: Little Brown, 1980.

Nye, Russel B. *William Lloyd Garrison and the Humanitarian Reformers.* Boston: Little Brown, 1955.

Sorin, Gerald. *Abolitionism: A New Perspective.* New York: Praeger, 1972.

Stewart, James Brewer. *Holy Warriors: The Abolitionists and American Slavery.* New York: Hill & Wang, 1976.

Tyler, Alice Felt. *Freedom's Ferment: Phases of American Social History to 1860.* Minneapolis: University of Minnesota Press, 1944.

## Abortion

**TYPE OF ETHICS:** Bioethics

**DATE:** 300 B.C.E. to present

**DEFINITION:** The technique of removing a developing embryo or fetus from the maternal uterus for the purpose of preventing the subsequent birth of a baby

**SIGNIFICANCE:** Raises the question of the morality of terminating a prenatal human life in response to the desire of others who would be adversely affected by the birth

**Background.** Childbirth should be a happy occasion. Yet other influences often prevent that ideal from being realized. Worldwide estimates suggest that 30 to 50 million women undergo abortions each year, of which almost half are illegal. In the United States, about 1.5 million women terminate their pregnancies each year, resulting in the statistic that about one pregnancy in four is ended with an induced abortion. Statistics on U.S. women who receive abortions show that about 26 percent of them are under nineteen years of age, 58 percent are under twenty-five years of age, and a little more than half of them are unmarried. The nonwhite abortion rate is 57 per 1,000 women, while the white abortion rate is 21 per 1,000 women.

Since the 1973 U.S. Supreme Court decision, *Roe v. Wade*, that made abortion legal, this medical procedure has been in popular use and has generated a sharp controversy between those who advocate a woman's right to have an abortion ("pro-choice") and those who oppose abortions ("pro-life"). The arguments have encompassed moral and medical issues as well as legal and social issues. Churches and religious denominations as well as politicians and political parties have been separated by the intensity of persons who oppose or defend abortion.

Abortions can be classified into two types: spontaneous and induced. Spontaneous abortions are those that result from unknown reasons that are attributed to "natural" causes. Estimates suggest that in normal, healthy women, more than half of fertilized embryos never implant and are spontaneously aborted. Furthermore, it is thought that about 10 to 15 percent of the implanted embryos spontaneously abort. Induced abortions are those that result from medical procedures designed to terminate development. When the word "abortion" is popularly used, as in this article, it refers primarily to induced abortions.

**History.** Abortions have been performed for centuries. The ancient Greeks advocated abortion as a method of birth control. Plato advocated that women after age forty should be compelled to have abortions. Early Roman law proclaimed that a "child in the belly of its mother" is not a person. Thus, abortion and even infanticide were permitted and practiced. Roman physicians described the use of abortifacient drugs in their treatment of patients. Early Christians in the first centuries C.E. largely prohibited the practice of abortion for their adherents, unlike the Greeks and Romans.

During the Middle Ages, the Roman Catholic Church objected to some abortions on the basis of ensoulment. It was thought that the soul entered the developing embryo about forty days after conception in the case of the male and eighty days after conception in the case of the female. Thus, abortions before ensoulment were accepted, but after that time were banned.

In the United States in the seventeenth and eighteenth centuries, abortions were neither prohibited by written laws nor prosecuted under common law. Abortion was regarded as immoral if it occurred after the time of quickening, when fetal movements were first perceived by the mother. Abortion become so widespread in the nineteenth century that the fertility rate of American women decreased by half, returning to what it had been in the previous century. Toward the end of the nineteenth century, most states had enacted anti-abortion statutes, the American Medical Association developed an anti-abortion committee to raise public awareness, and the Catholic church began to lay the ideological groundwork for its subsequent ban on abortion. Later considering abortion to be a violation of natural law, the Catholic church took a restrictive stance against abortion and prohibited it at any time of pregnancy.

In modern times, societal and religious groups are strongly divided regarding the acceptability of abortion. Many religious denominations have struggled in attempts to denounce or condone abortion as a women's rights issue. In many cases, such attempts have been moderated by opposing voices that presented the other side of the issue. Globally, about fifty-three countries with populations greater than 1 million (totaling 25 percent of the world's population) prohibit abortions except to save the life of the mother. Another twenty-three countries (40 percent of the world's population)

| Selected Country and State Abortion Legislation | | |
|---|---|---|
| **Country or State** | **Date** | **Event** |
| England | 1803 | Lord Ellenborough's Law made all abortions before quickening punishable |
| | 1828 | Revised 1803 statute to make abortion after quickening a capital offense |
| | 1838 | Modified abortion penalties; eliminated death penalty for abortions |
| | 1861 | Passed Offences Against Person Act, which mandated imprisonment for unlawful abortions |
| United States | 1880 | Forty states had antiabortion statutes that made induced abortions criminal |
| Canada | 1892 | Made it a crime to possess abortifacients |
| Japan | 1899 | Abortion becomes a crime |
| Soviet Union | 1920 | Legalized abortion on demand for all women, calling it a "necessary evil" |
| England | 1929 | Passed Infant Life Preservation Act, making it unlawful to terminate a viable fetus (viability was considered to be at twenty-eighth week of gestation), |
| Switzerland | 1942 | Became first nation in Western Europe to permit abortions for maternal health reasons |
| Germany, Third Reich | 1943 | Death penalty enacted for performing abortions |
| Japan | 1948 | Passed Eugenic Protection laws that allowed abortion to maintain race purity |
| China | 1958 | Open abortion policy |
| U.S.: Colorado | 1967 | Became first state to pass a liberalized abortion law |
| England | 1967 | British Abortion Act permitted abortion before time of viability |
| Canada | 1969 | Allowed abortion in selected hospitals with approval of a committee of three or more physicians |
| U.S.: Hawaii, New York, Alaska, Washingon | 1970 | Repealed abortion laws |
| India | 1971 | Medical Termination of Pregnancy Act permitted abortions for health reasons |
| United States | 1973 | Supreme Court decision on *Roe v. Wade* legalized abortion without restrictions in the first trimester or pregnancy and for maternal health in second and third trimesters |
| France | 1975 | Prohibited abortion as birth control; permitted early abortion in cases of distress |
| Ireland | 1983 | Popular referendum banned abortions on demand |
| France | 1988 | Approved the marketing of RU 486, the "abortion pill" |
| England | 1990 | House of Commons restricted abortions to the first eighteen weeks of pregnancy |
| Romania | 1990 | Legalized abortion after the fall of Communism, |
| Belgium | 1990 | Became last country in Western Europe to pass a liberalized abortion law |
| U.S.: Utah | 1991 | Passed the most restrictive abortion law in the nation |

permit abortions on the request of the woman. These countries include China, Russia, the United States, and about half of the countries in Europe. Most of the remaining countries of the world (35 percent of the world's population) permit abortion on broad medical grounds or for extreme situations such as rape. Some of these countries, such as Australia, Finland, Great Britain, Japan, and Taiwan, include "adverse social conditions" as justification for abortion.

**Personhood.** Some people have suggested that the controversy on abortion is actually a controversy on the view of the embryo/fetus. Is the developing fetus a mere piece of tissue or is it a person? Those who view the developing fetus as a conceptus, or piece of tissue, tend to place value and base their ethical arguments on the needs and rights of the mother. In most cases, they freely advocate abortion on demand in the attempt to support the pregnant mother's wishes. Individuals who view the embryo/fetus as a person ("a baby"), however, maintain a responsibility to protect the developing fetus. In that situation, abortion is viewed as a heinous crime that violently snuffs out the life of an innocent, defenseless, living person.

In the middle of the controversy stand a group of persons who are often uncomfortably changing their position and ethic. On the one hand, they recognize the emotional and psychological pain that an unwanted pregnancy can elicit. On the other hand, they believe that the developing embryo minimally bears the potential of personhood and thus has intrinsic value. A fetus is not a mere piece of tissue that can be harmlessly trimmed away for the sake of convenience.

Personhood is a fundamental issue in the abortion debate, and a cultural ethic colors attitudes toward personhood. For example, in some societies, personhood begins at a birth ceremony that is celebrated shortly after the birth event. The ceremony confers status and protection on the newly born child. Within such a view, abortion or infanticide that occurs after birthing but before the birth ceremony is considered to be legitimate means of birth control. Others see personhood as a developmental process that occurs in the uterus. Thus, aborting a third-trimester fetus may have moral consequences, while an early first-trimester abortion may be acceptable. Some mark the advent of conception as the origination of the person. In this view, all abortion is immoral and the embryo and fetus must be protected in the same way that a newborn baby is protected.

**Beginning of Life.** Frequently, the abortion debate centers on the question of when life begins. Historically, that moment has been placed at one of three points: (1) the moment of conception, (2) the time of "quickening," when the mother can first feel the fetal movements, or (3) the time of birth itself. From a biological perspective, however, life does not begin; instead, life is a continuum in which a living sperm fertilizes a living egg to form the unique first cell, the zygote.

The distinctiveness of the zygote is based on the reality that it contains a unique assortment of genes on its chromosomes that are a product of the specific genes carried by the fertilized egg and sperm. In the hours and days that follow fertilization, the zygote divides to form multiple cells that give rise to the mass of cells that will form the embryo as well as the tissues that will form the placental attachments of the embryo to the uterine wall. By the third week of development, the embryonic heart begins to beat and brain tissue is differentiating and forming. Early neural responses can be detected late in the first trimester; these responses become more sophisticated and complex as development progresses in the second and third trimester. Fetal behavior is an area of research that investigates the effects of environmental conditions—light, sound, maternal voice, temperature, and so forth—on fetal responses and subsequent developmental patterns. Research in this area indicates that postnatal behavior patterns are significantly affected by prenatal influences and that the fetus learns certain behaviors while it is developing in the uterus.

According to this understanding, a unique individual is formed at the point of conception that developmentally obtains the characteristics of personhood. Therefore, the embryo and fetus have intrinsic value because of their individuality and personhood. Thus, abortion becomes a moral issue when one considers the possibility of destroying a person or, at the very least, a potential person.

Medical Aspects. Numerous studies indicate that in societies in which abortions are illegal, the percentages of women who die from the illegal abortions are about ten times greater than those in societies in which abortions are legal and are regulated by medical practice. Nearly two-thirds of the world's women live in countries where abortion is available on request for social reasons.

Normally, a fertilized ovum or zygote, which forms a developing embryo, implants in the mother's uterus about ten days after conception. Early abortions are designed to prevent this implantation step in the development process. Such abortion procedures include the use of RU 486 (an abortive drug first developed in France in 1988), the IUD (intrauterine device) placed in the uterus by a physician, or the administration of the drug DES (often called the "morning after pill"). If abortion is desired between two to seven weeks after conception, a simple vacuum extraction is frequently used. The embryo at this time is less than three centimeters in length and can be removed easily from the uterus wall. After seven weeks until about the fifteenth week, the uterus is dilated before vacuum extraction is used. Following the fifteenth week of development, abortions generally consist of an induced labor that results from uterine injections of concentrated salt solutions (hypertonic saline) or prostaglandins (hormones that stimulate uterine contractions).

Complications of abortions may vary greatly, depending upon the timing of the abortion, the particular technique used, the skill of the abortionist, and the unique physiology of the woman involved in the procedure. For many women, only minor symptoms such as slight bleeding or cramps occur. For others, complications may include severe hemorrhage, infection from contaminated instruments, uterine perforation, cervical injury, or an incomplete abortion in which the fetal remains may induce infection. Some cases of psychosocial and emotional disturbances of women who have had abortions have been documented, although the percentage of women thus affected is not high.

**Fetal Research.** An ethical issue related to abortion is fetal research. If abortions occur, what should be done with the aborted fetuses? Should they be buried or might some of them be used for medical research and medical treatment? Legally, the fetus is not a protected entity, yet it is a growing human, which is why it is prized as a source for tissue and organ transplantation in humans. Such a valuable commodity brings in the issues of ownership and economics that frame additional ethical dilemmas. Does the mother who has undergone the abortion own the aborted fetus and thereby have the right to sell the remains to the highest bidder? What are the ethics of buying and selling body parts?

Experimental efforts to transplant fetal cells into Parkinson's patients have been very successful in alleviating this debilitating disease. This technology paves the way for transplanting fetal tissues in attempts to control diabetes, Alzheimer's disease, and Huntington's disease, as well as other diseases. Ethically, it seems wasteful to discard tissue that could improve the quality of life for another person. Yet the danger exists that persons might become pregnant so that valuable fetal tissues could be "harvested" from their bodies for the medical treatment of a parent or loved one, or even for sale for profit.

**Biotechnology.** Biotechnology has developed abortive techniques that are minimally traumatic to the mother. One example is the use of RU 486, an aborticide drug that was developed in France. This drug works by preventing a fertilized egg or early embryo from implanting into the uterine wall. RU 486, an antiprogestin, breaks the fertilized egg's bond to the uterus wall and thus induces a miscarriage. Tests of this drug on thousands of women show that it is about 97 percent effective in terminating very early pregnancies. The drug can be administered in the privacy of a doctor's office and therefore avoid the stigmatization of going to an abortion clinic. That fact alone arouses strong responses both from advocates and opponents of the drug.

With sophisticated embryo screening techniques such as ultrasound and amniocentesis, it is possible to determine the gender of an embryo. By using genetic screening, one can also determine specific genes that the developing embryo may have that are beneficial or undesirable. One of the ethical dilemmas of the use of this technology is that abortion may become a means for obtaining a child of perfect genotype and gender, discouraging the attitude of accepting all prenatal embryos as unique beings who are intrinsically valuable, regardless of their gene makeup or gender.

**Summary.** Two absolute moral positions directly oppose each other and prevent an easy resolution to the abortion controversy. One position maintains that abortion is the killing of human beings. The other position declares that a woman has the right to control her own body. For many who hold one position or the other, there can be no compromise. In the face of such irreconcilable attitudes, public policy about abortion must be formed. For such policy to endure, it must compromise both positions. Two areas of compromise have been seen historically and are continuing: (1) to allow abortion only for certain specific reasons, such as to save the life of the mother or in the situation of rape or incest, and (2) to permit early abortions but to forbid or strongly regulate mid-term or late abortions. Many abortion laws in various states of the United States or in other countries recognize and attempt to integrate some aspects of these two compromises in their structure. Trends indicate that public policy may move more deliberately toward these compromises, which carve out a middle ground between two absolutist postures. —*Roman J. Miller*

**See also** Bioethics; Birth control; Eugenics; Genetic counseling; In vitro fertilization; Pro-choice movement; Pro-life movement; *Roe v. Wade*.

**Bibliography**

Bajema, Clifford E. *Abortion and the Meaning of Personhood.* Grand Rapids, Mich.: Baker Book House, 1976. In this small paperback, the author focuses the abortion controversy on the issue of personhood of the developing fetus. He reflects on the dilemmas of the mother and of the legislation of morality.

Costa, Marie. *Abortion: A Reference Handbook.* Santa Barbara, Calif.: ABC-Clio, 1991. An informative handbook on various aspects of abortion. Facts and statistics, a chronology of historical and political events, biographical sketches of persons involved, and organizations and resources relating to abortion are listed in a very objective fashion.

Feinberg, Joel. *The Problem of Abortion.* Belmont, Calif.: Wadsworth, 1973. An anthology of readings from prominent philosophers and ethicists on the problem of abortion. Some are opposed to and others support abortion. The writing is largely argumentative and in support of a particular perspective or viewpoint.

Fowler, Paul B. *Abortion: Toward an Evangelical Consensus.* Portland, Oreg.: Multnomah Press, 1978. This popular paperback illustrates the divided opinions of one group of Christians, the evangelicals, over the issue of abortion. The author describes the basis for the differences in thought and points to a possible resolution of this controversy.

Larsen, William J. *Human Embryology.* New York: Churchill Livingstone, 1993. This well-written text on human development is clearly illustrated with diagrams and photographs. Larson presents the normal biological development of the embryo and fetus and provides references to clinical cases.

Miller, Roman J., and Beryl H. Brubaker, eds. *Bioethics and the Beginning of Life.* Scottdale, Pa.: Herald Press, 1990. This collection of writings attempts to demonstrate the complexity that biotechnology has brought to issues at the beginning of life, including abortion. Chapters are written from various perspectives, such as biological, ethical, theological, legal, historical, psychological, maternal, sociological, and others framed within a Christian communal consensus.

Rodman, Hyman, Betty Sarvis, and Joy Walker Bonar. *The Abortion Question.* New York: Columbia University Press, 1987. The authors attempt to present the bases of the controversy over the abortion issue by describing the moral positions of the contending sides within the context of their historical development. While the authors acknowledge their "pro-choice" position, they attempt to present each side objectively, without embellishment or bias.

## Absolutes and absolutism

**Type of ethics:** Theory of ethics

**Definition:** Absolutism is any ethical theory that claims there is only one correct ethical standard applicable to everyone everywhere; alternatively, it is any theory that claims there are ethical absolutes—that is, ethical values or principles that hold for all humans regardless of their society, culture, or religion

**SIGNIFICANCE:** Absolutism is one of the two mutually exclusive positions that one may adopt concerning the nature of ethical principles and values; the other is relativism, which claims that ethical principles and values vary from culture to culture and that no one is better than any other

As the foregoing definition of absolutism implies, any absolutist theory will acknowledge the existence of ethical absolutes. These will be values or principles that absolutists believe should be embraced by every moral agent. Part of the absolutist's task will be to convince people that the values or principles are in fact objective and universally binding. To make things simpler, what follows will be primarily a discussion about absolutism. The issue of absolutism versus relativism has existed since the beginnings of ethics. One could make the argument that ethics as a branch of philosophy got its start with the development of the absolutist ethical theory of Socrates in the fifth century B.C.E. It may be best, then, to explain absolutism from an historical perspective.

**History.** Socrates lived during a period that exhibited moral skepticism. A group of itinerant teachers known as sophists were advocating various versions of relativism claiming that right and wrong were ultimately determined by, and thus relative to, the individual. It is against this position that Socrates offers his account of right and wrong, which turns out to be the first major version of absolutism. What is interesting is that he relies on a grand metaphysical scheme to supply the justification for his absolutist claim. Socrates believed that human beings were composed of two radically different kinds of substance: bodies and souls, with the soul, because it is the seat of reason, being more important. In addition, reality is also a fundamental dichotomy. One part of that dichotomy is the world of appearance; the other, the world of form. For Socrates, the world of appearance is an imperfect copy and, hence, less real than the world of form. If one focused on the world of appearance, the ever-changing world of daily experience, the world the body is in, it is easy to believe that relativism is the case. The one constant is that there are no constants. Everything is transitory. The world of form, however, is timeless, changeless, and eternal. It is a world with which the soul is acquainted. Everything is permanent and stable. It is the world that supplies both knowledge and absolute moral values and principles, to which humans have access and which they recognize as absolutely binding in virtue of their rationality.

With a few minor exceptions, the issue of absolutism versus relativism did not pose a major problem to the Western intellectual tradition until well into the nineteenth century. This is so, in part, because of the dominant role that Catholicism played in this tradition. According to Catholicism, there are moral absolutes and there is one correct ethical theory that is applicable to everyone everywhere. Right and wrong are simply a matter of what God commands. What is of moral value is simply a matter of what God deems valuable.

With the coming of the Enlightenment came a rejection of the above-described theory of ethics but not a rejection of absolutism. Christian ethics were replaced with other absolutist theories that appealed to human reason instead of God. One example is the utilitarianism of Jeremy Bentham, which claims that right and wrong is simply a matter of calculating which action would produce the greatest good for the greatest number. This so-called "principle of utility" is applicable to everyone everywhere. Another example is the deontological ethics of Immanuel Kant. For him, right and wrong is a matter of whatever reason determines through use of the categorical imperative, which, again, is applicable to everyone everywhere.

**Current Challenge to Absolutism.** The most recent challenge to absolutism comes from the social sciences—in particular, cultural anthropology. Cultural anthropology is the study, observation, and description of the customs and morés of various cultures and societies. Cultural anthropologists have gone to all parts of the globe to study, observe, and describe the cultures they have found. They have also gone into the historical record to do the same for cultures past. If absolutism were true, one would expect that there would be some common values or principles. When the gathered data are compared, however, what strikes the observer is the mind-boggling diversity of values and principles. Given an action one culture sanctions as right, one would have little difficulty finding a different culture that would claim the same action wrong. It seems that all the empirical evidence supports relativism. There is no universal agreement. Values and principles vary from culture to culture.

**Absolutist Reply.** The absolutists have a rather sophisticated three-part reply to the claims of the cultural relativists. First, it is shown that the data do not support what relativists claim but rather something weaker. All the data show is that, at best, there is not now one correct ethical theory. It does not rule out, logically, the possibility that the one correct standard may be discovered in the future. Second, there may be less disagreement than there seems. This disagreement among cultures may be the result of differing physical circumstances or factual beliefs and not necessarily the result of differing values. In other words, there may be absolute values that are implemented in different ways. Finally, there may well be absolute values and principles; namely, those necessary for the preservation and continuation of the society or culture. For example, all societies have some rules that protect children. This will ensure that the culture or society will continue into the future. —*John H. Serembus*

**See also** Anthropological ethics; Relativism; Socrates.

**BIBLIOGRAPHY**

Brink, David. *Moral Realism and the Foundations of Ethics*. Cambridge, England: Cambridge University Press, 1989.

Mackie, J. L. *Ethics: Inventing Right and Wrong*. New York: Penguin Books, 1977.

Pojman, Louis, P. *Ethics: Discovering Right and Wrong*. Belmont, Calif.: Wadsworth, 1990.

Rachels, James. *The Elements of Moral Philosophy*. 2d ed. New York: McGraw-Hill, 1993.

Williams, Bernard. *Ethics and the Limits of Philosophy*. Cambridge, Mass.: Harvard University Press, 1985.

## Absurd, The

**Type of ethics:** Modern history

**Date:** Mid-twentieth century

**Associated with:** French philosopher and novelist Albert Camus (1913-1960)

**Definition:** That which points toward the ultimately meaningless character of human life

**Significance:** In Camus' view, the absurd presents philosophy with its most fundamental problem: justifying the value of human existence

Owing largely to World War II and its aftermath, it seemed to Albert Camus that traditional values and ways of life had collapsed. He dramatized that situation in novels such as *The Stranger* (1942) and *The Plague* (1947) and reflected on it philosophically in essays such as *The Myth of Sisyphus* (1942). Especially in the latter work, Camus explained that absurdity arises from the confrontation between "human need and the unreasonable silence of the world." The absurd exists partly because human beings ask "Why?" but that is only part of the story. The other key component is that answers to the question "Why?"—at least ones that are complete, final, and convincing to all—never appear. The collision between the questioning human consciousness and "the unreasonable silence of the world" brings the absurd into existence.

Camus could see no way to overcome the absurd and its "total absence of hope." He did not, however, conclude that the absurd dictated nihilism and death. On the contrary, he argued that humanity's task was to rebel against the absurd by making life as good as it can possibly be.

**See also** Camus, Albert; Existentialism; Sartre, Jean-Paul.

## Abû Bakr (c. 573—Aug. 23, 634): Caliph

**Type of ethics:** Religious ethics

**Achievements:** Succeeded the Prophet Muḥammad as the first caliph

**Significance:** Expanded the nascent Muslim empire by conquering neighboring states

One of the first persons to convert to Islam, Abû Bakr lent much-needed credibility to the cause of Prophet Muḥammad in the early days of Islam. He belonged to a rich trading family and was a crucial figure in providing moral and financial support to sustain Muḥammad in Mecca at the time that Muḥammad declared his prophethood. The close relationship between the two men was further strengthened by marital relations. Abû Bakr gave two of his daughters in marriage to Muḥammad. One of them, Khadîja, was only thirteen years of age when she married Muḥammad. Muḥammad gave Abû Bakr the title *Siddiq*, one who always speaks truth, because he became a disciple of Muḥammad at a time when it was not safe for Muslims to reveal their allegiance openly. Abû Bakr is supposed to have accompanied Muḥammad at the time of their flight from Mecca to the city of Medina, which provided a safe haven to Muḥammad and his followers. Abû Bakr remained close to the Prophet in Mecca as well as in Medina and assisted him in becoming established in Medina. Abû Bakr negotiated on behalf of the Prophet with other clans in and around Medina whose support was crucial in the struggle against the Meccans. The Quraish tribe of Mecca tried to march on Medina to destroy Muḥammad's forces three times but failed. After the death of Muḥammad, Abû Bakr was chosen to lead the Muslims. He assumed the title caliph or successor.

**See also** Muḥammad al-Muṣṭafâ.

## Abû Ḥanîfa al-Nuʿman ibn Tabi (c. 699, Kufa, Iraq—767, Baghdad, Iraq): Theologian and jurist

**Type of ethics:** Religious ethics

**Achievements:** Author of the theological treatise *Epistle to ʿUthman al-Batti*

**Significance:** As a theologian, Abû Ḥanîfa was the founder of the first of the four orthodox schools of law in Sunnî Islam; as a legal scholar, he was among the earliest to formulate judicial doctrines relating to questions that might arise in the future of the Islamic community

Born to a family of non-Arab converts to Islam, Abû Ḥanîfa was originally attracted to theology but soon turned to Islamic law. His principal teacher was Hammad ibn Abî Sulayman, the foremost representative of the Iraqi school of legal thought. Following the death of his mentor in 737, Abû Ḥanîfa was acknowledged as the head of the school. Throughout his career, he declined offers of governmental positions under the Umayyad and Abbasid dynasties, and there are indications that he harbored antigovernment sympathies. Indeed, he seems to have been imprisoned from 762 because of his support for an Alid revolt. As a theologian, Abû Ḥanîfa vigorously opposed the Khariji rigorist doctrine that sin rendered one an unbeliever. He declared that faith was the ultimate determinant of a person's membership in Islam. It was this doctrine that ultimately became the orthodox position in Islam. As a jurist, Abû Ḥanîfa spent many years reviewing the corpus of Islamic law; formulating new, systematic legal doctrines based on religious tradition and judicial precedent; and, most important, proposing legal responses to hypothetical situations that might arise later in the Islamic community.

**See also** Islamic ethics.

## Abuse

**Type of ethics:** Personal and social ethics

**Associated with:** Pediatrician Henry Kempe, who called attention to child abuse

**Definition:** Intentional, nonaccidental acts of commission or omission aimed at hurting, injuring, or destroying a person

**SIGNIFICANCE:** Legislation in all fifty states requires helping professionals to report suspected cases of child abuse and neglect; regarding other types of abuse, legal and ethical prescriptions of action are less clear

Physical abuse, which is nonaccidental injury to another person, includes actions that physically damage another person, such as pushing, shoving, hitting, slapping, and throwing things. The consequences of physical abuse can be minor, such as a bruise, or major, such as death. Physically abusive actions are fairly stable, so that a person who is physically abusive early in life usually stays that way. Young adults (under age thirty) are more likely to engage in domestic violence than are older adults (O'Leary, et al., 1989).

Because ordinary physical punishment is widely accepted as an appropriate form of discipline in the United States, it is typically excluded from definitions of physical abuse. Physical abuse is, however, often difficult to distinguish from physical punishment. When does spanking become abuse? One guiding principle in distinguishing physical punishment from physical abuse is the leaving of bruises. Physical punishment that leaves bruises on a child is often considered physical abuse. Parents who endorse physical punishment are more likely than are others to physically abuse their children. Physical abuse is widespread.

Sexual abuse includes any sexual behaviors that are forced upon a person. Sexual abuse includes any type of sexual fondling, touching, or other such behaviors of a sexual nature (such as being exposed involuntarily to someone's genitals); rape (involuntary sexual intercourse); and incest (sexual activity between close relatives).

Sexual abuse may be the result of physical force, threat, or intimidation. Sexual abuse violates community norms in an extreme way; therefore, it is typically viewed with abhorrence and is often punished with imprisonment. Nevertheless, some form of sexual abuse is reported by between 19 percent and 38 percent of adult women (Russell, 1989), and by between 5 percent and 30 percent of adult men (Finkelhor, 1986). Thus, even though sexual abuse is not condoned in society, it is experienced by a significant percentage of women and men.

The long-term consequences of sexual abuse are usually negative. Many adults who have been molested as children report feeling guilt, anger, depression, disordered sexual behavior, poor self-esteem, feelings of isolation and stigma, self-destructive behavior, difficulties trusting others, substance abuse, and a tendency toward revictimization.

Sustained physical or sexual abuse is now thought to be a primary culprit in the development of multiple personality, a psychological disorder in which a person has two or more distinctly different personalities, each of which has a unique way of thinking and behaving. Not all people who were physically or sexually abused as children, however, develop multiple personalities as adults.

Psychological abuse, which is also called emotional or mental abuse, includes actions that damage a person's behavioral, cognitive, emotional, or physical functioning. Psychologically abusive behaviors are those that ridicule, belittle, degrade, exploit, intimidate, and so forth. Psychological abuse may be the most prevalent form of child abuse, and it is also a widespread form of adult abuse. Often occurring in conjunction with other forms of abuse, psychological abuse may exist independently of other types of abuse.

Because its consequences are often invisible, psychological abuse is seldom reported. Despite this fact, many experts believe that psychological abuse is the most damaging of all forms of abuse. It lowers a person's self-image, distorts his or her relationships with others, and leads to increased fear, anxiety, helplessness, aggression, and self-destructive behavior.

In a comprehensive overview of domestic violence, Dutton (1988) suggested a nested ecological explanation of domestic violence, which includes at least four factors. First, the cultural values of the individuals involved may contribute to abuse. For example, are men and women considered to be equal? Is hitting one's wife considered to be an indication of affection? Second, the social situation may contribute to abuse. For example, are the individuals involved unemployed? Are they under severe economic or other stress? Third, the family unit may contribute to domestic abuse. For example, do the individuals communicate as a couple? Do the parents typically use physical punishment? Fourth, the level of individual development may contribute to domestic abuse. For example, does the couple excuse violence? Have they witnessed family violence in the past? The nested ecological approach suggests multiple levels of causes, with the importance of each level differing in each assault case. —*Lillian Range*

**See also** Child abuse; Sexual abuse and harassment; Violence.

**BIBLIOGRAPHY**

Dutton, Donald G. *The Domestic Assault of Women*. Boston: Allyn & Bacon, 1988.

Finkelhor, David, *A Sourcebook on Child Sexual Abuse*. Beverly Hills, Calif.: Sage, 1986.

National Committee for the Prevention of Child Abuse. *Child Abuse and Neglect Statistics*. Chicago: Author, 1992.

O'Leary, K. Daniel, et al. "Prevalence and Stability of Physical Aggression Between Spouses: A Longitudinal Analysis." *Journal of Consulting and Clinical Psychology 57 (April, 1989): 263-268.*

Russell, Diana E. H. *Sexual Exploitation: Rape, Child Sexual Abuse, and Workplace Harassment*. Beverly Hills, Calif.: Sage, 1989.

Van Hasselt, Vincent B., et al. eds. *Handbook of Family Violence*. New York: Plenum Press, 1988.

## Academic freedom

**TYPE OF ETHICS:** Beliefs and practices

**DATE:** Formulated after 1865

**Associated with:** University of Leiden, Thomas Cooper, John M. Mecklin, Arthur O. Lovejoy, and the American Association of University Professors

**Definition:** The state in which teachers are free to discuss their subjects in the classroom, to conduct research, and to publish the results of that research

**Significance:** Academic freedom makes it possible to question the status quo; the result of such freedom might be an improved moral order

The freedom of teachers to instruct and to do research is fundamental for civilization. The discovery and dissemination of knowledge form the basis for positive dialogue. Such dialogue can lead to consensus, which can serve to motivate people both individually and collectively to take action that can bring moral order. Such an ethical dynamic makes it possible for new ideas to be advanced and new, positive action to be taken on an ethical and moral level.

Academic freedom is inextricably intertwined with conflict. Socrates' incessant probing in search of the truth led to his execution on the charge of corrupting the youth of Athens. During the Middle Ages in Europe, academic freedom began its relationship with institutions of higher learning.

The medieval era displayed contradiction concerning academic freedom. The Roman Catholic Church preached and insisted on a single system of truth that was anchored in God. Most medieval scholars accepted this central body of authority, but some rejected the idea that the hierarchy represented the true Church. In the thirteenth and fourteenth centuries, the ecclesiastical authorities, through condemnations and censures, greatly hindered philosophical and theological inquiry. Nevertheless, scholars fought back in the pursuit of truth that would outlast and even reverse condemnations.

*Clarence Darrow (on desk at center) makes a plea during the 1925 Scopes "Monkey Trial." The trial constituted a major test of academic freedom.* (Library of Congress)

Italian thinkers enjoyed a remarkable degree of academic freedom during the Renaissance. For example, Professor Pietro Pompanazzi published a book questioning the immortality of the soul and also attacked the clergy. Far from being censured, Pompanazzi was protected by Pope Leo X, and his salary was increased.

During the Reformation, Protestantism both impeded and advanced academic freedom. Rigorous orthodox Calvinism held that freedom of thought was an obstacle to ethics. Arminianism brought a latitudinarian thrust. Leiden was the home of the first European university to follow an intentional and consistent policy of academic freedom.

In seventeenth century England, the Act of Uniformity led to ejections from academic institutions. Those who were purged founded academies noted for liberality in thought. The graduates of these academies contributed to the American Enlightenment, which supported secularism in ethics.

Academic freedom has had a precarious life in the United States. The seventeenth century college demanded religious conformity from its faculty. In 1654, Harvard University dismissed its first president, the Reverend Henry Dunster, for heresy.

The eighteenth century displayed a mixed tableau. The secularization of colleges introduced skepticism and inquiry into ethics. Between 1740 and 1766, however, Yale experienced illiberalism under the Reverend President Thomas Clap, who promoted orthodox Calvinist ethics. Nevertheless, the Reverend Edward Wigglesworth, the first person in American collegiate education to hold a major professorship, enjoyed notable academic freedom as Harvard's Hollis Professor of Divinity from 1722 to 1765. Wigglesworth's namesake son, who was Hollis Professor between 1765 and 1791, advanced the cause of liberal ethics. In 1756, the University of Pennsylvania acquitted the Reverend Provost William Smith of the charge of teaching irreligious ethics.

Prebellum nineteenth century America experienced various notable situations regarding academic freedom. For example, the Unitarian Reverend President Horace Holley, who raised Transylvania University to distinction, resigned because of Presbyterian charges that he had made that institution infidel. President Thomas Cooper of South Carolina College, a materialist ethicist, put forward the boldest and most advanced argument for academic freedom.

Later nineteenth century America made significant strides in academic freedom. Despite opposition, the teaching of evolution and attacks on transcendental ethics entered institutions. At Yale, Professor William Graham Sumner ably defended his rigid ethic of self-reliance. The introduction of the German concept of *Lehrfreiheit*—freedom of teaching and freedom of inquiry for the university professor—was profoundly significant.

Between 1890 and 1900, a number of academic freedom incidents occurred in which a professor was summarily dismissed after espousing reform or criticizing the social order. Such cases involved Richard T. Ely (University of Wisconsin), Edward W. Bemis (University of Chicago in 1895 and Kansas State Agricultural College in 1899), E. Benjamin Andrews (Brown University), Frank Parsons (Kansas State Agricultural College), and Edward A. Ross (Stanford University). Ross's views had antagonized Mrs. Leland Stanford, Sr.

In 1913, the dismissal of Professor John M. Mecklin (philosophy, psychology) at Lafayette College proved to be noteworthy. President Ethelbert D. Warfield detested Mecklin's philosophical relativism, his interest in pragmatism, and his teaching of evolution. The American Philosophical and American Psychological Associations failed to obtain justice for Mecklin. A body representing the entire professorate was needed to protect academic freedom.

That organization appeared in the form of the American Association of University Professors (AAUP). Founded in 1915, its principal promoter was Arthur O. Lovejoy of The Johns Hopkins University. The organization's *1940 Statement of Principles on Academic Freedom and Tenure* has since been accepted by 142 educational and scholarly organizations. AAUP's national office, however, grew weak, and in World War I, it chose not to defend academic freedom. Between 1949 and 1955, AAUP General Secretary Ralph Himstead gave no help to victims of the United States House Un-American Activities Committee and neglected more than a hundred casualties of Senator Joseph R. McCarthy's misguided witch-hunts in search of communists.

Later twentieth century America experienced attacks against academic freedom. Both secular institutions, public and private, and religious organizations, Jewish, Protestant, and Roman Catholic, have stifled or attempted to stifle professors. The Catholic University of America, for example, dismissed Father Charles E. Curran because of his views on ethics.

The battle over academic freedom continues, and there is no indication that it will be resolved in the foreseeable future.

—*Erving E. Beauregard*

**See also** American Civil Liberties Union; Book banning; Censorship; Cold War; Communism; Sedition.

**BIBLIOGRAPHY**

Beale, Howard K. *A History of Freedom of Teaching in American Schools*. New York: Octagon Books, 1966.

Beauregard, Erving E. *History of Academic Freedom in Ohio*. New York: Peter Lang, 1988.

Gruber, Carol S. *Mars and Minerva: World War I and the Uses of the Higher Learning in America*. Baton Rouge: Louisiana State University, 1975.

Hofstadter, Richard, and Walter P. Metzger. *The Development of Academic Freedom in the United States*. New York: Columbia University, 1956.

Schrecker, Ellen W. *No Ivory Tower: McCarthyism and the Universities*. New York: Oxford University, 1986.

## Accountability

**TYPE OF ETHICS:** Theory of ethics

**DATE:** Coined 1794; the relevant sense of "account" dates back to 1340

**ASSOCIATED WITH:** Compatibilism and metaphysical libertarianism

**DEFINITION:** The state of being responsible, liable, answerable, or obligated

**SIGNIFICANCE:** Moralities generally require accountability, either individual or collective, before ethical evaluations can assign praise or blame

Accountability can be either individual or collective, but the latter has been much more controversial (for example, the alleged collective responsibility of Germans for Nazi atrocities). Ethicists usually believe that individual accountability applies to any free or voluntary act. Accountability is thus a key concept in morality and metaphysics.

One key doctrine that is related to accountability is compatibilism, the view that the causal determination of actions is consistent with moral responsibility for those actions. For example, a compatibilist holds that one would still be accountable for one's actions even if a scientist or a god could predict all of those actions in detail. Compatibilism is a metaphysical doctrine that is relevant to ethics. Incompatibilists claim that the causal determination of one's acts would prevent one from having the freedom necessary for having moral accountability for one's acts. Metaphysical libertarianism (which is completely distinct from political libertarianism) endorses incompatibilism but allows for accountability by denying that acts are causally determined. Another key doctrine here is the idea that "ought" implies "can," which denies that an agent can be accountable for failing to do the impossible. Accountability assumes that there is a duty (that is, a responsibility or obligation) that one is to discharge. One can generally be held to account for failure to do one's duty. As Joseph F. Newton wrote, "A duty dodged is like a debt unpaid; it is only deferred, and we must come back and settle the account at last."

Accountability is a key concept in law, where ethical issues are often discussed in terms of liability. Strict liability implies that one is responsible even if one is not at fault. Thus, strict liability seems to be inconsistent with the doctrine that ought implies can. Vicarious liability is responsibility for harm done by another (for example, one's child). Product liability is a field of law that holds manufacturers and merchants accountable for defective goods that they sell. Legal liability is the most general term for exposure to being held to account by a court or other legal institution. To be legally liable is to be subject to punishment or to an order to provide compensation to at least help make up for one's infraction.

Accountability is a key concept in politics. The Left (liberals, socialists, and communists) often calls for increased social responsibility for corporations and social elites, and often criticizes the allegedly unaccountable power that corporations and elites wield. The Right (conservatives, traditionalists, and fascists) often calls for people to take more responsibility for their own actions, and often criticizes individuals for allegedly shirking their duties by claiming to be victims of circumstance or of society. The importance of accountability is thus something about which the political moralities of the Left and the Right seem to agree.

Some people argue that corporations cannot be accountable, because, first, they are not persons or agents that are distinct from corporate employees, and, second, praise and blame can apply only to distinct agents. Others argue that corporations are agents, since they have internal decision-making structures, which arguably provide enough of a chain of command for ethicists to attribute acts to corporations as distinct from merely attributing the acts to some individual or some subset of the corporation's employees. Some argue that the whole is greater than the sum of its parts in this case. Even if no single employee were held accountable for a bad result, for example, the corporation could still be held accountable. Synergistic effects of individual acts of employees can produce corporate accountability for an immoral outcome. To deny this possibility would seem to be to commit the fallacy of composition, which assumes that whatever is true of each part of a whole (in this case, unaccountability) must be true of the whole as well. —*Sterling Harwood*

**See also** Duty; Negligence; Responsibility; Social justice and responsibility.

**Bibliography**

Adkins, Arthur W. *Merit and Responsibility: A Study in Greek Values*. New York: Oxford University Press, 1960.

Erikson, Erik H. *Insight and Responsibility*. New York: Norton, 1964.

Fischer, John Martin, ed. *Moral Responsibility*. Ithaca, N.Y.: Cornell University Press, 1986.

French, Peter A. *Collective and Corporate Responsibility*. New York: Columbia University Press, 1984.

__________, ed. *Individual and Collective Responsibility: Massacre at My Lai*. Cambridge, Mass.: Schenkman, 1972.

__________. *The Spectrum of Responsibility*. New York: St. Martin's Press, 1991.

Glover, Jonathan. *Responsibility*. Atlantic Highlands, N.J.: Humanitarian Press, 1970.

Gorr, Michael J., and Sterling Harwood, eds. *Controversies in Criminal Law: Philosophical Essays on Liability and Procedure*. Boulder, Colo.: Westview Press, 1992.

Hart, Herbert L. *Punishment and Responsibility: Essays in the Philosophy of Law*. New York: Oxford University Press, 1968.

Kenny, Anthony. *Freewill and Responsibility*. Boston: Routledge & Kegan Paul, 1978.

May, Larry, and Stacey Hoffman, eds. *Collective Responsibility: Five Decades of Debate in Theoretical and Applied Ethics*. Savage, Md.: Rowman & Littlefield, 1991.

Morris, Herbert. *Guilt and Shame*. Belmont, Calif.: Wadsworth, 1971.

Nadel, Mark V. *Corporations and Political Accountability*. Lexington, Mass.: D. C. Heath, 1976.

Walton, Clarence C. *Corporate Social Responsibilities*. Belmont, Calif.: Wadsworth, 1967.

## Accuracy in Media (AIM)

**Type of ethics:** Media ethics

**Date:** Founded 1969

**Associated with:** Media reform; conservatism

**DEFINITION:** AIM identifies factual errors made by the news media and seeks public corrections

**SIGNIFICANCE:** AIM, one of the most visible of several U.S. national media reform groups, seeks to protect First Amendment rights by guaranteeing readers and viewers access to news media

Accuracy in Media, with more than 28,000 members and a budget of more than $1.5 million, is a news watchdog organization. Its staff monitors television, radio, and print news, and checks for inaccuracies. It also receives complaints from the public. When AIM determines that a factual error has been made, it asks for a public correction. Should the media fail to issue a correction, AIM publicizes that failure. AIM reaches the public through a daily radio program carried on more than 200 stations across the country. The organization also maintains a speakers' bureau and gives annual awards for fair and accurate reporting. AIM believes that big media corporations have abused their power. They report the news in ways that promote a political view that enhances their power. Average citizens are denied access to the media, and their concerns—and differing opinions—often go unheard. It is AIM's intention to promote fair reporting on important issues—fairness that, it believes, is often lost because of the media's liberal bias. AIM has been accused by others, however, of allowing its own conservative bias to influence its activity.

**See also** Fairness and Accuracy in Reporting (FAIR).

## Acquired immunodeficiency syndrome (AIDS)

**TYPE OF ETHICS:** Bioethics

**DATE:** Coined 1981

**DEFINITION:** A physical condition thought to be caused by a special type of virus, called a retrovirus, of indeterminate origin, which invades and seriously damages the body's immune system, leaving it vulnerable to a number of "opportunistic" infections and rare cancers

**SIGNIFICANCE:** The AIDS pandemic highlights a host of crucial policy issues including civil and human rights, confidentiality and privacy, accessibility to medical and social services, the drug trial and approval process, prisoners' rights, substance-abuse treatment, school-based sex education, equitable distribution of scarce resources, and international cooperation

With the development of polio vaccines in the 1950's, medical researchers thought that the day would soon be at hand when humanity would be virtually free from communicable diseases. AIDS changed all that.

By the close of 1980, doctors in the United States discovered an increasing number of relatively young patients, predominantly gay and bisexual men, who had a series of rare infections and cancers previously seen only in much older people with weakened immune systems. Not knowing what to call it, doctors first gave it the name "gay-related immune deficiency" (GRID).

As more became known, researchers found that GRID was not confined to gay men but had already reached epidemic proportions among heterosexual populations in west-central Africa.

Medical researchers in France and the United States simultaneously isolated the deadly virus thought to cause this constellation of diseases. Originally calling it "human T-lymphotropic virus type III" (HTLV-III) in the United States, researchers renamed it "human immunodeficiency virus" (HIV) in the United States, and "lymphadenophy associated virus" (LAV) in France.

Though the virus' origins are still not fully understood, much is known about its pathways of transmission. Experts agree that it is not transmitted through casual contact (for example, sneezing, shaking hands, sharing drinking glasses, sitting on toilet seats). The primary means of exposure involve engaging in "unprotected" (without the use of a condom or dental dam) intimate sexual relations with an infected person, being transfused or injected with infected blood or blood products, sharing infected drug needles, or through breast milk from an infected mother to a child. At present, no vaccines or cures exist.

Perplexing as it is medically, ethically AIDS raises a number of crucial issues, for it taps into an array of common fears concerning sickness and death, sexuality, drug addiction, and money.

In Europe throughout the thirteenth and fourteenth centuries, Jews were wrongly accused of poisoning drinking wells, thereby causing the Black Death. The syphilis epidemic in the sixteenth century was referred to in England as "the French Disease" and in France as "the German Disease." Likewise, although AIDS can attack anyone who engages in "high risk" behaviors, Africans and gay and bisexual people have been scapegoated for AIDS.

**AIDS CASES AMONG U.S. ADULTS AND ADOLESCENTS THROUGH 1991 CALCULATED BY MODE OF EXPOSURE**

| Mode of Exposure | Percentage of All AIDS Cases |
|---|---|
| Men having sex with men | 58% |
| Use of injected drugs | 23% |
| Male users of injected drugs having sex with men | 6% |
| Heterosexual contact | 6% |
| Other/undetermined | 4% |
| Receipt of blood transfusion, blood components, or tissue | 2% |
| Hemophilia or blood coagulation disorders | 1% |

*Source:* Centers for Disease Control and Prevention. *HIV/AIDS Surveillance Report.* Washington, D.C.: Author, 1993

Governments throughout the world have been slow in responding to this pandemic, some believe because a disproportionate number of people with AIDS (PWAs) are members of disenfranchised groups: gay and bisexual men, drug users, people of color, poor people, and sex workers (prostitutes). People already considered outside the mainstream became further marginalized in the age of AIDS.

Public fear undermines objective medical evidence that shows that the virus is not casually transmitted. An epidemic of discrimination against people with HIV has spread: schoolchildren are prevented from attending classes, homes have been torched, airlines have refused to fly PWAs, insurance companies have refused coverage, some doctors and dentists have refused treatment to people with HIV, some religious denominations will not accept HIV-positive people into their orders, the U.S. military bans HIV-positive people, employers have fired workers, landlords have evicted tenants, some governments (including the U.S. government) ban the entry of HIV-infected persons, and some parents and friends have abandoned loved ones. Some legislators have even called for mandatory HIV testing of certain groups and/or the quarantining of PWAs.

A grass-roots advocacy movement has developed around AIDS in many countries, one that has forced a basic reexamination of the inherent inequities in the overall health care delivery system, with increasing calls for "treatment on demand" for drug users and for "universal heath care" for all.

AIDS activists—including members of direct-action groups such as ACT UP (the AIDS Coalition to Unleash Power), AIDS educators, journalists and writers, PWAs, workers in AIDS service organizations, and others—have won important victories on a number of fronts.

Activists have challenged traditional ways in which scientific inquiry is conducted and disseminated, and, more important, have redefined the very meanings of "science." The approval time for most drug therapies in the United States, for example, before the age of AIDS was between seven and ten years. Activists have pressured the Food and Drug Administration (the government agency charged with drug approval) to expedite approval for certain drug therapies and have, in effect, redefined the ways in which treatments for AIDS and other physical conditions (for example, cancer and Alzheimer's disease) are approved. In addition, community advisory boards now hold pharmaceutical companies accountable for the prices they charge.

Relationships between health care providers and the people they are meant to serve has also been altered. The new politics of science in the age of AIDS has seen those who were traditionally referred to as "patients," "victims," or "subjects" transformed into active participants who very often know as much or more than their physicians and other "experts."

The urgency of the pandemic has forced a basic reevaluation of traditional school-based sexual education programs, placing a greater emphasis on frank and honest discussions in the classroom and the availability of condoms and other birth control devices in the schools.

AIDS research and funding has implications in other areas of medicine. As researchers begin to break the AIDS code, they will begin to unlock the long-held secrets of the human immune system. This in turn will enable them to understand better the broader areas of disease and the workings of the human body. Advancements in AIDS research will translate into advancements in biomedicine and genetics and will give new impetus to research in the additional areas of human sexuality and drug dependency. —*Warren J. Blumenfeld*

**See also** Illness; Sexual stereotypes; Sexually transmitted diseases.

**Bibliography**

Blumenfeld, Warren J. *AIDS and Your Religious Community: A Hands-On Guide for Local Programs.* Boston: Unitarian Universalist Press, 1991.

Crimp, Douglas, ed. *AIDS: Cultural Analysis, Cultural Activism.* Cambridge, Mass.: MIT Press, 1988.

Kramer, Larry. *Reports from the Holocaust: The Making of an AIDS Activist.* New York: St. Martin's Press, 1989.

Nussbaum, Bruce. *Good Intentions.* New York: Penguin Books, 1990.

O'Malley, Padraig, ed. *The AIDS Epidemic: Private Rights and the Public Interest.* Boston: Beacon Press, 1989.

Patton, Cindy. *Sex and Germs: The Politics of AIDS.* Boston: South End Press, 1985.

Shilts, Randy. *And the Band Played On: Politics, People, and the AIDS Epidemic.* New York: St. Martin's Press, 1987.

## Adultery

**Type of ethics:** Personal and social ethics; Religious ethics

**Date:** From antiquity

**Definition:** Sexual relations by a married person with someone other than the spouse

**Significance:** Adultery undermines the basic social institution, the family, causing the innocent spouse and children to suffer trauma

Taboos, or at least prohibitions, against adultery exist in virtually every society, both past and present—the taboo is about as common as marriage itself.

**Differing Definitions and Punishments.** Under Mosaic law, a married man who had intercourse with a single woman was deemed not to have committed adultery, but a married woman who had sex with someone other than her spouse *was* deemed guilty. Furthermore, punishment varied according to time and place, with women usually receiving harsher "discipline" than the male. Under the Code of Hammurabi (Babylonia, eighth century B.C.E.), the punishment for adultery was death by drowning.

In ancient Greece and Rome, men were not harshly dealt with, but an offending female spouse could be punished by death. Likewise, in the Old Testament and in the Qurian, offending women were killed, while punishment for men was much less severe. Under ancient Hindu law, marriage was so sacrosanct that even a wife's adultery was *not* grounds for ending a legal union. At the time of Oliver Cromwell in England (mid-seventeenth century), authorities put adulterers to death, but afterward, under English common law, adultery was held to be a private wrong, not an indictable offense.

Among the Senoufo and Bambara peoples of West Africa, a spouse may kill his adulterous wife and her lover, but among the Kaka in Cameroon, a man may freely have sex with the wives of certain relatives without punishment. Among many South Sea islanders, as among certain Pueblo Indians, nonincestuous adultery is common and is tolerated if the actors are discreet and secretive. Wife "lending" is a common practice among the Eskimos.

**Adultery in the United States.** Although "reform" laws passed by enlightened state legislators have "softened" legal punishments for adultery, in most states the practice is still grounds for divorce, especially when combined with the "general breakdown" charge or the "mental cruelty" charge. Until recently, Virginia fined adulterers twenty dollars for the first offense, while repeat offenders could be sentenced to prison for a term of from six months up to one year. Once, Vermont's legal code held adultery to be a felony punishable by up to five years in prison—for both offenders. Various other states, such as Oklahoma, once had "alienation of affection" codes (that is, an innocent spouse could sue and collect money damages from the guilty spouse's companion, who presumedly caused such "alienation of affection"); such laws amounted to a "seduction" code for all would-be seducers of married people. Most states, however, have repealed many of the old punishments; unfortunately, incidents of adultery in the United States seem to have skyrocketed—or at least the reporting of such behavior is now more widespread than was the case previously.

**Extent of and Effects of Adultery.** Many authorities in the United States agree that approximately 50 percent of all married folk commit adultery. In addition, more commit "infidelities" that may well stop short of intercourse. Such escapades include "flirting" (done in front of the spouse to make him or her insecure and upset) and "psychic infidelity" (a man telling his mate about the beautiful secretary whom he has just hired; a woman telling her spouse about the handsome young man who is her new tennis coach).

Although most people seem to cope well with psychic infidelity, others become jealous. Jealousy leads to more and more suspicions and may also lead to vitriolic quarrels, with the result that a marriage may be permanently undermined; when the adultery is "real," the strain on a marriage becomes even more pronounced. It is, then, no surprise that the contemporary American divorce rate is close to 50 percent, the same percentage as that of adultery. In the case of a parent who commits adultery, the children may suffer most by having to cope with a broken home and by living in a poisoned atmosphere created by the adulterer.

**Exceptions.** In some cases, adultery (by dictionary definitions) may be sanctioned by certain spouses; for example, some married women (and men) become prostitutes with the approval or at least the toleration of their mates. Sometimes, married "swingers" engage in mate swapping and/or group orgies. Likewise, psychologists have reported cases wherein heterosexual couples allow each other homosexual lovers, since "real" sex would not take place. Indeed, enough mutual adultery apparently occurs that psychologists and other therapists exempt such cases from the "body count" of adultery.

**Adultery and Ethics.** Clearly, adultery often destroys families, leaving spouses and children in disaster's wake. Certainly, the practice contributes to social disorganization in the United States and elsewhere. Many analysts hold, however, that adultery does not solve the problems of the adulterer (whatever they might be); to solve those problems likely would involve hours of counseling and a look at the previous life of the perpetrator. Adultery is a moral and medical problem of the first magnitude that society should examine more closely. —*James Smallwood*

**See also** Loyalty; Marriage; Sexuality and sexual ethics.

**BIBLIOGRAPHY**

Boylan, Brian Richard. *Infidelity*. Englewood Cliffs, N.J.: Prentice-Hall, 1971.

Caprio, Frank S. *Marital Infidelity*. New York: Citadel Press, 1953.

Edwards, John N. *Sex and Society*. Chicago: Markham, 1972.

Gross, Leonard. *Sexual Issues in Marriage: A Contemporary Perspective*. New York: Spectrum, 1975.

Levitt, Shelley. "Why Men Cheat." *New Woman* 20 (October, 1990): 74.

Mason, Georgia. "Female Infidelity: May the Best Sperm Win." *New Scientist* 129 (January 19, 1991): 29.

Pittman, Frank S. *Private Lies: Infidelity and the Betrayal of Intimacy*. New York: Norton, 1990.

## Adversary system

**TYPE OF ETHICS:** Legal and judicial ethics

**ASSOCIATED WITH:** Criminal law, trial by jury, and criminal procedure

**DEFINITION:** An adversary system of law is one in which opposing parties appear before a neutral tribunal; the parties have equal rights to present evidence, examine witnesses, and compel the attendance of witnesses

**SIGNIFICANCE:** The adversary system rests on the judgment that a neutral tribunal is more likely to be fair in both criminal and civil cases than a panel of judges or other government officials would be; this is a much debated proposition, since administrative law systems exist nearly everywhere in the world other than the English-speaking countries

In the adversary system of justice, a neutral, independent judge presides over a criminal trial. The judge is said to be independent because his or her tenure does not depend on executive or legislative officials. Federal judges in the United States are appointed for life; state judges are either elected or appointed for life or for other long terms. In trials of serious crimes, moreover, defendants have the right to have the facts determined by an impartial jury of laypeople. Both the prosecution and the defense have the right to present evidence, cross- examine witnesses brought by the other side, and argue their side of the case to the fact finders. The defendant need not testify in such a trial if he or she does not wish to. In the United States and England, this form of trial is believed to be the most just.

**See also** Civil rights.

## Affirmative action

**Type of ethics:** Civil rights; Business and labor ethics

**Date:** 1965

**Definition:** Activity designed to achieve a gender and racial balance in the workplace that closely reflects the surrounding labor pool

**Significance:** Raises questions of minority vs. majority rights, reverse discrimination, and compensatory justice for current specific discrimination vs. historic general discrimination

**Milestones is Affirmative Action**

| Year | Government Action/Court Case | Impact |
|---|---|---|
| 1965 | President Lyndon Johnson signs Executive Order 11246 | Required firms doing business with the federal government in excess of $50,000/year to submit timetables and goals for diversifying their workforces |
| 1978 | *Regents of the University of California v. Bakke* | Struck down a policy that established a quota for minority admissions on the grounds that it was unfair to a qualified white applicant (reverse discrimination) |
| 1979 | *United Steelworkers of America v. Weber* | Upheld an agreement between an employer and union establishing goals for minority inclusion in a training program on the grounds that any harm done to white employees was temporary and did not create an absolute barrier to advancement |
| 1986 | *Wygant v. Jackson Board of Education* | Held that right of seniority may take precedence over affirmative action plans when workforce is reduced |
| 1991 | Civil Rights Act | Modified effects of recent Supreme Court rulings that increased burden on plaintiffs |

The first general affirmative action program mandated by the U.S. federal government was established in 1965, when President Lyndon Johnson signed Executive Order 11246, requiring that all companies of fifty employees or more and doing at least $50,000 in business with the federal government file plans stating their goals for minority hiring and stipulating how and when they would reach those goals. Affirmative action plans can also be required by courts in order to correct the wrongful treatment of protected groups and can be adopted voluntarily by employers who believe that they are appropriate social policy. Affirmative action plans necessarily bring into conflict the rights of protected minority groups and of majority groups, usually white males, especially where seniority rights are recognized. The Supreme Court has wrestled with these issues, notably in *United Steelworkers v. Weber* (1979), which found that allocating a specified number of training slots to African American employees did not impose an unreasonable hardship on the white majority; and *University of California Regents v. Bakke* (1978), which found that Bakke, a white male applicant to medical school, had been harmed by reverse discrimination.

**See also** Civil rights; Hiring practices.

## African ethics

**Type of ethics:** Beliefs and practices; Religious ethics

**Date:** c. 4000 b.c.e. to present

**Definition:** The non-Christian, non-Islamic, indigenous, and traditional African views of the natural and supernatural worlds and their effect on morality and practices

**Significance:** The traditional African approach to ethics has grown out of religious, philosophical, and cultural beliefs shared by a significant percentage of the world's population

Though Africa is made up of many countries and societies, there is a common thread that runs through the peoples' religious and philosophical concepts; it is in practicing the concepts that each society establishes its distinguishing mark. Africa is the continent where humanity first originated, and religious and philosophical ethics in Africa date back to as early as 4000 b.c.e., when the priests and inhabitants of the Nile Valley reasoned that the best way to inculcate religion and morality in the minds of the people was through drama. The priests wrote hieroglyphic texts that established the existence of gods and goddesses and pondered the moral question of human mortality by viewing death as the ascent of the soul of the dead to immortality, and by posing the possibility of the physical resurrection of the dead. That belief that the dead live has continued through the ages in various African traditional and cultural practices, including deification, reincarnation, divination, prayers, ancestral masquerades, and the cult of the living-dead. Though most African civilizations did not develop writing until they interacted with Muslim and Christian missionaries, religious and ethical ideas were passed down orally and through practice and observance from one generation to another by parents, guardians, elders, age-groups, and socioreligious institutions.

**Chain of Existence.** In 1977, the second World Black and African Festival of Arts and Culture (FESTAC '77) was held in Lagos, Nigeria. As part of the festival, a colloquium on "Black Civilization and Religion" was held and its report was published among the proceedings of the *Colloquium on Black Civilization and Education* (1977). Among other things, the report determined that belief in a universe where everything is living and strong, in the existence of two worlds of which one is visible and the other invisible, and in the interdependence of being and a fundamentally vital unity in spite of the existence of hierarchy are essential elements of doctrine in African traditional religion. It also points out that the sacred, invisible world is made up of the Supreme Being, the spirits, the ancestors, and cosmic forces. This makes possible the creation of a chain of being in the level-belief system that stretches hierarchically from the highest—that of the Supreme Being (God)—through the supernatural world of spirits (divinities, spirits per se), ancestors, and cosmic or earth forces to the mundane world of humanity and of animate and inanimate beings.

The Supreme Being, who is omniscient, omnipotent, omnipresent, and immortal, is the ultimate creator of humanity and of everything in existence. He created male and female, and the color of a Person's skin is explained by the color of clay that the Supreme Being used in fashioning him or her. To ask about the Supreme Being's origin is deemed foolish and disrespectful, and it is fundamentally assumed, not argued, that he created the universe. Because the universe is the Supreme Being's by virtue of his creating it, it is a religious universe, and no strict separation is made between sacred and secular affairs. The seal of the Supreme Being is found in the most secular and the most sacred, as is seen, for example, in the person of the monarch, who is both secular (political figure) and sacred (divine deputy with religious rights).

Next to the Supreme Being are the spirits, who are referred to as divinities, deities, or simply gods. They are the Supreme Being's associates and ministers. Some of them are dead national heros or heroines and legendary figures who have been defined and are associated with aspects of nature and of cultural life. For example, Sango (Shango) of the Yoruba people of Nigeria is the god of thunder and lightning, who represents the Supreme Beings wrath, while the Zulu of southern Africa have a goddess described as the "Queen of Heaven," from whom emanates the beauty of the rainbow; she taught women the culinary arts, feminine responsibility, and gracefulness.

There is another category of spirits, next in hierarchy to the divinities, whose members are generally called spirits. They are superhuman beings that were created to assist the deities. Some of them are human ancestors who have lost touch with their earthly lineage over the ages and have risen to the spirit status, which is higher than that of the ancestors. There are myriad spirits, some of whom inhabit trees, animals, rivers, and mountains and are generally referred to as nature spirits. Spirits can possess human beings and do possess mediums when solicited. Though invisible, they can appear to humans, especially priests, diviners, and shamans,

Ancestral spirits (simply called ancestors or the living-dead) are deceased family elders who are still fondly remembered by name and deed and are honored with libations and prayers by the living. From their spiritual abode, they participate in the affairs of their descendants. They are revered as part of the family; they protect it and are called upon as guardians of morality and as witnesses at important events such as marriages and the resolutions of family feuds. They are humanity's closest links to the supernatural world, and they demonstrate in the African tradition that there is life after death.

Usually, human beings are next in the hierarchical structure, followed by animals, plants, earth, and water. There is some fluidity here, because when animate and inanimate objects are occupied by spirits or "cosmic powers," they assume a higher position than that occupied by humanity. In ordinary life, however, human beings rank higher. A child that is being formed in the womb is considered a human being; Banyarwanda women of Rwanda believe that the Supreme Being "shapes children" in the mother's womb. The chain of being is rounded out by rain, sun, moon, stars, and other natural objects and phenomena.

Each element of the chain of being is very important to the whole, because it helps to sustain harmony. This is underscored by the fact that what brings up the rear in the chain is linked to the Supreme Being directly. The Akan people of Ghana, the Galla of Ethiopia, the Nandi of Kenya, and the Ovambo of Namibia see the sun, moon, and stars as the eyes of the Supreme Being, while the Shona of Zimbabwe view the cotton softness of the cloud as his bed.

Irreligious, immoral, and antisocial activities such as murder, ritual impurity, incestuous relationships, adultery, wanton destruction of nature, irresponsible acts, and disrespect to the elderly could create disharmony in the chain of existence. This could cause epidemics, droughts, deaths, and natural disasters if not detected and corrected. Priests and priestesses, who may combine their vocation with rainmaking, divining, mediumship, and medicine, often function to restore harmony.

**The Orderly Universe.** John S. Mbiti has shown that Africans view the universe as one of harmony, order, and logic and that this orderliness comes from and is maintained by the Supreme Being. Natural laws govern everything. Among human beings there are moral and religious orders. It is believed that the Supreme Being instituted the moral order. The Zulu, Nuer, Ila, Lugbara, Nuba, Etsako, and Edo peoples believe that the Supreme Being established their customs, laws, and regulations so that people could live in harmony with one another and know what is right and wrong as they live a dutiful and responsible life.

Because the universe is created by the Supreme Being, it is necessarily imbued with a religious order. It is directly or

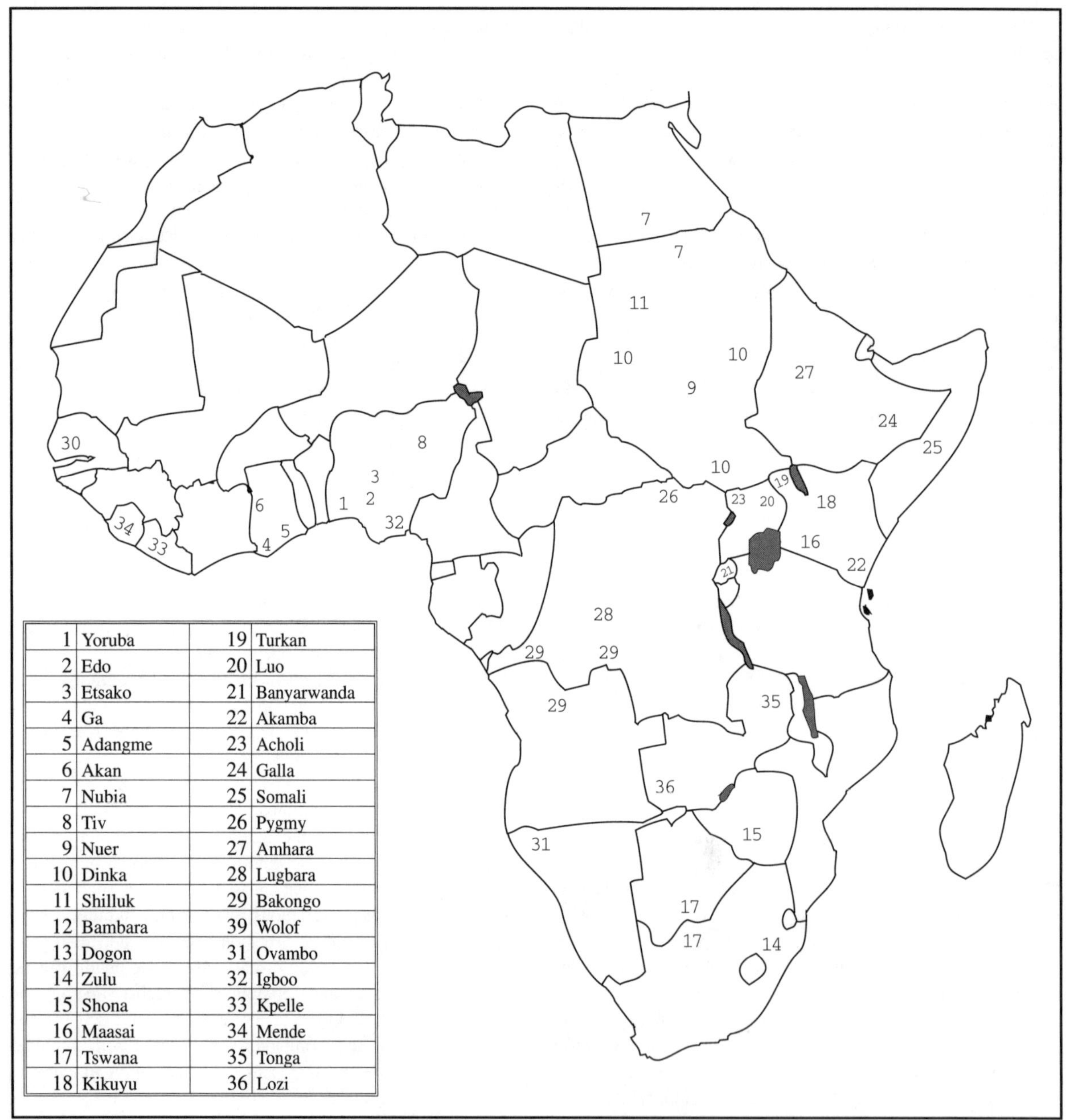


*Map of Africa showing some societies*

indirectly (through social institutions, sanctions, and natural law) controlled by him. Through prayers, ceremonies, rituals, blessings, sacred places, objects, and personages, humanity actively engages the religious order of the universe.

Africans also believe that there is a mystical order or power that is closely linked to the religious order of the universe because it comes from the Supreme Being; it can be tapped into by spirits and by some human beings. The order shows itself in the ability of some Africans to predict events accurately, to perform miracles and wonders, to be telepathic, and to ward off evil. It can also be negatively used to bring misfortune and harm to people and property. Africans believe in the reality of witches and sorcerers, and especially in their power to bring illness, infertility, suffering, failure, death, and general calamity. Their power comes from tapping into the mystical force of the universe and directing that energy toward evil deeds.

Though humanity is at the center of the African concept of the universe, the human being is not seen as the master of nature. The human being is simply nature's friend and the recipient of its riches which he or she must use judiciously. Humans are required to live harmoniously with the universe by obeying its natural, moral, and mystical laws. Humankind suffers when this harmony is upset.

**Corporate Values.** African religious and ethical behavior seem to be guided by the following philosophy: "I am because we are, and since we are, therefore I am." The individual does not exist except in a corporate manner. Each person exists because of other people, including that person's family and people of past and contemporary generations. Being a part of the whole, the individual is a product of the community and necessarily depends on it. In no better way is this corporate nature of the African society depicted than in rites of passage that are communally observed as one goes through birth, initiation (maturity), marriage, old age, and death. These changes that an individual goes through are regarded as challenging, upsetting, and at times dangerous to social and individual life. African rites of passage help to "cushion the disturbance," to ease the pains and difficulties that occur in the society's or the individual's transition from one status to another. Initiation rites provide an excellent example.

Among the Akamba people of Kenya, the first stage of initiation rites involves circumcision for boys and clitoridectomy for girls: The foreskin of the penis and a tiny portion of the clitoris are excised. As a group act, the rites are performed the same day in the same place. The activity symbolizes separation from childhood, just as the ritual cutting and disposal of the umbilical cord at birth symbolize mother-baby separation and the acknowledgment that the child belongs to the corporate society represented then by the family, and not only to the mother's family. Anyone who does not go through this first stage of initiation rites, even when he or she attains maturity, age, and position, is communally despised and regarded as a baby in most, if not all, African societies.

It is the belief among the Akamba that ritually cutting the skin from one's sexual organ moves the individual from the state of sexual dormancy and ignorance to one of action and knowledge, and therefore to the crucial stage of sexual reproduction, which, keeps the lineage and society going. The blood shed on Earth during the excision mystically forms a bond of unity between the initiates and the ancestors. The accompanying pains prepare the initiates for the pain, suffering, and difficulty they will inevitably encounter. They are encouraged to endure such discomforts and to overcome them instead of despairing. The reason that the initiation is a group act is to encourage the participants to seek help and solace from others when they encounter difficult times. A person can bear much suffering when he or she realizes there are people who will help. The initiates are then given presents an introduction to keeping and owning property. There is general merriment and dancing to emphasize communal solidarity. The initiates, for the first time in their lives, are officially allowed to join in public dances.

The second stage of initiation, which follows years later, is meant to help the initiates as they approach full maturity. The ceremony lasts about a week, during which time the initiates are sequestered in huts built outside the village and away from public interaction. Accompanied by watchful older people, the youths are taught all they need to know concerning womanhood and manhood. The process is referred to as "brooding over the initiates." They learn educational songs, are tested for bravery, and are taught the roles they are expected to play as adults and as future married people and parents. They are taught dances that symbolically imitate the performance of sexual acts. They also learn moral and corporate responsibilities, and are reminded of their religious obligations. They have full access to the wisdom of the elders and the secrets of their society. When they emerge from their seclusion on the last day, they are recognized in the society as people who may legally and morally establish families, and who are capable of protecting themselves, their dependents, and their society. A new generation capable of carrying on the life of the community thus comes into being, and the community is assured of immortality.

The maturity of those who emerge from the Akamba initiation rites helps to prevent the unhappy syndrome of "babies producing babies." When they eventually marry, they are responsibly fulfilling an African corporate requirement that ties marriage to procreation. To the African, marriage without procreation is incomplete. Humanity, through marriage and procreation, tries to recapture the lost gift of immortality, since husband and wife reproduce themselves in their children and by so doing perpetuate not only their family lineage but also the chain of humanity. In his *African Religions and Philosophy* (1990), Mbiti hits the mark when he points out that marriage is viewed in the African society as a "rhythm of life" that involves everyone. Anyone ignoring participation in it is a "curse to the community" and a rebellious lawbreaker. It is an immoral act to reject the society, and society is bound in turn to reject the person who does so.

The importance of marriage is underscored by the fact that it involves the entire family, all of whose members must give support and approval. Female virginity at the time of marriage is highly prized and rewarded. Monogamy and polygamy—especially polygyny—are legitimate; a widow may be remarried to a male adult member of the family of the deceased husband, who then assumes full responsibility for her and the children she brings along. Bride price and dowry are important parts of the custom: They symbolize the value and importance placed on the women as a person and as a wife, and they are a constant reminder that the bride and the groom are together under some mutual agreement between their families. They cannot simply terminate their marriage on their own, because people other than themselves are involved.

**Traditional Enforcement of Morality.** In an African

society in which traditions and customs have not been replaced by Christian and Islamic customs, people owe allegiance to a common founding ancestor and are bound by common hopes and fears and destiny. The social structure helps in the formulation and enforcement of moral ideals and ethical standards. Factors that determine morality in such a society include religious beliefs; practices and taboos; the desire for communal solidarity; the influence of proverbs, folk stories, and wise sayings; and the experiences, common sense, and conscience of the individual and of the group. Though each person regards himself or herself in some form of relationship to the other, human passions and interests do come into conflict, leading some members of the society to flout established norms. The enforcement of morality then becomes important. The examples listed have come from the religious and social methods used by the Ga and Adangme of Ghana, though similar methods are found among the Etsako, Ishan, Edo, and Yoruba peoples of Nigeria.

J. N. Kudadjie of the University of Ghana, Legon, points out that people's beliefs about the Supreme Being, the divinities, the spirits, and the ancestors are used to enforce morality. "The promise and expectation, coupled with actual experience, of the blessing and protection of the Supreme God and the other spirit-powers for those who kept the moral code, on the one hand, and the fear and threat, coupled with actual experience, of punishment and desertion by the spirit-powers kept people doing what was right and avoiding what was wrong." The practice of the religious and magical "cursing" of an offender in which supernatural agencies bring harm, misfortune, or even strange death to the culprit or his or her family keeps people on the right path. Even marital infidelity is checked through the curse, whose punishments for adulterers include barrenness and impotence, the inability to leave the scene of adultery or to disengage the sexual organs, insanity, incurable physical illness, and sudden death. In entrances to farms and homes, magical objects are buried, hung, or displayed to warn people that they will not go undetected and unpunished for any crime they may commit when the owner of the property is not present: The gods, spirits, ancestors, and mystical forces are ever-present law-enforcement agents.

Positive social sanctions such as parental gifts to a good, reliable, and well-behaved child; admission of the young to the presence of elders where they are given secret knowledge of herbs, spiritual powers, and activities well beyond their age; and the award of honors, chieftaincy, titles, and property are used by the society to reward people who have distinguished themselves. These sanctions are meant to "encourage and give incentive to the good life."

There are also negative sanctions that are meant to discourage unethical behavior. A family may hold a special meeting to correct a notoriously wayward member. If the person persists in bad behavior, the family severs all ties with him or her, including such family occasions as marriage, birth, and death. A family may even disinherit a member who brings material and spiritual disgrace to it. Initiates are made to swear oaths regarding specific things they should or should not do; the ancestors are invoked as witnesses. Other social sanctions include invoking a parental curse banning a disobedient and immoral child from attending the parent's funeral; ostracizing sorcerers, witches, hardened criminals, and morally perverse individuals from the society or excluding them from social intercourse; publicly disgracing a person by having his or her bad deeds announced or sung at public festivals and social gatherings; and finally, in extreme cases, making those considered "destroyers of society" to "disappear." At least once a year, in some societies, a day is set aside in which the traditional ruler is publicly insulted for various acts of inefficiency; the idea is to make him correct his mistakes and be a better leader. Formerly, in some African societies, such as the Banyoro, Shona, Luvedu, Amhara, and Yoruba, a bad ruler was ritually killed, usually through poisoning. In traditional African societies, it is not so much the physical punishments that keep people observing the moral codes as it is the threat of disgrace to one's self, family, relatives, friends, future and present offspring, and ancestors.

**Changing Africa.** Colonialism, Christianity, and Islam have also had an impact on Africa, contributing to new forms of religious and philosophical ethics. In the cities where these religions are most successful, traditional African ethics have been undermined and are practiced secretly. One interesting phenomenon is the emergence of new Christian and Islamic religious movements founded by Africans that merge aspects of the imported religions with aspects of African belief and cultural systems to form new distinctly syncretist African religious and philosophical ethics. Among such movements are the Falasha (Beta Israel) movement of Ethiopia, the Mahdist movement of Sudan, the Mourides (Islamic Brotherhood) movement of Senegal, the Kimbanguist movement of Zaire, the Zulu Zionist movement of South Africa, the Aladura movement of Nigeria, and the Eden Revival movement of Ghana. Behind these movements is an undying respect and a yearning for the traditional African moral universe, and in them the old gods and spirits are revitalized, not displaced, by the new ones. It is a dynamic universe.

*—I. Peter Ukpokodu*

**See also** Colonialism and imperialism; Family values; God; Guilt and shame; Honor; Moral education; Moral principles, rules, and imperatives; Morality; Multiculturalism; Natural law; Pan-Africanism; Pantheism; Religion; Right and wrong; Social justice and responsibility; Taboos; Values; Vice; *The Wretched of the Earth.*

**BIBLIOGRAPHY**

Adegbola, E. A. Ade, ed. *Traditional Religion in West Africa.* Ibadan, Nigeria: Daystar Press, 1983. An illustrated collection of essays on religious personalities, rites of passage, festivals, morality, mythology, and the concepts of humanity and God. Some comparison with world religions.

Bohannan, Paul, and Philip Curtin. *Africa and Africans.* 3d ed. Prospect Heights, Ill.: Waveland Press, 1988. Focuses on Africa in general, covering the people, institutions, and history; contains good maps and photographs.

Chidester, David. *Religions of South Africa.* London: Routledge, 1992. A comparative study of different religions in South Africa; particularly rich in its treatment of independent churches and their relationship to traditional religious practices.

Joint Symposium of Philosophers from Africa and from The Netherlands. *I, We and Body.* Edited by Heinz Kimmerle Amsterdam: Verlag B. R. Grunner, 1989. Various scholars of African philosophy, anthropology, and theology discuss the individual and the community in African thought, the perception of reality, and the notion of time, among other things. Examples are drawn from many African peoples: Dogon, Lingala, Akan, Turkana, Massai, Yoruba, Kikuyu, and Nuer.

Jules-Rosette, Bennetta, ed. *The New Religions of Africa.* Norwood, N.J.: Ablex, 1979. Various academic essays discuss the role of African religions in cultural transformation and the relationships between men and women in them; important in its treatment of new religions that are usually left out of other works.

Kamalu, Chukwunyere. *Foundations of African Thought.* London: Karnak House, 1990. A well-documented, illustrated book that discusses numerous aspects of African thought from the earliest times. Origins; being; ethics; arts and sciences; and ancient Egyptian, Dogon, and Bambara cosmology are among the many topics treated.

King, Noel Q. *African Cosmos.* Belmont, Calif.: Wadsworth, 1986. Presents some of "Africa's deepest wisdom" as an attempt to know the world better. The religious worlds of various African peoples—Dinka, Acholi, Nubia, Yoruba, Akan, and the Bantu-language groups—are presented along with Christianity and Islam.

Mbiti, John S. *African Religions and Philosophy.* 2d rev. ed. Portsmouth, N.H.: Heinemann, 1990. A comprehensive study of traditional religion in Africa and its supporting philosophy. African cosmology, rites of passage, witchcraft, ethics, sacred officials, and the presence of Judaism, Christianity, and Islam in Africa are among the topics examined. A valuable book that should be read by scholars and laypersons alike.

Parrinder, Edward Geoffrey. *African Traditional Religion.* 3d ed. London: Sheldon Press, 1974. A valuable, accessible book that shows, by describing and analyzing religious pantheons, social groups, and spiritual forces, that knowing African religion is essential to understanding the motive forces of African life.

Wiredu, Kwasi. *Philosophy and an African Culture.* Cambridge, England: Cambridge University Press, 1980. Using Ghanaian traditional culture, Wiredu's philosophical analysis tries to distinguish those aspects of African traditional culture that are worth preserving from those that should be discarded; also examines African philosophy vis-à-vis Western thought.

## Ageism

**TYPE OF ETHICS:** Older persons' rights

**DATE:** Coined 1969

**DEFINITION:** Ageism consists of either prejudice or discrimination against a particular age group, and generally involves the promotion of false stereotypes about the members of that group

**SIGNIFICANCE:** An ethic of justice calls for the elimination of ageism, since age discrimination inhibits the fair and accurate determination of each person's true potential

Although certain age groups have always been subjected to unfair treatment, the concept of ageism, or age discrimination, is a relatively recent one. Robert Butler, the first director of the National Institute on Aging, introduced the term "ageism" in 1969. Butler used this term to describe systematic prejudice or discrimination against the elderly. Butler believed that a pervasive youth culture had developed in the United States in which old people were frequently devalued and denigrated. Although the term "ageism" is still used primarily to describe society's negative view of the elderly, most social scientists now believe that other age groups, such as that of young children, can also be subject to ageism. Most contemporary social ethicists define ageism as prejudice or discrimination against any group of individuals on the basis of chronological age.

**Discrimination Against the Elderly.** Though any age group can be subject to unfair treatment, prejudice against the elderly appears to be the strongest form of ageism in the United States. Many researchers have discovered pervasive but erroneous beliefs that all old people are senile, cranky, physically unattractive, weak, and without sexual desire. Erdman Palmore, a sociologist and authority on aging, has suggested that many Americans have an extremely stereotyped view of the elderly in which old people are seen as useless individuals who place both an emotional and financial burden on the rest of society. Palmore believes that the numerous derogatory terms that are used to describe the elderly, such as " coot," "geezer," "old hag," "old buzzard," and "over the hill," are merely a reflection of the negative view that many Americans have toward elderly individuals.

Such terms fly in the face of research conducted by gerontologists, who study aging and the needs of the elderly. In a review of research on the aged, psychologist David Myers concluded in 1992 that many elderly individuals are physically healthy, socially active, and mentally alert. Although most individuals experience some decline in mental and physical abilities with advancing age, the vast majority of older adults remain capable of living happy and productive lives. Stereotypical beliefs about the frail and lonely elderly are often based on worst-case scenarios, and they should not be applied to the whole population of aged individuals.

**Practical Concerns.** In addition to developing a poor self-image because of the negative social stereotypes that abound in our society, many elderly individuals experience discrimination in practical matters as well. Perhaps the most blatant example of this is the common practice of mandatory retirement at age sixty-five, which forces many older adults to stop working when they are still competent and talented. While many organizations have begun to question this practice, it is still common for healthy individuals to be forced from their professions simply because of their chronological age.

In the past, many elderly individuals have suffered from not only forced retirement but also poverty and poor medical care. By joining forces, senior citizens have made significant progress in overcoming these difficulties. Groups such as the Amerićan Association of Retired Persons, the National Council of Senior Citizens, and the more radical Gray Panthers have lobbied to improve the fate of older adults. A number of factors, such as the Social Security Act of 1935, subsequent cost-of-living increases in Social Security benefits, and the accumulation of individual assets through home mortgages have gradually improved the economic status of older Americans. Senior citizens no longer constitute the poorest age group in American society.

In addition to financial gains, senior citizens have benefited from programs such as the Medicare Act of 1965, which provided basic medical care for all older Americans. Unfortunately, this act did not extend medical benefits to other members of the population. Some theorists, such as gerontologist Richard Kalish, have argued that special programs for the elderly create a "new ageism." Kalish believes that programs such as Medicare, which provide the elderly with special benefits, promote a new ageism by reinforcing the notion that old people are weak and ineffective and need the rest of society to care for them.

**Discrimination Against Children.** Other theorists have also suggested that society must redefine the standard notion of ageism to include any age group that lives in a disadvantaged position. In particular, scholars concerned with social justice have pointed out that young children now constitute the poorest age group in the United States, with approximately one-fifth living below the federal poverty level. Many children lack basic necessities such as adequate nutrition and proper medical care. Social critics such as Marian Wright Edelman, the director of the Children's Defense Fund, have argued that society devalues children and considers them to be unimportant because they are young.

Whether ageism affects children or the elderly, this form of discrimination always causes an ethical dilemma. Ageism contradicts America's democratic ideals of fairness and equal treatment for all. A society that strives to promote justice must treat people in an equitable fashion, regardless of their chronological age. —*Steven C. Abel*

**See also** Children's rights; Civil rights; Discrimination; Gray Panthers; Prejudice.

**BIBLIOGRAPHY**

Barrow, Georgia, and Paula Smith. *Aging, Ageism, and Society*. St. Paul, Minn.: West, 1979.

Butler, Robert. *Why Survive? Being Old in America*. New York: Harper & Row, 1975.

Friedan, Betty. *The Fountain of Age*. New York: Simon & Schuster, 1993.

Levin, Jack, and William C. Levin. *Ageism: Prejudice and Discrimination Against the Elderly*. Belmont, Calif.: Wadsworth, 1980.

Palmore, Erdman. *Ageism: Negative and Positive*. New York: Springer, 1990.

Rosenthal, Evelyn R., ed. *Women, Aging, and Ageism*. Binghamton, N.Y.: Haworth Press, 1990.

## Aggression

**TYPE OF ETHICS:** Theory of ethics

**ASSOCIATED WITH:** John Dollard, who developed the frustration-aggression hypothesis in 1939

**DEFINITION:** Any behavior that is intended to harm someone, either physically or verbally

**SIGNIFICANCE:** Violence in Western society is an intractable social ill; there are more than 685,000 violent assaults and 18,000 killings in the United States each year

Hostile aggression is intended solely to hurt another person. Instrumental aggression is intended to achieve some goal. Aggression generally declines with age, and changes in form as it does so. Younger children display more instrumental aggression; older children, more hostile aggression. With age, aggression tends to become less physical and more verbal.

Instinct theories are proposed as one cause of aggression. The Viennese psychoanalyst Sigmund Freud proposed that aggression is an instinct that gradually builds. He thought that the drive to return to an inanimate, lifeless state conflicted with the pleasure drive and was satisfied by being turned outward. The result was aggression toward others. If this drive turned inward for some reason, the person would become suicidal. Another proponent of an instinctive theory of aggression, ethologist Konrad Lorenz, argued that aggression is adaptive for animals, so it is the natural product of evolution. Although all animals, including humans, have an aggressive instinct, most have "built-in safety devices" such as exposing their throats to signal submission. Unlike Freud, however, Lorenz suggested that an environmental stimulus must be present in addition to the genetic predisposition. Studies of identical twins support the theory that there is a genetic or instinctive component to aggression. For example, identical twins are more similar to each other than fraternal twins are to each other in terms of measures of aggression.

Biological theories seek to identify the biological structures or processes responsible for the expression of aggression. Numerous areas of the brain influence aggression. Lesions of the septum, hypothalamus, amygdala, and related areas in lower animals are followed by defensive aggression. Mild electrical stimulation of a specific region of the hypothalamus produces aggressive, even deadly, behavior in animals. Hormones also influence aggression. Injections of the masculine hormone testosterone increase aggression in animals; criminals with higher testosterone levels commit crimes that are more violent than those committed by criminals with lower levels of testosterone. Neurotransmitters play a role in aggression as well. Aggression is associated with high levels of adrenaline and noradrenaline and low levels of serotonin. Thus, experimental evidence supports biological theories of aggression.

Learning theories explain aggression in terms of learning principles, noting that in two specific ways learning shapes aggression. First, aggression is learned by watching others (modeling). For example, in classic experiments with children and Bobo dolls, Albert Bandura and his colleagues found that the amount of violent content watched on television by eight-year-olds predicts aggressiveness in these children even ten years later. Further, children will imitate the behavior of live models, filmed humans, and cartoon characters all to about the same degree. Second, aggression depends greatly on the pattern of rewards and punishments that a person has received. People become more aggressive when they are positively reinforced for aggression and less aggressive when they are punished for aggression. Experimental support exists for learning theories of aggression, just as it does for instinctive and biological theories.

Emotional factors exist in aggression. One such emotional factor is frustration. Dollard's 1939 frustration-aggression hypothesis proposed that whenever a person's effort to reach any goal is blocked, an aggressive drive is induced that motivates behavior that is intended to injure the obstacle (person or object) that causes the frustration. Thus, frustration causes aggression and aggression is always a consequence of frustration. Leonard Berkowitz's 1981 modification of the hypothesis proposed that frustration produces a readiness toward aggression. Then, cues in the environment that are associated with aggression often lead a frustrated person toward aggression. Also, unexpected failure at some task creates a more intense reaction than does expected failure, and intentional attempts to annoy a person are more provocative than are unintentional acts. Research has supported Berkowitz's modification of the frustration-aggression hypothesis and the learning theory of aggression.

Another emotional factor in aggression is arousal. Transferred excitation is arousal from one experience that is carried over to an independent situation. For example, a person who was excited after riding a Ferris wheel would probably be more aggressive when struck than a person who was bored after reading an article about gardening would be. Generalized arousal alone does not lead to aggression. Rather, aggression occurs when the situation contains some reason, opportunity, or target for aggression.

Situational factors influence aggression. One situational factor is aggression itself. Participating in aggressive activities either increases aggression or maintains it at the same levels. For example, individuals who are given repeated opportunities to shock another person who cannot retaliate become more and more aggressive. Those who are angry react even more strongly. Thus, aggression breeds aggression rather than dissipates it, which provides an argument against catharsis as a value of watching television violence.

Other situational factors that influence aggression are temperature, noise, exposure to erotic stimuli, the presence of weapons, and deindividuation (loss of all concern for oneself as an individual and a focus instead on the present environment with little thought of past or future). When people are exposed to high temperatures, noisy environments, weapons, or erotic stimuli, they as a rule become more aggressive. As they become deindividuated by being lost in crowds, for example, they exhibit behaviors—such as aggression—that they would ordinarily inhibit. This principle explains the tendency for crowds to yell "Jump!" to a suicidal person on a high ledge. Overall, aggression has instinctive, biological, learning, emotional, and situational components.

Also, gender influences aggression. Boys are more aggressive than girls and are more affected by violence than girls. Boys who are low achievers and are unpopular at school are more likely than other boys to imitate aggression on television. Young males, who have the highest levels of testosterone, are most likely to be violent. Women behave as aggressively as men, however, when they are alone or when urged on by another person. —*Lillian Range*

**See also** Abuse; Anger; Child abuse; Genocide; Milgram experiment; Sexual abuse and harassment.

**Bibliography**

Deffenbacher, Jerry L., et al. "Cognitive-Relaxation and Social Skills Interventions in the Treatment of General Anger." *Journal of Counseling Psychology* 34, no. 2 (April, 1987): 171-176.

Grobel, Jo, and Robert A. Hinde, eds. *Aggression and War: Their Biological and Social Bases*. New York: Cambridge University Press, 1989.

Tavris, Carol. *Anger: The Misunderstood Emotion*. New York: Simon & Schuster, 1982.

Wood, Wendy, Frank Y. Wong, and Gregory J. Chachere. "Effects of Media Violence on Viewers' Aggression in Unconstrained Social Interaction." *Psychological Bulletin* 109, no. 3 (May, 1991): 371-383.

## Agreement for the Suppression of White Slave Traffic

**Type of ethics:** Sex and gender issues

**Date:** 1904

**Associated with:** Prostitution

**Definition:** The agreement committed thirteen nations, including the United States, to investigate and halt white slavery

**Significance:** This agreement, the first international accord on the issue of prostitution, marked the first time that men in power viewed prostitutes as potential victims

In most European countries, prostitution has long been considered a social evil, but it was generally tolerated through the nineteenth century. The early twentieth century brought a dramatic increase in young women migrating from one country to another to work as prostitutes. Many of them were brought to prostitution through deceptive offers for employment, or kidnapping, or even sale by their parents. These women became known as "white slaves." Government officials came to believe that the only way to stop the exploitation of young girls and women was to stop prostitution altogether. In 1904, France invited other nations to a conference; there, the International Agreement for the Suppression of White Slave Traffic was signed by thirteen nations. The signatory nations agreed to stop prostitution on their own soil and to share information with other countries. Late twentieth century critics of this and other antiprostitution legislation have argued that these laws do not take into account that many prostitutes—like their clients—have chosen their careers freely and have a right to do so.

**See also** Sexuality and sexual ethics; Slavery; Women's ethics.

## Ahiṁsā

**TYPE OF ETHICS:** Religious ethics

**DATE:** Attested in Chāndogya Upaniṣad, eighth to seventh century B.C.E.

**ASSOCIATED WITH:** Hinduism, Buddhism, and Jainism

**DEFINITION:** Doctrine of nonkilling or noninjury to living beings: Ahiṁsā is a compound that combines the word for injury (hiṁs) and the alpha privative

**SIGNIFICANCE:** A basic principle in Indian thought, ahiṁsā has influenced such behavior as vegetarian diet and pacifism; it served as the foundation for Gandhi's view of nonviolent resistance

The idea of noninjury appeared first in the Chāndogya Upaniṣad, which described the enlightened person as one who was nonviolent toward all things except the victim; that is, the victim of the Vedic sacrifice. The contradiction between noninjury and sacrifice led Hinduism to abandon such rituals in favor of knowledge. Noninjury also influenced Hindu thinking about warfare. The Bhagavad Gītā argued that since fighting belonged to the duties of the warrior caste, warriors could not avoid killing; however, they should fight without malice or desire. Mohandas K. Gandhi reinterpreted noninjury by incorporating it into his political program of nonviolent resistance. In Buddhism, the concept of ahiṁsā constitutes the first of five precepts or vows taken both by laypeople and monks, which is to abstain from taking life. That view precluded the devout Buddhist's eating meat or engaging in violent occupations. Jainism also demanded noninjury as the first of its Five Great Vows and extended it to preclude even unintentional injury to insects by accidentally swallowing or stepping on them.

**See also** Buddhist ethics; Hindu ethics; Jain ethics; Karma; Pacifism.

## Akbar, Jalâl al-Dîn (Oct. 15, 1542, Umarkot, Sind—1605, Āgra, India): Emperor

**TYPE OF ETHICS:** Religious ethics

**ACHIEVEMENTS:** Solidified the Mogul Empire in the Indian subcontinent and introduced his own religion

**SIGNIFICANCE:** Introduced a new religion that combined elements of Hinduism and Islam

The longest reigning Mogul emperor of India, Akbar, also known as Akbar the Great, was a man of great talent. He became the emperor of India at the age of fourteen. Despite the fact that he did not receive any formal education, Akbar acquired knowledge by having books read to him and through discussions among scholars belonging to different religions, including Christians, Zoroastrians, Hindus and Jains. He hosted several religious scholars belonging to different religions to acquire knowledge of these religions, and he held debates with them. He invited Portuguese missionaries to his court and discussed the Jesuit faith at length with them. Although Akbar became disillusioned by Islam and is said to have renounced it completely, he did not formally join any other religion. One of his concerns was to create harmony among the majority Hindu populations of India and the Muslims, who formed a small minority. One of the most important steps that he took in this regard was to repeal a religious tax called jizya, which all non-Muslims paid in exchange for protection. He also married into prominent Hindu families to forge close ties with the Hindus. Finally, he introduced his own religion, "Din-e-Ilahi," which sought to combine elements of the various religions to which he had been introduced over time. The divinity of the king was central to this new religion. Other important milestones of his reign were introduction of an elaborate revenue system, the introduction of land rights, and the creation of a civil bureaucracy to run the government.

**See also** Aśoka; Christian ethics; Hindu ethics; Islamic ethics; Jain ethics; Zoroastrian ethics.

## ʿAlî ibn Abî Ṭâlib (c. 600, Mecca, Arabia—661, Kufa, Iraq): Caliph

**TYPE OF ETHICS:** Religious ethics

**ACHIEVEMENTS:** Last of the four caliphs of Islam after the death of the Prophet Muḥammad

**SIGNIFICANCE:** One of the first converts to Islam, ʿAlî was a brave warrior and a scholar; Shiʿites contend that ʿAlî should have been chosen as the first caliph after the death of Muḥammad

**ʿAlî's Life.** ʿAlî, a first cousin of Muḥammad and later his son-in-law, was the youngest of the first three persons to convert to Islam. When ʿAlî's father, Abû Ṭalib, became unable to care for his son because of ill health and poverty, Muḥammad allowed ʿAlî to live with him. Muḥammad was returning a favor to Abû Ṭâlib, who had taken care of Muḥammad after the death of Muḥammad's grandfather, with whom Muḥammad had lived in his youth. Alî was only ten years old when Muḥammad declared his prophecy. The followers of the Shīʿite sect of Islam believe that ʿAlî was the first person to convert to Islam. Sunnis, however, believe that Khadîja, Muḥammad's first wife, was the first Islamic convert and that Abû Bakr was the second. During the difficult early period of Islamic history, ʿAlî stayed by Muḥammad's side as he struggled to spread the new religion.

ʿAlî is considered to be one of the most important persons in early Islamic history, because of his qualities as a warrior, a statesman, and a person with immense knowledge of Islam as a result of his close association with Muḥammad. Muḥammad entrusted ʿAlî with many important missions; for example, he used ʿAlî as a decoy when he escaped to Medina. It is popularly believed that Muḥammad would ask ʿAlî to take charge of battles when no one else could bring victory to the Islamic forces. ʿAlî is said to have possessed a magical sword given to him by Muḥammad that he used in battle and to have been able to subdue many warriors single-handedly. He is also revered for his patronage of the arts and sciences and for his alleged special insight and knowledge that ordinary humans did not possess. In the South Asian subcontinent, Sufis seek endorsement from ʿAlî for their beliefs. His wisdom was valued greatly by the first three caliphs, who sought advice from him regarding both religion and politics. Muḥammad is believed to have said that he himself was the city of knowledge and that Alî was the door to the city.

ʿAlî was chosen as caliph after ʿUthmân, the third caliph, was assassinated by those who claimed that ʿUthmân was guilty of favoritism toward his Banu Umayya clan. Rebellious forces from Egypt attacked and killed ʿUthmân. After ʿAlî became caliph, a rebellion against him was led by Aʿisha, the widow of the Prophet Muḥammad, who demanded swift punishment for those who had killed ʿUthmân. ʿAlî defeated Aʿisha and her followers, but his authority was seriously challenged by Amir Muʿawiyya, a relative of ʿUthmân's and governor of Syria. Muʿawiyya said that he would not recognize ʿAlî as caliph until those who killed ʿUthmân were punished. In fact, Muʿawiyya wished to lead the Muslim community himself. A battle between the two ensued, and although ʿAlî's forces were superior to his opponent's, Muʿawiyya tricked ʿAlî into accepting a truce. At that time, some of ʿAlî's followers deserted him and elected their own leader, which weakened ʿAlî's position. ʿAlî was assassinated in 661. Muʿawiyya foiled all attempts by ʿAlî's followers to appoint ʿAlî's son Ḥasan to lead the Muslim community. Muʿawiyya established himself as the leader of the Muslim community but never officially received the title of caliph. After Muʿawiyya's death, his son Yazid became the leader of the Muslims. At that time, ʿAlî's second and best-known son, Ḥusayn, challenged Yazid's authority. Ḥusayn's followers believed that he was the rightful heir to the seat that had belonged to ʿAlî, but Ḥusayn was defeated and killed in a battle with Yazid's forces near Karbala in present-day Iraq. This incident had a major impact on the subsequent history of Islam. Those who belong to the Shîʿa sect revere Ḥusayn as a martyr and a true hero of Islam. The death of Ḥusayn precipitated the schism between Sunnî and Shîʿa Muslims, who now have distinctly different interpretations of Islam and the teachings of Muḥammad. The death of Ḥusayn in Karbala is commemorated each year for ten days throughout the Muslim world, particularly in areas where the Shîʿites are in the majority.

**ʿAlî's Legacy.** Shîʿites believe that ʿAlî and his family were the rightful successors of the Prophet Muḥammad and that the first three caliphs conspired to deny ʿAlî the caliphate. The Sunnîs claim, however, that those caliphs took power because of their personal ability and their knowledge of Islam. ʿAlî actually had no desire to become caliph; he was too busy making arrangements for Muḥammad's burial to attend the assembly at which the successor was chosen. During ʿAlî's rule as caliph, clan rivalries began that pitted the Banu Umayya against the Banu Ḥashim, Muḥammad's clan, which ultimately led to ʿAlî's assassination and the victory of the Banu Umayya. ʿAlî and, later, his sons Ḥasan and Ḥusayn commanded a large, faithful group of followers, whose cause ultimately led to the emergence of the Shîʿite sect. Shîʿites believe that God sent imams to lead the Muslim community after the deaths of Muḥammad and ʿAlî. They believe that Ḥasan, ʿAlî's son, was the first imam. The last imam, it is believed, vanished at the age of three and will return again as the savior who will rescue the world and restore the glory of God and Islam.

*—Khalid N. Mahmood*

**See also** Islamic ethics; Muḥammad al-Muṣṭafâ; Shîʿa; Sunnîs.

**BIBLIOGRAPHY**

Momen, Moojan. An Introduction to Shiʿi Islam: The History and Doctrines of Twelver Shiʿism. New Haven, Conn.: Yale University Press, 1985.

Muir, William. The Caliphate: Its Rise, Decline, and Fall. Beirut, Lebanon: Khayats, 1963.

Nasr, Seyyed Hossein Hamid Dabashi, and Seyyed Vali Reza Nasr, eds. Shiʿism: Doctrines, Thought, and Spirituality. Albany, N.Y.: State University of New York Press, 1988.

Pinault, David. The Shiites: Ritual and Popular Piety in a Muslim Community. New York: St. Martin's Press, 1992.

## Alienation

**TYPE OF ETHICS:** Personal and social ethics

**DATE:** 1807

**ASSOCIATED WITH:** Hegelianism and Marxism

**DEFINITION:** Fundamentally, alienation denotes a separation between what the self is and what the self ought to be

**SIGNIFICANCE:** Alienation raises questions about the fundamental nature of human beings and the relationship that ought to exist between the self and society

Semantically considered, alienation may be understood as a

sense of loss, separation, estrangement, or self-denial. Metaphysically, alienation refers to a state of affairs in which the self suffers either from an internal split in the psyche or from an external separation from society. There are, therefore, two fundamental forms of alienation. Its corollary term, "de-alienation" refers to the process by which alienation is overcome. Jean-Jacques Rousseau, Georg Wilhelm Friedrich Hegel, and Karl Marx understood alienation, fundamentally, as an external split between the self and society. De-alienation, implied in this point of view, would consist of a social transformation resulting in an accord between self-determination and social conformity. Sigmund Freud, however, described alienation as an internal split. Following this line of thought, de-alienation would primarily consist of a pyschological process of restoring wholeness to the self.

**Social Contract Theory.** Jean-Jacques Rousseau employed the term "alienation" in On the Social Contract. Rousseau contended that society corrupted human beings by separating them from their natural state. He is widely remembered for his famous epigram: "Man is born free but everywhere he is in chains."

Rousseau grappled with the following problem: How can human beings form a society in which sovereignty would be legitimate yet in which the governed would not lose their autonomy or alienate their freedom? He believed that he found the solution in the social contract. In order to form a social contract, each person would alienate his or her rights to the entire community, to the general will. Such alienation would not entail the loss of autonomy or liberty, however, because each member, as a part of the general will, would be governed by laws to which each person consented. Legitimate authority and individual freedom would be guaranteed by the accord between private wills and the general will.

**Hegelianism.** Georg Wilhelm Friedrich Hegel (1770-1832) gave alienation a prominent place in his writings. In The Philosophy of History (1822), Hegel depicted alienation as the separation between the idea of freedom in itself and its realization or actualization in world history. In *The Phenomenology of Spirit* (1807), Hegel employed the concept of alienation to articulate the failure of human consciousness to recognize itself in the external world of nature and culture. Culture, the world of produced objects and human actions, represents the process of the transformation of the natural human being into the social being. Thus, culture alienates the socialized self from the naturalized self. Estrangement results from the split occurring in intellectual life. For example, law, a product of culture, divides the self into the legal person, from whom the law demands social conformity, and the self-conscious person who values freedom. De-alienation would result from the union of personal freedom and the objective rule of the state.

**Marxism.** Karl Marx (1818-1883) applied alienation to politics and economics. In *On the Jewish Question* (1843), Marx denounced the split existence of human beings in modern societies. In civil society, people function as egoistic, private, self-interested individuals. In the political community of the state, however, people are regarded as abstract citizens. Human emancipation, or de-alienation, requires the unification of the communal being and the real individual.

In the *Economic and Philosophical Manuscripts* (1844), Marx specified four forms of alienation in the section entitled "Alienated Labor." The first form of alienation is the separation between the laborer and the product of labor. Alienation occurs because the object, as the realization of the life activity of the worker under capitalism, does not belong to labor. Therefore, the loss of the object represents the loss of reality to the worker.

If it is the case that the worker is alienated from the product, then it logically follows that the worker is also alienated in the act of production. If the result of production is alienation, then the process is also alienating. In productive activity, the worker becomes self-alienated because labor is the life-activity of the worker. Rather than becoming self-affirming activity, work becomes self-denying activity. Rather than becoming the satisfaction of a need for human self-fulfillment, work becomes only a means to satisfy the basic needs of human survival.

The third form of alienation is that of alienation from species-being (society, social consciousness). Because labor serves only to further basic survival, the worker exists only as an egoistic individual and not as a social being; that is, he or she thinks egoistically, not communally.

The last form of alienation is the estrangement between the self and the other. Each person is equally estranged from his or her true human essence. Self-estrangement therefore manifests itself in estrangement with others. Under capitalism, the estrangement between the self and the other finds expression in the alienation between the labor and capital. De-alienation therefore entails the emancipation of the worker by abolishing private property. Private property is both the presupposition and the result of alienated labor.

**Freud.** Sigmund Freud posited alienation as the fundamental human condition. The self is split between the ego and the ego ideal. The latter, a social and conditioning factor, becomes a repressive mechanism. The conflict between the ego and the ego-ideal is alienation. Repression is the agency of alienation to the extent that it keeps away from consciousness those elements that are not approved by the superego.

**Ethical Problems.** In conclusion, several questions remain open: If there is such a universal phenomenon as self-alienation, is it necessary to presuppose a universal human nature? If alienation is not universal, is it relative to history and culture? If alienation is universal, de-alienation must be considered a psychological fantasy or a social utopia. If it is psychologically relative, its psychological causes must be discovered so that wholeness can be restored. If it is sociologically relative, then its social causes must be revealed so that they can be transformed. —*Michael R. Candelaria*

**See also** Hegel, G. W. F.; Marx, Karl; Rousseau, Jean-Jacques.

**BIBLIOGRAPHY**

Feuerbach, Ludwig. *The Essence of Christianity*. Translated by George Eliot. New York: Harper & Row, 1957.

Freud, Sigmund. *The Ego and the Id*. Edited by James Strachey. Translated by Joan Riviere. New York: W. W. Norton, 1962.

Hegel, Georg Wilhelm Friedrich. *The Phenomenology of Spirit*. Translated by A. V. Miller. Oxford, England: Oxford University Press, 1977.

Marx, Karl. *Selected Writings*. Edited by David McLellan. Oxford, England. Oxford University Press, 1977.

Meszaros, Istvan. *Marx's Theory of Alienation*. New York: Harper & Row, 1972.

## Altruism

**TYPE OF ETHICS:** Theory of ethics
**DATE:** Fifth century B.C.E. to present
**DEFINITION:** Disputed, but having to do with other-directed behavior and motivation for that behavior
**SIGNIFICANCE:** Absent in ancient ethical work, crucial according to modern ethicists

The concept of altruism can be developed in at least two different ways. It may be looked at historically, beginning with the opposition of altruism to egoism by Thomas Hobbes (1588-1679) and moving primarily forward, or it may be looked at with a view toward simple definition. The meaning of altruism, or, vaguely, other-directed behavior in ethics, is not as clear as it might be, as Lawrence Blum and others have noted. Simple definitional concerns will be taken first.

**Definition.** If the term "altruism" is taken to mean action that benefits others, immediately the problem arises that such behavior can quite easily be part of a scheme that is ultimately selfish. If, for example, creatures from an advanced civilization were to land on Earth, quell all international, civil, and family strife, and institute a plan of resource management, child-rearing, and government that ensured peace, tranquillity, and the development of learning for all, that behavior would have to be construed as altruistic according to this initial definition, whether the aliens were raising people for food or not.

To avoid this problem, one might consider some restriction regarding motivation. The word "altruism" applies to actions intended to benefit others. This definitional amendment raises the question of who decides what is of benefit to whom. A mother may consider it a benefit to her son to quash a relationship in which he is involved. The son may disagree. If she succeeds, then she does what she intended to do and may well continue to defend her action as beneficial to her son. Who is correct?

Since the mother seems to be serving her own interests, one might propose an amendment that altruism applies to behavior that is intended to benefit others and places the interest of others ahead of one's own interest. This, however, makes the definition worse. According to this definition, a morally altruistic woman who had been raped and beaten should not bring charges against the man responsible, because it is would not be in his best interest. Any other reason for not bringing charges would be more palatable than this one.

There are also general objections to placing restrictions regarding motivation in the definition of altruism. Psychologists state that people are often not aware of their own real motivations. Mates of alcoholics, for example, if the alcoholic begins to deal with the alcoholism, often sabotage the effort. They may buy alcohol for the alcoholic mate, for example. If one asks why, they may give one of any number of reasons, such as giving the alcoholic a break from feeling bad about his or her childhood. These reasons all have in common that they are focused on the alcoholic. In truth, however, according to psychology, the mates' own identities may be dependent upon helping the alcoholics with their problem, and these identities are threatened when the alcoholics begin to get better. Therefore, other-directed behavior according to the mates' lights turns out to be self-directed behavior according to the psychologists' lights.

Indeed, those who have paid any attention to their own decisions have found it difficult to know whether their motivations are simply self-serving or take others properly into account, particularly when there is disagreement with someone else on the point. This inability to isolate motivation accurately dims enthusiasm for restrictions regarding motivation in a functional definition of altruism.

Sociobiologists E. O. Wilson and Richard Dawkins offer a different reason for the inability to isolate and be certain of motivation. Their conjecture, based on the behavior of certain animals, is that people are genetically programmed to act in such a way as to bring about the greatest survival rate for their own genes. One might, then, sacrifice oneself for one's progeny much more quickly than for one's spouse or strangers. This action is not the result of a decision. It is the decision of the gene pool, according to the law of perpetuation of the species. If motivation cannot be determined, however, what are the ramifications for the definition of altruism?

At this point, one is foundering on the impossibility of deciding whether altruistic acts should all be reinterpreted as egoistic. What is peculiar here has to do with egoism as a theory of motivation. Any piece of behavior can be seen as egoistic. No human behavior can fail to be explained as motivated by self-interest. This fact makes the modern project of discovering an altruistic ethic in an egoistic human nature hopeless. The next step is to inspect historical uses of the word "altruism" in the hope of illumination.

**Hobbes.** The place to begin is with Hobbes, though he is not the earliest philosopher to be considered. Hobbes's view of the state of nature, in which life is "nasty, brutish, and short," is consistent with his belief that human beings are motivated only by fear of death and desire for dominance. According to this view, altruistic behavior is always a screen for egoistic behavior. This seems the point at which the modern problem in ethics mentioned above arises: finding a place for altruistic behavior in an egoistic human nature.

The strength of this position is not that Hobbes's premises concerning motivation are persuasive. One can easily reject the contention that persons are exclusively motivated by fear of death and desire for dominance by positing, for example, the independent power of compassion as a motivator of human behavior, as does Arthur Schopenhauer (1788-1860). Much of modern ethical philosophy can be seen as either affirming Hobbes's position concerning the impossibility of altruism or hypothesizing some independent, altruistic motivation as part of human nature. Examples of those who opt for some altruistic principle are, in addition to Schopenhauer, Søren Kierkegaard (1813-1855), the Third Earl of Shaftesbury, called simply "Shaftesbury," Anthony Ashley Cooper (1671-1713), Francis Hutcheson (1694-1746), the later David Hume (1711-1776), and Henry Sidgwick (1838-1900). Among those that opt for self-interest alone, in addition to Hobbes, are Bernard Mandeville (1670-1733), John Grote (1813-1866), and, with a twist, the theologian William Paley (1743-1805).

The twist with Paley is that he considered benevolence to be in a person's long-term self-interest rather than short-term self-interest. According to Paley, all persons are egoistic, but God has arranged that the only way to secure eternal happiness is to obey the fundamental (and, for Paley, utilitarian) moral rule. In this way, he makes the transition between egoistic human nature and altruistic moral behavior.

One thinker who perhaps deserves separate mention is Friedrich Nietzsche (1844-1900), who attacked altruism as a moral mistake.

**Nietzsche.** It was noted above that a definition of altruism that included a restriction on motivation to the effect that one should always place others' interests ahead of one's own is inadequate. Nietzsche thought so, too, but recognized large groups of persons who in fact upheld this definition in what he called a "slave morality." Nietzsche was passionately opposed to such morality, which glorified suffering as meaningful. His primary target was Christianity, though he also sideswiped Judaism and Greek ethics. He was apparently not, however, the virulent anti-Semite that some have made him out to be. Nietzsche saw the Judeo-Christian values of humility, passivity, and dependence as necessarily grounded in a value system built on fear, guilt, and a distortion of the will to power. Master morality, however, extolled the proper virtues of courage and self-grounded spiritual strength. Thus, altruism was condemned by Nietzsche as unworthy of highly evolved individuals.

Concern for others need not be a sign of poor self-esteem or any sort of escape from higher values. Such concern for others might well exist in very strong persons who need no rhetoric of a master mentality to know their worth, attending to the needs of others with utter confidence in their capacity to care also for themselves. Still, there is such a thing as the pathology of low self-esteem, a suppression or devaluing of the self, and it is correct to eschew such an attitude. This eschewing does not require the adoption of an attitude that demands individual dominance, however, as Nietzsche recommends. It is this recommendation of individual dominance, however, that made Nietzsche useless to the Third Reich until he was edited. Ethnic group dominance is not the same thing as individual dominance, even if both are misguided.

The total of all the developments since Hobbes does not seem to advance the problem significantly. There are exceptions, notably Joseph Butler (1692-1752), who takes a different direction. Even today, however, many ethicists presuppose the opposition between altruism and egoism as the fulcrum for allegedly historically informed discussions of ethical thinking and behavior. This is the case with, for example, Richard Norman's popular textbook *The Moral Philosophers: An Introduction to Ethics* (1983). Much of value is said in this intelligent book, but it ends without closure concerning its central tension: the problem of egoism and altruism. Ethics interpreted in terms of this narrow, insoluble problem cannot satisfy the desire to understand.

**Butler.** The significance of Butler, an Anglican clergyman, is that he reintroduced a larger model for ethical reflection than can be used if one limits oneself to issues of altruism and egoism. This broader model is presented primarily in Butler's "Three Sermons on Human Nature" (1726). It is a common claim among philosophers that Butler's sermons are the closest thing in English to Aristotle's (384-322) ethical thought. A larger model was standard during Classical times and in the thought of Thomas Aquinas (1224-1274) during medieval times.

Thomism, as Aquinas' thinking is called, is also a reintroduction of Aristotle's thinking into the Christian, European world, made possible by the Islamic scholars Averroës (1126-1198) and Avicenna (980-1037) and the Jewish scholar Moses Maimonides (1135-1204). Maimonides set forth, in his *Guide of the Perplexed* (1190), discussions of Aristotle's thinking that were especially influential on Aquinas and other medieval scholastics. Aristotle had been lost to Europe at the close of the Classical Age and was regained through these Islamic and Jewish scholars, primarily via paths between Moorish Spain and the rest of Europe.

The primary idea reintroduced by Butler is that self-love and benevolence, or egoism and altruism, are part of a larger motivational whole. It is not that Butler transcended his age without connection to it. He took himself to be looking, along with most other seventeenth and eighteenth century writers, for a foundation for morals that was independent of the divine will. He found it in the divine creation. Though Butler's ethical thinking is very similar to Aristotle's, it should not be forgotten that he writes as a Christian.

In the divine creation, Butler found human nature. As a creation of God, human nature could not be depraved, as John Calvin (1509-1564), Martin Luther (1483-1546), and perhaps even Immanuel Kant (1724-1804) held. Rather, human nature is a reasonable guide to the way in which God would have human beings behave. Furthermore, what human beings desire, or what motivates them, is a reasonable guide to what they should want, or that by which they should be motivated. The claim that what people actually want, overall, is a happy life is not necessarily egoism—at least not egoism as opposed to altruism.

Consider a happy life one that involves trusting relationships, friendship, and cooperative endeavors. Persons possessing a desire for this kind of life could not separate their interests and others' interests according to different motives. Allowing self-interests to outweigh others' interests, and vice-versa, will both be involved in a life in which decisions produce, overall, trusting relationships, friendship, and cooperative endeavors. Therefore, to allow the distinction between altruism and egoism to occupy a central place in ethical discussion or to consider that egoism might be an all-encompassing motivation is to narrow one's perspective on ethical behavior to a small class of conflict situations. This leaves behind both common sense and common life.

If what is good is what is desired by natural persons, then pursuing trusting relationships, friendship, and cooperative endeavors as a means to a happy life is good. The good of this kind of life is not good for a self only, except in the trivial sense that a self desires and pursues it. The good of this kind of life includes the good of other lives. Therefore, the model wherein two person's goals conflict and each person's goals connect to self-interest alone covers only a small area even of human conflict, and certainly not the entire arena of human ethical behavior. This small area is not qualified to serve as a model for ethics, and Butler understands this fact.

When challenged, Butler had recourse to his own experience. He claimed, and urged others to agree, that the vast majority of persons are motivated completely by neither self-interest nor benevolence. Exceptional individuals, such as conscienceless businessmen or servants with no detectable personal wishes, should be ignored in such an assessment. Furthermore, self-regard and other-regard exist side by side in the same person, most of the time without conflict, and even reinforce each other. Most people are much more integrated than the opposition between altruism and egoism would lead one to believe. This integration involves not only altruism and egoism, which have no relationship of priority of one over the other, but also many other affections or goal-oriented motivations.

In a short article such as this, there is reason to interrupt an analysis of Butler before completing it. A much fuller analysis of the problems of modern ethics that contrasts Butler's point of view, called an ethic of "virtue," with the modern presupposition that altruism and egoism are foundational to ethical discussions is available in Alasdair MacIntyre's *After Virtue* (1981). Butler himself traces his views to Epictetus (50-130), not Aristotle. As far as the present analysis goes to this point, he and Aristotle are agreed. Aristotle offers the more complete virtue ethic, so it will be instructive to discuss Aristotle at this point.

**Aristotle.** The first thing to understand about Aristotle's view of happiness is that it applies only to a whole life. A happy life is a whole life well lived. A life well lived is a life lived according to virtue and accompanied by the blessings of good fortune. Good fortune, which is a matter of luck, is necessary. The best overview of the function of luck in Greek philosophy and literature is available in Martha Nussbaum's *The Fragility of Goodness* (1986).

A virtuous person who meets a bad end, such as Socrates, cannot properly be called happy according to Aristotle. Aristotle took steps once to ensure that Athens did not have the opportunity to treat him as it had treated Socrates, and no doubt would have explained this behavior as pursuing a happy life.

This "happy life" is not to be experienced or enjoyed at any particular moment, but functions as a goal for the sake of which everything else works. The virtues, such as courage, temperance, prudence, and justice, are functional means toward the end of living a good life. Altruism is not taken into account by Aristotle, and it is not clear whether altruism should be treated as a virtue. Modern ethicists consider that only altruistic behavior can properly be called ethical. Aristotle considers that behavior in accordance with the virtues is a means to the unique, practical goal of all persons, happiness, offering a broader goal for virtuous activity than either the good of self or that of others, either egoism or altruism.

Aristotle is aware that not all persons pursue the same ultimate good, but he is convinced that the real goods that people naturally desire, which meet human needs, are the same for everyone. Some persons mistakenly acquire desires for goods that are not real goods. This explains why the word "good" is used differently by different persons, even when all admit happiness as the name for that which is always pursued as an end and never as a means.

Aristotle offers a flexible absolutism. He claims that a whole life is made good, or happiness is achieved, by the cumulative attainment of all real goods in the period of that whole life. Real goods are those to which natural desires lead. These natural desires are the same for all in view of their identical natures and needs as human beings. Individualistic relativism is rejected by Aristotle.

Such a complete view of ethics is difficult even to compare with modern, truncated discussions of altruism and egoism. It is very tempting to endorse MacIntyre's suggestion that one should move toward an integration of modern law and a virtue ethic in the post-modern predicament, whether one agrees with MacIntyre's particular attempt to construct such an ethic or not. *—Joe Frank Jones III*

**See also** Aristotelian ethics; Butler, Joseph; Egoism; Hobbes, Thomas; Human nature; MacIntyre, Alasdair; *Nicomachean Ethics*; Public interest; Religion; Self-interest; Virtue ethics.

**Bibliography**

Blum, Lawrence. "Altruism." In *Encyclopedia of Ethics*, edited by Lawrence C. Becker and Charlotte B. Becker. New York: Garland, 1992. A first-rate article overall, and with interesting material on Anna Freud's (1895-1982) work with not-really-altruistic mental patients.

Butler, Joseph. *Fifteen Sermons Preached at the Rolls Chapels*. London: W. Botham, 1726. This book, the best text available, contains useful introductory material.

Cooper, John M. "Aristotle on the Goods of Fortune." *Philosophical Review* 94 (April, 1985): 173-196. This article explains the essential role of luck in Greek ethics.

___________. *Reason and Human Good in Aristotle*. Cambridge, Mass.: Harvard University Press, 1975. An excellent preamble to Aristotle's ethics.

Hobbes, Thomas. *Man and Citizen: Thomas Hobbes's "De Homine" and "De Cive."* Translated by Charles T. Wood and T. S. K. Scott-Craig. London: Humanities Press, 1978. The text is accurate, and the introduction by Gert is excellent.

MacIntyre, Alasdair. *After Virtue*. Notre Dame, Ind.: Notre Dame University Press, 1981. This book contains a large picture of the nature of morality, along with smaller pictures of the historical circumstances in which morality has played its part.

___________. "Egoism and Altruism." In *The Encyclopedia of Philosophy*, edited by Paul Edwards. New York: Macmillan, 1967. This extended discussion, historically informed, is an excellent place to begin.

Maimonides, Moses. *The Guide of the Perplexed*. Translated by Shlomo Pines. Chicago: University of Chicago Press, 1963. This difficult work benefits from both an introduction by the translator, Pines, and an introductory essay by Leo Strauss.

Norman, Richard. *The Ethical Philosophers: An Introduction to Ethics*. Oxford: Oxford University Press, 1983. This book has many virtues, among which is the discussion of why neither Aristotle nor Plato is subject to the criticism that he is egoistic on the grounds that he argues that it is advantageous to the just person to act justly. It is ethics done well within an academic mindset, including an antipathy for Christianity.

Nussbaum, Martha C. *The Fragility of Goodness*. Cambridge, England: Cambridge University Press, 1986. An insightful, scholarly look at the notion of luck in ancient literature and philosophy. The next step after Cooper's article concerning "fortune" in Aristotle.

## American Civil Liberties Union (ACLU)

**Type of ethics:** Legal and judicial ethics

**Date:** Founded 1920

**Associated with:** Jane Addams, Clarence Darrow, Norman Thomas, and the U.S. Bill of Rights

**Definition:** The ACLU was established to protect the rights set forth in the Bill of Rights

**Significance:** The ACLU has played a leading role in increasing Americans' concerns for individual rights, including the rights of those holding minority positions

The ACLU has more than 375,000 members, a staff of more than one hundred, and offices in each of the fifty states. It argues more cases before the U.S. Supreme Court than any other group except the federal government itself. The ACLU defends the rights set forth in the Bill of Rights. Over the years it has worked to clarify and defend the freedoms of speech, press, assembly, and religion; the rights to due process and a fair trial; and equality before the law regardless of race, color, sexual orientation, national origin, political opinion, or religious belief. It has always taken an absolutist approach, believing that these freedoms are for all Americans, even those with unpopular opinions. Thus, it has represented extremist political groups including Communists, Nazis, and the Ku Klux Klan. It played an important role in the Scopes "Monkey Trial," and it defended Communists during the Cold War and interned Japanese Americans during World War II. In 1977, the ACLU supported the right of Nazis to stage a public demonstration in Skokie, Illinois. This absolutism has made the ACLU a subject of ridicule—even vilification—by mainstream Americans.

**See also** Bill of Rights, U.S.; Civil rights; *Goss v. Lopez*; *Miranda v. Arizona.*

## American Federation of Labor (AFL)

**Type of ethics:** Business and labor ethics

**Date:** Founded December 8, 1886

**Definition:** The AFL was the first permanent national-international federation of skilled trades

**Significance:** The AFL asserted the rights of workers to organize on their own behalf and upheld the dignity of labor against the impositions of the business community

A successor to the Federation of Organized Trades and Labor Unions, which was established in November of 1881 in Pittsburgh, Pennsylvania, the American Federation of Labor (AFL) became the first permanent American trade union federation. Earlier American national labor organizations, such as the National Labor Union (established in 1866) and the Knights of Labor (established in 1871), had been loosely structured industrial unions with polyglot memberships and broad economic and political programs. Despite some limited successes, they ultimately failed because of internal divisions, the dispersion of their energy, and the hostility of the public and the business community.

The AFL, founded largely through the efforts of Samuel Gompers and Adolf Strasser, both of whom were immigrant cigarmakers and socialists, was a pragmatic organization. It was tailored to American workers' lack of class consciousness and emphasized the improvement of wages, hours, and working conditions—that is, bread-and-butter unionism. Its constituents—carpenters, coal miners, building tradespeople, and railroad workers—enjoyed almost complete autonomy and enlisted skilled workers almost exclusively. The relatively high wages of skilled workers made it possible for the organization to accumulate substantial strike funds. AFL membership rapidly grew to two million by 1910 and more than tripled by 1950. Publicly, the AFL sought the mediation of labor disputes, the enactment of labor legislation, limits on immigration, protection from technological unemployment, and, whenever possible, collaboration with employers. The AFL's merger with its rival, the Congress of Industrial Organizations, in 1955 (founding the AFL-CIO) created the free world's largest labor union. The merger also resulted in diminished autonomy and the acceptance of industrial unionism and political action.

**See also** International Labour Organisation; Knights of Labor; National Labor Union.

## American Medical Association (AMA)

**TYPE OF ETHICS:** Bioethics
**DATE:** Founded 1847
**ASSOCIATED WITH:** Codes and principles of professional medical ethics
**DEFINITION:** The AMA was established at an 1846-1847 convention in New York City to develop standards of medical practice and behavior, and to lobby for laws licensing medical practitioners
**SIGNIFICANCE:** The AMA's 1847 *Code of Medical Ethics* was the world's first national code of medical ethics

The AMA's positions on medical ethics (rulings on, for example; the permissibility of physicians performing abortions, allowing patients to die, assisting patient suicide, divulging confidential information, euthanasia, owning laboratories, refusing to treat AIDS patients, splitting fees), as announced in the "Opinions" section of the *Principles of Medical Ethics*, in its *Newsletter*, or in the *Journal of the American Medical Association (JAMA)*, are considered important by all medical professionals. Courts of law often use these positions to determine the standard of care to which medical personnel are held accountable in malpractice and other cases.

**See also** Bioethics; Bills of rights, medical; Medical ethics; *Principles of Medical Ethics with Annotations Especially Applicable to Psychiatry.*

## American Society of Newspaper Editors (ASNE)

**TYPE OF ETHICS:** Media ethics
**DATE:** Founded 1922
**DEFINITION:** The ASNE encourages newspaper editors to concern themselves with the ethics, quality, and history of editorial and news policy
**SIGNIFICANCE:** Of the many groups monitoring the news media for fairness and accuracy, ASNE is among the most influential because it is made up of the editors themselves

The American Society of Newspaper Editors (ASNE) has more than one thousand members, who are the directing editors who determine editorial and news policy on daily newspapers across the country. The organization has several goals: to improve the quality of journalism education and of newspaper writing and editing, to help newspaper managers work more effectively with employees, to encourage adequate minority representation on newspaper staffs, and to protect First Amendment rights and freedom of information. To achieve these goals, ASNE publishes several periodicals for editors, educators, and others, and presents awards for excellence in editing and writing. ASNE monitors its own members to see how newspapers are responding to various needs. This often leads to controversy. In the late 1980's, ASNE began surveying daily newspapers to determine whether gay and lesbian journalists were being given fair treatment in hiring and promotion, and whether the AIDS epidemic was receiving fair and adequate coverage. During the same period, ASNE researched the hiring and promotion of members of racial and ethnic minorities, and debated whether to publicize the names of newspapers with poor minority-hiring records.

**See also** Journalistic ethics.

## Americans with Disabilities Act

**TYPE OF ETHICS:** Disability rights
**DATE:** Established July 26, 1990
**DEFINITION:** The Americans with Disabilities Act (ADA) is a civil rights law that was established in order to protect disabled people from discrimination
**SIGNIFICANCE:** Prior to the passage of the ADA, the civil rights of the disabled community were not protected; the ADA strictly prohibits discrimination against disabled people

The Civil Rights Act of 1964 did not prohibit discrimination against disabled people. The Rehabilitation Act of 1973 required that increased opportunities be made available for handicapped people, but discrimination against the disabled continued to be evident until the passage of the Americans with Disabilities Act in 1990. The Americans with Disabilities Act stands as a comprehensive civil rights law for people with disabilities. The ADA states that no individual shall be discriminated against on the basis of a disability in seeking employment, receiving state and local government services, or having full and equal enjoyment of public accommodations. Title I of the ADA prohibits discrimination against hiring a "qualified applicant" only on the basis of the applicant having a disability. The ADA public accommodation provisions, known as Title III, which became effective on January 26, 1992, require accessible wheelchair routes and signage identifying special services for the disabled. Such services may include braille materials and assistive listening devices. The effect of the passage of the ADA has been increased accessibility for people with disabilities and an increased awareness of disability civil rights.

**See also** Civil Rights Act of 1964.

## Amnesty International

**TYPE OF ETHICS:** Human rights
**DATE:** Founded 1961

**DEFINITION:** An international organization dedicated to releasing prisoners of conscience, ensuring fair and timely trials for political prisoners, and ending capital punishment and torture

**SIGNIFICANCE:** Amnesty International, while not the first international human rights monitoring organization, pioneered the use of such tactics as letter-writing campaigns and the selective use of publicity to put pressure on governments to release individuals detained solely because of their beliefs or origins

Amnesty International began as a temporary campaign, organized by British lawyer Peter Benenson in 1961, to put pressure on the dictatorial Portuguese Salazar government to release two students who had been sent to prison for seven years for the crime of drinking a toast to freedom in public. Since that time, the organization has monitored human rights violations throughout the world, consistently fighting for the rights and the very lives of oppressed people. Amnesty International's official purpose is to put an end worldwide to the illegal detention of "prisoners of conscience," who have neither used nor advocated violence, and to stop torture and capital punishment.

**See also** Capital punishment; Disappeared, The; Genocide; Human rights; Oppression; Universal Declaration of Human Rights.

**EXAMPLES OF AMNESTY INTERNATIONAL CAMPAIGNS**

| Year(s) | Advance in Human Rights | Type of Human Rights Abuse | Country |
|---|---|---|---|
| 1972 | Publication of report | Torture | Brazil |
| 1973-1976 | Release from prison of prisoners of conscience | Illegal detention and torture | Tanzania |
| 1975-1979 | Investigation of misuse of psychiatric hospitals | Illegal detention and torture | Soviet Union |
| 1977-1980's | Political and economic pressure to cease aid | Political assassination, illegal detention, and torture | El Salvador |
| 1979 | Exposé of Anastasio Somoza who was eventually overthrown | Dictatorship | Nicaragua |
| 1979. | Exposé of murders in prison of 50 to 100 school children | Assassination | Central African Republic |
| 1979-1980 | Increase in public awareness | Mass political executions | Guatemala |
| 1980 | Improvement of prison conditions for Baader-Meinhof gang | Isolation treatment | West Germany |
| 1980 | Suspension of death sentence of Madame Mao | Capital punishment | China |
| Ongoing | Campaign to save death-row inmates | Capital punishment | United States |

# Anarchy

**TYPE OF ETHICS:** Politico-economic ethics

**DATE:** Late nineteenth and early twentieth centuries

**ASSOCIATED WITH:** Mikhail Bakunin, a nineteenth century Russian revolutionary who argued for the abolition of the state

**DEFINITION:** Political theory that asserts that individual freedom has been destroyed by the coercive power of the state, and seeks to replace the state with voluntary associations

**SIGNIFICANCE:** Anarchy is a belief that the individual should never be forced to live according to values that are imposed through the power of the state

Anarchy, as the word is commonly used, refers to chaos that results from an absence of authority. The term has its roots in Greek and means, literally, "without a leader." Anarchy as a political philosophy, however, seeks to liberate the individual from the coercion of the state and to create a society of voluntary participation. This dual nature of anarchy—disorder and individual freedom—is reflected in the approaches taken by anarchists since its inception as a political philosophy in the nineteenth century.

**History.** Pierre-Joseph Proudhon (1809-1865), a French writer and social theorist, came from a lower-class background. "What is property?" he asked in his most famous work with that title (1840). His answer, "Property is theft," is one of the intellectual foundations of modern anarchism. Proudhon felt that one's labor was the basis of value in society. Property, in the form of capital or land, whose owners were supported by the state, denied the worker his or her fair share. This emphasis on the economic foundation of the state would be appropriated by syndicalist labor unions at the beginning of the twentieth century, and it provided the justification for revolutionary general strikes aimed at destroying the state.

Anarchism was popular among workers because it promised action. Revolutionaries, such as the Russian Mikhail Bakunin (1814-1876), and the Italian Enrico Malatesta (1850-1932), worked for the revolution that, sparked by an act of violence, would bring about the new society. At the end of the nineteenth century and the beginning of the twentieth century, some anarchists engaged in terrorism, which they called "propaganda of the deed." They thought that one dramatic act of violence, especially the assassination of a major political leader, would bring about the long-awaited revolution. President William McKinley of the United States, Antonio Cánovas del Castillo, the premier of Spain, and Umberto I, King of Italy all died at the hands of anarchist assassins. Assassinations and bomb-throwing attacks led to the image of anarchists as violent criminals plotting to destroy society.

The Russian-born American anarchist Emma Goldman (1869-1940) was a symbol of this terror in the minds of many Americans. Children were threatened with capture by "Red" Emma, and their fate was left to the imagination. Emma Goldman's life, however, was a testament to the ethics of anarchy as a way of life. She believed in her rights as a woman to work, to practice birth control, and to love without the bonds of marriage. She supported labor unions and openly opposed the entry of the United States into World War I. She was deported to Russia in 1917 but became disillusioned by the authoritarian nature of the revolutionary Bolshevik regime. Instead, she favored the anarchist revolution that occurred in Spain at the outbreak of the Spanish civil war in 1936. In Barcelona, workers took over factories and set up committees to oversee production. Factory committees then elected representatives to regional industry councils in an attempt to organize an economy and a society without exploitation. This worker control ended when the military, under Francisco Franco, defeated the Republican government and set up a dictatorship in Spain.

*The assassination of U.S. President William McKinley by an anarchist in 1901.* (Library of Congress)

**Ethical Principles.** There was another, intellectual approach to anarchy that focused less on the destruction of the state and more on the freedom of the individual. Several Russian intellectuals, among them Leo Tolstoy (1828-1910) and Peter Kropotkin (1842-1921), used the peasant village as an example of individual cooperation and moral authority. Kropotkin was an advocate of mutual aid, believing that individuals would spontaneously create groups for their mutual benefit and join voluntarily. The state existed to coerce individuals to conform to moral standards and economic organization that benefited those who controlled that state.

The ethics of anarchy is more than a protest against a particular state or society or economic organization. It is an expression of complete faith in the individual. In the twentieth century, the legacy of anarchy has influenced both violent demonstrations and scholarship. The worldwide student uprisings of the late 1960's owed much to the anarchist belief in direct action and mistrust of the state. In Chicago, Paris, and Mexico City, students battled police to protest government policies.

Herbert Read (1893-1968), an English writer, has sought to explain the ideals of freedom through anarchy. Read addresses the differences between individual freedom and the concept of liberty. Liberty, according to Read, is a doctrine that depends on the relationship of the individual to the state. Liberty is a civil right; freedom is a personal attribute. One is granted liberty but possesses freedom. Anarchy, according to Read, recognizes that freedom is innate and leaves the individual unfettered.

Paul Goodman (1911-1972) was an American scholar who wrote about education, society, and urban living. Goodman's human perspective envisaged educational communities, not mammoth universities, and cities on a human scale, designed around the individual rather than around a system of production and transportation.

Anarchy is not a system, and its adherents often exhibit contradictory behavior and ideas. It accepts spontancity and variety as attributes of freedom, and welcomes diversity. Anarchy opposes uniformity enforced by dictatorships or elected governments and supports the freedom of each individual. It is this respect for the value of the individual that marks the ethics of anarchy. —*James A. Baer*

**See also** Assassination; Class struggle; Communism; Revolution.

**BIBLIOGRAPHY**

Avrich, Paul. *Anarchist Portraits.* Princeton, N.J.: Princeton University Press, 1988.

Drinnon, Richard. *Rebel in Paradise: A Biography of Emma Goldman.* Chicago: Chicago University Press, 1982.

Horowitz, Irving L. *The Anarchists.* New York: Dell, 1964.

Joll, James. *The Anarchists.* 2d ed. Cambridge, Mass.: Harvard University Press, 1980.

Read, Herbert. *Anarchy and Order: Essays in Politics.* Boston: Beacon Press, 1971.

## Anger

**TYPE OF ETHICS:** Personal and social ethics

**ASSOCIATED WITH:** Charles Darwin (1809-1882), William James (1811-1882), and Sigmund Freud (1856-1939)

**DEFINITION:** A primary, reactive emotion or psychosomatic condition characteristic of both humans and animals

**SIGNIFICANCE:** Because emotions affect human behavior, anger may be a precondition of or motive for unethical or illegal acts

**Anger as Sin.** Modern psychology and psychoanalysis have to some measure removed the onus that medieval Christianity attached to anger when identifying it as one of the seven cardinal, or deadly, sins. It is now viewed as a natural, reactive, even a mature emotion experienced by all humans at some time in their lives, as unavoidable as other primary emotions such as fear, sadness, and joy. Still, orthodox moral philosophers knew that unabated anger, or wrath, could be destructive, particularly in the guise of vengeful fury, and argued that in that form it should be God's prerogative alone. As the Greek theologian Saint Basil (330-379) proclaimed, in mortals it was viewed as a reprehensible, "temporary madness."

**The Humors Theory.** The primitive, physiological "humors" theory that persisted from antiquity through the Renaissance and explained emotions as "passions" should have called into question the idea that anger per se could be deemed sinful. After all, if a person was disposed to choler because of an imbalance in body chemistry, an excess, specifically, of yellow bile, anger could arise without permission of the will, making sin a moot concept. Morality must hinge on both the cognitive distinction between good and evil and a voluntary choice between them—that is, free will.

The implications of the pseudo-scientific idea of the humors simply remained as remote from moral philosophy as contemporary physiological study is likely to remain. Knowing, for example, that under stress, as in an angry condition, there is a decrease of lymphocytes in the blood but an elevation of free fatty acid avails the moralist nothing. Knowing that anger can contribute to destructive behavior, however, provides some food for ethical thought. Moral principles based on emotions must therefore focus on their effects rather than on the emotions themselves.

**Anger as a Healthy Emotion.** Anger is engendered by some sort of stimulus, usually in the present but possibly recalled from memory. It is normally a conscious feeling accompanied by physical discomfort and tension, and may be outwardly expressed by glaring, gritting of teeth, clenching of the fists, or even quaking of the bodily frame, depending on its intensity. Most psychologists believe that it is a realistic, healthy emotion, unlike hostility, which is based in immature fear. It is, however, a delimited emotion, and unless it subsides or finds outlet in expression, it can yield to more destructive reactions such as anxiety, depression, and aggression. When sublimated through creative energy, however, it can lead to positive behavior, such as efforts to ameliorate social injustice.

**Anger's Destructive Potential.** Anger tends to become dangerous when it is suppressed, repressed, or displaced. Both suppression and repression work to deny its expression an outlet, while displacement, common in dreams, redirects the expression of anger from the actual stimulus to a surrogate or scapegoat. Repressed, seething anger may find sudden, explosive release, as it did in the 1992 riot in Los Angeles, which was prompted by the acquittal of the police officers in the Rodney King beating trial. The violence erupted because the demands of a collective anger aroused by the beating were not satisfied by the jury's verdict. The anger was then displaced as violence against persons and property that had no rational link to the King affair.

The widespread deflection of anger away from its actual cause toward a scapegoat has affected even whole nations. A prime example is Nazi Germany, where Jews were blamed for the economic ills of the nation and displaced anger gradually gave way to hatred and murderous, genocidal aggression. How that could have happened in such a highly developed culture remains something of a mystery, but the basic paradigm of hatred arising from anger joined to frustration is clear enough.

The vestiges of the idea of anger as a sort of madness persist in law, as, for example, in the "temporary insanity" defense, or as a mitigating factor in sentencing in "crimes of passion." Moreover, the cumulative effect of long-suppressed anger has increasingly been used as a defense in court, when, for example, a battered wife has killed her spouse under circumstances that would otherwise preclude a plea of self-defense. For some theorists, that defense has opened a legal version of Pandora's box.

Furthermore, as the Rodney King case revealed, the legal process is a potential hostage to collective anger. The videotape of King's beating, repeatedly aired by the media, aroused great public indignation, which could have intimidated and suborned the jury. It did not, but the lawlessness that followed in the wake of that jury's verdict may weigh heavily on some future jury.

Although modern psychologists can agree on the symptomatic behavior and physiological phenomena accompanying anger, they can provide no definitive conclusions regarding what it is or even where, anatomically, it resides. Practical ethics must take anger and other emotions into account, but using them as primary building blocks of moral principles is at best subjective and very risky.

*—John W. Fiero*

**See also** Aggression; Hate; Passions and emotions; Violence.

**BIBLIOGRAPHY**

Averill, James R. *Anger and Aggression: An Essay on Emotion.* New York: Springer-Verlag, 1982.

Callwood, June. *Emotions: What They Are and How They Affect Us.* Garden City, N.Y.: Doubleday, 1986.

Gaylin, Willard. *The Rage Within: Anger in Modern Life.* New York: Simon & Schuster, 1984.

Izard, Carroll E., Jerome Kagan, and Robert B. Zajon C., eds. *Emotions, Cognition, and Behavior.* New York: Cambridge University Press, 1984.

Sontag, Frederick. *Emotion: Its Role in Understanding and Decision.* New York: Peter Lang, 1989.

Stearns, Frederic R. *Anger: Psychology, Physiology, Pathology.* Springfield, Ill.: Charles C Thomas, 1972.

## Animal consciousness

**Type of ethics:** Animal rights

**Date:** From antiquity; revived in the 1970's

**Associated with:** Donald R. Griffin, American behavioral scientist and discoverer of bat sonar

**Definition:** The argument that mental experience probably exists throughout the animal kingdom, that animals may experience thought processes, self-awareness, and emotions similar to, though simpler than, those of humans

**Significance:** Used to argue for the ethical treatment of animals; may contribute to understanding the evolution of ethical systems

Early in the twentieth century, in response to exaggerated claims for mental abilities in animals, the behaviorist tradition came to dominate psychology and animal behavior. Behaviorists claimed that animals are probably not conscious of themselves or of their behavior; that if they were, the knowledge would not be important to them; and that this consciousness would be impossible for humans to measure, analyze, or understand. Through the following decades, behavioral scientists assumed that animals were incapable of thought, emotions, and self-awareness. Animals were treated almost as machines in behavioral studies.

Later in the century, some ethologists (people who study animal behavior under conditions as nearly natural as possible) began to question the assumptions of behaviorism. One of these was Donald R. Griffin, who was impressed by the number of animal capabilities that were initially considered to be preposterous by behavioral scientists but were later clearly demonstrated. His own discovery (with Robert Galambos) that bats use a sonarlike system for spatial orientation and insect capture is an example of such a capability. Griffin thought that animals might also have greater mental ability than behaviorists believed. Karl von Frisch had already described an elaborate dance of honeybees, with which scout bees direct their coworkers to sources of nectar. The dance uses symbolic representations for the direction, distance, and quality of the nectar source. Other examples of animal mental accomplishments ranged from navigation in birds to evidence of learning and language use in apes, monkeys, dolphins, sea lions, and parrots.

Griffin wrote *The Question of Animal Awareness* in 1976 to explore the possibility that reasoning and consciousness might exist in animals. The question of animal awareness has actually been in existence since people became conscious. Animal thought and awareness were assumed to exist by many scientists and most laypersons before the establishment of behaviorism. Griffin's book, supported by his impeccable scientific reputation, brought the idea back for serious consideration among behavioral scientists and initiated a new science: cognitive ethology.

Griffin argued that animals do many things that can be most easily explained if they are assumed to have at least a limited ability to think and plan. Also, given the fact that human anatomy and physiology—including the anatomy and physiology of the nervous system, the center of thought and consciousness—are very similar to those of animals, there is good reason to assume that human mental processes are also similar to those of animals. Further, he proposed that the ability to reason, even in a very rudimentary fashion, should be of value to animals, as it is to humans, and so should be favored by natural selection. He suggested that there is no more evidence demonstrating animals' inability to think and feel than there is demonstrating their ability to do so, and that it is foolish to assume they lack such abilities without evidence.

Griffin did not say that animal reasoning is on the same level as that of humans. Though whales and apes, especially chimpanzees, have been assigned near-human abilities by some investigators, these claims have always been unsupported when carefully investigated. Griffin argued that awareness and thinking ability are far greater in humans than in animals, but that the essential processes supporting consciousness are the same in the two groups. In other words, there are great quantitative differences, but no qualitative differences.

In some people's minds, the ethical treatment of animals hinges on the question of animal consciousness. If animals are aware of fear and pain, ethical consideration requires that any human use of an animal be designed to minimize the animal's distress. Assuming that animal consciousness exists, animal rights extremists argue that animals should not be used by humans in any way. Instead, as sentient beings, they should be given the same rights and respect as humans. Organisms that are not aware of their pain and fear, however, need not be so carefully treated. The most extreme animal use proponents assume that there is no animal consciousness and argue that unfeeling beasts can be used in any way humans see fit. Most cognitive ethologists agree that humans have a right to use animals, since all species use others in natural ecological interactions such as predation. Animal use should, however, be carried out with the animal's potential awareness in mind, and pain or discomfort should be minimized.

Animal awareness might also prove to be of importance to the study of ethics. Ethics, like consciousness, has been assumed to be the exclusive concern of humans. Some animals, however, appear to use deception to manipulate their fellows intentionally. If such behavior occurs widely among animals, the evolution of ethical systems might be profitably studied using these primitive systems. A problem with this prospect, and with the question of animal consciousness in general, is the difficulty of understanding what is going on in another species' mind. Behaviorist assumptions are still prevalent in psychology and animal behavior. Not everyone is convinced that animals think or are aware of themselves and their actions, let alone that they make conscious ethical (or unethical) decisions. —*Carl W. Hoagstrom*

**See also** Animal research; Animal rights; Cruelty to animals; Moral status of animals.

**Bibliography**

Cheney, Dorothy L., and Robert M. Seyfarth. *How Monkeys See the World: Inside the Mind of Another Species*. Chicago: University of Chicago Press, 1990.

Griffin, Donald R. *Animal Minds*. Chicago: University of Chicago Press, 1992.

Linden, Eugene. "Can Animals Think?" *Time* 141 (March 22, 1993): 54-61.

Ristau, C. A., ed. *Cognitive Ethology*. Hillsdale, N.J.: Lawrence Erlbaum, 1991.

Waal, F. B. M. de. *Chimpanzee Politics: Power and Sex Among Apes*. Baltimore: The Johns Hopkins University Press, 1989.

## Animal research

**Type of ethics:** Animal rights
**Date:** Fifth century B.C.E. to present
**Definition:** The practice of using animals in research for the purpose of acquiring new knowledge that could benefit humankind, education, and product testing
**Associated with:** Peter Singer
**Significance:** Raises questions regarding the moral acceptability of subjecting animals to pain, suffering, and sometimes death for the benefit of people

**History.** Using animals for purposes of research (also referred to as vivisection) has been practiced since the beginning of scientific medicine, when it was practiced by the ancient Greeks. The field of medicine benefitted from the study of living organisms, and the fields of experimental physiology, biology, and comparative anatomy could not have emerged as independent disciplines without the knowledge gained from animal laboratory research. Up through the seventeenth century, the scientific community had no moral, legal, or religious objection to vivisection. As Nicolaas Rupke, a scientific historian, points out in his book *Vivisection in Historical Perspective* (1987), it was not until the nineteenth century that vivisection became the focus of public controversy. This controversy grew out of the animal welfare movement of the 1820's and eventually led to the introduction in Britain of the Cruelty to Animals Act of 1876, which was the first law enacted to regulate animal research.

Although the public debate over vivisection continued throughout the next century, the publication of *Animal Liberation* (1975) by animal rights activist Peter Singer fueled and revived the antivivisection movement. Singer's book contained the most powerful arguments to date against the use of animals in research. He used the term "speciesism" to encapsulate the notion that it is morally indefensible for one particular species (humans) to dominate and abrogate the rights of another species for their own interests. One of the first books published by a member of the scientific community to rebut the antivivisection arguments was William Paton's *Man and Mouse: Animals in Medical Research* (1984).

**Arguments for and Against the Use of Animals in Research**

| | Pro | | Con |
|---|---|---|---|
| 1. | Animals provide good models for understanding fundamental human processes. | 1. | Inflicting pain and suffering on animals is unacceptably cruel and is therefore immoral. |
| 2. | Since animals are less complex organisms (both biologically and psychologically), they provide a good beginning point for exploratory research. | 2. | Animal research has no value or efficacy for understanding human processes or disorders. |
| 3. | Animals have shorter life-spans, which facilitates the study of genetically transmitted traits. | 3. | Most animal research serves no beneficial purpose for humans and is unnecessary. |
| 4. | Scientists are able to control an animal's environment effectively, reducing the number of confounding variables that plague research. | 4. | The cost of harming another animal in most cases does not outweigh the benefit to society. |
| 5. | Animals can be used for experiments that would be considered unethical to perform on humans. | 5. | Animals have intrinsic worth and deserve to live freely, unrestricted by selfish motives of another species. |

**The Extent of Animal Research.** Animals are frequently used for research in both the biomedical fields (for example, pharmacology, bacteriology, toxicology) and the social sciences (for example, psychology). Although estimates are difficult to come by, the National Research Council believes that approximately 17 million animals are used for research each year in the United States. The majority of these animals, roughly 85 to 90 percent, are either laboratory rats or mice. Primates appear to account for less than 7 percent of research animals. In comparison, the American Humane Association reports that approximately 12 million animals are killed in shelters each year.

**Arguments.** Many views exist concerning the moral acceptability of using animals in research. On one end of the continuum, a minority of scientists advocates the unrestrictive use of animals for experimental research, teaching purposes, or product testing, regardless of the value of that research for improving the welfare of the human condition. On the other end of the continuum, a minority of animal activists, such as Tom Regan of the Animal Liberation Movement, promotes the total elimination of the use of animals for science. Most scientists and activists hold positions in between these extremes.

Advocates of vivisection maintain that animal research has unlocked mysteries in the fields of physiology, biochemistry, neuroscience, and pathology, among others, which have allowed discoveries to be made that have led to the elimination or reduction of human pain and suffering for generations of people to come. These advocates point to progress in mental illness, neurological disorders, genetic disorders, pain management, vaccinations, and many other areas, all made possible by animal research. Antivivisectionists argue, primarily on moral or ideological grounds, that inflicting pain on another species is cruel and immoral. Many activists state that humans do not have the authority to usurp the rights of another species for their own purposes, holding that animals possess intrinsic worth and should be able to live freely, without restrictions imposed by an intellectually superior species. Singer asks: Is speciesism merely another form of blatant racism? Those who support animal research counter with the argument that animals are not morally equal to humans.

Most animal rights groups do not want to see all animal research abolished. They do, however, want to see the institution of more responsible research practices. Michael Fox, philosopher and author of *The Case for Animal Experimentation* (1986), states that animal rights groups have accused the scientific community of being reluctant to use humane research methods that are intended to reduce the number of animals being used and minimize or eliminate the pain or suffering that they experience. In addition, the animal rights groups maintain that much research serves no valuable purpose. Fox agrees that pain and suffering should be minimized whenever possible, but points out that in some instances, it may not be possible. Also, it is difficult to predict how valuable research is going to be before it is conducted.

**Regulations.** Guidelines created by a number of scientific organizations, along with state and federal laws, exist to help regulate the use of animals in research. Many of these documents address the humane treatment of animals, including the concern for the animals' comfort and health. The guidelines typically stress the need to reduce pain and discomfort by using anesthesia or analgesics and to use particularly invasive techniques only when no other alternatives can be found.

—*Bryan C. Auday*

**See also** Animal consciousness; Animal rights; Cruelty to animals; Moral status of animals; National Anti-Vivisection Society; People for the Ethical Treatment of Animals; Singer, Peter; Vivisection.

**BIBLIOGRAPHY**

Fox, Michael A. *The Case for Animal Experimentation: An Evolutionary and Ethical Perspective.* Berkeley: University of California Press, 1986.

Linzey, Andrew. *Christianity and the Rights of Animals.* New York: Crossroad, 1987.

Paton, William D. *Man and Mouse: Animals in Medical Research.* Oxford, England: Oxford University Press, 1984.

Rollin, Bernard. *Animal Rights and Human Morality.* Buffalo, N.Y.: Prometheus Books, 1981.

Rupke, Nicolaas, A., ed. *Vivisection in Historical Perspective.* New York: Croom Helm, 1987.

Singer, Peter. *Animal Liberation.* New York: New York Review Books, 1975.

## Animal rights

**TYPE OF ETHICS:** Animal rights

**DATE:** Last quarter of twentieth century

**ASSOCIATED WITH:** Philosophers such as Peter Singer and Tom Regan and organizations such as People for the Ethical Treatment of Animals

**DEFINITION:** "Animal rights" refers specifically to the extension of rights-based ethical theories to nonhuman animals and generally to a political movement with philosophical foundations in both the utilitarian and rights-based traditions in ethical theory

**SIGNIFICANCE:** The rhetoric of animal rights groups borrowed two basic concepts from ethical theory: Peter Singer's principle of equal consideration of interests and Tom Regan's analysis of what it means to have moral rights

The animal rights groups that became a potent and pervasive political force in the United States and Europe during the last quarter of the twentieth century were distinguished from earlier, more moderate animal protection groups by their rights-based rhetoric, but they also drew freely on the thinking of utilitarian ethicist Peter Singer.

**History.** The older "animal protection" groups, such as the American Society for the Prevention of Cruelty to Animals (ASPCA) and the Humane Society of the United States (HSUS), had as their primary focus the prevention of blatant mistreatment of work and companion animals. In 1975, the Australian philosopher Peter Singer published *Animal Liberation*, which subsequently became the bible of the animal rights movement, and in the early 1980's, a number of professional philosophers began devoting serious attention to the ethics of the treatment of nonhuman animals. The new animal rights groups, such as People for the Ethical Treatment of Animals (PETA), the Fund For Animals, and the Farm Animal Reform Movement (FARM), used ideas that emerged from the philosophical debate to question the very use of animals, especially in agriculture and science.

While some groups, such as the Animal Legal Defense Fund, worked within the system, the best known groups emphasized confrontation and "direct action," especially the clandestine Animal Liberation Front (ALF), which devoted itself solely to illegal actions such as stealing ("liberating") lab animals and destroying scientific equipment and data. In 1981 Alex Pacheco, who later founded PETA along with Ingrid Newkirk, volunteered as an assistant to Edward Taub, who was doing research on nerve damage using monkeys at Silver Spring, Maryland. Pacheco documented violations of state cruelty laws, and Taub was convicted on six counts. Then, in 1984, the ALF provided PETA with videotapes stolen from a laboratory at the University of Pennsylvania that was using baboons to study head injuries. The footage, which had been shot by the scientists themselves, showed researchers joking about the animals, which were being subjected to severe, brain-damaging whiplash, and showed what appeared to be inadequately anesthetized baboons left unattended. PETA edited the footage into a widely distributed video, *Unnecessary Fuss*, and the resulting publicity forced the closure of the lab.

Although Taub's conviction was subsequently overturned on the grounds that the state cruelty laws in question did not govern federally funded research, groups such as PETA capitalized on the publicity from such cases to become a potent political force. In 1985, the federal Animal Welfare Act of 1966 was amended to require all universities accepting federal funds to have an Institutional Animal Care and Use Committee (IACUC), and by the late 1980's there were persistent calls, from a number of scientists and in proposed legislation, for "The Three R's": *replacement* of animals with nonanimal models, *refinement* of experimental protocols to eliminate animal suffering, and *reduction* of the number of animals used.

The political success of animal rights groups was reflected in the birth of groups defending the use of animals, such as the Animal Industry Foundation, the Incurably Ill For Animal Research, and the Foundation for Biomedical Research (FBR). The FBR produced a response to *Unnecessary Fuss* called *Will I Be Alright Doctor?* featuring children whose lives had been saved with medical procedures first developed on animals, and it took out ads with photos of animal rights protesters captioned: "Thanks to animal research, they'll be able to protest 20.8 years longer."

Although most philosophers writing on the subject concluded that animal rights and environmental ethics are based on incompatible foundations (concern for individuals versus concern for ecological wholes) and environmental groups such as the Sierra Club and the Audubon Society took steps to distance themselves from animal rights groups during the late 1980's and early 1990's, some animal activists sought to forge coalitions with environmental concerns. From its founding in 1967, the Fund For Animals merged concern for animals and endangered species in its campaigns against hunting and trapping. Similarly, Animal Rights Mobilization (founded in 1981 as Trans-Species Unlimited) conducted an annual "Fur-Free Friday" the day after Thanksgiving in more than 100 cities, in an effort to meld animal rights and environmental ethics.

While emphasizing action and sometimes even disparaging philosophical reflection as a frivolous distraction, animal rights activists borrowed two notions from philosophers studying the ethics of the human treatment of nonhuman animals: Peter Singer's principle of equal consideration of interests and Tom Regan's analysis of the concept of moral rights. Although most activists read Singer's popular *Animal Liberation*, few read his more philosophical book *Practical Ethics* (1979) or Regan's lengthy and rigorous *The Case for Animal Rights* (1983). Yet it is in these latter two books that Singer and Regan provide careful analyses of the concepts that animal rights activists commonly invoked, and, in particular, Regan's book—not Singer's—is the source of the analysis of moral rights that activists used to question the very use of animals.

**Singer's Principle of Equal Consideration of Interests.** Singer wrote *Animal Liberation* for popular consumption, and in it he spoke loosely of animals having moral rights. In later, more philosophically rigorous work (summarized in *Practical Ethics*), however, he explicitly adopts a utilitarian stance and eschews talk of rights. Utilitarianism is the view that right actions maximize aggregate happiness. In principle, nothing is inherently or intrinsically wrong, according to a utilitarian; any action could be justified under some possible circumstances. One way of characterizing rights views in ethics, by contrast, is that there are some things that, regardless of the consequences, are simply wrong to do to individuals, and that moral rights single out these things. To defend the moral rights of animals would be to claim that certain ways of treating animals cannot be justified on utilitarian grounds.

As a utilitarian, however, Singer does not oppose all uses of animals. If the benefits to humans of scientific experimentation or animal agriculture sufficiently outweighed the harms to animals, then they would be justified in utilitarian terms. What Singer insists on is *equal consideration of interests*. Singer argues that what makes racism and sexism morally objectionable is that the racist does not give equal weight to the similar interests of members of different races and the sexist does not give equal weight to the similar interests of men and women. Borrowing a term from Richard Ryder, he defines a *speciesist* as one who ignores or gives different weights to the similar interests of humans and animals.

To insist on equal consideration of animals' interests is

not to claim that animals have all the same interests as human beings or that animals ought to be treated in the same way as humans. Singer illustrates these points with the following example. Because a pig has no interests that would be served by an education, whereas a child does, equal consideration for the interests of a pig and a child will lead to very different treatment.

What a child and a pig do have in common, however, is an interest in avoiding suffering. Singer argues that sentience, the capacity for suffering, is a necessary and sufficient condition for moral standing. Arguing that if a being suffers, there can be no excuse for refusing to take its suffering into account, Singer concludes that sentience is sufficient for moral standing. Arguing that if a being is incapable of suffering, there is no individual welfare to be taken into account, he concludes that sentience is a necessary condition for moral standing. Singer speculates that sentience may have vanished from the phylogenetic "scale" by the level of the mollusks (clams, oysters, and scallops), because these organisms' nervous systems and behaviors are so simple that they probably are not conscious at all.

Singer argues that the status quo in science and in agriculture is based on violations of the principle of equal consideration of interests. He argues that one would not subject a human being to the amount of pain routinely inflicted on sentient animals for the kind of results usually obtained. Similarly, he argues, one would not subject any human being to the pain and stress routinely inflicted on farm animals for the sake of nutritionally unnecessary meat.

Singer's *Animal Liberation* became the bible of the animal rights movement. PETA distributed it to new members and many who read it were inspired to political activism and vegetarianism. To the extent that the animal rights activists opposed *all* use of animals, however, Singer's utilitarian stance was not the philosophical foundation of their cause. As a utilitarian, Singer could countenance *some* uses of animals under *some* conditions, as he himself admitted in his later, more philosophical book *Practical Ethics*.

There he argues that if a happy animal is slaughtered painlessly and replaced with an equally happy animal, then the world is no worse off, in utilitarian terms. Singer denies, however, that this "replaceability argument" can be used to defend large-scale, intensive animal agriculture, for two reasons. First, he claims that the humaneness of living conditions, handling, and slaughter is inversely proportional to the scale of animal agriculture, so that the argument would apply only to an idealized, small-scale animal agriculture. Second, Singer argues that "self-conscious individuals, leading their own lives and wanting to go on living," are not replaceable, because when such an individual dies, its desires go unsatisfied even if another individual's desires are satisfied in its stead. Arguing that a case can be made that all mammals are self-conscious, Singer concludes that the replaceability argument would not apply to most types of farm animals (although he admits that it applies to both fowl and fish, which he thinks are not self-conscious).

Still, Singer's utilitarian position does not imply blanket, exceptionless opposition to animal agriculture. This is all the more clear in the case of medical research, where—at least sometimes—it is not only culinary taste but also the health and lives of self-conscious beings that are at stake. An animal rights activist adhering carefully to Singer's utilitarian position could endorse *some* types of experimentation under *some* circumstances.

**Regan's Analysis of "Having Moral Rights."** In *The Case for Animal Rights*, Tom Regan claims, for this reason, that it is his "rights view," rather than Singer's utilitarianism, which is the philosophical basis of the animal rights movement. Regan argues that respecting animals' moral rights would imply, not only improving the conditions under which they are kept but also the total abolition of animal agriculture and experimentation.

Although there is controversy as to the specifics, there is general agreement among ethicists about what it means to "have moral rights": To attribute moral rights to an individual is to assert that the individual has some kind of special moral dignity, the value of which is that there are certain things that cannot justifiably be done to him or her (or it) for the sake of benefit to others. For this reason, moral rights have been characterized as "trump cards" against utilitarian arguments. In *The Case for Animal Rights*, Regan explores the implications of recognizing moral rights so conceived in at least all normal mammals one year old or older.

Regan argues that in order to possess moral rights, an individual must be not merely sentient but also a "subject of a life," with self-consciousness, beliefs, memories, desires, and a sense of its future. Just as Singer argues that probably all mammals are self-conscious, Regan argues that at least all normal mammals one year old or older have these capacities. He argues that birds, reptiles, amphibians, and fish ought all to be treated *as if* they have rights, out of a spirit of moral caution (they *may* be subjects of a life, but the case for saying that they are is weaker than the case for saying that mammals are).

According to Regan, all subjects of a life have basically one moral right: the right not to be harmed on the grounds that doing so benefits others. Recognizing this right would, he argues, imply the total dissolution of animal agriculture and animal experimentation. If animals have moral rights, then the slaughter of an animal cannot be justified in terms of the benefits accruing to humans. Even experimentation calculated to save human lives cannot, Regan argues, be justified. If animals have moral rights, then humans are not justified in harming them for the sake of benefits to humans, no matter how great those benefits may be. Human beings can knowingly waive their rights and accept the suffering or additional risks involved in experimentation, but animals cannot. Regan's view is that the only permissible experiments on animals are those that impose no new risks on the animals involved, such as trials of new drugs on animals already suffering from currently incurable diseases.

**The Influence of Philosophy on Practice.** In practice, the animal rights activists of the late twentieth century drew freely on the ideas of both Singer and Regan. They often invoked the concept of moral rights, but they also commonly invoked Singer's principle of equal consideration of interests and claimed his *Animal Liberation* as their philosophical inspiration.

Although both philosophers opposed the status quo in agriculture and science, their professional philosophical writings dramatically illustrate the distinction between rights-based and utilitarian theories of ethics and the degree to which animal rights activists could differ over specific issues. An activist thinking in utilitarian terms might endorse animal experimentation that is likely to save lives, whereas one thinking in terms of animals' rights might oppose all research, no matter how beneficial to humans. An activist thinking in utilitarian terms might endorse the humane slaughter of some animals, whereas one thinking in terms of animals' rights might oppose slaughter under all circumstances.

**The Philosophical Response.** Just as the political successes of animal rights groups inspired the formation of groups defending various uses of animals, the attention given Singer's and Regan's work on the subject inspired opposing philosophical work. Two philosophers' works are especially noteworthy in this regard.

In 1980, Canadian Michael A. Fox published *The Case for Animal Experimentation*, the first book-length defense of animal experimentation by a philosopher. Fox's defense of experimentation turns on an anthropocentric conception of ethics. Fox argues that rights and duties apply only among individuals capable of recognizing reciprocal obligations, and that only humans are capable of this. He concludes that only human beings are full-fledged members of the moral community and that we have no duties directly to animals. He nevertheless opposes cruelty (deliberately inflicting unnecessary pain) because doing so makes us more likely to wrong our fellow human beings. Fox subsequently recanted his central argument, but his book nevertheless represents a systematic development of an argument commonly used by defenders of animal research.

A more persistent critic of animal rights philosophies was American philosopher Raymond G. Frey. In *Interests and Rights: The Case Against Animals* (1980), Frey expresses skepticism about the very usefulness of "rights" as a moral concept (Frey, like Singer, is a utilitarian), but for the sake of argument he accepts the view of rights theorists like Regan that having rights implies having desires. Frey's central argument in the book is that animals cannot have rights because they are incapable of having desires. In defense of this claim, Frey offers a subtle, original analysis of what it means to have desires. He argues that, in order to have desires, one must be capable of entertaining various beliefs, because what distinguishes conscious desires from mere needs is their sensitivity to the individual's beliefs.

Frey argues that animals that lack language lack beliefs, because it is only sentences that can be true or false, and only creatures with language can think about a sentence being true or false. Therefore, only creatures endowed with language can have desires, and hence, only they can have moral rights. Frey concludes that neither vegetarian nor antivivisectionist conclusions can follow from a rights-based philosophy. Frey's later *Rights, Killing, and Suffering: Moral Vegetarianism and Applied Ethics* (1983) is focused specifically on moral arguments for vegetarianism, and while less original, philosophically, than his earlier book, it probably contains a version of every argument ever offered in response to ethical arguments in favor of vegetarianism, including utilitarian arguments such as Singer's.

*—Gary E. Varner*

**See also** Animal consciousness; Animal research; Consequentialism; Cruelty to animals; Environmental ethics; Humane Society of the United States; Moral status of animals; People for the Ethical Treatment of Animals; Sentience; Singer, Peter; Society for the Prevention of Cruelty to Animals (SPCA); Vegetarianism; Vivisection; World Society for the Protection of Animals.

**Bibliography**

Fox, Michael E. "Animal Experimentation: A Philosopher's Changing Views." *Between the Species* 3, no. 2 (Spring, 1987): 55-82. Fox's recantation of his earlier argument and a sketch of the direction in which his views were evolving.

___________. *The Case for Animal Experimentation*. Berkeley: University of California Press, 1986. A systematic defense of animal experimentation, based on an anthropocentric conception of ethics.

Frey, R. G. *Interests and Rights: The Case Against Animals*. Oxford, England: Clarendon Press, 1980. A rigorous and original analysis of key concepts leading to the conclusion that animals cannot have rights because they have no interests.

___________. *Rights, Killing, and Suffering: Moral Vegetarianism and Applied Ethics*. Oxford, England: Basil Blackwell, 1983. An eclectic critique of all the main moral arguments for vegetarianism, including both rights-based and utilitarian arguments.

Regan, Tom. *The Case For Animal Rights*. Berkeley: University of California Press, 1983. A philosophically rigorous defense of the claim that animals have moral rights, with applications to experimentation and agriculture.

Singer, Peter. *Animal Liberation*. New York: Random House, 1990 Rev. ed. The bible of the animal rights movement; a popular but philosophically superficial overview of the animal rights issue.

___________. *Practical Ethics*. New York: Cambridge University Press, 1979 (revised edition, 1992). A rigorous introduction to applied ethics and the definitive statement of Singer's position on ethics and animals.

## Anthropological ethics

**TYPE OF ETHICS:** Scientific ethics

**DATE:** Nineteenth century to present

**DEFINITION:** The relationship between ethnographic fieldwork and moral decisions

**SIGNIFICANCE:** Tries to minimize negative impacts on ethnographic informants providing information that can be used to understand human culture and behavior

Anthropology studies human culture and behavior primarily through the observation of participants living intimately with and observing a community. Anthropologists risk negatively affecting a community or individuals within it by their presence, actions, or reportage of information.

Anthropology originated only in the mid-nineteenth century, and its early practice betrayed its colonialist roots. Field anthropologists often were government agents sent on espionage expeditions to colonies or territories, informants typically were misled regarding the uses to which information would be put, and concern for informants often was sorely lacking. As early as 1916, Franz Boas and other prominent anthropologists had decried these abuses in print.

World War II proved to be a watershed in terms of concern about ethics in anthropology. The second half of the twentieth century saw the development of formal ethical codes for most of the major anthropological organizations, including the American Anthropological Association, the Society for Applied Anthropology, and the Association of Social Anthropologists of the Commonwealth. These codes contain a core of generally-accepted principles, though controversy flourishes regarding other issues.

**Core Principles.** Formal ethical codes in anthropology emphasize the obligations of the anthropologist to the people under study, the discipline, and the sponsors of the research.

The anthropologist's greatest responsibility is to the people under study. These people are critical to the study and can be hurt by it. Furthermore, in some cases, cultural differences make people unlikely to understand fully the possible ramifications of their participation. Consequently, anthropologists must use extreme care to protect their informants-hosts.

Knowledge of the political or social structure of a community, even if it is divorced from the specifics of individual office holders, can be used by governments and others to control, terrorize, or punish a community, and individuals should be aware of what level of risk they are taking by providing that information to anthropologists. Only if the informants find these conditions acceptable should the research continue.

The anthropologists must be prepared to withhold information if necessary to protect the people under study. Many ethnographic reports use pseudonyms or nonspecific reporting in attempts to disguise informant and community identities. Recognizing the trust placed in them, anthropologists should be very sensitive to issues of confidentiality and reveal nothing that is likely to harm the study community or its individual members.

Ethical obligations to the discipline revolve around publication. Anthropologists are obligated to publish the results of their studies, lest they become mere self-indulgent "custom collectors." In order to achieve the greater goals of anthropology, the broadest possible corpus of evidence is necessary. Clearly, falsification and distortion are intolerable.

Sponsors of ethnographic fieldwork vary greatly. Academic funding agencies sponsor much research, and they typically are sympathetic to anthropological ethics. Other funding, however, may come from private foundations or government agencies that may be unfamiliar with ethical standards or even antagonistic toward them. Project Camelot, for example, was sponsored by the Special Operations Research Office of the U.S. Army between 1964 and 1967. As described in the prospectus, which was mailed to many anthropologists and other social scientists, the goal of this project was "to predict and influence politically significant aspects of social change in the developing nations of the world," particularly Latin America. This kind of a project can place an anthropologist in an untenable position, since it may require providing information that will harm (in the anthropologist's judgment) the people under study.

While many anthropologists argue that anthropologists should never accept funding from agencies with questionable motives, ethical codes typically are less dogmatic. They stress the need for a clear agreement regarding what information is to be made available to the sponsor. Obviously, the anthropologist should reject funding if agreement cannot be reached. If agreement is reached, the anthropologist has an obligation to provide accurate, though not necessarily complete, reporting.

**Intervention Versus Scholarly Neutrality.** Under the leadership of Franz Boas, early twentieth century anthropology was committed to preserving information about "traditional" societies before they were transformed by the spread of Western civilization. This led to a nonintervention ethic maintaining that anthropology should dispassionately describe and analyze societies but not try to change them.

The twentieth century, however, showed that these societies were changing in response to Western civilization and would continue to do so. An emerging cadre of applied anthropologists argued that anthropology properly should help direct this change in the manner least damaging to these societies.

Not all anthropologists, however, have accepted the tenets of applied anthropology, and critics argue that anthropological understanding is too rudimentary to permit control of cultural change. Further concern derives from the fact that most funding for applied anthropological research comes from governments that may not be particularly concerned about the welfare of the people under study; pressure placed on an anthropologist by such a sponsor can be considerable.

**Issues of Relativism and Cultural Conflict.** In response to ethnocentrism in early anthropology, Boas and others argued for cultural relativism, the recognition that all cultures are equally valid and worthy of respect. Cultural relativism remains entrenched in anthropology, but twentieth century ethnogenocide and human rights violations have led some anthropologists to reconsider, arguing that cultures advocating these and other unacceptable practices are not compatible with world values and must change.

Another related issue occasionally arises. The ethics of anthropology are culture-bound, closely tied to Western precepts, and they may conflict with the ethics of another society. When living in and studying a society whose ethics are very different, should anthropologists cling to their own culture's ethical standards?

**"The Delicate Balance of Good."** The ethical perspectives discussed above are full of contradictions. Obligations to the discipline require that studies be published fully; obligations to the people studied require that sensitive information be withheld. These and other conflicts should be resolved by reference to what Erve Chambers calls "the delicate balance of good." The anthropologist must examine the likely results of actions, assess their impact on all parties concerned, and follow the path that is most likely to lead to the best overall outcome. —*Russell J. Barber*

**See also** Professional ethics.

**Bibliography**

Beals, Ralph. *Politics of Social Research.* Chicago: Aldine, 1969.

Cassell, Joan. "Ethical Principles for Conducting Fieldwork." *American Anthropologist* 82 (March, 1980): 28-41.

Murphy, Michael Dean, and Agneta Johannsen. "Ethical Obligations and Federal Regulations in Ethnographic Research and Anthropological Education." *Human Organization* 49 (Summer, 1990): 127-138.

Rynkiewich, Michael, and James Spradley. *Ethics and Anthropology.* New York: John Wiley & Sons, 1976.

## Anthropomorphism

**Type of ethics:** Beliefs and practices
**Date:** First used in English in 1753
**Definition:** The description of God in terms of properties that are typical of human beings
**Significance:** The extent to which God is conceived to be similar to human beings determines the way in which people relate to God and to one another, providing the basis for ethical systems

In philosophy and ethics, anthropomorphism means believing that God has properties that are shared by human beings. These may be physical properties, such as having eyes and hands; psychological properties, such as feeling sadness or anger; or cognitive or intellectual properties, such as possessing knowledge or power. Insofar as anthropomorphic descriptions imply defects or limitations, monotheistic traditions (unlike polytheistic traditions) treat such descriptions figuratively. For example, physical properties are almost always taken to imply defects or limitations; therefore, references to "God's strong right arm" are typically taken to refer to divine power rather than divine right-handedness. Insofar as anthropomorphic descriptions do not imply defects or limitations, they are typically regarded as being literally true. Human beings typically possess some knowledge and power. Likewise, in monotheistic traditions, God is held to be omnipotent and omniscient. Being omnipotent entails having power and being omniscient entails having knowledge, so describing God in these terms is anthropomorphic in that it ascribes knowledge and power to God. Because the terms "omnipotent" and "omniscient" mean that there is no limit to God's power and knowledge, these concepts are taken literally. Typically, having psychological properties is thought to involve limitations and defects, either directly or by way of implication that having psychological properties also means that one has physical properties, although this implication is sometimes denied. Unless it is denied, descriptions of God as having psychological properties are also taken figuratively. The fact that having psychological properties also implies having intellectual or cognitive properties typically is not taken to imply any defect or limitation.

**See also** God.

## Anti-Semitism

**Type of ethics:** Race and ethnicity
**Date:** Coined 1870's
**Definition:** All forms of hostility toward Jews
**Significance:** Raises the issues of the "ethical justification" for anti-Semitism, the arguments of "moral responsibilities" posed by non-Jews to Jews in the Holocaust's aftermath, and "ethical demands" by Jews

**History.** Prejudice against Jews appeared in antiquity (pagan anti-Semitism), during the early Christian era, under Islam, during the Middle Ages in Spain, in early modern and modern Europe, in the contemporary Arab world, and in the Americas. Whether in Hellenistic/Roman times or, since 321 C.E., the year that Christianity emerged as the official religion of the Roman Empire, when accusations of blood libels against Jews intensified (the allegation that Jews murdered Christians to obtain blood for ritual purposes), as did their portrayal as the "executioners of Jesus"—the Jews were gradually excluded from society.

Under Islam the Jews, like the Christians, were often treated as second-class subjects. Nevertheless, they were regarded by the Qur'an (Islam's sacred book) as "people of the book," possessing scriptures of their own. Since Islam spread by physical conquest rather than by spiritual propaganda, it did not seek, initially at least, to conquer souls as early Christianity had done, displaying greater tolerance vis-à-vis the monotheistic religions.

Prevalent in Europe, anti-Semitism during the Middle Ages surfaced in the form of expulsions, inquisitions, and massacres. In addition, Catechism, then the only form of education, instilled into the minds of the children negative attitudes toward the "executioners of Christ."

The Enlightenment, on the other hand, offered mixed signals to the Jews. The Enlightenment's philosophers, as a group, were far from constituting a cohesive and unified force in their attitudes toward anti-Semitism. An important segment of philosophers denounced Christianity in the name of deism ("natural religion") and promoted secularism and tolerance toward ethnic minorities. This made them the natural allies of the Jews, the victims of Christian intolerance. Yet while prominent philosophers such as Lessing, Rousseau, and Montesquieu advocated tolerance, other philosophers, equally influential, albeit secular, did not hesitate to criticize "Jewish particularisms."

**ESTIMATED NUMBER OF JEWS KILLED IN THE FINAL SOLUTION**

| Country | Estimated Pre-Final Solution Population | Estimated Jewish Population Annihilated | |
|---|---|---|---|
| | | Number | Percent |
| Poland | 3,300,000 | 3,000,000 | 90 |
| Baltic countries | 253,000 | 228,000 | 90 |
| Germany/Austria | 240,000 | 210,000 | 90 |
| Protectorate | 90,000 | 80,000 | 89 |
| Slovakia | 90,000 | 75,000 | 83 |
| Greece | 70,000 | 54,000 | 77 |
| The Netherlands | 140,000 | 105,000 | 75 |
| Hungary | 650,000 | 450,000 | 70 |
| SSR White Russia | 375,000 | 245,000 | 65 |
| SSR Ukraine* | 1,500,000 | 900,000 | 60 |
| Belgium | 65,000 | 40,000 | 60 |
| Yugoslavia | 43,000 | 26,000 | 60 |
| Romania | 600,000 | 300,000 | 50 |
| Norway | 1,800 | 900 | 50 |
| France | 350,000 | 90,000 | 26 |
| Bulgaria | 64,000 | 14,000 | 22 |
| Italy | 40,000 | 8,000 | 20 |
| Luxembourg | 5,000 | 1,000 | 20 |
| Russia (RSFSR)* | 975,000 | 107,000 | 11 |
| Denmark | 8,000 | - | - |
| Finland | 2,000 | - | - |
| Total | 8,861,800 | 5,933,900 | 67 |

* The Germans did not occupy all the territory of this republic

The post-1789 revolutionary era in France, where the Jews acquired political rights through emancipation, was not devoid of anti-Semitic manifestations. In the 1880's, Edouard Drumont, the anti-Semitic author of the best-selling book *La France Juive* ("Jewish France"), clerical-royalist right-wingers, and socialists perpetuated the myth that the Jews controlled world governments and international money markets. The Dreyfus Affair of the 1890's—in which Captain Alfred Dreyfus of the French army, a Jew, was falsely accused of spying for Germany—revealed the extent of French Jewry's vulnerability. The trials and legal battles that finally led to Dreyfus' vindication nearly destroyed the Third Republic.

Eastern European anti-Semitism was the strongest, especially in the Russian Empire of the pre-1914 periods. The pogroms (massacres) of Odessa (1880's) and Kishinev (early 1900's), as well as the Stalinist anti-Semitism of the 1930's through the early 1950's, were either official policies or acts intentionally overlooked or condoned by the highest echelons of government.

Under Germany's Third Reich (1933-1945), the Jews were depicted as the corrupters of society, responsible for Germany's misfortunes after World War I. Coupled with the ascendance of European fascism and aryanization policies, these trends culminated in the Holocaust. The application of racial anti-Semitism and the *numerus clausus* (limiting the representation of Jews in the professions) in Germany, Italy, France, and North Africa exposed anti-Semitism at its worst.

Anti-Semitism and anti-Zionism—Zionism emerged since the 1890's as the Jewish national movement that contributed to the creation of a Jewish national home in Palestine and, eventually, the state of Israel—gained momentum in the Arab world of the 1930's and 1940's. Following each war fought between Israel and the Arab countries, anti-Jewish and anti-Zionist moods took the form of expulsions of Jewish communities (Egypt), pograms (Morocco), and allegations that Jews controlled Western governments, using Zionism and Israel to realize colonialist goals.

**Ethical Principles.** According to Wendy Stallard Flory, the legitimation of anti-Semitism (and racism in general) may be the result of a selfish attempt to inflate one's self-worth, and often to compensate for one's feelings of inadequacy, by choosing to treat differentness as though it were a moral failing. For example, any attempt to identify specific personality traits of Jews as "reasons" for prejudice is an attempt to rationalize the real motive: a narrowmindedness and defensive refusal to allow others the fundamental human right to be judged as individuals. Anti-Semitism, then, does not necessarily begin with hatred, but with selfish impulses to reinforce one's sense of worth at the expense of others.

After World War II, however, there emerged the "sense of guilt" phenomenon, evinced by Europeans. This is evident in France and Germany. When France was divided into a German-occupied zone and a French free zone at Vichy, the French police who collaborated with the Germans rounded up tens of thousands of Jews and transferred them to Nazi death camps. Following the liberation of France in 1944, a sense of guilt struck the French people. Julius Gould maintains that though in the postwar years French Jews were the targets of anti-Semitic activity, the perpetrators were punished and their organizations forced to disband. This is in marked contrast to the political climate and ethos of the 1930's and 1940's, when anti-Semitism was embraced by the state or disregarded.

The German sense of guilt has also become more pronounced since 1945. The German Federal Republic, under Konrad Adenauer's leadership, sought to convince the world that Germany was stepping out of Hitler's shadow. As Frank Stern contends, during the 1950's Germany moved from the one extreme of depicting the Jews as morally and physically inferior to the other extreme of philo-Semitism. This tendency included idolizing all things Jewish. Every Jewish child was supposed to be a genius; every Jewish woman turned out to be the beautiful Jewess.

Offering German financial and material reparations to Israel, to Holocaust survivors and their families, and to Jewish institutions was reciprocated with moral restitution. In the case of the latter, the Germans were eager to promote the image of the "new" Germany.

As time passed, however, the notion that the Jews and the Germans shared a collective memory of the Holocaust began to fade. Furthermore, a new generation of Germans that emerged in the 1960's and 1970's included elements that equated Israel's policies toward the Palestinian Arabs with pre-1945 Germany's treatment of its Jewish citizens. Frank Stern takes this one step further, suggesting that "a shift in intellectual consciousness took place, a shift that is prominently represented in the German democratic left. . . . In this way a latent cultural anti-Semitism was transformed into overt political anti-Zionism."

Just as support for the United Nations Third World/Soviet bloc-sponsored resolution in 1974 equating Zionism with racism won the approval of young leftist Germans, the total denial of the Holocaust by right-wing forces in the 1980's and 1990's has in fact penetrated academic circles in parts of the Western world. These are thorny issues for Jewish thinkers and scholars. For them, the Holocaust and Zionism are the two central reasons for the emergence of the state of Israel in 1948, the cradle for Jews in need of refuge. Israeli scholars in particular are profoundly concerned with what they regard as a current myth of "German innocence" about the Holocaust, as well as with comments by influential Germans such as Rudolf Augustein, editor of *Der Spiegel,* who, on April 23, 1992, commented that there is no way "of speculating that the young Germans, who know Auschwitz only from their school-books, can be forced into memory." The fear is that these developments could set the stage for the rise, legitimation, and institutionalization of large-scale anti-Semitism once again, particularly in the ever-changing and turbulent Europe of the post-1989 period and in the face of German reunification.

**Ethical Decision Making.** Since 1946, the National Conference of Christians and Jews in the United States and the World Council of Churches fought anti-Semitism with vigor, adopting papers, resolutions, and statements calling for the fostering of close Christian-Jewish cooperation.

Regarding Catholicism, as Norman Solomon observes, the Roman Catholic church, with its history of vilification and oppression of Jews, had waited two decades after World War II to grapple with anti-Semitism. It was in the mid-1960's, during the pontificate of John XXIII, that the Catholic church—through the medium of the Second Vatican Council—addressed itself realistically to the modern world. On October 28, 1965, the Vatican published the *Nostra Aetate*, a document on relationships with non-Christians. Though it contained no direct mention of the Holocaust and Israel, it condemned anti-Semitism explicitly with the backing of the church, and stressed that the Jews collectively, including their ancestors, must not be held accountable for the crucifixion of Jesus Christ.

Other ethical decisions of great magnitude include the role of the German churches in disassociating themselves from the Nazi past, after having been implicated in supporting the Third Reich, and the more recent measure in 1992 to rescind the aforementioned United Nations resolution equating Zionism with racism. The collapse of the Soviet Union and the Soviet bloc, the strengthened position of the United States and the West within the United Nations and the political orientation of the new Russia facilitated the reversal of this controversial and mildly anti-Semitic resolution.

*—Michael M. Laskier*

**See also** Hate; Holocaust; Racism.

**Bibliography**

Bauer, Yehuda. *The Holocaust in Historical Perspective.* Seattle: University of Washington Press, 1978.

Curtis, Michael, ed. *Antisemitism in the Contemporary World.* Boulder Colo.: Westview Press, 1986.

Katz, Jacob. *From Prejudice to Destruction: Antisemitism, 1700-1933.* Cambridge, Mass.: Harvard University Press, 1980.

Laskier, Michael M. *The Jews of Egypt, 1920-1970: In the Midst of Zionism, Anti-semitism, and the Middle East Conflict.* New York: New York University Press, 1992.

___________. *North African Jewry in the Shadow of Vichy France and the Swastika.* Tel Aviv: Tel Aviv University Press, 1992.

Wistrich, Robert S., ed. *Anti-Zionism and Antisemitism in the Contemporary World.* New York: New York University Press, 1990.

## Antitrust legislation

**TYPE OF ETHICS:** Business and labor ethics
**DATE:** Seventeenth century to the present
**DEFINITION:** Defines some actions of large companies, or combinations of companies, as illegal because they give the actors too much power in the marketplace
**SIGNIFICANCE:** Attempts to create marketplace conditions that are fair to all buyers and sellers

Antitrust legislation regulates the behavior of businesses, in particular large businesses and business combinations. The combinations that are regulated can take the form of agreements, formal contracts, and legally identified organizations such as trusts and holding companies. Through antitrust legislation, governments attempt to balance the goal of business, which is to control the market to earn profits, with the goal of providing all marketplace actors, including both buyers and sellers, with the

**LANDMARKS IN ANTITRUST HISTORY**

| Date | Action | Significance |
|---|---|---|
| 1623 | Statute of Monopolies | British law that voided monopolies, with many exceptions. |
| 1890 | Sherman Antitrust Act | Banned every "contract, combination . . . or conspiracy" in restraint of trade or commerce. |
| 1898 | *United States v. Addyston Pipe and Steel Co.* | Ruled an agreement to set prices to be illegal because it gave the parties power to set unreasonable prices. |
| 1904 | *Northern Securities v. United States* | Supreme Court ruled against holding companies that control the stock of competing companies. |
| 1911 | *Standard Oil Co. v. United States* | Supreme Court ordered the breakup of Standard Oil. |
| 1911 | *United States v. American Tobacco Co.* | Supreme Court ordered the breakup of American Tobacco Company. Along with the Standard Oil case, established the "rule of reason" approach to antitrust prosecution. |
| 1914 | Clayton Antitrust Act | Specified actions that were subject to antitrust prosecution. |
| 1914 | Federal Trade Commission Act | Established the Federal Trade Commission as an administrative agency to police "unfair methods of competition." |
| 1920 | *United States v. U.S. Steel Corp.* | Supreme Court ruled that size alone, in the absence of abuse of power, did not make a monopoly illegal. |
| 1921 | *American Column and Lumber Co. v. United States* | Ruled that competitors could be convicted if they had discussed prices and later set identical prices, even if no agreement to do so had been reached. |
| 1936 | Robinson-Patman Act | Specified the types of price discrimination that are illegal. |
| 1936 | *International Business Machines Corp. v. United States* | Established conditions under which it is illegal to tie the sale of one product to the sale of another. |
| 1937 | Miller-Tydings Act | Exempted manufacturers and retailers from prosecution for agreeing to set minimum prices if the states in which they operate allow such agreements. |
| 1938 | Wheeler-Lea Act | Strengthened enforcement powers of the Federal Trade Commission. |
| 1945 | *United States v. Aluminum Co. of America* (Alcoa) | Supreme Court ordered breakup of Alcoa, ruling that a monopoly is illegal even if not accompanied by abuse of power. |
| 1947 | Act Concerning Prohibition of Private Monopoly and Maintenance of Fair Trade | Japanese antitrust law drafted in cooperation with the U.S. government. More stringent than U.S. laws, but Japanese law has weakened over time. |
| 1948 | *Federal Trade Commission v. Cement Institute* | Supreme Court ruled illegal agreements by producers to base prices on manufacturing costs plus transportation from a given location (base-point pricing). |
| 1950 | Celler-Kefauver Act | Clarified the Clayton Antitrust Act, making it enforceable against mergers accomplished by sale of assets in addition to those accomplished by sale of stock. |
| 1952 | Combines Investigation Act | Canadian antitrust legislation. |
| 1967 | *Federal Trade Commission v. Procter & Gamble Co.* | Supreme Court forced Procter & Gamble to divest itself of Clorox because P&G's market power could have allowed Clorox to dominate the bleach market. |
| 1973 | Continental Can decision | International Court of Justice ruled that the company would have violated the European Economic Community Treaty by enhancing its already dominant market position. |
| 1976 | Antitrust Improvements Act | Allows state attorneys general to sue on behalf of residents. |
| 1976 | *United States v. American Telephone and Telegraph Co.* | Ruled that even though the company was subject to regulation it still was subject to antitrust prosecution. The decision forced the breakup of AT&T. |

opportunity to compete. By definition, noncapitalist societies do not have antitrust laws, since firms are owned and operated by the state rather than competing independently.

The law generally recognizes that size confers benefits on firms and can be beneficial to society, as in the case of "economies of scale." A firm with economies of scale can produce its product at a lower cost per unit the more it produces. The law also recognizes, however, that the existence of a large firm may make operation more difficult for smaller firms and that consumers generally benefit from having a choice among sellers. These considerations prompt the drafting of antitrust legislation.

**History.** One of the earliest pieces of antitrust legislation was the Statute of Monopolies, which was enacted in Great Britain in 1623. It stated that monopolies, or single firms producing a given product in a certain market, were not allowed. That law had many exceptions but did set the precedent for later antitrust legislation.

The United States developed the most comprehensive antitrust legislation in the world. The Sherman Antitrust Act of 1890 represented the first clear statement that the U.S. government disapproved of abuse of market power by large firms. That law led to an era of "trust busting" over the next thirty years, particularly under the presidential administrations of Theodore Roosevelt (1901-1909). The Sherman Antitrust Act was somewhat vague in its prohibitions. The Clayton Antitrust Act of 1914 clarified the actions that would be subject to antitrust prosecution.

Two major cases in 1911 clarified judicial thinking on antitrust policy. The Supreme Court ordered the breakup of Standard Oil and of the American Tobacco Company. It established the "rule of reason" approach, whereby the law proscribed only actions that were "unreasonable" restraints of trade. The Court ruled that largeness of a company was not necessarily an offense but that both of those companies had used the power associated with their size in "unreasonable" ways.

**Antitrust Issues.** The history of antitrust legislation, both in the United States and elsewhere in the world, has been uneven. Actions prohibited at one time have later been allowed, and actions that were legal have been prohibited. In general, the law has come to specify particular actions that are not allowed and has clarified the conditions under which various actions are allowed.

In the United States, the Robinson-Patman Act (1936) specified types of price discrimination that are illegal. Price discrimination consists of setting different prices for different customers when those differences are not justified by differences in the cost of serving customers. Price discrimination prevents each customer from being offered the best price on a product. Other laws and regulations concern tie-in sales, in which a consumer has to buy one product before being allowed to buy another; resale price maintenance, whereby a manufacturer forces distributors to charge a minimum price; and base-point pricing, under which competitors agree to set prices as if their products were delivered from a given "base point," thereby not using a location that allows lower transportation costs to offer lower prices to customers. The law covers both "horizontal" business combinations (those at the same stage of production or sale, such as a retailer forming a contract with or acquiring another retailer) and "vertical" combinations (those at different stages of production, such as a manufacturer buying a retail outlet for its product).

**Ethical Principles.** The most basic goal of antitrust legislation is to create a marketplace that produces the best results for society. Economists define an "efficient" marketplace as one that produces a given product at the least cost. In this sense of "good" results, a large firm can benefit society if it operates under economies of scale. A firm that has control over its customers because it is the only seller (or only one of a few sellers), however, may not pass those cost advantages on to customers. Antitrust legislation attempts to prevent that possibility. Some firms with economies of scale are allowed to operate under regulation by the government. Examples include telephone companies, cable television operators, and electric companies.

Most market economies respect freedom. Freedoms, however, can conflict. The freedom of businesses to get together and agree to charge the same price conflicts with the freedom of consumers to shop around to find the lowest price. Most governments that have consciously considered the issue have ruled in favor of the consumer, to at least some extent. The Sherman Antitrust Act, for example, outlaws every "contract, combination . . . or conspiracy" in restraint of trade. That means that firms are not allowed to hinder competition among themselves. Antitrust legislation seeks to clarify which actions constitute hindrances of competition.

*—A. J. Sobczak*

**See also** Business ethics; Capitalism; Communism; Economics; Monopoly; Price fixing; Profit economy; Sales, ethics of.

**BIBLIOGRAPHY**

Armentano, Dominick T. *Antitrust and Monopoly: Anatomy of a Policy Failure*. New York: Wiley, 1982.

Howard, Marshall C. *Antitrust and Trade Regulation: Selected Issues and Case Studies*. Englewood Cliffs, N.J.: Prentice-Hall, 1983.

Kintner, Earl W., and Mark R. Joelson. *An International Antitrust Primer*. New York: Macmillan, 1974.

Low, Richard E. *Modern Economic Organization*. Homewood, Ill.: Richard D. Irwin, 1970.

Posner, Richard A. *Antitrust Law: An Economic Perspective*. Chicago: University of Chicago Press, 1976.

Sherman, Roger. *Antitrust Policies and Issues*. Reading, Mass.: Addison-Wesley, 1978.

Whitney, Simon N. *Antitrust Policies: American Experience in Twenty Industries*. New York: Twentieth Century Fund, 1958.

## Apartheid

**TYPE OF ETHICS:** Race and ethnicity

**DATE:** Adopted in 1948

**DEFINITION:** A policy of racial segregation nurtured by political and economic discrimination against non-European groups in the Republic of South Africa

**SIGNIFICANCE:** Promotes racial discrimination and segregation based on the color of one's skin

Literally, the Afrikaans term *apartheid* means "apartness" or "separateness." It is a system whereby Africans have been stripped of power and control over their lives by whites, through an elaborate network of legislation and custom. Since 1948, successive governments have created a closed, compartmentalized society in which each racial group has prescribed living areas, kinds of work, levels of wages, and distinctive educational systems. In order to enforce the segregation policies of the government, beginning from 1949, various major apartheid laws were put into place. Among others, the Prohibition of Mixed Marriages Act (1949) and the Immorality Act (1950) made all marriages and sexual relations between whites and other races illegal; the Group Areas Act (1950) set aside specific areas for the exclusive occupancy of each racial group, with powers to remove forcibly African tenants (most of whom were confined to the so-called "homelands") from unwanted areas. In addition, all Africans over age sixteen were required to be fingerprinted and to carry a passbook. Opposition to any of these laws was crushed by means of the Suppression of Communism Act (1950) and the Internal Security Act (1982), both of which were enforced by a ruthless police force and an omnipresent secret police.

**Moral Issues.** While cases of racial discrimination occur in other parts of the world, it is the systematic official and legalistic character of apartheid that has made South Africa unique.

South Africa is divided hierarchically into four major population groups according to shades of skin color. Whites (15.6 percent) occupy the top rank, followed by "coloreds" (9.7 percent) and Asians (2.7 percent) in the middle, and Africans (72.0 percent) at the bottom. As the figures indicate, apartheid has been imposed by a minority on the majority, which brings into question the legitimacy of its authority. According to the political philosophy of Jean-Jacques Rousseau, governments should derive their just powers from the consent of the governed. Thus, from the politico-ethical perspective, a minority government without the consent of the majority of the governed would be diffi-

**APARTHEID TIME LINE**

| Time | Event |
|---|---|
| 1652 | Dutch expedition lands in Cape Town, South Africa, and establishes the first permanent white settlement in sub-Saharan Africa. |
| 1820 | Five thousand British colonists arrive at Port Elisabeth. |
| 1836 | *The Great Trek.* To escape the political and cultural influence of the British, twelve thousand Boers (Dutch farmers) move from the Cape in ox wagons to claim the resources and virgin islands of the interior. |
| 1910 | The Union of South Africa is created, as the British join with the Boer Republics to form one country. |
| 1912 | The first major African nationalist movement, the African National Congress (ANC), is founded. |
| 1948 | The Nationalist Party is elected to power and introduces the segregation policy of apartheid as the official policy of the Union. |
| 1958 | Some nationalists break away from the ranks of the ANC to form the Pan-African Congress (PAC). |
| 1960 | The Sharpeville massacre leaves 69 dead, most of them shot in the back, and another 178 wounded in a nonviolent protest against pass laws. The ANC and PAC are outlawed. The hopelessness of working through the system finally convinces the African nationalists to adopt the tactics of sabotage and guerilla war. |
| 1961 | Prior to an all-white referendum, South Africa becomes a republic and withdraws from the British Commonwealth of Nations. Albert John Luthuli wins the Nobel Peace Prize. |
| 1964 | Nelson Mandela, prominent member of the ANC, is sentenced to life imprisonment. |
| 1976 | *Soweto Riot.* A number of rioters are killed by police in a protest begun by schoolchildren against the imposition of Afrikaans as a medium of expression. |
| 1983 | The United Democratic Front (UDF), a multi-racial anti-apartheid movement, is formed. |
| 1984 | Constitutional reform establishes a three-parliament system that allows for a "cosmetic" participation of Indians and coloreds in decision-making but excludes blacks. Bishop Desmond Tutu wins the Nobel Peace Prize. |
| 1991 | Nelson Mandela is released from prison. Ban on nationalist movements is lifted. |
| 1993 | Africans are allowed to participate in the voting process for the first time in the history of the country. |

cult to justify through moral laws. Besides, as the most inclusive form of government, majority rule is more likely to have regard for the rights and best interests of most people than is a minority government. In addition, majority rule presupposes equality of all before the law as well as equal rights and liberties. In the light of these precepts, the South African government may be described as both illegal and immoral.

Over the years, supporters and detractors of this system have existed both within and without South Africa. Black resistance to the policy has been championed by such nationalist movements as the African Nationalist Congress (ANC), the Pan-African Congress (PAC), the United Democratic Front (UDF), the Azania Peoples Organization (AZAPO), and the Black Consciousness Movement, whose leader, Stephen Biko, died in detention under suspicious circumstances. Despite the government's cruelty, immorality, and absurdity, the Afrikaner-dominated Dutch Reformed church of South Africa, to a large extent, supports the government and condones its policies. The church's theological position is that equality between blacks and whites involves a misapprehension of the fact that God made people into different races and nations. The more liberal English-speaking churches and prominent African nationalist leaders have been at various times victims of the wrath of the government, which has been expressed through bannings, withdrawal of passports or visas, deportations, and often imprisonment. Nelson Mandela, one of the leading members of the ANC, was incarcerated for almost three decades as a political prisoner.

With the arrival of Frederick De Klerk as president, serious efforts were made to dismantle apartheid and to achieve majority rule in South Africa: Most of the apartheid laws were repealed; the ban on the nationalist movements was lifted; and Nelson Mandela, a prominent leader of the ANC, was finally released after having served twenty-seven years in jail as a political prisoner. The government of South Africa also announced that on July 27, 1993, for the first time in the history of the country, Africans would be allowed to participate in the voting process. The days of apartheid appeared to be numbered. —*Olusoji A. Akomolafe*

**See also** Mandela, Nelson; Racism; Segregation.

**BIBLIOGRAPHY**

Davis, Hunt R., Jr., ed. *Apartheid Unravels*. Gainesville: University of Florida Press, 1991.

Grundy, Kenneth W. *South Africa: Domestic Crisis and Global Challenge*. Boulder, Colo.: Westview Press, 1991.

McCuen, Gary E. *The Apartheid Reader*. Hudson, Wis.: Gary E. McCuen, 1986.

Motlhabi, Mokgethi B. G. *Challenge to Apartheid: Toward a Morally Defensible Strategy*. Grand Rapids, Mich.: Wm. B. Eerdmans, 1988.

Walshe, Peter. *The Rise of African Nationalism in South Africa*. Berkeley: University of California Press, 1971.

## Apology: Book

**TYPE OF ETHICS:** Classical history; Politico-economic ethics
**DATE:** Written between 399 and 390 B.C.E.
**AUTHOR:** Plato
**SIGNIFICANCE:** In his account of his mentor Socrates' decision to accept an unjust judicial verdict, Plato portrays a conflict of personal ethical values and the judicial system in the Western world's first democracy

Initially, it is important to understand two things about the *Apology*. First, it is Plato's dramatic, eyewitness account of the apology of his friend and teacher. Second, this apology is not an expression of regret for an error but a defense of Socrates' conduct and whole way of life.

**Background to the Trial.** In 399 B.C.E., a seventy-year-old Athenian citizen named Socrates went on trial for allegedly disrespecting the gods and corrupting the youth of Athens. It is clear from both the text of the *Apology* itself and from external evidence that Socrates' real "crime" was severely embarrassing important people in the Greek city-state by his habit of questioning them in public places with respect to matters about which they claimed expertise, exposing their true ignorance, and providing amusement to the onlookers who gathered to see the supposed experts confounded. Socrates regularly insisted that he was merely an earnest philosophical inquirer after truth asking those who presumably knew. In this insistence he was only half sincere. He was pursuing the truth, but he knew that his shallow interlocutors would fall victim to his superior logical and rhetorical skill. He chose the questioning method as an effective way of developing and presenting his own philosophy—a method later adopted in written form by Plato.

**Socrates' Defense.** Plato's account, the first literary "courtroom drama," purports to be a verbatim record of Socrates' defense. Far from corrupting youth by promoting atheism or belief in strange gods (for his accusers have vacillated on this point), Socrates explains that he philosophizes in obedience to a divine command. Since he has carried out his divine mission in a quasi-public way, Socrates feels obliged to explain why he has never made an effort to serve the state as an adviser, since the state would seem to need all the wisdom it can find. Here, he raises an ethical issue with which many later thinkers have struggled, including, notably, Sir Thomas More in his *Utopia* (1516).

Socrates has proclaimed himself a loyal Athenian. Why should not a loyal citizen use his primary talent for the benefit of the state? He argues that if he had gone into political life he would have long since "perished." The struggle for the right in his mind required "a private station and not a public one." He once held the office of senator and discovered that his efforts at promoting justice were futile and in fact on one occasion nearly cost him his life. He did not fear death, he explains, but realized that neither he "nor any other man" could effectively fight for the right in a political position. He could do Athens the greatest good in a private effort to inquire into virtue and wisdom. The state would profit most from citizens schooled in this sort of inquiry. He closes his defense by leaving the decision to the jury and to God.

**Socrates' Response.** According to the rules of an Athenian trial, the jury of 501 men must decide his guilt or innocence by majority vote. His opponents have taken every advantage possible of the prevailing prejudice against Socrates as a "clever" intellectual skilled in "making the weaker case appear to stronger." Such prejudice no doubt contributed substantially to what seems in retrospect a misguided verdict. Having been found guilty in a close vote, Socrates exercises his right to propose an alternative to the death penalty requested by the prosecution as a preliminary to the jury's choice of one of the two proposed punishments. When asked for his countersentence, Socrates banteringly suggests that he should be honored, not punished, but finally proposes a token fine that he then raises somewhat at the urging of his friends, whose expressions of dismay actually interrupt the proceedings. They realize that he is in effect condemning himself to death, but Socrates considers that as an unjustly convicted man he should not be punished at all.

To have offered the kind of alternative his enemies undoubtedly expected—exile—would have amounted to a repudiation of his vocation. He is aware that nowhere else would he be free to exercise this vocation as he has been doing in Athens for years before his enemies' conspiracy to silence him. To save his own life by leaving Athens or by accepting some other compromise such as agreeing to cease philosophizing would contradict the values that he has spent that life to date elucidating. Were he to compromise those values, he would give his shabby accusers a moral victory. Instead, he guarantees that his memory will be revered and—what surely is more important to him—that his work in pursuit of the truth will endure, thanks especially to Plato's decision to publish it. (Socrates himself never transcribed his dialogues.)

After the jury's inevitable vote in favor of the prosecution's request for the death penalty, Socrates rebukes his judges as men more interested in escaping the pressure of the accusers than in giving an account of their own lives. He believes that he is going to "another world where they do not put a man to death for asking questions." He does have a final request of them, however: that they punish his own still young sons if they show more interest in riches or anything else than in virtue. In this way, the judges can still do him and his sons justice. *—Robert P. Ellis*

**See also** Democracy; Freedom of expression; Justice; Plato; Socrates.

**BIBLIOGRAPHY**

Friedlander, Paul. *Plato.* Translated by Hans Meyerhoff. New York: Harper & Row, 1964.

Plato. *Apology*. Chicago: Bolchazy-Carducci, 1981.

Reeve, C. D. C. *Socrates in the Apology: An Essay on Plato's Apology of Socrates.* Indianapolis: Hackett, 1989.

Shorey, Paul. *What Plato Said.* Chicago: University of Chicago Press, 1978.

Taylor, A. E. *Plato: The Man and His Work.* 7th ed. London: Methuen, 1960.

## Applied ethics

**TYPE OF ETHICS:** Theory of ethics

**DATE:** From antiquity

**DEFINITION:** In the broadest sense, applied ethics involves the application of ethical and moral concepts to particular situations

**SIGNIFICANCE:** The ways in which ethics are applied in a society determine the nature of that society

There is no consensus regarding the meaning of the term "applied ethics." Some people believe that applied ethics involves methods of enforcing ethics. Others view it as a kind of ethics that is used up over a period of time. In academic circles, however, there is an increasing tendency to view applied ethics as the large body of codes that define desirable action and are required to conduct normal human affairs. These codes may produce rules that come to be regarded as formal, legal ethics.

Every kind of ethics has been applied at one time or another. A caveman, for example, who hit his wife or child with a club, was sorry about the results, and adopted it as an ethical rule to refrain from beating members of his family was developing an applied ethic. Such a rule remained in the realm of applied ethics until some prophet wrote it down or until a chieftain or legislative body adopted it as a law.

Many varieties of ethics have developed by themselves. As modern civilization developed, new applied ethics were developed for specific vocations or specific households. When Harriet Beecher Stowe wrote *Uncle Tom's Cabin*, she helped many men and women to realize that slavery was unethical because of its effects on men, women, and children; in doing so, she introduced an applied ethic. Later, a constitutional amendment changed this applied ethic to a permanent, legal ethic.

In the United States, many professional and vocational groups have established rules for conducting business. The rules that they devised probably grew out of applied ethics. Groups endeavor to secure in their work certain rules that initially do not have the force of law but can certainly be described as applied ethics. These ethics are used as the basis for determining which rules should become rules of law.

There are many published codes of applied ethical rules. Of these, one of the most important to the business and financial world is the code of the American Institute of Certified Public Accountants. This code requires members of the institute to exercise "professional and verbal judgments" in all accounting activities. In addition, they are told to maintain the "public trust" and "professionalism." They are also required to maintain "integrity and objectivity" and to avoid discreditable acts and advertising. Unfortunately, however, these rules have been violated fairly frequently. Suits brought chiefly by shareholders who found that their clients' stocks had been overvalued by auditors have resulted in multimillion-dollar fines being levied against auditing firms. The federal government and some state governments have at times tried to support rules of accounting ethics.

The American Association of Advertising Agencies created its own applied ethics banning false or exaggerated statements, recognizing an obligation to clients and the public. The standards also forbid unfair competition practices, disclaiming "suggestions or pictures offensive to public decency." Advertising agencies "should not knowingly fail to fulfill all lawful contracted commitments with media."

It should be noted that industry efforts to inculcate standards of applied ethics in the areas of accounting and advertising have not been fully realized. Governmental efforts have helped to move these applied ethics closer to the status of formal ethics.

The Direct Marketing Association enjoins its members to use applied ethics in advertising, solicitations, and special offers. The association may be moving toward developing an ethical code.

The American Institute of Architects has a code that has probably had some effect on the field of architecture. This code includes general obligations regarding knowledge and skill as well as specific obligations to the public, including involvement in civic activities and public interest service. Obligations to clients, to the profession, and to colleagues are fully outlined.

Applied ethics have not yet taken an adequate step toward genuine ethical values in the business world. New efforts are being made, however, to institute better ethics in business management. The federal government and the Business Roundtable, a thoughtful group of chief executive officers of large corporations, have recommended that corporations adopt written codes of conduct and well-defined corporate policies regarding executive compensation, fair play for employees, freedom of expression, and product quality. Corporate codes may do more than any other single policy to humanize business ethics.

The American Association of Engineering Societies has prepared a Model Guide for Professional Conduct that includes a number of applied ethics. Engineers are to be honest and truthful in presenting information and to consider the consequences of their work and the social issues that are pertinent to it. They should let affected parties know about potential conflicts of interest.

The American Society for Public Administration has prepared a code for its members to use. This code is not now actively promoted by the association, however, and for that reason the likelihood of developing new ethics is slim.

Bar associations have worked hard to enforce ethical considerations; Bar examinations include ethical questions; and law schools, some of them reluctantly, offer courses in legal ethics. State officials who regulate legal practice, however, note that ethical violations still occur all too often. A former worker on the staff of the Los Angeles County Bar Association, for example, has observed that there seems to be a trend toward light treatment of unethical behavior.

Similar problems arise in medical practice, and efforts to enforce ethical standards are sometimes hampered by problems of short staffing of local medical associations. Most physicians are relatively committed to following ethical standards, particularly because medical students are required, upon graduation, to take the Hippocratic oath, which dates from the fifth century B.C.E., a period during which the Greeks were greatly interested in ethics.

Banking is so basic in modern capitalist democracies that one would expect to see a host of applied ethics growing up in the field. Banking has been so much a creation of politics, however, that there has been little discussion of banking ethics. President Andrew Jackson probably made a basic ethical mistake when he killed the Second National Bank and its equalizing rules. President Woodrow Wilson tried to remedy Jackson's mistake with the establishment of the Federal Reserve System in 1914.

Clearly, banks that hold deposits of public funds should invest those funds carefully and pay interest to depositors. Some banks have maintained adequate resources, but many others have sought growth by endangering depositors' funds. Government regulators have tried to establish ethics of safe banking but have been unsuccessful in developing applied ethics.

The American Bankers Association has had a tough job outlining applied ethical demands on an industry that at times has helped to improve American economic life and at other times has caused the bankrupting of innocent citizens. The Revised Code of Ethics of 1985 lists basic ethical values that are needed in banking as well as a number of practices that should help to ensure the safety of depositors' money. It is unlikely, however, that the code places sufficient emphasis on establishing ethics that relate to maintaining bank safety. A more appropriate system of banking ethics must be developed, and this is particularly true of the savings and loan branch of the banking industry. —*George C. S. Benson*

**See also** Business ethics; Law; Marketing; Medical ethics; Professional ethics; Sales, ethics of; *Uncle Tom's Cabin*.

**BIBLIOGRAPHY**

Demarco, Joseph P., and Richard M. Fox, eds. *New Directions in Ethics: The Challenge of Applied Ethics*. London: Routledge & Kegan Paul, 1986.

Gorlin, Rena. *Codes of Professional Responsibility*. Washington, D.C.: Bureau of National Affairs, 1986.

Olen, Jeffrey, and Vincent Barry. *Applying Ethics: A Text with Readings*. 3d ed. Belmont, Calif.: Wadsworth, 1989.

Rachels, James, ed. *Moral Problems: A Collection of Philosophical Essays*. 3d ed. New York: Harper & Row, 1979.

Singer, Peter, ed. *Applied Ethics*. Oxford, England: Oxford University Press, 1986.

## Arbitration

**TYPE OF ETHICS:** Legal and judicial ethics
**DATE:** U.S. Arbitration Act enacted 1925
**ASSOCIATED WITH:** American Arbitration Association
**DEFINITION:** Arbitration is a mechanism for dispute resolution—often employed as an alternative to litigation—to which parties to a given controversy voluntarily submit
**SIGNIFICANCE:** Arbitration is part of a self-regulating process in that disputants agree to submit their disagreements to a mutually acceptable disinterested third party for settlement, rather than go through court proceedings

Although arbitration agreements were not favored in common, or judge-made, law, in recent times arbitration has come to be viewed as an expedient, less-expensive alternative to litigation that—not incidentally—helps to ease court docket congestion. Indeed, agreements to arbitrate are now protected by statute, at both state and federal levels. Contracts, or other written agreements between parties, often include an arbitration clause, and arbitration is used to settle disputes in such contexts as labor, insurance, and commerce. Because the rules of arbitration are not legally mandated but are set by the parties concerned, the process of settling disputes by this means is more informal than that of court proceedings. Arbitration does, however, proceed in accordance with rules agreed upon in advance—often those of the American Arbitration Association, founded in 1926—and unlike less-formal proceedings, its outcome is final and is enforceable in a court of law.

**See also** Adversary system; National Labor Relations Act.

## Arendt, Hannah (Oct. 14, 1906, Hanover, Germany—Dec. 4, 1975, New York, N.Y.): Philosopher

**TYPE OF ETHICS:** Politico-economic ethics
**ACHIEVEMENTS:** Author of *The Origins of Totalitarianism* (1951), *The Human Condition* (1958), *Eichmann in Jerusalem* (1963), and *On Revolution* (1963)
**SIGNIFICANCE:** Analyzed the characteristics of twentieth century totalitarianism and the essential conditions of a genuine political realm; coined the phrase "the banality of evil"

A student of philosophers Karl Jaspers and Martin Heidegger, Arendt, a German Jew, fled Europe for the United States in 1941. She taught at the New School for Social Research in New York City and at the University of Chicago. Arendt claimed that, beginning with Plato, the Western tradition has tended to denigrate human action by misconstruing it as production—that is, as something fabricated by a craftsman—and by valorizing the solitary life of contemplation rather than the plural realm of interaction. As a result, the political realm of human interaction is not given intrinsic value and is misconstrued as the mere execution of rules dictated by a "master," as in the workshop of the craftsman. Ethically speaking, Arendt claimed that those who are reliable are *not* those who "hold fast" to ethical codes or formulae but those who engage in critical self-examination and dialogue. Twentieth century totalitarianism rendered individuals "superfluous" and attempted to replace critical debate with abstract ideologies. What interested Arendt were the conditions that make political life possible or impossible.

**See also** Heidegger, Martin.

## Aristotelian ethics

**TYPE OF ETHICS:** Theory of ethics
**DATE:** Fourth century B.C.E.
**ASSOCIATED WITH:** Virtue ethics
**DEFINITION:** Concerns the nature of the good life for human beings
**SIGNIFICANCE:** Views analysis of character rather than analysis or particular actions as basic in ethical theorizing; stresses importance of moral education; develops concepts of golden mean and natural law

Aristotle's ethical theory is contained in two works: the *Nicomachean Ethics* and the *Eudemian Ethics*. The *Nicomachean Ethics* is later and more comprehensive than the *Eudemian Ethics*, and has been studied far more. A third book sometimes attributed to Aristotle, the *Magna Moralia*, is probably not authentic.

Aristotle's ethical theory was conditioned by his training as a biologist. He observed that every living thing tends to develop into a mature specimen of its kind that may be either healthy and flourishing or somehow stunted. His ethical theory is an attempt to describe the healthy, flourishing way of life for human beings (the "good life"). His motivation was political, since he believed that an understanding of the good life should guide lawmakers. He believed that since human beings are naturally social beings, a normal person whose natural inclinations are properly cultivated will be virtuous; hence, wrongdoing is a function of stunted development. In basing ethical behavior upon human nature (the essence of human beings), Aristotle largely founded natural law theory.

Aristotle followed Greek practice in calling the good life *eudaimonia*, often translated as "happiness." He observed that people agree that happiness is an intrinsic good and that attaining happiness is the guiding directive of life; however, they disagree concerning the nature or content of the happy life.

Aristotle criticized three popular candidates (then and now) for the happy life: sensual pleasure, pursuit of honors and recognition, and money- making. He assumed that human happiness must be unique to human beings. Hence, a life of sensual pleasure cannot be happiness, since sensual pleasures derive from behaviors—eating, drinking, sex—that animals also display; that is, they are not based upon human nature. He also assumed that happiness must be achievable through one's own efforts. Hence, receiving honors cannot be happiness, since merit is not necessarily recognized; it is not "up to us." Moreover, recognition is pursued as a warrant of excellence; therefore, excellence is valued more highly than recognition even by those who esteem recognition. Aristotle dismissed the life of money-making on the ground that money is essentially a tool and therefore cannot be an end in itself.

Aristotle recognized sensual pleasure, honors, and money as concomitants of the good life but held that genuine happiness is "an activity of the soul in accordance with excellence": Happiness consists in self-development, or the positive, habitual expression or realization of potentials inherent in human nature. Since human beings are both social and rational, they possess basic potentials for moral goodness and intellectual goodness (wisdom). Aristotle held that intellectual goodness is produced by training and moral goodness by habituation. Therefore, all persons are morally and intellectually neutral at birth and are subsequently shaped by their experiences and education. Modern criticisms that media violence leads to violence in society agree with Aristotle that character is shaped rather than inborn. In this view, the notion of education is expanded to include all character-determining experiences, moral education becomes the foundation for society, and censorship may seem attractive.

Moral goodness consists of possession of the virtues, which include courage, temperance, generosity, "greatness of soul," magnanimity, response toward small honors, mildness, friendliness, truthfulness, wit, "shame," and justice. Some commentators allege that this list specifies an ideal of the Greek upper class, so that Aristotle's ethics is relativistic. Aristotle believed, however, that he had grounded his theory upon human nature, and his intent was not relativistic.

A virtue is a trained disposition to express a particular emotion, through behavior, to a degree that is neither deficient nor excessive relative to a given agent in a given situation. For example, a generous rich person will donate more money than will a generous poor person. Aristotle coined the phrase "golden mean" to denote the midpoint between excess and deficiency to which virtuous actions conform. He probably arrived at this idea by analogy with Greek medical theory, according to which bodily health consists of a balance between opposite bodily states.

Aristotle held that character is fixed by repeated actions: One becomes like what done does. Hence, every virtue results from repetition of acts of the relevant sort, which train their corresponding emotions. For example, one becomes generous by, in effect, practicing to be generous through repeated instances of giving. Moral education consists in training persons to experience pleasure in doing virtuous acts and displeasure in doing vicious acts. Hence, a virtuous person will enjoy behaving well. The tie between virtuous behavior and pleasure solves the problem of motivation ("Why be moral?") to which more rationality-based theories tend to be subject, but it also invites the criticism that Aristotle's ethical theory is egoistic.

Intellectual goodness is of two kinds: Practical and theoretical. Practical wisdom is knowledge for the sake of action. It enables one to discern the golden mean in particular situations. Doing so is a complex process that cannot be reduced to rules; it requires experience. The rejection of a definite method for determining right actions distances Aristotle's theory from rule-based theories as varied as Kantianism and utilitarianism. Theoretical wisdom is knowledge of basic truths of philosophy and science solely for the sake of knowledge. Aristotle held that theoretical wisdom is the noblest part of life and that the happiest life is a life of moral goodness with a large admixture of study and learning. Critics respond that study tends to isolate one from society.

—*Joel Wilcox*

**See also** Aristotle; Character; Egoism; Excellence; Golden Mean; Human nature; Intrinsic Good; Kantian Ethics; Means/ends distinction; Moral Education; Motivation; Natural law; Platonic ethics; Psychology; Utilitarianism; Virtue ethics; Virtue; Will.

**Bibliography**

Aristotle. *Nicomachean Ethics*. Translated by Terence Irwin. Indianapolis: Hackett, 1985.

MacIntyre, Alasdair. *After Virtue*. 2d ed. Notre Dame, Ind.: University of Notre Dame Press, 1984.

Rorty, Amélie O., ed. *Essays on Aristotle's Ethics*. Berkeley: University of California Press, 1980.

Sherman, Nancy. *The Fabric of Character*. New York: Oxford University Press, 1989.

Urmson, J. O. *Aristotle's Ethics*. New York: Basil Blackwell, 1988.

## Aristotle

(384 B.C.E., Stagirus, Chalcidice, Ionia—322 B.C.E., Chalcis, Euboea): Philosopher

**Type of ethics:** Classical history

**Achievements:** Author of the *Nicomachean Ethics*, the first systematic treatment of ethics in Western civilization

**Significance:** Aristotle elaborates a definition of virtue that combines fulfillment of function, striving for a mean between extremes, and rational control of the appetites

Aristotle, an individual with encyclopedic knowledge, wrote on numerous topics, including physics, metaphysics, logic, ethics, politics, poetics, and rhetoric. In the area of ethics, his major works are the *Nicomachean Ethics*, the *Eudemian Ethics*, and the *Politics*. He claims that the purpose of the state is to provide for the intellectual and moral development of its citizens. The *Nicomachean Ethics* is considered to contain Aristotle's mature moral theory.

**The Good.** Aristotle begins the *Nicomachean Ethics* by claiming, "Every art and every inquiry, and similarly every action and pursuit, is thought to aim at some good; and for this reason the good has rightly been declared to be that at which all things aim." The good is what human beings are seeking. The Greek word for this goal is *eudaimonia*, which can be roughly translated as "happiness." *Eudaimonia* means much more, however, than mere transitory happiness. *Eudaimonia* can be equated with having a good spirit or with the fulfillment of function. Humans have many goals, but *eudaimonia* is that goal that is final, self-sufficient, and attainable.

Aristotle discusses the fulfillment of function in terms of a member of a species doing what is distinctive to that species. Other species share with human beings the ability to live and to experience sensation. Neither of these capabilities is unique to the human species. No other species, however, is able to reason. Therefore, when a human being is performing his distinctive function, he is using reason. Aristotle remarks that the human is potentially a rational animal. He attains *eudaimonia* only when he is actually engaged in activity according to reason. (The use of the masculine pronoun is necessary for the above discussion, since Aristotle was referring specifically to the male of the species.)

*Aristotle* (Library of Congress)

**Structure of the Soul.** Aristotle claims that the human soul has two parts: a rational element and an irrational element. The irrational part of the soul may also be divided into two parts: the part concerned with nutrition and growth, which is shared with other living species, and the appetites, which are shared with other animal species. The rational part of the soul likewise has two divisions: One part is concerned with pure contemplation, while the other part is occupied with control of the appetites.

There are proper virtues, or excellences, which belong to each of the rational divisions of the soul. A virtue is the performing of a proper function. Intellectual virtues, such as wisdom, belong to the contemplative part of the soul; moral virtues, such as courage, belong to the part of the soul that is concerned with control of the appetites. Intellectual virtues are attained through education, whereas moral virtues are a matter of habit. One becomes courageous by repeatedly behaving courageously. According to Aristotle, it is important to behave in such a way as to develop the moral virtues.

**Virtue as a Mean Between Extremes.** Aristotle claims that for many activities and ways of behavior there is an excess and a deficiency. Reason shows that the proper way of acting or being is to strive for a midpoint between these extremes. For example, cowardice is a deficiency of courage. There is also an excess of courage that may be termed rashness or foolhardiness. This is a jump-before-you-think way of behaving. Courage, the mean, is having the right amount of fearlessness so that one is neither a coward nor a fool. Reason determines midpoints such as this. These means are the virtues.

Virtue, however, is not an absolute mean. It is relative, varying from individual to individual and from time to time. Courage for one person might be cowardice for another. What one must do as a moral individual is to strive for behavior that is somewhere near the mean between the two extremes of excess and deficiency. This is often done by realizing to which extreme one is closer and aiming for the opposite extreme. This will result in the individual being closer to the mean.

**Responsibility.** Aristotle claims that one is responsible for one's voluntary actions. These are actions that are not committed out of ignorance. The individual is not externally compelled and is not acting to avoid a greater evil. Therefore, if an individual, with full knowledge, freely chooses an action, he may be held morally responsible for that action. Aristotle is here departing from the Socratic/Platonic position that to know the good is to do it. Knowledge is important, but so is making the right choice. Making the right choice is an activity of the soul that is in accord with reason. Reason controls the appetites and adds to the fulfillment of man's function by choosing rightly. Furthermore, this right choice will be a mean between extremes. For the moral individual, this will become habitual behavior.

*—Rita C. Hinton*

**See also** Aristotelian ethics; Golden mean; *Nicomachean Ethics*.

**BIBLIOGRAPHY**

Aristotle. *Nicomachean Ethics*. Edited by G. Ramsauer. New York: Garland, 1987.

__________. *The Politics of Aristotle*. Translated by Ernest Barker. Oxford, England: Clarendon Press, 1946.

Grene, Marjorie. *A Portrait of Aristotle*. Chicago: University of Chicago Press, 1964.

Hardie, William. *Aristotle's Ethical Theory*. 2d ed. New York: Oxford University Press, 1980.

Jaeger, Werner. *Aristotle: Fundamentals of the History of His Development*. 2d ed. Oxford, England: Clarendon Press, 1948.

Joachim, H. H. *Aristotle: The Nicomachean Ethics, A*

*Commentary*. Edited by D. A. Rees. Oxford, England: Clarendon Press, 1951.

Ross, W. D. *Aristotle*. 5th ed. London: Methuen, 1956.

Taylor, Alfred E. *Aristotle*. Rev. ed. New York: Dover, 1956.

Urmson, J. O. *Aristotle's Ethics*. New York: Basil Blackwell, 1988.

## Arms race

**TYPE OF ETHICS:** International relations
**DATE:** Began August 29, 1949
**ASSOCIATED WITH:** The United States and the Soviet Union
**DEFINITION:** The rapid competitive expansion of modern weapons among rival nations in order to gain military and political superiority

**MODERN ARMS RACE TIME LINE**

| Time | Events |
|---|---|
| 1900-1914 | Weapons innovations, military build-up, and entangling alliances precipitate World War I. |
| 1914-1918 | World War I utilizes and introduces new weapons of war. |
| 1939 | World War II officially begins; production of conventional weapons is increased. |
| 1942 | Manhattan Project is organized after U.S learns of German experiments to create a "superweapon". |
| 1945 | U.S. drops atom bombs on Hiroshima and Nagasaki. |
| 1946 | U.S. Strategic Air Command (SAC) is established as superpowers begin to rearm. |
| 1947 | Truman Doctrine is announced; informal declaration of Cold War increases tensions worldwide. |
| 1949 | NATO is formed, repeating the pattern of increased military alliances in pre-World War I Europe. Nuclear arms race begins as U.S.S.R. tests its first atom bomb. |
| 1950 | U.S. strategic nuclear warheads total 450. |
| 1952 | U.S. tests its first hydrogen bomb. |
| 1953 | U.S.S.R. tests its first hydrogen bomb. |
| 1954 | John Foster Dulles announces U.S. "massive retaliation" policy against Soviet aggression. U.S. deploys tactical nuclear weapons in Europe. |
| 1955 | Warsaw Pact is formally organized; other military alliances are strengthened. U.S. strategic nuclear warheads total 4,750. |
| 1957 | U.S.S.R. tests its first ICBMs; Western bloc countries fear a "missile gap," or Soviet rocket superiority. U.S.S.R. deploys tactical nuclear weapons in Europe. |
| 1959 | U.S. expands its strategic bomber force to include 1,350 B-47's and 500 B-52's. |
| 1960 | U.S. strategic nuclear warheads total 6,068; Soviet complement totals 300. |
| 1961 | U.S. begins accelerated ICBM production and build-up. |
| 1964 | Communist China tests its first atom bomb. |
| 1965 | U.S. strategic nuclear warheads total 5,550; Soviet complement totals 600. |
| 1966 | SAC inventory includes 6,000 atom bombs allocated to its 1,800- plus strategic bomber force. |
| 1967 | Communist China tests its first hydrogen bomb. |
| 1968 | U.S.S.R. sets up its first antiballistic missile (ABM) defense system. |
| 1970 | U.S. deploys MIRVs (Multiple Independently Targetable Reentry Vehicles). |
| 1972 | U.S. sets up ABM defense system. |
| 1974 | India tests its first nuclear device, signaling the entry of the Third World into the nuclear arms race. U.S. initiates the MX missile, a "first-strike" weapon. |
| 1975 | U.S.S.R. deploys MIRVs. Vietnam War ends; U.S. and European countries begin selling conventional "near nuclear" weapons to Middle East, African, and volatile Third World countries. |
| 1981 | U.S. creates neutron bomb. |
| 1982 | U.S. deploys long-range cruise missiles with nuclear capabilities. |
| 1983 | U.S. announces SDI ("Star Wars") defense system; Soviet Union responds with warnings of new escalation in offensive weapons. |
| 1985 | U.S. strategic nuclear warheads total 11,200; Soviet complement totals 9,900. |
| 1988 | Six nations are known to have nuclear weapons; thirty-five nations are capable of producing nuclear weapons. |
| 1991 | Dissolution of the Soviet Union puts nuclear weapons in the hands of unstable Asiatic republics. |
| 1993 | Soviet stockpiles of nuclear weapons are revealed to be much greater than previously estimated. Many countries continue to attempt to procure nuclear materials and conduct experiments. |

**SIGNIFICANCE:** A world filled with increasing numbers of progressively more destructive agents intensifies the possibility for human misery and threatens the very existence of the planet

Arms races have been a major factor in prompting war in modern times, especially since World War I (1914-1918). Demobilization immediately after the end of World War II was quickly followed by rearmament as the Cold War era unfolded. The nuclear arms race began on August 29, 1949, when the Soviet Union tested its first atomic bomb, and it intensified when the United States and the Soviet Union first tested hydrogen bombs in November, 1952, and August, 1953, respectively. This led to the strengthening of military alliances (the North Atlantic Treaty Organization, or NATO, and the Warsaw Pact) and the escalation of threats. In January, 1954, the United States warned that it would meet Communist aggression with "massive retaliation" using nuclear weapons.

In the late 1950's, the Soviet Union improved its ability to produce and deliver nuclear weapons, thus causing the Western bloc to fear a "missile gap" and motivating the Western nations to produce more missiles. Questions regarding the morality of pursuing such a course have received widely varying answers over time, ranging from the rightness of attempting to deter aggression to the position that the arms race is inherently wrong because it protects the power and wealth of the privileged. Nuclear tests aroused worldwide concern about radioactive fallout, but test bans were ignored by France and China, which acquired hydrogen bombs by 1968. After this occurrence, the nuclear arms race between the United States and the Soviet Union surged ahead. American officials announced in 1974 that the United States was capable of dropping 36 bombs on each of the 218 Soviet cities with populations of 100,000 or more. Ominously, after the 1980's, the focus of nuclear proliferation shifted to the smaller, sometimes less-industrialized countries that regarded nuclear weapons as simply another tool in the struggle for power and survival.

**See also** Campaign for Nuclear Disarmament; Cold War; Military ethics; Mutually assured destruction; Nonproliferation Treaty; SALT treaties.

## Art

**TYPE OF ETHICS:** Arts and censorship
**DATE:** From antiquity
**DEFINITION:** The production of art and the products of art as they relate to artistic freedom and human virtue in society
**SIGNIFICANCE:** This relationship concerns the artistic freedom necessary for creativity and the moral effect that the artistic product has on human beings and society as a whole

The earliest discussion of the relationship of art and ethics goes back to the Greek classical period, when philosophers such as Socrates, Plato, and Aristotle considered art and its goodness and importance in relationship to the search for truth and virtue in human life. Socrates believed that the beautiful is that which both serves a good purpose and is useful, therefore uniting the beautiful and the good. He viewed the arts as being only incidental to other concerns, however, not of primary importancelato considered the relationship of art to nature and truth, and its resulting ethical function, which led him to reject art. Art was imitation and therefore was not good because imitations were untruelato loved beauty but hated painting. Aristotle separated ethics and art by describing goodness as present in human conduct and beauty as existing in a motionless state. He saw moral good and aesthetic value as separate considerations.

In the modern understanding, art—specifically, the fine arts of drawing and painting, sculpting, dance, music, theater, photography, and creative writing—is the act and process of creating. Works of art are the creations of the artistic process. It is the contact of the artist's work—the painting, dance, musical composition, and so forth—with the lives of other people that creates an ethical responsibility for the artist. Such contact invites participation by persons other than the artist in the artistic product, and it is this participation that implies an ethical responsibility.

Artistic freedom is publicly determined by ethical values; art as a creative act is independent of morality, but the artist as a human being is not. By making artwork public, the artist involves himself or herself in the lives of others, necessarily resulting in accountability for the contribution he or she is making to their lives. While the artist is not responsible for every effect his or her work may have, tension can exist between the aesthetic interests of the artist and the moral interests of the community.

The relationship of art and ethics is different from the relationship of art and aesthetics in that ethics deals with the concepts of what is good or bad, while aesthetics deals with the concepts of what is beautiful or ugly. These relationships are different yet closely related, because ethics raises questions of morality and propriety and aesthetics helps judge the aims and values of art: Is the end product beneficial for human life? Does it elevate the human spirit? Does the work of art respect the common good in intellect and conscience?

Answers to these questions involve the public in the role of censor when ethical standards are violated by the artist. Public censorship and self-censorship can determine the success or failure of a work of art but not the success or failure of the artistic process.

It is generally not subject matter but the manner of its treatment that causes art to be subject to moral ethical considerations. The very nature of art requires complete artistic freedom for the artist in order to "create," to bring about something new that is highly personal and unique. To impose limits on the creative process often stymies the goal of the process. Many people believe that art in itself is amoral, that the process cannot be subjected to ethical judgment because of its very nature. It is, however, the result of this process, the creative work of art, that is subject to ethical judgment. Moral value is judged by its contribution to the richness of human experience. Is it honest and fair-minded as well as aesthetically pleasing? Does it elevate the human spirit?

The issues of artistic freedom and artistic responsibility and the subordination of one to the other are at the heart of art and ethics. Using sensitivity, imagination, and inspiration, it is the responsibility of the artist to nourish the human spirit and express human emotion. Certain types of subject matter, such as nudity, cultural social taboos, religious concepts, and sexual perversion, can be difficult for the general public to accept. Art that utilizes such subjects is often subject to ethical examination and/or censorship.

The issues of forgery, plagiarism, and honest business practices are also important to the relationship of art and ethicsrofessional artistic standards in the modern world require that works of art be original if presented as such and that ethical business standards apply to the marketing of works of art.

The relationship of art and ethics touches the lives of all artists who share their work with others. The artist is often on the edge of cultural and societal changes, supporting as well as challenging traditional and contemporary ethical standards, broadening and enriching the human experience.

*—Diane Van Noord*

**See also** Art and public policy; Book banning, Censorship; Christian ethics; Golden mean; Goodness; *Index librorum prohibitorum*; Mapplethorpe, Robert; Plagiarism; Public interest; Religion.

**Bibliography**

Barasch, Moshe. *Theories of Art: From Plato to Winckelman*. New York: New York University Press, 1985.

Hygen, Johan B. *Morality and the Muses*. Translated by Harris E. Kaasa. Minneapolis, Minn.: Augsburg, 1965.

McMahon, Ahilip. *Preface to An American Philosophy of Art*. Chicago: University of Chicago Press, 1945.

Maritain, Jacques. *The Responsibility of the Artist*. New York: Scribner, 1960.

Taylor, Harold. *Art and the Intellect*. Garden City, N.Y.: Doubleday, 1960.

Tolstoy, Leo. *What Is Art?* Translated by Aylmer Maude. New York: Bobbs-Merrill, 1960.

## Art and public policy

**Type of ethics:** Arts and censorship

**Date:** Twentieth century

**Associated with:** Public funding of works of art

**Definition:** The relationships among artistic freedom of expression and governmental and public policies and attitudes

**Significance:** Public funding of the arts raises issues of freedom of speech, cultural bias, and appropriate uses of taxpayers' money

The legislation creating the National Endowment for the Arts (NEA) and the National Endowment for the Humanities, passed by the U.S. Congress in 1965, maintained that "it is necessary and appropriate for the federal government to help create and sustain not only a climate encouraging freedom of thought, imagination, and inquiry, but also the material conditions facilitating the release of this creative talent." In a speech at Amherst two years earlier, President John F. Kennedy had pledged support for artistic achievement, stating, "I look forward to an America which commands respect not only for its strength but for its civilization as well."

**The Arts and American Culture.** In the 1960's, there was widespread agreement across the United States that the time had come for federal, state, and local government to subsidize the arts, but the notion that a small amount of public funds could properly be spent on art was never universally embraced. Traditionally, in the fabric of American life, the arts were marginaluritan contempt for artistry outlived Colonial times. Among the grievances held against the British by Boston patriots in the 1770's was that King George's soldiers put on plays. The anti-obscenity campaigns of Anthony Comstock and others in the nineteenth century masked profound mistrust of artists, art, and free expression. Until Franklin Roosevelt's Works Progress Administration created programs to get artists off the relief rolls, governmental support for the arts was restricted to funding for military bands, statuary in public spaces, and adornment of public buildings.

The National Endowment for the Arts, resulting from years of lobbying by arts organizations, was hailed as a wise first step toward cultural democracy. The Endowment immediately contributed to a flowering of the arts at the local level, nudging state arts councils into being and fostering unprecedented attention to arts education. When Richard Nixon came to power, however, his NEA Chairperson Nancy Hanks set about increasing the Endowment's funding by favoring well-endowed elitist institutions such as symphony orchestras and large urban museums. The Endowment began to back away from individual artists and small arts organizations. By 1981, when Ronald Reagan took office, there was a serious movement to relegate funding for the arts to the private sector. This was thwarted by pressure from major arts institutions, and the Endowment survived with some cuts.

**Culture Wars.** During Reagan's administration, powerful forces began to use the "immorality" of the arts as a rallying point for fundraising and political gain. The failure of any meaningful public arts education ensured that much contemporary art would remain incomprehensible to the masses and that isolated examples of publicly supported art works that were difficult, heterodox, or sexually explicit could be used to frighten people whose exposure to art was nonexistent. The propaganda of the religious right exploited the belief that art was at best a frill and at worst a cause of moral turpitude and treason. A typical advertisement from Pat Robertson's Christian Coalition asked members of Congress: "Do you want to face the voters with the charge that you are wasting their hard-earned money to promote sod-

| Federal Funding of the Arts in the United States: WPA to Jesse Helms | |
|---|---|
| **Time** | **Event** |
| 1935 | On April 8, the Works Progress Administration (WPA) is created by Congress. Included are programs intended to provide employment for artists. |
| 1935 | In August, Hallie Flanagan is named director of the WPA Federal Theatre, which employs about 3,500 people during the next four years. |
| 1938 | The press begins reporting allegations that the Federal Theatre is dominated by Communists. |
| 1939 | On June 30, the Federal Theatre Project is ended by act of Congress following investigations by the House Un-American Activities Committee and the House Appropriations subcommittee set up to investigate the WPA. |
| 1952 | President Truman's Fine Arts Commission issues its report "Art and Government." |
| 1955 | President Eisenhower proposes an advisory council on the arts. During the Eisenhower Administration, Senators Jacob Javits of New York and Claiborne Pell of Rhode Island urge government support for the arts. |
| 1958 | Freshman congressman John Brademas (D., Indiana) proposes federal arts legislation. |
| 1958 | A National Cultural Center in the District of Columbia is chartered by Congress. (This later opens as the Kennedy Center.) |
| 1963 | August Heckscher, special consultant to President Kennedy, issues a report on the arts, outlining government policies affecting arts institutions and artists. |
| 1963 | In October, at a ceremony honoring Robert Frost at Amherst, Massachusetts, President Kennedy gives a speech later cited by advocates as a commitment to provide support for the arts. "I look forward to an America which will reward achievement in the arts as we reward achievement in business or statecraft," he affirms. |
| 1964 | President Lyndon Johnson signs the National Arts and Cultural Development Act into law, creating the National Council on the Arts, which is allotted an initial budget of $50,000. |
| 1965 | Congress passes the National Foundation for the Arts and Humanities Act establishing both the National Endowment for the Arts and the National Endowment for the Humanities, with a shared initial budget of $5 million. |
| 1969 | Nancy Hanks is appointed Chair of the NEA by President Richard M. Nixon. Under her leadership, the NEA's budgetary allotments increase substantially. |
| 1969 | Congressman William Scherle cites Aram Saroyan's dadaist poem LIGHTGHT, included in the NEA-sponsored *American Literary Anthology/2*, as a waste of tax dollars. |
| 1969 | Fearing right-wing Congressional opposition as the NEA comes up for reappropriation, Nancy Hanks demands that one story, "The Hairy Table" by Ed Sanders, be deleted from the *American Literary Anthology/3*. Editor George Plimpton refuses. Hanks cancels the $60,000 grant that would have supported the next anthology, terminating the series. |
| 1972 | When author Erica Jong acknowledges that an NEA fellowship helped support the writing of her novel *Fear of Flying*, freshman senator Jesse Helms (R., North Carolina), complains that taxpayers' money has been used by the NEA to promote obscenity. |
| 1977 | President Jimmy Carter appoints Livingston Biddle, Jr., to head the NEA. Joan Mondale, the wife of the vice president, becomes Honorary Chairperson of the Federal Council on the Arts and Humanities. |
| 1981 | The archconservative Heritage Foundation recommends a major overhaul of the NEA and the NEH, suggesting that consideration be given to their elimination. President Ronald Reagan subsequently proposes a 50 percent budgetary reduction for the two agencies. The NEA is finally budgeted at $143.45 million for fiscal 1982, a reduction of $15.34 million from the previous year. |
| 1983 | Reagan's NEA chairperson Frank Hodsoll vetoes a grant approved by a peer panel for a proposed series of public forums featuring activist artists and critics such as Hans Haacke and Lucy Lippard, under the auspices of the Heresies Collective and PAD/D in New York. |
| 1985 | Republican Congressmen Steve Bartlett, Tom DeLay, and Dick Armey, all of Texas, complain that the NEA has been funding and promoting blasphemy and obscenity, citing poetry published by the Gay Sunshine Press and screenings of Jean-Luc Godard's *Hail Mary* at the NEA-supported New York Film Festival. |
| 1986 | Frank Hodsoll vetoes a panel-approved NEA grant to the Washington Arts Project for an installation created by Jenny Holzer as a forum on free expression. |
| 1988 | Artist Andres Serrano is among the winners of the Awards in the Visual Arts (AVA) sponsored annually by the Southeastern Center for Contemporary Art in Winston-Salem, North Carolina. The work reviewed by the AVA judges includes an untitled color photograph of a small plastic crucifix submerged in urine (part of a series involving bodily fluids). Serrano's prize is a $15,000 fellowship and a place in the AVA traveling exhibition showcasing the seven winning artists for 1988. Among many sources of funding for the AVA program is a grant from the NEA. |
| 1989 | When the AVA show appears at the Virginia Museum in Richmond, *Piss Christ* is brought to the attention of moral watchdog the Reverend Donald Wildmon, head of the American Family Association of Tupelo, Mississippi. Wildmon sends out a million-piece mailing to raise funds, start a citizens' letter-writing campaign against the NEA, and alert members of Congress. In May, Republican senator Alphonse D'Amato of New York concludes a tirade against the NEA by tearing up the AVA catalog containing a reproduction of Seranno's work. |
| 1989 | Senator Jesse Helms begins an anti-NEA campaign in which the work of photographer Robert Mapplethorpe, whose recently-assembled retrospective has partial NEA funding, figures prominently. In July, the first of a series of restrictive "Helms Amendments" is passed. |
| 1992 | After an embattled three-year tenure during which he has antagonized both arts supporters and the religious right, John Frohnmayer, George Bush's NEA chairperson, turns in his resignation. Anne-Imelda Radice, a far-right Republican, steps in for the remainder of the Bush Administration, during which her readiness to veto "offensive" art creates havoc within the agency. |
| 1993 | President Clinton appoints actress Jane Alexander to head the NEA. |

omy, child pornography, and attacks on Jesus Christ?" In Congress, the most powerful adversary of the arts was North Carolina Senator Jesse Helms, formerly a television personality given to taking the University of North Carolina to task for the teaching of such "filth" as Andrew Marvell's 1650 opus "To His Coy Mistress."

From 1989 through 1992, a succession of artists and arts organizations were effectively demonized, and NEA Chairpersons John Frohnmayer and Anne-Imelda Radice preemptively vetoed a number of grants that had been approved by peer panels. The artists most typically affected were gay men, lesbians, feminists, AIDS activists, and members of racial minorities: Robert Mapplethorpe, Andres Serrano, Tim Miller, Karen Finley, Holly Hughes, John Fleck, David Wojnarowicz, Todd Haynes, Mel Chin, Marlon Riggs, and others. At the heart of this cultural strife was enmity between those who saw the NEA as custodian to a Eurocentrist tradition and those who believed that the NEA should nurture art at the grassroots level, acknowledging the diverse cultures that constitute the United States. The real issue was a clash of incompatible American dreams. In this context, concern for "your hard-earned tax dollars" was disingenuous.

From the NEA's inception, the yearly per capita expenditure on "controversial" art was, in fact, infinitesimal; critics might more justly have accused the NEA of making safe, stodgy choices. In 1992, the combined budgets of the National Endowment for the Arts and the National Endowment for the Humanities, both minor subdivisions of the Department of the Interior, added up to about 0.024 of one percent of the total federal budget. At $174.45 million, the NEA represented less than 3 percent of the Department of the Interior's total budget, and the United States continued to spend less on the arts than any other Western industrialized nation.

The National Endowment and its state counterparts were not entirely innocent of the charges leveled at them by their enemies. Biases in the funding and presentation of work appeared in various guises. Charges of elitism, cronyism, and conflict of interest were not without foundation. Nevertheless, most arts supporters believed that the solution was reform that would hold the NEA true to its original intent, not curtailment or elimination of the agency.

At the close of the twentieth century, the future of public arts funding in America hinged on which vision of the United States would prevail, and on the availability of arts education. Former arts administrator Edward Arian assessed the struggle in his book *The Unfulfilled Promise* (1989): "The stakes in this contest are very high. The right to artistic experience cannot be separated from the quality of life for every citizen, the opportunity for full self-development for every citizen, and the creation of the open and tolerant personality that constitutes the underpinning of a democratic society." —*James D'Entremont*

**See also** Art; Book banning; Censorship; Freedom of expression; *Index librorum prohibitorum*.

**Bibliography**


Arian, Edward. *The Unfulfilled Promise: Public Subsidy of the Arts in America.* Philadelphia: Temple University Press, 1989.

Biddle, Livingston. *Our Government and the Arts: A Perspective from the Inside.* New York: ACA (American Council for the Arts) Books, 1988.

Bolton, Richard, ed. *Culture Wars: Documents from the Recent Controversies in the Arts.* New York: New Press, 1992.

Dubin, Steven C. *Arresting Images: Impolitic Art and Uncivil Actions.* New York: Routledge, 1992.

Frohnmayer, John. *Leaving Town Alive: Confessions of an Arts Warrior.* Boston: Houghton Mifflin, 1993.

Heins, Marjorie. *Sex, Sin, and Blasphemy: A Guide to America's Censorship War.* New York: New Press, 1993.


## Art of War, The: Book

**Type of ethics:** Military ethics
**Date:** Written c. 510 b.c.e. as *Ping fa*
**Author:** Sun Tzu
**Significance:** *The Art of War* provided the theoretical and strategic basis for the way in which war was waged by East Asian countries for many centuries

According to Sun Tzu, a state should not begin a war unless definite advantages are foreseen; indeed, aggressive war should be avoided unless the situation is absolutely critical and no alternative exists. In determining whether war should be waged, questions should be raised regarding not only its moral basis but also season and weather, the kind of terrain to be traversed, the qualities necessary to a competent commander, and army organization and discipline. Success also depends on the internal harmony (tao) of the state; without such harmony, the state's efforts in war will fail. One should never engage in a protracted war, which is likely to result in military defeat and heavy financial deficit.

In waging war, deception is the key to success and attacks should always be conducted according to a coherent strategy. Indeed, supreme military excellence consists of breaking the enemy's resistance without fighting. The best tactics involve blocking the enemy's plans. The worst tactics involve besieging walled cities and fighting in mountains. The best strategy is always a balancing of the possibilities for victory. The good commander places himself in an invulnerable position and then watches for a favorable opportunity to defeat the enemy. Good tactics involve varying the concentration and division of forces. No one should attempt to wage war without knowing the topography of the territory involved. Above all, if a general fails to acquaint himself with the character of the enemy, whatever he does will lead to ruin. What enables a general to employ stratagems and deception is his knowledge of the enemy. Such information can be obtained only by means of espionage. Captured spies should be well treated and should be turned into defectors and double agents.

**See also** Military ethics.

## Artificial intelligence

**TYPE OF ETHICS:** Scientific ethics

**DATE:** Coined 1970's

**DEFINITION:** Pertaining to the use of computer programming to mimic human problem solving

**SIGNIFICANCE:** Artificial intelligence presents three questions to those who study ethics: What is human personality? Do good intentions justify possible evil abuses? What rights do nonhuman identities have?

Mary Shelley's Frankenstein (1818) is one of the first books to deal with an artificially created intelligence. In her book, Shelley tells the story of an entity that is created with good intentions but is perceived as a monster by the society it is to serve. Shelley's creature forces the reader to contemplate the possible evil results of scientific discovery, because her creature is easily accepted as having some sort of intelligence and, therefore, rights because it is clearly of human origin. In a computer age in which it is possible to mimic organic human processes electronically, philosophers must debate the being or awareness and rights of electronic intelligences. Are computer constructs actual beings with rights and wills? How is "being" defined? What makes humans aware, intelligent, and cognizant? If some new Frankenstein monster takes the nonorganic form of a silicon chip, what rights will that chip have, and how will it affect society?

The primary debate concerning artificial intelligence involves the question of what constitutes personality or awareness for the computer intelligence. Is the computer intelligence to be viewed as humans view one another, with rights, responsibilities, and motives? Will humans accept computer personalities as intelligent individuals when they act human? One of the first people to address this issue was Alan Turing. Turing, lacking the computer technology to tackle this issue, turned to a thought experiment. In his thought experiment, Turing devised a machine that solved human problems using an intricate set of rules that could be applied to any data that the machine received. By applying the programmed rules to the data, Turing's machine was capable of supplying a human-like answer to any problem that was presented to it. For a human observer who was unaware of the machine's existence, the responses to the questions supplied to the machine would appear to be responses given by a fellow human. Several years after Turing's mind experiment, Joseph Weizenbaum created a Rogerian psychologist program called ELIZA. ELIZA was programmed to respond to human queries using the basic rules of Rogerian psychology. Those individuals who encountered the program without the knowledge that their psychologist was a computer were convinced that they were dealing with a fellow human being. Although these experiments might seem to argue for the existence of an intelligence within the program, there was a backlash to this supposition.

J. R. Searle responded to Turing's machine by pointing out that the machine does not actually think or engage the material with which it is involved. He did not believe that a mechanized application of rules without an understanding of the problem was truly intelligence. Searle responded with a thought experiment called the Chinese room. In the Chinese room, several non-Chinese-speaking people are given a rule book for responding to Chinese symbols. When a symbol is passed into the room, the occupants act based upon what the rule book says. Searle points out that the output from the room is perfect Chinese, although the occupants of the room have no understanding of their responses. The intelligence in the room is the book of rules, which clearly is inanimate. Searle's argument raises the question of what meaning symbols have for computers. Are symbols simply electrical stimuli that trigger certain responses? Are these electrical stimuli and responses similar to the chemical stimuli and responses of the human brain?

In response to Searle's Chinese room, Douglas Hofstadter and Daniel Dennett proposed that the Chinese room is simply a small part of a larger "aware personality." The Chinese room is simply one cell in a larger framework that as a whole is cognizant. Indeed, the Chinese room is much like a brain cell, which follows chemical rules to give chemical responses that, on a larger scale, have meaning. Dennett then argues that what goes on inside the machine is less important than is the way in which humans respond to the machine. It is human response that credits the machine with intelligence. The term "intentional stance" was coined to describe this stance. To illustrate the point, Dennett used a chess-playing program. When engaging the program in a game of chess, the human opponents responded to the program as they would have responded to a human opponent. Each move was considered in terms of what strategy the program was using, how the program would respond, and what weaknesses the program had shown. All these responses are typical of interhuman chess playing; therefore, the program was being engaged in a manner that gave it identity—it acted, reacted, and anticipated.

While Dennett may justify the intelligence of a program on the basis of human response, the question of what is human thinking and intelligence is left unanswered. Mary Shelley's Frankenstein monster is granted intelligence by the human society it affects, but will human society grant intelligence to nonorganic creation? Furthermore, what rights and responsibilities will these nonorganic creatures have? Shelley's novel is a warning of the need for public debate about the creating of nonhuman identities. Scientist and writer Isaac Asimov suggested rules for the created identities to follow; for example, they could not injure humans or disobey humans. While humans have rules for the creations, what laws will there be for the creator in terms of actions taken upon the nonhuman life? While original attempts at creating artificial intelligence are for human purposes and goals, what will happen if and when machines are able to break away from humans and create goals and meanings for themselves? Perhaps the argument about computer intelligence and being will be resolved when a computer is capable of demonstrating intentionality, but then how will humans respond to this new life? These and many other questions remain to be answered. —*Tod Murphy*

**See also** Autonomy; Computer technology; Individualism; Technology.

**BIBLIOGRAPHY**

Dreyfus, H. L. *What Computers Can't Do*. Rev. 2d ed. New York: Harper & Row, 1979.

Garnham, Alan. *Artificial Intelligence*. New York: Routledge & Kegan Paul, 1987.

Hofstadter, Douglas, and Daniel C. Dennett. *The Mind's I*. Toronto: Bantam Books, 1982.

McCorduck, Pamela. *Machines Who Think: A Personal Inquiry into the History and Prospects of Artificial Intelligence*. San Francisco: W. H. Freeman, 1979.

Sharples, Mike, et al. *Computers and Thought—A Practical Introduction to Artificial Intelligence*. Cambridge, Mass.: MIT Press, 1989.

## Asceticism

**TYPE OF ETHICS:** Religious ethics

**DATE:** 800-400 B.C.E.

**DEFINITION:** Asceticism refers to the theory and practice of using self- discipline to gain self-mastery, usually in order to fulfill religious or spiritual ideals

**SIGNIFICANCE:** Ascetical practices include the cultivation of virtue and the performance of good works; increased virtue and ethical conduct contribute to greater mastery of self, the immediate objective of ascetical practice

Although popularly associated with extreme forms of bodily penance such as the wearing of hair shirts or self-flagellation, asceticism in its broadest sense refers to practices of self-discipline designed to benefit body and mind and to gain self-mastery. Even today, people modify their lifestyles and make use of practices to care for body, mind, and spirithysical exercise routines, special diets, meditation, and relaxation techniques are examples of contemporary ascetical practices.

Traditionally, ascetical practices have been linked to religious or spiritual goals. Ascetical self-mastery has been sought in order to achieve salvation, expiate individual or communal guilt, or imitate the example of a divine figure. In its positive expression, asceticism has taken the form of the practice of virtues—such as patience, forgiveness, or generosity—to benefit others. Ascetical practices remove personal limitations so that a person is less egotistic and better able to serve others.

Asceticism is a feature of the major religious and philosophical traditions. The term "asceticism" is derived from the Greek word *askesis*, meaning "athleticism" or "athletic training." The Christian apostle Paul of Tarsus likens the renunciation that Christians practice to gain eternal life to the discipline that prepares athletes to win a perishable trophy. The earliest records of ascetical thought are found in the Upaniṣads, written between 800-400 B.C.E. in India. They urge the wise person to practice austerities, or *tapas*, in order to apprehend the Cosmic Self, the unmanifest source and ground of creation.

**Asceticism in Judaism.** The earliest Jewish thought valued asceticism little, limiting ascetical practices to the fasting and sexual abstinence required by the divine commandments. In later Jewish thought, an awareness of individual and communal guilt led believers to acts of penance and expiation for sin. In the aftermath of the expulsion of the Jews from Spain in 1492, ethical and ascetical practice fused with mystical thought. This fusion continues to influence Jewish ethical teaching. It can be summarized as follows: Every action in accord with the divine commandments and every ethical deed provide a way for each Jew to help bring redemption to the Jewish nation and the world.

**Christian Asceticism.** Christian asceticism takes the example of Jesus' life as its model for ascetical practice. Jesus did the will of his heavenly Father in his life of teaching and service and in his death by crucifixion. Christians follow his example by crucifying their selfish desires and sinful inclinations. They accept suffering in imitation of Jesus' suffering. Leaders of the Protestant Reformation attacked asceticism because salvation is God's free gift and cannot be merited by good works. In response Catholic teaching maintains that although salvation is a gift, the good Christian freely chooses to grow in unity with Jesus by trying to live and die as he did.

**Asceticism in Islam.** Muḥammad, the founder of Islam in the seventh century, stressed the need for asceticismrayer and fasting are two of the five Pillars of the Faith central to Islamic teaching. Many ascetical practices are associated with Sufism, the mystical movement in Islam. These include cleansing one's heart through the constant remembrance of God and through restraining the breath in the recitation of one's prayers. A clean heart brings conformity to the will of God, the basis of right action in Islam.

**Asceticism in Hinduism.** The traditional structure of Hindu life sets aside the last two of four stages in life for ascetical practices and spiritual development. While the individual is engaged in worldly affairs, the performance of social duties is emphasized and every aspect of life is governed by elaborate codes of behavior. After supporting a family, serving the community, and accomplishing the worldly aims of life, the householder is freed from those responsibilities to devote the rest of life to gaining *moksha*, or liberation, union with the transcendental Ground of Being. By setting aside a certain time in life for spiritual development, Hinduism makes asceticism an established part of life while guaranteeing that the needs of family and society are also met.

**Asceticism in Buddhism.** Buddha advocated moderation in ascetical practice. The Eightfold Path of Buddhism sets forth the ethical conduct and ascetical practices necessary to gain *nirvāṇa*, a state of absolute consciousness. Buddhist asceticism demands discipline, psychological control, and selflessness in order to develop compassion, the supreme virtue according to the Buddhist tradition. Certain livelihoods, such as the manufacture of weapons and the butchering and sale of meat, are considered illegitimate in Buddhist societies because they violate the rule of compassion.

**Asceticism for Today.** Asceticism has fallen out of favor because of its association in the past with philosophies that condemned the body and matter. The forms of physical torture some ascetics chose to discipline their bodies disgust people today. Asceticism is now advocated on much more positive grounds. Discipline can aid in gathering and focusing personal energy in a culture that distracts its members in countless ways. Quiet reflection can help a person locate negative cultural conditioning in order to confront it. Spiritual discipline can intensify and concentrate awareness in order to help one make sound choices in life. Asceticism means having the power to choose. Choice is essential for ethical conduct. Bodily and spiritual discipline not only benefit body and mind but also contribute to ethical decision making by increasing a person's options. —*Evelyn Toft*

**See also** Mysticism.

**BIBLIOGRAPHY**

Dan, Joseph. *Jewish Mysticism and Jewish Ethics.* Seattle: University of Washington Press, 1986.

Huxley, Aldous. *The Perennial Philosophy.* London: Triad Grafton, 1985.

Miles, Margaret R. *Fullness of Life: Historical Foundations for a New Asceticism*hiladelphia: Westminster Press, 1981.

Valiuddin, Mir. *Contemplative Disciplines in Sufism.* London: East-West Publications, 1980.

## Aśoka (Third century B.C.E., India—c. 230 B.C.E., India): Emperor

**TYPE OF ETHICS:** Religious ethics

**ACHIEVEMENTS:** Unified India and promoted the spread of Buddhism

**SIGNIFICANCE:** Redefined Buddhist ethics as they related to statecraft

Aśoka, emperor of India from approximately 270 to 230 B.C.E., is known to posterity through the rock and pillar inscriptions that he left across the Indian subcontinent and through various Buddhist chronicles. Aśoka, who was the grandson of Candragupta, was the third monarch of the Maurya dynasty. From his capital at Pataliputra (modern Patna), he governed the largest Indian empire that had existed up to that time.

Aśoka converted to Buddhism after a particularly bloody campaign to win the territory of Kalinga (modern Orissa). He is said to have been so distraught over the sufferings caused by war that he renounced violence as a tool of statecraft. The central concept in his political philosophy was *dhamma* (Pali; Sanskrit, *dharma*), a Buddhist and Hindu concept that, in one of its meanings, referred to a kind of civic morality.

Aśokan reforms, which have been valorized by Buddhists throughout history, included social services such as free medical aid and the development of rest houses for travelers. He also promoted vegetarianism, enacting laws that restricted animal sacrifices and limited butchering and hunting.

Although Aśoka was said to have given up military imperialism, the expansion of his influence continued, this time through *dhamma-vijaya, or* "moral conquest." This idea of winning over one's enemies by dint of sheer moral superiority is echoed in Mohandas K. Gandhi's twentieth century notion of *satyagraha*, or the "victory of truth."

Although much about Aśoka is wrapped up in legend, it is clear that he attempted to rule in a way that no other Indian ruler had attempted. He developed a concept of citizenship that was broader than those of the caste and local loyalties to which people had adhered before his rule. The modern symbol of India, four lions facing the four directions, is derived from the capital of one of Aśoka's famous pillars.

**See also** Buddhist ethics; Gandhi, Mohandas Karamchand.

## Assassination

**TYPE OF ETHICS:** Politico-economic ethics

**DATES:** "Assassin" coined 1200; "assassination" from eighteenth century

**ASSOCIATED WITH:** Radical political and religious movements, *coups d'état*, and covert operations

**DEFINITION:** The killing, often by stealth, of persons prominent in government, religion, or culture for the purpose of effecting change

**SIGNIFICANCE:** Whether and under what circumstances assassination is ever morally justified has perplexed ethicists for centuries, as has the search for practical and morally permissible methods of combating terroristic assassination

Assassination, which is as old as history, arose at least in part from the lack of mechanisms for the removal of rulers in antiquity and also from the need of subjects to protect themselves from oppression.

**History.** The Bible tells of numerous acts of assassination, many of which receive the approval of Holy Writ. In Judges, the prophet Ehad stabbed Eglon, King of Moab. Jael slew the retreating Canaanite general Sisera, and Judith decapitated general Holofernes. The tyrannical judge-king Abimelech died when a woman dropped a millstone on him. Under the monarchies of Israel and Judea, many tyrants were killed, including Nadab, Elah, Jehoram, Ahaziah, Jezebel, Zechariah, Jobesh, and Pekah.

In the ancient world, Hipparchus, a tyrant of Athens, was fatally stabbed by Harmodius and Aristogiton. That these tyrannicides acted more from personal motives than from love of political liberty did not cloud their godlike status in antiquity.

From the experiences of the Roman Empire, the West absorbed a deep ambivalence about assassination, since many targets were vicious tyrants, such as Caligula, Domitian, Commodius, Caracalla, and Heliogabalus, but the heroic reformer emperor Julius Caesar was also a victim.

| ASSASSINATIONS OF NOTABLE PERSONS | | | |
|---|---|---|---|
| **Date** | **Person(s)** | **Location** | **Motive or Responsible Party** |
| 514 B.C.E. | Hipparchus | Athens | Personal revenge, restoration of democracy |
| 44 B.C.E. | Julius Caesar | Rome | Restoration of republic |
| 661 C.E. | Caliph ʿAlī | Mecca | Religious rivalry |
| 924 | Emperor Berengar | Germany | Coup attempt and personal motives |
| 1127 | Charles the Good, Count of Flanders | Flanders | Political murder |
| 1170 | Thomas Becket, Archbishop of Canterbury | England | Church/crown struggles |
| 1192 | Conrad of Montferrat, King of Jerusalem | Tyre | Order of Assassins |
| 1327 | Edward II | England | Political coup and personal motives |
| 1400 | Richard II | England | Dynastic coup |
| 1584 | William the Silent | Holland | Religious and political war |
| 1610 | Henry IV | France | Religious motives |
| 1634 | Albrecht of Wallenstein | Bohemia | Killed by order of emperor |
| 1762 | Peter III | Russia | Coup by wife (Catherine the Great) |
| 1792 | Gustav III | Sweden | Aristocratic coup |
| 1801 | Paul I | Russia | Coup against insane tsar |
| 1865 | Abraham Lincoln | United States | Revenge for defeat of Confederacy |
| 1881 | James A. Garfield | United States | Angry job-seeker |
| 1882 | Lord Cavendish and Thomas Burke | Phoenix Park, Dublin, Ireland | Nationalist terrorism |
| 1900 | Umberto I | Italy | Anarchist terrorism |
| 1901 | William McKinley | United States | Anarchist terrorism |
| 1903 | Alexander and Queen Draga | Serbia | Dynastic coup |
| 1904 | Nikolai Bobrikov, Governor General | Finland (Russia) | Nationalist terrorism |
| 1911 | Pyotr Stolypin, Prime Minister | Russia | Anarchist terrorism |
| 1914 | Archduke Francis Ferdinand | Bosnia (Austrian) | Nationalist terrorism |
| 1919 | Rosa Luxemburg and Karl Liebknecht | Germany | Right-wing terrorism |
| 1922 | Michael Collins, Prime Minister | Ireland | IRA terrorism |
| 1922 | Walther Rathenau, Foreign Minister | Germany | Right-wing terrorism |
| 1934 | Alexander I of Yugoslavia (Croatian) and Jean-Louis Barthou, Foreign Minister (French) | France | Nationalist terrorism |
| 1934 | Engelbert Dollfuss, Chancellor | Austria | Nazi coup attempt |
| 1935 | Huey Long | United States | Personal motives |
| 1940 | Leon Trotsky | Mexico | Stalin's agents |
| 1948 | Folke Bernadotte, Count, U.N. Observer | Palestine | Pro-Israeli terrorism |
| 1948 | Mohandas K. Gandhi | India | Religious fanaticism |
| 1963 | John F. Kennedy | United States | Motive unknown |
| 1968 | Robert F. Kennedy | United States | Anti-Israeli terrorism |
| 1968 | Martin Luther King, Jr. | United States | Racist terrorism |
| 1981 | Anwar Sadat | Egypt | Anti-Israeli terrorism |
| 1984 | Indira Gandhi | India | Nationalist (Sikh) terrorism |

Ambivalence carried over to the Middle Ages, when scholastic theologians struggled with the divergent traditions of Christianity. Its early pacifism had evaporated, but the tradition of obedience to authority and of suffering evils meekly remained. Yet Old Testament support for assassination and the natural law tradition's support for a right of rebellion against wickedly unjust rule created support for the practice.

John of Salisbury, the English medieval theologian, held that any subject might kill an oppressive tyrant for the common good, but Saint Thomas Aquinas, like many later figures, retreated from the full implications of that view. Thomas Aquinas introduced the *melior pars* doctrine, which placed responsibility for elimination of a tyrant upon those in society who enjoy office, wealth, or rank.

A vital distinction drawn by the medieval schoolmen was between a tyrant by usurpation (*tyrannus in titulo*) and a tyrant by oppression (*tyrannus in regimine*). The former is one who has no legal right to rule but seizes power. The latter is one who rules unjustly. Thomas Aquinas, Francisco Suarez, and others maintained that private individuals had a tacit mandate from legitimate authority to kill a usurper to benefit the community.

During the Reformation, most Protestant reformers endorsed tyrannicide: Martin Luther held that the whole community could condemn a tyrant to death, Philip Melancthon called tyrannicide the most agreeable offering man could make to God, and John Calvin endorsed the *melior pars* doctrine. The Jesuit Juan de Mariana condemned usurpers and praised slayers of princes "who hold law and holy religion in contempt."

Renaissance drama often centered upon assassination; for example, Christopher Marlowe's *Edward II* and much of Shakespeare concentrated upon the morality of it—in historical plays such as *Richard II*, *3 Henry VI*, and *Richard III*, and also in *Macbeth*, *Hamlet*, and *Julius Caesar*. Julius Caesar was a tyrant by usurpation against the corrupt Roman Republic, but he ruled well. King Claudius in *Hamlet* was a tyrant by usurpation and oppression, as was Macbeth. A constant Renaissance theme involved the motivation for the tyrannicidal act. In *Julius Caesar*, all the assassins except Brutus have motives of jealousy, and Hamlet must struggle within himself, since he desires to kill the king because of private hatred rather than justice.

In the East, religion was often the motive, as with the Order of the Assassins in Muslim Syria in the twelfth and thirteenth centuries, and the Thuggees in India strangled travelers to honor the goddess Kalī until the British suppressed the cult in the 1830's.

In the modern era following the French Revolution, the main sources of assassinations have been nationalism, political ideology, and madness. Daniel McNaughtan, a Scot who killed the secretary of British Prime Minister Sir Robert Peel, represents an entire class of assassins. Because of McNaughtan's manifest insanity, the House of Lords created the McNaughtan Rule, which set the standard for the insanity plea in criminal law.

Nationalism motivated assassinations from the Phoenix Park murders in Ireland in 1882 and the calamitous slaying of Austrian Archduke Franz Ferdinand in 1914 to the killing of Indian premier Indira Gandhi by Sikhs in 1984. Finally, political ideologies, especially anarchism, claimed many victims, such as Russian Prime Minister Peter Stolypin and U.S. president William McKinley.

With both extreme nationalism and radical political ideologies, the moral arguments about assassination have tended to be focused upon the practical question of the effects of assassination rather than upon its abstract moral nature. V. I. Lenin, the founder of the Soviet Union, condemned assassinations of political figures and other terroristic acts as tactically inopportune and inexpedient.

Today, international terrorism uses random assassination as a tool to disrupt society by putting pressure upon targeted governments in order to alter policies.

**Ethical Issues.** As do personal self-defense, capital punishment, and just war, assassination raises general issues of whether homicide can ever be justified. Beyond this, there are special issues raised by the particular nature of assassination. Can the private citizen be trusted to wield the power of life and death, especially over his or her own magistrates?

Ethicists see assassination as destructive of the trust and loyalty that ought to exist between subject and ruler, and they dislike the fact that even when used upon vicious tyrants, it necessarily involves circumventing judicial forms, though the guilt of the tyrant may be manifest.

Practically speaking, attempted assassinations, like abortive revolts, may intensify the repression of a tyrannical regime. Additionally, it is notorious that democratic and even authoritarian rulers are more susceptible to assassination than are truly totalitarian despots. —*Patrick M. O'Neil*

**See also** Covert action; Homicide; International law; Tyranny.

**BIBLIOGRAPHY**

Ben-Yehuda, Nachman. *Political Assassinations by Jews: A Rhetorical Device for Justice*. Albany, N.Y.: SUNY Press, 1992.

Ford, Franklin L. *Political Murder: From Tyrannicide to Terrorism*. Cambridge, Mass.: Harvard University Press, 1985.

Lentz, Harris M. *Assassinations and Executions: An Encyclopedia of Political Violence, 1865-1986*. Jefferson, N.C.: McFarland, 1988.

Sifakis, Carl. *Encyclopedia of Assassinations*. New York: Facts on File, 1991.

## Atatürk, Mustafa Kemal (1881, Salonika, Greece—Nov 10, 1938; Istanbul, Turkey): First president of Turkey

**TYPE OF ETHICS:** Modern history

**ACHIEVEMENTS:** Between 1921 and 1923, Atatürk successfully drove out the Greeks, thwarted postwar partition by the allies, and established the modern nation of Turkey

**SIGNIFICANCE:** As the founder and first president of Turkey, Atatürk aggressively initiated a reform movement designed to Westernize and modernize Turkish social customs and law

The son of an Ottoman bureaucrat, the young Mustafa Kemal (Atatürk, meaning "father of the Turks," was added in 1934) was educated at the Istanbul military academy, where, like many other youths, he participated in subversive organizations. While initially allied with the Young Turk revolution, Atatürk in 1919 founded the rival Turkish Nationalist party and was elected its president. His military acumen and leadership, best illustrated by his engineering of the World War I victory over the British at Gallipoli, earned him a substantial and loyal following.

After his masterful ousting of the Greeks in 1923, Atatürk, as head of the Nationalist party, declared Turkish independence and was subsequently elected Turkey's first president. While serving for fifteen years as a virtual dictator, Atatürk initiated a program of modernization that fundamentally altered Turkish society. His reforms included the disestablishment of Islam, the abolition of the sultanate, the banning of polygamy, the institution of compulsory civil marriage, the enfranchisement of women, the replacement of Arabic script with the Latin alphabet, and compulsory literacy training for adults under age forty.

Atatürk also introduced economic reforms, including a policy of self-sufficiency and refusal of foreign loans.

**See also** Constitutional government; Dictatorship.

## Atheism

**Type of ethics:** Beliefs and practices

**Date:** Fifth century B.C.E to present

**Associated with:** Skepticism, rationalism, existentialism, humanism, and other nonreligious philosophies that try to define morality

**Definitions:** Atheism is an ideology based on unbelief in God (or gods), religion, and the supernatural

**Significance:** Though ethical systems in Western cultures have traditionally been grounded in religions, unbelievers also have value systems and seek to know and practice what is good and right

Though some ethicists—such as Thomas J. Higgins (1967)—find unbelief incompatible with ethics, many ethical views and practices grow from atheism. Because atheism is not institutionalized or codified in the same way that religions are, generalizations about the "ethics of atheists" are risky.

Paul Roubiczek (1969) restates three main ethical questions: How should people act? What does "good" mean? Are people able to do what they should? A fourth question, raised by G. E. Moore in *Principia Ethica* (1903), is "What kind of things ought to exist for their own sake?" Atheists, like believers, struggle to answer these hard questions.

**Who Are Atheists?** The term "atheism" was first used in 1571 to define an ideology "without theism." Many atheists do not deny the existence of God; instead, they find the term "God" meaningless. Atheists constitute a small minority in modern society: In 1989, only 10 percent of American adults had "no religious preference." This figure also includes agnostics and people without clear ideas about religion.

Unbelief places atheists outside the mainstream, because even in modern, secularized societies, most people have some sort of religion to guide them. Religions often prescribe traditional codes of conduct, such as the Ten Commandments of the Old Testament or the New Testament teachings of Christ. Atheists lack such institutionalized ethical codes.

Atheists are often well educated and trained in the humanities or sciences; they usually entertain scientific, not supernatural, theories about cosmic and human origins.

To religious believers, the term "atheist" may trigger the negative stereotype of one who is "against" something good and sacred; "atheist" may even suggest "demonically inspired," though "devil worship" is inconsistent with unbelief. The public image of modern atheists has been shaped by abrasive activists such as Madalyn Murray O'Hair, a crusader against Bible readings and prayer in American public schools, and author Ayn Rand, founder of a unique conservative ideology: objectivism.

**History.** Religious unbelief has a long history. One of the early figures to question religious orthodoxy and customs was Hecataeus, who ridiculed the Greek myths in the sixth century B.C.E. Herodotus and, later, the Sophists were also critical of justifying Greek customs as "the will of the gods." Socrates was sentenced to death in 399 B.C.E. partly for being "impious." Epicurus (341-270)—still popularly associated with an "eat, drink, and be merry" ethic—denied the gods' supernatural power and doubted the afterlife.

James Thrower (1971) traces the historic stages of unbelief: the breakdown of classical myths; the rise of science in the Renaissance; the rationalism of the Enlightenment, when such philosophers as Immanuel Kant and David Hume attacked the "reasonable" bases of religion; and more recent movements such as Marxism and existentialism. The moralist Friedrich Nietzsche (died 1900) declared, "God is dead," inaugurating what some call the "post-Christian" era.

**Varieties of Atheism.** Confusingly, modern atheists call themselves skeptics, utilitarians, objectivists, self-realizers, emotivists, relativists, Marxists, pragmatists, intuitionists, materialists, naturalists, empiricists, positivists, nihilists, libertarians, rationalists, hedonists, secularists, humanists, and existentialists. The principles of each ideology have ethical implications—but not easily predictable ones. Existentialism and ethical humanism are among the best-known atheistic philosophies.

**Modern Ethics.** Mary Warnock (1978), who surveys nonreligious ethical theories, says that modern ethicists have not built large metaphysical systems but have focused, instead, on human nature, social interaction, and language.

According to existentialists such as Jean-Paul Sartre, individuals confront isolation, impermanence, and the "burden of choice" in a stark, incomprehensible world. As Warnock notes, that view is not a very helpful ethical guide, but existentialist Albert Camus has urged humans not to give up the quest for right action in an absurd world.

Paul Kurtz (1983) says that the flexible ethics of modern humanism stands on basic principles: tolerance, courage, freedom from fear, respect for individuals, social justice, happiness and self-fulfillment, and the ideal of a world community. Kurtz believes that ethical conduct is possible without religious belief because certain "human decencies" are almost universally accepted: telling the truth; dealing fairly with others; being kind, sincere, honest, considerate, thoughtful, helpful, and cooperative; having friends; seeking justice; not misusing others; and not being cruel, arrogant, vindictive, or unforgiving.

Most modern philosophies and ethical theories leave humans free to make subjective, contingent, and relativistic choices; thus, students searching for specific, practical guides to personal morality may find modern writings theoretical, complex, and inconclusive. Ross Poole (1991) says, pessimistically, "The modern world calls into existence certain conceptions of morality, but also destroys the grounds for taking them seriously. Modernity both needs morality, and makes it impossible." John Casey (1990), however, affirms the persistent relevance of "pagan" virtues: courage, temperance, practical wisdom, justice, and respect for the personhood of all people. Such time-proven guides encourage honor, humanistic achievement, and proper kinds of pride and self-assertion. *—Roy Neil Graves*

**See also** *Beyond Good and Evil*; Camus, Albert; Hedonism; Humanism; Hume, David; Kantian ethics; Libertarianism; Marxism; Nihilism; Objectivism; Post-Enlightenment ethics; Pragmatism; Sartre, Jean-Paul; Secular ethics; Situational ethics; Utilitarianism.

**Bibliography**

Casey, John. *Pagan Virtue: An Essay in Ethics.* Oxford, England: Clarendon Press, 1991.

Gert, Bernard. *Morality: A New Justification of the Moral Rules.* New York: Oxford University Press, 1988.

Higgins, Thomas J. *Ethical Theories in Conflict.* Milwaukee, Wis.: Bruce Publishing, 1967.

Kurtz, Paul. *In Defense of Secular Humanism.* Buffalo, N.Y.: Prometheus Books, 1983.

Poole, Ross. *Morality and Modernity.* London: Routledge, 1991.

Roubiczek, Paul. *Ethical Values in the Age of Science.* London: Cambridge University Press, 1969.

Singer, Peter, ed. *A Companion to Ethics.* Oxford: Basil Blackwell, 1991.

Smith, George H. *Atheism, Ayn Rand, and Other Heresies.* Buffalo, N.Y.: Prometheus Books, 1991.

Stein, Gordon, ed. *The Encyclopedia of Unbelief.* 2 vols. Buffalo, N.Y.: Prometheus Books, 1985.

Thrower, James. *A Short History of Western Atheism.* London: Pemberton Books, 1971.

Warnock, Mary. *Ethics Since 1900.* 3d ed. Oxford, England: Oxford University Press, 1978.

## Atom bomb

**Type of ethics:** Scientific ethics
**Date:** 1939-1945
**Associated with:** The Manhattan Project
**Definition:** An extremely powerful bomb that utilizes the process of nuclear fission
**Significance:** Scientists ordinarily prefer to regard themselves as part of an international brotherhood devoted to the expansion of knowledge, but the two world wars revealed that scientific knowledge also has direct military applications

Among those caught in the ferment of World War I was the international scientific community. Early in the war, scientists in the United States were shocked to find that distinguished Germans such as Wilhelm Roentgen had signed a manifesto justifying the destruction of the famed library at Louvain, Belgium, by German armed forces. Soon, however, the imperatives of the war effort soon placed greater and more direct demands upon scientists, who generally were eager to use their abilities to advance the causes of their respective nations. Although chemists bore the moral burden most directly, thanks to their essential role in the development of increasingly lethal poison gases, physicists also shared in the war efforts of the various belligerents, making significant contributions to the development of acoustic devices for detecting enemy submarines and of flash-ranging and acoustic apparatuses for ascertaining the location of enemy artillery positions.

World War II demanded still more of scientists, and physicists in particular, for several of the war's most far-reaching new technologies demanded their expertise: the proximity fuze, radar, and the atom bomb. "Almost overnight," a scientist at a Midwestern state university remarked, "physicists have been promoted from semi-obscurity to membership in that select group of rarities which include rubber, sugar and coffee." Colleges and universities readily made their facilities available for various wartime endeavors, weapons research among them. In wartime, ethical distinctions between defensive and offensive weaponry can easily be blurred, for physicists who entered radar work labored over devices ranging from microwave apparatuses used to detect enemy submarines and approaching aircraft to equipment designed to enable Allied bombers to drop their bombs with greater accuracy.

At all stages of the conflict, ethical concerns about the war and its weapons were revealed in the thinking of various groups and individuals, including military personnel. Before the war and early in it, air force officers preferred to think of strategic bombing as so precise that only targets of direct military value such as the submarine pens at Wilhelmshaven, Germany, or the ball-bearing plants at Schweinfurt would be attackedrecision bombing was much more difficult to accomplish than prewar theorists had argued, however, and area bombing, in which not only the plants but also the surrounding communities were designated as target areas, was increasingly used. It was only a matter of time until the communities themselves became targets. Japan's great distance from Allied bases meant that sustained bombing of Japanese targets could not even be undertaken until well into 1944, by which time American forces had had more than a year of experience in the air war against Germany. Area bombing therefore played an especially large role in the air war against Japan. Would the use of an atom bomb represent something altogether different or would it simply expand the still uncertain boundaries of area bombing?

Almost as soon as the discovery of nuclear fission was revealed in 1939, physicists began to discuss an atom bomb. Such a bomb would be a weapon of enormous destructive potential, and using it would claim the lives of many thousands of individuals. First it had to be asked whether an atom bomb could be developed. American physicists and their emigré colleagues rallied to the war effort, nearly five hundred going to the Radiation Lab at MIT and many others entering the Manhattan Project (organized in 1942 to coordinate and push forward ongoing fission research) and its various facilities: among these were the Metallurgical Lab at Chicago, where a controlled chain reaction was first achieved; Oak Ridge, Tennessee, where weapons-grade uranium was processed; and Los Alamos, New Mexico, where work on the bomb itself—it was innocuously called the gadget for security reasons—was undertaken. Even when their own efforts seemed disappointing, Manhattan Project scientists could not know whether their German counterparts, such as Nobel laureate Werner Heisenberg, had achieved an insight that had eluded them and had therefore put the atom bomb into Hitler's hands.

Preoccupied with the work before them, these scientists rarely took time to reflect upon what they were doing. The surrender of Germany in the spring of 1945 was the occasion when scientists should have paused to ask themselves whether work on the atom bomb should continue. A young physicist at Los Alamos did raise the question of resigning from atom bomb work en masse, only to be told by a senior colleague that if work were suspended it would be easy for another Hitler to pick up where they had left off. At the Met Lab, where work was pretty much done by 1945, scientists did join in issuing the Franck Report, which asked that a demonstration of the new weapon be made on an uninhabited area before any use of it was made against Japan. Some half-dozen of the most eminent scientists involved in war work however,—those with access to policymakers in Washington—rejected such a recommendation. A direct use of the atom bomb against a Japanese city would be far more likely to bring the war to a prompt conclusion and to increase the likelihood of maintaining peace afterward, they reasoned. Although many of the scientists involved in the Manhattan Project did at one time or another speculate upon the ethical questions that the development of an atom bomb posed, their concern that Hitler might secure prior access to this weapon sufficed to keep their efforts focused on developing the atom bomb. Moreover, mastering the physics involved in creating an atom bomb was an immensely challenging and absorbing scientific and technological problem. "For most of them," Michael Sherry has observed, "destruction was something they produced, not something they did," an attitude that helps explain the wagers these scientists made on the magnitude of the explosive yield of the bomb used in the July, 1945, Trinity test.

Ironically, some German physicists might have pondered the ethical dimensions of the atom bomb more keenly than had their Allied counterparts. Unlike the Manhattan Project scientists, they knew that their research could give Hitler the atom bomb. After the war had ended, scientists were more likely to step back and ask what the atom bomb meant and whether international control of it or further development of nuclear weapons should take precedence. Among those who went on to develop a far more devastating weapon, the hydrogen bomb, the fear of Joseph Stalin and the Soviet Union provided the ethical justification that the thought of a Nazi atom bomb had provided for their Manhattan Project colleagues. By the same token, however, as historian Daniel Kevles put it, "To maintain their scientific, political, and moral integrity, the Los Alamos generation on the whole declared . . . that scientists could 'no longer disclaim direct responsibility for the uses to which mankind . . put their disinterested discoveries.'"

*—Lloyd J. Graybar*

**See also** Hiroshima and Nagasaki, bombing of; Military ethics; Nuclear energy; Research, weapons.

**Bibliography**

Batchelder, Robert C. *The Irreversible Decision, 1939-1950.* Boston: Houghton Mifflin, 1961.

Boyer, Paul. *By the Bomb's Early Light: American Thought and Culture at the Dawn of the Atomic Age.* New York: Pantheon, 1985.

Kevles, Daniel J. *The Physicists: The History of A Scientific Community in Modern America.* New York: Knopf, 1978.

Powers, Thomas. *Heisenberg's War.* New York: Knopf, 1993.

Rhodes, Richard. *The Making of the Atom Bomb.* New York: Simon & Schuster, 1986.

Rigden, John S. *Rabi, Scientists and Citizen.* New York: Basic Books, 1987.

Schaffer, Ronald. *Wings of Judgment: American Bombing in World War II.* New York: Oxford, 1985.

Serber, Robert. *The Los Alamos Primer: The First Lectures on How to Build an Atomic Bomb.* Berkeley: University of California Press, 1992,

Sherry, Michael. *The Rise of American Air Power: The Creation of Armageddon.* New Haven, Conn.: Yale University Press, 1987.

Smith, Alice Kimball. *A Peril and A Hope: The Scientists' Movement in America, 1945-47.* Chicago: University of Chicago, 1965.

## Atomic Energy Commission (AEC)

**Type of ethics:** Scientific ethics

**Date:** Founded 1946; superseded 1974-1975

**Definition:** The AEC established joint military and civilian supervision of uses of nuclear reactions

**SIGNIFICANCE:** After World War II, it was clear that nuclear energy called for special regulation; the AEC was designed to provide it

When World War II was ended by the atomic bombs that were dropped on Hiroshima and Nagasaki, nearly all that the public knew about nuclear energy was that it could be devastatingly destructive. The many medical and industrial uses of the atom lay mostly in the future, and only its horrific power was known. Furthermore, advocates of military applications of nuclear energy insisted on continuing development and testing of atomic weapons. In this atmosphere, the Atomic Energy Act of 1946 was signed into law. It provided for the formation of a presidentially appointed Commission, with separate military and civilian committees under it. The AEC devoted much attention to military weaponry in its early years, but the Atomic Energy Act of 1954 provided for civilian industrial participation in the research and manufacture of atomic materials, and the construction of atomic power installations, licensed by the AEC. In 1974, the AEC was disbanded, and in 1975 two new organizations took up its now changed functions: the Nuclear Regulatory Commission, charged with the investigation and licensing of all uses of atomic energy—medical, industrial, and power, as well as the health aspects connected with these uses; and the Energy Research and Development Administration, which later became the Department of Energy, with the narrower function implied by its name. The weapons applications have been less prominent since then.

**See also** Atom bomb; Hiroshima and Nagasaki, bombing of; Neutron bomb; Nuclear energy; Nuclear Regulatory Commission, U.S.; Research, weapons; Union of Concerned Scientists.

## Attorney-client privilege

**TYPE OF ETHICS:** Legal and judicial ethics

**DATE:** Codified 1975

**DEFINITION:** Attorney-client privilege is a testimonial privilege that permits a client or an attorney to refuse to disclose or to prohibit others from disclosing certain confidential communications between that client and attorney

**SIGNIFICANCE:** Although the disclosure of certain sorts of information that is exchanged between attorney and client is relevant to legal proceedings, the rules of attorney-client privilege are designed to ensure the confidentiality of this relationship

In the U.S. legal system, the following rules apply to the attorney-client privilege. First, in order for a communication to be covered by the attorney-client privilege, an attorney-client relationship in which the client or the client's representative has retained or is seeking the professional services of the attorney must exist at the time of the communication. Second, only communications that are intended to be confidential—that is, those that are not intended to be disclosed to third parties other than those who are involved in rendering the legal services—are protected by the privilege. Third, the privilege cannot be invoked by either the plaintiff or the defendant in a lawsuit when both are represented by the same attorney in the transaction that is at issue. Either party may, however, invoke the privilege against third parties. Fourth, the client holds the power to invoke or waive the privilege.

No privilege can be invoked in any of the following circumstances: when the attorney's services have been sought in connection with planning or executing a future wrongdoing; when the adversaries in a lawsuit make their respective claims through the same deceased client; or when the communication concerns a breach of duty between lawyer and client, such as attorney malpractice or client failure to pay legal fees.

**See also** Adversary system; Confidentiality; Jurisprudence; Privacy; Revelation.

## Augustine, Saint

(Aurelius Augustinus; Nov. 13, 354, Tagaste, Numidia [modern Souk Ahras, Algeria]—Aug. 28, 430, Hippo Regius, Numidia [modern Annaba, Algeria]): Theologian, philosopher

**TYPE OF ETHICS:** Religious ethics

**ACHIEVEMENTS:** Author of *Confessions* (401) and *City of God* (427), the most influential of his numerous writings

**SIGNIFICANCE:** His abiding importance rests on his unique understanding and interpretation of salvation history, human psychology, and Christian moral imperatives

For centuries, the immense influence of Augustine of Hippo has been felt in the life of the Christian Church in the West. Theologians, preachers, ecclesiastical officials, and laity alike have been guided by, or forced to respond to, the power of his ideas and ethical teachings. Thomas Aquinas, Martin Luther, and John Calvin, to name only a few, formulated their own theological positions with special reference to Augustinian thought. A prolific and brilliant writer whose works range from spiritual autobiography to biblical interpretation, Augustine was also a man of the people and a man of action. Born of a pagan father and a Christian mother, he received a first-rate education in the Roman province of Numidia and later became a teacher of rhetoric in Italy. Reconverted to Christianity in 386, Augustine went on to become bishop of Hippo Regius in 395/396 and served in that capacity until his death.

As with any great thinker, Augustine's ideas developed and changed somewhat over the years, but there is also a remarkable consistency to much of his thought, especially in the area of ethics. Augustine's views on ethics were conditioned by his own powerful, personal experiences as well as by the theological and ecclesiastical controversies that erupted during his period of service in the Church. Although he had some knowledge of the ethical theories of both Plato and Aristotle, his familiarity was derived second-hand from his reading of Cicero, Plotinus, and others. Nevertheless, his high regard for Platonic thought can be seen in his attempts to reconcile Christian ideals and Platonic teachings.

**God, Love, and Desire.** On the general issues of human conduct and human destiny, Augustine's thinking was naturally conditioned by the New Testament and by Church tradition. A person, he states, is truly blessed or happy when all of his or her actions are in harmony with reason and Christian truth. Blessedness, accordingly, does not mean simply the satisfaction of every desire. Indeed, the satisfaction of evil or wrong desires provides no ultimate happiness: "No one is happy unless he has all he wants and wants nothing that is evil." Central to Augustine's understanding here is his emphasis on God and love. Indeed, for Augustine, virtue can be defined as "rightly ordered love." Throughout his writings, he stresses that for the Christian an action or work can have value and be worthy only if it proceeds from the motive of Christian love, that is, love of God. Augustine's famous and often-misunderstood injunction "Love, and do what you will" is to be understood in this context.

For Augustine, there exists in humans a conflict of wills, a struggle between original human goodness and the later, inherited desire for lesser things. Although, as he states, "the guilt of this desire is remitted by baptism," nevertheless, "there remains the weakness against which, until he is cured, every faithful man who advances in the right direction struggles most earnestly." In time, as a person matures in the Christian faith, the struggle lessens. As long as humans allow God to govern them and sustain their spirits, they can control their lower natures and desires, and advance on the Christian path. As the concluding prayer of *The Trinity* (420) puts it: "Lord, may I be mindful of you, understand you, love you. Increase these gifts in me until you have entirely reformed me."

**Sin, Moral Conduct, and Society.** According to Augustine, the essential task of humans is to attempt the restoration of the image of God within themselves through prayer, meditation on Scripture, worship, and moral conduct. Sin, by its very nature, obscures and imprisons this image. Especially dangerous to people is the sin of pride, which opens the soul to other vices such as earthly desire and curiosity. Each is destructive of the human soul as well as of human society. A properly ordered moral life not only marks a person's individual movement toward God but also contributes to the improvement of earthly society. Although Augustine believed that humans are social animals by nature and that human potential can be realized only within such an environment, he did not agree that the machinery of political organization is natural. Rather, government institutions are at most a necessary check on the worst excesses of human behavior following the fall of Adam and Eve. The best government is one that provides a peaceful, stable environment in which people can work out their own salvation. For Augustine, as for other early Christian teachers, humans are earthly pilgrims in search of a final resting place. God is both the goal and the means of attaining such: "By means of him we tend towards him, by means of knowledge we tend towards wisdom, all the same without departing from one and the same Christ." —*Craig L. Hanson*

**See also** Christian ethics.

**Bibliography**

Battenhouse, Roy. *A Companion to the Study of St. Augustine. New York: Oxford University Press, 1955.*

Bonner, Gerald. *St. Augustine of Hippo: Life and Controversies*. London: SCM Press, 1963.

Bourke, Vernon. *Joy in Augustine's Ethics*. Villanova, Pa.: Villanova University Press, 1979.

Brown, Peter. *Augustine of Hippo: A Biography.* Berkeley: University of California Press, 1967.

Burnaby, John. *Amor Dei: A Study of the Religion of Saint Augustine*. London: Hodder & Stoughton, 1938.

Deane, Herbert. *The Political and Social Ideas of St. Augustine*. New York: Columbia University Press, 1963.

Gilson, Étienne. *The Christian Philosophy of Saint Augustine*. Translated by L. Lynch. New York: Random House, 1960.

Markus, R. A. *Saeculum: History and Society in the Theology of St. Augustine*. Cambridge, England: Cambridge University Press, 1988.

O'Connell, Robert. *St. Augustine's Early Theory of Man, A.D. 386-391*. Cambridge, Mass.: Harvard University Press, 1968.

Portalié, Eugene. *A Guide to the Thought of Saint Augustine.* Translated by R. J. Bastian. Chicago: H. Regnery, 1960.

TeSelle, Eugene. *Augustine the Theologian.* New York: Herder & Herder, 1970.

Trapé, Agostino. *St. Augustine: Man, Pastor, Mystic.* New York: Catholic Book, 1986.

## Aurobindo Ghose, Sri

**Aurobindo Ghose, Sri** (Aug. 15, 1872, Calcutta, India—Dec. 5, 1950, Pondicherry, India): Philosopher

**Type of ethics:** Religious ethics

**Achievements:** Author of *The Life Divine* (1914-1919) and *Synthesis of Yoga* (1915); in 1910, established an ashram, or retreat, dedicated to the practice of integral yoga in Pondicherry, India

**Significance:** Sri Aurobindo, one of the foremost twentieth century religious thinkers in India, helped to revitalize India both politically and spiritually

After being educated in England from the age of seven until he was twenty-one, Sri Aurobindo returned to India in 1893. He soon became involved in the nationalistic movement in India, and he was imprisoned for his activities in 1908. Realizing through visionary experience that real human liberation went far beyond the political liberation of India, he withdrew from the world and established an ashram, or retreat, in Pondicherry, India.

Aurobindo was very much influenced by the western philosopher Henri Bergson (1859-1941), and he created a synthesis of Bergson's evolutionary view and the Upaniṣads. According to Aurobindo, no evolution is possible without involution, which entails the descent of the divine to the world of matter. The Eternal Spirit is beyond all description, but it descends into the lower realms of being and then by evolution ascends until it returns to its source. This transition from the Eternal Spirit to the multiplicity of the phenomenal world is what Aurobindo calls Supermind. Though matter is the lowest level of being, it is nevertheless a low form of the Supreme. The practice of integral yoga, which consists of three steps, awakens the potentiality of self-perfection that exists in each person. The steps of integral yoga are (1) to surrender oneself totally to God, (2) to recognize that one's progress is a result of the Śakti energy working within oneself, and (3) to have the divine vision of the deity in all things.

**See also** Bergson, Henri; Hindu ethics; Śaṅkara; Upaniṣads; Vedānta.

## Authenticity

**Type of ethics:** Modern history

**Date:** Twentieth century

**Associated with:** Existentialism

**Definition:** Authenticity refers to an individual's autonomy in making moral choices that are not bound by society's norms

**Significance:** Authenticity replaces conformity and shifts moral choices from society to the individual

Lionel Trilling, who wrote *Sincerity and Authenticity* (1971), concurs with French philosopher Jean-Jacques Rousseau that society thwarts authenticity. Trilling analyzes the relationship between sincerity, which he defines as the similarity of what one says and what one feels, and authenticity, which is the essence of that person revealed. He finds that society often rejects authenticity when it conflicts with prevailing standards. Authentic individuals may find it difficult to remain true to themselves and still meet with social acceptance. Such alienation could lead to a form of madness—either clinical madness, as Sigmund Freud suggested could occur when one's ego is unable to reconcile primitive desires with social norms; or a spiritual form of madness-as-truth of the type suggested by Michel Foucault.

The authentic person acts from a sense of innate principles and does not depend on social acceptance for his or her standards of ethics. This emphasis on the individual has led some critics to claim that authenticity tends toward situation ethics. Jean-Paul Sartre has suggested, however, that the actions of the individual are not completely separate but link him or her with society, and Simone de Beauvoir believed that genuine authenticity requires a sustained commitment by the individual within a community.

**See also** Existentialism; Relativism; Sartre, Jean-Paul; Situational ethics.

## Autonomy

**Type of ethics:** Theory of ethics

**Date:** Ancient Greek political thought

**Associated with:** Eighteenth century philosopher Immanuel Kant

**Definition:** The word "autonomy," which comes from the Greek words *autos* ("self") and *nomos* ("law"), denotes the absence of external constraint plus a positive power of self-determination

**Significance:** Immanuel Kant clearly articulated the idea that individual persons must be treated with respect because they are autonomous moral agents; this claim has many implications for moral theory and practice

There are many levels at which autonomy can be said to operate. For example, nations can be said to be autonomous if they formulate and enforce their own laws and policies. (The original use of the word "autonomy," in ancient Greek political thought, designated the independence of city-states that created their own laws instead of having them imposed from without by other political powers.) Similarly, other groups of people can be said to be autonomous, including companies, universities, religious institutions, and even families.

The most important level at which autonomy is believed to be operative, however, is probably the level of the individual person. In Western thought, the ideal of individual autonomy has become enormously important for the evaluation of various political arrangements and for moral reasoning in general (at both the theoretical level and the level of practice). For example, the idea of a totalitarian state is often criticized by political philosophers because of the failure of such an arrangement to respect the autonomy of individual citizens. In a similar way, at the level of particular moral practices, people often appeal to individual autonomy in order to justify or criticize specific ways of behaving. For example, many people argue that in order to respect the autonomy of individual patients, medical professionals are typically obligated to obtain some kind of informed consent from patients before treating them. The notion of individual moral autonomy also plays a very significant role in contemporary moral theory; for example, many theorists insist that the morality of particular actions depends in part upon the self-determined moral outlook of the person acting, and others claim that some kind of individual autonomy in action is necessary in order for persons to be morally responsible agents.

In order to explore the notion of individual autonomy, it will be helpful to consider in some detail what it involves and to examine briefly the influential views of Immanuel Kant (1724-1804) concerning individual moral autonomy.

The notion of individual autonomy is often applied to the actions of individual people; in this sense, people are said to act autonomously to the extent that they determine for themselves what to do, independently of external influences (including the wishes of other people). This individual autonomy with respect to action is often viewed as essential for attributing actions to people as their own and for holding people morally responsible for what they do. It is a matter of great controversy, however, just how much independence a person must have from external influences in order to act autonomously. Some people claim that the actions of persons cannot be determined by environmental factors that are beyond their control if they are to act autonomously, whereas others claim that such independence is not necessary for individual autonomous action.

It is important to realize that the notion of individual autonomy is not applied only to the actions that people perform; it is also applied to the formation of individual beliefs, desires, and preferences, as well as of individual moral principles and motives for acting. Since Immanuel Kant's influential views concerning moral autonomy involve individual autonomy with respect to moral principles and motives for acting, perhaps it would be wise to consider his views at this point.

For Kant, people are distinctive because they are sources of value or ends in themselves, rather than mere means to ends. (In this respect, people are different from other things, such as tables and chairs, which can only be treated as means to other ends, not as ends in themselves.) People are autonomous, self-determining moral agents who are capable of adopting different principles of action. According to Kant, one ought to adopt only those principles that are universalizable; that is, principles that could be willed rationally to become universal laws of conduct for anyone, anywhere, at any time. (Such principles must be completely impartial and make no reference to any particular person's preferences, values, or circumstances.)

The following principle expresses one version of Kant's universally binding moral principle (or categorical imperative): One should always act so as to treat persons as ends in themselves, and never merely as means to ends. This principle reflects the emphasis upon respect for individual moral autonomy in Kant's moral philosophy, an emphasis that has had considerable influence upon later moral philosophers.

In conclusion, the idea of autonomy plays a very important role in political and moral philosophy. Although other notions of autonomy are important, Kant's account of individual moral autonomy has probably been the most influential, and it has served to focus the attention of many moral philosophers upon notions of individual autonomy.

*—Scott A. Davison*

**See also** Accountability; Censorship; Choice; Coercion; Democracy; Determinism and freedom; Diagnosis, ethics of; Dignity; Equality; Experimentation, ethics of; Exploitation; *Foundations of the Metaphysics of Morals;* Freedom/liberty; Human rights; Illness (definitions of, views of, reactions to); Impartiality; Individualism; International justice; Kant, Immanuel; Kantian ethics; Liberalism; Libertarianism; Means/ends distinction; Medical research; Moral principles, rules, and imperatives; Moral responsibility; Natural rights; *On Liberty*; Ought/can implication; Political liberty; *Principles of Medical Ethics*; Responsibility; Universalizability.

**Bibliography**

Dworkin, Gerald. *The Theory and Practice of Autonomy.* Cambridge, England: Cambridge University Press, 1988.

Kant, Immanuel. *Critique of Practical Reason.* Edited and translated by Lewis W. Beck. 3d ed. New York: Maxwell Macmillan, 1993.

__________. *Grounding for the Metaphysics of Morals.* Translated by James W. Ellington. Indianapolis, Ind.: Hackett, 1981.

__________. *Metaphysics of Morals.* Translated by Mary Gregor. Cambridge: Cambridge University Press, 1991.

Lindley, Richard. *Autonomy.* Atlantic Highlands, N.J.: Humanities Press, 1986.

Mill, John Stuart. *On Liberty.* Edited by Gertrude Himmelfarb. New York: Penguin Books, 1982.

__________. *Utilitarianism.* Edited by George Sher. Indianapolis: Hackett, 1979.

## Avalokiteśvara

**Type of ethics:** Religious ethics

**Date:** Depicted in art and literature in India by the third century

**Associated with:** Mahāyāna Buddhism

**Definition:** The personification of wisdom and compassion understood as a bodhisattva (an enlightened being who postpones entrance into *nirvāṇa* to help people achieve salvation)

**Significance:** A bodhisattva who destroys false views and passions

Avalokiteśvara is the bodhisattva of compassion par excellence, who preaches the way to Buddhahood, saves people from suffering and death, and leads them to safety and even enlightenment. The Sanskrit name perhaps meant "the Lord who looks in each direction"; hence, he is sometimes depicted iconographically as a being with eleven or more heads. He is believed to dwell on a mountain, from which he hears the cries of suffering people and brings them aid. In the *Pure Land* sūtras (scriptures), he is one of two bodhisattvas associated with the Buddha Amitābha, who dwells in the Western Paradise and saves those who call upon him. Avalokiteśvara escorts believers from their deathbeds to the Western Paradise. The *Avalokiteśvara Sūtra* teaches that he will intervene directly in human affairs to make fires burn out, enemies become kind, curses fail, and fierce animals calm. Originally conceived of as masculine, *Avalokite*śvara could take feminine forms to teach. In addition, believers thought that the bodhisattva could fulfill wishes, including the wish to bear children. By the fifth century, Buddhists in China had begun to view Avalokiteśvara (in Chinese, K'uan Yin) as feminine. In Japan, the bodhisattva is known as Kannon, a feminine figure; in Tibet, the bodhisattva is known as the male figure Chenrezig.

**See also** Bodhisattva ideal.

## Averroës (Abû al-Walîd Muḥammad ibn Aḥmad ibn Rushd; 1126, Córdoba, Spain—1198, Córdoba, Spain): Philosopher

**Type of ethics:** Religious ethics

**Achievements:** Author of numerous commentaries on Aristotle, criticisms of al-Fârâbî and Avicenna, and *al-*

*Tahâfut al-Tahâfut* (c. 1174-1180; *The Incoherence of the Incoherence*, 1954)

**SIGNIFICANCE:** Averroës' philosophical innovations and interpretations of Aristotle were important as far east as the Levant, and his European followers challenged Catholic orthodoxy

The most scrupulously Aristotelian of the medieval Islamicate philosophers, Averroës nevertheless introduced some significant innovations in his interpretation of Aristotle. His *Incoherence of the Incoherence* responded to al-Ghazâlî's attacks on demonstrative philosophy, which, Averroës argued, is independent of revelation and even is necessary for correct interpretation of revelation. Religion is useful for the masses, who can only attain a modicum of practical moral virtue at best, whereas philosophy is for the few who can attain intellectual contemplation of immaterial substance. Agreeing with Aristotle that only the intellectual part of the soul is immaterial, Averroës argued that the bliss of the soul is in its conjoining (*ittiṣâl*) with the (Neoplatonic) Active Intellect, returning the individual intellectual soul to the source from which it emanated. This apparent denial of the individual immortality of the soul was championed by Latin Averroists (such as Siger of Brabant), whose challenge to Catholic orthodoxy was so persistent that it was the professed target of Descartes in his *Meditations*.

**See also** Avicenna; al-Fârâbî, Muḥammad ibn Muḥammad ibn Ṭarkhân; al-Ghazâlî, Abû Ḥâmid; Islamic ethics.

**Avicenna** (Abû ʿAlî al-Ḥusayn ibn ʿAbdallâh ibn Sînâ, al-Sheykh al-Raîs; 980, Afshanah, Transoxiana Province, Bukhara, Persian Empire—1037, Isfahan, Iran): Philosopher

**TYPE OF ETHICS:** Religious ethics

**ACHIEVEMENTS:** Author of *al-Shifâ'* (c. 1023; *Book of Healing*), *al-Kitâb al-Ishârât wa al-Tanbîhât* (c. 1034; *The Book of Remarks and Admonitions*), and numerous other important works

**SIGNIFICANCE:** In the Islamic world, Avicenna is arguably the most widely discussed philosopher; in medieval Europe, his early works contributed to the understanding of Aristotle and the framing of twelfth through fourteenth century philosophical controversies

Avicenna happily acknowledged his debt to Aristotle and al-Fârâbî, but he was also an original thinker. His distinctive ethical concern with the relation between individual beings and Pure Being (which was to become important for Thomas Aquinas, John Duns Scotus, and others) focused on the fate of the soul after bodily death. The being of individual things is utterly dependent on Pure Being, from which one came and to which, if one is to attain bliss, one returns. That return is ensured only by rigorous study, which overcomes attachment to this world of change and purifies the soul so that it can be immersed in the Light of Being.

Although he was sometimes a commentator on Aristotle (frequently, in *al-Shifâ'*), Avicenna also wrote mystical allegories and poetry that suggest a strong affinity with his Sufi contemporaries.

*Avicenna* (Library of Congress)

**See also** Averroës; al-Fârâbî, Muḥammad ibn Muḥammad ibn Ṭarkhân; al-Ghazâlî, Abû Ḥâmid; Islamic ethics.

**Ayer, Alfred Jules** (Oct. 29, 1910, London, England—June 27, 1989, London, England): Philosopher

**TYPE OF ETHICS:** Modern history

**ACHIEVEMENTS:** Author of *Language, Truth, and Logic* (1936) and *Philosophical Essays* (1954)

**SIGNIFICANCE:** Combining the principles of Austrian logical positivism with the tradition of British empiricism, Ayer argued for a noncognitivist (emotivist) view of ethics

Ayer was Wykeham professor of logic at Oxford, where he completed his education in 1932. Through his early association with the Austrian group of philosophers known as the Vienna Circle, he became a logical positivist. In 1936, he published his best-known book *Language, Truth and Logic*, one of the most influential philosophical essays of the twentieth century. In it, Ayer defended the logical positivist doctrine known as the verification principle, which states that the meaning of any statement is its method of verification. According to this view, which was adopted in order to eliminate all metaphysics, a statement is meaningful if and only if it is either analytic or verifiable by empirical means. Thus, many utterances are pseudo-statements, since they do not express any matter of fact even though they have the grammatical appearance of doing so. Such utterances are therefore neither true nor false. Moral utterances conform to this analysis. So-called "judgments of value" of the form "*x* is good" are not factual judgments at all; instead, they are emotional judgments (reports) meaning "*x* is pleasant" or "*x* is desired." This view of the nature of moral judgments came to be called "emotivism." For Ayer, who was an atheist, moral philosophy is reducible to the metaethical analysis of the meaning of ethical terms.

—*R. Douglas Geivett*

**See also** Atheism; Cognitivism and noncognitivism; Emotivist ethics; Epistemological ethics; Metaethics.

**Bacon, Francis** (Jan. 22, 1561, London, England—Apr. 9, 1626, London, England): Philosopher

**TYPE OF ETHICS:** Renaissance and Restoration history

**ACHIEVEMENTS:** Author of *Colours of Good and Evil* (1597) and *Essayes* (1597, 1612, 1625), *Advancement of Learning* (1605), and *De Augmentis Scientiarum* (1623)

**SIGNIFICANCE:** Bacon inaugurated the naturalistic approach to ethics that came to dominate British moral philosophy into the twentieth century

Bacon's chief contribution to the history of philosophy was his effort to reconstruct completely the conception and practice of science. His own novel method of induction figures prominently in his reconstruction, which helped to launch the modern period of philosophy. His approach, however, was quickly surpassed by better accounts of scientific methodology. In ethics, the *Essayes* was Bacon's main work. These essays were published in three editions (1597, 1612, 1625), the second one an enlargement upon the first, and the third a completion of the whole. No systematic moral theory is presented; Bacon's style is more aphoristic than philosophical. The *Essayes* offers practical advice on moral and social questions. Bacon's major preoccupation as a philosopher was to point the way in which individuals could be restored to a position of superiority over nature. His views about ethics exhibit a hint of this same spirit. Thomas Hobbes, who is best known for his own elaborate political and moral philosophy, was Bacon's apprentice for a time. His emphasis on overcoming the state of nature may have been reinforced by his association with Bacon. On a personal note, Bacon pleaded guilty in 1621 to charges of political corruption. For this offense he paid a fine, was imprisoned in the notorious Tower of London for a brief time, and was permanently banned from political office. Although his particular actions clearly were illegal, the morality of a law that would impugn them has been disputed. As a happy consequence of the leisure thus afforded him, Bacon composed most of his writings during the last five years of his life.

**See also** Hobbes, Thomas.

*Sir Francis Bacon* (Library of Congress)

**Baḥya ben Joseph ibn Paḳuda** (fl. second half of eleventh century): Philosopher

**TYPE OF ETHICS:** Religious ethics

**ACHIEVEMENTS:** Author of *al-Hidâya ilâ farâʿid al-gulûb*, better known from the Hebrew translation *Ḥovot ha-levavot (1161*; *Duties of the Heart*, 1962)

**SIGNIFICANCE:** Baḥya ibn Paḳuda's *Duties of the Heart* is a classic statement of the inner response necessary for a true commitment of self to the service of God

Despite Arab and Islamic influence (notably, Muslim Sufism and Arabic Neoplatonism), the cosmological, ethical, and eschatological discourses of *Duties of the Heart* are essentially Jewish in both content and character. The introduction distinguishes between overt ceremonial rituals and commandments performed by organs and limbs of the body ("duties of the limbs")—such as prayer, charity, fasting, and so forth—and inward belief, intention, attitude, and feeling, which are accomplished by the human conscience. Each of the ten sections that follow highlights a specific duty of the heart, which serves as a gate through which the soul must ascend if it is to attain spiritual perfection. The ten gates are divine unity, divine wisdom and goodness as the foundation of creation and nature, divine worship, trust in God, unification of and sincerity in purpose and action in serving God, humility, repentance, self-examination, abstinence, and the love of God. Each duty of the heart is illustrated by both positive and negative precepts (for example, to attain nearness to God, to love those who love Him and to hate those who hate Him). All duties of the heart are informed by revealed *Torah*, tradition, and—especially—reason. Philosophical proofs are offered for the unity and incorporeality of God and for the creation of the world, including teleology and *creatio ex nihilo*. Total separation from the pleasures of the world is not encouraged; the recommended asceticism involves living in society and directing societal obligations toward the service of God. In summation, the communion of humanity and God is made possible by the duties of the limbs, but the further union of the soul of humanity with the "divine light" of God is by the synthesis of virtues gained by the duties of the heart. Baḥya's theological work, which is considered the most popular moral-religious work of the medieval period, has left an indelible mark on subsequent generations of Jewish ethical and pietistic writing.

**See also** Jewish ethics; Neoplatonism; Sufism; Torah.

**Beauvoir, Simone de** (Jan. 9, 1908, Paris, France—Apr. 14, 1986, Paris, France): Philosopher, novelist

**TYPE OF ETHICS:** Modern history

**ACHIEVEMENTS:** Author of *Pyrrhus et Cinéas* (1944; *Pyrrhus and Cineas*), *Pour une morale de l'ambiguïté* (1947; *The Ethics of Ambiguity*, 1947), *L'Existentialisme et la sagesse des nations* (1948; *Existentialism and Conven-*

*tional Wisdom*, 1948), and *Privilèges* (1955; reprinted as *Must We Burn Sade?*, 1972)

**SIGNIFICANCE:** Defended existentialist ethics as optimistic; identified ethics with politics; upheld the value of authentic individualism; propounded the concept that meaning (function, essence) is never fixed

Like Jean-Paul Sartre, her partner in philosophy and in life, Beauvoir maintained the existentialist point of view that the individual is free from every principle of authority save that which he or she consciously chooses, and that he or she is ineluctably free in a meaningless existence to determine the meaning, or essence, that his or her life is to have. She insisted that one's individual existence is authentic to the extent that it is defined by oneself in relation to, but never as prescribed by, others (or the Other).

***The Ethics of Ambiguity.*** According to Beauvoir, the difference between absurdity and ambiguity, as ethical directions, is that absurdity denies the possibility of any meaning, while ambiguity allows that existence, although it has no absolute meaning and no meaning that can achieve permanence, can be given meanings by individuals who do not deceive themselves about the arbitrariness of meaning: Those who do deceive themselves are inauthentic and in "bad faith" (*mauvaise foi*).

She illustrated "bad faith" by identifying eight types of man (*l'homme:* Beauvoir always used the generic masculine): the "sub-man," who limits himself to facticity and makes no move toward ethical freedom; the "serious man," who claims to subordinate his freedom to a movement or cause, the values of which he takes as the valorization of himself; the "demoniacal man," who rigidly adheres to the values of his childhood, a society, or a religious institution in order to be able to ridicule them; the "nihilist," who, in wanting to be nothing, rejects, as a corollary to rejecting his own existence, the existences of others, which confirm his own; the "adventurer," who is interested only in the process of his conquest and is indifferent to his goal once it is attained; the "passionate man," who sets up an absolute, such as a work of art or a beloved woman, that he assumes only he is capable of appreciating; the "critic," who defines himself as the mind's independence; and "artists and writers," who transcend existence by eternalizing it. In her categorization, authenticity, which is the self's full awareness and acceptance of its own responsibility for what it is and what it does, can be generated in the movements of only the last two types, each of whom accepts existence as a constant and recognizes the inconstancy of meanings; each is susceptible, however, to the self-deception that characterizes the other six types.

In *Pyrrhus and Cineas* Beauvoir had argued the ambiguity of ends: Every goal attained or every end reached becomes no more than a means to still another end, but not to act in the face of nonfinality is to deceive oneself about human reality. Life is inconclusive action, and action is one's relationship to the Other and to existence.

The existentialist ethics of ambiguity is individualistic in its opposition to conventional principles of authority, but Beauvoir insisted that it is not solipsistic, since the individual defines himself in relation to others. It is an ethics of freedom but not, she asserted, of anarchy, since the individual discovers his law by being free, not from discipline, but for constructive self-discipline.

***Existentialism and Conventional Wisdom.*** The nonsolipsistic character of existentialism is presented with broader scope in the collection of four essays originally written for *Les Temps modernes* during 1945 and 1946. The title essay—literally, "Existentialism and the Wisdom of Nations"—condemns conventional wisdom as resignation. Phrased in commonplaces such as "Possession kills love" and "Human nature will never change," it amounts, in Beauvoir's opinion, to a shirking of the responsibility of challenging the sources of pessimism. She contrasted it with existentialism, which is the directing of one's individual freedom toward the mastery of one's fate, along with the willingness to risk one's own existence in striving to improve the conditions of all existence.

The other three essays in this volume carry ethical risk to levels of abstraction, idealism, and metaphysics (for example, literature should "evoke in its living unity and its fundamental living ambiguity this destiny which is ours and which is inscribed in both time and eternity") from which she retreated in her next three essays.

***Must We Burn Sade?*** "Right-Wing Thinking Today" attacks bourgeois idealism and conservative ideology in favor of Marxist realism. "Merleau-Ponty and Pseudo-Sartrism" defends Sartre's Marxist philosophy against Maurice Merleau-Ponty's utopian reading of Marxism. Both essays revert to Beauvoir's identification of ethics with politics. The most challenging of the essays in *Must We Burn Sade?* is the title essay, which reemphasisizes individualist ethics, self-definition in relation to others without being dictated to by the Other. Beauvoir defended the eighteenth century aristocrat, from whose name the word "sadism" was coined, as one who fashioned a consistent ethics apart from a conventional moral system and in keeping with his self-identifying choice. She applauded neither his actions nor his fictional wish-fulfillments, but she saw his defiant flouting of conventional morality and his exercise of choice as prerequisites for authentic individualism.

**Implications for Ethical Conduct.** Beauvoir elaborated the existentialist concepts of living both for oneself and with others, accepting no situation or moral system that one does not make one's own, acting in commitment, being realistic about human limitations, and eschewing all modes of self-deception. —*Roy Arthur Swanson*

**See also** Existentialism; Feminism; Humanism; Individualism; Sartre, Jean-Paul; *The Second Sex*; Women's ethics.

**BIBLIOGRAPHY**

Appignanesi, Lisa. *Simone de Beauvoir*. New York: Penguin Books, 1988.

Bair, Deirdre. *Simone de Beauvoir: A Biography*. New York: Summit Books, 1990.

Brosman, Catharine Savage. *Simone de Beauvoir Revisited.* Boston: Twayne, 1991.

Keefe, Terry. *Simone de Beauvoir: A Study of Her Writings.* London: Harrap, 1983.

Whitmarsh, Anne. *Simone de Beauvoir and the Limits of Commitment.* New York: Cambridge University Press, 1981.

## Behavior therapy

**TYPE OF ETHICS:** Bioethics

**DATE:** Early 1950's

**ASSOCIATED WITH:** Joseph Wolpe, Hans Eysenck, and B. F. Skinner

**DEFINITION:** a collection of procedures for changing behavior based upon principles of learning

**SIGNIFICANCE:** Because behavior therapy techniques often involve extensive control of the patient's environment and can include aversive procedures, they raise concerns about manipulation, denial of rights, and dehumanization of people

Behavior therapy describes a set of specific procedures, such as systematic desensitization and contingency management, which began to appear in the early 1950's based on the work of Joseph Wolpe, a South African psychiatrist; Hans Eysenck, a British psychologist, and the American experimental psychologist and radical behaviorist B. F. Skinner. The procedures of behavior therapy are based upon principles of learning and emphasize the careful measurement of undesired behavior and the setting of objective goals. By the 1960's, behavior therapy and behavior-modification procedures were widely taught in colleges and universities, and widely practiced in schools, prisons, hospitals, homes for the developmentally disabled, businesses, and in private practice offices. By the early 1970's, the ethical and legal status of behavior therapy was being challenged from several sources.

**Ethical Challenges to Behavior Therapy.** Behavior therapy techniques have associated with them the same concerns raised by any form of psychotherapy; namely, that informed consent be obtained from the patient, that the patient play the central role in the selecting of therapy goals, that the patient be primary even when a third party may be paying for or requiring the services, and that the least restrictive means (those that least restrict the freedom of the patient) be employed.

Behavior therapy procedures have been challenged on a variety of ethical grounds. Humanistic psychologists, most notably the late Carl Rogers, argued that behavior modification as practiced by the followers of B. F. Skinner led to treating people as objects to be manipulated by contrived rewards and denied patients the opportunity to find solutions to their problems through their own resources. Behavior modifiers reply that contrived reinforcers are already a part of our culture, that the learning of self-control techniques increases the client's or patient's freedom, that the patient or client is already controlled by the current environmental consequences, and that the client can select the desired goals of the behavior modification program.

Behavior therapy procedures that involve deprivation (withholding of desired objects and events) or aversive conditioning have come under special criticism. Aversive procedures (such as contingent electric shock) have been employed most often to lessen physically self-abusive behavior in the developmentally disabled and, in the 1970's, in attempts to change the behavior of persons with lengthy histories of sexual deviance. Time-out (a procedure in which a person is removed from all sources of reinforcement for a brief period of time) has also received criticism. Its use by school districts has been restricted in some states.

Legal authorities at two levels have singled out behavior therapy for regulation (again, nearly always techniques that involve aversive procedures or depriving a patient in some manner). Federal courts in several decisions have restricted the kinds of reinforcers (rewards) that may be withheld from patients and have required that in all circumstances the "least restrictive alternative" be employed in treating a patient. In addition, state legislatures and state divisions of mental health have established regulations limiting the use of aversive procedures and requiring review committees for certain behavior-modification techniques.

The Association for the Advancement of Behavior Therapy has developed a set of ethical guidelines for behavior therapists and has, along with the Association for Behavior Analysis, assisted states in developing appropriate regulations that assure the patient the right to effective treatment and the right to decline treatment. The associations have also been concerned that persons instituting behavior modification and therapy programs in fact have the requisite training to do so. Standards for claiming expertise in the field have been developed.

One of the unique aspects of behavior analysis and therapy is the attempt to develop ethical principles based upon theories of behaviorism and behavior analyses of the situations in which ethical constraints are necessary. For the most part, these efforts have been undertaken by followers of B. F. Skinner, who have tried to develop his ethical ideas.

—*Terry Knapp*

**See also** Behaviorism; Family therapy; Group therapy; Therapist-patient relationship.

**BIBLIOGRAPHY**

Barker, Philip J., and Steve Baldwin, eds. *Ethical Issues in Mental Health.* London: Chapman & Hall, 1991.

Bellack, Alan S., Michael Herson, and Alan E. Kazdin. *International Handbook of Behavior Modification and Therapy.* 2d ed. New York: Plenum, 1990.

Keith-Spiegel, Patricia, and Gerald P. Koocher. *Ethics in Psychology: Professional Standards and Cases.* New York: McGraw-Hill, 1985.

Stolz, Stephanie B. *Ethical Issues in Behavior Modification.* San Francisco: Jossey-Bass, 1978.

Van Hoose, William H., and Jeffery A. Kottler. *Ethical Issues in Counseling and Psychotherapy.* 2d ed. San Francisco: Jossey-Bass, 1987.

## Behaviorism

**TYPE OF ETHICS:** Personal and social ethics

**DATE:** Early twentieth century to present

**ASSOCIATED WITH:** John Broadus Watson, Burrhus Frederic Skinner

**DEFINITION:** The central tenet of behaviorism is that behavior is controlled by the environment; behaviorism is the systematic study of how environmental factors effect behavior

**SIGNIFICANCE:** Behaviorism holds that traditional ethics should be replaced by an objective science of behavior, and that such a science should be applied to correct the ills of society and foster moral behavior in individuals

Behaviorism as a psychological theory can be distinguished from behaviorism as an ethical theory. Psychological behaviorism is a loosely knit collection of theories and doctrines concerning the nature of science and the study of humankind woven around the central idea that psychology should model itself on the objective methods of natural science. In particular, psychology should restrict itself to descriptions of observable behavior, the situations in which it occurs, and its consequences. Such descriptions should make clear, among other things, whether particular environmental conditions tend to positively reinforce (make more likely) or negatively reinforce (make less likely) certain behaviors. Behaviorism in this sense aims not so much at *explaining* behavior as it does *predicting* and *controlling* it. The methodological precept of psychological behaviorism is that this is *all* that a scientific psychology should study. Behaviorism as an ethical theory builds upon the prescriptions and insights of psychological behaviorism and argues that the only effective means of solving individual and social problems is by implementing environmental conditions that systematically encourage "desirable" behaviors and discourage "undesirable" ones. In what follows, the term "behaviorism" will refer both to the methodology of psychological behaviorism, and to the goals and procedures of ethical behaviorism.

**Theory of Human Nature.** The late Harvard psychologist B. F. Skinner is primarily responsible for the development of modern behaviorism. According to Skinner, much of what is called "human nature" refers not to inborn propensities (such as aggression or altruism), but to the effects of environmental variables on behavior. Like other behaviorists, Skinner is little concerned with innate determinants; for, if they exist at all (for example, as part of the genetic endowment), then they, too, can be traced back to the environment through our evolutionary history. The basic qualities of human nature, therefore, are neither good nor bad; they are merely the results of complex environmental interactions. Perhaps more important, what is called an individual's "personality" consists of nothing more than his or her overall behavior repertoire, which is itself a function of the individual's idiosyncratic history of reinforcement.

The behaviorist makes two important assumptions regarding the study of human nature and personality. First, the behaviorist assumes that all behavior is lawful and determined; that is, that behavior is governed by scientific laws of some kind or other. Call this the assumption of universal determinism. Second, the behaviorist assumes that these scientific laws relate environmental causes to behavioral effects. These so-called stimulus-response relations state causal connections that a properly scientific psychology will discover and exploit in the prediction and control of behavior. Call this the assumption of environmentalism. (Environmentalism is as important for what it *denies* as for what it *asserts*. In particular, environmentalism denies that internal mental or physiological processes play an important role in the production of behavior.)

**Social Policy.** The behaviorist's optimism in shaping human behavior by the manipulation of environmental variables is nowhere more evident than in J. B. Watson's famous claim that if he were given a dozen healthy infants, he could guarantee to take any one at random and train him to be a doctor, lawyer, beggar-man, or thief. This optimistic (and extreme) version of environmentalism forms the basis of behaviorism as a social policy.

*Behaviorist B. F. Skinner* (Alfred A. Knopf)

Skinner has repeatedly made the argument that the inescapable fact of the matter is that behavior is controlled either by factors that lie outside human knowledge and thereby intelligent control and manipulation, or by factors that people create and can thereby direct toward ends of their choosing. The choice is *not* between actions that are "free" and actions that are "determined," as perhaps a traditional ethicist might insist, for *all* human actions (behaviors) are under the control of the environment. Rather, Skinner insists, the choice is to allow arbitrary and unknown factors to shape behavior or to manipulate the environment in order to create the best possible humans.

Behaviorists are vague about how one should go about manipulating the environment, though a few steps immediately suggest themselves. First, science must elucidate the processes and factors that control behavior. Why is it, for example, that Peter becomes a doctor and Paul becomes a thief? Second, this knowledge must be utilized by governments, educators, parents, and so on to develop more productive and socially beneficial behaviors. Parenting and social policy must work in tandem in this (as yet unspecified) process.

Behaviorists are even more vague about what should count as desirable behaviors and who should decide them. To say that people ought to be "happy and productive" is platitudinous, and it hardly guarantees respect for human rights or democratic forms of government. Skinner claims that objective science can settle the matter of what should count as socially beneficial behavior, and he states that totalitarian societies would be inimical to the flourishing of human potential. The fact remains, however, that what is good for the individual may not be what is good for society, and neither may be what is good for the long-term survival of the species. How these competing conceptions of the good might be resolved by science is far from clear.

**Analysis.** Psychological behaviorism has been used with much success in behavior modification therapy, educational and industrial settings, prisons, and even advertising. Few would disagree that the behavioral sciences have made great progress in predicting and controlling behavior. The question of whether the principles and methods of behaviorism can be extended to deal with problems of enormous magnitude and complexity, however, is far from answered. Even if such principles and methods can be extended, one is still left with the question of whether they should be. Moreover, many philosophers and psychologists doubt either universal determinism or environmentalism, or both. Long-standing beliefs regarding human freedom and volition contradict the assumption of universal determinism, and modern cognitive science is committed to the view that internal mental processes are not incidental to intelligent behavior—that they are, in fact, essential to it. On either account, behaviorism may be deeply flawed. Even so, behaviorism's vision of a happier and more rational human order based upon the tenets of natural science and human reason remains the hope of many. —*James A. Anderson*

**See also** Human nature; Psychology.

**BIBLIOGRAPHY**

Nye, Robert D. *Three Psychologies: Perspectives from Freud, Skinner, and Rogers*. 4th ed. Pacific Grove, Calif.: Brooks/Cole, 1992.

Skinner, B. F. *Science and Human Behavior*. New York: Free Press, 1965.

__________. *Walden Two*. 2d ed. New York: Macmillan, 1990.

Stevenson, Leslie. *Seven Theories of Human Nature*. 2d ed. New York: Oxford University Press, 1987.

Watson, J. B. *Behaviorism*. New York: W. W. Norton, 1970.

## Being and Nothingness: Book

**TYPE OF ETHICS:** Modern history
**DATE:** Published 1943 as *L'Être et le néant*
**AUTHOR:** Jean-Paul Sartre
**SIGNIFICANCE:** According to *Being and Nothingness*, human beings are free, but freedom is given within the limits of historical existence; interhuman relationships are threatened by each person's ability to objectify others

For Sartre, human existence is conscious being, "being-for-itself" (*pour-soi*). Human existence as "being-for-itself" is temporal—always in some present, always on the way from some past toward some future. Another characteristic of human existence is its dependence on things. Things have a fundamentally different mode of existence: "being-in-itself" (*en-soi*). They have no consciousness, no possibilities, no freedom. Their being is complete as it is.

One danger for human existence is that it may be falsely reduced from free "being-for-itself" to unfree "being-in-itself." This threat may come from others or from oneself. One may intentionally avoid freedom and the anxiety of conscious decision making by convincing oneself that one has no options, but this is to reduce oneself to an object, to use freedom to deny freedom, to live in "bad faith" (*mauvaise foi*).

The existence of "the others" (*autrui*) is a fundamental fact of human existence. In Sartre's view, however, the constant factor in interpersonal relationships is not potential harmony, but inevitable alienation. Lovers, in his analysis, cannot avoid the objectifying will to possess, which denies freedom and reduces the loved one from "being-for-itself" to "being-in-itself."

**See also** Existentialism; Sartre, Jean-Paul.

## Benevolence

**TYPE OF ETHICS:** Theory of ethics
**DATE:** Coined 1384
**ASSOCIATED WITH:** Thomas Aquinas, Richard Cumberland, Jonathan Edwards, Carol Gilligan, William Godwin, Johann Friedrich Herbart, humanitarians, David Hume, Francis Hutcheson, Earl of Shaftesbury, Henry Sidgwick, and virtue ethicists
**DEFINITION:** Benevolence is a motivation to act sympathetically and altruistically
**SIGNIFICANCE:** Hume considered benevolence the foundation of ethics, and many people believe that the central task of ethics is encouraging benevolence, but ethical egoism and Friedrich Nietzsche consider benevolence unethical

Thomas Aquinas, David Hume, and many others consider benevolence or altruism a key virtue. As Michael W. Martin acutely observes, "Hume makes [benevolence] the supreme virtue, and of all virtue ethicists Hume most deserves to be called the philosopher of benevolence." Jonathan Edwards considers benevolence the supreme virtue in Christianity. Hume believes that benevolent acts are natural products of two features of human nature: sympathy and imagination. Sympathy generates altruistic desires, while imagination enables one to see oneself in the shoes of others in need and conclude, "There but for the grace of God or good fortune go I."

Charity is a virtue that involves benevolence. Martin reports some hard data on charity: (1) rich people and wealthy foundations account for only 10 percent of private donations; (2) the remaining 90 percent comes from individuals, half of them in families whose income is under $39,000; (3) about half of Americans older than thirteen volunteer an average of 3.5 hours of their time each week. Horace Mann used the concept of benevolence to try to distinguish between the ethical value of generosity during the prime of life (for example, teenage volunteers) and deathbed generosity. He said, "Generosity during life is a very different thing from generosity in the hour of death; one proceeds from genuine liberality and benevolence, the other from pride or fear."

In law, mortmain statutes forbid deathbed gifts, apparently out of concern that the gift may be motivated by desperate fear rather than genuine benevolence. Law often encourages benevolence by providing tax deductions for charitable donations, but traditional Anglo-American law (unlike Islamic law, for example) imposes no general duty to rescue strangers and thus fails to require much benevolence.

Regarding political and business ethics, some people argue that the welfare state institutionalizes benevolence and charity. They contend that welfare state programs such as those that mandate minimum wages and relief payments smooth some of the rough edges of laissez-faire capitalism, which is notorious for its cutthroat competition. The alternative of relying on private donations to charity, they believe, will tend to fail precisely when charity is needed most, during an economic recession or depression. During such hard times, people will have less to give for charity and will be less willing to give what they do have as a result of economic insecurity. These trends will intensify as the number of charity cases grows and the need for charitable giving grows with them.

In political ethics and in debates on sex and gender issues, benevolence plays a crucial role. While many feminists try to debunk stereotypes of women as the more emotional and illogical sex, other feminists support the idea that women have a special ethical outlook called Care Ethics. The latter feminists follow Carol Gilligan in suggesting that women are generally more cooperative and less confrontational than men. Care Ethics claims that women are generally less interested in dealing with abstract rules and impersonal ideals such as justice and impartiality and are more interested in nurturing personal relationships by attending to the specifics of the backgrounds or surroundings of particular people. This view seems self-contradictory, however, since so much of the specific backgrounds of particular people consists of rules, which Care Ethics was designed to deemphasize. Such contradictions do not deter some feminists, who openly embrace inconsistency while criticizing traditional ethics for being male-dominated and logocentric. Unfortunately, aside from its obvious illogic, this view has the defect of playing into the hands of those who would stereotype women as more prone to hysteria and inconsistent mood swings between emotional extremes (for example, the view that it is a woman's prerogative to change her mind). Some feminists thus regard Care Ethics as making a retrograde step in the women's movement.

Ethical egoism and the thinking of Friedrich Nietzsche condemn benevolence. Ethical egoists, such as Ayn Rand, think that each person should always act only in his or her own self-interest. In contrast, Johann Friedrich Herbart argued that benevolence involves the harmonization of one's will with others' wills. Nietzsche's concept of the will to power rejects such harmony between wills. One's will to power involves one's domination of the weak.

In conclusion, it would be appropriate to ponder Walter Bagehot's view that "The most melancholy of human reflections, perhaps, is that, on the whole, it is a question whether the benevolence of mankind does most good or harm."

*—Sterling Harwood*

**See also** Altruism; Charity; Christian ethics; Edwards, Jonathan; Feminism; Forgiveness; Generosity; Gratitude; Greed; Hate; Human nature; Hume, David; Love; Mercy; Nietzsche, Friedrich; Perfectionism; Rand, Ayn; Shaftesbury, Earl of; Sidgwick, Henry; Smith, Adam; Thomas Aquinas; Virtue ethics; Welfare programs; Welfare rights; Will.

**BIBLIOGRAPHY**

Broad, C. D. *Five Types of Ethical Theory*. London: Routledge & Kegan Paul, 1956.

Gauthier, David P., ed. *Morality and Rational Self-interest*. Englewood Cliffs, N.J.: Prentice-Hall, 1970.

Gilligan, Carol. *In a Different Voice: Psychological Theory and Women's Development*. Cambridge, Mass.: Harvard University Press, 1982.

Kaufmann, Harry. *Aggression and Altruism*. New York: Holt, Rinehart and Winston, 1970.

Martin, Mike W. *Everyday Morality: An Introduction to Applied Ethics*. Belmont, Calif.: Wadsworth, 1989.

Nagel, Thomas. *The Possibility of Altruism*. Oxford: Clarendon Press, 1970.

Peters, R. S. *The Concept of Motivation*. 2d ed. New York: Huntington Press, 1967.

Pojman, Louis P. *Ethics: Discovering Right and Wrong*. Belmont, Calif.: Wadsworth, 1990.

Prichard, H. A. *Duty and Interest*. Oxford: Clarendon Press, 1928.

Rand, Ayn. *The Virtue of Selfishness: A New Concept of Egoism*. New York: New American Library, 1964.

Rescher, Nicholas. *Unselfishness: The Role of the Vicarious Affects in Moral Philosophy and Social Theory*. Pittsburgh, Pa.: University of Pittsburgh Press, 1975.

Singer, Peter. *The Expanding Circle: Ethics and Sociobiology*. New York: Farrar, Straus & Giroux, 1981.

Wilson, Edward O. *On Human Nature*. Cambridge, Mass.: Harvard University Press, 1978.

**Bentham, Jeremy** (Feb. 15, 1748, London, England—June 6, 1832, London, England): Philosopher and economist

**Type of ethics:** Modern history

**Achievements:** A founder of English utilitarianism and author of *A Fragment on Government* (1776), *An Introduction to the Principles of Morals and Legislation* (1789), *The Rationale of Reward* (1825), and *The Rationale of Punishment* (1830)

**Significance:** Influenced by the impact of the rationalist tradition, the effects of industrialization and urbanization, and the French Revolution, Bentham developed an ethics based upon the "greatest happiness principle" and used it as the cornerstone of English utilitarianism

Frustrated by his inability to pursue a career in politics and law, Bentham developed a radical philosophy based upon the notion of the "greatest happiness principle." He argued that humankind by nature seeks pleasure and the avoidance of pain and that this principle should be the dominant value in society. Society should seek to promote the "greatest happiness for the greatest number." Furthermore, Bentham contended that the law should be based upon this ethical principle. The level of "evil" that results from a crime should be the basis for appropriate punishment; the motivation for the crime is fundamentally insignificant. Bentham maintained that some alleged crimes, such as homosexuality, were not criminal actions because they did not cause harm to anyone. The greatest happiness principle would be realized through an effective government that would be focused on four major concerns: subsistence, abundance, security, and equality. Bentham and James Mill (1773-1836) were the founders of English utilitarianism, which was a philosophic elaboration of the greatest happiness principle.

**See also** Utilitarianism.

**Berdyaev, Nikolai** (Mar. 6, 1874, Lipky, near Kiev, Ukraine—Mar. 23, 1948, Clamart, France): Philosopher

**Type of ethics:** Modern history

**Achievements:** Edited the journal *Put'*(path); wrote *Istori i smysl russkogo kommunizma* (1937; *The Origin of Russian Communism*)

**Significance:** Berdyaev's Christian existentialism explored the role of freedom in the improvement of humankind and society

A Marxist in his youth, Berdyaev moved steadily toward religious idealism. After failed attempts to revitalize Russian spirituality by reconciling the intelligentsia with the Russian Orthodox Church, he distanced himself from the main socialist and liberal reform movements and investigated teleological and eschatological approaches. While retaining traces of his early Marxism, he combined mystical elements taken from early Christian theology, the Reformation theologian Jacob Boehme, and the Moscow philosopher Vladimir S. Solovyov with the idealistic philosophy of Immanuel Kant to develop a Christian existentialist philosophy. In numerous writings, he criticized the materialism and spiritual impoverishment of the Russian intelligentsia, promoted intuitive, mystical modes of investigation, and rejected logic and rationality. To Berdyaev, the value of humanity lay in its capacity for creation. The act of creation illuminated truth and helped to bridge the gap between God and human being, Creator and created. The key element in Berdyaev's God/human relationship was the way in which freedom was used. If it was used in the service of enlarged awareness and capacity, God and humanity became co-creators in a continually progressing universe; if it was turned toward material products instead of being, humanity and society remained in turmoil and confusion.

**See also** Christian ethics; Determinism and freedom.

**Bergson, Henri** (Oct. 18, 1859, Paris, France—Jan. 4, 1941, Paris, France)

**Type of ethics:** Modern history

**Achievements:** Author of *Matière et mémoire* (1896; *Matter and Memory,* 1911), *L' Évolution créatrice* (1907; *Creative Evolution,* 1911), and *Les Deux Sources de la morale et de la réligion* (1932; *The Two Sources of Morality and Religion,* 1935), and the first person to advance a "process philosophy"

**Significance:** Influenced by the French philosophical tradition, which opposed materialism and the "mechanistic" worldview, Bergson's approach to ethics emphasized the primacy of personal actions within the context of evolutionary processes

Throughout his professional life, Bergson maintained that ethical questions, which are affected by myriad external fac-

*Henri Bergson* (Library of Congress)

tors, were fundamentally personal issues. During the latter part of his life, Bergson became absorbed in mysticism and religious thought. In *The Two Sources of Morality and Religion*, Bergson argued that human progress—including the ethical dimension—would be advanced by those few who gained intuitive insight into the mind of God. These "enlightened" individuals would contribute to the continuing progressive evolution of humanity by providing direction and leadership. Thus, Bergson moved in the direction of the authoritarianism of the Christian tradition in which mystics assume an obligation to control society and direct it toward the realization of its fullest potential (the good) in the evolutionary process. He noted that this process would be impeded by the seemingly endless effort to provide the requirements for sustaining physical life. Bergson's philosophy opposed "radical finalism"; in the ethical aspect as in all others, it supported a "progression," or "fulfillment," predicated upon the direction of overriding principles.

**See also** Christian ethics; mysticism.

## Beyond Good and Evil: Book

**Type of ethics:** Modern history

**Date:** Published 1886

**Author:** Friedrich Nietzsche

**Significance:** Sought to free humanity from value systems that encourage weakness and conformity rather than strength and achievement

Friedrich Nietzsche disputed the long-unexamined notion that morality was an absolute. He believed that morality was relative to the condition in which one finds oneself. In *Beyond Good and Evil*, he defined two moralities. The "master morality" encouraged strength, power, freedom, and achievement, while the "slave morality" valued sympathy, charity, forgiveness, and humility. Those qualities that the master morality deemed "good," such as strength and power, were a source of fear to the slave morality and were thus deemed "evil." Nietzsche believed that each person was motivated by the "will to power," the essential driving force behind human behavior, and that exploitation of the weak by the strong was the very nature of life. Reform movements such as democracy and Christianity, which he associated with the slave morality, tried to negate this basic life function and were thus "antilife." Nietzsche feared that Western society had been unduly influenced by the slave morality's resentment and fear of the life-affirming qualities of the master type. Because the achievements of the master class were necessary to human progress, the overall effect was a weakening of the human race. To solve the problem, *Beyond Good and Evil* suggested that the master class's will to power should be encouraged and that members of this class should be freed from the debilitating value system of the oppressed so that they could rise above the paradigm of the slave morality; that is, "beyond good and evil." Thus freed, they could metamorphose into a higher level of existence, which Nietzsche termed "the overman."

**See also** Nietzsche, Friedrich.

## Bhagavad Gītā: Hindu religious text

**Type of ethics:** Religious ethics

**Date:** c. 500-200 B.C.E.

**Author:** Unknown

**Significance:** A central text of Hinduism from the Vedic tradition, the Bhagavad Gītā contains practical guidelines for ethical living, acknowledging standard moral values but emphasizing that the particular situation determines the right course of action

The Bhagavad Gītā is the crown jewel of Vedic literature and has had a huge influence on Hindu thought, ethics, and practices. A short eighteen chapters in the epic Mahābāhrata, the Gītā consists of a dialogue between Lord Kṛṣṇa (an incarnation of the god Viṣṇu) and Arjuṅa, a great warrior. A battle between the Pāṇḍavas—Arjuṅa and his brothers—against the evil Kauravas is imminent, but Arjuṅa is suddenly transfixed when he realizes that he must wage war against relatives and close friends. He asks for Kṛṣṇa's guidance.

Kṛṣṇa's reply to this and subsequent questions constitutes the text of the Bhagavad Gītā, whose title translates literally as "divine song."

Kṛṣṇa begins by addressing Arjuṅa's problem, stressing that nothing with a soul really dies. People are immortal. Furthermore, Arjuṅa's duty as a warrior is to fight in a righteous battle. With these instructions, Kṛṣṇa reveals his relativistic ethics—right action must be appropriate to the specific situation.

Kṛṣṇa continues by revealing the central message of the Gītā: be without the three *guṇas,* the basic forces of nature that bind people to the temporal world. The first, *sattva*, or light, binds people to happiness and lower knowledge. The second, *rajas*, or fire, binds people to action with strong desires. The third, *tamas*, or darkness, binds people to sleepy dullness. In transcending the everyday world of the senses to gain a direct perception of God, or ultimate reality, one must resist being overcome by these forces. By working toward this transcendence, one can achieve liberation from the cycle of death and rebirth and live in eternal bliss consciousness.

At first, Kṛṣṇa describes two basic ways to transcend the three *guṇas*: Jñāna Yoga and Karma Yoga. Jñāna Yoga is the way of monks or renunciants—the path of wisdom on which one studies the sacred texts and lives life away from the pleasures of the world. Karma Yoga is the way of the householder—the path of action on which one is active in the world, meditates, and follows one's *dharma*, or duty. In terms of talent and temperament, people are suited to different roles in society; therefore, everyone has a duty that, however lowly, should always be followed. In later epochs of Indian history, this key concept gave rise to a rigid caste system.

Later, Kṛṣṇa talks about a third path, that of Bhakti Yoga, or the path of devotion, on which one practices Vedic rituals or simply offers anything one does to Kṛṣṇa or some lesser god. Kṛṣṇa emphasizes that everyone should practice all three Yogas, although one Yoga will tend to predominate in one's life.

**See also** Hindu ethics; Karma; Religion.

## Bigotry

**Type of ethics:** Race and ethnicity

**Date:** From antiquity

**Definition:** Obstinate and unreasonable attachment to one's own opinions or beliefs

**Significance:** Bigotry causes innumerable personal and social problems, raising many issues in ethics

Bigotry is the obstinate and unreasonable attachment to one's own opinions or beliefs. A bigot is intolerant of beliefs that oppose his or her own. This is the state of mind of a prejudiced person. Often, such a person is very emotional and may become stubbornly intolerant or even hostile toward others who differ with him or her regarding religion, race, sexual orientation, or other issues. This state of mind encourages stereotyping, overgeneralization, and other errors that suggest the absence of critical thinking.

Bigoted attitudes can be culturally transmitted as part of the education of children or adults. Bigotry is a learned prejudice that is founded on inaccurate and inflexible overgeneralizations. A bigot may believe, for example, that "all blacks are thieves," despite the fact that he or she has no experience on which to base this belief. He or she may even know a very honest black person. In such a case, the bigot will state that this person is the exception to the rule or has yet to reveal his or her truly degenerate character by being caught stealing. When confronted with new information that contradicts his or her beliefs, the bigot is unwilling to change. Instead, the bigot will become excited and emotional when his or her prejudiced beliefs are threatened.

Bigoted attitudes are learned from the social environment. Some people believe that economic competition creates conflict between groups and that this scenario may create hostility and prejudices. The probability of conflict increases if two groups differ in easily identifiable ways. Thus, those who pose the greatest threat to people's jobs or security become the targets of those people's prejudice and bigotry. For example, when Vietnamese immigrants to the United States bought fishing boats and began successfully to fish off the coast of Texas, many Texan fishermen called them names, threatened them, and physically attacked them. Their fishing boats were burned by Texan bigots who feared being displaced because they could not compete with the Vietnamese. Bigotry and unfair tactics were used to eliminate competition and reward inefficient fishermen.

Bigotry is not confined to race. Some bigots dislike fat people, redheads, or the elderly and discriminate against these populations without cause. It should not be forgotten that, in addition to persecuting African Americans, the Ku Klux Klan targeted Roman Catholics and Jews as objects of their hatred.

In societies such as the old American South or the white minority-ruled apartheid regime of South Africa, where racial prejudice was legally sanctioned and socially rewarded, people often manifested both prejudice and discrimination as a means of conforming to prevailing social norms, values, and beliefs. It was against the law for a black South African to become a boss or manager because it would have given him or her authority over a white worker, which was unthinkable to white South Africans. To them, a person's biological inheritance set limits upon that person's current position and what he or she would be allowed to achieve. Where social reward and reinforcement for such ethically reprehensible behavior are absent, bigotry and prejudice are likely to be exhibited by people who suffer from personal insecurity or psychological problems.

Bigotry is not immutable behavior. Social policy can be used to influence bigots in positive ways. Teaching bigots to avoid overgeneralizations and to think critically can provide a good beginning.

**See also** Anti-Semitism; Apartheid; Civil rights movement; Ethnic cleansing; King, Martin Luther, Jr.; Malcolm X; Racial prejudice; Racism.

## Bill of Rights, English

**Type of ethics:** Civil rights

**Date:** Enacted December, 1689

**Associated with:** The Glorious Revolution of 1688, English common law, and the U.S. Constitution

**Definition:** The law established fundamental rights of citizens by specifying limits of governmental power

**Significance:** The English Bill of Rights is an important landmark in the development of the concept of inalienable human rights and political freedoms

Originally proposed as the Declaration of Right, the English Bill of Rights was adopted under the title "An Act Declaring the Rights and Liberties of the Subject, and Settling the Succession of the Crown." Most of its provisions limiting monarchical power had long been supported as established liberties under English common law. By effectively limiting governmental power, it dealt a death blow to the monarchical concept of divine right. It limited monarchical action by forbidding the suspension of established laws, the formation of ecclesiastical courts, and the levying of taxes without parliamentary approval. It also required parliamentary approval for a standing army. As further enhancements of parliamentary power, it upheld freedom of elections and freedom of speech, and specified regular meetings of parliament. For all English subjects, the bill guaranteed the right of petition, the right of trial by jury, and the right of reasonable bail. It prohibited fines and forfeitures of property prior to conviction. It forbade cruel and unusual punishments and granted Protestant subjects the right to bear arms. By enshrining in law rights that are central to a concept of human rights, the Bill became important in the development of freedoms throughout the Western world.

**See also** Bill of Rights, U.S.; Civil rights; Constitution, U.S.; Freedom and liberty; Jury system; U.N. Covenant on Civil and Political Rights.

## Bill of Rights, U.S.

**Type of ethics:** Civil rights

**Date:** Adopted September, 1789—December, 1791

**Definition:** A collection of constitutional amendments that provide legal and civil rights to citizens of the United States

**SIGNIFICANCE:** Provides the legal basis for the protection of fundamental and procedural rights of all classes of citizens

The Bill of Rights, which comprises the first ten amendments to the U.S. Constitution, is the legal basis for the protection of the civil and legal rights of the people of the United States. Protection of those rights was not included in the Constitution itself because the majority of the framers did not feel it was necessary. The federal government was a government of limited powers and therefore could not violate the rights of the citizens. It was at the state level that protection was necessary, and most state constitutions included bills of rights.

When the Constitution was submitted to the states for adoption, however, objections centered on its lack of a bill of rights. Its proponents agreed to submit amendments after the adoption was completed. James Madison led the effort and persuaded the first House of Representatives and the Senate to submit twelve amendments to the states. Ten of the amendments were approved between 1789 and 1791. In December, 1791, the ten amendments were adopted and became known as the Bill of Rights. The first eight amendments state rights that cannot be abridged by Congress; freedom of speech, press, assembly, petition, and religion are included in the First Amendment. The right to keep and bear arms is in the Second Amendment. The Third Amendment prohibits the quartering of troops in private homes. The Fourth Amendment provides for persons to be secure in their person, homes, and papers against unreasonable search and seizure, and sets limits for search warrants. The Fifth Amendment rights are concerned with procedural guarantees. Indictment by a grand jury in criminal cases, a ban on double jeopardy, and a ban on self-incrimination are included in the Fifth Amendment. It also mandates that persons cannot be deprived of life, liberty, or property except by due process of law, and that private property cannot be taken for public use without just compensation. The Sixth Amendment ensures the right to a speedy and public trial by an impartial jury in the state and district where a crime was committed and in a court previously established by law. The accused shall be informed of the charge, be confronted with the witnesses, and shall have subpoena power and council. The right of trial by jury is included in the Seventh Amendment. The Eighth Amendment prohibits excessive bail and cruel and unusual punishment. The Ninth and Tenth Amendments were added to ensure that the Bill of Rights would not be used to deprive the people or the states of their implied rights or reserved powers. The Ninth Amendment says that the enumeration of rights does not mean that others not included are denied. Powers not delegated to the federal government or denied to the states are reserved to the states or to the people by the Tenth Amendment.

Initially, the Bill of Rights was not tested in the federal courts. Even the Alien and Sedition Acts, passed by the Fed-

### THE BILL OF RIGHTS

**Article I**

Congress shall make no law respecting an establishment of religion, or prohibiting the free exercise thereof; or abridging the freedom of speech, or of the press; or the right of the people peaceably to assemble, and to petition the Government for a redress of grievances.

**Article II**

A well regulated Militia, being necessary to the security of a free State, the right of the people to keep and bear Arms, shall not be infringed.

**Article III**

No Soldier shall, in time of peace be quartered in any house, without the consent of the Owner, nor in time of war, but in a manner to be prescribed by law.

**Article IV**

The right of the people to be secure in their persons, houses, papers, and effects, against unreasonable searches and seizures, shall not be violated, and no Warrants shall issue, but upon probable cause, supported by Oath or affirmation, and particularly describing the place to be searched, and the persons or things to be seized.

**Article V**

No person shall be held to answer for a capital, or otherwise infamous crime, unless on a presentment or indictment of a Grand Jury, except in cases arising in the land or naval forces, or in the Militia, when in actual service in time of War or public danger; nor shall any person be subject for the same offence to be twice put in jeopardy of life or limb; nor shall be compelled in any criminal case to be a witness against himself, nor be deprived of life, liberty, or property, without due process of law; nor shall private property be taken for public use without just compensation.

**Article VI**

In all criminal prosecutions, the accused shall enjoy the right to a speedy and public trial, by an impartial jury of the State and district wherein the crime shall have been committed, which district shall have been previously ascertained by law, and to be informed of the nature and cause of the accusation; to be confronted with the witnesses against him; to have compulsory process for obtaining Witnesses in his favor, and to have the assistance of counsel for his defence.

**Article VII**

In Suits at common law, where the value in controversy shall exceed twenty dollars, the right of trial by jury shall be preserved, and no fact tried by a jury, shall be otherwise reexamined in any Court of the United States, than according to the rules of the common law.

**Article VIII**

Excessive bail shall not be required, nor excessive fines imposed, nor cruel and unusual punishments inflicted.

eralists in 1798, were not taken into court, because people believed that the Supreme Court, staffed by Federalists in 1798, would not declare them unconstitutional.

The Supreme Court accepted cases involving the Bill of Rights in the 1830's. John Marshall's decision in *Barron v. Baltimore* in 1833 established the principle that the Bill of Rights did not apply to the states. This view dominated Court decisions, with only a couple of isolated exceptions, until the decade of the 1930's. In 1897, the due process clause of the Fourteenth Amendment was used to apply the Fifth Amendment right of protection of property to the states, and in 1925 in *Gitlow v. New York* the Supreme Court held that freedom of speech and press are among the fundamental liberties protected by the due process clause of the Fourteenth Amendment from impairment by the states.

During the 1930's, the Court began the "modernization" of the Bill of Rights by incorporating the Bill of Rights into the Fourteenth Amendment. The Court applied the federal guarantees to the states. The judicial principle used in *Palko v. Connecticut* became the basis for fully incorporating the First Amendment rights of freedom of speech, press, assembly and religion in the due process clause of the Fourteenth Amendment. During World War II and the Cold War era, however, some restrictions upon these rights were permitted in the interest of security; for example, federal and state loyalty programs.

Incorporation of the Bill of Rights accelerated after 1950. In a series of cases, the Supreme Court said that part of the Fourteenth Amendment that reads "no state shall . . . deprive any person of life, liberty, or property without due process of law" provides a guarantee of the fundamental liberties in the Bill of Rights that state governments must protect to the same extent as does the federal government.

By 1991, all the rights included in the first eight amendments were protected from state encroachment except the Second Amendment right to keep and bear arms, the Fifth Amendment right to a grand jury indictment, the Sixth Amendment requirement of twelve jurors in a criminal trial, and the Seventh Amendment right to a civil jury. The Supreme Court has held that state procedures are adequate to protect the values inherent in those Bill of Rights guarantees.

*—Robert D. Talbott*

**See also** Civil rights; Constitution, U.S.; Due process; First Amendment; Freedom of expression; *Gideon v. Wainwright*; *In re Gault*.

**Bibliography**

Alderman, Ellen, and Caroline Kennedy. *In Defense of Our Rights: The Bill of Rights in Action*. New York: Avon Books, 1991.

Brand, Irving. *The Bill of Rights: Its Origin and Meaning*. Indianapolis: Bobbs-Merrill, 1965.

Cortner, Richard C. *The Supreme Court and The Bill of Rights: The Fourteenth Amendment and the Nationalization of Civil Liberties*. Madison: University of Wisconsin Press, 1981.

Douglas, William O. *A Living Bill of Rights*. Garden City, N.Y.: Doubleday, 1961.

Goldwin, Robert, and William A. Schambra, eds. *How Does The Constitution Secure Rights?* Washington, D.C.: American Enterprise Institute for Public Policy Research, 1985.

## Bills of Rights, Medical

**Type of Ethics:** Bioethics

**Dates:** The term "rights" appears to have been coined in Britain in the eleventh or twelfth century; in medicine, however, patients' correlative rights precede the coinage of the term, dating to the Hippocratic oath of the fifth century B.C.E.

**Definition:** Bills of rights make explicit the rights that people may claim; rights are claims created by contracts, promises or other obligation or duty-generating commitments

**Significance:** Rights language shifts the focus of moral attention from the duty-bound party to the party to whom there is a duty—to the claims of the right holder

Although the express use of rights language in medicine is an artifact of the late twentieth century, deontological (duty-based) conceptions of medical ethics trace back to the Hippocratic oath, which explicitly obligates physicians to "abstain from all intentional wrong-doing and harm"—particularly "from [sexual] abus[e]"—and from "divulging [information about patients] holding such things to be holy secrets." Correlative to these obligations (although unstatable at the time, since the language of rights had yet to be invented) patients have the right not to be intentionally harmed, not to be sexually abused, and not to have confidential information divulged.

Duty-based conceptions of the patient-physician relationship were dominated by the Hippocratic oath until three eighteenth century British writers—the Reverend Thomas Gisborne (1758-1846), Doctor John Gregory (1725-1773), and Thomas Percival (1740-1804)—developed theories of obligation deriving from physicians' social responsibilities and from their sympathy with patients. In 1803, Percival published a syncretic version of all three theories in the form of a code of ethics; that code, in turn, became the basis of codes of medical ethics issued by nineteenth century regional and national medical associations throughout the world. Although these writers were familiar with rights language, their primary focus was stating the duties of physicians. Consequently, even though their theories on physicians' duties generate correlative rights (see table), they eschew the language of rights—as do the codes of medical ethics they inspired.

The first document to focus primarily on patients' moral claims is the 1947 *Nuremberg Code*, a set of ten principles issued by the Nuremberg Tribunal to justify their finding that the medical experiments conducted by twelve German physicians and their assistants were "crimes against humanity." The first Nuremberg principle opens by stating that for "moral, ethical, and legal [experimentation] . . . the voluntary consent of the human subject is essential." It closes by stating that "the duty . . . for ascertaining consent rests on each individual who initiates, directs, or engages in the experiment." The *Nuremberg Code* never uses the language of

| Historical Table of Patients' Rights | | | |
|---|---|---|---|
| **Document** | **Date** | **Author** | **Rights** |
| Hippocratic oath | 400 B.C.E. | Unknown | Not to be harmed.<br>Not to be sexually abused.<br>Confidentiality. |
| *Lecture on the Duties of Physicians* | 1772 | John Gregory | Sympathetic and humane care. |
| *On the Duties of Physicians* | 1794 | Thomas Gisborne | Diligent attention.<br>Confidentialty.<br>Honesty.<br>Punctuality.<br>Steadiness and sympathy. |
| *Medical Ethics* | 1803 | Thomas Percival | Attention and steadiness.<br>Humanity.<br>Confidentiality.<br>Authority and condescension (to be treated as equals). |
| *Code of Ethics* | 1847-1957* | AMA | Skill, attention, fidelity. Tenderness and firmness.<br>Authority and condescension (equal treatment).<br>Humanness and steadiness.<br>Confidentiality.<br>Not to be abandoned.<br>Treatment during epidemics (even if physician jeopardized). |
| *Nuremberg Code* | 1947 | Nuremberg Tribunal | To consent to, and to refuse to be, experimented upon.<br>To be informed of experiments.<br>To terminate experiments unilaterally. |
| *Patient's Bill of Rights* | Current | American Hospital Association | To considerate and respectful care.<br>To know the name of one's physician<br>To be informed of diagnosis, prognosis, treatment plans, and alternatives.<br>To consent to, and to refuse, treatment<br>To privacy and confidentiality.<br>To be informed of conflicts of interest.<br>To be informed of, and to refuse to participate in, research<br>To have continuity of care and appointments.<br>To examine bills and have them explained.<br>To be informed of hospital rules. |
| *Accreditation Manual* | Current | Joint Commission on Accreditation of Health Care Organization | Impartial access to treatment, regardless of race, cred, sex, or national origin, or sources of payment.<br>To condsiderate and respectful care.<br>To privacy and to wear personal clothing.<br>To request a change of room.<br>To know who is providing treatment.<br>To refuse to be treated by trainees. To be clearly informed of diagnosis. To visitors, phone calls, and letters.<br>To informed participation in health care decisions.<br>To consent to, and to refuse, treatment.<br>To be informed of, and to refuse to participate in, experiments.<br>To consult with a specialist and to continuity of care.<br>To receive itemized explanations of bills.<br>To be informed of a hospital's rules and complaint procedures |

* Most contemporary statements of medical and nursing ethics are formulated as standards or principles rather than duties or obligations, and thus do not generate correlative rights. In 1957, for example, the AMA replaced its *Code of Ethics* with *Principles of Medical Ethics*, the principles state standards of conduct rather than duties, but Principle IV of the current AMA *Principles* stipulates that: "A physician shall respect the rights of patients."

rights, yet most commentators treat it as the progenitor of patients' rights theory because its focus (exemplified in these quotations) is on the moral claims—the rights—of the subjects of research.

Rights language was first expressly used in major medical documents during the 1970's, when it surfaced in the American Hospital Association's 1972 *A Patient's Bill of Rights* and, concurrently, in the section "Rights and Responsibilities of Patients," in the *Accreditation Manual* of the JCAH(O), the Joint Commission on the Accreditation of Hospitals (later, Health Care Organizations)—the organization that accredits American medical hospitals, psychiatric hospitals, and nursing homes. —*Robert Baker*

**See also** Medical ethics; *Principles of Medical Ethics*.

**Bibliography**

Annas, George. *The Rights of Patients: The Basic ACLU Guide to Patients Rights*. 2d ed. Carbondale: Southern Illinois University Press, 1989.

Annas, George, and Michael Grodin, eds. *The Nazi Doctors and the Nuremberg Code: Human Rights in Human Experimentation*. New York: Oxford University Press, 1992.

Baker, Robert, Dorothy Porter, and Roy Porter, eds. *The Codification of Medical Morality: Historical and Philosophical Studies of the Formalization of Western Medical Morality in the Eighteenth and Nineteenth Centuries*. Dordrecht, The Netherlands: Kluwer, 1993.

Edelstein, Ludwig. *Ancient Medicine: Selected Papers of Ludwig Edelstein*. Edited by Owsei Temkin and C. Lilian Temkin. Translated by C. Lilian Temkin. Baltimore: The Johns Hopkins University Press, 1967.

## Biodiversity

**Type of ethics:** Environmental ethics

**Date:** Since 1960

**Associated with:** The United Nations, Earth Summit, and conservation groups

**Definition:** Biodiversity is the genetic diversity of all forms of life on earth, measured in terms of both numbers of species and genetic variability within species

**Significance:** An ethical mandate for the preservation of biodiversity can be derived either from the potential usefulness of the organisms to human beings or from the viewpoint that humans are stewards of the earth's resources and have no moral right to destroy a unique biological species

The importance of conserving biodiversity is an idea that attracted increasing international attention in the 1980's; previously, conservationists had concentrated their efforts on preservation of conspicuous and economically important organisms. The 1992 United Nations Conference on Environment and Development ("Earth Summit") arrived at a convention on biodiversity with protocols for protecting endangered species and international cooperation on biotechnology.

Species are undoubtedly becoming extinct at a rapid rate because of pollution, habitat destruction, deforestation, overexploitation, and other human activities. The approximately seven hundred extinctions that have been recorded in the last three hundred years are only a small fraction of the total, which is estimated by some scientists to be approaching fifty thousand species per year. Much of the world's genetic biodiversity is concentrated in inconspicuous insects, fungi, aquatic invertebrates, and herbaceous plants that have never been described. Efforts to conserve biodiversity involve balancing known present needs with projected future needs and balancing the conflicting demands of local, national, and international agencies. Frequently, corporate and national policy have favored overexploitation. The well-being of the indigenous population of an area is an important consideration. Resource management by stable traditional societies, which is more sophisticated than is commonly realized, favors biodiversity, but global upheaval and the population explosion have destroyed the delicate balance between society and the biosphere in much of the developed and developing world.

The rise of genetic engineering has served to highlight the economic value of biodiversity and raise the question of ownership. Historically, species have been regarded as common property, but advocates for the rights of indigenous peoples have suggested that something akin to patent rights should belong to the group of people on whose territory an economically important organism is discovered.

**See also** Conservation; Deforestation; Earth, human relations to.

## Bioethics

**Type of ethics:** Bioethics

**Date:** From antiquity

**Associated with:** American Medical Association (AMA), Environmental Protection Agency (EPA), ecology, conservation, genetic engineering, and gene transfer

**Definition:** The multidisciplinary study of ethical problems of humanity arising from scientific advances in medicine and technology examined in the light of moral values and principles

**Significance:** Seeks development of a set of guidelines for moral decision making utilizing the resources of medicine, biology, law, philosophy, theology, and social sciences, aiming to serve the best interests of individuals and society

While the rudiments of bioethics are ancient in origin, modern bioethics—medical, scientific, and environmental—is a relatively young field, that emerged about 1970. Its growth has been necessitated by increasingly complex dilemmas brought about by sophisticated technological knowledge and capabilities. Bioethics deals with questions of moral dimension and professional responsibility involving all forms of life: issues of medical decision making, living and dying, withdrawing and withholding medical care, conducting research on human subjects, allocating scarce resources, transferring cells from one or several organisms to produce another with particular characteristics ("cloning"), and preserving natural resources by efficient use of energy to protect the atmosphere and counteract the deleterious effect of pollutants.

These are issues to which there is no single clear-cut or mechanical answer. A proposed solution involves reviewing the parameters of various options and selecting the most beneficial. Superimposed on that seemingly facile solution are overriding considerations such as the identity of the decision maker, his or her values, legal capacity, and priorities. Bioscience is based on principles of natural science and risk assessment, while bioethics is based on moral principles developed and applied in the context of professional ethics.

**Historical Background.** Ethical medical guidelines are rooted in the writings of the Greek physician Hippocrates, who was born about 460 B.C.E. The Hippocratic oath reflects the traditional notions of paternalism of the medical profession, which regard the physician as the primary decision maker for the patient and the person best able to decide what course of action is in the patient's best interest. The oath requires physicians to act to benefit the sick and keep them from harm ("*primum non nocere*"), and it admonishes physicians to refrain from assisting patients in suicide or abortion. Most of the codes of ethics adopted by the AMA in 1847 and revised in 1903, 1912, 1947, 1955, and 1980 use a similar approach. In 1957, the AMA adopted "Principles of Medical Ethics," a set of ten principles outlining the ethical mandate of the physician and requiring the medical profession to use its expertise to serve humanity. In 1973, the American Hospital Association adopted a "Patient's Bill of Rights," which ensures patient privacy and confidentiality.

*Lectures on the Duties and Qualifications of a Physician*, written by John Gregory, professor of medicine at the University of Edinburgh, was published in 1772. The book emphasized the virtues and dignity of the physician and further defined his responsibilities and duties. In 1803 Thomas Percival, an English physician, wrote *Medical Ethics.* Pragmatic in approach, it stressed the professional conduct of the physician, and his relationships with hospitals, medical charities, apothecaries, and attorneys. Percival encouraged physicians to act to maximize patients' welfare. His influence is reflected in the AMA codes of 1847 and 1957.

A changed focus from a theological approach to a growing secularization of bioethics began with Episcopalian theologian Joseph Fletcher's *Medicine and Morals* (1954), which introduced "situation ethics," emphasizing the uniqueness of moral choice. Protestant theologian Paul Ramsey's *The Patient as Person* (1970) examined the emerging moral issues.

Environmentalism is derived from conservation and ecology. The former concept originated with forester Gifford Pinchot during the administration of President Theodore Roosevelt (1901-1909). At that time, the populace first became aware of conservation, but only in the context of how to manage natural resources; the consequences of the wasteful use of property were not considered. The term "ecology" was invented by Ernst Haeckel, a biologist and philosopher, and introduced in his 1866 book *General Morphology of Organisms.* Use of the term spread throughout the life sciences. Charles Elton, a founder of scientific ecology, explained that primitive men and women are actually ecologists who interpreted their surroundings. Therefore, environmentalism may be said to equate to primitivism. Ecology became a household word in the 1960's, when a public outcry arose concerning abuses of the environment.

Biotechnology evolved from biblical times. Noah's drunkenness, described in the Book of Genesis, indicates a requisite familiarity with the process of fermentation, which must have been used to produce the alcohol that Noah imbibed. Used in leavened bread, cheese, and pickling, the fermentation process was also later utilized to isolate organisms capable of producing acetone and butanol, and in 1928 penicillin and streptomycin.

In the late 1940's, the study of deoxyribonucleic acid (DNA) began, for scientists recognized that every inherited characteristic has its origin somewhere in the code of each person's DNA. The structure of DNA was discovered in the early 1950's. Viewed as one of the major scientific accomplishments of the twentieth century, the study of DNA has significantly widened the horizons of biotechnology.

**Principles of Biomedical Ethics Illustrated.** The U.S. Constitution guarantees persons the right to exercise their liberty and independence and the power to determine their own destiny and course of action. Autonomy is legally grounded in the right to privacy, guaranteed as a "penumbra," or emanation, of several amendments of the Bill of Rights. The philosophical origins of autonomy stem from John Locke's *Two Treatises of Government* (1690), Immanuel Kant's *Grundlegen Zur Metaphysik deu Sitten* (1785; *Groundwork for the Metaphysics of Morals),* and John Stuart Mill's *On Liberty* (1989).

There is an inherent tension at the core of biomedical ethics, which springs from the need to balance the right of the patient to act in his or her own best interest without constraint from others (autonomy) and the obligation of the health care professional to act to promote the ultimate good of the patient, prevent harm, or supplant harm (beneficence). A conflict between patient autonomy and beneficence may arise in the context of medical treatment, acute care, or chronic care. Acting in the patient's best interest may dictate a certain course of conduct that is medically indicated but whose result is unacceptable to the patient in terms of limitations in lifestyle. The President's Commission for the Study of Ethical Problems in Medicine and Biomedical and Behavioral Research (1983) declared that where a conflict between a patient's self-interest and well-being remains unresolved, respect for autonomy becomes paramount. A weighing or balancing of the benefits against the burdens must be considered in order to arrive at an acceptable solution. Often, notions of paternalism are raised.

The principle of nonmaleficence, or the noninfliction of harm or evil on the patient, may conflict with obligations to promote the good of the patient, because many medical courses of action may involve certain undesirable consequences yet result in an ultimate benefit. (An example is inflicting a negligible surgical wound to avoid death). In other circumstances, such as the continued futile treatment of seriously ill newborns, pointless treatment for the irreversibly comatose patient, or a decision to withdraw artificial nutrition or hydration from a patient in a persistent vegetative state, there must be a weighing of potential benefit versus potential harm. Quality of life considerations may influence the outcome of the analysis.

The principle of justice seeks a scheme whereby scarce resources may be allocated fairly and uniform criteria may be developed to determine, for example, an order for the allocation of organs for transplantation, space in intensive care units, participation as clinical research subjects, and access to health care for those who lack health insurance. Governed by a cost-benefit analysis, distributive justice issues arose as pressures for health care cost containment that emerged in the 1980's escalated in the 1990's.

**Informed Consent.** The most concrete example of autonomous decision making is contained in the doctrine of informed consent: an explanation of the patient's condition; an explanation of the procedures to be used, along with their risks and benefits; a description of available alternatives or options, if any; and reasonable opportunity for the patient to change his or her mind, withdraw consent, or refuse consent. Informed consent free from coercion or deception must be obtained before procedures that invade the body can be performed. In the normal setting absent an emergency, if proper consent is not obtained, a legal action for battery may ensue.

In the partnership model that characterizes the physician-patient relationship in pluralist Western society, variables may act as obstacles to the true exercise of autonomy. Individual circumstances and cultural, familial, and religious differences may color a person's moral judgment and influence that person's decision making capacity. Because of patient's limited understanding of their medical conditions, they may make decisions that are ambivalent, contradictory, or detrimental to their own health. At the same time, they may be harmed by the fears and anxieties induced by a more accurate understanding of the risks and options they face. The health care professional may be required to make a determination about the extent of disclosure and the degree of assimilation of the information conveyed.

The most controversial exception to informed consent is the therapeutic privilege, which permits medical personnel to withhold information intentionally if in the exercise of sound medical judgment it is determined that divulging certain information would be harmful to the patient. The use of placebos for the welfare of the patient is an extension of the therapeutic privilege. Another instance of intentional nondisclosure or limited disclosure occurs in the context of clinical research, where "adequate" disclosure for purposes of consent does not necessitate "complete" disclosure. Resolution of these and other dilemmas of this nature are the subject of debate in this area.

**Environmental Ethics.** The global environmental crisis is serving as a catalyst for the reexamination of human values and ethical concerns about moral responsibility for the common good. Questions of environmental concern include the propriety of exposing workers to substances whose toxicity is unknown or discharging pollutants into the air, the role of the government in preventing adverse activity, a determination of the steps to be taken to halt or slow the erosion of biological diversity, and the fair and equitable allocation of material resources.

Examples of serious environmental problems that threaten the earth and its inhabitants are overpopulation, an inadequate food supply, the threat of global warming or climate change caused by the release of greenhouse gases and the destruction of the ozone layer, deforestation, loss of biodiversity, threats of water and air pollution, and the depletion of mineral and energy resources. Wastes and poisons are threatening land, water, air quality, mineral resources, and energy resources. Soil erosion is the greatest threat to farmland. Chemical fertilization, once thought to provide a solution to the problem of the billions of tons of topsoil that are lost in runoff, is costly and does not accomplish its goal effectively. Worldwide dumping of litter has caused the loss of millions of sea birds and animals and contamination from crude oil residue. Freshwater lakes have become polluted from bacteria, sewage, groundwater contamination, and hazardous waste; drinking water has remained unprotected.

Acid rain is a damaging form of air pollution. Wind may cause acid rain to rise high in the air and travel many miles. A product of combustion, acid rain kills fish in lakes, destroys crops, corrodes pipes carrying lake water, and releases toxic metals from soil compounds into groundwater. The main sources of contaminants in acid rain are combustion fumes from industry and automobile and truck exhausts. Environmentalists have warned of a "greenhouse effect"—that is, a trend toward global warming—resulting from the buildup of carbon monoxide and other gases in the atmosphere. These climatic changes are expected to melt glaciers and ice caps, causing sea levels to rise, flooding cities and coastal areas. The decline in rainfall could potentially cause mass starvation and the extinction of plant and animal life unable to adapt to changed conditions. Depletion of the earth's ozone layer would permit potentially carcinogenic ultraviolet rays to escape into the atmosphere. Because of the worldwide deforesting of acres of trees, the earth's ability to reabsorb carbon dioxide has been reduced.

A general increase in energy efficiency is the fastest and cheapest solution to the problem. Energy efficiency reduces fuel consumption, thereby reducing the output of gases into the atmosphere. The development of automobiles that run on clean-burning natural gas or methanol will reduce emissions into the atmosphere. Using solar power, tidal power, and geothermal energy (natural steam produced by heat within the earth itself) as alternative energy sources have also been proposed as solutions. The use of atomic energy has also been debated.

In 1993, U.S. president Bill Clinton signed an international biodiversity treaty designed to protect plants and animals, committing the nation to reduce emissions of greenhouse gases to their 1990 levels by the year 2000. Earth Day, celebrated on April 22 of each year since 1970, calls attention to environmental problems. Community groups have instituted recycling programs. Activist groups such as the Sierra Club and Greenpeace and organizations such as Earthwatch and the Worldwatch Institute have flourished, alerting policymakers and the general public to emerging trends and the availability and management of resources.

The Environmental Protection Agency (EPA) is the governmental agency with the responsibility to enforce compliance with environmental standards through monitoring programs and inspections. Those who knowingly violate environmental laws may be subject to criminal sanctions. Under the Clean Water Act (1970), negligent acts can also be construed as criminal violations (felonies or misdemeanors punishable by fine, imprisonment, or both).

**Biomedical Technology.** The use of new technological powers brigs challenges to traditional notions of preserving human dignity, individual freedom, and bodily integrity. Scientific ability to prolong life through the use of respirators, pacemakers, and artificial organs; to conquer infertility and gestation through in vitro fertilization and fetal monitoring; and to practice birth control through abortion and techniques for reducing fertility make it possible to manipulate life. Genetic engineering and human genetic manipulation have unlimited potential. Overriding ethical considerations concerning problems of abuse and misuse of technological powers, must, however, be addressed.

**Genetic Engineering.** Ethical and social questions about experimenting on the unborn and the possible misuse and abuse of power have been raised since genetic engineering (also known as gene splicing, genetic manipulation, gene cloning, and recombinant DNA research) sparked the revolution in biotechnology. The debate was especially intense in the mid-1970's, when fear about the wisdom of interfering with nature in a fundamental way was thought to outweigh the possible benefits in biological and medical research. It was feared that genetic accidents could occur when someone with expertise deliberately constructed an organism with the potential to threaten human health. There was also the fear that gene therapy might be used to alter human attributes such as intelligence or physical appearance. As scientists demonstrated evidence of precautions and federal government guidelines regulating genetic engineering research and banning certain types of experiments were drafted, a majority of biologists concluded that the risks were negligible.

The industry most affected by biotechnology is the pharmaceutical industry. In September, 1982, insulin from bacteria became the first of many genetically engineered materials licensed for human consumption. The potential is enormous as better and cheaper antibiotics are developed, improved methods for matching organs for transplantation are found, and techniques for correcting body chemistry emerge. Transferring genes from one organism to another would reduce the cost and increase the supply of materials used in medicine, agriculture, and industry. Far-reaching benefits from the bioindustrial revolution include better health, more food, renewable sources of energy, more efficient industrial processes, and reduced pollution.

**Genetic Screening and the Human Genome Project.** The genome, or combination of genes acquired from one's biological parents, is central to a person's development. The three-billion-dollar, fifteen-year Human Genome Project, initiated in the 1990's to map human DNA, aims to study the total genetic endowment in the chromosomes, identify new markers for traits and diseases believed to have a genetic basis, and develop diagnostic tests to screen for hereditary diseases. Advances in human gene therapy could lead to the prevention of hereditary diseases and the alteration of inherited characteristics. Prenatal screening through amniocentesis or chorionic villus sampling to determine whether certain individuals are carriers of defective genes makes possible informed choices about child-bearing and alleviates the anxiety of noncarriers of diseases such as sickle-cell anemia and Tay-Sachs disease. Ethical issues and public policy dilemmas in this area involve the right to experiment, accessibility to organ and fetal transplants, and the imposition of controls in genetic testing. —*Marcia J. Weiss*

**See also** Eugenics; Euthanasia; Physician-patient relationship; Population control.

**BIBLIOGRAPHY**

Beauchamp, Tom L., and James F. Childress. *Principles of Biomedical Ethics.* 3d ed. New York: Oxford University Press, 1989. An important textbook and central resource in the study of bioethical theory.

Engelhardt, H. Tristram, Jr. *The Foundations of Bioethics.* New York: Oxford University Press, 1986. A critique of theoretical bioethics and a cogent issue-oriented explanation of the role of theories and values in the concepts of health and disease.

Gore, Albert. *Earth in the Balance: Ecology and the Human Spirit.* Boston: Houghton Mifflin, 1992. The vice president of the United States discusses the environmental crisis on a global scale and alleges that every aspect of society, including political leaders, is involved in its consequences.

Kass, Leon R. *Toward A More Natural Science: Biology and Human Affairs.* New York: Free Press, 1985. An issue-oriented discussion of the relationship between science and ethics in the light of new technologies and traditional democratic values.

Kogan, Barry S., ed. *A Time to Be Born and a Time to Die: The Ethics of Choice.* Hawthorne, New York: Aldine De Gruyter, 1991. Proceedings of a thought-provoking conference dealing with the impact of current medical and technological advances on the ethics of controversies concerned with the beginning and the end of life from philosophical, religious, medical, and legal perspectives.

Olson, Steve. *Biotechnology: An Industry Comes of Age.* Washington, D.C.: National Academy Press, 1986. A basic book on the advances in biotechnology and their implications.

Prentis, Steve. *Biotechnology: A New Industrial Revolution.* New York: George Braziller, 1984. A detailed book with diagrams and illustrations explaining basic concepts in biotechnology and their uses in medicine, agriculture, and industry.

Scheffer, Victor B. *The Shaping of Environmentalism in America.* Seattle: University of Washington Press, 1991. Explores the roots of environmentalism and examines progress in education, law, and politics in dealing with areas of concern.

## Biofeedback

**TYPE OF ETHICS:** Bioethics

**DATE:** Established early 1960's

**DEFINITION:** The discipline that teaches people to regulate physical functions of the body that are under involuntary control or are no longer under voluntary control

**SIGNIFICANCE:** Provides an alternative to painful and more extreme treatments for health problems but poses questions of ethics in areas of human and other animal research

Biofeedback has been used to treat a variety of health problems and to help people perform well. Among the health problems treated with biofeedback are gastrointestinal cramping, fecal incontinence, frequency and severity of epileptic seizures, high blood pressure, migraine headaches, tics, insomnia, bronchial asthma, bruxism (clenching and grinding of the teeth), sexual dysfunction, masticatory pain and dysfunction (MPD), temporomandibular joint (TMJ) syndrome, and Raynaud's disease (a functional disorder of the cardiovascular system characterized by poor blood circulation to the hands, feet, and face). Biofeedback has also been used to treat patients whose muscles are no longer under voluntary control because of a stroke or an injury. Among the uses of biofeedback to improve performance are controlling test anxiety, improving athletic performance, controlling motion sickness in Air Force pilots, and reducing space adaptation syndrome (SAS) for astronauts. Biofeedback has also been used to help people quit smoking and to help people lose weight.

Biofeedback teaches people to regulate physical functions of the body. It provides continuous information about physiological responses so that individuals can learn to regulate these responses. Three types of biofeedback are integrated electromyographic feedback (EMG), electrodermal response (EDR), and electroencephalographic response (EEG). EMG, in which muscular activity is recorded, is used for treatment of muscles and migraine headache. EDR, which records perspiration responses on the palms, is more often used for weight control, managing stress, or improved athletic performance. EEG biofeedback helps individuals gain voluntary control of their alpha rhythms.

Biofeedback is based on operant, rather than classical, conditioning. (In operant conditioning, desired behavior is rewarded with a stimulus; in classical conditioning, a conditioned stimulus precedes an unconditioned stimulus—for example, Pavlov's class heard the sound of the bell and then were shown food—until the conditional stimulus alone can elicit the desired behavior.) During the process of biofeedback, machines record physiological functions, such as muscle movement, alpha waves, heart rate, blood pressure, or body temperature. The machines feed this information back to the patient in the form of numbers, gauges on a meter, lights, or sounds. Through this process, the patient learns to focus attention on controlling physical responses. The result, in part, is training of alpha waves that results in the calming effects of meditation.

In the United States, experiments with operant conditioning of heart rate began in 1962. The first biofeedback studies of controlling blood pressure in humans were reported at Harvard in 1969. Such studies mark the early stages of biofeedback. Even though biofeedback, by historical standards, was first explored in the United States quite recently, Asian spiritual practitioners have, for centuries, been practicing conscious control of involuntary functions though meditation. Today, in clinics throughout the United States, biofeedback techniques are being taught to patients in as few as five to ten sessions.

According to Dr. Lilian Rosenbaum, in her 1989 book *Biofeedback Frontiers,* biofeedback research has moved into applications for diabetes, cancer, AIDS, physical rehabilitation, education, vision disorders, improving performance in space, and developing superior athletes. Biofeedback is also being used to treat social disorders in criminals who voluntarily participate in the experiments. As researchers move into new areas, the machines that record the individuals' responses become more sophisticated. Among the most sophisticated of these machines is the computerized automated psychophysiological scan (Capscan), developed by Charles Stroebel and his colleagues. The Capscan "combines advances in computers, computerized electroencephalography (brain-wave measurements) and biofeedback, according to Rosenbaum.

Concerning the ethics of biofeedback, it is relevant that much of the current information on biofeedback comes from those who practice biofeedback and believe in its effectiveness. Several researchers, however, are exploring the ethical concerns in biofeedback research. Much of their concern focuses on the need for human subjects, since human consciousness is involved in the control of muscle responses that are usually regarded as involuntary. Testing the validity of biofeedback involves, in part, establishing control groups so that researchers can determine whether biofeedback or a placebo effect of psychotherapy is responsible for the results. Researcher Martin T. Orne observes that not only drugs but also treatment procedures themselves have "placebo components" that have "powerful effects on their own."

In summarizing the effects of biofeedback, Orne concludes that the effects of biofeedback are similar to the effects of relaxation therapy, self-hypnosis, or meditation. Nevertheless, he concludes, each of these techniques shows "considerable therapeutic effect" for various individuals, and such approaches "have been overlooked for many years, at least in this country."

Another ethical issue in biofeedback research involves the use of animal subjects. Research in biofeedback has often involved animal experimentation, especially with curarized animals—that is, animals in a state of drug-induced immobility. Some of the first studies with curarized animals involved rats that responded to stimulation of the pleasure center in the brain to slow down or speed up involuntary body functions. When the pleasure centers in the brain were stimulated, some of the rats responded by slowing down involuntary responses so much that death resulted. Other animal studies involved learning visceral and glandular (autonomic) responses. Additional animal studies have involved mice, golden hamsters, and baboons in Kenya.

Modern researchers have posed a number of complex ethical questions related to research in biofeedback, particularly questions involving the "justification for withholding therapy for research purposes." John P. Hatch, in his discussion of ethics, lists a number of concrete ethical questions related to placebo therapy, fees for service, random selection of subjects, acceptable control treatment, and effects of biofeedback research on patients. He concludes that the "central ethical question is whether current knowledge allows a preferred treatment to be chosen, and whether the relative risk to a patient would be greater as a result of assigning treatments randomly versus basing treatment assignments on clinical judgment." —*Carol Franks*

**See also** American Medical Association (AMA); *Ethical Principles of Psychologists*; Holistic medicine; *Principles of Medical Ethics*.

**Bibliography**

Hatch, John P., Johnnie G. Fisher, and John D. Rugh, eds. *Biofeedback: Studies in Clinical Efficacy.* New York: Plenum Press, 1987.

Rosenbaum, Lilian. *Biofeedback Frontiers.* Vol. 15 in *Stress in Modern Society*. New York: AMS Press, 1989.

Schwartz, Mark Stephen, and associates. *Biofeedback: A Practitioner's Guide.* New York: Guilford Press, 1987.

Van Hoose, William H., and Jeffrey A. Kottler. *Ethical and Legal Issues in Counseling and Psychotherapy.* 2d ed. San Francisco: Jossey-Bass, 1985.

White, Leonard, and Bernard Tursky, eds. *Clinical Biofeedback: Efficacy and Mechanisms.* New York: Guilford Press, 1982.

## Biological warfare

**Type of ethics:** Military ethics

**Definition:** The introduction of disease into the military and/or civilian populations of one's enemies

**Significance:** The use of biological agents in warfare is generally regarded by international agreement, most particularly the Geneva Convention of 1925, as inhumane and a violation of human rights

The introduction of disease among the soldiers or general populations of one's foes is the focus of biological warfare. While extreme mortality is not vital—although the victims must be too sick to resist—high morbidity and rapid onset are. It is also important that the attacker be able to protect its own forces and civilian population from infection. The use of biological weapons, which cannot be controlled or focused on definably military targets, has long been regarded as particularly heinous and, unlike the use of nuclear devices, is outlawed by international agreements. Despite such agreements, biological warfare has been used deliberately, and on some occasions the outcome of military operations has been influenced as a result of diseases unintentionally introduced by one of the combatants. Although it may be argued that in moral terms the latter case is not actually warfare, the results are the same as would be desired in the case of the deliberate introduction of the disease. Since biological warfare has never been used on a large scale, studying such incidents provides the only picture of what such warfare would be like.

**History.** Although the effects were problematical, efforts at using biological warfare go back almost as far as the building of walled cities. There are records of besiegers up through the Middle Ages using catapults to throw the bodies of soldiers dead from various epidemic diseases into the cities and fortifications they were attacking. Since diseases such as typhus and plague often followed armies on the march and sanitation was in the best of times minimal, there is little hope of determining how often if ever efforts produced disease that would not have otherwise occurred among defenders.

There are, however, some examples of disease being a decisive factor in war. One such instance is the destruction of Charles VIII of France's failed invasion of Italy in the very late fifteenth century. More dramatic was the introduction of smallpox by the Spanish conquistadors in Mexico and Peru. The defense of the numerically greatly superior Aztecs and Incas was devastated, allowing the small number of Spaniards and some Indian allies to conquer. The impact was so great that the Amerindians proved to be much easier prey for missionaries than had other peoples subjected to imperial conquest. As Spaniard and Aztec agreed, the European God had proved to be superior in protecting his followers, while the Amerindian deities had failed.

The deliberate use of biological warfare has been rare. During the nineteenth century, there were occasions when the British army left items contaminated with smallpox to be taken by Africans who were resisting imperial expansion. The U.S. Army did the same thing during the Indian wars in the American West. Before the twentieth century, however, the technology for using biological weapons was limited, and the means for making, transporting, and storing them were even more so.

**The Modern Situation.** The development of modern biological science has made the potential for employing biological warfare much more serious. The major powers, including the United States, the former Soviet Union, the United Kingdom, Canada, and many others, have experimented with various biological agents. These include such bacterial diseases as pneumonic plague, anthrax, tularemia, and cholera, and viral plagues such as smallpox, yellow fever, and psittacosis. Other possible agents are the rickettsial diseases Q-fever and typhus and botulin toxin. The continuing development of genetic engineering makes the possibility of new and more deadly germs and toxins increasingly dangerous.

Biological weapons apparently have not been used in any major conflict, despite preparations for their use. During World War II, the Allies were prepared to use anthrax against their enemies. The Nazis were equally prepared to use tabun, the first nerve gas, and were manufacturing sarin, a more potent nerve agent. It was a situation, perhaps the only one, in which deterrence worked in an actual wartime situation. Each side refused to risk retaliation with chemical and/or biological war, though Hitler did send nerve gas to field commanders with orders that it be used at the very end of the war. It is unlikely that even had subordinates not prevented the use of gas, the Allies would have responded in kind (they had nothing comparable to nerve gas) or with their anthrax bombs.

During the peace negotiations that eventually ended the Korean War, North Korea charged the United States with attempting to spread disease among its people. A United Nations investigation produced ambiguous results. Washington, although it did eventually admit to having the capacity for biological war, insisted that no such technology was ever sent outside its own national borders.

**Implications for Ethical Conduct.** Despite international prohibitions that were supported by most United Nations members in 1966 and denials by most large states, research into biological weapons has continued. This has produced many ethical dilemmas. For soldiers, the principles that unnecessary suffering should be avoided and that noncombatants should not be attacked have long been respected. Both of these principles are jeopardized by biological warfare. Doctors drawn into the research to produce either the weapons or vaccines to protect their own people violate the Hippocratic oath that defines their professional ethics. Since biological agents are comparatively cheap and very difficult to detect, they are particularly tempting to small states. Politicians face the question of releasing plagues that may not be subject to control and are certainly indiscriminate in their effects. Although the use of such weapons is clearly a violation of human rights, the temptation for the leaders of a small state to balance the power of larger foes with such tools may be irresistible. While the dilemmas are clear, the research continues, leaving the ultimate answers in doubt.

—*Fred R. van Hartesveldt*

**See also** Deterrence; Limited war; Medical research.

**BIBLIOGRAPHY**

Cookson, John, and Judith Nottingham. *A Survey of Chemical and Biological Warfare.* New York: Monthly Review Press, 1969.

Harris, Robert, and Jeremy Paxman. *A Higher Form of Killing: The Secret Story of Chemical and Biological Warfare.* New York: Hill & Wang, 1982.

Hersh, Seymour M. *Chemical and Biological Warfare: America's Hidden Arsenal.* Indianapolis: Bobbs-Merrill, 1968.

McCarthy, Richard D. *The Ultimate Folly: War by Pestilence, Asphyxiation, and Defoliation.* New York: Knopf, 1969.

Rose, Steven, ed. *CBW: Chemical and Biological Warfare.* Boston: Beacon Press, 1969.

## Birth control

**TYPE OF ETHICS:** Bioethics

**DATE:** Nineteenth century B.C.E. to present

**DEFINITION:** The methodology of ethical population control by physical, surgical, and chemical methods, excluding abortion

**SIGNIFICANCE:** Seeks appropriate and ethical methods to control population growth by preventing conception rather than using infanticide and methods that kill the already conceived fetus

The question of birth control has faced humanity throughout history. In the modern world, overpopulation and Malthusian doctrine loom ever larger, making birth control a must. Consequently, equitable and ethical solutions to the problem are essential. Contemporary birth control consists of and combines physical methods, chemical methods, and surgical intervention that must be applied with good ethical judgment to provide results that prevent both overpopulation and the exploitation of individual population sectors.

**Methodology.** Among methods of birth control are coitus interruptus; the rhythm method; pessary condoms, diaphragms, and intrauterine devices (IUDs); chemical intervention via birth control pills; and surgical vasectomy or tubal ligation. Least satisfactory are coitus interruptus and rhythm methods, which involve male withdrawal prior to climax and intercourse during safe portions of the menstrual cycle. The difficulties here are adequate self-control and variation of the fertile period of the cycle. The problems associated with pessary condom, diaphragm, and IUD use are mechanical faults and incomplete understanding of the proper usage of these devices. Birth control pills have the disadvantages of causing health problems in some users and of often being used incorrectly. Surgical interventions via tubal ligation and vasectomy are usually irreversible, which often makes them psychologically inappropriate.

**History.** Birth control methods arose in the nineteenth century B.C.E. At that time, a wide range of methods—including incantations, crude chemical preparations (for example, animal dung, plant products, and crude spermicide salves), and pessaries—were used with questionable results. Such methodologies flourished until the Hippocratic school of medicine realized that there were fertile and safe times during menstruation that could be utilized for birth control.

During the following historical period, however, contraception was frowned upon by many people. Relatively flexible, Judaic theological doctrine proposed that "no man or woman among you shall be childless" but allowed birth control. In the Greek and Roman milieus, birth control was practiced but was controversial because high population went hand in hand with political security. A very powerful ethical judgement against its use was made by the Greek Stoics, who believed that intercourse was intended solely for the purpose of procreation and that all forms of birth control were wrong.

With the rise of Christianity, birth control practices were denounced as sinful, and practitioners of birth control were classed with murderers. The view of Christian ethics was that even coitus interruptus was wrong and that marital intercourse had to be procreative. In time, Christianity was to become the strongest ethical movement against birth control. In contrast, Islamic culture did not actively condemn birth control. In fact, the eleventh century Arab physician Avicenna described many ways to prevent pregnancy in an encyclopediac medical work.

The dichotomy of attitudes toward birth control continued until the end of the eighteenth century, despite the development of Protestantism and the doctrine of rationalism. Religious movements condemned birth control thunderously from the pulpit as opposed to Christian ethical principles, and the rationalists did not advocate it as rational behavior. One useful development during this period was the invention of the condom.

The beginning of the advocacy of birth control can be traced to development of Malthusian doctrine by Thomas Malthus, who proposed that famine and war would come to the world unless population growth was curbed. Malthus favored postponement of marriage, not birth control via contraceptives. Others advocated the use of birth control methods, however, despite unrelenting opposition from Christian churches and most governments. For example, America's 1873 Comstock law made the importation of contraceptives illegal, and many state governments forbade their sale.

The climate had begun to change, however, and by the 1920's many favored birth control. Particularly important was the American nurse Margaret Sanger, one of the strongest advocates of birth control. Furthermore, scientific and medical endeavors caused changes of opinion in the intellectual and biomedical community. This development was aided by the invention of diaphragms and birth control pills. Furthermore, the realization of pending overpopulation and possible apocalypse quickly led to the widely held view that it was unethical to oppose birth control measures.

By the 1970's, American laws fostered the development of family planning research and the Population Council had brought the technology of birth control to the world. Europe concurred, and while the responses of various countries in the less-developed areas of the world varied, birth control was generally accepted. In addition, the world's major religions began to endorse birth control practices to various extents. In response to the change of the ethical climate, techniques of voluntary sterilization by vasectomy and tubal ligation developed further, new contraceptive preparations were discovered, and state-endorsed birth control programs developed in many countries. In the 1980's and 1990's further progress along these lines occurred.

**Conclusions.** The ethical issue that has long caused disharmony concerning birth control is whether it is ever appropriate to prevent the occurrence of a human life. In part, the idea that it is never appropriate to do so was based on the fact that in an underpopulated world, the more humans in a society or religion, the safer that sociopolitical entity would be. It is perhaps germane to the ethical shift that now condones or fosters birth control that world population enhancement once protected. Therefore, the changed ethical paradigm now supports birth control procedures. Other negative ethical issues, however, remain. These issues include the ethical choice of individuals who will practice birth control, especially in instances in which a nation implements policies that lead to inequities (for example, limitation of birth control to the less-advantaged classes). In addition, there is the question of the ethics of irreversible birth control and informed consent, the understanding of which governs individual freedom when a choice of sterilization is made under duress and may be regretted later. Finally, there is the ethical question of whether birth control will diminish family ties, causing future societal and individual problems. Surely, answers to these ethical problems will come and new problems will arise when the paradigm changes again. —*Sanford S. Singer*

**See also** Bioethics; Christian ethics; Family; Islamic ethics; Jewish ethics; Pro-choice movement; Pro-life movement.

**Bibliography**


Baulieu, Etienne-Emile, and Mort Rosemblum. *The Abortion Pill.* New York. Simon & Schuster, 1991.

Lammers, Stephen E., and Allen Verhey, eds. *On Moral Medicine.* Grand Rapids, Mich.: W. B. Eerdmans, 1987.

Silber, Sherman J. *How Not to Get Pregnant.* New York: Charles Scribner's Sons, 1987.

Veatch, Robert M. *The Patient as Partner.* Bloomington: Indiana University Press, 1987.

__________. *A Theory of Medical Ethics.* New York: Basic Books, 1981.


## Birth defects

**Type of ethics:** Bioethics

**Date:** From antiquity

**Definition:** Malformation of body structures present at birth

**Significance:** Birth defects raise serious questions of prevention, responsibility, and treatment for the medical community and society as a whole

Birth defects are the primary cause of death of children under one year of age. Estimates of occurrence vary depending on what is classed as a defect, ranging from 2 percent to 15 percent of live births. Many defects result in spontaneous abortion or stillbirth and therefore are not included in these statistics.

**Causes.** In most cases, the cause of malformation is unknown. Since the 1960's, however, enormous advances have been made in the determination of factors that affect fetal growth. Of those cases in which etiology has been discovered, the anomalies are the results of genetic causes, environmental causes, or a combination of the two.

Genetic causes include mutation and abnormality of chromosomal material as well as inherited traits. Environmental factors range from maternal nutrition or disease to exposure of the fetus to toxic substances. These factors include certain drugs, such as alcohol; chemicals, such as mercury and lead; radiation, such as radon and X rays; maternal illness, such as diabetes or rubella (German measles); intrauterine infection, such as cytomegalovirus; and parasites, as in toxoplasmosis. Some of these environmental factors act by causing genetic anomalies, resulting in multifactorial defects. Also included as birth defects are birth injuries and low birth weight.

**BIRTH DEFECTS — HUMAN-MADE CAUSES**

| Year Recognized | Defect or defects | Cause |
|---|---|---|
| 1952 | Growth retardation, distinctive facial defects, shortened limbs, mental retardation | Aminopterin |
| 1957 | Intrauterine growth retardation, low birth weight | Cigarette smoking |
| 1961 | Severe physical malformations, especially of limbs | Thalidomide |
| 1963 | Mental retardation, microcephaly | Exposure to radiation, including X rays |
| 1968 | Mental retardation, fine motor dysfunction, irritability/hyperactivity (Fetal Alcohol Syndrome) | Ethanol |
| 1968 | Heart defects, microcephaly, growth and mental retardation, chromosomal abnormalities | Anticonvulsants |
| 1968 | Growth retardation, microcephaly, deafness, blindness | Mercury |
| 1970 | Malformations, growth and mental retardation | Lead |
| 1973 | Addicted babies, growth impairment, respiratory disorders | Heroin |
| 1977 | Uterine lesions, increased susceptibility to immune disorders | Female sex hormones, esp. diethylstilbestrol |
| 1982 | Various malformations, especially of the face, heart, central nervous system, and lungs | Retinoic acid (Accutane) |
| 1987 | Growth retardation, defects of heart, skull, and central nervous system | Cocaine |

**Ethical Problems.** The ethical issues involved in birth defects can be divided into three major areas: prevention, treatment, and responsibility.

**Ethics of Prevention.** In those cases in which the cause is known, there is a societal obligation to minimize the possibility of the occurrence of a particular defect. The question is, however: How far does this obligation extend? Does it supersede the rights of the mother, a competent autonomous adult? Consider this example: Hydantoin and phenobarbital are drugs commonly used to treat epileptic seizures. Hydantoin has been shown to cause mental deficiencies and abnormal body structures. Phenobarbital causes defects in laboratory animals, but it is not clear whether it does so in humans, although some studies have found a correlation. Ninety percent of women with epilepsy have as many or more seizures during pregnancy as they did before they became pregnant. Is it ethical to treat the mother with anticonvulsants that may endanger the fetus? Is it ethical to set the possibility of fetal problems above the actuality of maternal illness and not treat the disease?

Certain birth defects, such as Tay-Sachs disease and sickle-cell anemia, follow the strict laws of genetic inheritance. Genetic testing and counseling is generally available now for potential parents who carry the genes for these traits. These parents must make the decision to risk having an affected child or to not have children. What is an acceptable risk in these cases? Is it ethical to ask a couple not to have children when this violates their religious beliefs or personal aspirations?

Many abnormalities, including spina bifida and Down syndrome, can be detected as early as the fourth month of pregnancy. In these cases, the parents must decide whether to continue the pregnancy or to abort the fetus. If they choose to carry the fetus to term, who is financially responsible for treatment, the cost of which can go far beyond most individuals' abilities to pay?

**Ethics of Responsibility.** Abnormalities caused by environmental factors raise the question of societal and maternal responsibility. One of the earliest recognized causes of birth defects was exposure to lead. Does society have an obligation to eradicate the presence of lead where any pregnant woman could be exposed to it? Is it possible, physically and economically, to completely eliminate exposure to teratogenic agents (agents that cause birth defects)? Does this elimination of possible teratogenic exposure extend to the prohibition of pregnant women from jobs that might endanger the fetus? If so, is this ethical if a consequence is unemployment resulting in the woman being unable to obtain adequate prenatal care and nutrition? Should the prohibition extend to all women of child-bearing age?

Maternal drug use is becoming more of a problem all the time. Fetal alcohol syndrome, low birth weight caused by cigarette smoking, and cocaine- and heroin-addicted babies are all common problems. What legal responsibilities does the mother have during pregnancy? What responsibilities does society have to the children of these mothers? Should custody be rescinded at birth? Should these women be detained during pregnancy and be forced to conform to certain specifications of acceptable maternal behavior? Should they be prosecuted for child abuse?

**Ethics of Treatment.** When a baby is born with severe defects, issues arise regarding whether to treat the defect or to allow the child to die. Considerations include the quality and length of life the child will have if allowed to live, and the ability and desire of the parents to care for the defective child. If nontreatment is chosen, the question of active euthanasia (infanticide, or withdrawal of all life support including feeding) versus passive euthanasia (nontreatment but continuation of feeding) arises. Furthermore, who makes these decisions is a question which is becoming more prominent. Should the parents have the final word? Should the physician, who has more medical knowledge? Should a "disinterested party," such as a hospital ethics committee, make such a decision?

The ethical dilemmas regarding birth defects are endless. As medicine advances in its ability to diagnose and treat these problems, more issues will arise. One of the few things upon which most people agree is that prevention is preferable to treatment, whenever possible.

*—Margaret Hawthorne*

**See also** Euthanasia; Genetic counseling; Genetic engineering; Life and death.

**BIBLIOGRAPHY**

Arras, John D., and Nancy K. Rhoden. *Ethical Issues in Modern Medicine.* 3d ed. Mountain View, Calif.: Mayfield, 1989.

Capron, Alexander Morgan. "Fetal Alcohol and Felony." *Hastings Center Report* 22 (May/June, 1992): 28-29.

Persaud, T. V. N. *Environmental Causes of Human Birth Defects.* Springfield, Ill.: Charles C Thomas, 1990.

Schardein, James L. *Chemically Induced Birth Defects.* New York: Marcel Dekker, 1985.

Smith, David W. *Smith's Recognizable Patterns of Human Malformation.* Edited by Kenneth L. Jones. 4th ed. Philadelphia: W. B. Saunders, 1988.

## Bodhidharma

(c. 480, Conjeeveram, near Madras, India—520, place of death unknown): Buddhist monk

**TYPE OF ETHICS:** Religious ethics

**ACHIEVEMENTS:** Legendary founder of Chinese Ch'an (Japanese, Zen) Buddhism

**SIGNIFICANCE:** Taught that ethical living depends upon understanding and believing that there is no individual self

The legendary founder of the Ch'an (or Zen) School of Buddhism in China, Bodhidharma brought Indian meditation practices to China. His life and teachings have been reworked and expanded by later Buddhists that certainty about either is impossible. A saying attributed to him, though almost certainly from a latter period, may nevertheless capture one aspect of Bodhidharma's thinking:

> A special tradition outside the scriptures;
> No dependence upon words and letters;
> Direct pointing at the soul of man;
> Seeing into one's own nature, and the attainment of Buddhahood.

This passage links Bodhidharma to the Zen Buddhist practice of meditation leading to enlightenment. He seems also to have treasured particular sutras, or scriptures, that emphasized the unity of all things. Furthermore, ethical thinking that probably goes back to him is found in a text called *Two Entrances and Four Acts.* In "Entrance by Conduct" into the path of enlightenment, he emphasized (1) that karma (consequences adhering to deeds) causes adversity, (2) that pain and pleasure are the result of previous actions, (3) that escape from karma is possible by avoiding attachment to anything, and (4) that the Mind of enlightenment is above such attachments.

**See also** Dōgen; Hui-neng; Zen.

## Bodhisattva ideal

**TYPE OF ETHICS:** Religious ethics

**DATE:** c. sixth century B.C.E.

**ASSOCIATED WITH:** Mahāyāna Buddhism

**DEFINITION:** The Sanskrit word *bodhisattva* means "enlightenment being"; a bodhisattva is one who has postponed personal enlightenment in favor of remaining in the world of suffering to work for the enlightenment of all beings

**SIGNIFICANCE:** The primacy of the bodhisattva ideal in Mahāyāna Buddhism serves to refute the commonly held misconception that Buddhism is a religion of withdrawal from the everyday world; there is no higher ideal in Buddhism than that of working for the enlightenment of all sentient beings

The bodhisattva ideal is the highest ideal to which a Buddhist practitioner can aspire, the ultimate expression of the ethical tradition of Buddhism. The historical Buddha, Śākyamuni, the founder of Buddhism, is the ultimate bodhisattva. After he realized his own enlightenment, he could have enjoyed the great bliss of the enlightened state and had nothing further to do with his fellow beings. Instead, however, he chose to remain in the world to teach what he had learned. He made the choice to teach others the tenets of the religion that came to be called Buddhism out of a tremendous sense of compassion for all beings, whose existence is characterized by suffering of various kinds.

When Buddhists say that all life involves suffering, they do not mean that there is no pleasure to be experienced in ordinary existence. It is emphasized, however, that all pleasure is fleeting. No joy or sorrow lasts forever. All happiness must end, and therefore it is a mistake to make the search for happiness one's primary goal in life. All that is born must die, and everything that comes together must sooner or later come apart. It is possible, however, to live in such a way that one sees and understands the processes that operate in life. When one lives in this way, one gives up the vain search for worldly happiness and begins to see more clearly the way things really are.

All major schools of Buddhism recognize the importance of the bodhisattva ideal, which involves the commitment to work to bring all sentient beings to enlightenment, thereby ending the suffering that they experience in the fruitless search for happiness. In the Theravāda tradition, a tradition that is much like the Buddhism of the earliest followers of the Buddha, it is believed that to aspire to be a bodhisattva is beyond the capabilities of men and women. It is thought that the Buddha is the only bodhisattva, and that only by first aspiring to less lofty goals can Buddhist practitioners proceed on the Buddhist path toward ultimate enlightenment. Theravādins typically work toward the goal of individual liberation, of becoming *arhats*, who have conquered ignorance and desire and see reality as it truly is. In the Mahāyāna Buddhist tradition, however, it is believed that to aspire to become an *arhat* is inherently selfish, not realistic, and ultimately harmful to the practitioner who has such an aspiration. Mahāyāna means "great vehicle," and Mahāyānists use the term to differentiate themselves from the Theravādins, whom they call practitioners of the Hīnayāna, or "lesser vehicle." It should be clearly understood, however, that this simple differentiation is ultimately unfair to the Theravāda tradition. The Mahāyāna approach was developed at least partly in response to the selfish approaches and practices of early Buddhist splinter groups whose members did not practice Buddhism in a way that sincere Theravādins would recognize as true Buddhist practice.

There are three main stages of the path of the bodhisattva. The first is *anuttara-pūjā*, or supreme worship, which consists of various devotional practices that are intended to break down the practitioner's sense of self (Buddhism holds that no self truly exists) and prepare him or her for the later stages of the path. Supreme worship involves, among other things, obeisance before the image of the Buddha; the taking of refuge (the placing of one's faith) in the Buddha, the dharma (the teachings of Buddhism), and the *sangha* (the community of Buddhist practitioners); the confession of one's sins; and the act of rejoicing because of the spiritual attainments of others.

The second stage of the bodhisattva path is *bodhicitta-utpāda*, the generation of the thought of enlightenment. It is during this stage that the practitioner truly becomes a bodhisattva, vowing to save all sentient beings. This stage does not entail a simple wish to become enlightened, but represents the point at which the desire to realize enlightenment becomes so powerful that the practitioner is, psychologically, completely altered by it. The generation of bodhicitta necessarily involves an awareness of the suffering of all beings. Indeed, the bodhisattva feels that when any being suffers, he or she suffers as well. At this point, the bodhisattva has given up the illusion of self, the illusion that there is any such thing as an individual being. Although beings do not exist in any ultimate sense, however, beings do experience suffering, and it is the bodhisattva's aspiration to alleviate that suffering.

The third stage of the bodhiṣattva path involves the practice of the four *caryās*, or modes of conduct. These four are *bodhipakṣya-caryā*, or the practice of the constituents of enlightenment; *abhijñā-caryā*, the practice of the knowledges; *pāramitā-caryā*, the practice of the perfections; and *sattva-paripāka-carya*ā, the practice of teaching sentient beings. Of these four modes of conduct, the practice of the perfections is the most important.

In large part, the practice of the bodhisattva is the practice of the six *pāramitās,* or perfections

The first perfection is *dāna*, or giving. Giving does not simply mean giving alms to the needy or clothing to the unclothed, although such actions are certainly aspects of the first perfection. It can also mean sheltering a person from fear, thereby giving that person a sense of security. It can also mean helping a person to develop spiritual awareness.

The second perfection is that of *śila*, or morality. In essence, Buddhist morality involves refraining from doing harm to oneself or others. It also includes promoting goodness and being helpful to others.

The third perfection is *kṣānti*, or patience, which entails keeping one's mental balance in the face of difficulties, tolerating the way things are. It also involves having confidence in the Buddhist path.

The fourth perfection is *vīrya*, or effort, which means continuing one's spiritual practice without losing enthusiasm.

The fifth perfection is *dhyāna*, or meditation, the practice of which enables one to see more clearly and to gain spiritual stability, without which one's practice will degenerate.

| The Six Pāramitās (Perfections) | | |
|---|---|---|
| **English** | **Sanskrit** | **Description** |
| 1. Giving | Dāna | Physical and spiritual generosity |
| 2. Morality | Śila | Refraining from doing harm to oneself or others |
| 3. Patience | Ksānti | Accepting things as they are and having confidence in Buddhism |
| 4. Effort | Vīrya | Continuing one's spiritual practice without losing enthusiasm |
| 5. Meditation | Dhyāna | Seeing clearly and maintaining spiritual stability |
| 6. Understanding | Prajñā | Directly perceiving the truth of emptiness |

The sixth perfection is *prajñā,* or understanding. In addition to ordinary understanding, the sixth perfection entails the direct perception of the truth of emptiness, the truth that nothing exists in an ultimate sense.

By practicing the six perfections and the other practices that are part of the bodhisattva's path, the Buddhist practitioner who has raised the thought of enlightenment and taken the vow to work for the enlightenment of all beings travels through ten *bhumis,* or levels, of development, ultimately realizing buddhahood, which is complete enlightenment. —Shawn Woodyard

**See also** Buddha; Buddhist ethics; Five precepts; Four noble truths; Mādhyamaka; Nirvana.

**Bibliography**

Dharmasiri, Gunapala. "The Bodhisattva Ideal." In Fundamentals of Buddhist Ethics. Antioch, Calif.: Golden Leaves, 1989.

Gyatso, Geshe Kelsang. *Meaningful to Behold: A Commentary Guide to Shantideva's "Guide to the Bodhisattva's Way of Life."* London: Tharpa, 1989.

Sangharakshita. "The Bodhisattva Ideal." In *A Survey of Buddhism: Its Doctrines and Methods Through the Ages.* 6th rev. ed. London: Tharpa, 1987.

Shantideva. *A Guide to the Bodhisattva's Way of Life.* Dharamsala, India: Library of Tibetan Works and Archives, 1979.

Snelling, John. *The Buddhist Handbook: A Complete Guide to Buddhist Schools, Teaching, Practice, and History.* Rochester, Vt.: Inner Traditions, 1991.

## Boethius, Anicius Manlius Severinus (c. 480, Rome, Italy—524, Pavia, Italy): Philosopher

**Type of ethics:** Classical history

**Achievements:** Author of *De consolatione philosophiae* (*The Consolation of Philosophy*)

**Significance:** Boethius combined classical philosophical traditions with Christian morality and theology

A member of the Roman upper classes and a seminal Christian philosopher, Boethius served as a transition between the pagan classical world and the Christian one. An educated man, Boethius was among the first Western Christian writers to be well acquainted with classical Greek philosophical and ethical thought, including Aristotle's *Nicomachean Ethics.* He was also heavily influenced by Platonic thought and by the ethical views of the Stoics. Boethius combined these views with Christian morality to create a practical guide for living the moral life. Knowledge, according to Boethius, is based upon self-evident axioms revealed by God; building upon these axioms, humans can discover additional truths that bring them, ultimately, to the greatest good of all, which is God.

**See also** Aristotelian ethics; Aristotle; Christian ethics; *Nicomachean Ethics.*

## Bonhoeffer, Dietrich (Feb. 4, 1906, Breslau, Germany—Apr. 9, 1945, Flossenburg concentration camp, Germany): Theologian

**Type of ethics:** Religious ethics

**Achievements:** Author of *Nachfolge* (1937; *The Cost of Discipleship*, 1948); *Ethik* (1949; *Ethics*, 1955); and *Widerstand und Ergebung* (1951; *Letters and Papers from Prison*, 1958)

**Significance:** Bonhoeffer believed that ethical conduct is to be judged neither by absolute principles nor by the demands of changing conditions and situations, but rather by their consequences for the future

Bonhoeffer's ethical thought was forged in the furnace of Nazi Germany. As one of the founders of the Confessing Church, which refused to submit to Nazi ideology, and a member of the resistance movement inside Germany, Bonhoeffer was compelled by the conviction that Christian ethics consist not in trying to do good but in assuming responsibility for the future. His ethical theology is, therefore, "teleological" or "consequentialist." The focus is not upon motives (for example, adhering to some set of moral rules labeled "Christian") but upon living in light of the reality that in Jesus Christ God has reconciled the world to Himself. By rooting ethics in the person of Jesus Christ, the Christian is freed from the need to conform to the world's standards and is thus free to conform to Jesus Christ as Jesus Christ takes form in him or her. The individual, like the church, is then free to participate in the suffering of Christ in the life of the world.

In focusing on the resurrected Jesus Christ as the ultimate reality, Bonhoeffer is able to avoid legalism and moralism. If there is a moral or ethical code, a pattern of behavior, that can be labeled "Christian," then living a Christian life can be separated from Jesus Christ. It then becomes only a lifestyle, a universal moralism, which can be followed by anyone who is attracted to it, whether or not that person is conforming to Jesus Christ.

Bonhoeffer also avoids the dangers inherent in the traditional Lutheran doctrine of the two realms (or spheres). As originally formulated by the sixteenth century reformer Martin Luther, the doctrine states that God rules in both realms, the holy (the church) and the profane (the state). What was meant by Luther to be a duality (God ruling in both realms) became instead a dualism or dichotomy in which the state became autonomous. What is in fact one reality, "the reality of God, which has become manifest in Christ in the reality of the world," was split into two realities.

Once split off from the world, the Church becomes merely a "religious society" having only spiritual authority, while individual Christians pursue lives of personal piety. Bonhoeffer saw this development as a reversal of God's intent. Rightly understood, the church is the world redeemed by God through Jesus Christ. It exists to serve the world by witnessing to Jesus Christ. When the two spheres (church and state) become autonomous, as happened in Germany, the church abdicates its responsibility for the fallen world, while the state is free to become idolatrous.

Bonhoeffer saw a similar danger in the traditional Protestant orders of creation concept. In Protestant writings on ethics, the orders of creation serve a role similar to that of natural law in Roman Catholicism. Whatever the particular version of the concept, the orders always include church, state, and family. The danger latent in the orders concept became all too clear in its exploitation by the pro-Nazi "German Christian" movement. Referring to Romans 13:1, "the powers that be are ordained by God," the German Christians argued that Christians were obliged to support the Third Reich.

In their "Guiding Principles" of June 6, 1932, the German Christians declared that "race, folk, and nation" were "orders of existence granted and entrusted to us by God," which Christians were obligated by God's law to preserve. The danger in their argument, as Bonhoeffer saw it, was that almost any existing order could be defended by it, even a positively demonic one such as the Third Reich.

Bonhoeffer argued that the fallen nature of creation precludes the concept of orders from being used to discern the will of God for today. The central fact of the fall means that "each human order is an order of the fallen world, and not an order of creation." As an alternative to the orders of creation, Bonhoeffer developed his concept of the "divine mandates" in *Ethics,* which was written between 1940 and 1943. These divine mandates are social relationships, or structures, by means of which God brings order out of the chaos of the fallen world. The mandates include the church, family, labor, and government.

In the social relationships of the divine mandates, the individual Christian lives as a member of a community. There in the real world where God meets fallen humanity in the person of Jesus Christ, the individual is conformed to the image of Jesus Christ. By living responsibly as a Christian upon whose heart is written the law of God, the individual Christian becomes the means by which "the reality of Christ with us and in our world" is manifested. In focusing on the ultimate reality of Jesus Christ, the individual Christian finds both freedom and responsibility. He or she becomes free to live in obedience to God's commands, even though that may bring him or her into conflict with human laws. The individual must seek and do the will of God in the historic, space-time world, while living as a responsible member of the community though the divine mandates.

The Christian is free to live as a disciple of Christ in the world, but that discipleship can be costly. Sharing Christ's suffering for the lost always places the Christian on the side of justice. Like Jesus Christ, his Lord, the Christian becomes the advocate of the weak. By choice, he or she takes up the cross and follows Christ, even when, as in the case of Dietrich Bonhoeffer, it leads to a martyr's death in a concentration camp. —*Paul R. Waibel*

**See also** Christian ethics; Consequentialism; Deontological ethics; Natural law; Niebuhr, Reinhold; Religion; Situational ethics.

**Bibliography**

Bonhoeffer, Dietrich. *The Cost of Discipleship.* Translated by R. H. Fuller. New York: Macmillan, 1963.

___________. *Ethics.* Edited by Eberhard Bethge. Translated by Neville H. Smith. London: SCM Press, 1971.

___________. *Letters and Papers from Prison.* Edited by Eberhard Bethge. New York: Macmillan, 1972.

Burtness, James. *Shaping the Future: The Ethics of Dietrich Bonhoeffer. Philadelphia: Fortress Press, 1985.*

Hamilton, Kenneth. *Life in One's Stride: A Short Study in Dietrich Bonhoeffer.* Grand Rapids, Mich.: W. B. Eerdman's, 1968.

Huntemann, Georg. *The Other Bonhoeffer.* Grand Rapids, Mich.: Baker Book House, 1993.

Klassen, A. J., ed. *A Bonhoeffer Legacy: Essays in Understanding.* Grand Rapids, Mich.: W. B. Eerdman's, 1981.

## Book banning

**Type of ethics:** Arts and censorship

**Date:** From antiquity

**Definition:** The suppression of literary works deemed to be socially unacceptable for a variety of reasons (obscenity, religion, self-censorship, racial or sexual subordination)

**Significance:** Seeks to establish the social, political, and aesthetic bases that justify suppression of literary materials by a social group or agency

Book banning is an ancient activity practiced throughout history and the world (although this review will focus on book banning in the United States). The first book banning occurred in Western civilization in 387 B.C.E., when Plato recommended that Homer be expurgated for immature readers. Four hundred years later, the Roman emperor Caligula tried to ban Homer's *Odyssey* because he feared that the book's strong theme of freedom and liberty would arouse the citizenry against his autocratic rule. In 1559, Pope Paul IV issued a list of prohibited books, the *Index librorum prohibitorum*.

In the United States, the First Amendment to the Constitution seems unequivocally and absolutely to guarantee freedom of speech, no matter how that speech is expressed, without interference by the government. The First Amendment states in part that "Congress shall make no law . . . abridging the freedom of speech." In fact, however, this freedom is by no means absolute or unfettered. Donna E. Demac (1990) correctly pointed out that the history of freedom of expression in America is a complex mixture of a commitment to personal rights and intolerance of ideas deemed subversive, dissident, or obscene.

Certain books, by the very nature of their subject matter or writing style, will offend the values and attitudes of certain individuals or groups. As Kenneth Donelsen has observed: "Any book or idea or teaching method is potentially censorable by someone, somewhere, sometime, for some reason." A book's ideas may be disliked, the book may be perceived to ridicule certain individuals or to ignore others; or the book may be judged to be dangerous or offensive. If these parties believe the book has transgressed the bounds of acceptability, they may take action to have the book banned.

Book banning is in fact a common and everyday occurrence in the United States. More than a thousand incidents are recorded each year, and no doubt many other incidents go unrecorded or unrecognized. As William Noble (1990) so aptly stated the situation:

> [Book banning] is a pervasive ethic. . . . Book banning incidents arise in all parts of the country and play themselves out in many forums—school board proceedings, public libraries, legislative hearings, ad hoc parental complaints, governmental committees, private groups assessments, open court and even commercial publishing decisions. Book banning is as much a part of our lives as the morning newspaper or . . . television; its cultural influence is strong enough to affect the way we think and the way we communicate (p. xiii).

**Categories of Book Banning.** The primary reasons behind book banning seem to fall into four categories, according to Noble: (1) The book is deemed to be obscene. (2) The book promotes secular humanism or is antireligion. (3) Self-censorship in the publishing business or government. (4) Subordination of individuals belonging to a particular racial or sexual group. Examples of each category are presented in the next section, followed by discussion of the ethical implications of book banning and censorship.

**Obscenity.** The first antiobscenity law passed in the United States was in 1712 by the colony of Massachusetts. The "composing, writing, printing, or publishing of any filthy, obscene, or profane song, pamphlet, libel or mock sermon" was prohibited. The first obscenity case in America occurred in 1821 in Massachusetts, when Peter Holmes was found guilty for publishing and circulating a "lewd and obscene" book, John Cleland's *Memoirs of a Woman of Pleasure*. The federal government effected its first antiobscenity statute in 1842, and in 1865 Congress passed a law prohibiting the sending of obscene materials by mail.

The modern era of book censorship and book banning commenced after the Civil War, a period of urban upheaval, rootlessness, loosening of moral controls, and widespread circulation of graphic erotica. The most notable milestones of this era were the passage of the Comstock Act by Congress in 1873 and the passage of antiobscenity legislation by most states by 1900. The Comstock Act prohibited using the mails to send any "obscene, lewd, or lascivious, indecent, filthy or vile book" through the mails and was responsible for the seizure and destruction of thousands of tons of books and court prosecutions.

The 1920's marked the end of an era for the book banners. The liberalizing influences of 1920's American culture resulted in a change in attitudes and values among the population and judiciary toward what had been formerly considered obscene. Three landmark court decisions occurred between 1933 and 1973. In 1933, James Joyce's *Ulysses* was declared to be a work of art that was not written for the purpose of exploiting obscenity. Also, in determining whether a book was obscene, the entire book now had to be considered, whereas previously obscenity charges could be based on a single page or paragraph. In 1957 in *Roth v. the United States*, the Supreme Court specifically defined what constituted obscenity: "Obscenity is utterly without redeeming social importance." This definition was further refined in 1973 when the Supreme Court established three criteria to be used to determine if material is obscene: (1) "[The] average person, applying contemporary community standards would find that the work, taken as a whole, appeals to the prurient interest; (2) whether the work depicts or describes, in a patently offensive way, sexual conduct specifically defined by the applicable state law; and (3) whether the work, taken as a whole, lacks serious literary, artistic, political or scientific value."

These rulings had the effect of making it much more difficult to prove a work was obscene. Old bans were overturned (*Lady Chatterley's Lover* in 1959, *Memoirs of a Woman of Pleasure* in 1966), and although attempts at censorship and book banning still occur with frequent regularity, the current era is characterized by greater tolerance and openness in artistic and personal expression. To an extent, this greater tolerance and openness fostered by the judicial process can be circumvented by the political process. For example, a bill that prohibited the use of federal money for any obscene work of art was passed by Congress and signed into law by President Ronald Reagan.

**Secular Humanism and Anti-Religionism.** Secular humanism has been characterized by an attorney as "a godless religion which rejects any notion of the supernatural or a divine purpose for the world" and which also "rejects any objective or absolute moral standards and embraces a subjective 'anything goes' approach to morals based on personal

| FAMOUS BOOK BANNINGS | | | |
|---|---|---|---|
| **Year Banned** | **Book/Author** | **Group/Person Responsible** | **Stated Reason** |
| 387 B.C.E. | *The Odyssey* (Homer) | Plato | Harmful to immature readers |
| 35 C.E. | *The Odyssey* (Homer) | Caligula | Opposed autocracy |
| 1525-1526 | The New Testament | Church of England | Deemed irreligious |
| 1922 | *Ulysses* (James Joyce) | U.S. Post Office | Obscene |
| 1927 | *Elmer Gantry* (Sinclair Lewis) | Local officials in Boston | Religious hero depicted as obscene |
| 1929 | *Lady Chatterley's Lover* (D. H. Lawrence) | U.S. Customs | Obscene |
| 1931 | *The Merchant of Venice* (William Shakespeare) | Jewish organizations, New York | Fostered intolerance |
| 1934 | *Tropic of Cancer* (Henry Miller) | U.S. Customs | Obscene |
| 1939 | *The Grapes of Wrath* (John Steinbeck) | St. Louis public library | Vulgar |
| 1941 | *Tobacco Road* (Erskine Caldwell) | U.S. Post Office | Obscene |
| 1948 | *Sanctuary* (William Faulkner) | Vice Squad, Philadelphia | Obscene |
| 1955 | *From Here to Eternity* (James Jones) | U.S. Post Office | Obscene |
| 1955-present | *The Catcher in the Rye* (J. D. Salinger) | Various schools | Obscene |
| 1957 | *Ten North Frederick* (John O'Hara) | Detroit Police Commissioner | Obscene |
| 1960 | The Sun Also Rises (Ernest Hemingway) | San Jose and Riverside, Calif., public libraries | Obscene |
| 1965 | *The Naked Lunch* (William Burroughs) | Boston Superior Court | Obscene |
| 1972 | *Catch 22* (Joseph Heller) | Strongsville, Ohio, schools | Obscene |
| 1989 | *The Satanic Verses* (Salman Rushdie) | Ayatollah Khomeini | Offensive to Muslims |

needs and desires." According to plaintiffs, secular humanism has been advocated in public school textbooks. Since secular humanism is a religion, it violates the constitutionally mandated separation of church and state, and therefore the books should be banned. Plaintiffs were upheld in a court case in 1987, but this decision was reversed by the Court of Appeals.

A much broader and more widespread attack on school textbooks has been instituted by various watchdog groups that believe that a number of textbooks are antireligious. For example, Beverly LaHay of Concerned Women for America has expressed the necessity "to preserve, protect, and promote traditional and Judeo-Christian values through education, legal defense. . . . The sad fact is that educational systems in most American schools has already removed any reference to God or teaching of Judeo-Christian values that is the most important information a child can learn." In a famous case, LaHay's group supported seven families in Hawkins County, Tennessee, who were attempting to ban a series of textbooks. Purportedly, the books contained passages about witchcraft, astrology, pacifism, feminism, and evolution, while ignoring religion and creationism.

The trial judge agreed that the textbooks interfered with the parents' free exercise of religion, that the children were exposed to offensive religious beliefs that interfered with practice of their own religion and that put Tennessee in the position of favoring one religion over another. Ten months later, however, the Court Of Appeals reversed this decision, stating that the Constitution was not violated and that exposure to offensive religious beliefs is not identical to requiring them to be accepted.

**Self-Censorship by Publishers and Government.** William Noble (1990) observed that the absorption of many independent publishing houses into conglomerates has produced more reluctance to stir up controversy or to offend, resulting in self-censorship of what is published. Unlike the previously discussed situations, the publisher may be the only one who knows what has happened.

Self-censorship can take several forms. Probably the mildest form occurs when an author is asked (not ordered) to change or eliminate some text. For example, Judy Blume removed text at her publisher's request in her book *Tiger Eyes*: "There was just one line in the book [about masturbation], but my publishers said it would make the book controversial and limit the book's audience. I took it out but I wish I hadn't."

Similar to Judy Blume's encounter with self-censorship is bowdlerism, named for Thomas Bowdler, a nineteenth century British physician who excised text from Shakespeare's plays. These "bowdlerized" versions can still be found in schools, and in 1980 Harcourt Brace Jovanovich published an edition of *Romeo and Juliet* minus about ten percent of the text. About two-thirds of the omitted passages had sexual connotations.

A more severe form of self-censorship is to fail to publish a book or to withdraw it from publication under pressure once it has been published. Deborah Davis' unflattering 1980 biography of Katharine Graham, owner of *The Washington Post*, was pulled from circulation after Graham and the *Post*'s executive director, Ben Bradlee, protested in private to the publisher. When the Ayatollah Khomeini of Iran issued a death warrant on Salman Rushdie for his authorship of his "blasphemous" *The Satanic Verses* in 1989, worldwide book bannings and burnings occurred. In America, three of the largest book chains—Waldenbooks, B. Dalton, and Barnes and Noble—removed all copies of *The Satanic Verses* from open display (the book could still be bought by request). This action was justified in terms of protecting the safety and welfare of employees and patrons.

Frank W. Snepp, a former CIA agent, wrote a critical book (*Decent Interval*) about the CIA's involvement in the Vietnam War. The book was published in 1977 without prior CIA approval, to which Snepp had previously agreed in writing. In federal district court, Snepp's attorney argued that since no classified information was revealed in the book, the government was violating Snepp's rights under the First Amendment. The CIA argued that finding Snepp innocent would create a dangerous precedent and that the CIA would lose control and be unable to enforce the guarantee. Snepp was found guilty, but the decision was reversed in appeals court on the grounds that since no classified information was revealed, Snepp was protected by the First Amendment. The Supreme Court upheld the district court decision, however, stating that Snepp's book had "irreparably harmed the United States government," and Snepp was ordered to hand over more than $200,000 in royalties to the Department of Justice.

**Racial and Sexual Subordination.** Mark Twain's *The Adventures of Huckleberry Finn* (1884) was considered to be racist by the National Association for the Advancement of Colored People, who sought to have it banned from New York City Schools in 1957. The book was said to demean African Americans but not whites, resulting in a loss of respect by the reader for African Americans. The book continues to be attacked, and in 1984 an African American alderman in Illinois did succeed in having the book removed from a high school reading list for use of offensive language. William Golding's *Lord of the Flies* (1954) was branded as racist by the Toronto School Board for using the term "nigger" and for demeaning African Americans and was banned from schools.

Radical feminist writer Andrea Dworkin and lawyer Catherine McKinnon attempted to regulate pornographic literature on the grounds that it discriminated against women and therefore was under the jurisdiction of civil rights laws. According to Dworkin, pornography produced "bigotry and hostility and aggression toward all women," and promoted the idea that "the hurting of women is . . . basic to the sexual pleasure of men." Legislation intended to allow a woman who perceived herself to be hurt by pornography to sue the bookstore owner for civil damage and have the materials banned was proposed in three cities but was never put into law. In Indianapolis, the case was appealed to the Supreme Court, which upheld a lower court's ruling that "to deny free speech in order to engineer social change in the name of accomplishing a greater good for one sector of our society erodes the freedoms of all and, as such, threatens tyranny and injustice for those subjected to the rule of such laws."

**Ethical Issues.** The preceding presentation of the history of book banning was intended to bring into focus the issues and points of view related to book banning and censorship. It is apparent that book banning and censorship are more of a dilemma than a quandary. That is, various ethically defensible positions exist.

**The Case for No Censorship or Book Banning.** Freedom of expression is a cherished right that people are guaranteed by the First Amendment to the Constitution. Some people have interpreted the First Amendment literally to mean that book banning or censorship is not justifiable or permissible under any circumstances. The late Supreme Court justices William O. Douglas and Hugo Black and the American Civil Liberties Union (ACLU) stated that the First Amendment protected all publications, without qualification, against either civil or criminal regulation at any level of government. Douglas tolerated "no exceptions . . . not even for obscenity." To Douglas, the First Amendment can have meaning and significance only if it allows protests even against the moral code that is the standard in the community. The ACLU declared that all published material is protected by the First Amendment unless it creates a "clear and present danger" of causing antisocial behavior.

George Elliot (1965) stated the case for removing all censorship for pornography: (1) No law can be stated clearly enough to guide unequivocally those who decide censorship cases. The ACLU has called such laws "vague and unworkable." The Supreme Court has for years grappled with defining obscenity and pornography with considerable disagreement among justices and changes in definition over the years. (2) There is no clear and unequivocal evidence that in fact pornography does severely injure many people, even adolescents. (3) The less power government has the better. As Justice Hugo Black wrote in 1966: "Criminal punishment by government, although universally recognized, is an exercise of one of government's most awesome and dangerous powers. Consequently, wise and good governments make all possible efforts to hedge this dangerous power by restricting it within easily identifiable boundaries."

The essence of the belief that reading materials should not be banned under any circumstance rests on the assumption that the citizenry has free will and is intelligent. Therefore, each citizen is free and able to reject material that he or she finds personally offensive, but no person has the right to define what is personally offensive for anyone else or to limit anyone else's access to that material. To do so is, to paraphrase the words of federal judge Sarah Backer, to erode freedom for the entire citizenry and threaten tyranny and injustice for those at whom the laws are directed.

**The Case for Censorship.** An editorial in the April 2, 1966, issue of *The New Republic* commented on Justice Douglas' position: "It would be nice if we could have a society in which nothing that others sold or displayed made anyone fear for the future of his children. But we are not that society, and it is hard to protect Mishkin's [a convicted pornographer] freedom to make a profit any way he likes, when his particular way is a stench in the nostrils of his community, even though the community would perhaps be better advised to ignore him." The editorial advocated permitting Mishkin to cater to those who seek his product but not allowing him to display it in public.

This editorial represents the stance of most of the procensorship articles that have been published, as well as the position of the courts. It is a middle-of-the-road position. Censorship itself and the power vested in agencies to enforce it should be approached warily. Pornography does exist; however, it is a social evil that needs to be controlled. When material is perceived to destroy or subvert social and moral laws, undermine community standards, or offend decency without aesthetic justification, it may be banned.

The two situations of most concern are materials available to or directed at minors and material that is publicly displayed and available that is indecent and offensive to community standards. If such material is made unavailable to minors and kept from public view, it may be permissible to offer it to those who desire it. A more extreme and minority position is that the ban on pornography should be total, and the material should not be made available to anybody.

Most of the debate about censorship and the banning of books has focused on pornography and obscenity. The other areas of book banning (self-censorship, religion, and sexual and racial subordination), however, would no doubt find adherents to each of the above positions. Probably the only area of censorship that comes close to finding a consensus is the revelation of classified material that would endanger lives or national security. Most people support the censorship and banning of such material.

Defining what kinds of books and other reading materials should be banned and the subject of banning itself are slippery issues. The reason is, as George Elliott (1965) noted, that these issues are not amenable to scientific analysis. They cannot be numerically defined or objectively measured. They are ambiguous matters of personal preference and consensus opinion. Censorship and book banning are psychological, aesthetic, and political phenomena.

*—Laurence Miller*

**See also** Art; Art and public policy; Censorship; Freedom of speech; *Index librorum prohibitorum*; Song lyrics.

**Bibliography**

Demac, Donna A. *Liberty Denied.* New Brunswick, N.J.: Rutgers University Press, 1990. An excellent discussion of the different kinds of censorship and book banning and their effect on the authors and on society. Takes a strong anticensorship position.

Haight, Anne Lyon, and Chandler B. Grannis. *Banned Books.* New York: R. R. Bowker, 1978. A comprehensive list of book banning and related incidents through the years and in various countries.

McClellan, Grant S., ed. *Censorship in the United States.* New York: H. W. Wilson, 1967. An excellent collection of magazine and newspaper articles that argue the pros and cons of censorship.

Noble, William. *Bookbanning in America.* Middlebury, Vt.: Paul S. Erickson, 1990. Highly recommended. A lively, very readable, thorough, and thoughtful discussion of the various forms of censorship. Takes a strong anticensorship position.

Rauch, Jonathan. *Kindly Inquisitors: The New Attacks on Free Thought.* Chicago: University of Chicago Press, 1993. A leisurely and very personal but insightful essay on the evils of censorship.

Woods, L. B. *A Decade of Censorship in America: The Threat to Classrooms and Libraries, 1966-1975.* Metuchen, N.J.: Scarecrow Press, 1979. A detailed and thorough presentation of the censorship wars as fought in public schools and libraries. Presents both pro- and anticensorship points of view.

## Boycott

**Type of ethics:** Politico-economic ethics

**Date:** Coined 1880

**Associated with:** Consumerism

**Definition:** An organized attempt to achieve certain goals by convincing consumers not to buy specific products or not to buy products from specific stores

**Significance:** Boycotts are attempts to realize certain consumer or civil rights or to correct perceived imbalances of political and/or economic power among individuals and organizations

Although boycotts (named for Charles Boycott, a notoriously unfair Irish landlord) have been a recognized form of protest at least since the Boston Tea Party, which signaled the beginning of the American Revolutionary War, they did not become common until the late 1960's. Since that time, more and more groups have used boycotts to achieve increasingly diverse goals. By 1990, there were more than one hundred local or national consumer protests in progress at any given time. Some boycotts are organized by groups for their own benefit; for

| Prominent U.S. Boycotts | | |
|---|---|---|
| **Date** | **Boycott** | **Ideological Reason** |
| 1950's | Martin Luther King, Jr., leads boycott of Montgomery, Alabama, bus system | To protest racial discrimination |
| 1960's-1970 | The United Farm Workers urges a boycott against table grapes | To pressure the growers into recognizing the union |
| 1983 | The UFW renews the boycott | To protest dangerous working conditions, including the use of cancer-causing chemicals in the fields |
| 1972-1974 | ACWA union boycotts Farah Manufacturing Company | To protest alleged unfair labor practices. Notable because of the support of the boycott by the Roman Catholic church. |
| 1977-1982 | Consumers boycott all Nestle products sold in the U.S. | To protest unfair practices used to market Nestle's infant formula in Third World countries |
| 1980-1990 | Citizens boycott firms doing business in South Africa. Boycott organized by the Reverend Leon Sullivan | To protest the South African government's continuing policy of apartheid |
| 1990 | PUSH, headed by Jesse Jackson, boycotts Nike Shoes | To pressure the company to promote more African Americans to management positions and to use more African American-owned banks, suppliers, and so forth |
| 1992 | Gay rights supporters boycott all businesses in the state of Colorado, especially tourism | To protest Colorado citizens' unwillingness to pass legislation protecting gays and lesbians |

example, customers stop shopping at certain stores that they believe are charging unfair prices. Other boycotts are aimed at gaining benefits for third parties; for example, consumers in the United States refused to buy Nestle products until that company changed its infant formula marketing practices in Third World countries. Still other boycotts have been called against one company to put economic or social pressure on a different company, as when the United Farm Workers and their supporters boycotted stores that sold table grapes until the growers recognized the union. Organizations now use boycotts to achieve such wide-ranging political goals as animal rights, environmental protection, and the rights of women and minority groups.

**See also** Coercion; Consumerism; Economics.

## Bradley, Francis Herbert (Jan. 30, 1846, Clapham, Surrey, England—Sept. 18, 1924, Oxford, England): Philosopher

**Type of ethics:** Modern history

**Achievements:** Author of *Ethical Studies* (1876), *The Presuppositions of Critical History* (1874), *Principles of Logic* (1883), and *Appearance and Reality: A Metaphysical Essay* (1893)

**Significance:** Bradley stressed the significance of ideas, especially spiritual ideas, as the fundamental reality, and he criticized the utilitarian concept that happiness was the goal of ethical behavior

Francis Herbert Bradley was a nineteenth century British philosopher whose career spanned more than five decades at Oxford University, where he was first elected to a fellowship in 1870. His writing eventually earned him Britain's Order of Merit. Bradley's keen critical analysis of the dialectic between the importance of spirituality and that of reality stood in opposition to utilitarian thought, whose advocates, such as John Stuart Mill, wrote that the goal of humankind should be to do that which would bring the greatest good to the greatest number of individuals. Bradley's work was based on the ideals of Georg Friedrich Hegel, which stressed the social nature of morality and held that one's ethics was determined by one's place in society. Since Bradley focused on the place of the individual within society, some of his critics have suggested that his ideas lead to moral relativism. Bradley's most famous work, *Appearance and Reality: A Metaphysical Essay*, appeared in 1893. Although this book spoke of the spiritual nature of reality, Bradley recognized that the existence of that spiritual nature was impossible to prove intellectually because of the limitations of the human intellect.

**See also** Bentham, Jeremy; Mill, John Stuart; Utilitarianism.

## Brandeis, Louis Dembitz (Nov. 13, 1856, Louisville, Ky.—Oct. 5, 1941, Washington, D.C.): Jurist

**Type of ethics:** Legal and judicial ethics

**Achievements:** Supreme Court Justice (1916-1939); Chairman, World Zionist Organization

**Significance:** One of the leading progressives of the early twentieth century, Brandeis became the "people's lawyer,"

*Louis Dembitz Brandeis* (Library of Congress)

espousing an environmental view of law known as sociological jurisprudence whereby law is guided by reason From 1916 until his retirement in 1939, Brandeis served as an associate Supreme Court Justice. His progressivism on the Court was manifested by his use of the power of government to protect the interests of all Americans. Brandeis translated controversies in court into universal moral terms and incorporated those moral values into the framework of law. His leadership in the World Zionist Organization, as on the Supreme Court, demonstrated his consuming passion to create a just democracy for all individuals and to use every avenue of government to perfect and preserve a genuine equality. He wrote that democracy "demands continuous sacrifice by the individual and more exigent obedience to the moral law than any other form of government . . ." Deciding each case on the basis of moral rectitude within a democracy, he wrote opinions that were detailed, were intended to instruct, and reflected his beliefs in the maintenance of the federal system of government. He was willing to attempt social experimentation within the structure of the government to achieve a democratic equality and preserve the liberties of speech, press, and assembly—all of which are requisites for the maintenance of a free society.

**See also** Progressivism.

## Bribery

**TYPE OF ETHICS:** Personal and social ethics

**DATE:** The word "bribe" found in Geoffrey Chaucer's writings in the fourteenth century

**ASSOCIATED WITH:** Commerce, politics, and law enforcement

**DEFINITION:** Obtaining illegal or improper favors in exchange for the payment of money or other value

**SIGNIFICANCE:** The concept of bribery focuses attention upon the relationship of special duties to general moral obligations

Bribery involves paying somebody in money or other things of value, whether objects or favors, to violate a special obligation or duty. Payments to violate general ethical duties, such as to refrain from murder or robbery, would not ordinarily be classified as bribery. Very often, however, general ethical duties and special obligations may be yoked; for example, a prosecutor who through bribery is induced falsely to prosecute the briber's political opponent is violating both general and special obligations.

It might be tempting to analyze bribery in terms of extrinsic morality, in which a morally neutral act is made wrong (or obligatory) by some just authority for the common good. Modern industrial societies have found bribery to be inconsistent with efficiency and have, therefore, outlawed bribery. Most ethicists, however, see true bribery as a violation of intrinsic morality—a wrong in itself—because it aims at luring persons to neglect or to trespass the obligations they have taken upon themselves by acceptance of public or private office with inherent duties.

The moral impermissibility of bribery arises out of two primary considerations: First, the briber induces the bribee to violate his or her special duty, and second, evil consequences may flow from the action undertaken for the bribe. Consider the employment manager of a corporation who accepts a bribe to hire a particular candidate for a job. Even if the candidate is fully qualified, if the bribe causes the choice of a less-than-best candidate, that manager makes his company slightly less competitive in the free market, potentially costing jobs, profits, and even the future existence of the enterprise. In the case of a scrupulous bribee, who will accept a bribe only from the candidate he considers best qualified for the position, the evil of the bribe rests on the violation of the duty alone, or that violation plus a kind of fraud against the briber (although the latter is problematical).

Similar but more complex difficulties arise when one considers officials of illegal or immoral organizations. What of an SS officer who takes bribes from Jews to help them escape from Nazi persecution and extermination? Certainly, that SS officer is in technical violation of his official duty both to his specific organization and to his national government—Hitler's Third Reich—but there can be no morally binding special obligation to a thoroughly immoral organization, for one cannot morally bind oneself to do that which is ethically wrong.

Problems still arise, however, for the right to require payments for doing a good act remains uncertain. If the good deed is morally obligatory, it would seem that demanding payment for it would not be right unless the payment were actually necessary to carry on the good work. If, on the contrary, the good act were supererogatory, then perhaps a requirement of payment might be justifiable.

Another area of concern in regard to bribery involves payments made in response to demands by persons in authority (or otherwise influential) to prevent the conduct of business or to inflict other harms. Moral philosophers have established a useful distinction between bribery and extortion. Demands of payment to prevent harm are, properly speaking, extortion, and the theoretical considerations involved in such payments are extremely complex. Clearly, refusing to pay extortion must usually be regarded as praiseworthy, but under many circumstances such a principled approach must be judged to be supererogatory.

The customs of many regions and nations support the making of moderate payments to public officials to perform their ordinary tasks. Persons seeking permits, licenses, visas, passage through customs, and so forth, may be required to pay small "bribes" to the appropriate officials, but where sanctioned by long-standing custom (even though technically illegal), such payments are more akin to tips than to bribes. In much of the world, furthermore, such practices may be accepted on account of the unrealistically low salaries of officials, which necessitate the supplementation of pay. In addition, gift giving to public officials has the beneficial effect of giving an incentive for the performance of duty, when civic virtue does not suffice.

The offering of bribes, whether accepted or not, may be assumed to be morally reprehensible in circumstances in which the taking of bribes would be blameworthy. In a situation in which taking a bribe would be morally blameless, such as making nominal payments to public servants where custom sanctions it, the offering of such bribes must be held innocent.

In Plato's *Crito*, Socrates refused to allow his friends to bribe his guards in order that he escape into exile, avoiding his execution. Socrates had numerous reasons for his principled stance, and among these was that bribery would cause the guards to fail in the duties they owed by virtue of their office. Simply stated, the moral maxim would be that nobody ought to induce (or attempt to induce) another to do wrong—that is, to violate his or her special obligations and duties.

The U.S. Foreign Corrupt Practices Act was enacted by Congress to restrict both the payment of bribes and extortion by U.S. corporations operating overseas. Some ethicists praise the act as holding American corporations to the highest ethical standards, but others see it as an unrealistic imposition upon American businesses, damaging their competitiveness. —*Patrick O'Neil*

**See also** Business ethics; Cheating; Duty; Hiring practices; Inside information; Professional ethics; Sales, ethics of; White-collar crime.

**Bibliography**

Carson, Thomas L. "Bribery and Implicit Agreements." *Journal of Business Ethics* 6 (February, 1987): 123-125.

Noonan, John T. "Bribery, Extortion, and 'The Foreign Corrupt Practices Act.'" *Philosophy and Public Affairs* 14 (Winter, 1985): 66-90.

__________. *Bribes*. New York: Macmillan, 1984.

Philips, Michael. "Bribery." *Ethics* 94 (July, 1984): 621-636.

__________. "Bribery, Consent and *Prima Facie* Duty: A Rejoinder to Carson." *Journal of Business Ethics* 6 (July, 1987): 361-364.

## Brown, Louise

**Type of ethics:** Bioethics

**Date:** Born July 25, 1978

**Associated with:** In vitro fertilization

**Definition:** Louise Brown was the first baby born to be conceived outside a mother's body in a laboratory dish; the fertilized egg was then implanted into the mother's uterus, where development continued

**Significance:** This event increased public awareness regarding the power of technology to enable conception when normal biological means have failed

Gilbert Brown and Lesley Brown were childless because Lesley's fallopian tubes were blocked with adhesions and had to be surgically removed. Consequently, eggs from her ovaries could not migrate down these tubes, which prevented their possible fertilization and uterine implantation. To overcome this biological problem, doctors used in vitro technology, in which an egg was surgically removed from the mother and was combined with ejaculated sperm from the father in a laboratory dish to induce conception or fertilization. The fertilized egg was then implanted into the mother's uterus, where its devel-

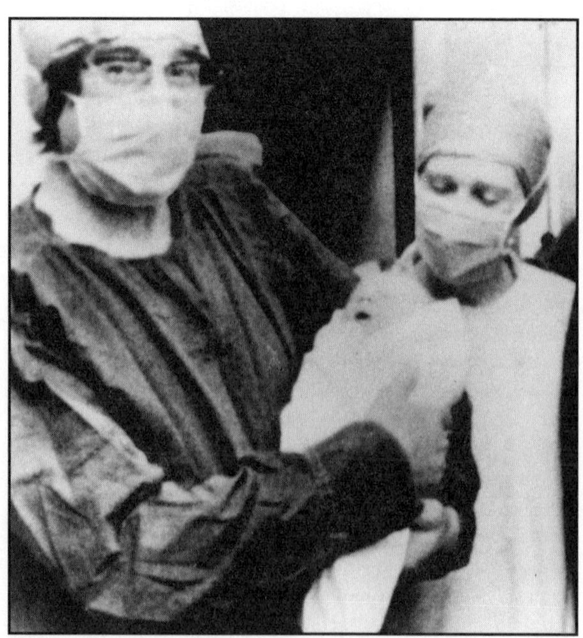

*Doctor Robert Edwards holds Louise Brown, the first "test-tube" baby.* (UPI/Bettmann Newsphotos)

opment culminated in the birth of Louise Joy Brown. Ethical considerations involved the fact that for the first time, sexual intercourse had been separated from conception. Some questioned whether this "artificial procreation" would hinder the normal physical, psychological, and social development of the child. Other ethical dilemmas emerged regarding the appropriate use of discarded embryos, as well as the problem of technological containment. It is conceivable that in vitro technology could be routinely used as a genetic screen for desirable traits or to exclude embryos that have an undesired gender.

**See also** Bioethics; In vitro fertilization; Sperm banks; Surrogate motherhood.

## Brown v. Board of Education of Topeka

**TYPE OF ETHICS:** Race and ethnicity

**DATE:** May 17, 1954

**DEFINITION:** U.S. Supreme Court decision that overruled the *Plessy v. Ferguson* (1896) "separate but equal" law

**SIGNIFICANCE:** Found that segregated public schools were not "equal," could not be made "equal," and that they had a psychologically detrimental effect on African American children

Segregated public schools dominated education for African Americans until 1954, when the U.S. Supreme Court decision *Brown v. Board of Education of Topeka, Kansas*, rejected the *Plessy v. Ferguson* (1896) "separate but equal" law. *Brown v. Board of Education* inspired several years of struggle by African Americans, the courts, and supporters of equal rights to force its implementation. In the years preceding *Brown*, education throughout the South had constituted an effective means of discrimination.

**History.** Until the 1950's, *Plessy v. Ferguson* (1896) continued to justify all segregation, including school segregation. In *Plessy*, the Supreme Court upheld a Louisiana law requiring equal but separate accommodations for "white" and "colored" railroad passengers. The Court assumed that legislation was powerless to eradicate racial dispositions or abolish distinctions based upon physical differences, and that any attempts to do so could only complicate the issue. Laws requiring the separation of African Americans and whites in areas of potential interaction did not imply the inferiority of either race, according to the Court.

Besides the fact that racism was inherent in *Plessy*, it was clear by the 1950's that the separate schools, transportation, and public facilities that were provided for African Americans were not equal to those provided for whites. Oliver Brown, whose daughter Linda was denied entrance to a white school three blocks from their home and ended up at an African American school twenty-one blocks away, questioned the constitutionality of the Topeka Board of Education's policies. Authorities, citing state laws permitting racial segregation, denied Linda Brown admission to the white school.

In *Brown*, the District Court found segregation to have a detrimental effect on African American children; however, African American and white schools were found to be substantially equal. The plaintiff took the case to the U.S. Supreme Court, arguing that segregated public schools were not equal and that they constituted denial of equal protection of the laws. The Fourteenth Amendment (1868) grants equal protection, stating, "no state shall deprive any person of life, liberty, or property, without due process of the law; nor deny to any person within its jurisdiction the equal protection of the laws."

In the first cases following the adoption of the Fourteenth Amendment, the Supreme Court interpreted it as proscribing all state-imposed discriminations against the Negro race. The Court, led by Chief Justice Earl Warren, chose this perspective in handling the *Brown* case. In deliberations, the Court focused on the effect of segregation, not on whether the schools were considered equal.

**Ethical Principles and Issues.** The Supreme Court detailed the importance of education and posited education as the foundation of good citizenship. Thurgood Marshall (who later became a U.S. Supreme Court Justice), the National Association for the Advancement of Colored People's chief counsel for *Brown*, argued on the basis of the inequalities of segregation, noting the findings of social scientists on segregation's negative effects. Chief Justice Warren's majority opinion expressed doubt that any child could reasonably be expected to succeed in life when denied educational opportunity, and further, that such an opportunity, where the state has undertaken to provide it, is a right that must be made available to all on equal terms. The Court found that the doctrine of "separate but equal" has no place in the field of public education.

The Court's decision to take a substantive look at the *Brown* case, along with the procedural approach, led to a 9-0 decision in favor of Brown. Arguments alluding to the negative psychological impact of segregation on African American children keyed the decision. A public school system that was erected for the betterment of all citizens but denied certain segments of the citizenry access to the system's best public education was held to be unethical. The *Brown* decision, (which says, in effect, that no matter how equal the physical qualities of separate schools or any other public facilities may be, their segregated nature has negative effects on the psyche of African American children, hindering their ability to learn and consequently to become productive citizens), provided the Court with a precedent on which to build and ensured that public education would be conducted on an ethical basis at least in theory.

**Post Brown v. Board of Education.** Implementing and enforcing the *Brown* decision proved to be infinitely more difficult than had been arriving at the decision itself. Public officials, especially in the South, openly, aggressively, and consistently defied the Court. This reaction did not, however, prevent the Court from ruling on a desegregation order. Thus, on May 31, 1955, the Court, in *Brown v. Board of Education II*, ruled that school authorities have the primary responsibility for dismantling segregationist policies. Courts were given the responsibility of considering whether the actions of school authorities constituted good-faith implementation of the governing constitutional principles. The Court required that desegregation be carried out "with all deliberate speed."

The intention of "deliberate speed" was to assist school authorities in making smooth transitions from segregation to integration; however, school officials throughout the South interpreted it to mean little or no action. Several southern school districts closed down public schools rather than integrate, while others, such as the Little Rock, Arkansas, district, were forced to deploy armed soldiers to ensure successful integration. By the late 1960's, most southern schools settled into a pattern of integration. After the *Brown* cases, the Supreme Court dealt little with desegregation, allowing the lower courts to handle such cases.

The *Brown v. Board of Education* decision had an influence that reached well beyond the desegregation of public schools. It inspired court cases involving the segregation of public transportation, hotel accommodations, restaurants, and other public facilities. Although the *Brown* decision did not explicitly outlaw racial discrimination in areas other than education, the decision influenced the rulings of lower court judges in other discrimination cases. The impact of *Brown v. Board of Education* on the lives of African Americans, and all Americans, cannot be overemphasized.

—*Gregory Freeland*

**See also** Bigotry; Evers, Medgar; King, Martin Luther, Jr.; Racial prejudice; Racism; Segregation.

**Bibliography**

Chandler, Ralph, Richard Enslen, and Peter Renstrom. *Individual Rights*. Vol. 1 in *The Constitutional Law Dictionary*. Santa Barbara, Calif.: ABC-CLIO Information Services, 1985. An excellent reference text containing summaries of court decisions and their significance.

Gunther, Gerald. *Constitutional Law*. 11th ed. Mineola, N.Y.: The Foundation Press, 1985. Provides very informative, specific references to important cases.

Mason, Alpheus Thomas, and Gordon E. Baker, eds. *Free Government in the Making*. 4th ed. New York: Oxford University Press, 1985. A text on the democratic process that reveals how various cases shaped democracy.

Murphy, Walter, and C. Herman Pritchett, eds. *Courts, Judges, and Politics*. 3d ed. New York: Random House, 1979. A scholarly book that examines important court cases, providing important dialogues among judges deciding cases.

Nieman, Donald G. *Promises to Keep: African Americans and the Constitutional Order, 1776 to the Present*. New York: Oxford University Press, 1991. A concise book on the history and effects of critical court rulings affecting African Americans.

## Buber, Martin

**Buber, Martin** (Feb. 8, 1878, Vienna, Austro-Hungarian Empire—June 13, 1965, Jerusalem, Israel): Philosopher

**Type of ethics:** Religious ethics

**Achievements:** Author of *Ich und du* (1922; *I and Thou*, 1937)

**Significance:** Interpreted the foundation of ethics and morality as the personal "I-Thou" (as opposed to the impersonal "I-It") relationship of people to one another, existence, and God

**I and Thou.** For Buber, the two primary ways in which people relate to their world are characterized by the words "I-It" and "I-Thou (or You)." The "I-It" way of seeing life is one in which people objectify the reality they see and deal with into *things*—mere objects to be used, understood, manipulated, and controlled. In such a way of relating to life, perhaps characterized best by the business or scientific approach to existence, there is little opportunity for a true personal connection between the individual and the rest of reality. Instead, life is spent trying to attain goals, analyze and control others, and organize reality into something that can be used or consumed.

While the "I-It" approach to reality might be necessary to conduct the everyday affairs of life or create intellectual circumstances for technological advancement, Buber believed that its aggressive domination of modern culture had created a painful and pitiful climate that fostered human isolation. As a result, people had become alienated from their fellow human beings, their world at large, and their God. To Buber, such a life was not authentic, not genuine, and not fully human.

The "I-Thou" attitude is characterized in terms of an honest and open "dialogue" between the "I" and the "Thou." A mutual and dynamic, though intimately personal, connection ensues in the "I-Thou" mode, in which there is a marrying of the subjective "I" and the objective other, which is now no longer a dominated "It" but instead a responsive partner in a profoundly communicative and respectful meeting of the two: "I-It" becomes "I-Thou."

In Buber's "I-Thou" relationship, people are relieved of their isolation and alienation from those around them and the world at large, because they no longer relate to what is not themselves as merely means to purposes or goals ("Its"), but instead as respected and appreciated ends in and of themselves ("Thous"). People no longer live life as detached and solitary but are connected and "whole" with everything in the realm of their "I-Thou" encounter.

The most basic example of the "I-Thou" relationship for Buber is that between two people in honest, dialogic communication in which both encounter the essential integrity and *being* of the other. Yet Buber also believes that this relationship can exist between humans and nature. A tree, for example, is no longer a commodity to be made into lumber for a house; it is, in the "I-Thou" relationship, a significant object with which, perhaps as a thing of beauty or simply as a "being" itself, one can have an intimate connection. In the same way, an artist can have such a relationship with those things that become objects in the artist's works.

Buber's perspective also has social implications. If a community of people is to succeed, it must be based on an "I-Thou" dialogue that nurtures a humanizing, unselfish climate of respect for individuals and the common good. In this regard, Buber was an advocate of utopian social models such as the Israeli *kibbutz,* which promoted mutual cooperation among all members of the community at every level of life.

Finally, there are the religious dimensions of Buber's thought. For him, every "I-Thou" relationship brings individuals in touch with the eternal "Thou," or God. In fact, Buber asserts that it is impossible to relate to God in a manipulative "I-It" mode. He believed that it was only through the direct, dialogic encounter with the otherness of objective existence in the respectful "I-Thou" mode that the qualities and presence of God became actual in the world. It is only in such personal, and finally mysterious, circumstances (so alien to traditional theologies that seek to make God an "It" by explaining and dogmatizing) that the living God can be discovered.

**Implications for Ethical Conduct.** Buber's philosophy demands that people take the risk of opening themselves up to "I-Thou" relationships, no matter how fleeting they may be. It is only in the experience of such profoundly personal relationships with their fellow human beings, the world at large, and God that humans, even momentarily, become able to escape the propensity to transform everything into an object of "I-It" use and scrutiny. It is only through the "I-Thou" dialogue that human beings can move out of a life of lonely impersonality and into a mode of existence that keeps them personally involved with the uniqueness of their fellow human beings, communities, and God. Without such an "I-Thou" foundation, there is no possibility for a moral life of meaning and purpose.

*—Richard M. Leeson*

**See also** Existentialism; Heidegger, Martin; *I and Thou*; Jewish ethics; Kierkegaard, Søren; Tillich, Paul.

**Bibliography**

Arnett, Ronald C. *Communication and Community: Implications of Martin Buber's Dialogue*. Carbondale: Southern Illinois University Press, 1986.

Diamond, Malcolm L. *Martin Buber: Jewish Existentialist*. New York: Oxford University Press, 1960.

Friedman, Maurice S. *Martin Buber and the Eternal*. New York: Human Sciences Press, 1986.

___________. *Martin Buber: The Life of Dialogue. 3d ed. Chicago: University of Chicago Press, 1976.*

Manheim, Werner. *Martin Buber*. New York: Twayne, 1974.

Silberstein, Laurence J. *Martin Buber's Social and Religious Thought: Alienation and the Quest for Meaning*. New York: New York University Press, 1989.

Smith, Ronald G. *Martin Buber*. Richmond, Va.: John Knox Press, 1967.

## Buddha

**Buddha** (Siddhārtha Gautama, c. 566 B.C.E., Lumbinī, Nepal—c. 486 B.C.E., Kuśinārā, India). Religious leader

**Type of ethics:** Religious ethics

**Achievements:** Founded Buddhism, one of the world's major religious and ethical systems

**Significance:** From a rigorously experiential perspective, the Buddha provided a comprehensive moral discipline designed to liberate humankind from an existence characterized by impermanence, suffering, and delusion

**Biography.** The son of a chief of the warrior clan of the Śakyas, Siddhārtha Gautama was born in approximately 566 B.C.E. at the edge of the Himalayas, in what is now Nepal. His father, Śuddhodana, although not the king he was once thought to be, nevertheless provided Gautama with all of the elements necessary for a comfortable, luxurious existence. Legend and myth cloud much of the surviving information regarding Gautama's early years, but at approximately the age of nineteen, he was married to his cousin Yaśodharā, by whom he had one child, Rāhula.

At the age of twenty-nine, according to some accounts, he was exposed to the basic realities of existence. While being driven around his father's estate in his chariot, he saw four things that would ultimately change his life: a man suffering from disease, a man weakened and reduced by age, a corpse, and a wandering ascetic. Questioning his charioteer about these sights, he learned that although no one can escape disease, age, and death, asceticism might at least offer some sort of alternative.

Having realized the fate of all living things, Gautama resolved to leave the luxurious life of his youth in order to seek the cause of the horrors of human existence and, if possible, to discover a solution. In this homeless, wandering existence, Gautama sought instruction from adepts in the art of meditation, but finding little of real value there, he began to practice the most extreme forms of asceticism for the next six years, almost starving himself to death in the process. At last, seeing the inadequacy of this approach, he decided to abandon asceticism and, by the pure force of will, achieve his goal.

At Bodh Gayā, Gautama sat down at the foot of a tree, resolving not to leave until he had achieved enlightenment. Passing beyond all previously attained meditative states and conquering manifold temptations in the process, he at last attained complete liberation and found the answers that he had sought. He was thirty-five years old.

Having resolved to proclaim his message of enlightenment to the world, Gautama, now the Buddha, or Enlightened One, spent the next forty-five years teaching his doctrine up and down the Ganges and establishing his monastic order, or *sangha*, of Buddhist monks and nuns. At the age of eighty, the Buddha died at Kuśinārā, India, in approximately 486 B.C.E.

After his enlightenment at the age of thirty-five, the Buddha proposed both a diagnosis of the human condition and a response to it. The human condition is characterized by impermanence, suffering, and false consciousness. Throughout his career, the Buddha claimed to teach but two things: suffering and the end of suffering.

**The Nature of Existence.** With systematic, scientific rigor, the Buddha began his analysis of existence by citing three of its basic characteristics: impermanence (*anitya*), suffering (*duḥkha*), and the lack of an abiding self (*anātman*). Why is existence bound up with suffering and impermanence? The Buddha saw life in terms of a "chain of dependent origination" (pratītya-samutpāda). This chain begins with ignorance (avidyā), which leads to choices both negative and positive (saṃskāra), which in turn result in a will to live. This will takes the form of consciousness (vijñāna), and consciousness is followed by a material mind and body (nāma-rūpa). Mind and body connect with the external world through the sense organs (*ṣaḍāyatana), the most prominent of which is touch (sparśa*). Once the consciousness is active, feelings (*vedanā*) that are associated with sensations follow, giving the impression of pleasure, pain, or neutrality. The combination of these feelings produces desire (tṛṣṇā) and attachment (upādāna), finally resulting in becoming (*bhava*). Becoming, in turn, inevitably results in birth (*jāti*) and decay (*jāra*).

*Buddhist image at Ryusenji, Japan.* (Diane C. Lyell)

The Buddha employed the Hindu concept of karma, the law of cause and effect following both thought and action, to explain the cycle of life. Through many lifetimes and many rebirths, positive and negative thoughts and actions have karmic reverberations, either shortening or prolonging the round of rebirths (*saṃsāra*). The practical aim of moving beyond karma is to free oneself from the round of saṃsāra and all of its suffering. Once this liberation is achieved, nirvana (Sanskrit, nirvāṇa), the cessation of desire, of karmic residue, and of a sense of self ensues. Although it is not extinction, nirvana is clearly a transcendental, unconditioned, and ineffable state—the final goal of Buddhism.

**The Moral Life.** With this analysis of existence, the Buddha developed a comprehensive moral code intended to bring about happiness and liberation. He began his moral superstructure with the four noble truths: (1) all is suffering (*duḥkha*); (2) suffering has a cause, which is desire, or craving (*tṛṣṇā*); (3) suffering has an end (duḥkha-nirodha); (4) the end of suffering is achieved by means of the noble eightfold path (*ārya-astāṅga-mārga*).

The noble eightfold path consists of (1) right understanding (*samyag-dṛṣṭi*), (2) right aspiration (*samyak-samkalpa*), (3) right speech (*samyag-vācā*), (4) right action (samyak-karmanta), (5) right livelihood (*samyag-ājīva*), (6) right effort (samyag-vyāyāma), (7) right mindfulness (samyak-smṛti), and (8) right concentration (*samyak-samādhi*).

The Buddha's emphasis on systematic, cause-and-effect analysis makes practical morality the core of Buddhist doctrine. In order to follow the advice given in the Dhammapada—"Cease to do evil,/ Learn to do good,/ Purify your mind"—one must begin with a series of freely adopted precepts to address the grosser physical defilements of life. The five precepts (*pañca-śila*), once internalized, set the stage for more advanced levels of endeavor. They exhort one to:

1. Refrain from taking life
2. Refrain from taking what is not given
3. Refrain from engaging in sexual misconduct
4. Refrain from telling lies
5. Refrain from taking intoxicants

The five precepts apply to all who consider themselves to be Buddhists. The list of precepts is expanded and applied more rigorously to Buddhist monks and nuns.

In Buddhism, a virtuous or proper ethical action is simultaneously a rational action. Rationality, or wisdom, is directly connected to morality, and the one generates the other. According to Maurice Walshe's translation of the *Digha Nikāya*,

> For wisdom is purified by morality, and morality is purified by wisdom; where one is, the other is, the moral man has wisdom and the wise man has morality, and the combination of morality and wisdom is called the highest thing in the world. Just as one hand washes the other, or one foot the other, so wisdom is purified by morality and this is the highest thing in the world.

Once the negative dimensions of life have been addressed in an honest attempt to cease to do evil, a positive reconstruction can begin and one can learn to do good. This positive reconstruction will take such forms as generosity (dāna), loving kindness (maitri), compassion (*karunā*), sympathetic joy (*muditā*), and equanimity (*upeksā*).

**Theravāda and Mahāyāna.** In time, Buddhist ethics developed the different ideals of the arhat, the accomplished individual of the older Theravāda tradition, and the *bod-*

*hisattva*, the heroic world-savior of the later Mahāyāna tradition. For the arhat, individual salvation culminating in nirvana is primary; for the bodhisattva, the salvation of all beings is foremost. With its wider focus (all of suffering existence), the Mahāyāna tradition has tended to be less strictly concerned with specific precepts, occasionally permitting the transgression of certain rules to attain the final goal. The bodhisattva ideal represents the most extreme extension of Buddhist compassion, integrating all existence into its perspective.

In those countries in which Buddhism is a living social and religious tradition, a practical ethics has developed over time in which sincere practitioners may, through careful attention to the four noble truths, the eightfold path, and the five precepts, attain a morally pure and productive state in this life with at least the hope of ultimate liberation.

—*Daniel W. O'Bryan*

See also Bodhisattva ideal; Buddhist ethics; Five precepts; Four noble truths; Hindu ethics; Karma; Nirvana.

**BIBLIOGRAPHY**

Buddha. *The Dhammapada.* London: Oxford University Press, 1950.

__________. *Thus Have I Heard, The Long Discourses of the Buddha Digha Nikaya.* Translated by Maurice Walshe. London: Wisdom Publications, 1987.

Conze, Edward. *Buddhism: Its Essence and Development.* New York: Harper & Row, 1975.

Keown, Damien. *The Nature of Buddhist Ethics.* New York: St. Martin's Press, 1992.

King, Winston L. *In the Hope of Nibbana: An Essay on Theravada Buddhist Ethics.* Lasalle, Ill.: Open Court, 1964.

Rahula, Walpola. *What the Buddha Taught.* New York: Grove Press, 1974.

Saddhatissa, H. *Buddhist Ethics: Essence of Buddhism.* London: Allen & Unwin, 1970.

## Buddhist ethics

**TYPE OF ETHICS:** Religious ethics

**DATE:** Sixth century B.C.E. to present

**DEFINITION:** The diverse sets of beliefs or opinions about behavior that have grown out of the teachings of Siddhārtha Gautama

**SIGNIFICANCE:** Seeks to define ethical conduct for Buddhist monks and laity

Moral teachings of Buddhists can be understood as extensions of the insights of Siddhārtha Gautama (d. 486 B.C.E.). The heart of his teachings as handed down by Buddhist tradition includes the four noble truths: (1) Life is suffering; (2) Suffering has a cause; (3) That cause is self-seeking desire; (4) There is a way of escape), the eightfold path (the path of escape), and the five (or ten) precepts. Buddhists have developed these teachings in terms of proper behavior for both the laity and the monks, basic virtues, and social ethics.

**Rules for Proper Behavior.** The first two steps on the eightfold path involve right knowledge and right aspiration; that is, recognition of the four noble truths and the will to relinquish anything that interferes with gaining liberation. The fourth step, right behavior, includes the basic ethical teachings for the laity known as the five precepts. (1) Abstain from taking life. This precept goes beyond a prohibition against killing fellow humans to include taking the life of any sentient being. As a result, most Buddhists are vegetarians. (2) Abstain from taking what is not given, and practice charity instead. (3) Do not engage in sexual misconduct, but practice self-control. (4) Practice right speech (step 3 on the eightfold path) by refraining not only from lying but also from gossip and back-biting. (5) Abstain from intoxicating drinks and drugs. The fifth step on the eightfold path is right livelihood. For the layperson, this meant following no occupation precluded by these precepts.

A monk would be held to an even stricter application of these rules. In connection with the second precept, for example, he would own nothing but the robes, toilet articles, and begging bowl given him at ordination. In addition, the monk would agree to as many as five more precepts: to eat moderately and not at all after noon, to refrain from attending dramatic performances, to refrain from self-decoration, to refrain from luxurious living, and to refrain from handling money. The rules derived from these precepts, along with the rules for monasteries, eventually numbered 227. The normative collection of these rules is called, in Pali, the *Patimokkha*.

Buddhists analyzed behavior carefully to determine when the precepts were violated. In connection with the injunction against taking life, for example, the following five conditions had to be present: (1) the thing destroyed must have actually been alive; (2) the Buddhist must have known that the thing was alive; (3) the person must have intended to kill the thing; (4) the person must have acted to carry out that intention; and (5) death must have resulted from the act. Hence, Buddhism was concerned both about the facts of the deed and the motives behind it.

**Basic Virtues.** Theravāda Buddhism emphasized four "cardinal" virtues: love, compassion, joy, and equanimity (defined as the absence of greed, hatred, and envy). All these virtues derived from the basic Buddhist insight that there is no underlying self, so self-seeking is inevitably futile. Later, Mahāyāna Buddhism enjoined several basic virtues, including generosity, righteousness, patience, and wisdom. The Mahāyānist virtue par excellence, however, is compassion, which is embodied in the bodhisattva, the enlightened being who postpones entrance into the bliss of nirvana in order to help other beings reach salvation.

**Social Obligations.** Wherever one finds Buddhism, one finds monks. Even in Shin Buddhism, which allows monks to marry, the distinctions between monks and lay people are only minimized, not eliminated. For many Buddhist laypeople, therefore, the first social obligation is to feed and otherwise support the monks. A layperson can also build a pagoda or perform other meritorious acts that benefit the larger

Buddhist community. At the same time, the monks have the responsibility to share with the laity the results of their study and meditation through teaching and to officiate at various public ceremonies.

Over the years, Buddhism has addressed other areas of social responsibility. Two examples must suffice. First, one of the early figures to address social responsibility was King Aśoka, who became king of Magadha, which dominated the Indian subcontinent. Penitent over suffering caused by his wars, he looked to Buddhism for help in ruling. His inscriptions advocated living peacefully, and he sent Buddhist missionaries to a number of other countries. Second, in 1946, the monks of Sri Lanka joined ongoing efforts to free their country from British rule, thus injecting themselves into political dispute, if not revolt. The monks distributed seeds and vegetables, settled disputes that would otherwise have gone to court, gave out medicines, supported the arts, and helped fuel Sinhalese nationalism. Although not all Buddhists (even in Sri Lanka) have agreed that such behavior is appropriate for monks, it shows how seriously they take social ethics.

**Ethics and Enlightenment.** The ultimate goal of Buddhist teachings is to lead people to enlightenment, not to define ethical behavior. Both Theravāda and Mahāyāna Buddhism portray the enlightened person as one beyond the categories of right and wrong, moral and immoral. This is so because such persons have achieved a level of equanimity and insight at which calculations such as those discussed above are left behind. The person who sees that there is no abiding self and who sees the suffering that will result from selfish behavior will naturally feel no inclination to act in such a destructive fashion. Those who have not yet achieved such a state, however, benefit from ethical rules.

*—Paul L. Redditt*

**See also** Aśoka; Avalokiteśvara; Bodhisattva ideal; Five precepts; Karma; Nirvana.

**Bibliography**

Davids, T. W. Rhys, ed. *The Questions of King Milinda*. Sacred Books of the East 35-36. New York: Dover, 1963.

King, Winston L. *In the Hope of Nibbana: An Essay on Theravada Buddhist Ethics*. LaSalle, Ill.: Open Court, 1964.

Rahula, Walpola. *The Heritage of the Bhikku*. Translated by K. P. G. Wijayasurendra. New York: Grove Press, 1974.

Saddhatissa, H. *Buddhist Ethics: Essence of Buddhism*. London: Allen & Unwin, 1970.

Tachibana, Shundo. *The Ethics of Buddhism*. London: Oxford University Press, 1926.

## al-Bukhârî, Abû ʿAbdallâh Muḥammad

(July 19, Bukhara, Central Asia—Aug. 3, 870, Khartank, near Samarkand): Islamic scholar

**Type of ethics:** Religious ethics

**Achievements:** Author of *Al-jami al-sahih* (*The Sound Epitome*), a compendium of traditions (*ḥadîth*) relating to the life and times of Muhammad and the early Islamic community

**Significance:** Through his establishment of rigorous standards for the evaluation of *ḥadîth*, or traditions, al-Bukhârî helped to place Islamic ethics and jurisprudence on a new, historically documented level

From an early age, al-Bukhârî took an interest in the study of oral and written traditions hearkening back to the days of the first Muslims. By his late teens, he had traveled extensively in the Near East and had made a pilgrimage to Mecca and Medina. Because of the pressing need in contemporary Muslim society for explicit ethical and legal precepts that could be said to derive from Muḥammad's teachings and actions, it was vital that the historicity and accuracy of popular *ḥadîth* be determined. It is to al-Bukhârî's credit as a painstaking scholar and devoted traveler that he is said to have examined more than 600,000 *ḥadîth* during his lifetime. Of these, he designed 2,602 as authentic *(sahih)*. *Al-jami al-sahih* was intended to provide future generations of Muslims with verified historical, legal, and ethical material from which their societies could draw in times of need. This work still stands as the most respected collection of *ḥadîth* in the Islamic world.

**See also** Ḥadîth; Islamic ethics.

## Burke, Edmund

(Jan. 12, 1729, Dublin, Ireland—July 9, 1797, Beaconsfield, Buckinghamshire, England): Politician

**Type of ethics:** Politico-economic ethics

**Achievements:** Author of *The Speech on Moving His Resolutions for Conciliation with the Colonies* (1775) and *Reflections on the Revolution in France* (1790)

**Significance:** Offered a pragmatic organic model for the development of citizen's rights that became a pillar of modern conservatism

Burke's career, which began in 1759, was devoted to politics and journalism. He rose to prominence as a member of the Marquis of Rockingham's political faction, but his real fame was the result of his becoming the spokesman for the new Whig Party view of the constitution. Burke drew from the Revolution of 1688 a conception of the rights of citizens that was based on a combination of tradition and evolution. The natural order, set by God, would inevitably have inequalities, but the need to unify the nation led to rules that evolved into rights and privileges. Those with better situations were obligated by their privileges to act in the public interest, with respect for traditional rights. Burke's seemingly contradictory support for the rights of the Americans and the Irish and his savage denunciation of the French Revolution become quite consistent in view of his ideas of rights. The Crown, the power of which Burke was always eager to reduce, was infringing on traditional rights in America and Ireland, whereas the revolutionaries in France were attempting to create a wholly new society based on a utopian rationalistic model that, like all such models, could never exist in practice. In such a case, the existing good would be destroyed in pursuit of a pipe dream. It should be allowed to evolve over time in the natural order. Burke's *Reflections on the Revolution in France* (1790) was read all over Europe, provoking opposition to the revolution and giving his ideas a wide audience.

**See also** Conservatism; Human rights.

## Bushido

**Type of ethics:** Military ethics

**Date:** Coined seventeenth century in Japan

**Associated with:** Yamaga Soko (1622-1685), Japanese master of religion and military science

**Definition:** The term *bushido* literally means the "Way of the Warrior." This "Way" incorporates strict ethical responsibilities with a code of physical sacrifice

**Significance:** Bushido requires systematic training of mind and body, emphasizing absolute loyalty, spontaneity, collective responsibility, and personal sacrifice; this training has been adapted to business and religious practices

**History.** The "Way of the Warrior" derives from three early sources. First, the ancient animistic belief of the Japanese, known as Shintoism (the Way of the Gods) emphasized naturalness, sincerity, and the spirituality of all things Japanese. This tradition suffused bushido with the sense of a sacred link to one's peers, the soil, and the mission of Japan.

Second, during the twelfth century, a warrior class (*bushi*) emerged near present-day Tokyo. The bushi usurped power from the aristocratic elite in the capital of Kyoto, and conquered new territory in eastern Japan. Some of these bands gave allegiance to their lords through total self-renunciation and personal loyalty; others constantly shifted their allegiance for materialistic gain. Gradually, a code of ethics developed that stressed the samurai's unconditional willingness to die for his master. By the mid-seventeenth century, this code supported an attitude toward death that idealized and romanticized the warrior who was honor-bound to die for his lord, or even to commit ritualistic suicide (*seppuku*).

Third, the major religious influence on the warrior class was Zen Buddhism, which teaches that the goal of life is personal enlightenment through ascetic selflessness, rigorous discipline, and repetitive effort. Religious discipline must not, however, become lost in the drudgery of the rituals. Enlightenment is achieved through spontaneous, intuitive revelations, or single acts of self-awareness that can erupt from toilsome tasks. Enlightenment is not a consequence of rational judgment, but of sudden personal discovery.

**Principles of Bushido.** Yamaga Soko (1622-1685) synthesized the thinking of the various religious and military schools to describe what became known as "The Way of the Warrior." Yamaga related the traditional values of sincerity, loyalty, self-discipline, and self-sacrifice to the Chinese values of a sage. To be a real warrior, one needs to be cultivated in humanistic arts—that is, poetry, painting, calligraphy, and music—while in service to the master. The true sage combines the virtues of "wisdom, humanity, and valor" to perform his service to his lord's government.

During the peaceful Tokugawa era (1602-1868), the ethics of bushido prevented the military from becoming a warlike and oppressive elite. Rather, the samurai became administrators, accountants, artists, scholars, and entrepreneurs. Miyamoto Musashi combined the roles of warrior, artist, and intellectual. In 1643, he wrote a classic work on military strategy, *A Book of Five Rings*. As an artist, he became noted for the intensity of his extraordinary monochromatic ink paintings. Other samurai such as Uragami Gyokudo (1745-1820) renounced or neglected their military role and concentrated on the humanistic arts of music, painting, and literature. The Mitsui Company, one of Japan's largest business enterprises, was one of many Tokugawa businesses operated by a samurai family. These contributions to civil society helped Japan to develop economically and intellectually into the twentieth century.

There was also a non-Chinese or indigenous influence. The samurai classic *Hagakure* (1716), by Yamamoto Tsunetomo (1659-1719), provided the famous aphorism "bushido is a way of dying." Contrary to Yamaga's emphasis on public service or the balance between the military and civic role of the samurai, Yamamoto idealized and spiritualized the role of death. The loyal and self-abnegating samurai is expected to give his life spontaneously and unquestioningly for his master. A life that ends in death on the battlefield with unswerving hard work and dedication, or in ritualistic suicide, is glorious.

Yamaga and Yamamoto agreed that only through action could one pursue truth and self-enlightenment. The "Way of the Warrior" emphasized human performance, intuition, and spontaneity. Training in the martial arts (*bujutsu*) was an important technique to promote group cohesiveness and self-awareness. Through bujutsu the samurai discovers and overcomes his spiritual and physical weaknesses, thereby deepening his self-awareness and ultimately preparing himself for a life of service and a readiness to sacrifice.

The abolition of feudalism and the samurai class in 1872 did not also end the appeal of bushido. The rise of militant nationalism and Imperial Shintoism created a militaristic bushido. The publication of *Fundamentals of Our National Polity* by the Ministry of Education in 1937 declared in unequivocable terms that bushido was the "outstanding characteristic of our national morality." The new bushido "shed itself of an outdated feudalism . . . [and] became the Way of loyalty and patriotism, and has evolved before us as the spirit of the imperial forces." The Japanese soldier was called upon to sacrifice his life for the emperor. A strong central government and a fascist military system forcefully made the new bushido a significant part of Japan's imperialist expansion.

**Legacies.** Bushido is no longer a military force in Japan. The vainglorious attempt by the writer Yukio Mishima (1925-1970) to revive the martial spirit of Japan ended in his brutal and meaningless act of *seppuku*. Bushido's ethical foundations are, however, still part of Japanese culture and society. Bushido's stress on loyalty to the head of a group is still evident in the strong sense of loyalty workers have to their employers, students to their teachers, and apprentices to their masters. Corporate groups imitate the samurai system by dovetailing the personal values of their members with common group and public goals. Ethical training camps (a direct legacy of Zen martial arts training) for workers are week-long intensive seminars combining physical exertion with a type of group therapy. These consciousness-raising exercises are designed to create a loyal, harmonious, and ethical workforce.

**Conclusion.** The term *bushido* unfortunately invokes images of Japanese soldiers dashing off into suicidal missions against the enemy and committing atrocities of every kind. Since World War II, cartoons have depicted the Japanese businessman as a samurai (Japanese warrior) in a business suit. The relationship of bushido with the military nationalism of World War II and its alleged association with Japan's postwar economic expansion have obscured its ethical contributions of loyalty, frugality, and dedication to Japanese society and culture. —*Richard C. Kagan*

**See also** Chu Hsi; Military ethics; Wang Yang-ming; Zen.

**Bibliography**

Addiss, Stephen, and Cameron Hurst III. *Samurai Painters*. Tokyo: Kodansha, 1983.

De Bary, Theodore, with Ryusaku Tsunoda and Donald Keene. *Sources of Japanese Tradition*. New York: Columbia University Press. 1958.

Mishima, Yukio. *Way of the Samurai: Yukio Mishima on Hagakure in Modern Life*. Translated by Kathryn Sparling. New York: Basic Books, 1977.

Yamamoto, Tsunetomo. *Hagakure: The Book of the Samurai*. Tokyo: Kodansha, 1983.

## Business ethics

**Type of ethics:** Business and labor ethics

**Date:** From antiquity

**Definition:** The study of moral behavior in business and organizational circumstances; the application of ethical concepts to business relationships

**Significance:** Examines business goals and values, such as profit and power, in the light of traditional ethical principles and concepts

Business ethics enjoys a long history. Questions regarding inequalities of wealth have stirred ethical deliberation for every generation in all cultures. For example, the Old Testament, from the fifteenth century B.C.E., states that when buying from or selling to one another, "ye shall not *oppress* one another" (Leviticus 25:14) and that one must use "a perfect and just [weight and] measure," one that is neither too large nor too small, in one's business dealings (Deuteronomy 25:13-15). As civilizations have evolved from pastoral and agrarian to highly industrialized societies, and as humans have become increasingly interdependent, concerns about the proper way in which to conduct business have grown more complex. Especially since the Industrial Revolution, as business units have adopted corporate identities and have grown to be huge, and as rapid changes in technology have led to the development of extremely complex products and processes for manufacturing them, imbalances in power between buyer and seller, employer and employee, and business and community have focused increased attention on business ethics.

Since the late 1960's and early 1970's, as U.S. society increasingly questioned established institutions, business ethics and the concept of "corporate social responsibility" have been given ever-greater importance by business critics, in business school curricula, and inside corporate boardrooms. As environmentalism, consumerism, feminism, and the civil rights movement gained strength, it was natural that society would examine the extent to which the business community had been exacerbating these problems and would begin to expect that businesses would begin contributing to their solutions. Also at that time (1973-1974), the widespread corporate practice of bribing foreign officials and the numerous illegal corporate contributions to Richard M. Nixon's presidential campaign came to light, leading to more calls for a higher level of ethical standards among business executives.

**Frameworks of Analysis.** Ethicists generally have used three ethical concepts—utility, rights, and justice—to analyze and judge the morality of business behavior. Utilitarianism, a teleological approach, focuses on the results, or consequences, of any business decision. It requires managers first to identify all the costs and all the benefits to all of society of a given set of alternative business actions and then to choose that alternative that will provide society with the greatest net benefit. An important aspect of this framework is that it requires business managers to consider not only the consequences for their business—that is, the economic effects on their companies—but also the consequences to other elements of society. An advantage of the utilitarian approach for business ethics is that it corresponds closely to cost/benefit analyses, which managers are very accustomed to using in making normal business decisions. There are also, however, several disadvantages. First, it is difficult for managers to identify all costs and benefits, especially to all of society, as is required by utilitarianism. Second, it is extremely difficult to assign weights—that is, to measure the costs and especially the social benefits of a given alternative course of action. Benefits include an improvement in the general level of health, a greater enjoyment of life, and aesthetic improvements, which are notoriously difficult to measure. Third, utilitarianism ignores questions of individual or group rights and can sometimes lead to conclusions that seem unfair.

Using rights as the framework for analyzing business decisions requires that managers identify what stakeholders—that is, affected individuals or groups—will be involved in a particular decision, what rights those individuals or groups including the business may have, and what corresponding duties accompany those rights. As the German philosopher Immanuel Kant (1724-1804) stressed, people must be considered as ends in themselves and not merely as means toward some other end. This approach, which is called deontological, is quite different in that it ignores the consequences of a decision and focuses instead on principles. Thus, it has as its advantage the fact that it satisfies the disadvantage of the utilitarian approach. It has, however, several disadvantages. There will seldom be agreement regarding whether an individual or group has a right and regarding what the extent of that right may be. For example, do employees have a right to continued employment and to be terminated only "for cause"? To what extent do consumers have a right to safe products? Another disadvantage of a rights framework is that the rights of two or more stakeholder groups often compete or conflict with one another. This conflict necessitates a decision regarding whose rights will have priority.

A third framework for assessing the appropriateness or morality of business decisions involves focusing on justice or fairness. Justice requires an equitable distribution of life's benefits and burdens. Using this approach, managers would ask which of their alternative courses of action would be the most fair to all affected parties. The advantage of this framework is that justice and fairness are universally accepted as desirable qualities. The disadvantage is that there is very little agreement in defining these principles. A free, democratic, capitalistic system assumes that individuals pursue their own goals—in business terms, accumulate wealth—according to their individual and differing abilities. This necessarily leads to unequal distribution of income and assets and, therefore, of benefits and burdens. There are no precise, commonly accepted standards regarding what degree of inequality can still be considered fair and just.

**Relevant Issues.** The field of business ethics is most often organized around specific issues, and these issues can be grouped according to the stakeholders that are most affected. Business managers are faced with many questions. What is the nature of my company's relationship with this particular group of stakeholders? What rights do they have? What rights does the company have? What responsibilities does the company have to them? How does one resolve conflicting and competing claims among the various stakeholders?

A company's employees are one of its most important stakeholder groups, and there are a number of different issues that relate to employees. Discrimination in all of its many forms is one of the most common. Since the passage of the Civil Rights Act of 1964, along with certain subsequent legislation, employers are prohibited from discriminating on the basis of sex, race, national origin, religion, age, or disability in any of their employment policies: hiring, pay, promotion, benefits, or termination. Decisions in these matters must be made on the basis of an individual's ability to perform his or her job, with only a minimum number of exceptions, such as seniority. From an ethical point of view, this is seen as necessary to satisfy society's view of fairness and to protect each individual's right to equal opportunity. The issue is complicated, however, by such issues as affirmative action programs, which can lead to the possibility of reverse discrimination against majority groups; discrimination against groups left unprotected by the law; the nature of sexual harassment (a form of sex discrimination); and the determination of whether corporate ethical behavior requires equality of results, not merely equal opportunity.

Another set of ethical issues involves the question of employees' rights to privacy. Testing for employee drug use is the most common problem. On the one hand, employers have the right to insist on a drug-free workplace, to avoid the heavy costs (loss of productivity and so forth) that drug usage imposes, to protect other employees, and to ensure the high quality of their products. On the other hand, drug testing is sometimes seen as an invasion of employees' private, off-the-job lives; it is not directly related to job performance; it is particularly invasive, since it usually requires urine samples and the validity of those samples requires supervised urination; it may be imposed on some job classifications that are deemed especially sensitive in terms of public safety (for example, airline pilots and bus drivers) but not on others; managers are sometimes exempted; and tests are sometimes unannounced and conducted randomly, which may be perceived as unfair. Other privacy issues involve employees' political activities and their lifestyles in terms of sexual preferences; in these cases, the question is what right the employer has to intervene when and if profitable operation is adversely affected.

Employer-employee issues also include relationships and responsibilities to union organizations; whistle blowing; large-scale layoffs or plant-closing situations; the question of whether employees acquire over time some rights to retain their jobs; the question of whether employers have the duty to provide a minimal level of health insurance, child care, pension plans, and other benefits; and the question of whether workers have some rights to participate in management decisions that affect their jobs. In all these issues, managers must face the question of how far beyond minimum legal standards they are expected by prevailing social expectations to go.

**Customer Relationships.** Customers also represent a vital stakeholder group that defines yet another set of ethical issues. One of the most complex of these is product liability: a company's responsibility for any harm caused by its products or services. Although there is a considerable body of law, both statutory and court-determined, that applies to this subject, managers still face very difficult problems in deciding just how safe their products must be.

*Caveat emptor* ("Let the buyer beware") is no longer the guiding principle in transactions between buyers and sellers or between manufacturers and their customers. The courts and some state laws have moved steadily in the direction of placing on the manufacturer more and more of the responsibility for any harm done by its products or services. Under the concept of *strict liability*, it is no longer necessary

| BUSINESS ETHICS ISSUES AND CORRESPONDING U.S. LEGISLATION | | |
|---|---|---|
| **Issue** | **Date** | **Laws Affecting** |
| Discrimination in employment | 1963 | Equal Pay Act of 1963 |
| | 1964 | Civil Rights Act of 1964; Title VII |
| Employee privacy | 1988 | Polygraph tests: Federal legislation banning polygraphs for screening applicants and random testing of employees except in certain security situations |
| | | Drug testing: Various state and city laws prohibiting or limiting random testing |
| Sexual harassment | | EEOC guidelines interpreting Title VII |
| Employee safety and health | 1970 | Occupational Safety and Health Act |
| Consumer product safety | 1938 | Food; Drug; and Cosmetic Act |
| | 1958 | Delaney Clause |
| | 1966 | Hazardous Substances Labeling Act |
| | 1969 | Child Protection and Toy Safety Act |
| | 1972 | Consumer Product Safety Act |
| | 1976 | Magnuson-Moss Warranty Act |
| Truth in advertising | 1968 | Consumer Credit Protection Act; Title I; Truth in Lending Act |
| | 1993 | New labeling requirements from the FDA for all processed foods |
| Environmental protection | 1969 | National Environmental Protection Act |
| | 1971<br>1991 | Clean Air Act |
| | 1972 | Clean Water Act |
| | 1976 | Toxic Substances Control Act |
| | 1976 | Resource Conservation and Recovery Act |
| | 1980 | CERCLA (Superfund) |
| Bribery of foreign officials | 1977 | Foreign Corrupt Practices Act |
| South Africa: trade and investment | 1986 | Comprehensive Anti-Apartheid Act |
| Plant closings | 1988 | Worker Adjustment and Retraining Act |
| | 1988 | Economic Dislocation and Worker Adjustment Assistance Act |

for a claimant to prove that the manufacturer was negligent in the production or the design of the product. Courts routinely expect manufacturers to anticipate any potential problems and commonly hold manufacturers responsible for harm done even when it is shown that state-of-the-art scientific knowledge at the time of production could not have predicted such harm.

Another major category of ethical problems associated with the seller-buyer relationship stems from the advertising and other promotional tactics that the seller employs. Even most critics of business would agree that advertising serves a necessary and useful purpose in carrying out the marketing function. Advertisers are often tempted, however, to make claims about their products and services that are either blatantly fraudulent or can be easily misconstrued by the public. Various governmental agencies, such as the Food and Drug Administration and the Federal Trade Commission, have the statutory responsibility for protecting against dishonest advertising, and industry groups such as the Better Business Bureaus provide a self-policing function.

As the persuasive power of advertising messages has become more subtle, some businesses have been accused of exploiting certain "vulnerable" groups. Advertising directed at children, especially for such products as breakfast cereals and toys, has frequently been criticized. The argument is made that children lack the experience and the maturity to evaluate advertising messages, especially when manufacturers blur the lines between commercials and entertainment programs. Cigarette, alcoholic beverage, and handgun advertisers have also been sharply criticized, especially when they have "targeted" such groups as women and racial minorities with their product designs and advertising strategies.

**Environmental and Other Issues.** Another major category of business ethics problems is related to environmental or ecological concerns. It is now widely reported and understood that business, in its normal functions of manufacturing and transporting products, and the subsequent use of products such as automobiles and chemicals, contributes to all the various forms of pollution: air, water, and solid wastes. The ethical question is then posed: What responsibilities must business assume for the clean-up of polluted water and dump sites, in redesigning its products and processes, and in the liability for environmental damage done? Other subcategories of environmental problems include the wise use and conservation of nonrenewable resources (for example, proper forestry, mining, and agricultural techniques), the protection of endangered species, and animal rights (for example, the fur-garment industry and the use of laboratory animals to test the safety of cosmetics and other consumer products).

Two of the most widely reported instances of unethical (and illegal) business behavior, the trials and convictions of Ivan Boesky and Michael Milken, have involved the practice of *insider trading*. This term refers to the buying and selling of a company's securities by company officers and others who have access to privileged, not-yet-publicized information. Top management faces other ethical issues relating to corporate governance. Here, the question is raised whether managers, in their agency role, are acting in the best interests of shareholders or are acting primarily out of self-interest. The question is especially pertinent during mergers and acquisitions and when a manager's salary, incentive package, and termination package are determined. Critics argue that too much power has slipped away from shareholders and the board of directors and has been usurped by management. More outside (nonemployee) directors and more voting rights for shareholders are the usual recommended solutions.

**Transnational Problems.** There are two important business ethics issues involving a corporation's overseas operations. The first is the dilemma that sometimes arises regarding the need to be sensitive to a host country's customs and values and at the same time to hold true to fundamental ethical principles. The problem of bribery in certain countries and cultures is one example. This was highlighted during the 1970's by the revelation that Lockheed and other companies had been routinely bribing foreign government officials in return for certain business contracts and favors. This resulted in the passage of the Foreign Corrupt Practices Act of 1977. Another example is the often acrimonious debate during the 1970's and 1980's over whether U.S. corporations should do business in South Africa.

The second international issue is whether a business headquartered in an industrialized country has some special responsibilities when doing business in a developing economy. The marketing tactics of Nestle's infant formula in Third World countries were widely criticized during the late-1970's and led to a boycott of the company's products in the United States. Indiscriminate free sampling, heavy consumer advertising, and dressing the sales force in nurses' uniforms were seen as exploiting impoverished and often illiterate mothers. Another example of this issue is the legal exportation by U.S. manufacturers to Third World countries of toxic chemicals that have been banned for use in this country.

Interest in business ethics has increased since the mid-1980's in the academic community. Colleges and universities have incorporated ethics courses into their graduate and undergraduate business programs, sometimes as requirements for the degree. A number of professional academic societies, such as the Society for Business Ethics, hold annual meetings and encourage the writing and publication of scholarly papers. The Center for Business Ethics at Bentley College has sponsored a series of national conferences.

In the business community, there has also been a marked increase in the recognition of ethical problems. A number of companies have created the new position of "ethics officer." Most large companies have implemented programs that are designed to clarify their policies regarding ethical behavior, which are often referred to as corporate codes of conduct, and to inform their managers and employees at all levels of these policies. Johnson & Johnson credits the understanding of and respect for its credo throughout the organization with helping the company through its Tylenol crisis in 1982; its handling of the crisis was widely accepted as the quintessential example of positive ethical behavior by a corporation.

A number of corporate executives and scholars have investigated the possible linkage between "doing good and doing well." Can a manager actually improve the company's economic performance through ethical policies and practices? To date, there is no conclusive empirical data to support such a theory. There are also suggestions that the cause and effect are actually reversed—that only when corporations enjoy robust profits can they afford to be leaders and trend-setters in ethical practices. International Business Machines (IBM) Corporation, for example, maintained a no-layoff policy throughout its long and profitable history; in 1992, however, when the company sustained a large loss, it was forced to abandon this policy. —*D. Kirk Davidson*

**See also** Boycotts; Corporate responsibility; Hiring practices; Insider trading; Whistleblowing; White-collar crime.

**BIBLIOGRAPHY**

Acton, H. B. *The Morals of Markets: An Ethical Exploration.* Harlow, England: Longmans, 1971. This work covers the systemic level of business ethics in presenting a defense of capitalism, especially as it has developed in the United States.

De George, Richard T. *Business Ethics.* 3d ed. New York: Macmillan, 1990. An exposition on moral reasoning in business that includes good coverage of most of the important issues by a widely respected professor in the field.

Donaldson, Thomas. *The Ethics of International Business.* New York: Oxford University Press, 1989. Donaldson is one of the leading business ethicists in the United States. This work focuses only on international issues and develops positions based on the author's philosophical training and style of reasoning.

Smith, N. Craig, and John A. Quelch. *Ethics in Marketing.* Homewood, Ill.: Richard D. Irwin, 1993. An excellent collection of business case studies and articles from business periodicals on all aspects of marketing ethics: advertising, pricing, product policy, research, and so forth.

Velasquez, Manuel G. *Business Ethics: Concepts and Cases.* 3d ed. Englewood Cliffs, N.J.: Prentice-Hall, 1992. A very good all-purpose text on the subject. Explains in readable, straightforward language the three ethical frameworks for analyzing business behavior and the most important of the issues.

## Butler, Joseph (May 18, 1692, Wantage, Berkshire, England—June 16, 1752, Bath, England): Minister

**Type of ethics:** Religious ethics

**Achievements:** Author of *Fifteen Sermons* (1726) and *The Analogy of Religion, Natural and Revealed, to the Constitution and Course of Nature* (1736)

**Significance:** A pastor and bishop in the Church of England, Butler stressed the complexity of human nature and moral life and the importance of the conscience in decision making

In his sermons, Butler focused on various topics, including human nature and the love of one's neighbor. Humans and animals both have instincts, but humans also have a conscience, a superior inner sense of direction that holds authority over all other principles. Indeed, human government is possible only because people have this moral nature. One's conscience will direct one toward behavior that is most appropriate in the long run. It is possible, Butler conceded, to violate one's conscience in favor of some passion, but such behavior that gratifies the appetites at the expense of the conscience is unnatural. Conversely, acting in one's long-term self-interest is both rational and natural. Likewise, Butler contended, the conscience urges one to act benevolently toward other people, since such behavior is also in one's long-term best interest. Thus, love of one's neighbors is as natural as love of oneself. Virtues such as temperance and sobriety are traceable to the exercise of benevolence, and vices to ignoring it. Butler disagreed with Francis Hutcheson (1694-1747), however, that benevolence is the sum of virtue in human beings, though he thought it to be so in God. In humans, conscience dictates that one should never approve on the grounds of benevolence such acts as falsehood, violence, and injustice.

**See also** Altruism; Conscience.

**Calvin, John** (July 10, 1509, Noyon, Picardy, France—May 27, 1564, Geneva, Switzerland): Theologian

**TYPE OF ETHICS:** Religious ethics

**ACHIEVEMENTS:** Led the Swiss Reformed branch of the Protestant Reformation; author of *Christianae religionis institutio* (1536; *Institutes of the Christian Religion*, 1561)

**SIGNIFICANCE:** Calvin emphasized the sovereignty of God, seeing the ultimate fate of all humans as determined

Calvin studied theology, law, and classics, and he wrote his *Commentary on Lucius Anneas Seneca's Two Books on Clemency* (1532) by the age of twenty-three. His sympathies with emerging Protestant thinking caused him to flee Paris in 1534. He wrote the first edition of his *Institutes of the Christian Religion* in 1536 in Basel, Switzerland. That same year, he settled in Geneva, where he acted as both its civil and its religious leader. His own conversion experience gave him a sense of God's direct dealings with people. Calvin emphasized the sovereignty of God. He believed that knowledge of God came only through revealed scriptures, not through unaided human reason. Humans were created morally upright, but through Adam's sin human nature became "totally depraved"; that is, all human faculties have been corrupted, and as a result humans are incapable of any act that God would deem good. Salvation is thus necessary but is wholly the act of God. Jesus died to effect the salvation of those God elects, and even the faith to accept salvation is God's irresistible gift. God alone chooses who will and who will not receive the faith to accept forgiveness. Further, those whom God saves, God preserves. The responsibility of the Christian is to lead a moral, temperate life. Max Weber (*The Protestant Ethic and the Rise of Capitalism,* 1904-1905) has argued that Calvinism has given rise to a work ethic and capitalism, although that conclusion is debated.

**See also** Fatalism; God.

**Camus, Albert** (Nov. 7, 1913, Mondovi, Algeria—Jan. 4, 1960, near Villeblevin, France): Journalist and author

**TYPE OF ETHICS:** Modern history

**ACHIEVEMENTS:** Author of *L'Étranger* (1942; *The Stranger*, 1946), *Le Mythe de Sisyphe* (1942; *The Myth of Sisyphus and Other Stories*, 1955), *La Peste* (1947; *The Plague*, 1948), *L'Homme révolté* (1951; *The Rebel*, 1956), and *La Chute* (1956; *The Fall*, 1957), among other works

**SIGNIFICANCE:** Camus was an opponent of totalitarianism in any form and a proponent of the individual

Camus went to Paris in 1940 to work as a journalist. In 1943, he became a reader for the publishing firm Gallimard. He worked there until the end of his life to subsidize his writing. His writings can be divided into three periods: first, the period of the absurd or the antihero; second, the period of man in revolt, or the hero; and finally, the period of man on the earth. During the period of the absurd, which is best exemplified by the novel *The Stranger*, man kills and is killed in turn by the state in a relatively senseless existence. During the second period, characters who are larger than life defy the world's absurdity and find meaning in life. In both *The Plague* and *The Rebel,* heroic men fight to overcome the evils of totalitarianism. The struggle reveals possibilities of goodness and principled existence hitherto not present in Camus' work. During the final period, Camus often portrays characters who are wounded by their existence in the world. Yet these characters are often able to find some measure of human happiness and redemption in everyday life. Camus received the Nobel Prize in Literature in 1957. He died in an automobile accident in 1960.

**See also** Existentialism; Human rights; Moral realism; Moral responsibility.

## Cannibalism

**TYPE OF ETHICS:** Beliefs and practices

**ASSOCIATED WITH:** Tribes of so-called "primitive people" and survival situations that compel people to ingest human flesh in order to live

**DEFINITION:** The ingestion of human flesh by a human

**SIGNIFICANCE:** The morality of the practice of cannibalism is a matter of some controversy, especially because of the different kinds of circumstances in which it might occur

When investigating the morality of cannibalism, it is important to keep in mind several crucial distinctions. First and most important, there is the distinction between *lethal cannibalism,* which involves the cannibal's killing of the person whose flesh is eaten by the cannibal, and *nonlethal cannibalism,* which does not involve the cannibal's killing of the person whose flesh is eaten by the cannibal. Clearly enough, since it involves killing a person, lethal cannibalism is nearly always morally wrong. (Cases of morally permissible lethal cannibalism would be cases involving some special circumstance that justified killing another person; although this is very controversial, there may be cases in which lethal cannibalism is justified as a form of self-defense.)

Whereas it seems clear that lethal cannibalism is nearly always morally wrong, the moral status of nonlethal cannibalism is less clear. How might nonlethal cannibalism occur? One kind of case involves people who are stuck in places without food and are forced to consume the flesh of other people, with or without permission.

Thinking about this possibility (or about cannibalism in general) probably causes disgust or revulsion in many people. It is important, however, to recognize the distinction between what people find disgusting or repulsive and what people sense to be morally wrong. Many things are disgusting although they are not morally wrong (for example, the consumption of human waste). One must be careful not to infer that nonlethal cannibalism is morally wrong merely because one finds it disgusting or repulsive.

What should one say about the morality of nonlethal cannibalism? Perhaps what one should say here depends in part upon one's view of the relationship between human beings and their bodies. For example, if people are really nonphysical souls that are "attached" to physical bodies until the moment of death (when souls "leave" their bodies), then nonlethal cannibalism might seem to be morally permissible after death. After the soul has left the body, in this view, the dead person's body is very similar to the dead body of an animal, and it seems morally permissible to many people to consume dead animals.

(Of course, this argument could be reversed; if one believed that it was morally impermissible to consume dead animals, then one could draw the same conclusion about dead persons. There are interesting similarities between arguments concerning nonlethal cannibalism and arguments concerning the consumption of animals; it is important in both cases to observe the lethal/nonlethal distinction.)

A similar argument is suggested by the very different view that persons are physical creatures without nonphysical souls. In this view, death involves the cessation of bodily function. While a person is alive, she is identical to her body; once she has died, however, she ceases to exist and her body becomes a physical object much like the body of a dead animal. As previously mentioned above, if it is morally permissible to consume the flesh of a dead animal, then it might seem morally permissible to consume the flesh of a dead person.

Another consideration that suggests this conclusion is the fact that, typically, the bodies of dead persons naturally decompose and become changed into other organic substances. Sometimes these same bits of matter eventually become parts of new plants or animals, which are consumed by human persons in morally permissible ways. At what point in this transition does it become morally permissible to consume the matter in question? It seems hard to offer a nonarbitrary answer, which suggests that it is morally permissible to ingest the matter in question at any stage in the process, even when it is still recognizable as part of a dead person's body. (Of course, this argument could also be reversed: One might conclude instead that it is morally impermissible to ingest the matter in question at any stage in the process.)

There are other considerations, however, that must be weighed against these arguments on behalf of the moral permissibility of nonlethal cannibalism. For example, it might be suggested that unless the lives of other people are at stake, respect for dead people requires that their bodies not be ingested by others. It also might be argued that religious prescriptions concerning the treatment of dead persons' bodies make nonlethal cannibalism morally impermissible. Finally, it might be unwise to permit nonlethal cannibalism because such a policy might encourage lethal cannibalism, which is almost always morally wrong.

Because of the arguments on both sides and the controversial issues that surround them, it is very difficult to settle the dispute over the morality of nonlethal cannibalism in a brief article such as this one. Hence, people should consider carefully the arguments on both sides in order to arrive at a well-informed opinion. —*Scott A. Davison*

**See also** Animal rights; Death and dying; Dominion over nature, human; Immortality; Life and death; Moral status of animals; Taboos; Vegetarianism.

**Bibliography**

Hogg, Garry. *Cannibalism and Human Sacrifice.* New York: Citadel Press, 1966.

Read, Piers Paul. *Alive: The Story of the Andes Survivors.* Philadelphia: Lippincott, 1974.

Sanday, Peggy Reeves. *Divine Hunger.* Cambridge: Cambridge University Press, 1986.

Simpson, A. W. Brian. *Cannibalism and the Common Law.* Chicago: University of Chicago Press, 1984.

Tannahill, Reay. *Flesh and Blood.* New York: Stein and Day, 1975.

## Capital punishment

**Type of ethics:** Legal and judicial ethics

**Date:** From antiquity

**Associated with:** Supporting capital punishment: Washington Legal Foundation; Opposing: Amnesty International, American Civil Liberties Union, and the National Association for the Advancement of Colored People

**Definition:** Execution for a crime on the grounds of justice and/or deterrent benefit to society

**Significance:** An ethical and legal life-and-death issue that may be seen in the contexts of justice, deterrence, and the progress of society

**History.** Capital punishment is present in the earliest criminal codes and is probably as old as civilization itself. Hammurabi's code, in the eighteenth century B.C.E., provided for capital punishment for a number of offenses, including murder, putting a death spell on another, lying in a capital trial, and adultery. At the time of the Industrial Revolution, England employed the death penalty for more than two hundred offenses, including cutting down a tree and picking pockets. Throughout history, capital punishment has been applied more readily to the lower economic and social classes.

The history of the practice raises the question of "cruel and unusual punishment." Execution has occurred through boiling, burning, choking, dismembering, slicing away the body bit by bit, impaling, disemboweling, crucifixion, hanging, stoning, and burying alive. Today's gas chambers, electric chairs, and lethal injections are seen by many as humane advances; others respond that the guillotine also was once seen as humane.

Because of constitutional challenges, no executions took place in the United States between 1967 and 1977. The U.S. Supreme Court in 1972 (*Furman v. Georgia*) ruled that capital punishment was a violation of the Eighth Amendment's prohibition against "cruel and unusual punishment" because the penalty was being administered in an "arbitrary and capricious manner." Many states then began to redraft their statutes on capital punishment. In 1976 (*Gregg v. Georgia*), the Supreme Court ruled that the death penalty is not unconstitutional as long as there is a system (such as Georgia's list of aggravating circumstances) that is intended to prevent juries from imposing the sentence in an arbitrary or capricious manner.

Since capital punishment resumed in the United States in 1977, all those executed have been found guilty either of murder or of committing an action that, although not classified as murder, led to the death of another person. Various state statutes also allow capital punishment for treason, aircraft piracy, and train-wrecking.

**Retributive Justice.** One argument for capital punishment appeals to the desire for a retribution to fit the offense, as expressed by the saying "an eye for an eye, and a tooth for a tooth." It has been argued, most eloquently by Immanuel Kant in the eighteenth century, that the only fitting repayment for murder is the life of the murderer, for to permit any other punishment would be to devalue the unconditional worth of a human being. Kant takes the unusual tack of arguing that it also would be an offense to the murderer *not* to take his life, for not to do so would imply that the murderer was not responsible for his actions and was thus not a human being.

Several objections are made to the retributive justice arguments. First, it may be argued that on Kant's own grounds of the unconditional worth and dignity of the individual, execution should not take place, for surely the concept of unconditional worth applies even to a murderer. Second, many social scientists would argue that two centuries of empirical investigation since Kant have shown that murderers are often *not* responsible for their actions. Third, it is clear that by Kant's insistence that the murderer not be maltreated in his death, Kant is saying that justice requires not an identical act as retribution, but one of likeness or proportion. Therefore, would not a life sentence without the possibility of parole be proportionate, and in addition allow for the reversal of erroneous verdicts?

**Deterrence.** The reform movements of the eighteenth and nineteenth centuries, led intellectually in Great Britain by the utilitarians Jeremy Bentham and John Stuart Mill, questioned the logic behind the widely varying punishments set forth in the legal codes. The utilitarians questioned the authority of religion and tradition, pointing to the often inhumane results of such reasoning by authority. Instead of basing legal Penalties on retribution, the utilitarian agenda of maximizing the pleasure and minimizing the pain of a society called for penalties based on deterrence: penalties should be only as harsh as necessary to prevent an undesirable activity from occurring, and no harsher. This utilitarian approach has been used to argue both for and against capital punishment.

Some argue that capital punishment is necessary as a deterrent against further murders. Surely, they reason, having one's life taken is the greatest fear that a person should have, and a swift and just application of the death penalty would prevent many future murders from occurring. Execution would obviously deter convicted murderers from committing later offenses, and would also deter potential murderers who would fear the consequences.

Numerous objections have been raised to the deterrence argument. First, while deterrence seems to be a modern, progressive view that is far more reasonable than an "eye for an eye," opponents point out that society is still engaging in the barbaric practice of taking human life. In addition, the argument from progress can well be used against capital punishment, since only two Western countries still have capital punishment: the United States and South Africa. Second, it is not at all intuitively clear that one would fear a relatively painless death, say by lethal injection, more than one would fear the prospect of unending days in prison. Third, there is great question about the empirical claim that the death penalty actually *does* deter potential murderers. Opponents argue that of the many studies done, none has ever showed convincing evidence that the death penalty is an effective deterrent. Many murders are crimes of passion in which the murderer does not rationally assess the penalty he or she might face if apprehended and convicted.

Others argue that the death penalty continues to be "cruel and unusual punishment" because it is disproportionally given to minorities and the poor. Of the 199 executions from 1977 through April 21, 1993, only one was for the execution of a white person killing a black person. Several studies conclude that a prime factor in determining whether the death penalty will be imposed is the race of the victim. Regardless of the race of the defendant, the death penalty is imposed far more often if the victim is white.

*—Norris Frederick*

**See also** Criminal punishment; Homicide; Punishment.

**BIBLIOGRAPHY**

Amnesty International. *The Death Penalty*. London: Amnesty International, 1979.

Bedau, Hugo Adam, ed. *The Death Penalty in America*, 3d ed. New York: Oxford University Press, 1982.

Berns, Walter. *For Capital Punishment*. New York: Basic Books, 1979.

Van den Haag, Ernest, and John P. Conrad. *The Death Penalty: A Debate*. New York: Plenum Press, 1983.

## Capitalism

**TYPE OF ETHICS:** Politico-economic ethics

**DATE:** Late eighteenth century, generally coinciding with the Industrial Revolution

**DEFINITION:** An economic system based on the concepts of private property and individual liberties

**SIGNIFICANCE:** Profoundly affects standards of living and levels of personal freedom

An economic system is a set of arrangements by means of which people living in a relatively large group, generally a country, make decisions about how they will produce, distribute, and consume goods and services. Broadly speaking, those decisions can be made by means of either central planning by the government or consumer choice in a free market.

The existence of the capitalist economic system that prevails in the United States is made possible by the political system, which is based on the idea of the highest possible level of individual freedom and responsibility. Capitalism emphasizes three principles: the private ownership of property, including the means of production; the dominance of the consumer, who is free to buy or not, as he or she pleases; and individual rewards for those producers whose products please the consumer.

**A Frame of Reference.** In every field of human activity, ethics involves determining what types of human behavior are right, good, and to be encouraged, and what types are wrong, bad, and to be avoided. In order to make such determinations, there must be standards against which to judge specific actions and sets of rules that are used to guide the personal decision-making process.

The most appropriate ethical system by which to judge capitalism is, as it happens, also the ethical system that has exerted the most influence over the past several hundred years: utilitarianism. Developed during the nineteenth century by John Stuart Mill, utilitarianism has as its *summum bonum*, its highest good, the principle of the greatest good for the greatest number, which, Mill said, "holds that actions are right in proportion as they tend to promote happiness, wrong as they tend to produce the reverse of happiness." (Each ethical system has its own *summum bonum*. What has been described here applies specifically to Mill's utilitarianism.)

Matters of human happiness and well-being generally bring to mind conditions that are measured by degrees of political liberty and freedom from oppression. If people in a society are enjoying political freedom and democratic government, if they are not living under a military dictatorship or in a police state, and if they have elections that are fair and honest, the spectrum of activities in which day-to-day freedom is a major factor would seem to be covered. Yet that may not be the case. In a democracy, it is true that the majority rules, and that would appear to be consistent with the principle of the greatest happiness for the greatest number. A closer look, however, gives rise to a question: How is the minority represented? Consider, for example, that, even with the greatest degree of political freedom, an individual voter generally is faced with only two choices. An issue passes or fails. A candidate wins or loses. It is a fact that, although the supporters of an unsuccessful issue or candidate may not be completely ignored, they are not represented in the same way that the majority is. To say this is, to be sure, not to disparage democratic freedoms or personal liberties or free elections. It is simply to state that, by their very nature, political (government-developed) responses to human needs usually have one great limitation: They provide a single or a very limited selection. That limitation applies also to government-developed responses to economic questions involving the production, distribution, and consumption of goods and services, to the arrangements for the actual day-to-day business of providing for oneself. It affects the standard of living and the quality of life.

**Consumer Happiness.** Capitalism, however, once established as an economic system within a free political system, can offer the individual consumer, who is voting with dollars at the cash register with each purchase, a huge number of choices. Free entry into markets brings out multiple producers, all of whom offer their wares and are able to satisfy, together, virtually all consumers by satisfying separately a large number of very small markets, producing in the end the greatest happiness for the greatest number and achieving the *summum bonum* of Mill's utilitarianism.

The incentive for producers to enter any market in a capitalist system is to try to satisfy as many people as possible in order to make a profit, which comes to a producer as the result of sufficient voluntary patronage by free consumers. That tangible reward for producers induces them to put forth their best efforts, to produce the best product, and to attempt to capture the largest share of their market. The principal beneficiary of profit, therefore, is not the producer but the consumer. Building a better mousetrap will certainly make the producer prosperous, but the real payoff for society at large is that the better mousetrap will catch everyone's mice, and in that way everyone will be better off. In other words, the *summum bonum,* the greatest happiness, is achieved.

Nevertheless, it is still often said that capitalism, with its emphasis on the profit incentive, has no ethics or principles. That view misunderstands, however, the real and fundamental nature of profit as it relates to the consumer. Profit is a means of communication from consumer to producer. It is the consumer's voice and the producer's ears. Because it is communication that cannot be ignored by the producer, who wants to stay in business, it is a device that enables the control of the producer by the consumer. Profit exists only when a sufficiently large segment of a producer's market has chosen to buy the product being offered for sale. If customers are not happy, they do not buy, and there is no profit. Profit is a real-time indicator of the degree to which a producer is serving the greatest-happiness principle.

**The Real Test.** The true test of any economic system, however, asks but one question: How well are those who are using it able to provide for themselves and their families? Even a cursory glance around the world will reveal at once that capitalism has proved itself best able to improve the human condition. When the question of the unequal distribution of wealth in a capitalist society is raised, it should be noted that people in noncapitalist states are working very hard indeed to establish capitalism. Capitalism is the economic system of choice when people are free to choose their own economic system. —*John Shaw*

**See also** Communism; Economics; Marxism; Socialism.

**BIBLIOGRAPHY**

Beaud, Michel. *A History of Capitalism: 1500-1980.* Translated by Tom Dickman and Anny LeFebvre. New York: Monthly Review Press, 1983.

Friedman, Milton, with Rose D. Friedman. *Capitalism and Freedom.* Chicago: University of Chicago Press, 1962.

Heilbroner, Robert L. *The Nature and Logic of Capitalism.* New York: Norton, 1985.

Rand, Ayn. *Capitalism: The Unknown Ideal.* New York: New American Library, 1966.

Wright, David McCord. *Capitalism.* Chicago: Regnery, 1962.

## Caste system, Hindu

**Type of ethics:** Beliefs and practices

**Date:** First millennium B.C.E. to present

**Definition:** A social order indigenous to India in which society is divided into hierarchically ranked, occupationally specialized, endogamous groups

**Significance:** Founded on the principle that ethics are not universalist but are relative to one's niche in society

The Hindu caste system is one of the most ancient forms of social organization in the world. It is based on the conception of society as an organic whole in which each group serves a particular function. The social order of caste emphasized hierarchy and interdependence rather than equality and independence. Though the idea of caste is most fully elaborated and justified in the Hindu religious tradition, elements of caste organization have permeated South Asian society generally. The caste system is being eroded by urbanization, industrialization, and the increasing influence of Western ideas.

**Characteristics of Caste.** From a sociological viewpoint, the caste system can be defined as a form of social stratification based on hierarchically ranked, occupationally specialized, endogamous (in-marrying) groups. Caste is an ascribed rather than an achieved status, meaning that an individual is born into the caste niche that he or she will occupy throughout life.

There are four basic caste levels, or *varṇa* in the Hindu system. The highest ranked level is that of the *brāhmin*, traditionally associated with the priesthood. The second level is that of the *kṣatriya*, warriors and rulers, and the third is that of the *vaiśya* or merchants. The bottom level is that of the *śūdra*, the commoners. Beneath the four major *varṇa* of the system are the outcastes, or untouchables.

Within the *varṇa* categories of Hindu society are numerous smaller groupings called *jāti.* (The English word "caste" is used, somewhat confusingly, to refer to both *varṇa* and *jāti.*) Like the *varṇa* themselves, *jāti* are also ranked strictly in terms of social prestige. Intricate rules govern the interactions of the *jāti* in daily life; for example, some groups may not accept food from other groups, some groups have access to sacred scriptures and some do not, and some groups must indicate humility and subservience before other groups. In addition to rules that divide and separate people, however, there is another principle that unites them: *jajmani,* or the exchange of services. Through a *jajmani* relationship, a *jāti* of shoemakers might exchange services with a *jāti* of potters, for example, however separate they may be in other areas of social life.

**History of Caste.** Though some scholars search for the roots of India's caste system in the ancient civilization of the subcontinent, the Indus Valley or Harappan civilization, the earliest clear evidence for caste is found in the texts of Indo-European groups who migrated into the area in several waves beginning about 1500 B.C.E. These texts, collectively called the *Vedas*, or books of knowledge, which became the sacred texts of the Hindu religion, describe three classes of society roughly corresponding to the top three *varṇa* of the later system. Though archaeological and historical evidence for this ancient period is scanty, most people believe that the fourth, or *śūdra*, *varṇa* was added to the three Indo-European classes as these immigrants moved into the subcontinent, encountering indigenous people who were pushed to the lowest position in the social hierarchy. Supporting this scenario is the fact that the top three *varṇa* are called *ārya*, or "pure" (from "Aryan," another name for the Indo-Europeans), while the *śūdra varṇa* is *anārya,* "impure" (un-Aryan). The untouchable stratum, with its particularly despised status, would have been added to the system as the migration southward forced the Indo-Europeans into contact with even more remote indigenous peoples.

Buddhism and Jainism, which arose during the fifth century B.C.E., were in part rebellions against Vedic society with its unequal social divisions. Both religions renounced the institution of caste, and Buddhism became particularly popular in India by about the third century B.C.E. Afterward, however, there was a revival of Vedic tradition with its attendant social order, which became codified in legal treatises such as the Code of Manu. While it is unclear whether the rules prescribed for caste behavior in such texts were enforced, certainly the conception of what caste meant and how a caste system should function was solidified by the middle of the first millennium C.E. The religious tradition of Hinduism, which arose out of a synthesis of Vedicism, Buddhism, Jainism, and other strands of thought and culture, developed an intricate philosophical justification for caste that remains viable for many Hindus today.

**Religious Justification for Caste.** The Hindu understanding of caste is tied to the notion of reincarnation, an eschatology that sees souls as being reborn after death in an endless cycle. Dependent on the *karma* an individual has accumulated during his or her lifetime, he or she might be reborn at a higher or lower level than during his or her previous life. One implication of this vision is that the respect that one owes to high-caste individuals has been earned by them in previous lifetimes, and that the scorn heaped upon those of low birth is deserved because of similar past deeds.

Linked to this understanding of *karma* is the notion of *dharma*, or duty, meaning in the Hindu sense duty to one's caste niche. "One's own duty imperfectly performed is better than another's duty perfectly performed," is the wisdom offered by the Bhagavad Gītā, a text holy to many Hindus. In one scene in this text, a *kṣatriya* prince named Arjuna hesitates on the eve of battle out of an ethical concern for killing, and is advised by his charioteer Kṛṣṇa that since he is of *kṣatriya*, or warrior, status, his *dharma* is to kill. The highest ethic for him is to do what he was born to do (that is, to fight), which will then accrue positive rather than negative *karma.* Another's *dharma*, and hence his or her *karma,* would be different. This is the particularism of Hinduism's ethical tradition, which leads to an unwillingness to generalize about rights and wrongs of human action in the universalist way familiar to most Westerners.

Another component of Hinduism's conceptualization of caste involves the traditional cosmogony in which the various levels of society were created out of the primordial cosmic being, the *brāhmin* arising from his mouth, the *kṣatriya* from his arms, the *vaiśya* from his thighs, and the *śūdra* from his feet. This vision of the divine spirit being equivalent to the social order itself leads to a sense of division and difference as themselves holy. Combined with the notion of a moral duty to accept one's caste position as discussed above, this image contributes to a deep resistance to change in the caste system.

Although caste has been abolished in legal terms in modern India, it continues to function on many levels of social life. In recent years, there has been some attempt on the part of the government of India to uplift those of lower-caste backgrounds through preferential admissions and hiring policies, but caste conflict remains a potent force in Indian politics.

**Interpretations of Caste.** Among many perspectives on the caste system, two general trends can be discerned. Some prefer to emphasize the consensus that is implicit in the conceptualization of society as an organic whole, contrasting this with the individualist and competitive character of social relations in Western societies. Others focus on the degree of conflict that is inherent in the caste model, which privileges some groups and subordinates others. The first of these is most common in the Indian Hindu community and is favored by many Indian and Western social scientists, while the second is expressed most vociferously by non-Hindu minorities and by Marxist scholars. Western interpretations of caste are tied into the notion of cultural relativism—the idea that other cultures have to be understood in their own terms and not in those imposed by the West. While this concept leads many to respect caste as an indigenous form of social organization, others believe that it needs to be circumscribed by a cross-cultural commitment to human rights and basic equality. The caste system of India therefore provides an entry point to some of the key issues facing those who are interested in the study of other cultures.

*—Cynthia Keppley Mahmood*

**See also** Bhagavad Gītā; Hindu ethics.

**Bibliography**

Das, Veena. *Structure and Cognition: Aspects of Hindu Caste and Ritual.* 2d ed. Delhi, India: Oxford University Press, 1990.

Dumont, Louis. *Homo Hierarchicus: The Caste System and Its Implications.* Translated by Mark Sainsbury, Louis Dumont, and Basia Gulati. Chicago: University of Chicago Press, 1980.

Freeman, James M. *Untouchable: An Indian Life History.* Stanford, Calif.: Stanford University Press, 1979.

Joshi, Barbara, ed. *Untouchable! Voices of the Dalit Liberation Movement.* London: Zed Books, 1986.

Kolenda, Pauline. *Caste in Contemporary India: Beyond Organic Solidarity.* Menlo Park, Calif.: Benjamin/Cummings, 1978.

McGilvray, Dennis B., ed. *Caste Ideology and Interaction.* New York: Cambridge University Press, 1982.

Naipaul, V. S. *India: A Million Mutinies Now.* London: Heinemann, 1990.

## Casuistry

**Type of ethics:** Theory of ethics
**Dates:** Prominent 1200 to 1650, 1970 to present
**Definition:** A method of resolving ethical dilemmas through the analysis and comparison of individual cases of decision making
**Significance:** For millennia, casuistry was an influential method in Judaic and Christian ethics; it reemerged in the 1970's as a dominant approach in professional ethics and especially in bioethics

Casuistry focuses on cases of decision making in which agreed-upon moral principles do not provide obvious answers about what would be the right action. The method involves comparing a difficult case with settled cases and using these comparisons, along with agreed-upon principles, to debate what should be done in the difficult case. Casuistry is a natural method that is employed by nearly every human culture. It was self-conciously developed and taught in Greco-Roman rhetoric and in Judaism, and it was dominant in Christianity from 1200 to 1650. Casuistry decreased in influence thereafter, partly as a result of its abuse by some medieval authors to justify whatever decision they preferred, and partly as a result of the rise of systematic moral theory. Since a consensus on moral theory did not develop, however, and modernity brought new moral problems, casuistry continued to be employed. It has been especially prominent since the 1970's in professional ethics.

**See also** Applied ethics; Intuitionist ethics; Situational ethics.

## Censorship

**Type of ethics:** Arts and censorship
**Date:** c. 360 B.C.E. to present
**Associated with:** Conflicts regarding the importance of freedom of expression relative to the importance of public standards of morality and public welfare
**Definition:** The official scrutiny and consequent suppression of publications, performances, and various art forms that fail to meet institutional standards concerning religion, morality, or politics

| Legislation Related to Censorship and Freedom of Expression in the United States | | | |
|---|---|---|---|
| **Date** | **Medium** | **Case** | **Result of Case** |
| 1868 | books | *Regina v. Hicklin*, L.R. 3 Q.B. 360 | First legal standard for obscenity: tendency to corrupt minds of those most susceptible. |
| 1919 | circulars | *Abrams v. U.S.*, 250 U.S. 616 | Conviction for conspiracy to advocate resistance to war was affirmed. In dissent Justice Holmes cited "argument from truth": Truth can only be found in the marketplace of ideas. |
| 1934 | books | *U.S. v. One Book Entitled Ulysses*, 72 F.2d 705 | Ending of Hicklin rule; entire work judged by dominant effect on average people. |
| 1942 | speech | *Chaplinsky v. New Hampshire*, 568 U.S. 571 | Insulting or fighting words unprotected by the First Amendment. |
| 1952 | film | *Joseph Burstyn, Inc. v. Wilson*, 343 U.S. 495 | Film could not be banned as sacrilegious; film is expressive communication protected by First Amendment. |
| 1957 | books, circulars, ads | *Roth v. U.S.*, 354 U.S. 476 | First set of standards to determine obscenity beyond First Amendment protection. |
| 1958 | speech | *Speiser v. Randall*, 357 U.S. 513 | Mandatory loyalty oath a violation of free speech. |
| 1961 | film | *Times Film Corp. v. Chicago*, 365 U.S. 43 | Screening prior to permit not void as prior restraint. |
| 1963 | books | *Bantam Books v. Sullivan*, 372 U.S. 58 | Procedure used to police books for obscenity violates First and Fourteenth Amendments. |
| 1964 | film | *Jacobellis v. Ohio*, 378 U.S. 184 | Film found not obscene under *Roth* standard. |
| 1965 | film | *Freedman v. Maryland*, 380 U.S. 51 | Procedural requirements in case of film censorship unconstitutional; this case terminated film censorship as such in the U.S. |
| 1966 | book | *Memoirs v. Mass.*, 383 U.S. 51 | Refined the *Roth* standard; *Fanny Hill* found not obscene. |
| 1968 | "symbolic speech" | *U.S. v. O'Brien*, 391 U.S. 367 | Burning draft card was "symbolic speech." |
| 1971 | words on clothing | *Cohen v. California*, 403 U.S. 15 | Epithet printed on jacket did not constitute obscenity but was protected speech. "One man's vulgarity is another man's lyric." |
| 1973 | film | *Paris Adult Theatre I. v. Slaton*, 413 U.S. 49 | Companion case to *Miller*, below; material found to be hard-core pornography not protected under First Amendment. |
| 1973 | books, photos, and brochures | *Miller v. California*, 413 U.S. 15 | Conviction of obscenity upheld; three-pronged test for obscenity established, overruling previous standards. |
| 1974 | film | *Jenkins v. Georgia*, 418 U.S. 153 | Application of *Miller*; film "Carnal Knowledge" not obscene. |
| 1975 | film | *Ernoznik v. Jacksonville*, 422 U.S. 205 | Ordinance prohibiting film with nude scenes at drive-in unconstitutional. |
| 1982 | film | *New York v. Ferber*, 458 U.S. 747 | Statute prohibiting sexual performance of children was upheld; child pornography passed *Miller* test. |
| 1982 | books | *Board of Education v. Pico*, 73 LEd 2d 435 | Divided majority of the Court found that removal of books from school libraries on grounds of being anti-Christian, anti-Semitic, and just plain filthy violated terms of First Amendment. |
| 1990 | dance | *Miller et al. v. Civil City of South Bend*, 904 F2d 1081 | Nude dancing not obscene and protected expression under First Amendment. |
| 1991 | dance/grants | *Bella Lewitzky Dance Foundation v. Frohnmayer et al.*, 754 F Supp 774 | Decency oath unconstitutional condition for grant funds. |
| 1991 | performance artists | *Karen Finley et al. v. NEA and Frohnmayer*, 795 F Supp 1457 | Denial of grant funds based on decency provision of grant enabling statute in violation of First Amendment. |

**SIGNIFICANCE:** Justification of censorship in virtually all cultures is founded upon policies concerning public welfare and morals; ethical arguments are at the core of any controversy about censorship

Since classical times, proponents of censorship have invoked religion or government to promote the repression of material that purportedly threatened public morals or controlling institutions. In this context, artistic expression has been targeted as potentially harmful by ancient philosophers, religious organizations, special-interest groups, and governmental bodies. Throughout the ages, the basic arguments for and against freedom of expression have remained remarkably the same.

**History.** Plato (428-348 B.C.E.) was among the earliest proponents of censorship of the arts. His *Laws* (360 B.C.E.) argued for strict censorship of the literary and visual arts, particularly poetic metaphor, which he claimed interfered with achieving pure, conceptual truth.

Early Christianity took a similar position concerning mythology and art. The Roman Catholic church eventually utilized censorship to control philosophical, artistic, and religious truth generally. In 1521, Holy Roman Emperor Charles V issued the Edict of Worms, which prohibited the printing, dissemination, or reading of Martin Luther's work. The *Index librorum prohibitorum* (1564), which was published by the Vatican, condemned specific books. The *Index* included such works as Galileo Galilei's *Dialogue Concerning the Two Chief World Systems* (1632); Galileo was subsequently prosecuted for heresy during the Inquisition.

The scope of governmental censorship in Europe changed with the separation of powers between the church and state. When church courts were abolished and religious beliefs and morés were no longer subject to government control, censorship laws focused on political speech and writing. Works criticizing government practices ran the risk of prosecution for seditious libel in England; in France, Napoleon censored newspapers, publications, theatrical productions, and even private correspondence at will.

Politically motivated censorship became common in countries with totalitarian governments, from communism to dictatorships. *The Communist Manifesto* (1848) of Karl Marx and Friedrich Engels was banned throughout Europe, yet subsequently communist leaders from Lenin to Mao Tse-tung to Fidel Castro routinely practiced political censorship. In the Soviet Union, political censorship targeted the arts when it imposed the doctrine of "socialist realism" in 1932. The following year in Germany, Adolf Hitler organized nationwide book burnings in the name of the National Socialist government. Soviet-bloc writers, artists, and scientists have been imprisoned, exiled, and have had their work confiscated, when it has been deemed ideologically impure. Aleksandr Solzhenitsyn was arrested in 1945 for a pejorative remark about Joseph Stalin, spent eleven years in prison, and was finally exiled in 1974. In Muslim fundamentalist countries, religious censorship is the norm. For example, the publication of Salman Rushdie's *The Satanic Verses* (1989) prompted Iran's Ayatollah Khomeini to pronounce a *fatwa*, calling for Rushdie's death and forcing the author into seclusion. Public political debate was given constitutional protection in some jurisdictions. Article 5 of the Basic Law of West Germany (1949) and Article 10 of the European Convention on Human Rights and Fundamental Freedoms (1953) specifically provided for free speech rights. The First Amendment to the U.S. Constitution, ratified in 1791, expressly prohibited Congress from making any law that abridged freedom of speech, press, religion, assembly, or the right to petition the government for redress of grievances. This right to free speech was not, however, absolute. The First Amendment has generated an enormous amount of litigation over its interpretation, particularly when it has collided with other rights in American society.

The degree to which the principle of free speech has been extended to the arts has been a matter of case law in all jurisdictions in which censorship has been scrutinized. Most troublesome for the courts has been the issue of the protection of allegedly obscene or pornographic material.

When free expression has come into conflict with potentially overriding public policy concerns, the courts have engaged in complex legal reasoning, often guided by philosophical and political arguments, in order to determine which interests dominate. Despite the evolution of cultural values, vestiges of several arguments remain common to most court deliberations of the free speech principle.

The argument from truth (also referred to as the libertarian argument) has been associated with the works of John Stuart Mill, but it was also articulated by John Milton two hundred years earlier. It emphasizes the importance of open discussion to the discovery of truth as a fundamental good and invaluable to the development of society. To some extent, this philosophy has been utilized by the U.S. Supreme Court, first in Justice Oliver Wendell Holmes's now-famous dissent, in *U.S. v. Abrams* (1919), although its application is limited to speech with political, moral, aesthetic, or social content.

The argument from democracy views freedom of speech as a necessary component of any democratic society, in which public discussion is a political duty. Alexander Meiklejohn is one of its leading proponents, and similar theories are found in the works of Immanuel Kant, Baruch Spinoza, and David Hume. Meiklejohn considered the First Amendment a protection of the right of all citizens to discuss political issues and participate in government. Similarly, the German Constitutional Court and the European Court have recognized the importance of public debate on political questions. The argument from democracy has had little success in cases involving nonpolitical speech.

Unlike the previous two arguments, the argument from individuality is rights-based rather than consequentialist, recognizing the interest of the speaker, rather than society, as being paramount. It asserts that there is an individual right to freedom of speech, even though its exercise may conflict with the welfare of society. A free expression rationale based solely on individual fulfillment has raised philosophical and legal quandaries when it has come into conflict with other equally important liberties.

The argument from the paradox justifies censorship in cases in which freedom of speech is exercised by those who would use it to eliminate the free speech principle itself. For example, in England, it was used to set regulations restricting the activities of the National Front. In the United States, those seeking to prohibit the marching of the Nazi party in Skokie, Illinois, a predominantly Jewish suburb of Chicago, relied on this argument without success. The European Convention on Human Rights employed it as a fundamental consideration in Article 10, and it has been cited as authority for outlawing the German Communist Party.

The utilitarian argument suggests that the speech in question should be weighed for the balance of pleasure and pain. Its value is limited in assessing the extent of free speech protection contemplated by the U.S. Constitution, or other legislation with similar provisions.

The contractualist argument is a rights-based conception that excludes certain rights from state power, particularly the right to conscience. This argument asserts that the government violates this right when it superimposes its own value judgment on the speech at issue.

**Censorship and the Arts in Europe.** Artistic freedom is protected in Europe in all countries adhering to the European Convention of Human Rights and Fundamental Freedoms. Article 10 guarantees everyone the right to freedom of expression. Any prior restraints on publication must be justified as necessary in a democratic society in order to constitute permissible restraints on the free expression principle.

West Germany's Basic Law, Article 5, provides for freedom of expression rights, specifically designating art, science, research, and teaching. This freedom of expression is, however, subject to a fundamental right to dignity and is limited by the provisions of the general laws. As a result, the German Constitutional Court has balanced the interests of free expression and other specific laws in a manner similar to that used by the U.S. Supreme Court.

Great Britain does not constitutionally protect speech; instead, it relies upon common law and administrative agencies to resolve issues involving free expression. Courts often articulate a common law principle of freedom of speech to limit the scope of other rules that impinge on this freedom. Prior restraint by licensing of the press was abolished in 1694, but films remain subject to scrutiny under the Video Recordings Act of 1985.

In 1979, a special committee, popularly known as "The Williams Committee," presented to the government its report containing studies and policies on obscenity and film censorship. Its findings, which recommended the restriction of material that is offensive to reasonable people, are frequently cited by the courts as well as by legal scholars.

Obscenity is prosecuted under the Obscene Publications Act of 1959, provided that the work is not justified as being for the public good or in the interest of science, literature, art, learning, or any other area of general concern. This exception to the obscenity law bears a strong resemblance to the balancing of interests tests utilized by American Supreme Court justices.

**Censorship and the Arts in the United States.** The constitutional guarantee of free speech was articulated in one simple phrase, yet its interpretation has been a matter of intricate, strenuous legal debate since its inception. When state laws are challenged as unconstitutional restraints on free speech, the ultimate determination of their legality rests with the U.S. Supreme Court. This court has established, on a case-by-case basis, both the scope and limitations of the free speech doctrine as well as its applicability to the states through the Fourteenth Amendment.

It has been argued that the drafters of the First Amendment contemplated only the protection of political speech. The path that the Supreme Court took in extending the free speech principle to the arts was long, arduous, and occasionally winding. Most instances of repression of the literary and visual arts have occurred under the guise of preservation of moral standards, pertaining to blasphemy and obscenity. Anti-vice movements and groups have operated on the basis of the premise that society needed protection from exposure to material that those movements and groups considered threatening to public morals. Although not necessarily acting under the color of state law, organizations such as the Legion of Decency, the New England Watch and Ward Society, and various independent groups constituting what became known as the "Moral Majority" have pressured municipalities and businesses into tacitly censoring material deemed offensive.

The Supreme Court began to address the extension of First Amendment protection beyond political speech in the 1940's. Blasphemy prosecutions are all but obsolete in the United States, but it was not until 1952 that the Supreme Court ruled that a film (*The Miracle*) could not be censored for sacrilegious content. The Court also ruled that motion pictures were included within the free speech and press guaranty of the First and Fourteenth Amendments; the importance of films as organs of public opinion was not lessened by the fact that they were designed to entertain as well as inform.

Literary and visual arts in the form of erotica have been afforded the least First Amendment protection. Obscenity has always been criminally sanctioned and subjected to prior restraints in the United States, based on numerous policy considerations: that it corrupts the individual, that it leads to sex-related crime and illegal sexual activity, that it serves no socially redeeming purpose, and that it is lacking in any viable element of the search for truth.

Until 1934, American courts relied on the English common law "Hicklin Rule" when determining whether a given work was to be considered illegally obscene. *Regina v. Hicklin* (1868) defined the test of obscenity as whether the tendency of the matter is to deprave and corrupt those whose minds are open to such immoral influences and into whose hands a publication of this sort may fall. Thus, a publication was judged obscene if any isolated passage within it could corrupt the most susceptible person.

The "Hicklin Rule" was replaced by the "Ulysses standard," first articulated in *United States v. One Book Entitled Ulysses* (1934), which required that the entire work, rather than an isolated passage, be evaluated for its libidinous effect. The Supreme Court continued to proclaim in Chaplinsky v. New Hampshire (1942) that there were certain well-defined and narrowly limited classes of speech that are of such slight social value as to be clearly outweighed by the social interest in order and morality. Such classes of speech included the lewd and obscene, the profane, the libelous, and insulting words that by their utterance inflict injury.

The first landmark case setting forth a standard for determining whether a work was to be considered obscene, and therefore undeserving of First Amendment protection, was *Roth v. United States* (1957). The Court, in upholding convictions for violations of California and federal obscenity statutes, found that the statutes did not violate constitutional standards. The Court stated that the test for obscenity was whether the average person, applying contemporary community standards, would find that the dominant theme of the material, taken as a whole, appealed to prurient interest.

Three years later, the Supreme Court found that a Chicago city ordinance requiring submission of film for examination as a prerequisite to obtaining a permit for public exhibition was not void as a prior restraint under the First Amendment. In *Times Film Corp. v. City of Chicago* (1961), the Court indicated that there is no complete and absolute freedom to exhibit, even once, any and every kind of motion picture. The Court limited the scope of the First Amendment, based on the overriding societal interest in preserving the decency of the community, assuming that the ordinance was directed at obscenity.

In applying the "*Roth* standard" in *Jacobellis v. Ohio* (1964), the Court found the motion picture *Les Amants* not to be obscene and overturned the prosecution of a theater manager who had exhibited the film. The court stated that obscenity is excluded from constitutional protection only because it is utterly without redeeming social importance, and that the portrayal of sex in art, literature, and scientific works is not in itself sufficient reason to deny material the constitutional protection of freedom of speech and press.

In 1970, a Presidential commission appointed to study the statistical correlation, if any, between crime and pornography published its conclusions, finding that there was no direct correlation. There was, however, considerable dissension among the members of the committee, who sought to lodge their conclusions separately.

In 1973, *Miller v. California* was decided, again refining an earlier standard set in *Memoirs v. Massachusetts* (1966). The test for obscenity established three standards that must be independently met in order for a work to be removed from the umbrella of First Amendment protection: whether the average person, applying contemporary community standards, would find that the work, taken as a whole, appeals to prurient interest; whether the work depicts or describes, in a patently offensive way, sexual conduct specifically defined by the applicable state law; and whether the work, taken as a whole, lacks serious literary, artistic, political, or scientific value.

Consequently, a work that had political value was protected, regardless of its prurient appeal and offensive depiction of sexual activities. Sexually explicit art was immune if it demonstrated serious artistic value. Subsequent cases have made it clear that works found by a reasonable person to have serious artistic value are protected from censorship, regardless of whether the government or a majority approve of the ideas these works represent.

A companion case to *Miller*, *Paris Adult Theater I et al. v. Slaton*, held that a state could prohibit hard-core pornographic films. Although there were extensive dissenting opinions, the majority categorically disapproved the theory that obscene, pornographic films acquire constitutional immunity from state regulation simply because they are exhibited for consenting adults; they stated further that the states have a legitimate interest in regulating the use of obscene material in local commerce and in all places of public accommodation. The Court concluded that a legislature could quite reasonably determine that a connection between antisocial behavior and obscene material does or might exist.

In October of 1989, the "*Miller* standard" of obscenity became controversial outside the courts. A censorious bill proposed by Senator Jesse Helms, which sought to restrict and punish the National Endowment for the Arts (NEA) for allegedly funding "obscene" art, was defeated. Congressional critics had assailed the NEA for funding two controversial projects: a photography exhibit by Robert Mapplethorpe that included homoerotic images and an exhibit by Andres Serrano entitled "Piss Christ," which was criticized as sacrilegious. Congress passed instead a compromise bill that removed most penalties against specific artists and institutions but required that the NEA observe legal bans on obscenity by employing standards reminiscent of the language in *Miller.* Further, grant recipients were required to sign a nonobscenity oath.

Subsequently, many organizations and artists refused to sign the oath, and several initiated lawsuits against the NEA. *Bella Lewitzky Dance Foundation v. Frohnmayer et al.* (1991) held that the nonobscenity oath requirement was unconstitutional. Artists and legal scholars alike voiced strenuous objections to the *Miller*-style decency standards of the legislation, particularly because the determination of obscenity was made by NEA panelists and administrators rather than by peer review, and because the standards ignored the nature and purpose of postmodern art, which rejects the previous definition that art must be "serious."

In June, 1992, a United States District Court heard the suit of *Karen Finley et al. v. National Endowment for the Arts and John Frohnmayer*, in which four performance artists whose grant applications were denied by the NEA brought suit alleging improper denial of the grant applications. The governing statute as amended in 1990 provided that artistic merit was to be judged taking into consideration general standards of decency and respect for the diverse beliefs and values of the American public. The Court found that the decency provision violated the Fifth Amendment's due process requirement. It further held that the public funding of art is entitled to First Amendment protection and that the decency clause on its face violates the First Amendment on the basis of overbreadth.

The influence of ethical arguments throughout the constitutional case law concerning censorship and the arts is unmistakable. Throughout the twentieth century, the Supreme Court has labored to give contemporary meaning to the terms of the First Amendment, affording broad freedom of expression to the arts while balancing various community values and shifting interests in a pluralistic society.

*—Kathleen O'Brien*

**See also** Art; Art and public policy; *Index librorum prohibitorum*; Intellectual property; Motion picture ratings systems; Song lyrics.

**BIBLIOGRAPHY**

Barendt, Eric. *Freedom of Speech*. Oxford: Clarendon Press, 1985. A comparative treatment of the protection afforded speech and other forms of expression in the United States, the United Kingdom, Germany, and countries adhering to the European Convention.

Gerber, Albert B. *Sex, Pornography, and Justice*. New York: Lyle Stuart, 1965. A complete study of the topic from the Middle Ages to the twentieth century, including exhibits of the items that came before the courts. Updated supplements are available.

Hurwitz, Leon. *Historical Dictionary of Censorship in the United States*. Westport, Conn.: Greenwood Press, 1985. An overview of the types of expression subjected to repression in the United States, with cases, concepts, terms, and events listed alphabetically with brief summaries. An extensive bibliography and a table of cases make the book a useful reference tool.

Richards, David A. J. *Toleration and the Constitution*. New York: Oxford University Press, 1986. Provides a contractualist account of U.S. constitutional law regarding religious liberty, free speech, and constitutional protection of privacy.

Schauer, Frederick. *Free Speech: A Philosophical Enquiry*. Cambridge, England: Cambridge University Press, 1982. Draws extensively on legal rules and examples to present the author's political philosophy as well as his analysis of the right to free speech principle and the variety of communication that it includes.

## Cesarean section

**TYPE OF ETHICS:** Bioethics

**DATE:** First U.S. procedure 1794; routine use began in the 1960's

**DEFINITION:** Surgical removal of a viable fetus from the mother through an incision in the uterus

**SIGNIFICANCE:** Obstetricians claim that the cesarean section is a life-saving procedure, but its opponents claim that it is dangerous major surgery and that 80 percent of its use is for the convenience of physicians

In Roman times, cesarean sections (C-sections) were legally required if a pregnant mother was dead or dying. Today, C-sections are necessary to save the life of mother and baby when a baby cannot be born vaginally. This happens in a total of 5 percent of births. In the United States, however, C-sections are performed in 30 percent of births. Obstetricians defend the high rate by saying that it is better to have an unnecessary C-section than to risk losing a baby and that a C-section can end the pain of a long and difficult labor. Opponents of C-sections, such as the Cesarean Prevention Movement, attribute the high rate to obstetricians' fear of lawsuits, poor training in managing the natural process of birth, lack of patience for the variations in and length of normal labor and birth; and naive enthusiasm for using the latest technological interventions. As a result of these deficiencies, opponents allege, obstetricians subject mothers to unnecessary surgery, including unnecessary pain, recovery time, scarring, and financial expense, as well as the risk of infection, adhesions, and bad reactions to anesthesia.

**See also** Medical ethics.

## Character

**TYPE OF ETHICS:** Theory of ethics

**ASSOCIATED WITH:** Hugh Hartshorne and Mark May's Character Education Project, Frank Goble and David Brook's Character Education Curriculum, and Thomas Lickona's Integrated Approach to Character Development

**DEFINITION:** A person's pattern of behavior related to the moral qualities of self-discipline and social responsibility

**SIGNIFICANCE:** Character is the manifestation of a system or code of ethics in persons who practice morality in their daily lives

The terms "character" and "personality" are sometimes used interchangeably, although character is more apt to be associated with behavioral and attitudinal characteristics that are consistent with the ethical standards of the community. It is thought that a wholesome character is not inherited but begins to form during the early years of the child's life and continues to form into adulthood.

In the mid-1920's, Hugh Hartshorne and Mark May were funded by the Institute of Social and Religious Research to conduct a study that came to be known as the Character

Education Project. The purpose of the project was to ascertain the effect of character education programs on the ethical behavior of children. The study took five years and produced three volumes, all published under the title, *Studies in the Nature of Character.* Almost 11,000 children, ages eleven through sixteen, in both private and public schools were tested for behaviors that could be labeled "character."

Tests included situations in which the children had a chance to cheat by copying answers, situations in which they had the opportunity to lie by answering in the affirmative such questions as "I always obey my parents cheerfully" and "I always smile when things go wrong," and situations in which it was possible for them to steal by taking money out of a coin box on their desk. More than 17,000 tests were given. The purpose was not to counter any student regarding his or her behavior but rather to determine for the group as a whole the variables that correlate with good character.

It was found that almost all children were dishonest under some circumstances but not under others. Moral behavior tended to be specific to the situation. Age and gender were not relevant. Furthermore, children who participated in organized programs of religious education or other programs emphasizing character development were not more honest than children without this training. What did make a difference was that children who were less apt to cheat or lie or steal were more intelligent and came from homes that were better off socioeconomically. Siblings also tended to resemble each other, showing the influence of the family.

The Hartshorne and May study has been used to discredit organized programs in character education. Simply telling the child what is right and what is wrong was not sufficient to produce good character. Methods other than direct instruction would need to be implemented. Moral educators came to believe that children must understand why it is important to be honest or brave or kind. Children also need to be actively involved in learning how they can show these favorable characteristics in their day-to-day dealings with others. Participatory decision making and opportunities to practice the desired character traits are essential.

The American Institute for Character Education, which developed the Character Education Curriculum in 1970, based its program on "a worldwide study of value systems" and identified fifteen basic values "shared by all major cultures and world religions." These values are courage, conviction, generosity, kindness, helpfulness, honesty, honor, justice, tolerance, the sound use of time and talents, freedom of choice, freedom of speech, good citizenship, the right to be an individual, and the right of equal opportunity.

Almost all character education programs list individual character traits. Boston University's Character Education program emphasizes such basic virtues as honesty, courage, persistence, loyalty, and kindness, which students learn from studying the lessons of history and reading good literature. The Heartwood Project in the Pittsburgh Public Schools has seven universal values developed for children at the elementary grades. Courage, loyalty, justice, respect, hope, honesty, and love are learned through stories, songs, art, and saying the seven virtue words in another language. The development of character comes not only from knowing what society expects of its members but also from a desire to incorporate that expectation into one's daily life.

Thomas Lickona writes that good character consists of knowing the good, desiring the good, and doing the good—habits of the mind, habits of the heart, and habits of action. His integrated approach to character development consists of fifteen components. Moral *knowing* is composed of awareness, values, perspective-taking, reasoning, decision making, and self-knowledge; moral *feeling* includes conscience, self-esteem, empathy, loving the good, self-control, and humility; and moral action incorporates competence, will, and habit. For each of these fifteen components, illustrations are given and suggestions are offered as to how they can be taught to children.

There have always been persons in every society who are so deficient in their moral makeup that they are said to have a "character disorder." These persons are average or above average in intelligence, are neither neurotic nor psychotic, and can verbalize the rules of society. Yet they seem unable to understand why they should obey the rules or conform to the expectations of others. Sometimes called "sociopath," they tend to project blame onto others, taking no responsibility for their own failures. They act impulsively, are unconcerned about the rights and privileges of others, are pathological liars, are unable to form deep attachments to other persons, display poor judgment and planning, and lack emotional control. The prognosis for such persons who are in therapy is poor, since they experience little anxiety or distress because of their social maladjustment and are unwilling or unable to see why they should change.

*—Bonnidell Clouse*

**See also** Personal relationships; Responsibility.

**BIBLIOGRAPHY**

Clouse, Bonnidell. *Teaching for Moral Growth: A Guide for the Christian Community.* Wheaton, Ill.: Victor Press, 1993.

Hartshorne, Hugh, and M. A. May. *Studies in Deceit.* Vol. 1 in *Studies in the Nature of Character.* New York: Macmillan, 1928-1930.

Hartshorne, Hugh, M. A. May, and J. B Maller. *Studies in Service and Self-Control.* Vol. 2 in *Studies in the Nature of Character.* New York: Macmillan, 1928-1930.

Hartshorne, Hugh, M. A. May, and F. K. Shuttleworth. *Studies in the Organization of Character.* Vol. 3 in *Studies in the Nature of Character.* New York: Macmillan, 1928-1930.

Lickona, Thomas. *Educating for Character: How Our Schools Can Teach Respect and Responsibility.* New York: Bantam Books, 1991.

Pritchard, Ivor. *Moral Education and Character.* Washington, D.C.: U.S. Department of Education, 1988.

## Charity

**TYPE OF ETHICS:** Theory of ethics

**DATE:** From antiquity

**DEFINITION:** Sharing one's property and person with others in order to alleviate their basic needs

**SIGNIFICANCE:** Unless people share what they have and who they are, community and personality disintegrate; charity is a recognition of the interdependence of humans, and ethics is a working out of that recognition

Every culture and religion recognizes the necessity of charity to healthy social and personal living. The unconditioned giving of oneself and one's possessions to alleviate the basic needs of others is the foundation of a good society.

The experience of receiving an unexpected gift is one that is enjoyed by most people. The experience of giving an unsolicited gift has been known by many people. These experiences of giving and receiving are fundamental to being charitable, since charity is both the act of giving and the act of receiving the basic necessities of life. Sharing is always a mutual action.

Contemporary Western culture is ambivalent about the place of such gift-giving in personal and social affairs. To clarify the reasons for this ambivalence, it will first be necessary to review the etymology of the word "charity" and the history of the practice of charity in Western culture. Next, this article will review the paradoxical nature of charity in contemporary American culture.

**Etymology and History.** The word "charity" comes from the old French *charité* and the Latin *caritas.* The Latin word is a translation of the Greek New Testament word *agape.* Most modern translators of the Bible translate *agape* as love. Love of one's neighbor and charity toward one's neighbor originally, and until recently, meant the same thing. Charitable acts such as feeding the hungry, giving water to the thirsty, providing homes for the homeless, educating the ignorant, giving medicine to the sick, burying the dead, and visiting those in prison were seen as acts of love to those in need. These acts of love were performed in imitation of the God who freely gave humans life.

The following of Christ's command to love, or be charitable to others, was institutionalized by placing some Church officials, deacons, in charge of these institutional acts of charity/love and by establishing institutional means, such as collecting food, to aid those in need. Every Christian had the obligation to love his or her neighbor. The community of Christians, the Church, understood love of neighbor as essential to its mission. During the Middle Ages (500-1500), groups of men and women, religious orders, organized themselves to continue this mission of the Church and thus dedicated themselves to educating the ignorant, feeding the hungry, clothing the unclothed, caring for the slaves and imprisoned, healing the sick, and caring for orphans.

With the advent of the modern state in the eighteenth century and that of the social sciences in the nineteenth century, the questions of who should care for the needy, how to train those who cared for the needy, and whether to care for the needy arose. In general, the care of the needy began to be seen in Europe as an obligation of the state in the eighteenth century and gradually began to be accepted as a governmental obligation by many people during the first quarter of the twentieth century in the United States. The obligation to love or be charitable toward one's neighbor continued to be recognized as an essential ingredient of an individual's life—and certainly of the Church's existence—but the means for fulfilling this command gradually became part of the government and came under the control of professionals.

The evolving social sciences and the ideologies that supported them developed a different view of gaining and possessing wealth. Before 1830, the possession of great wealth was seen as a danger to the individual and society. Wealth was for sharing. The poor were acknowledged and cared for because, it was understood, anyone could become poor. Life, riches, and personal abilities were all gifts from God that could easily be lost. Thus, both rich and poor acknowledged the tenuousness of their position. With the advent of entrepreneurial capitalism and Social Darwinism, everyone began to be seen as destined to be rich and to possess the goods of this earth. The poor were seen as poor because they did not work hard enough or had bad habits or genes or some other fault. It was their own fault that the poor were poor, it was claimed. The rich were rich because of their own initiative and work. Since being in need was one's own fault, the poor should not be rewarded by being given the basic necessities of life. They needed a stimulus for work. That stimulus was poverty. If, for whatever reason, the state did help individuals with the basic necessities of life, the state should never deprive the rich of the wealth that they had gained through their hard work. The command to love and the command to share was replaced by the demand for the ideological means to reduce one's guilt in the face of the starving, unclothed, and homeless. Institutions were developed in order to professionalize and economize the care of the needy. Thus, the needy were gradually segregated into institutions according to their specific needs: hospitals, orphanages, schools, and prisons. One result of such institutionalization was the invisibility of those in need. Charity became professionalized, love eroticized, and the possession of wealth individualized. Consequently, the original command to love one's neighbor through acts of charity/love lost all meaning, and with it the sense of community and self changed. Charity was no longer the sharing of one's goods with those in need, but rather the giving of one's leftovers to those who had failed.

**Competition and/or Cooperation.** The goal of competition is to win. Life, as competition, results in winners and losers. What part does charity play when one wins or loses? Should one accept the necessities of life from the winner? Should one provide the loser with the necessities of life, knowing that these provisions may enable that person to challenge one again? If one never aids the losers, what kind of a human being is one? If everyone always and everywhere acts only out of selfishness, what becomes of community?

**Self-sacrifice and/or Self-gratification.** Some contemporary authors argue that humans always act out of selfishness. Even at one's most giving moments, it is claimed, one is actually seeking self-gratification. This psychological claim is reflected in philosophical studies that make a distinction between *agape,* or disinterested love, and *eros,* or sensual love. True charity is then disinterested charity, something no human can do on his or her own. Only God can provide the ability to act out of *agape.* Followers of these contemporary authors are left with a cynical distrust of anyone who does good.

Actually, love can be both gratifying and sacrificial. It is paradoxical but nevertheless true that people act against every obvious self-interest in performing such heroic acts as jumping in front of a speeding car to save a child and jumping on a live hand grenade to save the lives of fellow soldiers. To risk death or to die for others may be interpreted as inherently pleasurable to the risk taker or the dead hero, but these theories seem to be held in the face of obvious contradiction. Even if true, they should not be used to destroy all charity, if only because of the obvious result: A world without love and charity would be a world devoid of humanity as people now know it. —*Nathan R. Kollar*

**See also** Benevolence.

**BIBLIOGRAPHY**

Amundsen, Darrel W. "Medical Ethics, History of Medieval Europe: Fourth to Sixteenth Century." In *Encyclopedia of Bioethics,* edited by Warren Reich. New York: The Free Press, 1978.

Gaylin, Willard, et al. *Doing Good: The Limits of Benevolence.* New York: Pantheon Books, 1978.

Outka, Gene. *Agape: An Ethical Analysis.* New Haven, Conn.: Yale University Press, 1972.

## Cheating

**TYPE OF ETHICS:** Personal and social ethics

**DATE:** From antiquity

**DEFINITION:** Willful violation of known standards of behavior with the intent to benefit oneself

**SIGNIFICANCE:** Cheating reduces the value of social contracts and rules, thus preventing some mutually beneficial behavior

Broadly speaking, cheating can be taken to mean any violation of known social norms, therefore encompassing all deliberate deception and lawbreaking. A narrower interpretation restricts cheating only to situations in which an individual has voluntarily agreed to behave according to a set of rules and willfully violates those rules for personal gain. Examples of such cases are games and marketplace behavior. In the former, rules are usually explicit; in the latter, rules may be implicit—taking the form of customs—or may be explicit or even established by law. Often, the punishment for cheating is limited to expulsion from the activity. Cheating is similar to breaking a personal promise in that a person willfully breaks an expected standard of behavior; it differs in that the standard was set socially rather than individually.

**Forms of Cheating.** All immoral action can be taken to constitute cheating, but most discussions limit cheating to several broad areas. Cheating is taken to mean willful breaking of rules. The breaking of formal established rules, such as laws, most often falls outside discussions of cheating. The innocent violation of rules is not considered to be cheating; even though "ignorance of the law is no excuse," a person is not said to have cheated by violating a rule of which he or she was unaware. Cheating is deliberate behavior.

The clearest cases of cheating are those in which individuals deliberately violate rules that they have willingly chosen to follow. Games provide some examples. By participating in a game, a player agrees to follow the rules of the game. Cheating takes place when a player violates the rules with the intention of winning. This behavior takes advantage of other players who follow the rules. Clearly, if everyone cheated, games would cease to have any meaning and would cease to exist. This would deprive people of any enjoyment they derive from playing games.

Societies have rules in the forms of laws and social conventions. Lawbreaking is usually, but not always, a clear violation of social norms. The exceptions occur in cases in which there is a perception that the law is widely violated or is irrelevant to the situation. Such cases include speeding, jaywalking, and cheating on taxes. Even though all of those behaviors are violations of laws, many people do not believe themselves to have behaved unethically by performing those behaviors, since "everyone does it." Unwritten social conventions include positive reinforcement for helping those in need and prohibitions against eavesdropping, spreading gossip, and skipping ahead in lines, to name only a few.

Ethical issues arise when people argue that they did not enter into social contracts voluntarily and thus are not bound by those contracts. Examples include taxpayers who argue that they did not vote for the tax laws and students who state that they are in school against their will and thus are not subject to its rules. As in games, when people violate social contracts, even those entered into implicitly (through citizenship in society) or against individuals' will, those contracts become meaningless and people become less certain of what they can expect of others. Behavior becomes less cooperative and more self-serving and protective.

**Misrepresentation.** Misrepresentation, or lying, is a particular case of violation of rules. One of the most basic social conventions is that people should tell the truth. In some cases, as in courts of law or on legal documents, that convention is enforced by threat of legal sanction. In many cases, people simply rely on each other to tell the truth.

In the United States, laws specifically cover many types

of misrepresentation, including that in many sales contracts, employment contracts, and even the marriage contract. Cheating behavior involving any of these contracts gives the damaged party the right to dissolve the contract and possibly to claim damages. Other countries that rely less on the legal system to settle disputes have not codified prohibitions against misrepresentation to the same extent, instead relying on social conventions and social sanctions against those found to misrepresent themselves.

**Ethical Implications.** Cheating involves taking advantage of a situation to gain an unfair advantage. In competitions of all sorts, the objective is to win, but winning carries less meaning when the rules of the game are violated. A student who cheats on a test, for example, appears to have proved attainment of knowledge but instead has proved only the ability to defeat any monitoring system. To the extent that cheating is successful, it punishes those who behave ethically and honestly by giving rewards to those who cheat. This harm to society is one reason that many social conventions have been codified into law. The same reasoning helps to explain why payment of taxes is not voluntary and is subject to rules, with punishment for violation. Individuals would believe themselves to be gaining by violating any voluntary system of taxation, but the society as a whole would lose because there would be insufficient money to allow the government to provide goods for the benefit of everyone. In cases where conventions are important to society, governments tend to mandate behavior through laws rather than relying on people to behave ethically.

*—A. J. Sobczak*

**Cheating**

| Situations in Which Cheating Occurs | Types of Cheating |
|---|---|
| Criminal | Forgery<br>Bribery of officials<br>Tax fraud<br>Tax evasion<br>Misrepresentation on tax forms |
| Games and gambling | Marking cards<br>Stacking the deck<br>Altering dice<br>Bribing athletes to underperform<br>Drugging animals<br>Use of steroids or other disallowed substances by athletes<br>Signaling a bridge partner or other gaming partner |
| Marriage | Infidelity |
| Employment | Lying on a resume or employment application<br>Filling out a false expense account<br>Taking credit for work done by others |
| Schoolwork | Stealing exams<br>Looking at another student's exam paper<br>Having someone else do one's homework<br>Plagiarism |
| Driving | Speeding<br>"Rolling stops" at intersections |
| Shopping | Purchasing a mispriced item at a price known to be too low |
| Self-discipline | Dieting or other regimens<br>Cheating at solitaire |

**See also** Conscience; Fairness; Fraud; Integrity; Lying; Moral education; Temptation.

**Bibliography**


Brandt, Richard B. *A Theory of the Good and the Right.* Oxford, England: Clarendon Press, 1979.

Gert, Bernard. *The Moral Rules: A New Rational Foundation for Morality.* New York: Harper & Row, 1970.

Harman, Gilbert. *The Nature of Morality: An Introduction to Ethics.* New York: Oxford University Press, 1977.

Lande, Nathaniel, and Afton Slade. *Stages: Understanding How You Make Your Moral Decisions.* San Francisco: Harper & Row, 1979.

Langone, John. *Thorny Issues: How Ethics and Morality Affect the Way We Live.* Boston: Little, Brown, 1981.

Weiss, Paul, and Jonathan Weiss. *Right and Wrong: A Philosophical Dialogue Between Father and Son.* New York: Basic Books, 1967.


## Chemical warfare

**Type of ethics:** Military ethics

**Date:** From antiquity

**Definition:** The use of chemical substances as military weapons

**Significance:** Seeks to establish whether the use of chemical weapons can be morally justified

A nation engaged in military aggression inevitably causes human casualties on the opposing side, but the development of toxic chemical agents against an enemy poses special moral problems for a nation. Chemical weapons can be effective in a variety of military situations. When used against unprotected individuals, they cause painful, lingering death and injuries.

**History.** The use of toxic chemical substances in warfare dates to ancient times. This includes the use of toxic substances to poison soldiers' drinking water and the production of poisonous clouds of sulfur dioxide by burning sulfur and pitch during battles. Condemnation of these primitive forms of chemical warfare also dates from these early times, as reflected in an ancient Roman quotation: "War is waged with weapons, not with poison." Modern chemical warfare began during World War I. Germany released deadly chlorine gas from thousands of cylinders against French and British troops at Ypres in Belgium in 1915. As a result, more than 5,000 men were killed in the attack. Later, Germany also employed phosgene and mustard gas. By the end of the war, both sides had used chemical weapons, causing more than 1.25 million casualties, including 90,000 deaths. After the war, families and friends of veterans exposed to chemical weapons were shocked to see their effect—coughing and gasping for breath and horrible scars on the victims. Public outrage sparked a worldwide drive to eliminate the use of these weapons in future conflicts, leading to the Geneva Protocol of 1925 prohibiting the use of poison gas in warfare. This agreement was signed by all the world's major powers except the United States and Japan.

Although they were never used in combat, highly toxic nerve agents were developed by Germany during World War II. With the surrender of Germany, the United States army came into possession of one such substance, Sarin, an incredibly lethal compound; one drop could kill fifty men. Since the end of World War II, some countries, including the United States, have continued to manufacture and store chemical weapons, but they have been employed in only a few of the more than 200 wars fought since World War II. They were used in Ethiopia and China in the 1930's and 1940's, in Yemen in the 1960's, and in the Iran-Iraq conflict during the 1980's.

**Ethical Principles.** The ethics of using chemical weapons focus on several important issues. Proponents of chemical weapons cite several arguments justifying the use of these weapons: First, military strength is a deterrent to a nation or state contemplating aggression toward another nation. If the types of weapons potentially available for use are restricted, this may reduce the deterrent factor. Therefore, all kinds of weapons—conventional, nuclear, chemical, and biological—should be available for use. Second, while chemical weapons produce human casualties, they do not, like conventional weapons, destroy inanimate objects such as roads, houses, hospitals, and bridges. Reconstruction of cities devastated by chemical weapons is therefore likely to be quicker and less costly. Third, chemical weapons can be effective in a variety of situations. For example, they can be used against concentrated or dispersed troops, against troops that are above or below ground, or against concealed troops. Fourth, if an enemy is believed to possess a chemical weapon capability, it forces soldiers to wear cumbersome protective devices that may hinder their effectiveness. The fear of chemical weapons may also affect the morale of soldiers. Fifth, unlike biological weapons, which are impossible to contain, the application and control of chemical weapons are relatively easy to maintain. Sixth, injuries inflicted by chemical weapons are not necessarily more terrible than those inflicted by the weapons of conventional warfare. Flying fragments of hot metal from conventional weapons can produce horrible injuries comparable in severity to those caused by chemical weapons.

By contrast to the above arguments, opponents of chemical weapon use cite the following arguments. First, many political and military leaders have had an aversion to employing chemical warfare because of the insidious nature of these substances and their effects on humans. In the case of nerve gases, they produce intense sweating; the filling of bronchial passages with mucus; decreased vision; uncontrollable vomiting, defecation, and convulsions; and eventual paralysis and respiratory failure leading to death. Other less lethal agents can produce painful blisters and blindness. In addition, the long-term effect of exposure to some chemical weapons is difficult to quantify. Second, while chemical weapons are effective when used against unprotected individuals, they have minimal effect against soldiers wearing gas masks and protective clothing. Third, although chemical weapons are more predictable than biological weapons, weather conditions and human error may still result in chemical weapons reaching unprotected nonmilitary targets. Fourth, compared to conventional weapons, chemical weapons are somewhat easier and cheaper to obtain and manufacture. Consequently, they are more likely to be used in conflicts within Third World countries. This was the case in the Iran-Iraq conflict in the 1980's, in which Iraq employed chemical weapons not only against its enemy but also within its own border on the civilian Kurdish population.

Military operations—whether they involve conventional or chemical weapons—that cause the widespread injury and death of civilians are condemned by most nations. For the reasons outlined above, most nations possessing chemical weapons could justify their use only in retaliation if they themselves were subject to a chemical weapons attack. Because of the many problems of chemical weapons, including their safe manufacture, storage, transportation, and disposal, most nations are reluctant to acquire these weapons of destruction, let alone use them. —*Nicholas C. Thomas*

**See also** Bioethics; Military ethics.

**BIBLIOGRAPHY**

Aspen Strategy Group. *New Threats: Responding to the Proliferation of Nuclear, Chemical, and Delivery Capabilities in the Third World.* Lanham, Md.: University Press of America, 1990.

Beckett, Brian. *Weapons of Tomorrow.* New York: Plenum Press, 1983.

McCarthy, Richard D. *The Ultimate Folly.* New York: Knopf, 1969.

Stockholm International Peace Research Institute. *Chemical Weapons: Destruction and Conversion.* London: Taylor & Frances, 1980.

Wakin, Malham M., ed. *War, Morality, and the Military Profession.* Boulder, Colo.: Westview Press, 1979.

## Child abuse

**TYPE OF ETHICS:** Children's rights

**DATE:** Coined 1950

**ASSOCIATED WITH:** American Humane Society, National Child Abuse Hotline, U.S. Department of Justice, Child

Welfare League of America, and U.S. Department of Health and Human Services

**DEFINITION:** Inadequate care, neglect, or other acts that put a child in danger or that cause physical harm or injury or involve sexual molestation

**SIGNIFICANCE:** Laws in many states require attorneys, physicians, dentists, interns, residents, nurses, psychologists, teachers, social workers, school principals, childcare givers, ministers, law enforcement officers, or any other persons having reasonable cause to report all cases of suspected child abuse

In 1988, the National Center on Child Abuse and Neglect estimated that 500,000 children are physically abused each year in the United States. The American Humane Society estimated that 2.2 million children were abused or neglected in 1986. The incidence of reported child abuse tends to be highest in the lower socioeconomic groups, where opportunities are most limited and stress is greatest. Between 1976 and 1986, reported child abuse tripled, indicating an increased willingness to report mistreatment, an increased incidence of mistreatment, or both.

Most child abuse occurs in the home. Although parents may abuse their children at any age, abused and neglected children are most often younger than age three. Signs of sexual abuse include extreme changes in behavior, such as loss of appetite; sleep disturbance or nightmares; regression to bed-wetting, thumb-sucking, or frequent crying; torn or stained underclothes; vaginal or rectal bleeding or discharge; vaginal or throat infection; painful, itching, or swollen genitals; unusual interest in or knowledge of sexual matters; and fear or dislike of being left in a certain place or with a certain person. Abuse is most traumatic if a nonabusive parent is unsupportive on hearing of the abuse, if the child is removed from the home, and if the child suffered from more than one type of abuse (for example, physical and sexual).

Explanations for child abuse include personality and behavioral characteristics of the parents, stresses on the parents, personality and behavioral characteristics of the child, and cultural values and institutions. Personality traits of parents that contribute to increased likelihood of abuse include low self-esteem, frustrated dependence needs, low family satisfaction, low need to give nurturance, and low ability to recognize or admit feelings of rejection of the child. Behaviorally, parents who abuse their children are more likely than nonabusing parents to be young and poorly educated, and they are often grossly ignorant of normal child development. For example, they may expect their children to be neat or toilet-trained at an unrealistically early age.

Stresses on the parents that contribute to increased likelihood of child abuse include unemployment or other chronic financial hardships, marital difficulties, social isolation, large families, poor living conditions, being isolated from the child at birth, and having been abused as children themselves. Approximately 30 percent of abused children actually become abusive parents.

A personality characteristic of children that contributes to increased likelihood of child abuse is difficult temperament (fussy, irritable, dependent). Behaviorally, children who are abused are more likely than nonabused children to be premature or low-birth-weight, to have colic, to have a serious illness during their first year of life, to have a mental or physical handicap, to be hyperactive, to have other behavioral abnormalities, and to be unattractive in appearance.

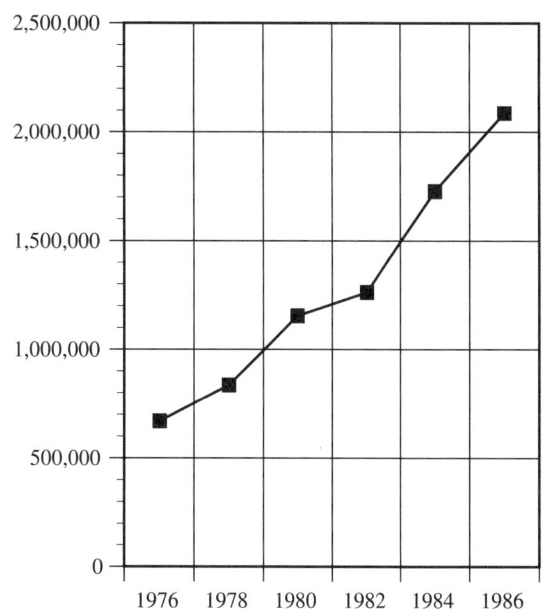


*Instances of Child Abuse Reported to U.S. Authorities, 1976-1986.*

Cultural values and institutions that contribute to increased likelihood of child abuse include acceptance of violence, approval of physical punishment and power assertion as methods of discipline, high levels of social stress, isolation, and absence of community support systems for individuals and families.

Abuse is a complex phenomenon that results from an interaction between the child's problematic traits, the parents' personality problems and social stresses, and cultural values and institutions. Compensatory factors that can prevent an abused child from repeating the abuse as a parent include having a history of positive attachment to a caregiver, resolving not to repeat the abuse, having an awareness of one's early abusive experiences and being openly angry about them, experiencing fewer stressful life events than the abusing parents did, being aware of one's own inner needs, and having a supportive spouse or committed relationship or social network.

At the individual level, child abuse prevention programs, which involve some combination of personal therapy and behavioral modification, have proved to be relatively successful in decreasing child abuse. Abusive parents need help in learning about and developing social relationships, including relationships with their own children. They also need training in caregiving, including learning how to meet the physical, social, and emotional needs of their children. Abusive parents are less likely than nonabusive ones to smile, praise, and touch their children, and they are more likely than nonabusive parents to threaten, disapprove, and show anger toward their children. Treatment includes helping the parent identify specific situations that trigger abuse, modeling how to reward appropriate behaviors, using timeout periods instead of physical punishment and threats, and learning how to settle problems and arguments through negotiation rather than violence.

At the community level, child abuse prevention programs involve identifying high-stress families and high-risk infants, providing crisis services and home support assistance, providing social support networks (such as Parents Anonymous), and offering public education. Also, people who are arrested for family violence are less likely to continue the maltreatment than are those who are not arrested. Many social agencies offer free services to those in need of help and/or counseling about child abuse. *—Lillian M. Range*

**See also** Abuse; Child labor legislation; Children; Children's rights; Sexual abuse and harassment.

**BIBLIOGRAPHY**

Bergman, A. B., R. M. Larsen, and B. A. Mueller. "Changing Spectrum of Serious Child Abuse." *Pediatrics* 77 (January, 1986): 113-116.

Browne, Angela, and David Finkelhor. "Impact of Child Sexual Abuse: A Review of the Research." *Psychological Bulletin* 99 (January, 1986): 66-77.

Cicchetti, Dante, and Vicki Carlson, eds. *Child Maltreatment: Theory and Research on the Causes and Consequences of Child Abuse and Neglect.* Cambridge, England: Cambridge University Press, 1989.

Wolfe, D. A. "Child-abusive Parents: An Empirical Review and Analysis." *Psychological Bulletin* 97 (May, 1985): 462-482.

## Child labor legislation

**TYPE OF ETHICS:** Children's rights

**DATE:** Late eighteenth century to present

**DEFINITION:** Laws designed to protect children from exploitative and dangerous conditions of employment

**SIGNIFICANCE:** Attention to children's rights, in the workplace or elsewhere in the social system, involves the ethical issue of protecting the defenseless or most vulnerable members of society

By the late decades of the twentieth century, nearly all countries in the world had developed some form of legislative protection to guard against the abuse of child labor in the workplace. General (but clearly not complete) acceptance of the role of the International Labor Office of the United Nations in establishing guidelines for international standards of child labor legislation, however, can be considered the result of more than a century of reform efforts that originated in only a few Western countries.

**Precedents Set in Selected Western Countries.** The most notable examples of countries that were first to address child labor in legislation include those areas that first experienced industrialization on a significant scale, particularly England, France, and the United States.

Indeed, one aspect of transition from the latter stages of what is called the Agrarian Age to the Industrial Age was the movement of large segments of the rural population into more concentrated wage-earning zones, either in cities or in areas where raw materials for newly established industries, especially coal and minerals from mines, were produced. Other sites that typically attracted cheap wage labor from economically depressed agricultural hinterland zones as the eighteenth century gave way to the nineteenth century were processing mills, especially in the textile manufacturing sector.

The issue of child labor in England was the object of several legislative reform efforts in the nineteenth century. In the words of Robert Oastler, one of the earliest reformers to denounce (in 1830) what he called "Yorkshire slavery," children were being "sacrificed at the shrine of avarice . . . compelled to work as long as the necessity of needy parents may require, or the cold-blooded avarice of . . . worse than barbarian masters may demand!" Responding to claims of inhumanity in conditions of work, a Parliamentary Act of 1833 banned children between the ages of nine and thirteen from factory labor, limited working hours for those between thirteen and eighteen, and required that all child workers must receive two hours of schooling each day. From this point, reformers aimed not only at near-slave-level pay, long hours, and harsh physical conditions and standards of hygiene, but increasingly at one of the things that became generally recognized as a harmful social effect of child labor: deprivation of minimal opportunities for education.

This factor was visible in England's 1844 Child Labor Act (which called for certificates proving a half-time education schedule daily) and especially the Education Acts of 1870, 1876, and 1891. The latter, soon backed up by a law making twelve the universal minimum age for leaving school, provided free elementary education for all children for the first time. The main motivation in this combination of child labor and education reform legislation was to provide what otherwise would be a totally ignorant youthful labor force with basic knowledge that could protect young workers from being dependent on exploitative offers coming from the lowest levels of the employment market.

In the second country to pioneer child labor legislation—France—information on actual conditions in factories and mines after 1837 had to be gathered by governmental authorities from local chambers of commerce and appointed labor arbitration boards, who encountered a clear unwillingness on the part of private employers to reveal what could only be described as exploitative conditions. Some even claimed that if harm was occurring to children who came to work in factories or mines, it came from unhealthy home environments. Basing this judgment partially on considerations of how children get into the situation of having to seek work, even under the worst conditions, child labor reformers in France during the rest of the century sought to legislate better general social and family environmental laws.

Examples of French laws that would be taken over by other European countries and that were even assumed to be applicable in France's foreign colonies include the Child Labor Laws of 1841, 1851, and 1874. These laws carried varied emphases.

1. In 1841: a maximum eight-hour work shift mandated for children between eight and twelve; proof of school attendance required until the age of twelve; specification of certain factories where danger or hygienic conditions would prevent hiring of any laborers under sixteen.

2. In 1851: Conditions of apprenticeship defined, obligating mutual commitments. Children work under predefined conditions in return for a guarantee of training that would eventually allow "full" integration, under agreed-upon conditions, into the "adult" trained labor ranks.

3. In 1874: Child labor for wages before the age of twelve banned unless guarantees of continued schooling apply; fifteen state inspectorates are established to oversee application of proper standards of work for children and to report to a national "High Commission" in the Ministry of Commerce to judge and penalize employers when complaints arise.

*Child labor legislation helped to improve the lot of young workers such as these oyster shuckers.* (Library of Congress)

**Attempts to Internationalize Legislative Models.** Eventual legislative reactions to the exploitation of child workers in most Western countries represent an uneven record even where nineteenth century laws existed and were updated to try to meet twentieth century expectations; conditions in less developed countries would constantly lag far behind. In some cases there could be a claim of "double standards."

In what came to be called a "neocolonial" situation following generations of actual colonial domination of many Asian and African countries, Western consumer markets for items produced under deplorable physical and near-slave labor conditions of child labor in other countries might have abandoned responsibility for obvious inequities had it not been for certain twentieth century humanitarian-inspired international agencies.

One of these agencies, the International Labor Office (ILO), originally under the League of Nations, now under the United Nations, has attempted since 1919 to obtain acceptance by member states of a number of international conventions on child labor. The formal reports of literally dozens of ILO conferences contain descriptions of key industrial and commercial activities throughout the world in which problem cases can be identified. In order to obtain a degree of international moral authority to "shame" potentially negligent countries into accepting general standards (regarding age, schooling, safety standards, and so forth), the ILO circulates questions to all member nations, who are expected to vote openly, giving their reasons for either accepting or rejecting suggestions of amendments (where needed) to individual country law codes with respect to child labor.

—*Byron D. Cannon*

**See also** Child abuse; Children; Children's rights.

**BIBLIOGRAPHY**

Bennett, Alan. *A Working Life: Child Labor through the Nineteenth Century.* Dorset, England: Waterfront, 1991.

Gollan, John. *Youth in British Industry.* London: Victor Gollancz, 1937.

International Labor Office (57th). *Minimum Age for Admission to Employment: Fourth Item on the Agenda.* Geneva, Switzerland: Author, 1972.

Mendelievich, Elias, ed. *Children at Work.* Geneva, Switzerland: Author, 1979.

Weissbach, Lee S. *Child Labor Reform in Nineteenth Century France.* Baton Rouge: Louisiana State University Press, 1989.

## Child psychology

**TYPE OF ETHICS:** Bioethics

**DATE:** Twentieth century

**DEFINITION:** The diagnosis and treatment of children with mental, emotional, or behavioral disorders

**SIGNIFICANCE:** Raises questions about consent; confidentiality; values conflicts among parents, child, and therapist; guidelines for research, and the role of the professional in court cases

**Consent.** Since persons under the age of eighteen (minors) are considered by law to be incompetent to make decisions for themselves, proxy consent from parents or guardians is required for medical treatment. Involving the child in the decision when possible respects the child as a person and has the practical advantage of giving the child information and enlisting his or her cooperation, which may be very important for the success of the treatment. Parents may commit children to hospitalization against their will, however, and still have the admission labeled as "voluntary" (*Parham vs. J.R.* 1979, U.S. Supreme Court).

While the law seems to assume that parents always decide in the best interest of the child, ethical dilemmas may arise when parents refuse consent for treatment of a child deemed in need by school officials or others. This raises the question of whether children have a right to needed treatment. Exceptions to the parental consent requirement may be made in cases of older adolescents who are legally emancipated minors—that is, living independently of parents, married, or in the armed services—or who are considered by the therapist to be mature minors and thus able to decide for themselves.

**Confidentiality.** The maintenance of confidentiality between a therapist and an adult patient is recognized as an important ethical rule, and there are many reasons why confidentiality should be respected for children, as well. Much of the material that becomes known to the therapist is very personal and may involve issues that are sensitive for the child or family. A pledge to honor confidentiality can enhance trust between child and therapist.

Also, harm may be done to a child by "labeling." Revealing past status as a psychiatric patient can, unfortunately, be a factor in denying later educational or job opportunities.

Despite the value of confidentiality, parents often think that they have a right to know everything, and sometimes a therapist may have to break confidentiality to protect the child or others. A therapist should be honest and state ground rules before beginning treatment and inform the child or family before revealing information.

**Conflict in Values.** Who should set the goals for psychiatric or behavioral therapy for a child? Parents may have unrealistic expectations for their children or want help in making them conform to cultural ideals of behavior that are different from societal norms or that the therapist may find inappropriate for a particular child. The therapist must decide whether to accept the family's values and help the child adapt to them or to help the child develop the strength to stand against parental pressures. Even using the best interest of the child as the standard, this can be a difficult decision. It is the right of parents to make decisions for their children and to bring them up as they see fit, and many child rearing practices and behavioral expectations are accepted in a pluralistic society. Although society does set limits and require that certain basic needs be met, and has legal standards of abuse or neglect, therapists must be careful not to impose their own personal values on families.

**Research.** Research in child psychology and psychiatry can run from totally nonintrusive observation of normal children in public places to surveys by questionnaire and interviews all the way to trials of new behavior modification techniques or clinical trials of psychotropic drugs. The use of children as research subjects presents ethical problems because as minors they cannot legally volunteer and because in many studies it is very difficult to assess potential risk. Thus, some questions are virtually unexplored and data about causes and effective treatment are lacking. The picture is improving, however, since in 1991 Congress approved a national initiative for increased research on child and adolescent mental health.

Ethical guidelines for medical research with children were adopted as federal regulations in 1983, and they provide that research be well-designed in order to give valid, nontrivial results, that trials be made on animals and adults rather than on children when possible, that risks be outweighed by expected benefits, and that informed consent of parents or guardian be given. It is recommended that children older than age seven be asked for their assent, as well. Nontherapeutic research, whose main goal is to obtain scientific information, has stricter standards than does therapeutic research, whose primary goal is to benefit the child-subject. Despite parental consent, in nontherapeutic research any child over age seven may refuse assent and veto participation, any child may withdraw from the research at any time for any reason, and except under very special conditions, no child may be subjected to anything greater than "minimal" risk, defined as the sort of experience likely to be encountered in everyday activities.

**Forensic Issues.** Courts often depend on the professional evaluations of psychiatrists or psychologists to determine the "best interest of the child" in custody or adoption suits, the reliability of child witnesses, or the competency of juvenile offenders to stand trial as adults. One must beware of potential bias or conflict of interest in such cases, since the professional may be hired by one party and be expected to give favorable testimony. There is no general agreement on the age or standards of competency that apply to adolescents or tests to determine the truthful reporting of young children; thus, professionals may offer conflicting judgments, and there may be no clear way to resolve the conflict.

*—Rosalind Ekman Ladd*

**See also** Children's rights.

**BIBLIOGRAPHY**

Forman, Edwin N., and Rosalind Ekman Ladd. *Ethical Dilemmas in Pediatrics.* New York: Springer-Verlag, 1991.

Graham, Philip. "Ethics and Child Psychiatry." In *Psychiatric Ethics,* edited by Sidney Bloch and Paul Chodoff. Oxford, England: Oxford University Press, 1981.

Koocher, Gerald P., ed. *Children's Rights and the Mental Health Professions.* New York: Wiley, 1976.

Koocher, Gerald P., and Patricia C. Keith-Spiegel. *Children, Ethics, and the Law.* Lincoln: University of Nebraska Press, 1990.

Melton, Gary B., G. P. Koocher, and M. J. Saks, eds. *Children's Competence to Consent.* New York: Plenum, 1983.

Stein, Ronald. *Ethical Issues in Counseling.* Buffalo, N.Y.: Prometheus, 1990.

## Child support

**TYPE OF ETHICS:** Children's rights
**DATE:** Common law, 200 C.E. to present
**ASSOCIATED WITH:** Changes in U.S. divorce legislation during the 1970's
**DEFINITION:** Concerned with the moral and legal obligations of parents to children over whom they do not have legal or physical custody
**SIGNIFICANCE:** Seeks to protect minor children from the financial consequences of family disruptions, balancing the obligations of the involved adults and society

Children have a legitimate expectation of protection and nurturance from adults. As society became increasingly complex during the twentieth century, that responsibility grew to cover a longer period of time and a wider range of obligations. Traditionally, the adults responsible for providing this nurturance have been the child's parents. While there have always been children who have not had two parents, owing to death, divorce, and out-of-wedlock childbirth, the number of children in single-parent households grew significantly during the late twentieth century. Simultaneously, changes in gender roles challenged traditional assumptions about the delegation of moral and legal obligations to children. The consequence was the nonsupport of many children and the insufficient support of far more.

**History.** Common law assumed that the physical care of children was the responsibility of the mother, while the financial support of the children (and, in support of that end, the mother) was the responsibility of the father. Courts adjudicated divorces and child support awards with this assumption until the 1960's. Two related trends altered this longstanding approach.

California passed the first "no-fault" divorce law in 1970. The intent was to minimize acrimony in divorce proceedings, with the anticipated consequence of alleviating the financial and emotional disruptions to children, as well as adults, imposed by an adversarial system. Cultural changes in gender role expectations led to additional changes in the division of responsibility between parents. These changes were reflected in the courts in the initiation of "joint custody" arrangements and an increase in contested custody.

Research by Ron Haskins showed that noncustodial fathers continued in the 1980's to recognize verbally a moral responsibility to support their children. Nevertheless, critics such as Lenore J. Weitzman, in *The Divorce Revolution* (1985), and Ruth Sidel, in *Women and Children Last* (1986), argued that changes in the application of divorce law in fact had the unanticipated effect of impoverishing women and children. First, "no-fault" laws made divorce easier to obtain. Second, growing legal assumptions of gender equality led to equal divisions of property, even when the mother had neither the education nor the job history to allow her to earn an equal income. Child support awards were based not only on unjustified assumptions about the mother's earning potential but also on the implicit assumption that she would continue the traditional role of sole physical care while assuming half of the financial responsibility. As noted, the law also changed to allow for joint custody. In practice, however, this applied to a tiny fraction of children during the 1980's.

The situation was further exacerbated by a trend of noncompliance with legally adjudicated child support. Recognition of social responsibility to the involved children was embodied in national legislation, notably the Child Support Enforcement Act, which passed in 1975. Nevertheless, critics charged that enforcement of child support payments remained insufficient.

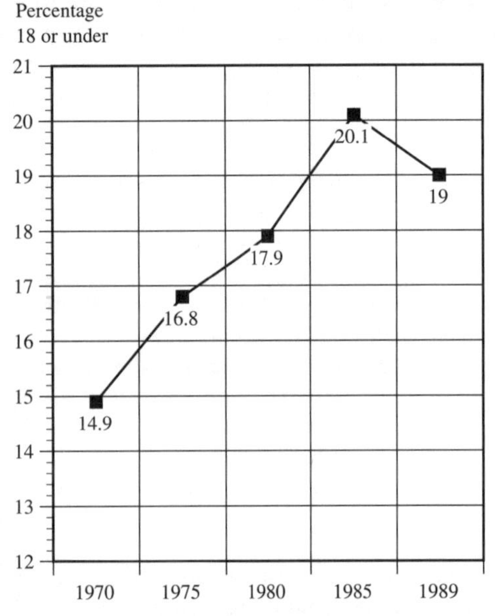


*Children in the United States Living Below the Poverty Level.*

These social changes created a situation that has been called the "feminization of poverty." While the term refers to adult women impoverished by circumstances such as divorce, in fact, the largest growing segment of the population trapped in poverty in the 1980's were *children*, in particular the children of these women. These children were effectively denied their right to appropriate nurturance in the form of proper nutrition, medical care, and education.

**Areas of Contention.** There were several specific areas that created disputes among lawyers and social policy analysts, as well as among the involved parties. The legal determination of the appropriate amount of child support weighed a number of complex factors, including the ability to pay and previous lifestyle. Many of these issues were determined from the perspective of the adult's concerns rather than from that of the child's rights. When that perspective was included, additional issues arose. Appropriate support included medical care; in practice, this entailed paying for health insurance. Educational needs were frequently a point of controversy, particularly since the age of majority usually determined the extent of legal child support obligation. In 1972, California changed that age from 21 to 18, with tremendous consequences for the support of college-age children.

Other disputes centered on how best to encourage noncustodial parents to meet their responsibilities. Legally, in the 1990's, there was no link between visitation arrangements and child support, but research by Mavis Hetherington suggested that fathers retained a greater sense of responsibility to their children when visitation was more frequent and/or extended. The organization Equal Rights for Fathers developed as a goal the greater enforcement of visitation and other policies to enhance visitation.

Most social policy analysts in the 1980's and 1990's focused efforts on enforcement of child support awards. Methods included attachment of wages, attachment of income tax refunds, and public humiliation of the worst offenders. Child advocates also noted that the size of awards at that time needed to be increased substantially to meet the real needs of children. Additionally, Ruth Sidel argued, in *Women and Children Last* (1986), that social policies needed to be designed to enable custodial parents to meet the obligations they could neither escape nor fulfill. Programs such as job training and childcare, and an end to wage discrimination against women, were deemed critical to that end.

The United States in the late twentieth century confronted a major ethical dilemma. Those who had reached adulthood had to find a way to meet their obligations to those who had not. —*Nancy E. Macdonald*

**See also** Children's rights; Divorce; Family values; Wage discrimination; Welfare programs.

**BIBLIOGRAPHY**

Cassetty, Judith, ed. *The Parental Child-Support Obligation: Research, Practice, and Social Policy.* Lexington, Mass.: Lexington Books, 1983.

Garfinkel, Irwin. *Assuring Child Support: An Extension of Social Security.* New York: Russell Sage Foundation, 1992.

Kahn, Alfred J., and Sheila B. Kamerman, eds. *Child Support: From Debt Collection to Social Policy.* Newbury Park, Calif.: Sage Publications, 1988.

Sidel, Ruth. *Women and Children Last: The Plight of Poor Women in Affluent America.* New York: Penguin Books, 1987.

Weitzman, Lenore J. *The Divorce Revolution: The Unexpected Social and Economic Consequences for Women and Children in America.* New York: Free Press, 1985.

## Children

**TYPE OF ETHICS:** Children's rights

**DATE:** From the eighteenth century Enlightenment to the present

**ASSOCIATED WITH:** *Parens patriae*, the nineteenth century child saving movement, and modern juvenile justice and child welfare agencies

**DEFINITION:** The ethical significance of "childhood" and attitudes toward children and their treatment is a social creation that has varied throughout history and across cultures

**SIGNIFICANCE:** Ethical views and practices that prevail toward children provide substantial insight into the larger social ethics of changing societies

The treatment of children by adults differs discernibly from culture to culture and has continually changed throughout history, as have general attitudes toward childhood. The social status of "childhood" is culturally defined and cannot be precisely identified through strictly biological or any other type of universal criteria. All culturally accepted conventions are, ultimately, arbitrary, so they gain their normative or legal validity only by social fiat.

Despite the commonsensical understanding of a child as a "biologically immature" adult, it is the social recognition of this "immaturity" that defines the child status. For example, while the achievement of childbearing age may signify full maturity and thus adulthood among females of certain indigenous peoples of South America, it emphatically does not among industrialized North American societies. Indeed, the very fact that many modern states legally specify a certain age to define childhood/adulthood contradicts the biological fact that human beings "mature" (however that is socially defined) at significantly different ages.

**Children's Ethics.** In moral terms, the norms of "acceptable" treatment of those people socially recognized as "children" are equally subject to historical and culturally relative criteria. The most common ethical issues that arise relate either to the extent to which full social obligations can be placed upon children or to the moral responsibilities of adults toward children, including the respective legal rights of both parties.

The ethical content of child status versus adult status can attain a profound social significance, determining the eligibility of people to perform certain types of work, consume alcoholic beverages, exercise control over their own health treatment, fight in wars, engage in legitimate sexual activity, vote in elections, and so on. In modern criminal law codes, the recognition of child status usually determines the extent to which one is legally punishable or even culpable for criminal behavior.

**Historical Attitudes.** The specification of "childhood" as a special social category is relatively recent in human history. As a legally recognized status, it is only a few hundred years old. The apparent social indifference toward young people prior to this specification is thought by some experts to be related to their high mortality rate. Up to the 1600's, more than half of the twenty-one-year-old and younger population died before entering what many contemporary societies now define as "adulthood." In such societies, it is reasoned, there was no strong argument for becoming too interested in members of a population who could not be reliably expected to survive. Comparative perspectives call these assertions into question, however, citing evidence from non-Western cultures that challenge the universality of these historical stereotypes.

Most experts agree that the general unifying characteristic from ancient times up to the sixteenth century, at least in European societies, was the virtual absence of societal institutions aimed specifically at children. In short, Western societies were "adult centered" for centuries, and children simply grappled with society by mixing with adults and eventually learning how to function as adults. Up into the eighteenth century, childhood in the contemporary sense essentially referred to pre-five-year-olds. Those individuals who were older became immersed in the normal work responsibilities of the household, though stratified by gender.

The origin of the social status of childhood as defined in Western societies is most frequently attributed to the eighteenth century Enlightenment. The Enlightenment weakened many of the most traditional religious notions that had governed human self-understanding, including the presumption of an inherent "evil" that resided in people as described in the biblical metaphor of "after the fall." With the rise of social "progress" theories that would in turn lead to the development of the social sciences, more sanguine images of human nature began to trickle down into the Western mindset, and notions of the perfectibility of the human race became widely disseminated.

Philippe Aries' seminal work on the history of childhood, *Centuries of Childhood: A Social History of Family Life* (1962), chronicles how social attitudes toward children began to change during this period. Using content analysis of portraits, early writings on pedagogy and pediatric medical care, and other cultural artifacts, Aries uncovered the various ways in which the developmental phases of childhood and the passage into adulthood became reconceptualized.

Examining the affluent classes of European societies, Aries shows how portraits began to appear as early as the sixteenth and seventeenth centuries in which children were depicted as having a distinct and "innocent" character and were no longer made to look like miniature adults. This notion of childhood innocence became one of the defining features of children in the post-Enlightenment period, which in turn helped fuel a shift in social attitudes. Children became increasingly thought of as "pure" and "good" people who needed protection from rude, dangerous, and immoral social processes that could harm their development. Social attention turned decisively toward child upbringing and the need to instill morality into children under the protection of adults. Activities formerly common among young people as well as adults, such as cursing, drinking alcoholic beverages, and sexual activities, all became increasingly regarded as antithetical to childhood and became socially prohibited among children.

Greater emphasis on structured childrearing gradually became the norm among the middle classes during this period. During the seventeenth century, the apprentice system routinely took young males and females between the ages of ten and fifteen out of the household, whereupon they became members of another in order to learn a trade from a skilled artisan. The apprentice earned his or her keep but remained under the strict control of the master. This was viewed socially as a means by which parental coddling could be defeated, since children completed the rearing process under the more detached supervision of an unrelated master. The apprentice system was ultimately dismantled by the onset of the Industrial Revolution and had largely disappeared by the nineteenth century.

**Child Welfare in the United States.** In the United States, social attitudes became more child-centered following the rise of the factory system in the early 1800's. Once seen as little more than the waiting period before becoming an adult, childhood became more idealized and regarded as an end in itself, an object of increasing social attention.

New social institutions designed to address the special needs and characteristics of children began to proliferate and expand in importance during the nineteenth century, with the most important being formal education. The eventual rise in popularity of kindergartens previsioned the subsequent social concern with progressive educational reform that aimed to nurture the spontaneity and creativeness of children rather than repress it. All such trends provide evidence of the continuous evolution in American attitudes toward recognition and respect of a "child's world."

Of equal ethical importance was the creation of social agencies aimed at dealing with child deviance. With deviance committed by children becoming increasingly regarded as a reflection on the social environment rather than as evidence of the "evil" lurking in the young person's soul, social forces arose to intervene in the lives of failed or defunct families so as to "rescue" children from their defective environment. "Houses of refuge" were opened for children throughout the United States during the 1820's, becoming the first generation of "child-saving" institutions that would later culminate in the expansion of state child protection services during the twentieth century.

Child refuges attempted to create a "properly structured environment" in which the negative influences of poverty, neglectful parents, and/or a syndrome of poor behavior on the part of the child could be corrected through military-like discipline and the learning of model social roles. The state was frequently called upon by charitable institutions to facilitate their child-saving activities by granting them legal rights of supervision over the children, a process that gradually drew the state into greater involvement in child welfare.

After the Civil War, social reformers began to criticize the prison-like model of child refuge centers, calling instead for more humanistic interventions that aimed to restore family life settings and to focus on teaching skills to errant children. With child saving emerging as a major ethical concern in the latter 1800's, many feminists began to enter into the child advocacy movement, emphasizing child welfare over child punishment.

Largely because of child welfare reformers, the juvenile court system was formed during the turn of the century, with the first court instituted in Illinois in 1899. Within three decades, virtually every state had a juvenile court system that typically exercised its jurisdiction over children "in trouble" under the age of sixteen. Invoking the principle of *parens patriae*, a notion dating back to feudal times that asserts that the state is the ultimate parent to children, the juvenile courts established the power of the state to designate as "wards of the state" those children who had broken laws, been improperly treated by their parents, or had engaged in behavior considered immoral for children, and to thus assume full legal responsibility for their welfare.

Many experts argue that the juvenile justice system as it developed acted primarily to address the concerns of the middle and upper classes by enabling the state to intervene in the lives of poor families. While the overarching ideology governing the court was child welfare through therapeutic action rather than a punishment ethic, critics over the years argued that the court routinely violated the civil rights of children, particularly those of the lower classes. The 1967 U.S. Supreme Court decision *In re Gault* reaffirmed the constitutional impropriety that pervaded the juvenile justice system in practice, its good intentions notwithstanding, and ruled that juveniles were entitled to the full legal protection of the due process enjoyed by adults.

Along with the increasing specialization of the legal system designed to differentiate children from adults, the social sciences gradually developed specialized research traditions in the area of juvenile delinquency. Institutes for the study of juvenile delinquency were formed and became influential in consulting with the state on the expansion of state social welfare agencies. By the early twentieth century, children received a variety of public services, usually for their material support in cases in which a need was recognized. State-sponsored foster homes and a variety of residential facilities were created to offer childcare and child protection. The eventual creation of specialized state child protection agencies led to the development of comprehensive systems of family welfare, with intervention into child abuse and neglect cases, emerging as systems that would coexist with legal and medical authorities.

**Ethics of Child Maltreatment.** The social recognition of child maltreatment and the "discovery" of child abuse provide a dramatic example of changing social attitudes toward children and their proper ethical treatment. In Ancient Rome, the principle of *patria potestas* established the complete control of fathers over their children, including decisions concerning their right to live, regardless of age. Infanticide was widely practiced there, as it was in virtually all ancient societies, including ancient Egypt and Greece. Often, a particular ritual was practiced that established the social expectation that a particular child was to be raised to maturity. Prior to the event, unwanted children could in most cases be disposed of without social sanction. Among the most common situations in which infanticide was practiced were cases of birth deformities and cases of children who were "illegitimate," conceived by incest, or considered likely to become a drain on the state in the absence of a conducive family setting.

During the Middle Ages, the Christian doctrine of parental love tempered somewhat the brutality latent in the absolute authority it granted parents over children in cultures where it predominated. Nevertheless, severe corporal punishment remained a norm in most Christian cultures. For example, historical data show that when French Jesuits first encountered the eskimo societies of North America in the 1600's, they observed with horror that the aborigines refused to hit their children for any reason. To the French missionaries, the taboo on child beating was evidence of the primitive and paganistic ways of the eskimos. Once the conversion to Christianity began, the Catholic missionaries placed special emphasis on preaching the necessity to beat children so that they would "learn to fear God."

In no way unique to France, the physical punishment of children, often in an extreme form, was considered fully legitimate in Western societies until the late nineteenth century. In the 1870's, the Society for the Prevention of Cruelty to Children (SPCC) was formed to advocate for legislation in the United States designed to protect children from abusive employers and surrogate caretakers. While the success of the SPCC and other child-saving institutions is shown by the formation of the juvenile justice system, it was the parallel development of social welfare agencies that pioneered the emphasis on direct intervention within conflictual families. Child protective services (CPS) exhibit a paternalistic and therapeutic model of intervention. With their legislative authority based in juvenile and criminal court statutes, CPS bureaucracies are firmly controlled by government agencies, primarily at the state level. The Child Abuse and Prevention Act of 1974 mandated that state CPS agencies follow certain federal guidelines with respect to creating open channels of reporting child maltreatment.

The expansion of CPS during the 1970's and 1980's emphasized the provision by social caseworkers of services that could repair and restore the family, with removal into state foster homes as a last recourse; this contrasted with the early child-saving movement, which emphasized removal and the creation of alternative arenas of socialization.

**Medicalization and Child Ethics.** Another important shift in social attitudes toward children grew out of changes in the medical establishment. The early development of pediatric medicine had paralleled the increasing social recognition of childhood. In the 1960's, the discovery of the "battered child syndrome" by pediatric radiologists helped fuel social concern about child abuse. During the same decade, an explosion of pediatric medical research occurred concerning the phenomenon of child hyperactivity, providing another example of the impact that modern medicine has had on social attitudes and the treatment of children.

Hyperactive children have a long history of being socially defined in adverse terms, either as "possessed" by the devil or other "evil spirits," or as malicious, disorderly, rebellious, and so on. Nurtured by the specialized study of children among psychiatric researchers, medical research in the second half of the twentieth century began to discover various biological factors that influence child hyperactivity, along with an array of pharmacological treatments that proved to be effective in controlling it. This led to the clinical designation of child hyperactivity as an illness known as "hyperkinesis."

The "medicalization" or general social recognition of hyperactive child behavior as an "illness" constituted a qualitative break from earlier conceptions. From a moral category of "bad" or "evil" activity, the medical profession has largely succeeded in shifting the larger social understanding of a whole set of aberrant child behaviors into the more "neutral" terrain of a "sick" condition that rests outside the control of the afflicted child. The medicalization of this form of child deviance helps to illustrate the continuing erosion of traditional conceptions of children and childcare as much as it demonstrates the power of the medical community to alter the perceptions and ethical standards of child treatment.

The celebrated "childrearing manual" of Benjamin Spock, *Common Sense Book of Baby and Child Care* (1957), provides yet another example of the direct impact that medical authorities have had upon attitudes toward and the treatment of children. Spock's instructive emphasis on preserving "happiness" in childhood socialization helped contribute to the social recognition of a "science" of parenting, initiating a trend in which adults look to medical experts for advice on the optimal technique for raising their children.

**Persistent Ethical Dilemmas.** The ethical issues that surround the social attitudes and treatment of children must be continually reexamined and considered in their overarching complexity. At all levels, the socially acknowledged rights and obligations accorded to children as well as the transgressions against them have historically been stratified by social class, race, and gender. Young females are sexually abused at a rate six times that of young males. The rate of physical neglect of impoverished children is invariably higher and unlikely to improve merely through therapeutic means of treatment.

Just as maltreatment exhibits its social biases, so too do the various institutions that are involved in the professional treatment of children. If socio-historians have shown how child savers of the nineteenth century enacted reforms that disproportionately affected poorer families, contemporary child protection agencies can likewise be seen to enforce white, middle-class standards in their practices at the expense of poor women and people of color. Any perspective that claims to grasp the tremendous complexity of child ethics must continually and critically evaluate how childhood is intertwined with the dynamics of social class, gender, and racial inequalities.

*—Richard A. Dello Buono*

**See also** Child abuse; Child labor legislation; Child support; Children's rights; *In re Gault*; Society for the Prevention of Cruelty to Children, American (ASPCC); U.S. Declaration of the Rights of the Child.

**Bibliography**

Aries, Philippe. *Centuries of Childhood: A Social History of Family Life*. Translated by Robert Baldick. New York: Knopf, 1962. A classic work in the history of childhood. The author attempts to make a comprehensive study of social attitudes toward children throughout the entire span of recorded history.

Bernard, Thomas J. *The Cycle of Juvenile Justice*. New York: Oxford University Press, 1992. A very readable review of the changing historical conceptions of justice and legal rights regarding children. The author shows how the breakdown of traditional social controls led to the social creation of "juvenile delinquency."

Binder, Arnold, Gilbert Geis, and Dickson Bruce. *Juvenile Delinquency: Historical, Cultural and Legal Perspectives*. New York: Macmillan, 1988. A well-written text that provides useful information on the historical conceptions of children and the social construction of "child deviance." The historical background of virtually all of the principal social institutions that affect children are considered.

Platt, Anthony. *The Child Savers*. Chicago: The University of Chicago Press, 1969. An excellent empirical study of the changing social definitions of child deviance and how the label of "juvenile delinquent" is unevenly applied to different social classes. Considerable historical information is presented on the "child savers movement" of the nineteenth century.

Rabb, Theodore K., and Robert I. Rotberg, eds. *The Family in History: Interdisciplinary Essays*. New York: Harper & Row, 1971. An extremely useful collection of interdisciplinary essays that includes several in-depth chapters on the changing conceptions of children and a bibliographic note on the literature concerning the history of childhood.

## Children's Bureau, U.S.

**Type of ethics:** Children's rights

**Date:** Founded 1912

**Associated with:** Social Security Act

**Definition:** The Children's Bureau investigated and reported on "all matters pertaining to the welfare of children"

**Significance:** The Children's Bureau was America's first institutional recognition of children as individuals—not as property—with their own rights and needs

In the late nineteenth century, children's health became an issue in the United States. Mortality was very high, largely because neither parents nor physicians knew much about the specific needs of children. Doctors had begun to understand that simply providing adult treatments in smaller doses was not adequate. Gradually, new thinking about child psychology and development spread. In 1912, Congress established the Children's Bureau to deal with infant mortality, preventive medicine, orphanages, the juvenile justice system, and child labor. The Bureau quickly became a strong force for the improvement of children's lives. It established national birth registration to make possible the first useful study of infant mortality. The Bureau produced two booklets, *Prenatal Care* (1913) and *Infant Care* (1914), which were updated and distributed for decades. For the first time, mothers had access to sound advice. By disseminating information and training new professionals, the Bureau greatly expanded public health services for mothers and children. After the passage of the Social Security Act in 1935, the Bureau added services for new populations, including disabled, abandoned, and delinquent children, the mentally retarded, and specific minority groups.

**See also** Children; Children's rights.

## Children's rights

**Type of ethics:** Children's rights

**Date:** Early nineteenth century to present

**Definition:** That area of legislation and work of social agencies that seeks to protect children from discriminatory or abusive practices

**Significance:** Since the rise of the Industrial Revolution and modern mass societies, it has become apparent that special forms of exploitation apply to children of both sexes; a need for specially adjusted concepts of ethic to guard against such abuses therefore exists

When the Universal Declaration of Human Rights was passed by the United Nations General Assembly in 1948, the wording of Article 2 provided ideally for the protection of rights "without distinction of any kind, such as race, color, sex, language, religion, political or other opinion, national or social origin, property, birth or other status." Thus, as in the famous French Revolutionary Declaration of the Rights of Man (1789), formulators of identifiable categories of persons with unalienable rights omitted specific mention of age (either old age or youth). Such omissions may have stemmed from a general assumption that children are automatically an essential component of any population. Historical experiences before those famous declarations, however, and many key social developments, particularly in the second half of the twentieth century, suggest that there should be a specific sphere of concern for the rights of children in all regions of the world.

**Historical Precedents.** It was the spreading mid-nineteenth century impact of the Industrial Revolution that brought a desire by mine and factory owners to cut unskilled labor costs and, in the process, ushered in an entire era of employer exploitation of child workers. In several countries where such exploitation (long hours, very low pay, hazardous work conditions) became the object of public and political outrage, special child labor legislation acts were passed. An important part of such legislation in England and in France (see table) was to oblige employers to guarantee that working children could receive enough education to "free" them from the bonds of ignorance (and therefore near "slavery" in the unskilled workplace). In most cases, the question of whether the wider social and family environment in which disadvantaged children had to live could be addressed and resolved by laws was hardly posed in this era of early child labor legislation.

**The Question of Majority Age in the Twentieth Century.** Various societies have defined "rights" or "rites" of passage from childhood in different ways. In some traditional tribal settings, for example, important cultural distinctions have been made between what constitutes becoming a "man" and what constitutes becoming a "woman." These tend in general to be linked with puberty and "qualification" for marriage and family responsibilities. In modern Western societies, however, passage from adolescence to early adulthood tends to relate to a number of legal rights. Characteristic rights here might be the right to make legally binding decisions (including marriage and the establishment of a separate place of residence) without necessary parental consent, the right to vote, and the right to purchase "controlled substances" such as alcohol or tobacco. In addition to such rights, there may also be certain obligations attached to the attainment of a certain age. These include, according to the country in question, obligatory military service and the obligation to be tried in court according to the same conditions that apply to persons of full adult status.

**IMPORTANT EVENTS IN THE HISTORY OF CHILDREN'S RIGHTS**

| Year(s) | Law or Event | Impact |
|---|---|---|
| 1833 | British Parliamentary Act | Ages and hours limited for children in factories |
| 1844 | British Child Labor Act | Requires guarantee of minimal education for working children |
| 1851 | French Child Labor Law | Defines rights of apprentices |
| 1874 | French Inspectorates placed over employers of children | Provides for fines when minimal standards not met |
| 1890's | Education Curriculum Reforms passed in United States | Emphasizes social democratization of all classes of pupils |
| 1900-1910 | Juvenile Court System introduced | Establishes different courts, procedures, and punishments |
| 1950's, 1960's | U.S. Aid to Families with Dependent Children introduced | "Welfare" to needy children |
| 1960's, 1970's | Child Welfare System created | Public assignment to foster homes to protect children's rights |

In the United States, a division between juvenile and adult criminal jurisdictions has existed only since about 1900. The juvenile court system was established on the assumption that children are more likely to reform themselves if "instructed" rather than punished to the full limits of penal law. Because the juvenile system functions according to procedures quite different from those of the regular courts (notably in its emphasis on the judge's role, with less attention given to formal representation of the accused by an attorney), critics from the 1960's forward have called for its reform. In addition, some specialized agencies, including the National Legal Resource Center for Child Advocacy and Protection in Washington, D.C., and the National Center for Youth Law in San Francisco, have taken it upon themselves to serve as "watchdogs" to assure that juvenile justice, while remaining separate, provides adequate guarantees of equality of rights within the total penal system.

**Concern for Children's Rights in Modern Mass Societies.** The concerns of lawmakers and courts over the phenomenon of child abuse in many modern countries have had many historical precedents. Extreme cases of systematic infanticide can be found in a number of historical cultures. One example only among others appears in the Islamic Qur'ân itself, in passages exhorting Arab tribes living in ignorance of God's ways to abandon the custom of preferring male over female infants, some of whom might be killed at birth. The physical abuse of children, ranging from beatings by one or both parents to sexual exploitation either in the family (the object of anti-incest laws) or commercially (the object of special laws against child prostitution or pornography) has existed in one form or another from antiquity to the present. The compounded negative effects of mass societies, however, combined with the increasingly intensive examination of such problems by the media, seem to have focused more attention in the second half of the twentieth century than in any other period on the need to address protective rights for children.

After experiencing rather distressing early campaigns for special legislation to protect children's "external" rights in the workplace and in the penal justice system, contemporary society seems to have identified a general ethical need to look more closely at the internal functioning of the family to determine whether one of the key contributors to the eventual "external" abuse of children's rights is the home (or the absence of a real home).

In cases in which children do not receive the "normal" nurturing experience of a nuclear family (orphans, for example, or those who are assigned by public authorities to foster homes), there may be less difficulty in establishing certain objective criteria for determining whether children's rights are being respected: Specific legislation exists in most modern countries that defines exact procedures for meeting required standards of care for dependent children who do not live with their own families. If shortcomings are discovered, these same laws provide for terminating a foster care contract, for example, or even for closing down specialized childcare institutions, be they orphanages or part-time day-care centers.

Determining whether children are fully safe in their own families, however, is a very different matter. Here, the legal rights of privacy stand as protective barriers intended to keep the public authority of the state from infringing on personal freedoms (guaranteed, in the United States, under the Bill of Rights). Certain forms of legislation have been passed that, on the surface, at least, aim at protecting children living in families experiencing deprivation.

Perhaps the best-known (and most controversial) packet of social legislation targeting children is the Aid to Families with Dependent Children (AFDC) program, also referred to as "welfare." Although AFDC does not speak directly to questions of children's rights in ethical terms, it is the only government cash-disbursing program in the United States that assumes that the primary beneficiaries of special assistance are children who would otherwise go without many essentials. Part of the process of determining the effectiveness of AFDC aid involves social workers' intervention in determining how families manage the funds they receive. In extreme cases, such intervention can take forms that are resisted by families who, although desperate for aid, resent interference in the private sphere of family-child relations.

A second agency that is meant to serve as a "watchdog" over children's rights is the Child Welfare System. Its responsibility is to remove children from family situations that may be detrimental to their personal development and even personal safety. As the main authority referring children to foster homes, the Child Welfare System comes closest to executing public responsibility to protect the private rights of children despite the will of their own families.

Until the mid-1980's and into the 1990's, the assumed typical dilemmas of child deprivation or abuse (alcoholism, drugs, dysfunctional families also confronted with poverty-level existence, and so forth) seemed to lend themselves to the programmatic actions provided for in the Child Welfare System. By the 1990's, however, a series of quite different issues began to attract the attention of the media and the court system. The most controversial, which was just entering the courts in 1993, involved recognition that children themselves might, under particular circumstances, exercise the legal right to "divorce" their parents. This issue promised to invite a critical turning point, since it implied transfer of the decision-making process in children's rights from the public to the individual private sphere.

—*Byron D. Cannon*

**See also** Child abuse; Child support.

**BIBLIOGRAPHY**

Boulding, Elise. *Children's Rights and the Wheel of Life.* New Brunswick, N.J.: Transaction Books, 1979.

Cohen, Howard. *Equal Rights for Children.* Totowa, N.J.: Rowman and Littlefield, 1980.

De Lone, Richard. *Small Futures.* New York: Harcourt Brace Jovanovich, 1979.

Vittachi, Anuradha. *Stolen Childhood.* Cambridge, England: Polity Press, 1989.

White House Conference on Children. *Report to the President.* Washington, D.C.: White House Conference on Children, 1970.

## Chivalry

**TYPE OF ETHICS:** Medieval history

**DATE:** Influential from the eleventh century to the end of the fourteenth century in western Europe

**DEFINITION:** A code of conduct that stressed loyalty, wisdom, courage, generosity, religious fidelity, and the virtues of courtly love

**SIGNIFICANCE:** Forms of chivalry contributed to feudal Europe's social coherence, particularly among the nobility, for several centuries

The dissolution of the Carolingian empire in the ninth century completed the decentralization of political authority in western Europe. Although there would soon be signs of newly evolving nation-states, nearly four hundred years passed before strong central monarchies were again dominant in France, Spain, and England. During the intervening years, a complex network of local authorities arose to maintain small subsistence economies and to secure them against attacks and invasions. Never a "system," these local arrangements, based on varying personal and contractual agreements, loosely described western European feudalism. It was in this context that, between the ninth century and the eleventh century, codes of chivalry evolved, reaching their refinement in the thirteenth and fourteenth centuries. Whatever the immediate intent of these codes, over time they set ethical standards for both personal conduct and social relationships. They applied only to nobles, most of whom at some point in life fulfilled their chief social functions as warriors. (For maximum military effectiveness and to bear the weight of his armor, each noble warrior required a horse. The French word *cheval,* which means "horse," is the source of the English word "chivalry.") Consequently, among the nobility, most chivalric standards derived from military obligations. Others especially concerned the conduct of lords, knights, and their vassals in relation to the ideals or needs of Europe's remaining universal institution, the Catholic Church. Additional rules of behavior, which developed later, pertained to courtly, or romantic, love. Chivalry affected the lives of peasants only indirectly, although peasants were by far the largest segment of Europe's population.

**Military Chivalry.** Feudal society generally was based on a division of labor that was essential for life because of the scarce resources available in the Middle Ages. A handful of nobles thus devoted themselves to providing security for the peasants, who, in turn, furnished the means to feed, arm, and maintain the nobles. Chivalry therefore reflected the centrality of the warrior in feudal society and warrior virtues—loyalty above all, but also courage, wisdom, physical skill, individual prowess in battle, and a longing for glory.

Chivalric behavior was also pragmatic, however, and was intended to make the warrior's tasks easier. For example, knights were armored—over time, more and more heavily. Armor was cumbersome, uncomfortable, and hot. Few nobles chose to wear it at all times. Accordingly, an armored knight was forbidden to ambush an unarmored one; ambush was permissible, but the armorless victim had to be allowed to suit up before battle legitimately could begin. Then, too, since the purpose of taking prisoners was to ransom them, and since the prospect of any captor—including a king—becoming a captive himself was good, knights began to treat their captives as honored guests. By the thirteenth century, if captive nobles were unable to raise ransoms, their captors frequently released them and accepted their children or other relatives as hostages. On other occasions, if captives were unable to meet their ransoms, they were released after a simple pledge to return if they were unable to secure the sums demanded. An example of this was the voluntary return of France's Jean I to captivity in England when his countrymen failed to raise his ransom.

Military chivalry reached polished forms in tournaments, which were arranged mock battles. Their original goals were to maintain knightly skills and to profit from the capture of those who were defeated in jousts. The principal objective of the participants, however, soon became the achievement of glory; for example, to win admiring attention from higher nobles, to charm ladies, to bear the flags or colors of noble houses into jousts with panache, or to distinguish themselves by means of various gallantries. The English word "gallant," in fact, derives from the French *galant*, a thirteenth century word associated with chivalric dash and spiritedness.

**Religious Chivalry.** The Catholic Church persistently sought to mitigate the perpetual violence of European aristocracies by diverting knightly energies to more peaceful or more obviously religious ends. Gradually, the Church's sermons and literature sketched out fresh knightly ideals. The ideal knight should become the ideal Christian. If fight he must, he should fight for God, not for personal aggrandizement, land, or booty. He should observe Church-decreed periods of truce. He should serve the Church and his secular lords faithfully. He should suppress crime and bring order to his realms. He should also care for the weak and helpless. Scholars have noted that Church-sponsored crusades against infidels were partially attempts to steer knightly energies toward religious goals and divert them from self-destruction and the disruption of daily life.

**Chivalry and Courtly Love.** The songs and poems of French and Spanish troubadours during the thirteenth century successfully celebrated the notion that the leading nobility could derive great benefit by conducting themselves in ways that led ladies to admire and adore them. Thus, incentives were provided for the cultivation of gentler manners, for elevating the status of women, and for making them the center of the actions of such figures as Richard the Lion Hearted, Roland, or Galahad. In addition, the troubadours, whose livelihoods depended on lordly patrons, did much to exalt generosity by making it a cardinal virtue in their lengthy songs and poems. —*Clifton K. Yearley*

**See also** Bushido; Etiquette; Generosity; Heroism; Honor; Loyalty; Mercy; War and peace.

**BIBLIOGRAPHY**

Bédier, Joseph. *The Romance of Tristan and Iseult.* Translated by Hilaire Belloc and Paul Rosenfield. New York: Vintage Books, 1965.

Campbell, Joseph. *The Masks of God: Creative Mythology.* New York: Penguin Books, 1968.

Painter, Sidney. *French Chivalry.* Ithaca, N.Y.: Cornell University Press, 1957.

__________. *Medieval Society.* Ithaca, N.Y.: Cornell University Press, 1968.

Sayers, Dorothy, trans. *The Song of Roland.* New York: Penguin Books, 1975.

Stephenson, Carl. *Medieval Feudalism.* Ithaca, N.Y.: Cornell University Press, 1942.

## Choice

**TYPE OF ETHICS:** Theory of ethics

**DATE:** From antiquity

**DEFINITION:** The ability to do one thing rather than another for the purpose of achieving some goal

**SIGNIFICANCE:** Choice is fundamental to any ethical discussion; an act becomes one's act, whether right or wrong, when one chooses to do it

When one congratulates individuals for a job well done or punishes them for harming another, one does so because what they have done is their action. They chose to act this way rather than that way and, as a consequence of that choice, they accepted the responsibility of that action—it became their act. Legal, ethical, and everyday culture are founded on the responsibilities that are the consequences of free choice. At the same time, one is surrounded by those who wish to control one's choices to achieve their ends. Modern free choice must always be considered within the context of personal responsibility and communal control. As a result, in any discussion of choice in its ethical context, it is necessary to consider the nature of choice itself, its freedom, and the various theoretical and practical attempts to destroy or control this freedom of choice.

**The Nature of Choosing.** Every living thing moves: birds fly, dogs bark, wasps build nests, and bees sting. Within a certain range of activity, living things move in a purposeful manner: There is a pattern to their movement and a selection from among possible movements. Living things seem to do this action rather than that action because of some inner purpose. The human observer easily projects onto all living things both human feelings and thought. When one sees the dog bark, the bee sting, the bird fly, one may presuppose that the dog, bee, and bird are doing something like what one does oneself—they choose to bark, sting, or fly. Such a projection upon the surrounding world is part of those magic years of childhood when the child talks to the doll and listens to its answer. It is part of primitive tribal life, in which the whole world is viewed as being animistic and filled with life.

Some contemporary scientific methods reverse this common experience by suggesting that human actions are like animal actions. Behaviorism, a type of determinism, suggests that all living things act as a consequence of the causes that surround them. There is no such thing as free choice; everything is already determined by forces outside of one's control. Religious determinists claim that God determines what humans do, psychological determinists claim that mental and emotional makeup determine what people do, and sociological determinists claim that society determines what people do. For determinists, human free choice is purposeful activity performed as a result of the inanimate forces that surround people.

Although these deterministic theories are favored by many in the social sciences, contemporary culture is based on an entirely different principle. The prison, education, legal, and political systems are based on the principle of responsible free choice. Culture demands an answer to various questions: Whose fault is it? Who performed such a wonderful job? The answers determine reward and/or punishment. The system of rewards and punishment is based on the presupposition that people, not circumstances, are responsible for actions. Ethical theory has the same presupposition. All ethical theory is based upon responsible free choice. People act as a consequence of freely chosen goals and purpose. Culture, as well as ethical theory, recognizes that humans can do things that are unexpected and different, things that are beyond scientific systems and attempts to explain. There is something about the human being that enables him or her to say no whenever everyone expects a yes and yes whenever everyone expects a no. There is something about human beings that enables them to create something new. People have not made their homes the same way throughout time because they have freely chosen to do otherwise. Activity by animals and humans is not the same: People choose to act. Somehow, people can take what is outside them, bring it inside them, and, because of certain ideas, choose to change what is outside them.

**Choice Is an Action.** Choice is not only internal, it is also an action—what one does. Choosing and doing are internally linked. Certainly, people think about things, reflect upon things, imagine things. Choosing, however, is an intimate link between one's personal, internal goals, principles, and habits and how one affects the world around one by operationalizing and creating one's own world through choosing what will make it up.

**Choice Is an Intended Action.** What one chooses to do is purposeful—one wants to do it. It is not necessary that one have the intention of doing something every time one does it. Many choices are not intentional in terms of the here and now. Most choices are part of a more extensive intentionality of wanting, for example, to be a good person, a generous person, or an industrious person. In the light of these general intentions, people build habits of goodness or virtue, and these good intentions constitute the intention for specific actions.

Because ethical individuals make choices based on such general intentions, their lives have a consistency to them such that one can say "This is a good person" and expect a consistency of ethical actions.

**Ethical Choice Is Free Action Freely Intended.** Freedom is the possibility and ability of making choices. Such a definition of freedom is easy to read but difficult to apply. Certainly one is not more free the more choices one has or makes. It is not possible to quantify freedom. Certainly, a blind person does not have to wait for sight to live freely. Those who are surrounded by the constant attempt to control their political, economic, educational, food, drink, and dress choices through advertising should not say that they were forced to vote for a U.S. senator or drink a soft drink because advertising dominated the air waves and limited their choices.

At the same time, people should realize that there is a great deal of subtle manipulation of choices. Advertising is sold on the basis of the claim that consumers' choices can be manipulated by the advertiser. In modern technological consumer culture, choice is never had without someone trying to influence it. Most of the social sciences, which began as disinterested attempts to understand human behavior, are now used to attempt to control human behavior for economic or ideological purposes. One must develop a strong character in order to choose freely in the modern world. When one accepts the necessity and the possibility of free choice in contemporary society, one also accepts the responsibility that accompanies it. Ethical life is not freedom alone or choice alone, but free choices that result in acceptance of responsibility for one's actions. A free choice may be a bad choice or a good choice. —*Nathan R. Kollar*

**See also** Behaviorism; Determinism and freedom.

**Bibliography**

Farrer, A. M. *The Freedom of Will.* London: A. & C. Black, 1958.

Feinberg, Joel. "Freedom and Behavior Control." In *The Encyclopedia of Bioethics*, edited by Warren Reich. New York: The Free Press, 1978.

Kant, Immanuel. *Critique of Practical Reason and Other Writings in Moral Philosophy.* Edited and translated by Lewis W. Beck. New York: Garland, 1976.

Macmurray, John. *The Self as Agent.* Atlantic Highlands N.J.: Humanities Press, 1991.

Neville, Robert. "Behavior Control and Ethical Analysis." In *The Encyclopedia of Bioethics*, edited by Warren Reich. New York: The Free Press, 1978.

Oldenquist, Andrew. "Choosing, Deciding, and Doing." In *The Encyclopedia of Philosophy*, edited by Paul Edwards. New York: Macmillan, 1967.

## Christian ethics

**TYPE OF ETHICS:** Religious ethics

**DATE:** First century C.E. to present

**ASSOCIATED WITH:** Jesus of Nazareth, the various Christian churches and sects, and the many world cultures shaped by Christianity

**DEFINITION:** The beliefs and practices of Christianity, generally emphasizing the oneness and primacy of God, the prevalence of human sin, redemption in Christ, and self-giving love as the highest virtue

**SIGNIFICANCE:** Christianity acknowledges the depth of suffering in all life yet affirms life's ultimate meaningfulness; no longer dominant in Western culture since 1800, it nevertheless continues to be broadly influential in most world cultures

Christianity is a rich and complex religion; it exists in many divergent and even contradictory forms. It draws upon many resources: the Jewish scriptures, Jesus of Nazareth (whom Christians call Christ), Zoroastrianism, Stoicism, and Neoplatonism (to name a few). The following portrait must therefore be painted in very broad strokes.

**Jesus of Nazareth.** The whole of Christian ethics (called moral theology in Roman Catholicism) can be seen as a series of footnotes to the Sermon on the Mount (Matthew 5-7). In this collection of sayings attributed to Jesus, Jesus calls upon his followers to reject the dominant values of their culture and to live according to a different vision. Calling them "the salt of the earth" and "the light of the world," he urges them to trust in God rather than money, to pray in secret and not to broadcast their piety before others. He condemns not only murder but hatred as well; not only adultery but also lust. In one of the most famous moral sayings of all time, he instructs his disciples to "turn the other cheek" to those who strike them, to "repay evil with good," to "love your enemies," and to "pray for those who persecute you."

It is commonplace to say that Christian ethics is an ethics of *love*—love of God, love of neighbor, and love of self. When asked to summarize the Law, Jesus quoted the Jewish scriptures: "You shall love the Lord your God with all your heart, soul, mind, and strength, and your neighbor as yourself." This is not the same love as desire (*eros*) or kinship (*philia*); it is a self-giving love (*agape*) that creates and finds fulfillment in the other.

Even more important than Jesus' teachings, however, are what he *did* and what happened to him—his life, death, and resurrection. His life, characterized by healing, power, suffering, forgiveness, obedience, and ultimate submission to a humiliating death by crucifixion—followed by the ultimate triumph of resurrection—has been taken by countless Christians as the pattern for their own lives.

**The Primacy of God and the Universality of Sin.** Jesus, a pious Jew, took for granted Judaism's belief in one powerful, just, and merciful God who was God of all the world even if all the world did not acknowledge him. This included a belief in the primacy of divine action over human action—the belief that human beings are neither self-made nor accidents of nature but creatures of the God before whom the nations of the world are mere drops in a bucket. The God of Jesus is active and enmeshed in the world and all human history, even though still above it.

One of the most controversial of all Christian teachings is the *universality of sin*, which is sometimes described as Original Sin. Broadly speaking, it is the belief that everything that human beings do—and particularly the *good* that they do—is infected by an evil for which they are responsible but over which they have little control. Hence all human actions fall short of the good; although some are clearly worse than others, none is wholly good.

**Conflict with Culture.** These beliefs and teachings have put Christians in conflict with both their cultures and themselves. Most cultures value self-preservation and self-assertion, and use violence and coercion to achieve justice and maintain order; but the Sermon on the Mount is in profound contradiction with such a view, as was Jesus' refusal to resist the Roman soldiers who arrested him. Christianity seems to require the impossible: Who can avoid hating some people and lusting after others? The inner tension between the commandment to love one's enemies and normal tendencies toward self-preservation is equally profound. How can a soldier, a judge, or a ruler, all of whom must make use of violence, be a Christian?

Thus, Christianity finds itself in the midst of overwhelming contradictions and tensions between religion and culture, tensions mirrored in its own history. The new religion grew from a persecuted and illegal sect (c. 30 to 300 C.E.) into a rich and powerful church that dominated European culture and politics (c. 300 to 1800 C.E.), only then to find itself bitterly criticized, put on the defensive, and transformed into one voice among many in a pluralist world (c. 1800 C.E. to present). How has Christianity responded to these tensions?

Christian ethics seems to have taken one of three basic responses to these tensions: (1) it can take the path of cooperation and compromise, becoming part of the power structure and working through the culture, as have medieval Roman Catholicism and nineteenth century American Protestantism; (2) it can take the path of withdrawal, separation and purity, removing itself into separate communities and then either attacking the surrounding culture (as the Jehovah's Witnesses do) or ignoring it (as the Amish do); or (3) it can take the path of inner withdrawal into the self, as medieval mystics and contemporary intellectuals who emphasize personal spirituality have done. In technical terms, these three approaches are called (1) the church, (2) the sect, and (3) mysticism. All three of these "types" are authentically Christian, all have great strengths, and all have weaknesses. The church engages the world and society but tends toward hierarchy, conservatism, and compromise with the great evils of the age (slavery, for example); the sect usually appeals to oppressed members of society and tends toward purity and radicalism (sometimes liberal, sometimes conservative), but at the cost of self-righteousness and fanaticism; and the mystic can combine a tremendous inner liberation with profound tolerance of others but often becomes an utter relativist, profoundly indifferent to most serious moral questions. For the past two or three hundred years, the church type has been in relative decline, while the sect type and mysticism have increased.

**Present and Future Debates.** Although confident predictions of religion's demise have clearly failed, Christian ethics is nevertheless undergoing massive changes. Christian ethics is no longer identical with the ethics of Western civilization, in two senses: Western civilization no longer regards itself as Christian, and the majority of Christians now live in the Third World. Two hundred years ago, Christianity was criticized for being too pessimistic; today, it is criticized for being too optimistic! Several vigorous debates arising from these and other changes will both enliven and frustrate Christian ethics for the foreseeable future.

The growth in the number of Third World Christians and the worldwide increase in minority populations in the developed world will fuel continuing debates over the extent to which salvation entails *liberation* from economic and social oppression. Does God clearly side with the poor, as liberation theology insists? What does that mean? At the same time, the rapid growth in charismatic and conservative Christianity, particularly in South America and perhaps in the former Soviet Union, will require reevaluation of an ethics that emphasizes personal morality and responsibility over social change (which it nevertheless unintentionally produces). The growing importance of women in culture and religious institutions will intensify debates over gender and oppression, as can be seen in the growth of feminist liberation theology.

New debates have also arisen over the role of *love* and *suffering* in the Christian life. Christian love has often been described as self-sacrificial, and human suffering has been viewed as an opportunity to share in Christ's suffering; but now many question whether Christianity should be in the business of prescribing self-sacrifice and suffering for women and the poor. Nevertheless, it is impossible to remove all suffering from human life; everyone must suffer and die. Must we resist all pain and suffering at all costs? Are there times when they should be accepted and even embraced? These questions are also relevant to the euthanasia debate and to the growing cost of health care.

Concern over Christian teachings regarding the *environment* will also grow, as the Christian ethic of Earth stewardship wrestles with various forms of biocentrism and recent attempts to revive some pagan religions.

Finally, one may continue to look for debates over the primacy and power of God's involvement in nature and history, apart from which it will be impossible to sustain Christian ethics. *—Garrett E. Paul*

**See also** Augustine, Saint; Calvin, John; Ethical monotheism; Hegel, Georg Wilhelm Friedrich; Jesus; Kierkegaard, Søren; King, Martin Luther, Jr.; Luther, Martin; Niebuhr, Reinhold; Sin; Thomas Aquinas; Tillich, Paul.

**Bibliography**

Boff, Leonardo, and Clodovis Boff. *Introducing Liberation Theology*. Translated by Paul Burns. Maryknoll, N.Y.: Orbis Books, 1987.

Gutierrez, Gustavo. *We Drink from Our Own Wells*. Translated by Matthew J. O'Connell. Maryknoll, N.Y.: Orbis Books, 1984.

Hauerwas, Stanley. *The Peaceable Kingdom: A Primer in Christian Ethics*. Notre Dame, Ind.: University of Notre Dame Press, 1983.

Niebuhr, H. Richard. *Christ and Culture*. New York: Harper & Row, 1975.

Niebuhr, Reinhold. *An Interpretation of Christian Ethics*. New York: Meridian Books, 1956.

Ruether, Rosemary. *Gaia and God: An Ecofeminist Theology of Earth Healing*. San Francisco: HarperSanFrancisco, 1992.

Tillich, Paul. *Love, Power, and Justice*. New York: Oxford University Press, 1972.

## Chu Hsi

(Oct. 18, 1130, Yu-ch'i, Fukien Province, China—Apr. 23, 1200, Chien-yang County, Fukien Province, China): Philosopher

**Type of ethics:** Medieval history

**Achievements:** Revised Ssu-ma Kuang's history of China, *Tzu-chih t'ung chien* ("The Mirror of Good Government"), as *T'ung-chien kang-mu* (1172; *Outline and Digest of the General Mirror*); with Lu Tsu-chien, compiled the *Chin-ssu lü* (1175; *Reflections on Things at Hand*, 1967), an anthology of the writings of the foremost Neo-Confucian philosophers; published, in 1177, commentaries on Confucius' *Lun yü* (*Analects*) and Mencius' *Meng Tzu*, which he followed with commentaries on the *Ta hsüeh* (1188; *The Great Learning*) and the *Chung yung* (1189; *Doctrine of the Mean*)

**Significance:** Chu Hsi's principle of extending knowledge "through the investigation of things" ("*tao chin tsai ke wu*") referred particularly to the study of ethical conduct in and out of government; his neo-Confucianism dominated the intellectual life of China into the first decade of the twentieth century and was influential in Korea and Japan

Chu Hsi's neo-Confucianism embraces cosmology and metaphysics as well as ethics and a theory of evil. What he calls the supreme ultimate (*t'ai chi*) is the summation of emptiness, or the realm of no-things (*li*), which is "above shapes"; it is the ideal prototype and standard that determines the nature of things. The concrete physical world is determined by the vital force (*ch'i*; literally, "breath"), which is "within shapes." It individuates each thing. In this way, each thing has a nature (*li*) and a specific character (*ch'i*). Every single thing is instilled with the supreme ultimate, which is the totality of *li* in all things. Every man can cultivate *t'ai chi* through earnest investigation of things and extend his knowledge of *li*; such research includes the study of the *Four Books (Ssu shu)* of Confucianism and the study of ethical conduct. People are born with either good or bad *ch'i*: If it is pure and clear, they are talented and wise; if it is impure and turgid, they are foolish and degenerate. In China, Chu Hsi's philosophy was called the school of *li* (*li hsüeh*). From a Western point of view, it is a species of idealism.

**See also** Confucian ethics; Taoist ethics.

## Chuang Chou

**Chuang Chou** (c. 365 B.C.E., Meng, Kingdom of Sung, China—c. 290 B.C.E., Nan-hua Hill, Ts'ao-chou, Kingdom of Ch'i, China): Philosopher

**TYPE OF ETHICS:** Classical history

**ACHIEVEMENTS:** Author of *Chuang Tzu*

**SIGNIFICANCE:** Developed relativism and introduced naturalism and individualism into Taoism

Chuang Chou, who is also known as Chuang Tzu, or "Master Chuang," criticized the other schools of thought in feudal China, such as Confucianism, Moism, and Legalism, for their artificiality. He argued that their political and social ethics were conducive to the very disharmony that their proponents appeared to be combating. Words such as "duty" and "righteousness," as well as concepts of "good and evil," were the unnatural products of thinkers who were ignoring the real nature of humanity and its place in the universe. The way, or *tao*, of the universe was nonjudgmental. Nothing was either good or bad. In fact, the concept "good" could not exist without the concept "bad," and thus any effort to promote one of these concepts led to the unwitting encouragement of the other. As the *Chuang Tzu* states, "The Tao is hidden by meaningless disputation, and speech is subsumed by artificiality. The Confucians and Mohists argue endlessly that each school is 'right' and the other 'wrong,' but the Tao is universal and does not recognize right or wrong."

***Chuang Tzu.*** The text of the *Chuang Tzu* has been corrupted by additions and emendations, and there is much controversy regarding which parts constitute the inner core of Chuang Chou's thought. Despite this uncertainty, it is possible to perceive several consistent themes in the work. Chuang Chou was continuing the Taoist relativism of the *Tao Te Ching*, a work attributed to a philosopher by the name of Lao Tzu ("Master Lao"). The essence of this work is that there is a *tao*, or "way of the universe," which encompasses all things and cannot be reduced into words, which have parameters. The tao is not subject to parameters of any kind. The first paragraph in this short work states that the tao that can be spoken about or identified cannot be the true tao. Nevertheless, Lao Tzu's book has eighty subsequent chapters that attempt to identify the manifestations of the tao. The *Tao Te Ching* infers that if left alone, people are naturally peaceful and harmonious, but if they are harangued by moral argumentation, they can change for the worse. Just as concepts of shape, size, and aesthetics are all relative, so too are ethical dictates that become counterproductive because of the relativity of language.

In a sense, Chuang Chou's writing is more consistent with Lao Tzu's injunction against trying to verbalize or even conceptualize the tao than is any other work of Taoism. Instead of sermonizing, Chuang Chou's work primarily relates anecdotes and parables, leaving the reader to intuit the universality of the tao. Reality and illusion are integral parts of the tao, and the sage does not try to distinguish between the two. Thus, Chuang Chou states simply that, on a given night, he dreamed that he was a butterfly but wondered if he were a butterfly dreaming that he was a man. In order for skepticism to be in accord with the tao, it must be an all-inclusive skepticism that doubts even doubt itself.

Instead of despairing at this uncertainty, Chuang Chou suggests that one should act as if what one is doing is real and important but should also know that it might be an illusion. This is an important point in understanding Chuang Chou's ethics. He does not dismiss moral behavior, and he frequently suggests that one should live simply and harmoniously with others. What he does dismiss, however, is the act of attributing much importance to what one does. According to Chuang Chou, therefore, ceremonies and sermons do nothing to induce moral behavior. Simplicity, and by inference what is "good," can be achieved only by "getting closer to the tao."

When Chuang Chou's wife died and he beat on a drum instead of mourning for her, he answered his critics by explaining that perhaps his wife had evolved into a happier existence than that which she had enjoyed while in human form. It was not wrong to have loved her and to miss her, but it was wrong to mourn her change from one form to another. Chuang Chou's parables point out that one cannot be certain what is best for other people and that one should therefore avoid imposing tentative and uncertain values on others.

In several tales in the *Chuang Tzu*, men who because they are criminals have been punished by amputation seem to possess considerable wisdom, most of which has to do with not valuing things, including their limbs. Chuang Chou suggests that these men are in some ways more honest than others and have attained contentment and even "virtue" by losing that which other people strive so desperately to keep.

Chuang Chou also ridiculed those who would try to define the tao as a philosophy of action or ethics, perhaps anticipating the plethora of "The Zen of . . . " and the "Tao of . . . " literature that abounds today. A famous bandit by the name of "Robber Chih," to whom an entire chapter of the *Chuang Tzu* is devoted, is said to have argued that there is even a tao of stealing: "There is cleverness in locating the booty, courage and heroism in taking it, and the intelligence of plotting the theft. Finally, there is the honesty of dividing it fairly."

Although Chuang Chou calls for individualism and skeptical relativity, he does not argue in favor of selfishness or dissipation. Instead, his ethics consist of leaving other people to decide for themselves what is right and wrong and having no state, religion, or social organization make such determinations. To Chuang Chou, one could best perfect oneself by blending with nature and not competing with it. Only when people ceased to interfere with nature or with other people could there be peace. —*Hilel B. Salomon*

**See also** Confucian ethics; Confucius; Lao Tzu; Taoist ethics.

**Bibliography**

Allinson, Robert. *Chuang-Tzu for Spiritual Transformation*. Albany: State University of New York Press, 1989.

Giles, Herbert Allen, trans. *Chuang Tzu: Taoist Philosopher and Chinese Mystic*. 2d rev. ed. London: Allen & Unwin, 1961.

Waley, Arthur. *Three Ways of Thought in Ancient China*. Garden City, N.Y.: Doubleday, 1956.

Watson, Burton, trans. *The Complete Works of Chuang Tzu*. New York: Columbia University Press, 1968.

Wu, Kuang-ming. *The Butterfly As Companion: Meditations on the First Three Chapters of the Chuang Tzu*. Albany: State University of New York Press, 1990.

## Chuang Tzu. *See* Chuang Chou.

## Cicero, Marcus Tullius (June 3, 106 B.C.E., Arpinum, Latium—Dec. 7, 43 B.C.E., Formiae, Latium): Orator and politician

**Type of ethics:** Classical history

**Achievements:** Author of *De republica* (*On the Republic*), *De legibus* (*On the Laws*), *De finibus bonorum et malorum* (*On the Chief End of Man*), *Tusculanae disputationes* (*Tusculan Disputations*), and *De officiis* (*On Duty*)

**Significance:** A leading figure in the tumultuous final days of the Roman Republic, Cicero articulated and attempted to practice his belief that the good man gave himself to unselfish public service

The author and orator Cicero was one of the most eloquent exponents in the Roman world of the stoic belief that there is an inherent natural order in the universe and that this order requires human beings, as rational creatures, to follow natural law. This natural law, which can be apprehended through a calm and philosophical survey of the world, clearly indicates that humans are morally obliged to conform to the universal rule of reason. This is particularly true in social relationships, since Cicero shares the Greek belief in the natural brotherhood and equality of man; this belief makes serving the common good of humanity the highest duty of every individual. For Cicero, enlightened patriotism is an ethical as well as a political duty.

**See also** Common good; Duty; Natural law.

## Citizenship

**Type of ethics:** Politico-economic ethics

**Date:** Fifth century B.C.E.

**Associated with:** Concepts of rights and responsibilities

**Definition:** A status held by individuals born or naturalized into a community or state that confers upon the individual certain rights and duties in relationship to other members of the community and to the community itself

**Significance:** Imposes on individuals the duty to respect and observe the rights of others and to recognize the legitimate rights of the community at large as they assert their own rights as individual citizens

The idea of citizenship is central to any conception of ethics. Human beings, by necessity, live in or rely on social and political communities. To avoid conflict and promote cooperation in these communities, it is necessary that individual members of it learn how to accommodate their own interests and needs with those of the collective whole. The earliest systematic treatment of politics and the ethical comportment of citizens in political contexts undertaken by the ancient Greeks recognized that necessity drove individuals into the social context and held that duty was the primary content of citizenship. To Greeks and Romans, citizens enjoyed certain privileges or rights denied to outsiders, but the notion of an individual right, a natural right inhering in the individual, as opposed to a positive customary or statutory right that might be granted or withdrawn by the state, was not conceived until the seventeenth century. Political and ethical theory now posits that rights are inherent in the individual as individual, and one

*Cicero.* (Library of Congress)

of the rights now affirmed is the right to citizenship itself. If rights have become the primary focus of much thinking about modern citizenship, however, there can be little doubt that duty must remain a significant feature of citizenship if the concept is to have any genuine content, since rights have no meaning if no one has a duty to respect the rights of others.

**History.** The earliest conceptions of citizenship stressed the importance of the individual's duty to the state. Not all persons were considered citizens in the fullest sense of the term, even in the most democratic of states, such as Athens in the fifth century B.C.E., where active citizenship was limited to propertied men. With the privileges of citizenship came responsibilities: to participate in assemblies, to hold office, to defend the city from external enemies, to serve in the army or navy, to pay taxes, to outfit a naval vessel, or to subsidize a public festival. In the intimate confines of the Greek polis the citizen might enjoy certain privileges, but above all the citizen was duty bound to the state. Still the Greeks, as evidenced in Sophocles' story *Antigone* and in Plato's accounts of the trial and death of Socrates, were alive to the contradictions that the citizen might face in honoring civic duty on one hand and the dictates of individual conscience on the other.

In Rome, a more extensive body of rights was enjoyed by its citizens, although, as in Greece, citizenship carried with it certain duties, such as paying taxes and serving in the legions or navy. Moreover, the rights of Roman citizens were not conceived as natural or human rights, but rather were rooted in the custom or statutes of the city, and could be revoked. As Rome expanded beyond a republic to an empire, its conception of citizenship also enlarged, and under Caracalla in 212 C.E., citizenship was extended to all the Empire's inhabitants. By that time, the rights of the citizen had been substantially diluted. The coming of Christianity created new tensions for the citizen. In general, Christianity taught that the good Christian should obey and serve the political ruler except in matters that called for the Christian to violate fundamental tenets of faith or scruples of conscience. In these circumstances, passive disobedience and the acceptance of punishment for such disobedience was counseled. Violent rebellion was considered wrong. Christians were urged to respect the need for political authority and civil order. Duty, as in the classical ages, still dominated thinking about the individual citizen's relationship with the state. Not until the Religious Wars of the seventeenth and eighteenth centuries did philosophers (such as Thomas Hobbes and John Locke) posit the notion that individuals had inherent human rights that no state in principle should violate. Not until after World War II, however, did governments begin to adopt human rights treaties stipulating what those rights were or how they might be guaranteed.

**Current Issues.** Modern issues concerning the ethical content of citizenship include the nature of citizenship as a human right, the problem of civil disobedience, the scope of freedom in which citizens may act in face of the community's need for order, and the problem of citizens and outsiders. Modern human rights treaties suggest that individuals have a right to citizenship. No state, however, has a duty to extend citizenship to any particular person, which leaves many people, including refugees, in precarious situations. States also have the power to take away citizenship. Citizenship, then, is still governed by sovereign states and has only a tenuous claim to status as a human right. Within democratic systems, however, citizens are guaranteed civil rights and individual freedoms in domestic law. Even aliens are guaranteed individual freedoms by most governments, although civil rights, such as the right to vote and hold office, are reserved for citizens alone. The citizen also has duties, such as supporting the state, serving in its defense, and obeying its laws. On occasion, the individual's religious beliefs or personal conscience come into conflict with the law. This may lead an individual into acts of protest or civil disobedience. Modern examples of movements that espouse civil disobedience include the civil rights movement, the sanctuary movement, and the Operation Rescue faction of the pro-life movement. Citizens practicing civil disobedience risk punishment for violation of the law.

The tendency in many democratic countries has been for citizens to claim an expanding body of rights and personal freedoms. This overemphasis on rights has often ignored the importance of duties to others and to the community as a whole. A perpetual clash of rights without a sense of corresponding duties can lead to disorder and eventually to the endangerment of rights. An increasingly important ethical question for modern democratic societies, then, is how to ensure a balance between rights and duties.

Finally, what duties do the citizens of a society have toward aliens, illegal immigrants, refugees, or asylum seekers? In an era of substantial migration, questions about how to deal with outsiders—whether to grant them admission or citizenship or to exclude or deport them—become increasingly important. Decision rules about who should or should not be admitted raise ethical issues for public policy makers regarding the needs and rights of the existing citizen body and the predicament of asylum seekers and prospective immigrants who wish to become members of it.

*—Robert F. Gorman*

**See also** *Apology*; Conscientious objection; Democracy; Human rights; *Leviathan*; *Nicomachean Ethics*; Politics; Sovereignty; *Two Treatises of Government*.

**BIBLIOGRAPHY**

Aristotle. *The Politics*. Edited by Stephen Everson. New York: Cambridge University Press, 1988.

Augustine, Saint. *The Political Writings of St. Augustine*. Edited by Henry Paolucci. Chicago: Gateway Editions, 1987.

Paine, Thomas. *Rights of Man*. New York: Penguin Books, 1984.

Plato. *The Apology and Crito*. Edited by Isaac Flagg. New York: American Book, 1907.

Rousseau, Jean-Jacques. *The Social Contract.* Translated by Maurice Cranston. Baltimore: Penguin Books, 1968.

Sophocles. *Antigone.* Translated by Michael Townsend. San Francisco: Chandler, 1962.

Thoreau, Henry David. *Civil Disobedience.* Boston: David R. Godine, 1969.

Von Glahn, Gerhard. *Law Among Nations.* 6th rev. ed. New York: Macmillan, 1992.

## Civil disobedience

**TYPE OF ETHICS:** Civil rights

**DATE:** Nineteenth century to present

**ASSOCIATED WITH:** Mohandas Karamchand Gandhi, Martin Luther King, Jr.

**DEFINITION:** A nonviolent form of protest defying the law for moral and ethical reasons with the aim of changing the law

**SIGNIFICANCE:** A check to authoritarian tendencies in a political system and a means of effecting social change

Most civil disobedience movements have been nonviolent, hence the term "civil" (disobedience to the law in a civil, or nonviolent, manner). Civil disobedience has been used by people in various societies as a vehicle to seek changes in the laws considered unjust to those participating in these movements. The resistance by the state to such protests is based on the moral and political legitimacy claimed by the rulers in the name of the people. The fundamental philosophical issue here is that although the rule of law must be maintained in order for the society to function and to protect life and property, civil disobedience movements represent a challenge to the legitimacy of that rule of law. Participants in actions of civil disobedience recognize a higher moral authority than that of the state, asserting that the laws do not reflect the ethical norms of the people. They believe that it is therefore justifiable to disobey the law.

**Philosophical Background.** Political philosophers since Socrates have discussed and debated the rule of law and the legitimacy sought by the state in demanding obedience to its laws from its citizens. Socrates was accused of corrupting the minds of young people by preaching atheism. He thought it was his moral duty to disobey laws that he thought were immoral. Thomas Hobbes considered it the prerogative of the sovereign to institute laws that must be obeyed. He considered all laws to be just laws. John Locke, however, considered that the citizens did not completely surrender their right to resist a law they considered unjust. Henry David Thoreau advocated the right of citizens to resist laws they considered immoral or laws that forced people to commit injustice to others. Thoreau is considered the pioneer in the United States in advocating civil disobedience on moral grounds.

An important element of civil disobedience is conscientious objection. In conscientious objection, the objector is defying a law he or she considers repugnant to his or her moral principles. Unlike civil disobedience, in which the participants are seeking to change a certain law or laws, in conscientious objection, an objector seeks exemption from a law for himself or herself only. For example, many individuals have refused to pay the portion of their federal taxes that would be used for defense expenditures. An important distinction here is the fact that these people are disobeying the law to pay taxes but they are not necessarily urging others to not pay taxes.

**Civil Disobedience in India.** A key civil disobedience movement in recent history was led by Mohandas K. Gandhi of India, popularly known as Mahatma Gandhi. He led protest movements in South Africa in the early twentieth century to challenge laws of racial discrimination by the whites against the indigenous peoples and nonwhites of South Africa. The technique he developed, based on ancient Indian philosophical ideas, focused on the notion of *satyagraha*, or "moral victory." According to this concept, the protesters would win their campaigns because they stood on higher ethical ground than did the laws they chose to disobey. After winning many legal battles in South Africa, Gandhi returned to India to take part in the movement for national independence from the British. This is where he perfected the art of nonviolent civil disobedience. He soon realized that the most effective way of hurting the British was to deny them the revenue they earned by selling products manufactured in Britain to Indians. Gandhi launched a movement to boycott goods made in Britain. Two important milestones in Gandhi's civil disobedience movement were the boycott of British-made cloth, which Gandhi reinforced by encouraging Indians to weave their own cotton, and the second was the defiance of the ban on making salt from saltwater. These two movements mobilized millions of people in boycotting British-made goods and defying British laws in a nonviolent manner.

**Civil Disobedience in the United States.** The civil disobedience movement in the United States was essentially the struggle of African Americans to gain equal rights. An important milestone in the civil rights movement in the United States was the refusal of Rosa Parks to vacate her bus seat to a white passenger in Selma, Alabama. This act of civil disobedience led to widespread agitation in the southern United States. Martin Luther King, Jr., who organized and led the protests, is considered the father of the civil disobedience movement in the United States. King adopted Gandhi's idea of nonviolent noncooperation. He led protesters in challenging "Jim Crow" laws that segregated whites and nonwhites in education, public facilities, and other arenas. This civil disobedience movement led to the dismantling of most of the racially discriminatory laws in the United States and the passage of the Civil Rights Act in 1964.

Another important civil disobedience movement in the United States was the opposition to the United States' involvement in the Vietnam War. Many young people refused to join the armed forces. There were protests all over the

| MAJOR EVENTS IN THE HISTORY OF CIVIL DISOBEDIENCE | |
|---|---|
| 1849 | Henry David Thoreau publishes "Resistance to Civil Government" (later known as "Civil Disobedience"). |
| 1906 | Mohandas K. Gandhi urges Indians in South Africa to go to jail rather than accept racist policies. This is the beginning of the *satyagraha* strategy. |
| 1919 | Gandhi leads nationwide closing of businesses in India to protest discriminatory legislation. |
| 1928 | Gandhi organizes on behalf of indigo workers in Bihar, India, and initiates fasting as a form of *satyagraha.* |
| 1920-1922 | Gandhi leads boycott of courts and councils in India and develops noncooperation strategies. |
| 1932-1933 | Gandhi engages in fasts to protest untouchability. |
| 1942 | Gandhi arrested for *satyagraha* activities. |
| 1955 | Martin Luther King, Jr., leads boycott of transit company in Montgomery, Alabama. |
| 1956-1960 | King leads protest demonstrations throughout the South. |
| 1963 | King leads the March on Washington for civil rights. |
| 1965 | King leads the "Freedom March" from Selma to Montgomery and organizes voter registration drive. |
| 1968 | King initiates a "Poor People's Campaign" but is assassinated before it can be carried out. |

country, mainly in educational institutions, demanding the withdrawal of U.S. troops from Vietnam. Resistance to the draft was a key form of civil disobedience in this era.

The civil disobedience movement poses a serious challenge to the authority and the claim of the state for total compliance of laws by its citizens in the name of maintaining peace and order in society. By defying laws considered morally repugnant, civil disobedience movements have played a key role in changing numerous unjust laws in the United States and abroad. —*Khalid N. Mahmood*

**See also** Gandhi, Mohandas Karamchand; Thoreau, Henry David.

**BIBLIOGRAPHY**

Fullinwider, Robert K., and Claudia Mills, eds. *The Moral Foundations of Civil Rights.* Totowa, N.J.: Rowman & Littlefield, 1986.

Gandhi, Mohandas K. *An Autobiography, or the Story of My Experiments with Truth.* Translated by Mahadev Desai. Ahmedabad, India: Navajivan, 1959.

Gans, Chaim. *Philosophical Anarchism and Political Disobedience.* New York: Cambridge University Press, 1992.

Thoreau, Henry David. "Civil Disobedience." In *Thoreau: People, Principles, and Politics,* edited by Milton Meltzer. New York: Hill & Wang, 1963.

Williams, Juan. *Eyes on the Prize: America's Civil Rights Years, 1954-1965.* New York: Viking, 1987.

## Civil rights

**TYPE OF ETHICS:** Civil rights
**DATE:** Coined in English 1483
**ASSOCIATED WITH:** History and development of law
**DEFINITION:** The original meaning of "civil right" or "civil law" was *jus civile*, the law of Roman citizens; in England, the term was first used to distinguish civil law from canon law, and over the years it has come to signify the laws establishing the private rights and duties of citizens
**SIGNIFICANCE:** The system of civil rights is intended to permit every member of a polity to seek liberty, property, and happiness, free of interference from others or from the government

Civil rights in the broadest sense permit one to live one's life free of fear of being victimized by other members of the community or by the government. Thus, laws that establish and protect property and personal rights are an important part of civil liberty. The common usage of the term, however, encompasses both the rights of individuals in relationship to government and those rights that are enforceable in courts. In this sense, there are two types of rights: substantive and procedural.

**Substantive Rights.** Substantive rights are those things that one can do as a matter of right without interference from the government or public officials. In the United States, there is constitutional and customary protection for many of the most basic aspects of life; for example, the rights to citizenship, to own property, to choose one's spouse, to choose an occupation, to be protected by laws, and to make and enforce lawful contracts. There is additional constitutional protection for other substantive rights. Most of the limits on government are found in the Bill of Rights. The First Amendment freedom of speech, press, and assembly and the right to the free exercise of one's religion protect the individual's conscience and allow him or her to associate with whomever he or she chooses. The Fourth Amendment, which has both procedural and substantive aspects, forbids agents of the government to enter one's home or other places where one can reasonably expect privacy, except under narrowly defined circumstances. The First and Fourth Amendments combined establish additional rights of privacy that protect access to birth control information, access to abortion for a pregnant woman in the first trimester of pregnancy, privacy in the choice of one's reading matter, and privacy in intimate marital matters. Under the Second Amendment, there is still a limited private right to keep and bear arms.

There are also substantive political rights in the United States. In general, political rights are conferred only on citizens; most of the other substantive rights discussed above are conferred on citizens and noncitizens alike. Political rights include citizenship itself, the right to vote, and the right to hold public office or to participate in other ways in the administration of government.

**WHERE TO FIND CIVIL RIGHTS IN THE U.S. CONSTITUTION**

| Right | Amendments to the Constitution | | | | | | | | | | | | | |
|---|---|---|---|---|---|---|---|---|---|---|---|---|---|---|
| | 1 | 2 | 3 | 4 | 5 | 6 | 7 | 8 | 9 | 10 | 14 | 19 | 24 | 26 |
| Freedom of religion | ✓ | | | | | | | | | | * | | | |
| Freedom of speech | ✓ | | | | | | | | | | * | | | |
| Freedom of the press | ✓ | | | | | | | | | | * | | | |
| Freedom of assembly/petition | ✓ | | | | | | | | | | * | | | |
| Right to bear arms | | ✓ | | | | | | | | | | | | |
| No unlawful quartering | | | ✓ | | | | | | | | | | | |
| No unreasonable searches or seizures | | | | ✓ | | | | | | | * | | | |
| Right to due process | | | | | ✓ | | | | | | ✓ | | | |
| Speedy trial by jury | | | | | | ✓ | | | | | * | | | |
| Jury trial in civil cases | | | | | | | ✓ | | | | | | | |
| No excessive bail or cruel and unusual punishments | | | | | | | | ✓ | | | | | | |
| Recognition of unnamed rights | | | | | | | | | ✓ | | * | | | |
| Powers reserved to the states and to the people | | | | | | | | | | ✓ | * | | | |
| Equal protection under the law | | | | | | | | | | | ✓ | | | |
| Voting rights | | | | | | | | | | | | ✓ | ✓ | ✓ |

*Rights that have been incorporated into the Fourteenth Amendment by Supreme Court decisions.

**Procedural Rights.** Procedural rights are those procedures that the government must afford an individual whose life, liberty, or property it proposes to take. The foremost expression of procedural rights is found in the due process clause of the Fifth Amendment, which promises that no "person will be deprived of life, liberty, or property without due process of law." At a minimum, then, the government must afford the individual a fair hearing before imposing any kind of punishment or deprivation. The Constitution is full of provisions that specify the contents of fair procedure. An arrested person must be brought before a magistrate soon after arrest and, except under certain narrowly defined circumstances, is entitled to be released on bail while awaiting trial. The defendant in a criminal case is entitled to a trial by an impartial jury; the government may not force him to stand trial away from the area in which the crime occurred. No one can be forced to incriminate himself or herself either before a tribunal or during a police interrogation. A defendant has the right to confront and cross-examine opposing witnesses as well as the right to have illegally seized evidence excluded from consideration at trial, thus making good the procedural side of the Fourth Amendment. Hearsay evidence is inadmissible in court. A defendant cannot be tried twice for the same crime if acquitted and cannot be subjected to cruel or unusual punishment. An indigent defendant has the right to representation by court-appointed counsel at public expense.

The crime of treason is narrowly defined by the Constitution, thus preventing the government from using treason charges against its political opponents. The writ of habeas corpus, which is the main procedural safeguard against unlawful arrest, may not be suspended by the government except in time of war or other emergency.

**Conclusion.** The guarantees discussed above reflect centuries of ethical thought and also incorporate the legal and political wisdom of bench and bar over the years. The fundamental principles that emerge are that people should be allowed to do and think as they see fit so long as they do not injure public peace or order, that only the guilty should be punished, that the powers of the government should never be used to injure people who are not guilty of crimes, and that fair evidentiary rules must be applied in the search for the truth when someone is accused of a crime.

*—Robert Jacobs*

**See also** Bill of Rights, U.S.; First Amendment; Freedom of expression; *Griswold v. Connecticut*; *Miranda v. Arizona*; Supreme Court.

**BIBLIOGRAPHY**

Abraham, Henry J. *Freedom and the Court*. New York: Oxford University Press, 1967.

*The Declaration of Independence and the Constitution of the United States*. Scarsdale, N.Y.: Lion Books, 1987.

Locke, John. *The Second Treatise of Government*. Edited by Thomas P. Peardon. Indianapolis: Bobbs-Merrill, 1952.

McLaughlin, Andrew C. *A Constitutional History of the United States.* New York: Appleton-Century-Crofts, 1935.

Mendenhall, Michael J., ed. *The Constitution of the United States of America: The Definitive Edition.* Monterey, Calif.: Institute for Constitutional Research, 1991.

Mill, John Stuart. *Utilitarianism, Liberty, and Representative Government.* New York: E. P. Dutton, 1951.

Smith, Goldwin. *A Constitutional and Legal History of England.* New York: Charles Scribner's Sons, 1955.

## Civil Rights Act of 1964

**TYPE OF ETHICS:** Civil rights

**DATE:** 1964

**ASSOCIATED WITH:** Congress of the United States and the civil rights movement

**DEFINITION:** This statute, the first true civil rights law in the United States since Reconstruction, made racial, religious, and ethnic discrimination in places of public accommodation unlawful

**SIGNIFICANCE:** Passage of the law signaled that the American public had accepted that racial discrimination and the "Jim Crow" system were evils that should be eliminated; the statute and its successor acts set American race relations on a new course

The Civil Rights Act of 1964 passed after decades of Southern resistance to any new civil rights laws. Public opinion in the United States had changed as a result of violent Southern resistance to demonstrations such as the sit-ins and freedom rides of the civil rights movement. The assassination of President John F. Kennedy and the murders of several civil rights activists strengthened the public sense that it was time to reform American race relations. The bill was powerfully pressed by President Lyndon B. Johnson, who, as a Southerner, was able to generate a great deal of support for it. The law prohibited discrimination on account of race, color, religion, or national origin in access to places of public accommodation such as hotels, restaurants, shops, and theaters. Later amendments to the law added age, gender, and disability as forbidden grounds for discrimination; employment and education were later added as protected activities.

**See also** *Brown v. Board of Education of Topeka*; Civil rights movement.

*Lady Bird Johnson, Robert F. Kennedy (third from left) and members of Congress look on as President Lyndon B. Johnson signs the Civil Rights Act of 1964* (National Archives)

## Civil rights movement

**TYPE OF ETHICS:** Civil rights
**DATE:** Twentieth century
**ASSOCIATED WITH:** The African American struggle for equality
**DEFINITION:** The movement dedicated to actualizing the rights to personal liberty guaranteed by the Constitution, the Thirteenth and Fourteenth Amendments, and acts of Congress
**SIGNIFICANCE:** Changed the status of race relations in the United States, especially between African Americans and whites

The civil rights movement in the United States represents a broad and protracted struggle in the effort to establish constitutional liberties for African Americans and other oppressed groups. A liberal interpretation suggests that the civil rights movement could date as far back as the Emancipation Proclamation of 1863. Some scholars maintain that the Montgomery bus boycott of 1955 represents the genesis of the civil rights movement. Yet this assessment tends to ignore the contributions of many individual activists (for example, William E. B. Du Bois and A. Philip Randolph) and organizations such as the National Association for the Advancement of Colored People and the National Urban League that took place prior to 1955. These and other initiatives gave rise to countless efforts over the next twenty years or so by African Americans and their supporters.

**Brief History.** The 1954 *Brown v. Board of Education* decision augured a dramatic shift in the status of race relations in America. "Separate but equal" had been declared unconstitutional in education. The system of segregated education in the South was ordered to be dismantled.

The *Brown* decision did not go unchallenged. In 1956, the White Citizens Council of America was formed. Its expressed purpose was to provide "massive resistance" against the desegregation effort in the South. The organization was successful in pressuring school boards, business leaders, and politicians to maintain a hard line against the desegregation effort. In 1957, massive resistance emboldened Governor Orval Faubus to use the National Guard to prevent African American students from integrating Central High School in Little Rock, Arkansas. As the civil rights effort broadened in scope, so did the violence caused by some whites. Freedom riders were sometimes brutally beaten; peaceful demonstrators were frequently attacked by local police with dogs and pounded with water hoses; some demonstrators were jailed for marching and sit-ins; and some civil rights leaders were physically abused, while others had their homes bombed.

The 1955 Montgomery bus boycott, however, appeared to have begun a spirit of social activism that could not be easily deterred. The refusal of Rosa Parks, an African American seamstress, to give up her seat to a white passenger sparked a protest that lasted more than a year, paralyzing the city buses. The significance of the bus boycott was that it kept the Supreme Court involved in the desegregation debate, gave national prominence to Martin Luther King, Jr., and demonstrated that direct action could bring about desired change.

The movement appeared to have gained momentum following the Montgomery bus boycott. Soon after, challenges to Jim Crow began to spring up in various places throughout the South. In Greensboro, North Carolina (1960), four African American college students sat at a lunch counter, challenging Woolworth's policy of serving only white customers. The sit-in became a powerful weapon of nonviolent direct action that was employed by the Congress of Racial Equality (CORE), the Student Nonviolent Coordinating Committee (SNCC), the Southern Christian Leadership Conference (SCLC), and other nonviolent activist groups and organizations fighting discriminatory practices.

Also during this time, CORE began the "freedom rides," while the SCLC began organizing a major voter rights drive (Voter Education Project), both in the South. All such efforts were met with resistance from whites who were determined to hold on to the advantages that racial discrimination afforded and to the traditions of segregation.

Some significant legislation supporting the civil rights effort was passed by Congress. The 1964 Civil Rights Act and the 1965 Voting Rights Act are often viewed as the most important legislation of the period. Together, they enhanced the Fourteenth and Fifteenth Amendments to the Constitution, guaranteeing equal protection of the law and the right to vote. Legislation did not, however, readily translate into a more open society. Frustration over the lack of opportunity for jobs, better housing, and greater educational opportunity resulted in a series of riots from 1965 to 1967. In 1968, the Kerner Commission (The National Advisory Commission on Civil Disorders) concluded that white racism was responsible for the conditions leading up to the riots.

**Retrenchment.** Some observers suggest that the civil rights movement began to wane in the late 1960's and early 1970's. There are indications that as the movement became more militant, whites were hard pressed to find common ground with some organizations. There are also indications that the Vietnam "antiwar" movement became the focus of attention, detracting from the civil rights effort. Still others suggest that the death of Martin Luther King, Jr., in 1968 deprived the movement of its most influential leader, causing disarray and abandonment by liberal whites. Others maintain that the civil rights movement is still underway but that it has experienced only moderate support from liberals and outright hostility from conservatives.

Despite the ups and downs of the struggle, the civil rights of all citizens have been enhanced by the efforts of African Americans and their supporters. Women have gained tremendously, as have other minority groups, such as Hispanics, Native Americans, Asian Americans, and gays and lesbians. The tactics and strategies employed by African Americans during the 1950's and 1960's have become standard operating procedure for many activist groups.

| **Chronology of Significant Civil Rights Events** | |
|---|---|
| **Date** | **Event** |
| 1909 | The National Association for the Advancement of Colored People (NAACP) is established. |
| 1911 | The National Urban League is established. |
| 1915 | The Supreme Court strikes down "grandfather" clause in *Guinn v. United States.* |
| 1941 | A. Philip Randolph calls for a march on Washington by African Americans to end discrimination in the defense industries, federal employment, and the armed forces.<br>President Franklin Delano Roosevelt temporarily establishes the Fair Employment Practices Committee (FEPC) through Executive Order 8802 as a result of the proposed march on Washington. |
| 1942 | The Congress of Racial Equality (CORE) is established. |
| 1945 | President Harry Truman's attempt to establish a permanent FEPC is stymied by a Senate filibuster. |
| 1946 | The Supreme Court rules in *Morgan v. Commonwealth of Virginia* that segregated seating on buses engaged in interstate commerce is unconstitutional.<br>Executive Order 9808 is issued by Truman, establishing the President's Committee on Civil Rights. |
| 1947 | Journey of Reconciliation is initiated by CORE to test the decision handed down in *Morgan v. Commonwealth of Virginia.*<br>The President's Committee on Civil Rights issues its first report: "To Secure These Rights." |
| 1948 | The Supreme Court rules in *Sipeul v. Board of Regents of the University of Oklahoma* that African Americans cannot be excluded from state (law) schools because of their race.<br>Truman issues Executive Order 9980, establishing employment in federal agencies based on merit. |
| 1950 | The Supreme Court rules in *Mclaurin v. Oklahoma State Regents* that a state cannot deny access to facilities to African Americans who have been admitted to law school.<br>The Supreme Court rules that a state cannot deny African Americans access to law school on the grounds that there is an African American law school available. |
| 1951 | Truman creates a government Compliance Committee to confer with government contract officials and oversee all government contracts. |
| 1953 | Executive Order 104790, issued by President Dwight D. Eisenhower, establishes the Government Contract Committee. |
| 1954 | The Supreme Court rules in *Brown v. Board of Education of Topeka, Kansas* that "separate but equal" is inherently unequal in public education facilities. |
| 1955 | The Supreme Court hands down its "all deliberate speed" decision in the implementation of school desegregation in the South.<br>Emmett Till, a fifteen-year-old African American youth from Chicago, is kidnapped and killed by two white men in Money, Mississippi, for allegedly flirting with a white woman.<br>Racial segregation is banned on interstate buses and trains by the Interstate Commerce Commission.<br>When Rosa Parks refuses to give up her seat to a white passenger on a city bus, she is arrested. This act initiates the Montgomery bus boycott, which lasts for fifty-four weeks. |
| 1956 | Eisenhower, in his state of the union address, requests the establishment of a bipartisan commission on civil rights.<br>The home of Martin Luther King, Jr., in Montgomery, Alabama, is bombed.<br>Autherine Lucy gains admission to the University of Alabama but is expelled following comments to the press regarding her effort to gain admission.<br>Martin Luther King, Jr., is convicted of conspiracy because of his participation in the Montgomery bus boycott.<br>The Supreme Court rules unanimously that ordinances requiring segregation on Montgomery city buses are unconstitutional.<br>The Montgomery bus boycott ends with victory for Martin Luther King, Jr., and the Montgomery Improvement Association. |
| 1957 | The Southern Christian Leadership Conference (SCLC) is founded by Martin Luther King, Jr., and other African American leaders from southern cities.<br>A. Philip Randolph, Martin Luther King, Jr., and Roy Wilkins lead approximately 37,000 people in a prayer vigil to commemorate the 1954 *Brown* decision.<br>Governor Orval Faubus attempts to use the National Guard to prevent the integration of Little Rock Central High by nine African American students. He is later forced to recall them by a federal court injunction. They are later used to protect the nine African American students.<br>Eisenhower signs the bill that establishes the Civil Rights Commission. It is the first civil rights bill signed in eighty-two years. |

*(Continued)*

*(Continued)*

| Chronology of Significant Civil Rights Events | |
|---|---|
| **Date** | **Event** |
| 1958 | The Supreme Court rules that the NAACP has the right to keep its membership list private. |
| 1959 | Four Little Rock, Arkansas, schools close to avoid desegregation.<br>The Civil Rights Commission issues its first report, which emphasizes the scarcity of African American voters in the South. |
| 1960 | The student lunch-counter sit-in begins in Greensboro, North Carolina.<br>The Student Nonviolent Coordinating Committee (SNCC) is founded.<br>The Supreme Court upholds the right of the Civil Rights Commission to hold a hearing in Louisiana and take steps to prevent the intimidation of African American voters.<br>The Supreme Court denies appeals to delay the integration of public schools in Delaware, Houston, and New Orleans.<br>Lunch counters in W. T. Grant, Kresge, McCrory-McLellan, and Woolworth stores are integrated in more than one hundred cities in the South.<br>Martin Luther King, Jr., is jailed in Atlanta. President John F. Kennedy uses his influence to gain King's release. |
| 1961 | Executive Order 10925, issued by Kennedy, establishes the Committee on Equal Employment Opportunity.<br>CORE initiates its "freedom rides" to test ban on segregation in interstate bus terminals. Along the way, a bus is burned and riders are beaten in Birmingham, Alabama.<br>Federal marshals are sent to Alabama after freedom riders are injured.<br>A two-year extension of the Civil Rights Commission is passed by Congress. In a mass campaign against segregation in Albany, Georgia, Martin Luther King, Jr., and more than seven hundred demonstrators are arrested. |
| 1962 | The Supreme Court rules that no state can establish laws requiring segregation in interstate or intrastate travel.<br>The Council of Federated Organizations (COFO) begins voter-registration drives in the South.<br>Governor Ross R. Barnett is found guilty of civil contempt in barring James Meredith from enrolling at the University of Mississippi.<br>James Meredith enrolls at the University of Mississippi and causes a full-scale riot in which more than two hundred people are arrested. |
| 1963 | The SCLC begins a campaign against segregation in Birmingham, Alabama. School children are utilized in the effort.<br>Eugene (Bull) Connor, commissioner of police, orders the police to use dogs and fire hoses on demonstrators in Birmingham.<br>Birmingham's white leadership agrees to a desegregation plan proposed by the SCLC. The headquarters of the SCLC in Birmingham is bombed, as is the home of the brother of Martin Luther King, Jr.<br>More than six African American children are arrested in Jackson, Mississippi, because of their involvement in demonstrations against segregation.<br>Governor George Wallace of Alabama attempts to block the enrollment of the first African American student at the University of Alabama.<br>The Supreme Court rules that state and local governments cannot prevent peaceful sit-ins to protest racial segregation.<br>Medgar W. Evers, field secretary for the Mississippi NAACP, is assassinated following a mass demonstration in Jackson.<br>A massive march on Washington is sponsored by a coalition of civil rights organizations, unions, churches, and other religious organizations. More than 200,000 people participate in the march.<br>The Sixteenth Street Baptist Church in Birmingham, Alabama, is bombed; four African American girls are killed, and many others are injured.<br>A one-day "freedom day" boycott of Chicago's public schools is held in which more than 225,000 students protest "de facto" desegregation. |
| 1964 | The Twenty-fourth Amendment to the Constitution, which outlaws the use of the poll tax in federal elections, is ratified.<br>Eleven steel companies agree to end discriminatory practices in the industry.<br>Three civil rights workers, James Chaney, Mickey Schwerner, and Andrew Goodman, are killed near Philadelphia, Mississippi.<br>President Lyndon B. Johnson signs the 1964 Civil Rights Bill, which closes loopholes in voting legislation and allows for the desegregation of public facilities.<br>Johnson signs the Economic Opportunity bill, which calls for a decrease in poverty, illiteracy, and unemployment, and an increase in public services. |

| Chronology of Significant Civil Rights Events | |
|---|---|
| **Date** | **Event** |
| 1964 (Continued) | The Mississippi Freedom Democratic Party challenges the all-white delegates of the Mississippi Democratic Party and stages a demonstration on the convention floor.<br>Martin Luther King, Jr., is awarded the Nobel Peace Prize. |
| 1965 | Malcolm X is assassinated at the Audubon Ballroom as he prepares to deliver a speech.<br>About 525 marchers are attacked by state troopers and sheriff's deputies on horseback with tear gas, nightsticks, and whips as they attempt to cross the Edmund Pettus Bridge on their march from Selma to Montgomery.<br>Johnson signs into law the Elementary and Secondary Education Bill, which is designed to withhold categorical aid for civil rights violations.<br>The U.S. Commissioner of Education announces that public schools in the South will be required to desegregate by the fall of 1967.<br>Johnson signs into law the Voting Rights Bill, which eliminates literacy tests and other qualifications that hinder the right to vote. |
| 1966 | The SCLC begins its "Open City" campaign in the North in Chicago, attempting to draw attention to the plight of ghetto residents.<br>Julian Bond is denied a seat in the Georgia legislature because of his affiliation with the SNCC.<br>The Supreme Court rules against the use of the poll tax in state elections.<br>Stokely Carmichael introduces the term "black power" to the public.<br>The SNCC votes to exclude whites from policy-making positions and from the recruitment organizing of African Americans.<br>CORE endorses "black power" and calls for the withdrawal of the United States from Vietnam.<br>James Meredith is shot on his one-man march against fear in Mississippi.<br>The Black Panther Party is created in Oakland, California, by Bobby Seale and Huey P. Newton.<br>The Supreme Court overturns the Georgia legislature's decision not to seat Julian Bond. |
| 1967 | The Southern Education Reporting Service states that only about 16 percent of African American students in the South are attending integrated schools.<br>In New York City, Martin Luther King, Jr., leads a massive march against the Vietnam War.<br>The U.S. District Court orders an end to de facto segregation in Washington, D.C., public schools.<br>National Conference on black power is held in Newark, New Jersey.<br>Johnson appoints a National Advisory Commission on Civil Disorders, headed by Otto Kerner, to investigate the cause of urban riots.<br>Thurgood Marshall becomes the first African American Supreme Court Justice.<br>Two African American mayors, Richard Hatcher and Carl Stokes, are elected in northern cities: Cleveland, Ohio, and Gary, Indiana. |
| 1968 | The National Advisory Commission on Civil Disorders issues its findings: It concludes that white racism caused the riots and is heading America toward two societies—one white and one African American.<br>The Department of Health, Education, and Welfare turns its attention to northern schools and de facto segregation.<br>Martin Luther King, Jr., is assassinated in Memphis, Tennessee.<br>Johnson signs into law the 1968 Civil Rights Bill, which bars discrimination in the sale and rental of housing.<br>Resurrection City campsite is established near the Washington Monument following the "Poor People's March."<br>African Americans are included in the Democratic Party's delegation to the National Convention for the first time.<br>CORE excludes whites from the organization.<br>Fifth Circuit Court rejects "freedom of choice" in desegregation suit in *Green v. County School Board of New Kent County.* |
| 1969 | Black Panther Party members are indicted on charges of conspiring to bomb stores and public buildings.<br>The Civil Rights Commission charges the federal government with complicity in racial discrimination in employment. |

*(Continued)*

*(Continued)*

| **Chronology of Significant Civil Rights Events** | |
|---|---|
| **Date** | **Event** |
| 1969 (continued) | Attorney General John Mitchell announces that the Nixon administration will oppose the extension of the Voting Rights Act of 1965. |
| | The Civil Rights Commission charges the Nixon Administration with retreating from the enforcement of school desegregation. |
| | The Supreme Court declares that all southern schools must end their dual school systems "with all deliberate speed." |
| | The Supreme Court denies the request for delays in implementing desegregation plans by thirty-three school districts in Mississippi. |
| 1970 | Yale University students boycott classes to show support for Bobby Seale of the Black Panthers who is awaiting trial on murder charges. |
| | Two African American students are killed by police during demonstrations at Jackson State College. |
| | The 1965 Voting Rights Act wins approval for five additional years. |
| | The Black Panther Party holds a (Revolutionary People's Constitutional) convention in Philadelphia with other protest groups. |
| | The Congressional Black Caucus is created. |
| 1971 | The Supreme Court rules that tests not related to job performance that disproportionately discriminate against African Americans are illegal. |
| | In *Swann v. Charlotte-Mecklenburg Board of Education*, the Supreme Court upholds the right of district courts to use busing. |
| | The prohibition against involuntary busing is struck down by the Supreme Court in *North Carolina State Board of Education v. Swann.* |
| | Black Panther Party members in New York are acquitted of all charges of conspiracy to bomb public places. |
| 1972 | Busing is ordered across district lines to achieve desegregation in Richmond, Virginia. |
| | The National Black Political Convention is held in Gary, Indiana. |
| | Nixon asks Congress to pass legislation to end busing as a desegregation tool. |
| | Barbara Jordan of Texas and Andrew Young are elected to Congress. They are the first African Americans elected in to Congress in the twentieth century. |
| 1974 | A plan to bus students across city lines in Detroit is struck down by the Supreme Court. |
| 1975 | President Gerald Ford signs a seven-year extension of the Voting Rights Act. |
| 1976 | The Supreme Court rules that racial discrimination by private nonsectarian schools is prohibited by the 1866 Civil Rights Act. |
| 1977 | The U.S. Senate confirms Andrew Young as United States Ambassador to the United Nations. |

**Significant Organizations.** There have been a number of organizations that have helped to lead the struggle for civil rights. The more successful of these organizations have been the National Association for the Advancement of Colored People (NAACP), the National Urban League (NUL), the Congress of Racial Equality (CORE), the Southern Christian Leadership Conference (SCLC), and the Student Nonviolent Coordinating Committee (SNCC).

The NAACP, founded in 1909 by African Americans and white liberals, assumed leadership in the struggle during the first half of the twentieth century. From its inception, the NAACP began the struggle to achieve legal redress in judicial systems around the country on behalf of African Americans. Throughout most of the twentieth century, the NAACP has fought for anti-lynching legislation, the fair administration of justice, voting rights for African Americans in the South, equal educational opportunity, and the ending of discriminatory practices in the workplace.

The NUL was founded in 1911. Although it is considered a proactive civil rights organization, it stood on the periphery of the civil rights struggle until about 1960. Prior to the 1960's, the Urban League concentrated almost exclusively on improving employment opportunities for African Americans migrating from the South.

CORE, founded in 1942, did not become actively involved in the civil rights movement until about 1961. It was one of the first civil rights organizations to employ the strategy of nonviolent direct action. It began utilizing the sit-in as a protest strategy following the initiation of the Journey of Reconciliation (freedom rides).

The SCLC was founded in 1957, under the leadership of the Reverend Martin Luther King, Jr., and often worked hand in hand with the NAACP. It grew out of an effort to consolidate and coordinate the activities of ministers and other civil rights activists in southern cities.

The SNCC was organized by the SCLC and African American student leaders in 1960 to help guide anti-segregation activities in the South. It broke away from Martin Luther King, Jr., and the SCLC within a year, arguing that its tactics for achieving integration were too conservative. Over the years, as the leadership of SNCC became more militant, it began to exclude whites from decision making and the recruitment of new black members. This militant posture culminated in the call for "Black Power" by SNCC in 1966. —*Charles C. Jackson*

**See also** Civil rights; King, Martin Luther, Jr.; Racism; Segregation.

**BIBLIOGRAPHY**

Blumberg, Rhoda L. *Civil Rights: The 1960s Freedom Struggle*. Boston: Twayne, 1984.

Bosmajian, Haig A., and Hamida Bosmajian. *The Rhetoric of the Civil-Rights Movement*. New York: Random House, 1969.

D'Emilio, John. *The Civil Rights Struggle: Leaders in Profile*. New York: Facts on File, 1979.

Price, Steven D., comp. *Civil Rights, 1967-68*. Vol. 2. New York: Facts on File, 1973.

Sobel, Lester A., ed. *Civil Rights, 1960-66*. New York: Facts on File, 1967.

## Class struggle

**TYPE OF ETHICS:** Politico-economic ethics

**DATE:** Since French Revolution of 1789

**ASSOCIATED WITH:** Socialist and Communist movements such as those of Gracchus Babeuf, Karl Marx, Karl Kautsky, and Vladimir Ilich Lenin

**DEFINITION:** Belief that all societies are divided into social classes based on their relation to the economy and that these clash over the direction of society

**SIGNIFICANCE:** Rejects notion that all members of a society share common interests and believes instead that there is a constant conflict between classes

The ethical concept of class struggle revolves around the notion that more or less clearly defined classes exist in every society. These classes are defined by their relationships to the predominant means of production, with one class dominant in its ownership or control of society's assets. Since different policies will affect various classes in diverse manners, each class inherently has its own set of interests. Since resources are limited, each class will struggle, albeit at times unconsciously, against others to attempt to gain benefits.

While social conflict has doubtlessly existed since the formation of social classes, "class struggle" as a concept dates back to the French Revolution of 1789. Before this time, awareness of social classes was certainly widespread, but conflict was seen as primarily being between different groups or peoples. First articulated by Gracchus Babeuf within his small "Conspiracy of Equals," the concept of class struggle was fully developed in the nineteenth century by Karl Marx and Friedrich Engels.

Marx denied that he had discovered class struggles, pointing to various historians before him who "had described the historical development of this struggle between classes." Yet it remained for Marx and Engels to take these empirical observations and transform them into a theory. They came to the conclusion that at the root of all conflicts was a struggle between different social classes, no matter in which arena a conflict might occur: religious, political, or ideological. That the participants themselves did not see the conflict in explicit class terms was immaterial. What counted was that there was always an underlying class interest that motivated various social group, even if the conflict was expressed in nonclass language.

Therefore, even an event such as the Reformation, which appears at first glance to be almost wholly religious in nature, is in the final analysis the disguised expression of class conflict. This struggle is not solely an economic one. For Marx, the struggle between competing classes has taken many forms. Its expression is constrained by the ideology of the day. For example, class struggles during medieval times naturally cloaked themselves in the language of Christianity because that was the common shared culture of all contending classes.

The cause and intensity of class struggles in different areas and at diverse times vary widely in terms of specifics. Still, they all share a root communality. Whenever a portion of society has ascendancy in terms of the means of production, that dominant class will exploit the common people. This exploitation may be open and direct as in the case of slavery or less obvious as is the situation with modern workers. All the same, the antagonism generated by the opposed interests of owners and workers will result in class conflict.

In the modern era, the main protagonists of class struggle were the capitalists on one side and workers on the other. Put crudely, employers desire high profits and workers want high wages. This is the source of struggle between the classes. This conflict is not simply between the opposing classes; the governmental apparatus or the state is always a major player.

For Marx and Engels, no government or state is really above, or neutral in, the class struggle. Far from being impartial, the state is itself the historical product of class society. That is, the state was established (and later its power expanded) because of the need the dominant class had for protection from the exploited. Thus, in ancient Rome, slave revolts led to a battle not so much between slaves and their owners per se as between slaves and the Roman state.

Although the state was seen by Engels "in the final analysis as nothing more than a body of armed men," governmental apparatuses function as more than repressive institutions. They can mediate class conflicts with an eye to reducing their intensity. In addition, governments serve an ideological function in that they legitimize the dominant system of wealth and power.

Although Marx hoped that class struggle would lead to a consciousness among workers that would lead them to overthrow capitalism, he realized that this was far from automatic or assured. Further, he argued that the only solution to the history of class conflict would be the establishment of a classless society that was free of exploitation. With the abolition of private property, the basis for classes and class struggle would disappear.

Karl Kautsky argued that social conflicts need not always be between classes, saying that struggles have often taken place between status groups. By contrast, V. I. Lenin and the Russian Bolsheviks took a more strict interpretation of the primacy of class struggle. Subsequent socialist thinkers have often stressed that classes are by no means homogeneous and that gender, racial, and occupational divisions are a counterweight to general class cohesion.

In the final analysis, the significance of the concept of class struggle goes beyond nuances of interpretation. As an ethical formulation, it suggests a view of the world that seeks to go beyond platitudes of common interest. Moreover, it is an ethical tool for a certain type of understanding of the world. —*William A. Pelz*

**See also** Communism; *Communist Manifesto*; Marx, Karl; Socialism.

**Bibliography**

Beer, Max. *The General History of Socialism and Social Struggles.* 2 vols. New York: Russell & Russell, 1957.

Callinicos, Alex, ed. *Marxist Theory.* New York: Oxford University Press, 1989.

Kautsky, Karl. *The Class Struggle.* Chicago: C. H. Kerr, 1910.

Marx, Karl, and Freidrich Engels. *The Marx-Engels Reader.* Edited by Robert Tucker. 2d ed. New York: W. W. Norton, 1978.

Milliband, Ralph. *Divided Societies: Class Struggle in Contemporary Capitalism.* Oxford, England: Oxford University Press, 1991.

Poulantzas, Nikos. *Classes in Contemporary Capitalism.* London: Verso, 1978.

## Clean Air Act

**Type of ethics:** Environmental ethics

**Date:** 1963

**Definition:** A federal law that directs the states to take action to control and prevent air pollution, on the premise that air pollution is essentially a state or local problem

**Significance:** The Clean Air Act acknowledged that air pollution was a problem of the commons rather than an individual problem, requiring action by the community (the federal government) to protect the health of the public

The Clean Air Act of 1963 replaced the Air Pollution Act of 1955, which had authorized studies of air pollution and recognized air pollution as an emerging national problem. The 1963 Act was passed as a result of a report by the U.S. surgeon general that found that motor vehicle exhaust can be dangerous to human health. The 1963 Act, however, did not permit action by the federal government; instead, grants were made available to state and local governments to undertake initiatives to control pollution in their areas. The Act was amended in 1970 and again in 1977, both times to set or change national standards for air quality in response to state and local government inaction. In 1990, significant changes were made to the 1963 Act to deal with remaining lower atmosphere pollution and, particularly, to act against upper atmosphere problems such as acid rain and the thinning of the ozone layer, which could damage forests, animal life, and the ability of humans to live a healthy life.

**See also** Biodiversity; Environmental Protection Agency (EPA), U.S.; Global warming; Greenhouse effect.

## Clean Water Act

**Type of ethics:** Environmental ethics

**Date:** 1972

**Definition:** A United States law amending the Federal Water Pollution Control Act of 1956 (FWPCA) to enable broad federal and state campaigns to prevent, reduce, and eliminate water pollution so that the biological integrity of the nation's waters could be restored

**Significance:** The nation's waters were acknowledged as a part of the commons, of benefit to all, and the federal government accepted the responsibility for ensuring the safety of those waters for human health and for maintaining the biological diversity of the waters

The Federal Water Pollution Control Act (FWPCA) of 1972 (known as the Clean Water Act) continued a line of federal legislation of water pollution that began with the Rivers and Harbors Act of 1899, which required a permit to discharge pollutants. In the FWPCA, responsibility was generally left to the states to control pollution, with the federal government providing grants for local construction of sewage treatment plants. Other Acts (the Water Pollution Control Act of 1956 and the Clean Water Restoration Act of 1966) set federal standards for water quality and imposed fines on source point polluters. The goals of the Clean Water Act were to achieve waters clean enough for recreation use by 1983 where such uses had been discontinued because of pollution, and, by 1985, to have no discharge of pollutants into the nation's waters. The Act established a National Pollutant Discharge Elimination System that required permits for all source points of pollution, focusing attention on specific polluters rather than on specific bodies of water. The Clean Water Act criminalizes the act of pollution by imposing fines and prison terms for persons found guilty of polluting the waters.

**See also** Biodiversity; Environmental Protection Agency (EPA), U.S.

## Coercion

**TYPE OF ETHICS:** Personal and social ethics

**DATE:** Since Aristotle in the fourth century B.C.E.

**DEFINITION:** The concept of coercion attempts to account for a form of power that is expressed through a threat to affect a person in a way that the person does not want unless that person acts in a way that the coercer proposes but that is also against the person's desires

**SIGNIFICANCE:** A determination of coercion is crucial in assigning responsibility for personal and group behavior, civil and criminal violations, international relations, and actions in war

Reinhold Niebuhr, the most politically influential American theologian of the twentieth century, wrote in *Moral Man and Immoral Society* (1932) that "all social co-operation on a larger scale than the most intimate social group requires a measure of coercion." Contemporary ethicists agree that coercion is present if not necessary in every area of social life. The task of ethicists is to lead in critical discussions that will help to identify the nature of coercion, assess responsibility for coerced acts, determine if and when coercion can be appropriately employed, and control coercion.

**The Nature of Coercion.** Though coercion is sometimes considered to be synonymous with force, they are in fact distinct. When force is used, the person is acted upon; the forced person does not act. In the case of a forced deed, the victim has no freedom to act otherwise. The victim of force is a medium of another person or power. Personal physical force (for example, being manacled or shot) and natural forces (for example, hurricanes, gravity, or illness) can override or remove the agent's ability to act. If I push you out of the way of an oncoming car, I have forced you to move; I have not coerced you. Coercive threats are, however, obstacles to self-determination. They limit one's freedom to act, but they are not overwhelming or insuperable. Some choice remains. A coerced person still acts. Though autonomy is diminished, a measure of autonomy remains.

A coercive threat is intended to motivate a person to act by stimulating in the person an irresistible desire to avoid a penalty although the act is also contrary to the person's will. Offers also intend to motivate a person to act by stimulating in the person an irresistible desire, though here the similarity stops. Scholars agree that threats and offers are different types of proposals. Threats can coerce; offers cannot.

Even so, threats and offers (also incentives, rewards, bribes, and so forth) can be linguistically structured in terms of one another. A merchant could threaten a customer, saying, "Give me your money or I will deprive you of the merchandise." One could also construe a mugger's proposal, "your money or your life," not as a threat but as an offer to preserve one's life for a fee, but such machinations obscure the issues. The meaning of a proposal, not its linguistic structure, determines whether it is an offer or a coercive threat.

Coercive threats can be further understood and distinguished from offers by means of other characteristics. First, and most fundamental, is that the recipient of coercion perceives a coercive threat as a danger, penalty, or some kind of loss. An offer is considered a beneficial opportunity. Second, a coercive threat cannot be refused without unwanted consequences. Moreover, the consequences of acting in accordance with a coercive threat are also undesired. Regardless of a coerced person's actions, an unwanted consequence is unavoidable. The recipient of an offer, however, can refuse without the recipient's life conditions being altered. Third, a coercive threat requires an imbalance of power, while an offer is usually proposed in a more egalitarian relationship. Fourth, with coercion, the will of the coercion predominates. The threat's recipient submits reluctantly with mitigated freedom. With an offer, the will of the recipient dominates, is freer, and more readily accepts or rejects the proposal.

**Responsibility.** To be responsible for one's acts is to be accountable for their impact on oneself and on others. If a person were forced to perform certain actions, that person would be relieved of moral responsibility for those actions. Neither praise nor blame would apply. By contrast, when persons freely act, they are responsible for their behavior. Between these two poles is the moral territory of responsibility for coerced acts.

Not forced, but not wholly free, coerced persons are only partially accountable for their actions. Coerced persons act with less freedom than normal, contrary to their will, and subject to the influence—not control—of a coercer. All apparent options are rendered morally undesirable. A coerced person's responsibility is therefore limited. The degree of this limitation depends upon the cultural context, the historic background, the immediate situation, and the moral framework.

**Beneficial Coercion.** Some acts of coercion can be considered beneficial if they are directed toward the coerced person's well-being and are compatible with his or her autonomy. Some theologians have even written that coercion may be an act of love if it leaves the beloved one with more freedom than would have been secured otherwise. If a child, for example, were riding his bike in the middle of the street as a car approached and the child refused to move despite parental warnings, a loving parent could coerce him, shouting, "Nathan! If you don't get out of the street this minute, I'll ground you till you're twenty-one!"

**Limiting Coercion.** Because coercion can be personally beneficial and socially necessary, efforts must be made to control it, not eliminate it. To restrain coercion, regardless of the coercer's claim to benevolence, it must be subject to an impartial, third-party evaluation. Human beings are simply too self-interested to weigh their own acts of coercion impartially. Reducing the number of incidents of unjust coercion, however, is more fundamental than is controlling coercion. Unjust coercion can be limited by redressing the inequality from which it grows. History has shown that egalitarian social institutions such as democracy, income redistribution, and public education enhance equality and thereby reduce coercion. —*Paul Plenge Parker*

**See also** *Nicomachean Ethics*; Niebuhr, Reinhold; Responsibility; Will.

**Bibliography**

Frankfurt, Harry G. "Coercion and Moral Responsibility." In *Essays on Freedom of Action.* Edited by Ted Honderich. Boston: Routledge & Kegan Paul, 1973.

King, Martin Luther, Jr. *Why We Can't Wait.* New York: Harper & Row, 1964.

McCloskey, H. J. "Coercion: Its Nature and Significance." *Southern Journal of Philosophy* 18 (Fall, 1980): 335-352.

Nozick, Robert. "Coercion." In *Philosophy, Science, and Method.* Edited by Sidney Morgenbesser, Patrick Suppes, and Morton White. New York: St. Martin's Press, 1969.

Wertheimer, Alan. *Coercion.* Princeton, N.J.: Princeton University Press, 1987.

Williams, Daniel Day. *The Spirit and the Forms of Love.* New York: Harper & Row, 1968.

## Cognitivism and noncognitivism

**Type of ethics:** Theory of ethics

**Date:** Primarily twentieth century

**Definition:** Cognitivism is the view that moral statements make genuine moral judgments of fact that are either true or false; noncognitivism is the denial of cognitivism

**Significance:** The possibility of normative ethics depends upon the cognitive status of moral statements

The cognitivism/noncognitivism distinction arises within twentieth century metaethics as a result of disagreements about whether moral statements have truth values. Indeed, if moral statements are neither true nor false, as noncognitivists believe, then they are not really statements at all. That is, moral expressions of the form "X is right" or "X is wrong," though they have the grammatical appearance of making factual claims, really do not make factual claims. Noncognitivists are divided over how such expressions actually do function. There are relatively few noncognitivist metaethical theories.

All other moral theories are cognitivist theories. They have in common the view that locutions of the form "X is right" and "X is wrong" are either true or false. Cognitivist theories differ at two levels. At the most general level, there is a distinction between objectivist theories and subjectivist theories. Each of these categories of moral theory can be further subdivided according to what a given theory says makes an action right or wrong, or an agent good or bad.

**Some Cognitivist Theories.** Cognitivists hold that a statement of the form "X is right" is just what it appears to be: a statement that some action exemplifies an important and desirable moral property. The statement is true if the property in question is exemplified by the action and false if it is not. A statement of the form "X is wrong" is a statement that some action fails to exemplify a moral property that should be exemplified, or that it exemplifies a property that it should not exemplify. It too is either true or false. In any case, there is a class of actions whose members have moral properties.

Cognitivists differ about what makes an action right or wrong. If one believes that the feelings of some person or persons determine whether an action has the relevant moral property, then one is a subjectivist. Private subjectivists would hold that "X is right" means "I (the speaker) approve of X, and that is what makes X right." Social subjectivists hold that the moral quality of an action is relativized to the feelings of approval or disapproval of a group or society of persons rather than some individual.

If one denies that the moral quality of an action depends upon the feelings of some person or persons, then one is an objectivist. There are many different types of objectivist theories of ethics. Again, they can be distinguished in terms of what makes an action right or wrong. Thus, for the hedonistic utilitarian, "X is right" can be translated as "Among all alternative courses of action, X will produce the most happiness for the largest number of people." A divine command theorist would hold that "X is right" means "God wills X." The ethical egoist takes "X is right" to mean that "X is in my own best interests." Each of these theories looks like an attempt to define what is right or good in terms of something else.

G. E. Moore repudiated any attempt to define the good in terms of some other property, but he was still a cognitivist and an objectivist. He hold that "X is right" means something like "Among all alternative actions, X will be most productive of the nonnatural property goodness." Thus, while good is a property, it cannot be analyzed in terms of something else.

**Some Noncognitivist Theories.** Noncognitivists agree with Moore that goodness cannot be analyzed in terms of something else. They explain that this is because moral terms (such as "good," "evil," "right," and "wrong") are not genuine predicates that stand for independently existing properties of any kind. For this reason, noncognitivists have sometimes been called subjectivists. This form of subjectivism is quite radical, however, for according to the noncognitivist, moral terms do not refer to anything. There is no question of the ultimate source of the property of goodness, since goodness is not a property of any kind. Obviously, the noncognitivist offers a very different analysis of moral statements and of the moral terms embedded in them.

The best-known type of noncognitivist theory is the emotivist theory of ethics, which was developed by A. J. Ayer, Charles L. Stevenson, and others. According to emotivism, moral utterances merely express the feelings of their speakers. Thus, an expression of the form "X is right" can be translated as "Hurrah for X!" There is nothing more to the meaning of the utterance than that.

Prescriptivists have argued that moral utterances do more than simply express the feelings of the speakers. They also prescribe or commend behavior. Thus, "X is right" means "Do X!" and "X is wrong" means "Avoid doing X!" Yet to say that X is right is not to say that X has a certain property.

—*R. Douglas Geivett*

**See also** Ayer, A. J.; Emotivist ethics; Goodness; Hare, R. M.; Metaethics; Moore, G. E.; Objectivism; Prescriptivism; Subjectivism; Truth.

**BIBLIOGRAPHY**


Alston, William P. "Moral Attitudes and Moral Judgments," *Nous* 2 (February, 1968): 1-23.

Ayer, A. J. "On the Analysis of Moral Judgments." In *Philosophical Essays.* London: Macmillan, 1959.

Hare, R. M. *Freedom and Reason.* Oxford, England: Clarendon Press, 1963.

___________. *The Language of Morals.* Oxford, England: Clarendon Press, 1952.

Moore, G. E. *Principia Ethica.* Cambridge, England: Cambridge University Press, 1903.

Snare, Francis. *The Nature of Moral Thinking.* London: Routledge, 1992.

Stevenson, Charles L. *Ethics and Language.* New Haven, Conn.: Yale University Press, 1944.

Taylor, Paul W., ed. *The Moral Judgment: Readings in Contemporary Meta-Ethics.* Englewood Cliffs, N.J.: Prentice-Hall, 1963.

Urmson, J. O. *The Emotive Theory of Ethics.* London: Hutchinson, 1968.


## Cold War

**TYPE OF ETHICS:** International relations

**DATE:** 1946-1989

**ASSOCIATED WITH:** The United States and the Soviet Union

**DEFINITION:** The rivalry between the United States and the Soviet Union after the end of World War II

**SIGNIFICANCE:** Posed the problem of how foreign and domestic policy ought to be pursued in the age of the atomic bomb and of the national security state

As John Lewis Gaddis states in *The Origins of the Cold War,* President Harry S Truman and his advisers decided by early 1946 that the Soviet Union threatened the security of the United States. The reasons for this decision have been debated intensely by historians, who have argued about the extent to which a Cold War was necessary and about the motivations of both superpowers. How the Cold War is viewed depends upon how historians have assessed the moral validity of each side's arguments, policies, and actions.

**History.** Traditionalist historians posit an aggressive, totalitarian Soviet Union, as revealed in events such as the Berlin Blockade (1948-1949), in which the Soviet Union closed down all routes to West Berlin, so that the United States and its allies had to airlift supplies to the city; the institution of Soviet-dominated governments in Poland (1944), Romania (1945), Yugoslavia (1945), and East Germany (1945); the rapid Communist takeover of Albania (1946), Bulgaria (1947), Czechoslovakia (1948), and Hungary (1949); Communist insurgency in Greece (1946-1949); the later victories of Communists in China (1949), Cuba (1959), and Vietnam (1975); and several Marxist-inspired governments in Africa. Traditionalists contend that the United States was justified in opposing Communist subversion of governments throughout the world—not only by producing weapons of mass destruction but also by establishing security organizations, such as the Central Intelligence Agency (CIA), to monitor and to thwart the "Communist conspiracy" in secret operations conducted by spies.

Revisionist historians hold that the United States, beginning with the Truman administration, overreacted to the Soviet Union's drive to secure its borders and to maintain a sphere of influence guaranteeing that it would never again be invaded by a militaristic Germany, which had attacked the Soviet Union in both world wars. Similarly, the development of Soviet atomic bombs and missiles is regarded as a defensive measure, necessitated by the fact that the United States did not share its knowledge of atomic energy with the Soviet Union, its wartime ally, and that, indeed, the dropping of two atomic bombs on Japan was an effort to intimidate the Soviets, who had agreed to invade Japan after the conclusion of the war in Europe. For reasons of domestic politics, the Truman and subsequent administrations inflated the Soviet threat, inventing a witch-hunt at home for Communist subversives in government, in the schools, in Hollywood, and in other institutions, in order to maintain a huge defense establishment and to exercise conservative policies that strengthened the U.S. grip on the global economy. Even the Marshall Plan (1948-1951), which successfully helped Western European economies rebuild after World War II, is viewed by revisionists as an effort to isolate the Soviet Union's economy and the socialist economies of Eastern Europe and the Third World.

**Ethical Interpretations.** Many historians, of course, do not fit into either category; that is, they draw away from both the traditionalist and revisionist interpretations in order to raise ethical and moral questions about the tactics of both sides. Was it necessary, for example, for the CIA to participate in the overthrow of the Guatemalan government in 1954 because of that government's supposed Communist ties? Historians have also questioned the CIA-inspired efforts to embarrass and even to assassinate Fidel Castro. By the same token, Soviet premier Nikita Khrushchev's introduction of missiles into Cuba in 1962, the invasion of Afghanistan in 1979, and the Soviet Union's supplying of arms to various regimes around the world have been roundly attacked by historians who do not fit into any single ideological camp.

**Ethical Issues.** No matter how responsibility for the Cold War is distributed, it seems undeniable that neither the United States nor the Soviet Union achieved what it undertook to guarantee in the establishment of the United Nations: a respect for human rights everywhere and the establishment of a concept of collective security that would govern the world and prevent nations from acting unilaterally in war.

**Ethical Questions.** With the fall of the Berlin Wall in 1989 and the dissolution of Communist governments in Eastern Europe and in the Soviet Union itself, historians will continue to debate the extent to which each party was culpable in the Cold War. Was the Cold War necessary? If so, did it have to last as long as it did? Did the arms race itself bankrupt the Soviet Union and lead to its breakup? Did the actions of the Federal Bureau of Investigation (FBI) during the Cold War period, when it kept lists of so-called subversives, undermine individual liberties? Does the massive security state itself represent a threat to freedom at home and abroad? Is there a justification for the abrogation of certain human rights in the quest to combat what is regarded as the absolute evil of Communism? Did the United States and its allies "win" the Cold War, and if so, can it be deemed a moral victory? —*Carl Rollyson*

**See also** Arms race; Communism; Covert action; Deterrence; Espionage; Human rights; Intervention; Limited war; Marshall Plan; Marx, Karl; Marxism; Mutually Assured Destruction (MAD); Neutron bomb; North Atlantic Treaty Organization (NATO); Potsdam Conference; Realpolitik; Revolution; Solzhenitsyn, Aleksandr; Stalin, Joseph; Treason; Truman Doctrine.

**Bibliography**

Dudley, William, ed. *The Cold War: Opposing Viewpoints.* San Diego, Calif.: Greenhaven Press, 1992.

Gaddis, John Lewis. *The Long Peace: Inquiries into the History of the Cold War.* New York: Oxford University Press, 1987.

___________. *The United States and the Origins of the Cold War, 1941-1947.* New York: Columbia University Press, 1972.

Hyland, William G. *The Cold War Is Over.* New York: Times Books/Random House, 1990.

Kolko, Gabriel. *The Politics of War: The World and United States Foreign Policy, 1943-1945.* New York: Random House, 1968.

Kolko, Joyce, and Gabriel Kolko. *The Limits of Power: The World and the United States Foreign Policy, 1945-1954.* New York: Harper & Row, 1972.

Lynn-Jones, Sean M., ed. *The Cold War and After: Prospects for Peace.* Cambridge, Mass.: MIT Press, 1991.

Maddox, Robert James. *The New Left and the Origins of the Cold War.* Princeton, N.J.: Princeton University Press, 1973.

Maier, Charles S. *The Cold War in Europe.* New York: M. Wiener, 1991.

Naylor, Thomas H. *The Cold War Legacy.* Lexington, Mass.: Lexington Books, 1991.

## Colonialism and imperialism

**Type of ethics:** International relations

**Date:** From antiquity

**Definition:** The conquest and imposition of a nation's rule over a foreign territory

**Significance:** Colonialism and imperialism involve political domination by alien powers, economic exploitation, and cultural and racial inequalities

Colonialism and imperialism are two of the major forces that have shaped and influenced the modern world. Yet the two regions of the world that have been largely involved in colonialism and imperialism—the West and the "Third World"—have been affected differently by the two phenomena. The Western world has generally been the colonizer and beneficiary, whereas the "Third World" has been the colonized and the exploited.

Colonialism and imperialism are interrelated systems; both involve the conquest, settlement, and imposition of rule over a foreign territory. Hence, colonialism is not only often associated with imperialism but also typically results from a policy of imperialism. Whereas imperialism often involves the political and economic integration of the subordinate territories into the dominant nation to create a single imperial system, colonialism entails the territorial separation of colonies from the mother countries.

Historically, colonialism as a political-economic phenomenon was associated with Europe from the time of the so-called "Age of Discovery" in the fifteenth century. Various European nations explored, conquered or settled, and exploited other parts of the world. The major colonial powers were Spain, Portugal, England, France, and The Netherlands. In the nineteenth century, Belgium, Germany, Italy, the United States, the Soviet Union, and Japan also became colonial powers. The victims of colonial penetration were the Americas, Africa, Asia, and Australia.

Theoretical distinctions can sometimes be made between two broad types of colonialism: colonies of settlement and colonies of exploitation. In practice, however, these are distinctions of degree rather than of kind, since most colonial structures involved both immigrant settlement and political control. Furthermore, colonial systems everywhere were essentially identical. They were headed by a representative of the sovereign nation, usually a governor or viceroy; their governments were nonrepresentative because legislative power was monopolized by colonialists to the exclusion of the native populations; and their underlying philosophies sought to pattern the colonies after the mother countries and assimilate the subordinate populations into the culture, language, and values of the metropolitan nations. In consequence, colonialism and imperialism entail not only political control but also economic and cultural domination.

Although the concept of empire and its practice have a long history going back to ancient times, it was not until about the 1870's that the ideology of imperialism was formulated and came into common usage. Among the earliest theoretical formulations was A. J. Hobson's *Imperialism* (1902), which established that imperialism served the needs of capitalism, such as the provision of raw materials, cheap labor, and markets. This thesis was further advanced by V. I. Lenin's *Imperialism: The Highest Stage of Capitalism*

(1917), which held that capitalist expansion would lead to imperialist wars that would in turn destroy capitalism itself and pave the way for socialism. Critics have pointed out the weakness of this thesis in that imperialist expansion long preceded the rise of capitalism. Nevertheless, Marxist interpretations of imperialism inspired underdevelopment theorists such as André Gundar Frank to emphasize capitalist expansion as the root cause of "Third World" underdevelopment. To African nationalists such as Kwame Nkrumah, imperialism was a powerful political slogan that fueled independence movements. What is clear is that imperialism has a variety of meanings.

Three phases in imperialism can be identified. The first is the early period from ancient times to the end of the fifteenth century. Early imperialism was characterized by the despotic rule of emperors. Examples of early empires included Egypt, Babylonia, Assyria, and the Greek, Roman, Ottoman, and Mongolian empires. The second phase of imperialist expansion spanned the period from the fifteenth to the early nineteenth centuries. It was ushered in by the European exploration of Africa and Asia and Christopher Columbus' voyages to the Americas, and it resulted in the colonization of the entire Western Hemisphere and much of Asia by various European nations.

A number of motivations inspired imperial expansion. There was a strong drive to obtain gold and other precious metals as well as the desire for cheap colonial products such as spices, sugar, cotton, and tobacco. In some cases, imperialism was spurred on by appeals to religious zeal. Above all, however, the possession of colonies was linked to European political rivalries and prevailing economic doctrines, especially mercantilism. In this respect, chartered companies that received trading monopolies and the protection of the mother country became prime instruments in colonial expansion and exploitation.

The third phase, "New Imperialism," covers the period from about 1880 to 1914 and is marked by the subjugation of practically all of Africa and parts of the Far East by Europe. As before, motivations were varied. Not only were colonies considered indispensable to national glory, but imperialism was fed by an atmosphere of jealousy in which one European nation grabbed overseas colonies in fear that another might do so first. Additional justification was found in racist theories regarding the presumed inferiority of some races and the belief in colonies as markets for the sale of surplus manufactured goods produced through the Industrial Revolution. At the same time, strategic considerations, missionary activities, and advances in European military technology were all linked to imperialist expansion.

In the decades immediately following World War II, the proliferation of democratic ideas around the world, the rise of self-determination in Africa and Asia, and United Nations condemnations did much to undermine imperialist concepts. With the advance of nationalism in Africa and Asia, most of the imperial regimes in these regions crumbled. Some manifestations of colonialism, however, persist. One of these is the phenomenon of internal colonialism, whereby one segment of the state that is politically and economically powerful dominates another segment in a subordinate, peripheral relationship; one example of internal colonialism is the system of apartheid in South Africa. Another is neocolonialism, the continued domination and exploitation of postcolonial independent states by the technologically advanced world, often through foreign investment capital, the provision of technical skills, and trade expansion, which tends to lead to an increase in influence without actual political domination. A further legacy of colonialism, especially in Africa, is the artificially created political boundaries that do not conform to indigenous ethnic patterns, an issue that continues to undermine political integration. —*Joseph K. Adjaye*

**See also** Capitalism; Communism; Totalitarianism.

**BIBLIOGRAPHY**

Amin, Samir. *Imperialism and Unequal Development.* New York: Monthly Review Press, 1977.

Larrain, Jorge. *Theories of Development: Capitalism, Colonialism, and Dependency.* Cambridge, Mass.: Basil Blackwell, 1989.

Mommsen, W. J. *Theories of Imperialism.* Translated by P. S. Falla. London: Weidenfield & Nicolson, 1981.

Robinson, Ronald E., and John Gallagher. *Africa and the Victorians: The Official Mind of Imperialism.* London: Macmillan, 1961.

Warren, Bill. *Imperialism: Pioneer of Capitalism.* Edited by John Sender. London: NLB, 1980.

## Commission on Civil Rights, U.S.

**TYPE OF ETHICS:** Civil rights

**DATE:** Established 1957

**ASSOCIATED WITH:** Voting Rights Act of 1965

**DEFINITION:** The U.S. Civil Rights Commission investigates charges that citizens have been deprived of their civil rights

**SIGNIFICANCE:** The establishment of the Civil Rights Commission in 1957 was the first federal civil rights action taken in eighty-two years

The U.S. Commission on Civil Rights was formed as part of the demands of the Civil Rights Act of 1957. President Dwight D. Eisenhower had called for such a commission in 1956, and previous president Harry Truman's Committee on Civil Rights had called for a formal congressional committee as early as 1947. Southern senators and congressmen, however, blocked the establishment of the Commission until 1957. Initially, the Commission was charged with investigating allegations that American citizens had been denied equal treatment because of their color, race, religion, or national origin. In 1972, the Commission also began investigating discrimination based on sex. It also acts as a national clearinghouse for information about discrimination. The Commission does not prosecute offenders or pass laws protecting those who are discriminated against. It simply gathers information, investigates charges,

*The President's Commission on Civil Rights is sworn in as President Dwight D. Eisenhower looks on.* (Library of Congress)

and reports its findings to the Congress and the president. Still, recommendations made by the Commission are often enacted. The Commission played a major role in the passage of the 1965 Voting Rights Act. Important protections for minorities in the areas of education, housing, and economic opportunity have been signed into law because of its reports and recommendations.

**See also** Civil rights; Discrimination.

## Common good

**Type of ethics:** Personal and social ethics

**Date:** From Greek antiquity

**Definition:** A humanistic philosophy that focuses on the good of all

**Significance:** The common good is a system of ethics that encourages people to be less selfish and self-centered and to identify more with all humanity and with nationwide and worldwide problems that cause much human suffering

The common good is, simply, a holistic, humanistic philosophy that considers the good of the whole or the good of all. It should be the first virtue of the state and its institutions, as well as the first virtue of society and of society's individuals. Its greatest manifestation would likely be worldwide "voluntary" socialism wherein people would abandon selfishness and act for the good of all humanity. For the common good, when personal goals collide with communal needs, sometimes personal goals must be sacrificed for the good of all. For example, when monopolistic corporations have a "stranglehold" on consumers, government regulations are necessary (and, depending on the amount of abuse, corporations may well need to be nationalized).

In the 1990's, after the collapse of the Soviet Union, socialism appears to be "on the run," while capitalism is in the ascendancy. Ironically, the economic philosophy that apparently "won" is the only one worldwide that is based entirely on human greed. Many thinkers view the capitalistic "victory" as especially heinous because capitalism is completely unconcerned about the justice of its means and ends and, indeed, is unconcerned about the ends of human life, as well.

As opposed to selfishness, the common good is nothing less than the realization of the social, economic, and spiritual qualities inherent in the word "civilization." It is nothing less than the "goodness" of a community and goodness for the sake of all community members. The concept asks that individual liberalism as well as individual conservatism be laid aside; in their places come the common good and a form of communitarianism.

In small social groups, action that emphasizes the common good might well be simple friendship and fellowship, whereas on the political level that action might be the passage of reform laws that seem to help and protect all people;

on the worldwide level, that action could involve the United Nations or another international agency that, for example, seeks to end war, which condones the practice of mass murder. A national or international group dedicated to saving the world's environment would also be working for the common good.

Another way to examine the common good is to consider its antithesis. For example, gender discrimination (degradation of women) is not the common good, nor is discrimination based on race or ethnicity. Forever fouling the environment is not the common good, nor is insensitivity to world hunger and poverty; international terrorism, wars, and strife in general are not; anything that hurts human beings physically or mentally is not. Allowing elderly people to die because they cannot afford health care not only is not the common good but also is a disgrace.

Albert Camus, a noted twentieth century French philosopher and a Nobel Prize winner, seldom used the phrase "common good," but he captured the essence of the term when he held that the worth of an individual could be measured by observing what he or she will allow other people to suffer. Likewise, Camus believed that the worth of a society could be measured by observing how that society treats its most unfortunate people. One might also add that the worth of any international agency, movement, or institution can be gauged by observing what that agency, movement, or institution allows any world citizen to suffer. Many other philosophers, past and present, have agreed with Camus.

**Individuals, Society, and the Common Good.** To achieve the common good, individuals must, of course, respect the rights of all others; however, individuals must also "put away" egotism and create a just society wherein all people have their basic needs—economic, social, political, and spiritual—met. Society must also examine itself and remove contradictions between what it professes and what it actually does—in other words, society should remove the contradictions between appearance and reality. So long as a society reproduces patterns of living that harm some of its members (poverty and discrimination, for example), the common good cannot be realized; instead, continuing alienation will take place until even the "in" group or the affluent are hurt.

As one example, in the United States of the 1990's, 20 to 25 percent of the people live in self-esteem-crushing poverty (with racial, ethnic, and gender minorities suffering disproportionately). Given such suffering, American society cannot call itself just and certainly cannot say that the common good is being realized. Likewise, as the world faces the next century, the United States—while bespeaking world peace—manufactures 50 percent of the world's armaments, which are used to kill and maim human beings. Until it renounces armament production, the country will not be a significant factor in increasing peace on the planet.

**Conclusions.** It is remotely possible that in the indefinite future American society might promote the common good. To do so, however, people must release selfishness and personal greed, because when people hurt others they eventually ruin their own society as well. —*James Smallwood*

**See also** Capitalism; Communism; Communitarianism; Utopia.

**BIBLIOGRAPHY**

Amoia, Alba della Fazia. *Albert Camus*. New York: Continuum, 1989.

Diggs, Bernard James. *The State, Justice, and the Common Good: An Introduction to Social and Political Philosophy*. Glenview, Ill.: Scott, Foresman, 1974.

Held, Virginia. *The Public Interest and Individual Interests*. New York: Basic Books, 1970.

Leys, Wayne A. R., and Charner M. Perry. *Philosophy and the Public Interest*. Chicago: Committee to Advance Original Work in Philosophy, 1959.

Meyer, William J. *Public Good and Political Authority: A Pragmatic Proposal*. Port Washington, N.Y.: Kennikat Press, 1975.

Phenix, Philip H. *Education and the Common Good*. New York: Harper, 1961.

Sturm, Douglas. *Community and Alienation: Essays on Process Thought and Public Life*. Notre Dame, Ind.: University of Notre Dame Press, 1988.

Wallach, Michael A., and Lise Wallach. *Rethinking Goodness*. Albany: State University of New York Press, 1990.

## Communism

**TYPE OF ETHICS:** Politico-economic ethics

**DATE:** From antiquity

**ASSOCIATED WITH:** Radical social critics such as Thomas More, Thomas Münzer, Gracchus Babeuf, Étienne Cabet, Karl Marx, and Vladimir Lenin

**DEFINITION:** A classless society of equality and freedom in which private property has been abolished and replaced with communal co-ownership of material possessions

**SIGNIFICANCE:** Maintains that a classless society will end social strife and oppression while nurturing a community based on mutual human interdependence

Communism, the idea of a society based on communal rather than private property, was advanced long before the birth of Christ. There were elements of this idea present in some of the writings of ancient Greek philosophers. Plato, for example, argued in his *Republic* that ruling Guardians should be prohibited from owning property. Further, communism was raised by some radical critics of the status quo in the days of the Roman Republic. There is evidence that some of the slave insurgents involved in the slave rebellion led by Spartacus in 73 B.C.E. wanted their future "Sun Republic" to be without private ownership.

During the early years of Christianity, the followers of Christ practiced a type of communism based on communal ownership of material possessions. For the first Christians, private property was to be forsaken as a sign of their faith. Any number of Christ's teachings appear to argue that private property was, at best, a dangerous distraction from the process of earning salvation and, at worst, a sin. When the son of God said, "It is easier for a camel to walk through the eye of a needle than for a rich man to enter the kingdom of heaven," the early Christians took him at his word.

By the time of the collapse of the Western Roman Empire, the Christian Church had adapted itself to a world based on social classes and private property. Still, the ethical belief in communism as the truly Christian way of living persisted in various forms. During the era of feudalism, monasteries were based on a vow of poverty with monks held up as examples of Christian rejection of material wealth. Within the monastery, the members were to practice a type of communism in the communal sharing of all possessions.

Toward the end of the feudal period, this tradition asserted itself in the sixteenth century in the work of Saint Thomas More. More wrote his famous *Utopia* to show an ideal society based on a common community of possessions. More's views were in no way unique, since during the Reformation a number of religious rebels, such as the Taborites in Bohemia, came to the conclusion that God had meant the earth to be shared equally by all.

During the Reformation, a German priest named Thomas Münzer helped to lead revolt of thousands of peasants. In 1525, Münzer formed an "Eternal League of God," which was not only a revolutionary organization but also fought for a radically egalitarian Christian society. Basing himself on his interpretation of the Bible, Münzer preached that a classless society was God's will and the princes should be replaced with democratically elected leaders.

Communism appeared again as an important idea during the French Revolution, which began in 1789. Some radical republicans believed that the revolution would not be complete until political freedom was complemented by social equality. The revolutionary Gracchus Babeuf organized a "Conspiracy of Equals" that sought unsuccessfully to establish a society in which all land would be held in common and all would receive equal diet and education.

With the Industrial Revolution, earlier theories of communism that had stressed common ownership of the land became updated to accommodate the new mode of production. In the 1840's, the term "communism" became fairly well known as a result of the writings of Étienne Cabet, who favored the use of machinery on collectivized land as well as large communal factories. Despite such innovations, Cabet considered his theory of communism to be based on "true Christianity."

With Karl Marx, the concept of communism was further modernized. Marx argued against what he deemed the primitive communism of past thinkers who would merely extend ownership of land to the entire population. Marx argued that a classless society had to be based on a cooperative economy, not merely a diffusion of private property. This future communist society would unleash the forces of production to maximize efficiency and reduce the amount of labor necessary. In addition, it would eliminate the rigid division of labor so that people would be free to do both mental and physical work and rotate jobs. With the end of private property, humanity would no longer be alienated from work. Labor would be cooperative and technology would allow people to avoid unpleasant tasks. Therefore, people would be able to take pride in labor and the resulting self-fulfillment would increase the general happiness.

Marx saw these changes as creating a world in which authentic, moral relationships between people would exist. Moreover, humanity would be able to work with nature rather than being intent on conquering the environment. Freedom would be the basis of this new society, in which "the free development of each is the prerequisite for the free development of all."

Marx's vision was taken up by numerous later socialists, including V. I. Lenin, who outlined his views in *State and Revolution.* Following the Russian Revolution, Lenin attempted to implement some of these idea, but the material conditions for the construction of a communist society were absent. By the late 1920's, with the isolation of Soviet Russia, communism became an empty political slogan under the dictatorship of Joseph Stalin. Despite its popular association with the Russian dictatorship, the concept of communism remains appealing as an ethical concept that promises to free humanity from exploitation, poverty and oppression.

*—William A. Pelz*

**See also** Class struggle; *Communist Manifesto*; Marx, Karl; Socialism; Stalin, Joseph.

**Bibliography**

Beer, Max. *The General History of Socialism and Social Struggle.* 2 vols. New York: Russell & Russell, 1957.

Cole, G. D. H. *Socialist Thought: The Forerunners of 1789-1850.* Vol. 1 in *A History of Socialist Thought.* London: Macmillan, 1953.

Engels, Friedrich. *The Peasant War in Germany.* Translated by Moissaye J. Olgin. New York: International, 1926.

Lenin, Vladimir I. *The State and Revolution.* Moscow: Progress, 1974.

Marx, Karl, and Friedrich Engels. *The Marx-Engels Reader.* Edited by Robert Tucker. 2d ed. New York: W. W. Norton, 1978.

More, Thomas. *Utopia.* New York: Penguin Books, 1965.

## Communist Manifesto, The

**Type of ethics:** Modern history

**Authors:** Karl Marx and Friedrich Engels

**Date:** Published 1848 as *Manifest der Kommunistischen Partei*

**Significance:** Rejected the idea that private property was a positive force and argued that class conflict could lead to a just and equal society

Written by Karl Marx and Friedrich Engels for the Communist League, *The Communist Manifesto* has become a classic formulation of socialist political ethics. The authors base their

**Marxist Beliefs Espoused in *The Communist Manifesto***

1. All societies since early communal times have been inequitable class societies.
2. All history has been the history of class struggle.
3. The institution of private property has exploited and oppressed the majority of people.
4. Capitalist societies, like other class societies, do not allow people to develop freely.
5. To create a just and ethical world, the institution of private property should be eliminated. Bourgeois society uses labor to increase capital, whereas the future society will use capital to benefit workers.
6. Individuals should be free to choose their social relationships, free of outside interference. Therefore, the family in its present form should be abolished.
7. Workers have no nation, and as exploitation ceases, so will the need for nationalities.
8. All instruments of production should be centralized in the workers' state.
9. Because workers are in the majority, they must rule themselves democratically.
10. Because no one should possess unearned wealth, there should be no right of inheritance.
11. Credit, communications, and transportation should be placed in the hands of the people.
12. Factories should be government owned, and the government should protect the environment.
13. All able-bodied persons should work.
14. The differences between cities and rural areas should be eliminated gradually by means of population redistribution.
15. Free public education should be provided for all children.

work on the ethical belief that all people should live in a condition of equality and democracy. They contend that all previous societies have been marked by class struggle. This conflict between different social classes is rooted in the classes' economic relationships to the means of production. Classes themselves are seen as an inherent result of the institution of private property. Thus, for Marx and Engels, some people have always owned property while forcing those without to work for them. Although the form of this exploitative relationship has changed over time from master/slave to lord/serf and then bourgeois/worker, the inequality has remained present. This injustice has led world history to be the history of class struggle.

With the rise of capitalism, the new ruling class (the bourgeoisie) constantly revolutionizes the way things are produced and exchanged. As capitalism grows, the need for a constantly expanding market causes the bourgeoisie to expand borders until capitalism has engulfed the world. In the process of this ever-growing expansion, there is, of necessity, more economic and political centralization. This centralization of economic and political power further reduces the actual power of the majority of the population.

Marx and Engels note that this expansion is by no means a smooth process and is constantly beset with crisis. Since workers as a whole produce more in value than they are paid in wages, there are periodic periods of overproduction. These crises of overproduction take the form of business downturns or depressions that the bourgeoisie can overcome only by mass destruction of productive property (such as war) or by conquest of new markets (imperialism). Even when a crisis has been surmounted, the seeds of a future disaster remain within the very nature of capitalist society.

Further, the workings of the capitalist economy exploit the vast majority of people who increasingly have only their labor to sell to the capitalists. Labor is a component of production, so it becomes a commodity that is bought and sold like any other on the market. Thus, the worker becomes subject to the whims of the market and may fall from employment and relative comfort into unemployment and poverty without warning. As labor becomes simplified by machines, there are more workers who are capable of any one job; therefore, the oversupply of labor causes a decline in demand and thereby a decrease in real wages. In addition, the ever-increasing reliance on machines means that work loses its individual character for the worker, who becomes a mere appendage to the machine. This is profoundly unjust, unfair, and undemocratic, according to Marx and Engels.

Even for small businesspersons and professionals, capitalism ultimately spells disaster, since they find themselves unable to compete with the always-growing big bourgeoisie. As these new social layers are forced into the working class, many people will help fight against this unjust system. Because the entire capitalist society is based on exploitation and oppression and promotes the values of greed and inequality, the increasingly large working class will fight to destroy the dictatorship of the bourgeoisie. For Marx and Engels, this fight is historically unique because it is a movement of the vast majority against an ever-decreasing minority. Thus, only a workers revolution will allow true democracy to prevail.

To achieve this just and democratic society, Marx and Engels believe, the most conscious workers should band together and fight for the interests of the world's people, regardless of nationality. While struggling against the bourgeoisie, these "communists" must always consider the interests of the working-class movement as a whole. The first step is to make the working class, which is a class in itself, a class for itself. Then, the now-united workers must combat the bourgeois control of society. Moreover, when fighting against any form of injustice, communists must always raise the property question, since private property is at the root of all oppression. Ultimately, workers will need to take power themselves, since the bourgeoisie will manipulate any system of government, even a parliamentary one, to maintain class rule. Thus, the abolition of capitalism and the establishment of workers' rule is the only ethical path according to Marx and Engels. —*William A. Pelz*

**See also** Class struggle; Communism; Marx, Karl; Socialism.

**Bibliography**

Draper, Hal. *Karl Marx's Theory of Revolution.* 4 vols. New York: Monthly Review Press, 1977-1990.

Drennen, D. A. *Karl Marx's Communist Manifesto.* Woodbury, N.Y.: Barron's Educational Series, 1972.

Fischer, Ernst. *Marx in His Own Words.* Translated by Anna Bostock. New York: Penguin, 1984.

Mandel, Ernest. *From Class Society to Communism: An Introduction to Marxism.* London: Ink Links, 1977.

Marx, Karl, and Friedrich Engels. *The Marx-Engels Reader.* Edited by Robert Tucker. 2d ed. New York: W. W. Norton, 1978.

## Communitarianism

**Type of ethics:** Theory of ethics

**Date:** Since the 1980's

**Associated with:** American philosophers, political theorists, social scientists, and theologians who criticize excessive individualism and seek a community-based ethic

**Definition:** Communitarianism derives its name from the high value it places on community; it insists that the good of the community must not be subordinated to that of the individual; it rejects Western culture's one-sided emphasis on individual rights and seeks to balance rights with responsibilities

**Significance:** Communitarianism may represent the most powerful challenge to individualism since the Enlightenment; if it continues its impressive intellectual development and can extend its influence to social institutions, it could become the most important moral theory to originate in the West in the last two hundred years

**The Social Emergency.** Communitarianism carries with it a sense of profound urgency. As one leader of the movement, Robert Bellah, has declared, society is no longer merely in crisis: It is in a state of emergency. The social fabric has deteriorated to the extent that morality has become a virtual impossibility. The communities, institutions, and social relationships that make morality possible are quickly succumbing to a pervasive individualism. Although this social deterioration may be most visible in poverty-stricken urban areas where gangs, violence, and homelessness are commonplace and children must attend school in fear of their lives, it is nevertheless rampant throughout American society. Important social institutions such as families, churches, community groups, and even towns and cities have been drastically weakened, leaving society as a mere collection of individuals who have nothing in common but self-interest and the fear of death. Ironically, these developments threaten individualism itself, for community is the very basis of individuality. Because of this emergency, communitarians believe that it is necessary to nurture and foster constructive communities wherever they can still be found.

Although communitarianism has roots that extend deep into the past, it has existed as a self-conscious school of thought and moral theory only since the 1980's. Two important books published in that decade, *After Virtue* (1983), by the philosopher Alasdair MacIntyre, and *Habits of the Heart* (1985), by the sociologist Robert Bellah, signaled the appearance of a new ethic that repudiated both modern individualist liberalism and the rejuvenated conservatism of the Reagan era.

MacIntyre, a former Marxist who became a Roman Catholic, argued that moral discourse in the modern West has become incoherent and meaningless. He traced this incoherence to the Enlightenment, which tried to develop a morality that was based entirely on individuality and reason. The attempt was bound to fail, MacIntyre argued, because morality requires the very things that the Enlightenment took away: community, tradition, and narrative. That is why Immanuel Kant, Søren Kierkegaard, and John Stuart Mill all failed to develop a genuine morality, and why all attempts that do not repudiate the Enlightenment concept will fail.

MacIntyre's book ends on a pessimistic note, concluding that there is little to do except to wait for a new Saint Benedict (the founder of Catholic monasticism) to lead society out of its predicament. *Habits of the Heart,* though influenced by MacIntyre, is more hopeful in tone. Robert Bellah gathered a team of researchers to investigate "individualism and commitment in American life." After interviewing numerous people about their lives and commitments, the researchers concluded that, while many forms of community were being undermined in American life, there were still signs of a remarkable resilience. The research focused in particular on "voluntary associations," or nonprofit institutions that embody various forms of community: churches and synagogues, community service organizations, youth organizations, activist organizations, charities, and the like (but not including political parties). This "third sector" of American society (as distinguished from the governmental sector and the for-profit business sector), according to Bellah and his researchers, is essential to democracy and human flourishing, and must be encouraged.

Communitarianism rejects ordinary political liberalism, which emphasizes personal freedom at the expense of community, but it also rejects political conservatism, which emphasizes personal property and wealth at the expense of community. Bellah and his coauthors issued a powerful call to reaffirm the importance of community in American life, to form anew a "culture of coherence." Similar calls have been issued by the religious historian Martin E. Marty and the political scientist Amitai Etzioni. (One of the most impressive things about communitarianism is its broad interdisciplinary base.)

**Specific Issues.** Communitarianism as a self-conscious movement is in its infancy. Some communitarian positions, however, are readily apparent. In the realm of economics, communitarians are less interested in maximizing individual personal income and more interested in how economic production can foster and support human communities and relationships. With respect to children and the family, communitarians are less interested in the abstract "rights" of children and parents, and more interested in improving the human ecology of the family—including discouraging divorce. Communitarians point with alarm to the fact that, since the 1950's, all measurable indices of child welfare in America have declined—even during periods of economic growth. Similarly, with respect to women's issues, communitarians are less interested in simply maximizing women's freedom and more concerned with advancing women's well-being in the context of community and relationships, including relationships with men and children. With respect to diversity and multiculturalism, communitarians support measures that would enable diverse communities to flourish, but they reject those measures that seek to divide society into separate cultural fiefdoms. A communitarian approach to the environment might likewise be skeptical of animal or species "rights" but would strongly emphasize the community of nature and humankind's important and dangerous part in it. With respect to the health care crisis, communitarians would recognize the impossibility of obtaining the "best" health care for every individual and would ask what types of health care would foster human flourishing in the midst of the natural trajectory from life to death. Communitarians generally also have more sympathy for a public role for religion in our common culture.

**Challenges.** Like any other movement, communitarianism faces numerous challenges and dangers as it works out its implications. Perhaps its greatest peril is nostalgia for a past that never was, or worse, for a past that embodied specific evils. Many communities embody racist and sexist practices and traditions that are morally outrageous. Communitarians who strongly reject the Enlightenment also run the risk of disregarding the Enlightenment's great achievements—abolition of slavery, establishment of civil liberties, freedom of the press, popular elections, religious tolerance, emancipation of women, human rights. Much of the communitarian movement, too, has a strongly American focus, and needs to develop a broader international perspective. The collapse of Soviet-style communism may offer an opportunity to internationalize communitarianism; voluntary associations may be just the thing to fill the vacuum left by the collapse of communist parties.

Despite these challenges, however, communitarianism remains one of the most promising contemporary moral philosophies. —*Garrett E. Paul*

**See also** Common good; MacIntyre, Alasdair.

**BIBLIOGRAPHY**

Bellah, Robert N., et al. *Habits of the Heart.* Berkeley: University of California Press, 1985.

Elshtain, Jean Bethke, Enola Aird, and Amitai Etzoni. "A Communitarian Position of the Family." *National Civic Review* 82 (Winter, 1993): 25-36.

Etzioni, Amitai. "Communitarian Solutions/What Communitarians Think." *Journal of State Government* 65 (January/March, 1992): 9-11.

___________. *The Spirit of Community: Rights, Responsibilities, and the Communitarian Agenda.* New York: Crown, 1993.

Hauerwas, Stanley. *Naming the Silences.* Grand Rapids, Mich.: Eerdmans, 1990.

MacIntyre, Alasdair. *After Virtue.* Notre Dame, Ind.: University of Notre Dame Press, 1983.

Marty, Martin E. *The Public Church: Mainline, Evangelical, Catholic.* New York: Crossroad, 1981.

## Comparative ethics

**TYPE OF ETHICS:** Theory of ethics

**DEFINITION:** The discipline that studies the ways in which human morality and conduct are defined and practiced in various communities

**SIGNIFICANCE:** Attempts to analyze the varied constructs of ethics in diverse groups of people, both religious and otherwise, in different parts of the world

Ethics incorporates the scope and purport of morality and associated conduct. Ideas of morality may be determined by rational judgments or by inspired transhuman monistic notions. When the moral worth of an action or a person is determined according to a conscious ideal in any society, rationally determined moral laws guide and define well-being, order, harmony, and security. Both the explicit formulation of and implicit obedience to normative laws, codes, and decrees ensure the maintenance of individual and community well-being. Thus, socially useful regulations, juxtaposed with morally right rationalistic ideals, become the operative ethical norm of the community. When morality and virtue are contextualized in the orderly harmony of the universe, however, and when human life and actions are recognized as factors of that order, the monistic element rather than the rational is given primary cognizance in the definition of ethics.

Generally, in societies that are not avowedly theocratic, ethical ideals are defined according to a rationally determined context. By contrast, in myriad religious communities, the essential ethical directives that govern religious adherents are both defined and enforced on the basis of a monistic ideal of its intrinsic worth. As a survey of various traditions will portray, ethics at a comparative level is essentially a construct of a society or culture or religion that defines and formulates particular moral norms and values. Evaluations of morality thus depend on the estimation of conduct or norms according to specific values and notions—hence the importance of comparative ethics.

**Ethics in Ancient Greek and Egyptian Traditions.** Though the ethics (both theoretical and practical) of ancient Greece has many trends and representatives, Plato, Socrates, and Aristotle may be regarded as thinkers who exemplify the norms, conduct, and values of their society. According to Plato, Socrates regarded moral obligation as a construct of rational insight. Plato himself identified morality and virtue as normative conduct that reflected heavenly prototypes or the eternal ideas of the good. In contrast, ethical norms for Aristotle were bound by the social and empirical character of people.

In ancient Egypt, the theory of the soul and its divisions dictated ethics and conduct. The norms for different strata of the society were varied; for example, priests, kings, and shepherds had specific criteria for their own ethical conduct.

**Ethics in Monotheistic Traditions (Judaism, Christianity, and Islam).** In diverse religious traditions, the ethical code that dictates the conduct of a moral agent and the compulsion that ensures its maintenance are regulated by injunctions that are presumed to originate not from rationality or societal utilitarianism but from a monistic or suprahuman transcendent source. Thus, in the monotheistic religious traditions, ethics is dominated by a theocentric ideology. The authority of divine law or God is both the source and the aim of the moral realm.

In the Judaic tradition, for example, the authority of the Torah as moral law is based on divine proclamation. The *ought* of actions is primarily associated with the appeasement of God, and individual or collective pleasure is incidental. Virtue and ethics become aspects of the nexus between God and humanity as embodied in the notion of a covenant. Though many detailed regulations have been codified and accepted over the centuries, in the main the Ten Commandments form the salient ethical grid for all other injunctions. To be conscious of the identity of God, to be aware of obligations to parents, to maintain the Sabbath, and to refrain from bearing false witness or being adulterous or coveting are some of the moral imperatives contained in the Ten Commandments. Over the centuries, prayer, neighborliness, generosity, dietary regulations, learning, and purity became the essential ethos that governed the lives of the adherents of Judaism.

In Christianity, the person of Jesus Christ is the governing inspiration of all ethical norms. According to general Christian theology, Christ's descent and crucifixion represents *love*—God's love for humanity and the redemption of souls. The account of Christ, his passion and resurrection, become the standards for normative ethics. Thus, to imitate Christ is the moral goal and destination of devout Christians. Ideas of Christian fellowship, altruism, and humility are derived from the idea of the sacrifice of Christ in order to redeem humanity.

In Islam, the relationship of the human soul to God—to submit to God's command and gain peace—is the governing ethos of normative ethics. The Qur'ân situates the divine-human connection in a primordial covenant between God and human souls. Ethical imperatives (both practical conduct and moral intent) hence revolve around a transcendent authority that *ought* to be complied with by the core of one's being. Ethical obligations and responsibilities extend toward a transcendent power, the individual self, society, and nature, and they include personal qualities such as generosity, humility, and kindness. Sectarian differences aside, the five essential "pillars of faith" of Islam are testimony of acceptance of God's being and the prophecy of Muḥammad, prayer, charity, fasting, and pilgrimage to the Kaʾba (the Abrahamic shrine in Mecca).

**Ethics in Eastern Traditions (Hinduism, Buddhism, Confucianism).** In Hinduism, India's main religious tradition, the ideals of ethics are incorporated in the salient notions of *dharma* and *karma* which are mandated by a transcendent monist predicate. On an individual level, one's *dharma*, or sacred duty, is determined as a factor of birth by one's place in society. Accordingly, *karma*, actions and consequences, are evaluated according to individual dharma. Society is divided into four groups, each with a differentiated dharma—*brāhmins* as priests, *kṣatriyas* as warrior/rulers, *vaiṣnavas* as traders or farmers, and *śūdras* as performers of menial tasks. Merit was accrued to karma by fulfilling the moral imperatives of personal dharma. On a cosmic level, maintenance of individual dharma precludes chaos and causes harmonious balance.

The focal notion of Buddhist ethics is the "middle way," a way of conduct and morals that will enable the adherent to attain transcendent enlightenment, represented by the term *nirvāṇa.* These norms are monist in form, since their avowed purpose is a self-ennobling conduct that maintains and designates the cosmic value of human existence per se, though, in content, the norms are apparently rationalistic. The suffering (*dukkha*) of life is presented as a given, and the purpose of conduct and ethics is to transcend it. One may achieve this transcendence by following the "eightfold path," which includes right understanding, thought, speech, action, livelihood, effort, mindfulness, and concentration. Both monks and laypeople are to follow these general precepts, though the requirements are more stringent for the former.

In China, Confucian evaluations of morality and conduct are essentially governed by the ideals associated with the "sage." The *perfected virtues* or ethics of the sage include benevolence, righteousness, propriety, sincerity, loyalty, reciprocity, wisdom, and filial piety. When inculcated and adhered to, these ethics of the sage lead to harmony and well-being. These virtues are evidently rationalistic, since the notion of a revealed transcendent source is not a basis for the ethical imperatives; however, millennia of traditional acceptance have conferred upon them a *sacred* monistic value.

**Transtraditional Western Ethics**. In modern secularistic communities, especially in the West, a humane rationalistic idiom provides the essential grid for normative ethics. For example, Ethical Culture is a movement that is dedicated to the ethical growth of the individual. The nondenominational New York Society for Ethical Culture was founded in May, 1876, by Felix Adler, son of rabbi Samuel Adler of New York's Temple Emanu-El. He espoused the necessity of using morality and ethical regulation to address issues of societal malaise, such as inner city crime, education, welfare, health, and housing. In such a context, values and morals are generally based on a sense of the responsibilities of being human.

At the end of the twentieth century, issues such as abortion, euthanasia, capital punishment, race relationships, and gender relationships (in and out of wedlock) have ethical nuances which require resolutions. The solutions are proffered both by the monistically oriented religious traditions and by diverse forms of rationalistic secular thought. The normative moral resolutions so proffered are sometimes convergent but are frequently antithetical. —*Habibeh Rahim*

**See also** Aristotelian ethics; Buddhist ethics; Confucian ethics; Hindu ethics; Islamic ethics; Mādhyamaka; Platonic ethics.

**BIBLIOGRAPHY**

Crawford, S. Cromwell, ed. *World Religions and Global Ethics*. New York: Paragon House, 1989.

Navia, Luis E., and Eugene Kelly, eds. *Ethics and the Search for Values*. New York: Prometheus Books, 1980.

Singer, Peter, ed. *A Companion to Ethics*. Cambridge, Mass.: Basil Blackwell, 1991.

Smart, John Jamieson C. *Ethics, Persuasion, and Truth*. Boston: Routledge & Kegan Paul, 1984.

Smurl, James F. *Religious Ethics: A Systems Approach*. Englewood Cliffs, N.J.: Prentice-Hall, 1972.

Robertson, Archibald. *Morals in World History*. Reprint. New York: Haskell House, 1974.

## Compassion

**TYPE OF ETHICS:** Personal and social ethics

**DATE:** First occurrence in English, fourteenth century

**ASSOCIATED WITH:** Feminist ethics, Joseph Butler, David Hume, Arthur Schopenhauer, and Nel Noddings

**DEFINITION:** An emotion involving the feeling of others' troubles or sorrows combined with a disposition to alleviate or, at least, share in them

**SIGNIFICANCE:** Raises questions concerning the origin and ethical significance of an emotion that arises out of concern for others

**What Is Compassion?** Compassion is a combination of emotional and volitional elements that are also referred to by such words as "care," "sympathy," "pity," and "empathy." Compassion refers not only to the emotional ability to enter into another's feelings but also to an active will to alleviate and/or share in the other's plight.

The emotional element plays a large role in compassion. Theorists who, like Plato, Aristotle, and Kant, argue that reason must rule over emotion in ethics give compassion at best a secondary role in their systems. Others, such as Joseph Butler, David Hume, and many utilitarians, argue that ethics is rooted in human emotion. They give compassion a larger role. Feminist theorists such as Carol Gilligan and Nel Noddings have argued that care and compassion should be at the center of moral reasoning.

Persons working in applied ethics have also often suggested that human emotions deserve focused attention in ethical decision making. Those who seek to apply ethical theories in everyday settings, such as clinical medicine, have often urged that the common human experience of compassion for others deserves a larger place in decision making. They suggest that without a focus on compassion, ethical theorizing is in danger of neglecting what is most human in favor of satisfying abstract rational standards.

Emotions such as compassion must nevertheless also be served by rational assessment of situations. Compassionate persons employ reason to assess the source and significance of the troubles that are to be confronted, to weigh alternative ways of alleviating those troubles, and to relate projected actions to other ethical considerations, such as those concerning justice and/or self-interest.

Compassion includes not only the feeling of others' troubles and sorrows but also an active will to alleviate and/or share in them. Thus, compassion also includes a volitional element.

**What Is the Origin of Compassion?** Joseph Butler and David Hume both thought that compassion is a feature of human life that arises naturally. Using the word "compassion" as a verb, Butler wrote in the 1720's that human beings "naturally compassionate all . . . whom they see in distress." He also argued that concern for others is not motivated by self interest. In the 1980's, Nel Nodding spoke of a foundational experience of "natural caring."

*Mother Cabrini, the first American saint of the Catholic faith, worked with Italian immigrants in the 1930's.* (Library of Congress)

Sociobiologists, such as E. O. Wilson and Richard Dawkins, have argued that evolutionary natural selection may favor other-directed dispositions such as compassion. Behavior that is not in an individual's self-interest can nevertheless be favorable to the survival of the species. Thus, an individual bird risks its own survival as it cries out to warn others.

Others suggest that, whatever natural basis there may be, compassion and concern for others must be nurtured. For example, health care professionals are advised to play the role of patient from time to time in order to develop compassion for patients' suffering.

Some Christian thinkers claim that genuine compassion "goes right against the grain" (McNeill et al., 1982). They assert that "compassion is not . . . the outcome of our hard work but the fruit of God's grace."

**What Is the Ethical Significance of Compassion?** Human beings experience many different emotions, including anger, envy, and lust. Why should compassion be ranked as a primary human virtue and thus cultivated?

Plato, Aristotle, and Kant worried that the emotions generally are too unsteady and nonrational to be given first rank. Friedrich Nietzsche rejected the priority of compassion on the grounds that concern for others is often based upon a retreat from the higher discipline required to live a fully human life. He worried that compassion is too often expressed as concern for "the 'creature in man,' for what must be formed, broken, forged, torn, burnt, made incandescent, and purified—that which *necessarily* must and should suffer."

Other thinkers, such as Butler, Hume, Wilson, Dawkins, and Noddings, have based the ethical priority of compassion and care upon one or another type of appeal to nature. Alternatively, some religious thinkers appeal to what is revealed in the life of a person such as Jesus Christ or in God's revelation and gift of this virtue. While they may all agree with critics that reason is needed to guide one to effective compassion, they all also say that reason must be informed by compassion. They would agree with Nietzsche that compassion ought not to be a retreat from fully human living, but they assert that genuine human compassion arises from a positive sense of the meaning and purpose of one's own and others' lives.

**Who and What Are the Objects of Compassion?** Should compassion follow a path of care for those near at hand only or should it express itself equally in care for the far removed and unfamiliar? Some see a general and impartial compassion as the highest good, while others argue that compassion is inherently partial and best focused on particular individuals.

The word "object" suggests a difficulty. Many worry lest compassion reduce the individual being helped to the status of an object to be manipulated without concern for the individual's dignity or autonomy.

Who are the appropriate others upon whom compassion should focus? Many discussions presume that the objects of compassion are fellow human beings. Some argue, however, that compassion should extend to animals and/or to the entire environment. —*James V. Bachman*

**See also** Altruism; Benevolence; Butler, Joseph; Charity; Cruelty to animals; Euthanasia; Generosity; Hume, David; Mercy; Moral status of animals; Passions and emotions; Personal relationships; Physician-patient relationship; Schopenhauer, Arthur; Shaftesbury, Earl of (Anthony Ashley Cooper); Women's ethics.

**BIBLIOGRAPHY**

Butler, Joseph. *Five Sermons, Preached at the Rolls Chapel.* Edited by Stephen L. Darwall. Reprint. Indianapolis: Hackett, 1983.

Hume, David. *A Treatise of Human Nature*. 3 vols. Oxford, England: Clarendon Press, 1960.

McNeill, Donald, Douglas A. Morrison, and Henri N. M. Nouwen. *Compassion: A Reflection on the Christian Life*. Garden City, N.Y.: Doubleday, 1982.

Midgley, Mary. *Beast and Man: Roots of Human Nature*. Ithaca, N.Y.: Cornell University Press, 1978.

Noddings, Nel. *Caring: A Feminine Approach to Ethics and Moral Education*. Berkeley: University of California Press, 1984.

Schopenhauer, Arthur. *On the Basis of Morality*. Translated by E. F. J. Payne. Indianapolis: Bobbs-Merrill, 1965.

## Compromise

**TYPE OF ETHICS:** Personal and social ethics

**DEFINITION:** Compromise is an arrangement for settlement by mutual concession

**SIGNIFICANCE:** Negotiation by mutual concession is based on recognition of the moral legitimacy of an opponent's interests

Negotiation is the process used by parties or groups to come to terms or reach agreement regarding issues about which they are in conflict. Compromise is a subprocess of negotiating that involves making mutual concessions to reach an acceptable agreement. Compromise implies conflict—either an open disagreement or a difference leading to a disagreement that must be resolved. Compromise requires all parties to alter their claims or positions in order to reach an accommodation. If only one party or group alters its position, the result is not compromise but capitulation; even if one of the parties eventually agrees with the other, it may constitute appeasement. Compromisable conflicts exist when there is a partial coincidence of interests resulting in a setting of both competition and cooperation between parties. Such a situation can occur only when there is a recognizable and relatively stable social order in which there are explicit rules about compromising that are known and accepted by the parties involved in the negotiations.

Compromising to resolve conflicts is not the same as bargaining, although both processes involve each party's agreeing to give up something in order to get the other to give up something. At each stage of the negotiating process in both compromising and bargaining, one party proposes a resolution and argues for it. There is, however, a marked difference between bargaining and compromising that revolves around the attitude of the negotiating parties. In bargaining, each side assumes that the other will try to get the best for itself, and each knows that the other knows this, so the situation is mostly strategic. In a compromise, the parties have a certain level of respect for each other and therefore are willing to agree to an accommodation rather than make the best deal for themselves that they can. The distinction between bargaining and compromise can be seen clearly where one negotiating party is more powerful than the other. If the more powerful party is able to impose on its opponent a solution that is favorable to itself and uses its power to do so, the two parties are bargaining. Also, the fact that a negotiation's outcome may be equally favorable to both parties does not indicate that a compromise was reached; it merely demonstrates that the two parties shared relatively equal bargaining power during the negotiations.

Compromise involves acknowledging the moral legitimacy of the interests of one's opponent. To reach a compromise, each party must give its opponent's interests due consideration during negotiation. If a party has no ground for assuming that its opponent is morally inferior, then compromise is morally possible. If both parties' interests are similar, neither party has grounds for not recognizing the moral legitimacy of the other. When opponents' interests are at odds, compromise is possible only if a plurality of interests can be recognized or some level of tolerance can be exhibited. Fanatics do not recognize a plurality of interests or an environment of toleration, and although fanatics may bargain and make deals, they do not compromise. By the same token, idealists, while not rejecting the existence of mutual interests, invariably regard some negotiating points as illegitimate and also are unable to compromise.

Negotiating a compromise is more difficult when the principles, rather than the interests, of the opposing parties are in conflict. A compromise involving a conflict of interests means giving an opponent's interests due consideration in attempting to negotiate a resolution. When principles are in conflict, however, neither party can give due consideration to the other's principles, because at least one of the parties is presumed to be fundamentally wrong in its stance and hence entitled to no consideration. When a conflict of principles exists, there is no requirement to consider the opposition's principles as being as important as one's own in negotiating toward compromise. In many instances, cultural or philosophical principles may present insurmountable barriers to compromise. For example, a society's principles of right and wrong may limit what can be legitimately compromised; from a philosophical and moral standpoint, some points are thus nonnegotiable. It is usually the conflict of principles that limits the ability to negotiate compromises, but compromises can be achieved if the parties believe that their opponents are sincere and earnest about the principles they present to defend their negotiating position.

Negotiating in the spirit of compromise requires both parties to consider the legitimate interests of the opposition as morally equal to their own, and this may depend either on the recognition of a plurality of interests or on simple toleration. Reaching a compromise also involves understanding the principles that formulate an opponent's negotiating position and trusting the sincerity of an opponent's stance regarding principles governing the ability to reach a compromise. If during a negotiation of compromise either party fails to acknowledge the legitimacy of the opponent's interest or fails to understand the basis for the opponent's commitment to guiding principles, the parties are not negotiating a compromise, but engaging in a morally questionable palaver.

*—Randall L. Milstein*

**See also** Conflict of interest.

**BIBLIOGRAPHY**

Hall, Lavinia, ed. *Negotiation: Strategies for Mutual Gain.* Newbury Park, Calif.: Sage Publications, 1993.

Pennock, J. R., and J. W. Chapman, eds. *Compromise in Ethics, Law and Politics.* New York: New York University Press, 1979.

Strauss, Anselm. *Negotiations: Varieties, Contexts, Processes, and Social Order.* San Francisco: Jossey-Bass, 1978.

## Computer crime

**TYPE OF ETHICS:** Scientific ethics

**DATE:** 1950's to present

**DEFINITION:** Direct or indirect use of computer technology in conjunction with illegal or immoral activity

**SIGNIFICANCE:** Computer technology has provided a new tool and target of opportunity for criminals, spies, hooligans, and others

**Ethical Issues.** Instances of computer crime primarily involve breaches of well-defined ethical issues, but one aspect of the nature of computers raises the possibility of new interpretations of these issues. This is true because computers represent and exchange information as electronic signals rather than as tangible objects. Is the theft of a program or information from a computer really theft if what was taken remains in place? Is a person really trespassing if he or she remains thousands of miles away from the computer system on which he or she intrudes?

**Motivations.** The psychological motivations of persons and groups who engage in computer abuse fall into three categories. The first is personal gain of money, goods, services, or valuable information. The second is revenge against another person, a company, institution, government, or society at large. A variation on the motive of revenge is political motivation. The third type of motivation is to gain stature in one's own mind or those of one's peers by demonstrating mastery over complex technology.

These motivations serve as the basis for several types of activity, which include theft, fraud, espionage, vandalism, malicious mischief, and trespassing.

**Theft and Fraud.** Theft in computer crime takes many

forms. Embezzlement is one of the most publicized. One type of scheme involves the transfer of very small amounts of money from bank accounts over a period of time into an account established by the thief.

Another common and well-known form of theft is software piracy, which is the unauthorized copying of proprietary programs. The scope of piracy is broad. Well-organized groups mass-produce "bootleg copies" of popular personal computer programs. These are then sold to unsuspecting people as legitimate copies. At the other end of the piracy spectrum is the person who makes a copy of a computer game for a friend and may not even realize he is breaking the law.

Sometimes computers themselves are the targets of theft, either for their intrinsic value or for information they may contain. One celebrated case involved the theft of a staff officer's portable computer from his car in the Middle East late in 1990. The computer contained strategic plans for the upcoming U.S. Operation Desert Storm. The thief was evidently unaware of the computer's contents, and the act did not result in a serious breach of security.

**Vandalism.** Computer systems are often the targets of vandalism, either by disgruntled individuals or by organized groups. Some of the most serious cases of vandalism against computers were committed in France and Italy by the radical Red Brigades in the late 1970's. One of their attacks resulted in the loss of all records of automobiles and drivers' licenses in Italy.

**Malicious Mischief.** Perpetrators of malicious mischief on computer systems have come to be known as "hackers." Hackers are motivated by a desire to demonstrate mastery over computer technology, especially among their peers. One of their methods is to write a program that, when executed, causes damage to other programs and data files or causes the computer to stop running, or "crash." These programs vary widely in their nature and are variously known as Trojan Horses, worms, and viruses.

Worms and viruses are usually programmed to replicate themselves to every computer system they come in contact with. One of the most notorious was the Internet Worm, the work of a young computer scientist who placed it on the world's largest computer network in 1988. Within a matter of hours it spread to thousands of computer installations, including those of the U.S. Defense Department and many universities, causing tens of millions of dollars in damage.

**Trespassing.** In the context of computer crime, trespassing is unauthorized access to a computer system. The most common form of trespassing is committed by hackers, who often have no intention of causing damage to the systems they break into but are lured by the challenge of overcoming a system's security measures. Once inside a system, they are often content to view the system's contents. Some hackers, however, have been prosecuted for such acts as breaking into telephone company installations and circulating private access codes.

Another form of trespassing is committed by persons engaging in espionage. Companies engage in industrial espionage by breaking into rival companies' systems to look for trade secrets and other proprietary information. A rarer variant occurs when agents of a country break into the computer systems of another government. This occurred in the late 1980's, when West German hackers were discovered using the Internet to access classified information from the U.S. Defense Department.

**Legislation.** Computer crime has become so widespread that most Western industrialized countries have enacted laws against it. In the United States, much of this legislation has occurred at the state level; most states had computer crime laws on the books by the late 1970's or early 1980's. The rapidly developing countries of eastern Asia have lagged behind in efforts to police computer crime, and in many of those countries software piracy has become a flourishing business.

**Prevention.** Attention to security by programmers, systems managers, corporate management, and government agencies is the single most effective method of computer crime prevention. Many recorded cases of computer crime have been committed by previously honest individuals who noticed opportunities created by lax security methods and succumbed to temptation. The trend of replacing large mainframe computer systems with networks of personal computers raises further problems, because the network and personal computer operating systems do not have security features as sophisticated as those present on large systems.

Personal computers are also the most vulnerable to attacks by viruses. Virus detection and "disinfection" programs are available from a variety of vendors, sometimes on a free trial basis.

If the ethics of computer use were routinely incorporated into computer science and vocational training, people would have a better understanding of responsible behavior. They should know it is wrong to duplicate copyrighted programs and that it is wrong to access a computer system without proper authorization. Although it is difficult to change people's ethical values, it is not so difficult to teach them the difference between right and wrong. —*Charles E. Sutphen*

**See also** Computer technology.

**BIBLIOGRAPHY**

Betts, Mitch. "What About Ethics?" *Computerworld* 27 (June 7, 1993): 84.

Lundell, Allan. *Virus!* Chicago: Contemporary Books, 1989.

McAfee, John, and Colin Haynes. *Computer Viruses, Worms, Data Diddlers, Killer Programs, and Other Threats to Your System*. New York: St. Martin's Press, 1989.

Parker, Donn B. *Crime by Computer*. New York: Charles Scribner's Sons, 1976.

__________. *Fighting Computer Crime*. New York: Charles Scribner's Sons, 1983.

Whiteside, Thomas. *Computer Capers*. New York: Thomas Y. Crowell, 1978.

## Computer technology

**TYPE OF ETHICS:** Scientific ethics
**DATE:** Late 1960's to present
**DEFINITION:** The discipline that analyzes the social impact of computer technology and formulates policies for the ethical application of this technology
**SIGNIFICANCE:** Strives to protect the privacy of individuals, guard against misuse of personal information, avoid the disenfranchisement of workers, encourage the use of computers to enhance human values, and define ownership of intellectual property

Computer professionals face ethical dilemmas in their work. These dilemmas relate to protecting people's privacy by guarding against unauthorized access to confidential data and preventing the misuse of personal data. Computer professionals are obligated to design and program systems that ensure the accuracy of data, since critical decisions are made based on the output of their systems. Inaccurate information can have grave economic consequences and in some situations can even place people's lives in danger.

Computer professionals have opportunities to enrich people's lives. Conversely, through the improper application of their knowledge and talents, they can have devastating effects on large segments of society. This reality makes clear the necessity of an ethics for computer technology.

**History.** Traditionally, computers and their use were looked upon as value-neutral. By the late 1960's, however, some ethicists and computer professionals were questioning this assumption. By the late 1980's, computer ethics was being recognized as a legitimate academic pursuit and a professional necessity. As a field between science and moral studies, computer ethics has attempted to define the values inherent in computer technology. Some of the pioneers in this field are Walter Maner, Donn Parker, Deborah G. Johnson, James H. Moor, and Terrell Ward Bynum.

**Privacy Issues.** Computers are used to store massive amounts of information, much of which is personal and the subjects of which are deserving of protection against misuse of these data. Computer networking over various communication facilities, including ordinary telephone lines, allows electronic access to this confidential information. This environment requires a heightened awareness of the potential for political abuses of personal liberties and commercial exploitation through insensitive misuse and inappropriate manipulation of personal information.

**Surveillance.** Computers can and are used to monitor activities in the workplace. They track work done on computer terminals, monitor phone calls, and browse electronic mail without the individual's knowledge of this activity. While some of these activities may be historically grounded in efficient business management practices (Fred Taylor introduced time and motion studies at the beginning of the twentieth century), the intensity of monitoring activities with computers raises ethical issues. Awareness of monitoring produces stress and contributes to health problems; employees who know that they are monitored feel that they are in an electronic straitjacket.

The invasion of privacy threat posed by computer monitoring is very real. Improperly applied, monitoring is nothing short of eavesdropping on individuals' private lives. Employers may argue that *every* act by an employee while "on the clock" is their concern. This ethical dilemma needs to be evaluated on the basis of principles of fairness and quality of life in the workplace.

**Poor System Design.** One of the greatest obstacles to the ethical uses of computers is caused by incompetent system designers, however well intentioned, who develop and program systems that do not accomplish the required tasks, create frustration and aggravation for the users of the systems, and even generate erroneous information. In terms of their cumulative cost to organizations, individuals, and society, poorly designed systems that fail to utilize properly the power of the technology create the greatest and most persistent ethical quandaries. Error-prone, inflexible, unimaginative, and insensitive systems are an ethical issue because of the toll they take on human well-being.

**Assigning Responsibility.** Computers do not have values: They do not make independent decisions, they do not make mistakes, and they can do only what they are programmed to do. The *utilization* of computer technology, however, is not a value-neutral activity. Faulty programs, invalid data, or lack of proper controls creates computer errors. It is unethical for computer professionals and users to attempt to transfer blame for errors away from themselves. This constitutes denying responsibility and lying.

Also key to this issue is that ethical norms must be applied to situations in which the computer is *essentially* involved, not *passively* involved; that is, where computer technology is used, or misused, in the actual perpetration of moral wrongdoing. For example, using a computer to gain unauthorized access to company secrets *essentially* involves the computer; stealing computer equipment, wrong though it may be, only *passively* involves the computer.

**Disenfranchisement of Workers.** Using computers to do dull, repetitious, noncreative tasks is useful. Using them to replace workers simply for the purpose of reducing payrolls raises serious ethical questions of fairness and obligation. Computer technology ought to be applied in the workplace in ways that allow time for and actually encourage the pursuit of more creative activities.

**Intellectual Property.** Computer technology focuses attention on the whole issue of intellectual property because computer software is often viewed as such. Some people argue that programmers who write software create in much the same way that an author or an artist creates. Others argue that programming is simply stringing together series of instructions and algorithms that are in the public domain. Therefore, programming is not truly creative, and the end product is not someone's intellectual property.

For those who subscribe to the argument that software is intellectual property, the question of ownership must be answered. Does the programmer, as creator, own the software? Does her employer, who is paying her to create the software, own it? Should those who work to develop software or pay others to develop it expect to be reimbursed by those who use it? Still others argue that all software is in the public domain, since it is nothing more than ideas and thoughts, actualized on a computer, and therefore is not intellectual property at all. Proponents of this latter view oppose exclusive "ownership" of any software.

If the ownership of software can be established, however, then unauthorized use of the software raises serious ethical questions. —*Edwin R. Davis*

**See also** Computer crime; Robotics; Technological ethics.

**Bibliography**

Dunlop, Charles, and Rob Kling, eds. *Computerization and Controversy*. Boston: Academic Press, 1991.

Forester, Tom, and Perry Morrison. *Computer Ethics*. Cambridge, Mass.: MIT Press, 1990.

Hoffman, W. Michael, and Jennifer Mills Moore, eds. *Ethics and the Management of Computer Technology*. Proceedings of the Fourth National Conference on Business Ethics, sponsored by The Center for Business Ethics, Bentley College. Cambridge, Mass.: Oelgeschlager, Gunn & Hain, 1982.

Johnson, Deborah G. *Computer Ethics*. Englewood Cliffs, N.J.: Prentice-Hall, 1985.

Parker, Donn B., Susan Swope, and Bruce N. Baker. *Ethical Conflicts in Information and Computer Science, Technology, and Business*. Wellesley, Mass.: QED Information Sciences, 1990.

## Comte, Auguste (Jan. 19, 1798, Montpellier, France—Sept. 5, 1857, Paris, France): Philosopher

**Type of ethics:** Modern history

**Achievements:** Author of *Cours de philosophie positive* (1830-1842; course on positive philosophy); *Système de politique positive* (1851-1854); and *System of Positive Polity* (1875-1877); founder of positivism and sociology

**Significance:** Having advanced an elaborate argument predicated on his "law of the three stages"—in which the history of humankind took the sequence of a theological phase, a transitional metaphysical period, and then the modern age—Comte argued that "moral progress" was the primary focus of all human activity and was primarily a societal activity and responsibility

Although Comte developed the philosophic system that resulted in the establishment of sociology, he was concerned with the fate of the individual within modern society. Comte recognized the problems associated with modern society and the impact of science and the industrial order. He searched for elements of a good and ethical society that could command a consensus in the midst of varying individuals' beliefs. Further, he looked for a common ground for agreement on values in spite of the turbulent alterations in the structures of modern society. Finally, although Comte advanced the concept of a communal or societal order, he recognized the need for personal fulfillment in this ethical society. Comte has been criticized for his pro-Catholic and anti-Protestant statements and sentiments.

**See also** Morality.

## Confidentiality

**Type of ethics:** Personal and social ethics

**Date:** Fifth century B.C.E. to present

**Definition:** The state or quality of communications being secret; the expectation that disclosures in certain relationships will remain private

**Significance:** A person (usually the client in a professional relationship) reveals sensitive information only because of trust that the disclosed information will remain private

Many professions today have ethical rules requiring their members not to disclose confidential communications—roughly the same thing as keeping a secret—under most circumstances. A secret is information that is told to someone else with the reasonable expectancy that it will be private. Anything disclosed when other people can overhear it is not confidential. The ethical rules do not attempt to control general gossip. They cover only secrets revealed to professionals during professional work. Some laws (privileges) protect professional confidences. Other laws (exceptions to privilege and reporting statutes) permit or force the betrayal of confidentiality. These laws create new ethical dilemmas.

**History.** The concept of a professional having an ethical obligation to maintain confidentiality dates back to writings known as the *Corpus Hippocraticum*, attributed to the Greek physician Hippocrates about 400 B.C.E. Hippocrates is credited with stating: "Whatever I shall see or hear in the course of my profession . . . if it be what should not be published abroad, I will never divulge, holding such things to be holy secrets." This rule of confidentiality became a core concept in the medical ethics of the sixteenth century, when physicians discovered that infectious diseases were being spread by diseased persons who feared that disclosure of their condition would be punished by social isolation.

Physicians continued to apply the rule of confidentiality and, with time, the ethical codes of all mental health-related professions incorporated it. Today, it is a universal ethical concept in the helping professions and is seen as vital to promoting the full client disclosure necessary for effective treatment.

**Confidentiality and the Professions.** Psychotherapy is assumed to require the honest communication of clients' secret private feelings and the subsequent treatment of clients' symptoms. Clients will not reveal such matters if they do not trust the professional to keep them secret. Such trust, which is assumed to be essential for effective treatment, requires firm rules requiring that things that are said in confidence be kept confidential. Violating the client's expectations of privacy violates professional ethical rules, the

| PROFESSIONAL CONFIDENTIALITY | |
|---|---|
| **Professionals** | **Confidential Subject Matter** |
| Physicians | Medical information except that regarding child abuse, some contagious diseases, and most sexually transmitted diseases |
| Lawyers | Almost everything except information regarding future crimes |
| Journalists | Identity of the source of news information |
| Mental-health professionals | All information except that related to dangers to self or others or to child abuse |
| Clerics | All information |
| Accountants | Normal business data unless blatantly fraudulent |

client's constitutionally based civil rights, and most state laws that govern professional conduct. Violations can give rise to lawsuits.

Hippocrates' basic insight that physicians can best perform their duties if their clients trust them enough to reveal sensitive information also applies to other nonmedical professions. Legal clients will not discuss sensitive details of their cases if they do not trust their attorneys. Penitents will not bare their souls to clerics if they fear gossip about their confessions. News sources will not speak to reporters if they fear that their lives will be disrupted by disclosure of their identities. Business clients are reluctant to allow accountants access to sensitive business data without assurances of privacy. Therefore, all these professions have also developed ethical traditions of confidentiality to reassure clients that it is safe to speak freely with members of these professions.

**Beyond Confidentiality: Legal Privilege and Its Exceptions.** All traditions of confidentiality in the ethics of professions thus arise out of utilitarian considerations. Many of these considerations are considered so important that laws have been passed creating legal rights (privileges) for some professions to protect some types of confidences even against court orders. The attorney-client privilege, the oldest such privilege, is universal in the Anglo-American legal tradition. Most U.S. states also recognize the physician-patient, cleric-penitent, and psychotherapist-client privileges. The psychotherapist-client privilege does not apply to all mental health professions in all states. Communications with other professionals, such as divorce mediators and accountants, are privileged in some states. Members of professions having a privilege are ethically required to assert that privilege to protect confidential information when they are served with subpoenas. Communications in certain nonprofessional relationships, such as marriage, may also be privileged.

In recent years, courts and legislatures have decided that the social benefits of privileges are not as important as access to information in some types of situations, and they have created exceptions to privilege (preventing protection of information) and reporting statutes (requiring disclosures). Examples of exceptions to privilege include a therapist's duty to disclose threats made by a client against another person. Further, both medical and mental health professionals are legally required by reporting statutes to violate confidentiality when the subject matter is child abuse.

These exceptions to privilege and reporting statutes create new ethical dilemmas for professionals and for professions. Jail terms and fines have been used to punish the defiant. Obeying has put professionals in opposition to the ethical standards of their professions. The professional associations have retreated after fierce opposition. Today, the ethical codes of most professional groups say that the professional must protect confidentiality to the extent allowed by laws and legal duties. The Principles of the American Psychological Association (APA) state that confidentiality should be maintained unless to do so would clearly increase danger to the client or to another person or unless the client or the client's legal representative has given consent to disclose. The American Counseling Association (formerly the AACD) requires members to take reasonable personal action or to inform responsible authorities when they are faced with clear and imminent danger to the client or others.

Although the new flexibility in the ethical rules solves one set of problems, it also creates another set. Clients may feel betrayed when a professional discloses confidential information for legal reasons. Required disclosures can violate professional ethical duties to help clients (beneficence) and not to harm them (nonmaleficence). Revealing a client's past child abuse because of a reporting statute may betray that client's trust and make further therapy impossible. One solution is to have the professional explain to the client, in advance of any professional services, what is confidential and what is not. Many professionals reject this approach because they believe that prior warnings make the therapy process seem too legalistic and inhibit client trust.

Another approach is to keep required disclosures as limited as possible. Ethical guidelines for school counselors call for reporting information disclosed by pupil clients that reveals circumstances that are likely to have negative effects on others without revealing the identity of the student.

*—Leland C. Swenson*

**See also** Professional ethics.

**BIBLIOGRAPHY**

American Association of Counseling and Development (AACD). *Ethical Standards of the American Association of Counseling and Development*. 3d ed. Alexandria, Virginia: AACD Governing Council, 1988.

American Psychological Association (APA). "Ethical Principles for Psychologists." *American Psychologist* 45 (March, 1990): 390-395.

Denkowski, Kathryn, and George Denkowski. "Client-Counselor Confidentiality: An Update of Rationale, Legal Status and Implications." *Personnel and Guidance Journal* 60 (February, 1982): 371-375.

Feldman, James H. "Testimonial Privilege: Between Priest and Penitent, Doctor and Patient, Lawyer and Client . . . Which Confidences Are Protected?" *Family Advocate* 14, no. 2 (Fall, 1991): 20-24.

Slovenko, Ralph. *Psychiatry and Law.* Boston: Little, Brown, 1973.

Swenson, Leland C. *Psychology and Law for the Helping Professions.* Pacific Grove, Calif.: Brooks/Cole, 1993.

Taylor, Linda, and H. S. Adelman. "Reframing the Confidentiality Dilemma to Work in Children's Best Interests." *Professional Psychology: Research and Practice* 20 (April, 1989): 79-83.

## Conflict and conflict resolution

**Type of ethics:** Personal and social ethics

**Date:** Early 1960's

**Associated with:** "Win-win" or principled negotiations; mediation; and Roger Fisher, professor of law at Harvard Law School and director of the Harvard Negotiation Project

**Definition:** Conflict is a struggle between at least two interdependent parties

**Significance:** Trust and a high level of ethical behavior are essential to successful conflict resolution

Arguments, yielding, yelling, stalling, threats, coercion—these are all images of conflict. It is understandable that some people try to avoid dealing with any conflict. Yet there are techniques for resolving conflict productively and ethically. Many people are familiar with the concept of "win-win" negotiation, but few actually practice it. It seems, however, that "principled conflict management," as some call win-win negotiation, is finally moving into the mainstream. Universities are granting advanced degrees in conflict management. Nonadversarial, alternative dispute resolution methods, such as mediation, are now required in many contracts. Empowerment management styles such as Total Quality Management and Self-Directed Work Teams require win-win conflict management to be successful.

**Conflict Is a Natural Process.** Authors Joyce L. Hocker and William W. Wilmot, in their book *Interpersonal Conflict* (1991), find that "One of the most dysfunctional teachings about conflict is that *harmony is normal and conflict is abnormal.*" Some people think of conflict as the result of "personality clashes." In fact, however, conflict is a natural process that is inherent in all important relationships. Conflict is here to stay. No one can change that, but people can change their perceptions of conflict and the ways in which they manage it.

**Avoidance.** There are three basic styles of conflict management: avoidance, competitive negotiation, and principled negotiation. Many people use more than one style, depending on the situation. Avoidance is very common when people perceive conflict as a negative and conflict resolution as an unpleasant problem. Avoidance can be useful when open communication is not possible, when the issue or relationship is not important to one—something one regards as trivial and not worth the energy required to reach a mutually agreeable solution—and when the costs of confrontation are too high. Continual avoidance of conflict is highly destructive.

### Guidelines for Principled Negotiation

1. Attack problems, not people.
2. Build trust.
3. Start with a discussion and analysis of the interests, concerns, needs, and whys of each party. This is the essence of principled negotiation. Begin with interests, not positions or solutions.
4. Listen.
5. Brainstorm. Suggesting an idea does not mean you agree with it. Solve problems. Develop multiple options.
6. Use objective criteria whenever possible. Agree on how something will be measured.

**Competitive Negotiation.** Competitive negotiation is the familiar win-lose style. In this approach, each party pressures the other to change. Control, coercion, threats, walkouts, and lying are techniques that are employed. One pursues one's own concerns at the expense of another. Competitive negotiations work with set positions or predetermined solutions. Each party comes to the negotiations with a "solution" to the conflict and attempts to get the other to change or give up something. With this style someone always loses. Someone is disappointed. Someone may leave angry and wish to "get even" the next time. Competitive negotiation can be useful if the external goal is more important than the relationship or if the other party really has one's detriment at heart; for example, when there has been physical abuse in a divorce case. Relationships are rarely enhanced by competitive negotiation. The goal has to be so important that one is willing to sacrifice the relationship.

**Principled Negotiation.** Principled negotiation, also called collaborative negotiation, is the win-win style. With this model, one strives for a mutually favorable resolution to the conflict by inducing or persuading the other party to cooperate. While competitive negotiations start with positions or solutions, in principled negotiations the parties do not come with predetermined solutions. Instead, they come with interests, specific needs, or underlying concerns that may be met in several ways. The parties may have ideas about solutions, but they are not attached to them. They are open to different solutions, provided that their key interests, concerns, and needs are met. Principled negotiation takes the approach that the parties have both diverse and common interests and that, in the end, both parties will have their interests satisfied. The needs of each party are revealed, and both work to find mutually agreeable, and often new, solutions.

Although principled negotiation can be empowering for both parties and can lead to a long-term solution to the conflict, it has some disadvantages. It requires keen perception, good communication skills, and creativity. It also takes time and requires trust.

**Communicating Effectively.** Conflict is more often than not a product of communication behavior. Therefore, resolving conflict starts with improving communication skills. For most people, listening is "waiting to talk" rather than listening and validating (not necessarily agreeing with, but acknowledging) what the person is saying. Listening is more effective when the listener demonstrates that he or she understands by using phrases such as "I hear you saying that . . . " It is also effective to ask questions and to speak from the "I" position, saying what he or she thinks, rather than attacking the other party. It is more effective to say "I feel discriminated against" than it is to say "You are a racist." When one party takes a stance and "attacks" from a positional view, it is wise for the other party to break the cycle by refusing to participate in that destructive style of conflict management. In such a case, it is often effective for the party who is being attacked to express his or her own interests, to ask why the other party has this view, and to listen to the response. Often, when people are "heard," they soften their positional stands. Understanding need not imply agreement. When one party understands the other, then that party can calmly explain his or her concerns, needs, and interests, inviting the other party to cooperate to find a solution. It should be kept in mind that the two parties have a relationship and that it is better for both parties to resolve the conflict in an agreeable manner.

Principled negotiation is not appropriate for all conflicts, but it is a technique that deserves to be used more widely. It is the only style of conflict management that gets results and maintains and even enhances relationships.

—*Kathleen D. Purdy*

**See also** Business ethics; International justice.

**BIBLIOGRAPHY**

Fisher, Roger, and Scott Brown. *Getting Together: Building Relationships As We Negotiate*. New York: Penguin Books, 1989.

Fisher, Roger, and William Ury. *Getting To Yes: Negotiating Agreements Without Giving In*. Boston: Houghton Mifflin, 1981.

Hocker, Joyce L., and William M. Wilmot. *Interpersonal Conflict*. 3d ed. Dubuque, Iowa: Wm. C. Brown, 1991.

Raiffa, H. *The Art and Science of Negotiation*. Cambridge, Mass.: Harvard University Press, 1982.

## Conflict of interest

**TYPE OF ETHICS:** Personal and social ethics
**DATE:** c. 400 B.C.E. to present
**DEFINITION:** A situation in which two or more interests are not mutually realizable
**SIGNIFICANCE:** Raises the issues of whether human interests are compatible and whether social intercourse requires sacrifices

In pursuing their lives, individuals must establish goals and put into practice plans to achieve them. A goal to which an individual is committed is commonly called an "interest" of that individual.

Not all goals can be achieved. Individuals can set impossible goals, goals that conflict with the nature of reality—for example, the goal of discovering the secret of instantaneous interplanetary travel. Individuals can also set goals that conflict with each other—for example, a student of below-average intelligence setting the goals of getting A's in all of his courses while working a full-time job and playing a sport. Individuals can set goals that conflict with the goals of other individuals—for example, a burglar's goal of stealing a television conflicts with the owner's goal of keeping it.

Conflicts of interest can also arise in professional agent/client relationships. An agent can be hired by two clients with conflicting interests or can have a personal interest arise that conflicts with his or her professional role. An example of the former is a corporate director who is offered a job in a government agency that regulates her corporation. An example of the latter is an attorney who is hired by the plaintiff in a case in which the defendant turns out to be an old school friend.

Professional agent conflicts of interest raise moral concern because such conflicts make it more difficult for the agent to be objective in evaluating the interests of both sides; thus, the clients are less certain that the agent will act in their best interests.

The above cases present no intractable moral problems, since all of them arise either because of ignorance (instantaneous travel), unrealistic expectations (the student), illegitimate goals (the burglar), or happenstance that makes objectivity more difficult but not impossible (the attorney and the director).

Throughout most of the history of philosophy, however, the standard view has been that conflicts of interest must necessarily exist. This thesis is a conclusion derived from premises about human nature and the creation of values.

**Human Nature.** In dualist theories of human nature (such as those of Plato, Christianity, and Sigmund Freud, to take three influential examples), one part of the self (for example, the appetites, body, or id) is said to have innate interests that are absolutely opposed to those of another part of the self (for example, reason, the soul, or the superego). International conflicts of interest are thus built into human nature.

Reductive materialist theories tend to necessitate conflicts of interest among individuals. In Thomas Hobbes's theory, for example, human nature is constituted by drives for gain, safety, and glory that can be satisfied only at the expense of others. In the absence of social mechanisms created to mediate these conflicts of interest, life is "solitary, poor, nasty, brutish, and short."

**Zero-sum Economics.** In economics, the premise that someone's gain is always balanced by someone else's loss is called the "zero-sum" premise. Competitive games are often offered as zero-sum metaphors for life. Someone wins and someone loses; both parties want to win, but a conflict of interest exists since only one can.

**Ethical Implications.** If conflicts of interest are fundamental to human social relationships, then ethics is about resolving conflicts. Since such fundamental conflicts of interest can be settled only by someone's interests being sacrificed, however, it follows that ethics is about deciding whose interests must be sacrificed.

**Legitimate Interests as Harmonious.** Against the standard view is the position that all conflicts of interest are a result of error, not of human nature or zero-sum theory. The harmonious thesis holds that human nature is at birth a set of integrated capacities rather than an aggregation of innate, conflicting parts. The capacities exist to be developed so as to be able to satisfy one's needs, and it is by reference to one's needs that one's interests are defined. Since one's ultimate need is to maintain one's life, one's interests are defined by reference to maintaining one's life. Because life is a long-term endeavor, it follows that one must adopt long-range principles by which to guide one's actions.

Many principles are involved, but of special relevance to the question of conflicts of interest are the principles that life requires individual effort and that each individual's life is an end in itself. If these principles are true, then since other individuals are not one's property, one's interests must be specified by what one can do by one's individual effort. In a society based on the division of labor, this means that one must produce goods for trade. Since trade is a voluntary exchange, the long-range social principle is to interact with others on a mutually voluntary basis. If this broad, long-range context is established as the framework for defining interests, then social cooperation rather than conflict is a consequence of pursuing one's interests.

**Win-win.** The zero-sum account of production and distribution can also be challenged. If one purchases gasoline, the exchange is win-win for oneself and the gas station owner. Michelangelo's sculptures and Thomas Edison's inventions were not produced at the expense of those who did not create them; therefore, the sculptures and inventions are a net gain for everyone.

If legitimate interests are not in conflict, then it follows that personal and social harmony are possible without the sacrifice of legitimate interests. Accordingly, the task of ethics will not be to decide who must be sacrificed, but rather how to identify and fulfill legitimate interests.

*—Stephen R. C. Hicks*

**See also** Freud, Sigmund; Hobbes, Thomas; *Leviathan*; Nietzsche, Friedrich.

**BIBLIOGRAPHY**


Freud, Sigmund. *Civilization and Its Discontents.* Translated by James Strackey. New York: W. W. Norton, 1961.

Hobbes, Thomas. *Leviathan.* Edited by Richard Tuck. New York: Cambridge University Press, 1991.

Nietzsche, Friedrich. *Beyond Good and Evil.* Translated by Walter Kaufmann. New York: Vintage, 1966.

Plato. *The Republic.* Translated by A. D. Lindsay. New York: Knopf, 1992.

Rand, Ayn. "The 'Conflicts' of Men's Interests." In *The Virtue of Selfishness.* New York: New American Library, 1964.


## Confucian ethics

**TYPE OF ETHICS:** Classical history

**DATE:** Sixth century B.C.E. to present

**ASSOCIATED WITH:** Confucius, Mencius, Hsün Tzu, Tung Chung-shu, and subsequent neo-Confucian thinkers

**DEFINITION:** Maxims and prescriptions for social and political behavior based on writings by Confucian philosophers and canons dealing with filial piety, rituals, and social behavior

**SIGNIFICANCE:** Served as guidelines for personal and professional conduct for rulers, officials, and the upper classes in China, Korea, Vietnam, and Japan

First postulated during the feudal period in China (771-221 B.C.E.), Confucian ethics sought to effect peace and harmony in Chinese society. Starting with simple maxims, the school gradually developed into a comprehensive system of ethics that was primarily political but also emphasized social and religious conduct. Never a popular religion, its rites and ethical dictates were practiced by elites in several East Asian countries.

**History.** The first thinker in China to address the problem of the wars and uncertainty that characterized the breakdown of the feudal system was Confucius (K'ung Fu Tzu), who lived from 551 B.C.E. to 479 B.C.E. His solution to the problem of societal breakdown was to return to an idealized form of feudalism. Such a system would be based on the family; the king would act as father and role model for his subjects, who in turn would behave like filial children. While emphasizing hereditary rights, Confucius also called upon kings to act in a kingly fashion and upon noblemen to act with noble integrity. If this were done, laws would be unnecessary.

The next major Confucian, Mencius (371-289 B.C.E.), in response to the accelerated decline of feudalism, added to the responsibilities of the king welfare projects and the requirement to hire officials on the basis of merit and education rather than birthright. Mencius stipulated that those who worked with their minds were entitled to be the ruling class, thus creating the idea of a literocracy rather than a hereditary aristocracy. A ruler who did not provide for his people should be replaced by another member of his family.

The next major Confucian, Hsün Tzu (298-238 B.C.E.) expanded on Confucian themes, but unlike Confucius and Mencius, who either implied or asserted that human nature was good, Hsün Tzu argued that human beings were born evil. It was human nature to seek to be good in order to protect oneself, thereby engaging in a form of social contract with the state. All three philosophers considered that human beings could be good. To Confucius, the ruler and the nobility had to provide the proper role models. Mencius added the obligation to provide education and welfare to the weak and needy. Hsün Tzu's ideal ruler, however, could also mete out rewards and punishments in order to weed out incorrigibles and promote social harmony.

During the Eastern Chou and Ch'in Dynasties (771-210 B.C.E.), the Confucian school was neither large nor powerful. In fact, the prime minister of the Ch'in (221-210 B.C.E.) persecuted Confucians despite the fact that he had been Hsün Tzu's student. During the Han Dynasty (206 B.C.E. to 9 C.E.), Emperor Han Wu Ti (140-86 B.C.E.) made Confucianism the official school of China. This action was primarily the result of efforts of the emperor's minister Tung Chung-shu (179-104 B.C.E.), who combined Confucianism with other schools and also suggested that a ruler was a cosmic figure who coalesced the forces of Heaven, Earth, and Humanity. No doubt the prospect of having well-behaved citizens who were loyal to the throne also contributed to the emperor's decision.

By the end of the seventh century C.E., there was a regularized examination system that required prospective officials to know the Confucian canon by memory. In this way, the imperial throne sought to ensure that its officials would all adhere to the high moral standards of Confucianism. Subsequent neo-Confucian thinkers cemented the symbiotic relationship between the absolute throne and the Confucian literocracy by assuming responsibility for many of the failures of any given monarch or dynasty. Confucians accepted the displacement of one dynasty by another, ascribing such changes to the moral deficiencies of dynastic family. They did, however, fight tenaciously against any efforts to alter the system itself.

In 1911, when the last dynasty fell, an already weakened Confucian literocracy fell as well, although the religious and social practices of Confucianism have survived to some degree in many places in Asia.

**Ethical Principles.** In addition to requiring a monarch to set a proper moral example for his subjects, Confucius stressed that all humans should strive to be *jen*, which generally means "humane." Expressed by the character combining the meanings "man" and "two," this concept called for people to be considerate and compassionate toward one another. One method of developing one's *jen* was to observe the proper rituals and ceremonies. It was essential that people be obedient and loving toward their parents and superiors, who, in turn, should be kind and nurturing. Other concepts presented by Confucius and developed by his disciples included *li* ("principle") and *yi* (righteousness), both of which connoted acting in accordance with ancient precedents.

Mencius and Hsün Tzu further developed the concept of the five cardinal human relationships. These involved affection between father and son, respect between husband and wife, hierarchy between the old and the young, propriety between ruler and minister, and loyalty between friend and friend. All three of the Eastern Chou philosophers stressed ritualistic behavior in order to achieve discipline and nurture moral principles.

With the syncretism of Tung Chung-shu and of later neo-Confucians, other concepts of ethical behavior were incorporated from Taoism and Buddhism into Confucianism. Concepts such as *ch'i* ("inner spirit") crept into Confucian theory and practice. Nevertheless, the basic principles of Confucian morality were evident by 250 B.C.E. and have remained fairly consistent to this day. —*Hilel B. Salomon*

**See also** Confucius; Hsün Tzu; Mencius.

**Bibliography**


Creel, Herrlee Glessner. *Confucius and The Chinese Way.* New York: Harper, 1960.

Legge, James, trans. *The Four Books: Confucian Analects, The Great Learning, The Doctrine of the Mean, and the Works of Mencius.* Shanghai: Chinese Book, 1933.

Shryock, John Knight. *The Origin and Development of the State Cult of Confucius: An Introductory Study.* New York: Century Press, 1932.

Taylor, Rodney Leon. *The Religious Dimensions of Confucianism.* Albany: State University of New York Press, 1990.

Tu, Wei-ming. *Humanity and Self-Cultivation: Essays in Confucian Thought.* Berkeley: Asian Humanities Press, 1979.


## Confucius

(K'ung Fu Tzu or K'ung Tzu; 551 B.C.E., China—479 B.C.E., China): Philosopher

**Type of ethics:** Classical history

**Achievements:** Founder of Confucianism

**Significance:** Confucius integrated governing with the teaching of morality; he developed the moral category of the "elite scholar," the moral principles of *jen* (humanity) and *li* (rites), and the basic virtues, such as "filial piety"

Confucius lived at a time when the ancient empire of China was being broken up into numerous feudal states, whose struggles for power or survival created an urgent need for able state officials. For the first time in Chinese history, it became possible for a commoner to attain high court position and to effect political changes. A new class of literati was thus formed in Chinese society. As one of the forerunners of that class, Confucius was greatly distressed by the chaotic situation of his time, which was characterized by corruption, conspiracy, and usurpation in courts; harsh measures of oppression carried out against the people; and aggressive wars between states. He believed that this was a result of the moral degeneration of the rulers and that the only way to correct it was to teach and to practice morality.

Unable to persuade the rulers of his time to listen to his morally oriented political advice, Confucius devoted his life to teaching a large number of private students, in order to foster a special group of elite scholars (*chün tzu*, or superior people) who would serve the needs of the time and realize his political ideals. His teaching was made authoritative by the Han emperors in the second century B.C.E. and became the official Chinese ideology until the beginning of the twentieth century. The earliest biography of Confucius was written by Ssu-ma Ch'ien in his *Shih chi* (*Records of the Historian*) at the beginning of the first century B.C.E.

The *Analects* is a collection that consists mainly of Confucius' teachings, comments, and advice, along with some contributions from his main disciples. Also included are short records and descriptions of issues that concerned Confucius. The work was compiled and edited by the students of Confucius' disciples a century or so after his death. It was beautifully written, and many of the sayings contained in it became proverbs and everyday maxims. It is one of the most reliable texts among the Chinese classics, and it provides the most accurate information about Confucius and his teachings. The primary text of Confucianism, the *Analects* was the most influential book in China until the early twentieth century.

**Chün Tzu and Self-cultivation.** *Chün tzu* originally meant the son of a nobleman. Confucius used the term to mean a person with a noble character. It means an elite, superior man in a moral sense. The way to be a *chün tzu* is not by birth but by self-cultivation, which for Confucius is a synonym for learning. A *chün tzu* is a true scholar—that is, an elite scholar.

Confucius was famous for not discriminating on the basis of the social origins of his students. Anyone could choose to engage in learning, and thus to cultivate himself and become an elite scholar. It was not Confucius' aim, however, to turn everybody into *chün tzu*. He was characteristically practical and accepted the fact that his society was a hierarchical one. The majority belonged in the category of the inferior man, who was not required to espouse the high morals of the *chün tzu*. In fact, to be a *chün tzu* means to sacrifice one's own interests for the benefit of others. It is only natural to allow the majority to concentrate on their own interests instead of asking them to sacrifice themselves for morality's sake, given the social condition that the majority was governed by the rulers through the hands of elite scholars.

**Jen and Li.** *Jen* (humanity or benevolence) is the leading principle for self-cultivation. To be *jen* is to love others, though one should still differentiate in the degree of love among different social relationships. The love that is advocated is ultimately, however, and in its highest sense, directed toward the majority. In other words, one should never do to others what is undesirable to oneself.

*Li* is the principle of acting in accordance with custom, of preserving a special code of ceremony, and of performing the rites appropriate to one's social status. The emphasis on *li* is not only a way of guiding one's moral behavior for self-cultivation but also plays an important role in integrating governing with the teaching of morality.

**Governing by Morals Rather than by Law.** For Confucius, the ideal government is a moral government. It does not govern by rules, regulations, or laws, but by taking care of people's interests and teaching people to be moral. The rulers themselves must act morally, in order to set a good example for the people to follow. *Li* dictates the norm of proper social behavior for both rulers and the people. Observing *li* keeps all people in their social positions and thus makes the society stable. Confucius believed that a stable society would naturally become prosperous.

—*Weihang Chen*

**See also** Chu Hsi; Confucian ethics; Mencius; Mo Tzu; Taoist ethics; Wang Yang-ming.

**Bibliography**

Confucius. *The Analects (Lun Yü)*. Translated by D. C. Lau. New York: Penguin Books, 1979.

Dawson, Raymond. *Confucius*. Oxford, England: Oxford University Press, 1981.

Fung Yu-lan. *A Short History of Chinese Philosophy*. New York: Macmillan, 1948.

___________. *The Spirit of Chinese Philosophy*. Translated by E. R. Hughes. London: K. Paul, Trench, Trubner, 1947.

Lin Yutang, ed. *The Wisdom of Confucius*. New York: The Modern Library, 1938.

Liu Wu-chi. *Confucius, His Life and Time*. Reprint. Westport, Conn.: Greenwood Press, 1972.

___________. *A Short History of Confucian Philosophy*. Westport, Conn.: Hyperion Press, 1979.

## Congress of Racial Equality (CORE)

**Type of ethics:** Civil rights

**Date:** Founded 1942

**Associated with:** Marcus Garvey and the black nationalism movement

**Definition:** CORE is an organization that, looking to Africa for inspiration, seeks the right of African Americans to govern and educate themselves

**Significance:** From its origin as a broad-based organization with white and black membership, CORE evolved into one of America's first important black separatist groups

CORE was founded in 1942 by James Farmer and a group of University of Chicago students. Its membership included African Americans and whites, and its primary purpose was to combat segregation. CORE used various peaceful but confrontational techniques to achieve its aims. In 1943, its members began sitting in at segregated lunch counters, demanding to be served and willing to face arrest. CORE moved into the national spotlight in 1963, when the Freedom Rides challenged Southern segregated bus stations. Freedom Riders rode public buses to Southern cities, where white riders entered the "coloreds only" waiting areas and black riders entered "whites only" rooms. Although they sat quietly and peacefully, they were met with mob violence time after time. CORE also worked for voter registration in the South through the early 1960's. In 1966, CORE leadership adopted the new slogan "black power" and began a shift toward black separatism that alienated many of its members, both white and black. The organization struggled through the next decades but in the early 1990's was still operating a national office and several local groups, with a budget of $750,000.

**See also** Civil disobedience; Civil rights; Civil rights movement.

## Conscience

**Type of ethics:** Personal and social ethics

**Date:** First century B.C.E.

**Associated with:** Psychological studies of moral development and casuistical methods of solving moral problems

**Definition:** Subjective awareness of the moral quality of one's own actions as indicated by the moral values to which one subscribes

**Significance:** Since a person always chooses either against or in accord with the dictates of conscience, such dictates are the immediate basis for the evaluation of intentional human actions

Though they may not be explicitly aware of doing so, human beings everywhere and always have evaluated their own actions in the light of their own moral values. The earliest attempt at a philosophical analysis of this type of self-assessment—that is, of conscience—is found in the *Tusculan Disputations* of the Roman orator Cicero (first century B.C.E.). The most famous early casuistical employment of this notion is found in the letters of the apostle Paul (first century C.E.). It was not until the Middle Ages, however, that the understanding of conscience that is still employed was articulated. In their commentaries on St. Jerome's exegesis of scripture, Philip the Chancellor, St. Bonaventure, and St. Thomas Aquinas developed an analysis of conscience that made explicit several crucial distinctions. Awareness of the moral quality of one's own actions involves two aspects: first, the awareness of an act, and second, the awareness of one's values as exemplified (or not) by the act. This general knowledge of one's own values was distinguished by medieval moral theologians from conscience proper. "Conscience" itself was regarded as the activity of one's mind in bringing those values to bear upon one's own individual actions. It is thus a species of self-consciousness or a way of being aware of oneself.

**Development of Conscience.** A person's disposition to engage in this type of self-reflection develops as part of his or her general moral upbringing. People are taught how to identify their acts as examples of types and are taught that certain types of acts are good, bad, or morally indifferent. After a certain point in the person's development (the precise age varying greatly from culture to culture and from individual to individual) the individual becomes aware of this labeling process and of the good, bad, and other types in terms of which the labeling is carried out. From this point on, the person's general values are reflected upon and either endorsed or rejected. In this developmental sequence, the conscience of the person becomes a mental activity that is distinct from the functioning of the "superego" (which contains unreflected-upon and repressed prohibitions, injunctions, and so forth). The mature conscience of an adult involves applying values of which the individual is fully aware.

People differ greatly, however, with regard to the degree and extent of their awareness of the moral qualities of their own actions, just as people differ with regard to the degree and extent to which they are self-aware in general. Someone who is "hyper-aware" of the moral quality of all of his or her actions is said to be "scrupulous." Such a condition can become very problematic if the person becomes incapable of acting without severe apprehension that he or she is doing something wrong or scrutinizes the most trivial action for its possible moral significance. The opposite condition is exemplified by the "lax" person. Such an individual consistently fails to concern himself or herself with the morality of his or her own actions. The point at which scrupulosity or laxity becomes immoral in itself depends upon the moral values to which the particular individual subscribes: Some moralities demand strict solicitousness, while others allow for much greater lack of moral concern.

**Acts of Conscience.** The acts of a person's conscience have traditionally been divided into four types. First is the mental act of "command," whereby one senses that an act is "to be done." Second is the act of "forbidding," whereby one senses that an act is "not to be done." Third is the act of "permitting," in which one regards an act as "allowed" by one's own moral values. Fourth is the activity of "advising," in which one is aware that an act is either probably better to do or probably worse to do (the act is not sensed as being strictly required or strictly forbidden). Furthermore, the specific actions of the person to which these states of mind are directed can be in the future (in which case the act of conscience is referred to as "antecedent conscience"), in the past ("consequent conscience"), or in the present ("occurrent conscience"). If the past or current action is in accord with the dictates of conscience, the person is said to be in "good conscience" (or "to have a good conscience" or to be "acting in good conscience"). This state of mind is characterized phenomenologically as one of peace, quiet, self-contentment, and ease. If the past or current action is not in accord with the dictates of conscience, then the person has a "bad conscience." This condition is characterized subjectively as apprehensive, conflicted, anxious, and guilt-and-shame-filled.

Two points are crucial with regard to these various activities of the mind. First, in all these acts, the dictate of conscience pertains only to one's own actions: "Conscience" does not refer to evaluations of other people's acts. Second, the "voice of conscience" must be distinguished from other ways of evaluating one's own actions (other "voices," as it were). Conscience is most often confused with self-admonitions of a merely prudential nature. For example, I may admonish myself for stealing simply because I am in trouble after having been caught. A sure indication that it is not my conscience that is bothering me is that if I had not been caught, I would not have admonished myself. In effect, I am berating myself for having been caught, not for having stolen.

In these various acts of moral self-reflection, the individual may be either "certain" or "doubtful" concerning the moral quality of the deed at issue. Since a person only performs a deed on the basis of her awareness of what she is doing, if the individual is assured that the act she is contemplating has a particular moral quality, then she is morally required to act on that assuredness. If what is truly or objectively wrong appears to be the right thing to do, one must do it. In such a case, assuming that one does the deed, the act is objectively wrong but subjectively right (one performed in "good conscience"). A primary and purely formal rule of all morality, then, is to "do what conscience demands." This rule is the only guarantee that people will choose rightly when their beliefs about right and wrong are accurate. All people are under an obligation to ensure that the evaluation of their own actions is accurate. Hence, an even more important purely formal rule of morality is to "ensure that conscience is accurate."

**The Doubtful Conscience.** If one is in doubt about the accuracy of the dictates of one's own conscience, then it is morally imperative to eliminate the doubt before acting. If I act although I am uncertain of the morality of my own act according to the values to which I subscribe, I thereby express a lack of concern for those values. My acting while in doubt is tantamount to disdain for those values even if I happen to do what those values demand. The problem is how to move from doubt to certainty about the morality of a contemplated act.

When one is uncertain about the moral value of an anticipated act, one must first attempt to remove the doubt directly, perhaps by pausing to think about what one is doing, by consulting "experts" (people of practical wisdom), or by reading about similar cases. Often, such attempts fail or are not possible because of time constraints. In order to resolve remaining doubts about the right thing to do, people employ what moralists refer to as "reflex principles" of conscience, which stipulate what is required of one in such a condition. Though there is disagreement among moralists about the degree of probability required to ground the shift from doubt to certainty, most people in Western culture adhere to principles of roughly the following nature. If not doing something would result in grievous harm to oneself or to others or would result in failing to fulfill some other important moral obligation, then it is certain that one must do the deed regardless of how improbable the outcome might appear to be (this improbability is the source of the doubt about the morality of the action). A traditional example of this is the pharmacist who thinks it is possible that a deadly poison has been accidentally mixed in with some medicines. Most people in such a situation would regard themselves as bound to refrain from dispensing the medicines. Another such principle is that if not doing something would *not* result in harm, then it is certain that one must do the deed only if there is an overwhelming probability that so acting is morally required (in other words, only an overwhelming probability is sufficient grounds for acting). Finally, if the moral reasons for doing something are as good as the reasons for not doing it and no grievous harm is involved either way, then it is certain that either course of action is morally acceptable. What is to be avoided through the use of such guidelines for becoming certain of acting correctly while under conditions of uncertainty are the extremes of "laxism" and "rigorism." Laxism results from adopting the attitude that if there is any doubt about the morality of the matter at hand, then moral considerations may be completely ignored. Rigorism results from adopting the attitude that if there is the slightest chance that one's morality demands that one act in a particular way, then it is certain that one must act in that way. The problem with rigorism is that there is always a possibility, however slight, that one is required to do something in any situation. This attitude leads immediately to extreme scrupulosity.

**The Erroneous Conscience.** The distinction between a certain and doubting conscience is different from the distinction between a "correct" and an "erroneous" conscience. An erroneous or false conscience is the state of mind of someone who believes an action to have a moral quality that in fact it does not have. If such an error is culpable, then the person can and should "know better" and is held accountable for whatever wrong is committed (because the person is held accountable for being in error about the act's morality). For example, the person could have easily found out that the item taken belonged to someone else. If the error is inculpable, then the person cannot know better and is not held accountable for whatever wrong is done. These errors, which lead the person into wrongdoing, are either factual or moral. Factual errors concern simply the facts of the situation or action. For instance, the person is unaware that the suitcase taken from the conveyor belt at the airport belongs to someone else. Moral error is about morality itself—that is, the moral rules that apply to the situation (about which there may be no factual misunderstanding). For example, one knows that the suitcase belongs to another, but taking other people's belongings is not something the individual regards as wrong. People tend to regard inculpable error about basic principles of morality as being simply impossible (assuming no mental abnormality). For example, no adult is regarded as being ignorant of the immorality of killing people for utterly no reason. With regard to the application of principles in specific situations and with regard to less-general principles, however, inculpable error is quite possible. In other words, people can in good conscience disagree about the morality of certain types of actions or about the morality of a particular act in a specific situation even if they are in complete accord concerning the basic principles of morality.

If the "other" party to a moral dispute is regarded as *not* acting in "good conscience," then he or she is taken to be either acting in culpable moral error or acting unconscientiously. In the former case, the other person's difference of opinion is regarded as being caused by negligent ignorance for which he or she is held accountable. If the dissenter is regarded as being unconscientious, then in effect the person is held to be a moral fraud who is merely using the profession of conscience as a rationalization for acting out of sheer self-interest. Hence, in conditions of moral dispute, the virtue of conscientiousness becomes of paramount importance. These disagreements are about issues of vital moral importance, and the sincerity of others' moral allegiances determines the response to their dissension. If those with whom I disagree are not being sincere—that is, if they do not really believe in the morals in terms of which they justify their opposing point of view—then I have no reason to respect their merely apparent moral stand on the issue. In fact, if they are unconscientious, then their morals may not really differ from mine: They might "really" agree with my moral evaluation of the issue and merely invoke (in bad faith) different "morals" in order to justify their self-interest.

**Conscientiousness.** If the possibility of disagreement in good faith is accepted, then it becomes vitally important to clarify the distinguishing marks of being in good conscience. How can one tell that someone else is sincere when he or she takes a moral stand on an issue that differs from one's own? A common instance of this problem is that of the "conscientious objector" to military conscription. Insincerity of an objector's moral appeal to exemption from military service means that the individual does not really "believe in" the moral values in terms of which the exemption is being demanded. Two general characteristics of sincerity (or conscientiousness or "really believing") are a willingness to make sacrifices for the sake of adherence to one's values and a willingness to make an effort to abide by the values professed. If no effort is forthcoming or no sacrifice is willingly undergone, then that counts as evidence that the person is not acting in good faith. Someone who is willing to face a firing squad rather than serve in the military is most certainly quite sincere in his or her moral dissension from conscription. Another individual who would rather serve in the military than be forced to spend the same amount of time in prison is probably not dissenting in "good conscience." Therefore, the general virtue of conscientiousness involves a disposition to do what one judges ought to be done regardless of the sacrifice of other interests that may be entailed by so acting.

What must be kept in mind, however, is that this virtue is compatible with at least occasional failure to live by one's moral ideals. It is true that if one is not conscientious then one will fail to abide by one's own moral convictions. It is *not* true that if one has the habit of abiding by the dictates of conscience one will never fail to do so. The difference between conscientious failure and unconscientious failure to act according to the dictates of one's conscience is that the former is followed by repentance and a renewed effort to abide by those dictates, whereas the latter is not followed by such acts. Failure to live according to one's moral convictions may be the result of the fact that the person has established moral ideals that are too "high" for any human to achieve. Furthermore, consistent success in living according to the dictates of one's conscience may be indicative of establishing moral standards for oneself that are too "low."

**Conscientious Dissent.** These distinctions plus the formal principles of conscience previously noted create an intractable dilemma. Since one must act in accord with the dictates of an assured conscience, it is wrong for others to coerce someone into acting against the dictates of his or her conscience. In order to test the moral sincerity of dissenters, however, it is necessary to observe how they respond when prompted to act in a way that is contrary to the dictates of their conscience. The assumption in this situation is that if the person caves in to very little pressure, then his or her moral conviction is insincere. Thus, to ensure that a person's moral objection to conscription is conscientious, society must, in effect, prompt the individual to act against the dictates of conscience. Because of increasing sensitivity to the fact that coercing people in this manner is actually a species of scandal, conscientious objection is no longer severely punished in most countries.

Nevertheless, there are limits to what can be tolerated in the name of respecting conscientious action. If an individual's conscience dictates that he harms the innocent, then others are justified in protecting the innocent by forcing that person to act against the dictates of his conscience. The classic historical example of this is the outlawing of the practice of *thuggee* by the British colonialists in India during the nineteenth century. The Thugs believed that they had a moral obligation to waylay and murder travelers. The general principle in terms of which the British occupying force justified punishing the Thugs was (roughly) that "it is wrong to coerce someone to act against sincere moral conviction unless allowing the person to act according to the dictates of conscience would result in harm to the innocent."

—*Mark Stephen Pestana*

**See also** Casuistry; Guilt and shame; Intention; Moral education; Motivation; Self-deception; Vice; Virtue.

**Bibliography**

D'Arcy, Eric. *Conscience and Its Right to Freedom.* London: Sheed & Ward, 1979. Contains an excellent presentation of the history of the concept of conscience and the defense of the right to religious freedom.

Davis, Henry. *Moral and Pastoral Theology.* New York: Sheed & Ward, 1952. A good source for the standard Catholic teachings on conscience and the methods of casuistry. Contains a lengthy discussion of probabilism, probabiliorism, and equiprobabilism.

Donagan, Alan. *The Theory of Morality.* Chicago: University of Chicago Press, 1979. Most of chapter 4 is devoted to the problems of the erroneous conscience and the corruption of conscience. A superb updating of the traditional conceptions.

Donnelly, John. *Conscience.* Edited by John Donnelly and Leonard Lyons. Staten Island, N.Y.: Alba House, 1973. A collection of articles on the nature, existence, meaning, and authority of conscience by contemporary analytic philosophers. Fairly advanced material.

Kirk, Kenneth. *Conscience and Its Problems: An Introduction to Casuistry.* London: Longmans, Green, 1948. A twentieth century classic in the study of "cases of conscience" by the Anglican Bishop of Oxford. Contains chapters on doubt, error, loyalty, and moral perplexity.

Nelson, C. Ellis. *Conscience: Theological and Psychological Perspectives.* New York: Newman Press, 1973. A large collection of articles, many of which are devoted to the development of conscience in childhood and the distinction between conscience and superego.

Wallace, James D. *Virtues and Vices.* Ithaca, N.Y.: Cornell University Press, 1978. Chapter 4 of this work is an outstanding analysis of the meaning of conscientiousness and the reason for its preeminence as a virtue in pluralistic societies.

## Conscientious objection

**Type of ethics:** Politico-economic ethics

**Date:** Fifth century B.C.E. to present

**Associated with:** Historic peace churches, anti-war movements, National Interreligious Service Board for Conscientious Objectors, and civil disobedience

**Definition:** Refers to an individual's moral opposition on the basis of conscience to the demands or requirements of some external authority, usually the state; the objection typically relates to military service or participation in war

**Significance:** Recognizes the value of individual conscience as part of the process of making moral decisions; the focus on conscience lays the foundation for dissent, refusal, or resistance to the demands of the state

Conscientious objection establishes a moral relationship between the individual and external authority. The key element of the relationship is the claim that authority is not absolute; it cannot demand total obedience, especially when obedience would violate the individual's conscience. Conscientious objection, then, stands as a limit to the extent of the power of the state. In claiming conscientious objection, an individual seeks to justify opposition to an action or demand that the state deems necessary and may require of others.

**History and Sources.** One of the major concerns of the Greek philosophers Plato (427?-347 B.C.E.) and Aristotle (384-322 B.C.E.) was that of the relationship of the individual to the state. They noted that human life was fundamentally social, which entailed duties to the state. It was possible, however, for the demands of the state to come into conflict with an individual's own moral values. The source of the conflict was the assertion that the state did not totally control the conscience of an individual. Conscience was a person's moral self-understanding, the combination of values and ideals that provided the individual with a sense of ethical self-definition that also demanded loyalty. Violating an individual's moral integrity could lead to a crisis of conscience. A person might want to serve the state, but in this particular case could not without violating the sense of self.

The play *Antigone* (first produced 441 B.C.E.), by Sophocles (496?-406 B.C.E.), offers an explicit example of the conflict between the individual and the state. Antigone follows her conscience and refuses to obey King Creon's orders concerning the burial of her brother. In moral terms, the tension between the individual and the state rests on whether the state should recognize the demands of conscience when an individual cannot in good conscience obey the state's demands. In order to avoid breaking the law, the conscientious objector often seeks an exemption from obedience. The exemption would grant legal recognition to the disobedience, and the individual would escape punishment. For Antigone, escape was not an option, and the play serves as a stark reminder of the tension between individual conscience and the demands of the state.

The question of loyalty and obedience to the state became more acute with the rise of Christianity. Given the pacifist views of some early Christians and the resulting opposition to war, many refused to serve in the military. The refusal to participate in war on moral grounds rested on the teachings of Jesus. The conscience of the Christian, formed by the values associated with Jesus and out of loyalty to those values, would not permit military service or participation in war. Yet not all Christians were pacifists or conscientious objectors, and military service became more likely as Christianity became the dominant religion in the West. Still some Christians steadfastly refused to serve in the military. During the Protestant Reformation, the Anabaptists held to a pacifist view and sought exemption from the state's demands to participate in war. These exemptions, when granted, were only at the pleasure of the prince or ruler in whose territory the exemption seekers resided.

There have been dimensions of conscientious objection throughout American history. People fled Europe during the colonial period to escape persecution, and many were pacifists. As a result, conscientious objection entered into American wars and politics. James Madison wanted to add recognition of conscientious objection to his version of what was to become the Second Amendment to the Constitution. He wanted to allow persons with religious and moral objections to bearing arms the freedom not to serve in the military. Madison's suggestion was not approved in later debates, but it did serve to provide a basis for the legal recognition of conscientious objection in U.S. law.

The Selective Service Act of 1917 established guidelines for conscientious objection; specifically, the requirement that an applicant needed to show membership within a religious tradition that upheld conscientious objection as part of its teachings. This rule made it very difficult, if not impossible, for those outside the peace church tradition to be granted conscientious objector status. Although the guidelines were more flexible during World War II, the insistence on a religious basis for conscientious objection remained. The refusal of military service was not recognized unless an applicant equated moral and religious reasons. Two United States Supreme Court decisions, handed down during the Vietnam War, changed the basis for asserting conscientious objection. In *U.S. v. Seeger* (1965) and *U.S. v. Welch* (1970), the Court ruled that sincere and strongly held moral beliefs were a sufficient basis for granting an individual status as a conscientious objector to military service. While the requirement for opposition to all wars remained, there was no longer a religious test for conscientious objection.

**Types of Conscientious Objection.** There are two major types of conscientious objection with reference to the opposition to war. The first is absolute or universal conscientious objection (ACO or UCO). Usually based on a pacifist perspective, it leads to the moral conclusion that all wars are wrong. The ethical argument centers on the immorality of war and killing. The nature and purpose of the war are irrelevant to the moral opposition to the war. A second type is selective conscientious objection (SCO). The focus of selective conscientious objection is on the particular war, hence the notion of selection. An individual may not be morally opposed to all wars as such, but to a specific war. The moral basis for selective conscientious objection is just war theory, which is designed to differentiate between wars that are just and those that are unjust. This selection equates just with moral and unjust with immoral. An individual would hold that it is wrong to fight in an unjust war. Selective conscientious objection rarely, if ever, receives legal recognition. It is possible for both absolute conscientious objectors and selective conscientious objectors to accept military service as noncombatants such as medics. The moral opposition would center on the refusal to bear arms, not on military service itself. —*Ron Large*

**See also** Civil disobedience; Conscience; Pacifism; Private vs. public morality; Thoreau, Henry David; War and peace.

**BIBLIOGRAPHY**

Childress, James. *Moral Responsibility in Conflicts: Essays on Nonviolence, War, and Conscience*. Baton Rouge: Louisiana State University Press, 1982.

Finn, James, ed. *A Conflict of Loyalties*. New York: Pegasus, 1968.

Flynn, Eileen. *My Country Right or Wrong?: Selective Conscientious Objection in the Nuclear Age*. Chicago: Loyola University Press, 1985.

Gioglio, Gerald. *Days of Decision: An Oral History of Conscientious Objectors in the Military During the Vietnam War*. Trenton, N.J.: Broken Rifle Press, 1989.

Zahn, Gordon. *War, Conscience and Dissent*. New York: Hawthorn Books, 1967.

## Consequentialism

**TYPE OF ETHICS:** Theory of ethics

**DATE:** First used in philosophy in 1958

**ASSOCIATED WITH:** Thomas Hobbes, Ayn Rand, Jeremy Bentham, and John Stuart Mill

**DEFINITION:** The idea that the rightness or wrongness of an action is determined by the goodness or badness of its result

**SIGNIFICANCE:** This ethical theory provides individuals with a moral standard in which the end justifies the means; if the result of an action is right, or good for an individual's long-term self-interest or for the greatest number of people, then that action should be considered as right

As a moral standard, consequentialism can be divided into two varieties: In the first, the desired end is the long-term self-interest of the individual; In the second, the desired end is the greatest happiness of the greatest number. The first variety is called the theory of ethical egoism, and Thomas Hobbes and Ayn Rand are associated with it. The second is called utilitarianism, and it is associated with Jeremy Bentham and John Stuart Mill. Ethical egoism claims that before making a moral decision, one should consider the end of long-term self-interest, and if by using a reasonably moral means the long- term self-interest can be achieved, then that action should be performed. This means that short-term self-interest should be sacrificed for the sake of long-term self-interest. Utilitarianism, however, considers the desired end to be the greatest happiness of the greatest number of people; an action that achieves this end by using a reasonably moral means should be performed.

**See also** Hobbes, Thomas; Rand, Ayn.

## Conservation

**TYPE OF ETHICS:** Environmental ethics

**DATE:** 1902

**ASSOCIATED WITH:** Gifford Pinchot and Theodore Roosevelt

**DEFINITION:** Prudent use of resources

**SIGNIFICANCE:** Considers humanity as a part of nature rather than its ruler

The conservation ethic has its American roots in colonial times with the imposition of game limits at Newport, Rhode Island, in 1639, the limitation of timbering in Pennsylvania in 1681, and many other similar regulations that were intended to protect resources for the future. Later, authors such as Henry David Thoreau and Ralph Waldo Emerson emphasized the ethical interrelationship of humankind and nature. At the beginning of the twentieth century, Theodore Roosevelt and Gifford Pinchot wrote extensively on the conservation ethic; they are widely considered as the founders of modern conservationism. Their programs, such as the Reclamation Act of 1902, the Inland Waterways Commission of 1907, and the massive expansion of National Forest lands, reflect their emphasis on wise use of resources. They also were concerned with the preservation of natural and cultural assets, as in passage of the Antiquities Act of 1906. Harold Ickes, Henry Wallace, and their associates continued the advocacy of the wise consumption ethic in the 1930's, emphasizing land planning and soil management. Again, wise use was the principal concern. Preservation of unique natural entities, however, continued to be part of the mainstream conservation ethic. Preservationism as a part of conservation, however, has been more heavily promoted since World War II, leading to the vigorous reevaluation of many conservation-for-use programs.

**See also** Deforestation; Ecology; Leopold, Aldo; Muir, John; National Park System, U.S.; Sierra Club; *Walden*.

## Conservatism

**Type of ethics:** Theory of ethics

**Date:** First articulated in 1790

**Associated with:** Edmund Burke, the American founding fathers, and various political figures

**Definition:** Belief that the traditional institutions of the existing social order must be respected and preserved, particularly by governments

**Significance:** Skeptical that humanity has the moral or rational capacity to rule itself, conservatives argue that one's duty is to conform to natural law by dutifully following time-honored practices based on the wisdom accrued through the ages

"Political problems, at bottom, are religious and moral problems." Thus does Russell Kirk, the author of *The Conservative Mind,* emphasize the nexus of politics and morality to be found in philosophical conservatism. A term most often used in political theory, "conservatism" designates a belief that traditional ways of living and believing must form the foundation of any successful system of government.

One of the major differences among conservatives, liberals, and socialists lies in their estimation of the ethical nature of humankind. Conservatives believe that humans are imperfectible and that government, to be effective, must work hand in hand with other institutions, such as church and family, to restrain human behavior. To assume that humans are perfectible and that government is the means by which perfection can be achieved is, according to the conservative, a serious miscalculation that can lead to disastrous consequences. For example, conservatives regarded the French Revolution as chaotic, bloody, and predictable, the result of too much faith in pure reason and the capacity of a revolutionary new government to restructure a society that took centuries to build.

**Origins in Britain.** Conservatism as a political philosophy was first articulated in Edmund Burke's *Reflections on the Revolution in France* (1790), in which the British statesman denounced the radical practice of eliminating institutions and customs that over the centuries served to stabilize humankind's relationships and foster moral development. He also exposed as a fraud the notion that the elite group that engineered the French rebellion, the Jacobins, enhanced liberty. This quotation from the French Committee on Public Safety clarifies Burke's point that the freedoms of the people were actually sacrificed to a radical political agenda: "You must entirely refashion a people whom you wish to make free, to destroy its prejudices, alter its habits, limit its necessities, root up its vices, purify its desires." In fact, Burke argued, by forcing equality on society, abolishing the right to private property, attacking the church, and executing the royal family and others who disagreed with them, the Jacobins proved to be more despotic than the monarchy they replaced.

Burke believed that the radicals' promise of social and material equality to the common people was "a monstrous fiction" that simply aroused an insatiable discontent. He thought that the perpetuation of civilization depended on acceptance of the divine plan decreeing that human beings were equal neither in their characteristics nor their possessions. To him, the only natural equality was a moral one attainable by persons living virtuously in whatever condition they found themselves. The purpose of government, like that of other institutions, was to help every citizen find happiness in his or her assigned position in the diversity of creation. Far from trying to provide equal things to all people, a major role of government was to deny excessive demands: "the inclinations of men should frequently be thwarted, their will controlled, and their passions brought into subjection."

**American Conservatism.** The American founding fathers, in their struggle at the end of the eighteenth century to create a government, largely shared Burke's view of human nature and the likely misuses to which political power could be put. Few modern Americans are aware of the distrust with which humanity was regarded by the founding fathers. John Adams said bluntly, "Whoever would found a state, and make proper laws for the government of it, must presume that all men are bad by nature." To Adams, Alexander Hamilton, and James Madison, a successful government would have to be secured from the irrationality, selfishness, and passions commonly exhibited by human beings. They regarded notions of direct, widespread democracy and majority rule with skepticism. The people, as Adams put it, could be "as unjust, tyrannical, brutal, barbarous and cruel as any king or senate possessed of uncontrollable power." Consequently, built into the American government were various checks and balances to prevent radical change and tyranny. Clinton Rossiter calls the American Constitution "perhaps the most successful conservative device in the history of mankind."

Modern conservatives have generally continued to oppose revolutions and "planned" socialist governments, both of which, they believe, are designed to enforce egalitarianism at the expense of the traditional foundations of society. They have raised objections to movements that they believe either ruthlessly enforce their ends, as in the case of Communism, or slowly but inexorably chip away at basic freedoms, as in the case of America's growing, liberally oriented bureaucracy. They object to the elite movers of these revolutions, just as Burke objected to the Jacobins, because they uproot traditional structures and replace them with the flawed products of their own ideology.

American "neoconservatism," which arose from the turbulent 1960's, much as Burke's philosophy arose from the French Revolution, held that the breakdown of traditional institutions had contributed to social upheaval. The neoconservatives, many of whom were once liberals or socialists convinced of government's necessary role as a social equalizer, came to recognize what Nathan Glazer called "the limits of social policy" and to realize that governmentally imposed solutions often created more harm than good. They also reasserted the notion of individual responsibility. Irving Kristol, observing that America of the post-1960's era had degenerated into "self-seeking, self-indulgence, and just plain aggressive selfishness," felt that popular government could succeed only when it was "firmly linked" to the individual citizen's self-discipline.

After the demise of the Soviet Union in the early 1990's, American conservative attention turned inward to the phenomenon of "political correctness," particularly as it existed on college campuses. Protesting the hegemony of intellectual "leftism," various conservatives pointed out the irony that even as the peoples of Eastern Europe were rejecting Communism and state-controlled radical egalitarianism, American colleges, staffed with "tenured radicals," were inculcating those concepts in American students. The conservative saw on college campuses an arrogant elite that was largely ignorant of, or insensitive to, historical complexities and sought to impose an egalitarian conformity on the diversity of human life. Far from solving the problem, the new orthodoxy simply reduced America to "a nation of victims" in which a continually expanding aggrieved class and their advocates demanded limitations on the freedoms of others, a situation reminding conservatives of the proscriptions accompanying the French and Russian revolutions. Manipulation of traditional social structures, codes prohibiting free speech, and preferential treatment of aggrieved groups created resentment and, to many conservatives, a weakened intellectual environment. In the tradition of conservatism, opponents of political correctness argued that programs designed to force equality on society only destroyed liberty and created conformists who had lost sight of their responsibilities and freedoms. —*William L. Howard*

**See also** Burke, Edmund; Egalitarianism; Liberalism; Libertarianism; Natural law; Political correctness; Politics.

**Bibliography**

Burke, Edmund. *Reflections on the Revolution in France.* Edited by Conor Cruise O'Brien. Harmondsworth, England: Penguin Books, 1969.

Glazer, Nathan. *The Limits of Social Policy.* Cambridge, Mass.: Harvard University Press, 1988.

Kimball, Roger. *Tenured Radicals: How Politics Has Corrupted Our Higher Education.* New York: HarperPerennial, 1991.

Kirk, Russell. *The Conservative Mind: From Burke to Eliot.* 7th ed. Chicago: Regnery Books, 1986.

Nash, George H. *The Conservative Intellectual Movement in America: Since 1945.* New York: Basic Books, 1976.

Nisbet, Robert. *Conservatism: Dream and Reality.* Milton Keynes, England: Open University Press, 1986.

Rossiter, Clinton. *Conservatism in America: The Thankless Persuasion.* 2d ed. New York: Knopf, 1962.

Sykes, Charles J. *A Nation of Victims: The Decay of the American Character.* New York: St. Martins Press, 1992.

## Consistency

**Type of ethics:** Theory of ethics

**Date:** Sixth century B.C.E. to present

**Definition:** A property of an ethical system whose principles are individually and jointly coherent

**Significance:** Consistency is an essential component of any rational discipline, and ethics is that discipline that applies reason to the discernment of moral obligations

Given that the discipline of ethics involves reasoned reflection upon moral issues and that consistency is a necessary condition of any system, theory, or activity that is governed by reason, consistency must play an important role in the development of ethical theories. The two most important respects in which reason's commitment to consistency manifests itself in the development of an ethical theory are systematic consistency and nomothetic consistency.

**Systematic Consistency.** Systematic consistency is a characteristic of any ethical system whose fundamental principles may all be true. Put negatively, systematic consistency does not apply to a system that has two or more principles that are contradictory. The reason that ethical systems must exhibit this property is that one can prove absolutely anything from an inconsistent set of premises. An inconsistent set of ethical principles would therefore counsel both for and against every action and thus offer no guidance to the morally perplexed.

**Nomothetic Consistency.** If a particular course of action is said to be morally permissible, it would be arbitrary and irrational to claim that the action would not be permissible on a distinct occasion when all the relevant factors were the same. In this way, reasoned reflection on morality implies a commitment to general rules that specify classes of morally correct and morally incorrect behavior. The presupposition that moral judgments apply universally gives rise to the requirement of nomothetic consistency, the demand that a specific moral judgment can be coherently transformed into a general law.

The importance of nomothetic consistency to ethical theory is seen in the fact that one of the oldest and most prevalent of moral principles, the Golden Rule, demands that one treat others as one wants to be treated, a requirement that imposes a certain degree of generality on one's moral judgments. Though concern with nomothetic consistency thus goes back at least as far as the sixth century B.C.E. Confucian formulation of the Golden Rule, it was in the eighteenth century that German philosopher Immanuel Kant focused attention on it to an unprecedented level by arguing that it alone is sufficient to generate an entire moral code.

The primacy of nomothetic consistency to Kant's ethics is clearly expressed in that version of his fundamental ethical principle (the "categorical imperative"), which commands that one should act only according to that plan of action that one can will at the same time to be a universal law. According to Kant, a sufficient test of the moral permissibility of a specific action is found in the attempt to will that the action be universalized. If willing such universality can be consistently achieved, then one knows that the action is morally permissible. If the attempt to will the universality of some plan of action leads to an inconsistency, however, then one knows that the action is impermissible.

To grasp the full force and scope of this version of the categorical imperative, it is important to note that there are two ways in which a plan of action can fail the test of universalizability. The first occurs when the content of the law that results from the attempted universalization is internally inconsistent. A standard Kantian example to illustrate this kind of inconsistency is found in the attempt to universalize the activity of promise-breaking. When one wills that all promises be entered into with the intent that they be broken, one also wills that there can be no promises insofar as one wills the impossibility of trust, a necessary condition for the practice of promising. In this way, willing that promise-breaking be a universal law entails both the existence and the nonexistence of promises.

The second way in which some proposed plan of action can fail the universalizability test does not involve an inconsistency within the content of the universal law that is willed. Instead of the conflict being internal to the universalized plan of action, the conflict in these cases obtains between the universalized plan of action and the very activity of willing. The possibility of this second kind of inconsistency depends upon Kant's conviction that willing is an inherently rational activity and his acceptance of the fact that it would be irrational to will certain universal laws even though these universal laws are not internally inconsistent. A standard Kantian example used to illustrate this second type of inconsistency involves the intention to neglect the development of all of one's talents. It is, says Kant, possible to conceive that all human beings neglect the development of their talents without contradiction; however, it is not possible to *will* that this be the case, for willing is an activity that affirms one's rationality, an affirmation that conflicts with the fact that the universal law being willed is one that it is irrational to will. —*James Petrik*

**See also** Golden rule; Impartiality; Kant, Immanuel; Universalizability.

**Bibliography**

Ashmore, Robert B. *Building a Moral System*. Englewood Cliffs, N.J.: Prentice-Hall, 1987.

Donagan, Alan. *The Theory of Morality*. Chicago: University of Chicago Press, 1977.

Feezell, Randolph M., and Curtis L. Hancock. *How Should I Live?* New York: Paragon House, 1991.

Kant, Immanuel. *The Moral Law; Or, Kant's "Groundwork of the Metaphysic of Morals."* Translated by H. J. Paton. 3d ed. London: Hutchinson, 1956.

McNaughton, David. *Moral Vision: An Introduction to Ethics*. Oxford, England: Basil Blackwell, 1988.

Rawls, John. *A Theory of Justice*. Cambridge, Mass.: Harvard University Press, 1971.

Rost, H. T. D. *The Golden Rule*. Oxford: George Ronald, 1986.

## Constitution, U.S.

**Type of ethics:** Civil rights

**Date:** Written 1787

**Associated with:** The U.S. government and the U.S. Supreme Court

**Definition:** The document that established the national governing system for the United States of America preventing governmental tyranny and guaranteeing democratic elections

**Significance:** Provided the basis for political and economic liberty by defining and limiting the powers of a resilient democratic governing system

The design of governments depends on the political values and interests of the people who hold power. Individuals' desires for political liberty, civil rights, and democratic elections within a country may be thwarted by the will of militarily powerful dictators or by ethnic, religious, or geographic conflicts that divide a nation. The founders of the United States of America sought to avoid both divisive conflicts and the risk of dictatorship by drafting the United States Constitution in 1787. By electing officials to a government of limited powers and by guaranteeing representation to each geographic subdivision within the nation, the founders sought to create a governing system that would ensure political liberty and social stability for years to come.

**History.** After the American colonists' Declaration of Independence from Great Britain in 1776 and the concomitant revolutionary war, the newly independent American states attempted to govern themselves through a document called

**We the People** of the United States, in Order to form a more perfect Union, establish Justice, insure domestic Tranquility, provide for the common defence, promote the general Welfare, and secure the Blessings of Liberty to ourselves and our Posterity, do ordain and establish this Constitution for the United States of America.

# Article. I.

Section. 1. All legislative Powers herein granted shall be vested in a Congress of the United States, which shall consist of a Senate and House of Representatives.

Section. 2. The House of Representatives shall be composed of Members chosen every second Year by the People of the several States, and the Electors in each State shall have the Qualifications requisite for Electors of the most numerous Branch of the State Legislature.

No Person shall be a Representative who shall not have attained to the Age of twenty five Years, and been seven Years a Citizen of the United States, and who shall not, when elected, be an Inhabitant of that State in which he shall be chosen.

Representatives and direct Taxes shall be apportioned among the several States which may be included within this Union, according to their respective Numbers, which shall be determined by adding to the whole Number of free Persons, including those bound to Service for a Term of Years, and excluding Indians not taxed, three fifths of all other Persons. The actual Enumeration shall be made within three Years after the first Meeting of the Congress of the United States, and within every subsequent Term of ten Years, in such Manner as they shall by Law direct. The Number of Representatives shall not exceed one for every thirty Thousand, but each State shall have at Least one Representative; and until such enumeration shall be made, the State of New Hampshire shall be entitled to chuse three, Massachusetts eight, Rhode Island and Providence Plantations one, Connecticut five, New York six, New Jersey four, Pennsylvania eight, Delaware one, Maryland six, Virginia ten, North Carolina five, South Carolina five, and Georgia three.

When vacancies happen in the Representation from any State, the Executive Authority thereof shall issue Writs of Election to fill such Vacancies.

The House of Representatives shall chuse their Speaker and other Officers; and shall have the sole Power of Impeachment.

Section. 3. The Senate of the United States shall be composed of two Senators from each State, chosen by the Legislature thereof for six Years; and each Senator shall have one Vote.

Immediately after they shall be assembled in Consequence of the first Election, they shall be divided as equally as may be into three Classes. The Seats of the Senators of the first Class shall be vacated at the Expiration of the second Year, of the second Class at the Expiration of the fourth Year, and of the third Class at the Expiration of the sixth Year, so that one third may be chosen every second Year; and if Vacancies happen by Resignation, or otherwise, during the Recess of the Legislature of any State, the Executive thereof may make temporary Appointments until the next Meeting of the Legislature, which shall then fill such Vacancies.

No Person shall be a Senator who shall not have attained to the Age of thirty Years, and been nine Years a Citizen of the United States, and who shall not, when elected, be an Inhabitant of that State for which he shall be chosen.

The Vice President of the United States shall be President of the Senate, but shall have no Vote, unless they be equally divided.

The Senate shall chuse their other Officers, and also a President pro tempore, in the Absence of the Vice President, or when he shall exercise the Office of President of the United States.

The Senate shall have the sole Power to try all Impeachments. When sitting for that Purpose, they shall be on Oath or Affirmation. When the President of the United States is tried, the Chief Justice shall preside: And no Person shall be convicted without the Concurrence of two thirds of the Members present.

Judgment in Cases of Impeachment shall not extend further than to removal from Office, and disqualification to hold and enjoy any Office of honor, Trust or Profit under the United States: but the Party convicted shall nevertheless be liable and subject to Indictment, Trial, Judgment and Punishment, according to Law.

Section. 4. The Times, Places and Manner of holding Elections for Senators and Representatives, shall be prescribed in each State by the Legislature thereof; but the Congress may at any time by Law make or alter such Regulations, except as to the Places of chusing Senators.

The Congress shall assemble at least once in every Year, and such Meeting shall be on the first Monday in December, unless they shall by Law appoint a different Day.

Section. 5. Each House shall be the Judge of the Elections, Returns and Qualifications of its own Members, and a Majority of each shall constitute a Quorum to do Business; but a smaller Number may adjourn from day to day, and may be authorized to compel the Attendance of absent Members, in such Manner, and under such Penalties as each House may provide.

Each House may determine the Rules of its Proceedings, punish its Members for disorderly Behaviour, and, with the Concurrence of two thirds, expel a Member.

Each House shall keep a Journal of its Proceedings, and from time to time publish the same, excepting such Parts as may in their Judgment require Secrecy; and the Yeas and Nays of the Members of either House on any question shall, at the Desire of one fifth of those Present, be entered on the Journal.

Neither House, during the Session of Congress, shall, without the Consent of the other, adjourn for more than three days, nor to any other Place than that in which the two Houses shall be sitting.

Section. 6. The Senators and Representatives shall receive a Compensation for their Services, to be ascertained by Law, and paid out of the Treasury of the United States. They shall in all Cases, except Treason, Felony and Breach of the Peace, be privileged from Arrest during their Attendance at the Session of their respective Houses, and in going to and returning from the same; and for any Speech or Debate in either House, they shall not be questioned in any other Place.

No Senator or Representative shall, during the Time for which he was elected, be appointed to any civil Office under the Authority of the United States, which shall have been created, or the Emoluments whereof shall have been encreased during such time; and no Person holding any Office under the United States, shall be a Member of either House during his Continuance in Office.

Section. 7. All Bills for raising Revenue shall originate in the House of Representatives; but the Senate may propose or concur with Amendments as on other Bills.

Every Bill which shall have passed the House of Representatives and the Senate, shall, before it become a Law, be presented to the President of the

the Articles of Confederation. The Articles of Confederation established a weak national government that depended on the cooperation of the various states for economic and military matters. Because each state retained the primary power to govern itself, there were frequent disagreements between the states. Their failure to fully cooperate with one another made the new nation economically and militarily vulnerable.

The failure of the Articles of Confederation led representatives from each state to meet in Philadelphia, Pennsylvania, during 1787 to draft a new document that would provide a fundamental structure of government for a cohesive United States of America. The document produced in Philadelphia, the United States Constitution, was the product of extensive debate and compromise among men who feared the prospect of granting too much power to government. They had fought a war of independence against Great Britain because they believed that the British king had trampled on their civil rights and prevented them from effectively participating in democratic decision making concerning taxation, tariffs, and other policies. They sought to diminish the risk that any individual or branch of government would accumulate too much power and thereby behave in a tyrannical fashion.

The document produced in 1787 provides the basis for the governing system of the United States. Although specific aspects of the Constitution have been changed through the enactment of amendments, the basic words and principles of the Constitution remain the same. As American society changed over the years, the U.S. Supreme Court interpreted the words of the Constitution to give them applicability to new and changing social circumstances.

**Ethical Principles.** The Constitution seeks to avoid the risk of governmental tyranny through the principle of *separation of powers*. The legislative, executive, and judicial branches of government are separate from one another, and each possesses specific powers that enable it to prevent excessive actions by the other branches of government.

Political liberty and democratic decision making are guaranteed through the Constitution's provisions mandating elections for representatives in the legislative branch (Congress) and for the president and vice-president in the executive branch. The Constitution also grants the broadest list of specific powers to the legislative branch so that representatives from throughout the nation can enact laws rather than having one person be responsible for authoritative decision making. The legislative branch is divided into two chambers, one providing representation according to each state's population (House of Representatives) and the other providing equal representation to each state (Senate) in order to prevent the largest states from dominating all decisions.

The Constitution sets specific terms in office for elected officials in the legislative and executive branches. The voters have the opportunity to select new officials every two years for the House of Representatives, every four years for the president and vice-president, and every six years for the Senate. This accountability mechanism helps to preserve political liberty by preventing individuals from staying in office when they are no longer accountable to the citizens.

**Ethical Issues.** The U.S. Constitution, as drafted in 1787, did not specifically address several important ethical issues. Some of these issues were addressed later through amendments added to the Constitution. For example, the Constitution did not address the issue of slavery except to say that any congressional decisions on that issue must wait until twenty years after the document first went into effect. Slavery was eventually abolished through the Thirteenth Amendment in 1868 after a bloody civil war was fought over this unresolved issue. The original Constitution also did not guarantee specific civil rights for citizens. Freedom of speech, freedom of religion, criminal defendants' rights, and other civil rights were guaranteed in 1791 when the first ten amendments to the Constitution, known as the Bill of Rights, were ratified.

Although the Constitution's design for a representative democracy was intended to protect citizens' political liberty, several aspects of the Constitution are undemocratic. Because the drafters of the Constitution feared that the voters could be swayed by a charismatic demagogue, citizens do not elect the President directly. They vote instead for electors, known as the Electoral College, who can select someone other than the leading vote getter as president if they believe that the people have made an unwise choice. In addition, because representation in Congress is determined by state, people who live in the District of Columbia, although they outnumber the populations of several small states, do not have voting representation in Congress. The citizens residing in the nation's capital city lack the basic political liberty to elect representatives to the national legislature. Thus, although the Constitution has been effective in creating a stable democratic governing system, it remains imperfect as a document seeking to guarantee political liberty and participation in decision making for all citizens.

—*Christopher E. Smith*

**See also** Bill of Rights, U.S.; Civil rights; Constitutional government; Democracy; Political liberty.

**BIBLIOGRAPHY**

Ackerman, Bruce. *We The People*. Cambridge, Mass.: Harvard University Press, 1991.

Levinson, Sanford. *Constitutional Faith*. Princeton, N.J.: Princeton University Press, 1988.

Levy, Leonard W., Kenneth L. Karst, and Dennis J. Mahoney, eds. *American Constitutional History: Selections from the Encyclopedia of the American Constitution*. New York: Macmillan, 1989.

Mead, Walter B. *The United States Constitution: Personalities, Principles, and Issues*. Columbia: University of South Carolina Press, 1987.

Urofsky, Melvin I. *A March of Liberty: A Constitutional History of the United States*. New York: Knopf, 1988.

## Constitutional government

**TYPE OF ETHICS:** Politico-economic ethics

**DATE:** Sixth century B.C.E. to present

**ASSOCIATED WITH:** Western tradition, the Greek polis, the Roman Republic, the great codes of classical antiquity, and especially the rise of the modern secular state

**DEFINITION:** A formal contract between the governors and the governed concerning the rules and structures of the political system

**SIGNIFICANCE:** Constitutional government is based on the principles that government must be limited and that leaders and citizens alike are governed by the rule of law

The idea of constitutional government is that the social contract, or that system of social relationships that constitutes the origin of any community, is given concrete manifestation in a constitution. In sum, the legitimacy of a constitutional regime is based on formal agreement between the rulers and the ruled. Government accepts limitations based on citizen consent and the rule of law will govern all. In modern politics, few governments maintain legitimacy without a constitutional foundation. A constitution guarantees that the government rules in the name of the many (not the few or the one, as in dynastic or despotic regimes) and is limited in scope by agreement on the rules and structure of governance. Nevertheless, in practice a constitution is only as valid and effective as the citizens and leaders believe it to be and make it.

**History of the Concept.** Constitutions can be considered power maps that give form to the distribution of power within a political system. Although this conception emphasizes institutions, these power maps also reflect the political culture and the ideologies that undergird a society. In ethical terms, the constitutional idea expresses an ideological principle itself—that of government limited by law, government that emanates from the culture, customs, and mores of a community.

The principle of government founded on code and law can be traced back to antiquity. The covenant of the Hebrew people was one expression of this idea. The legal codes of Hammurabi (1792-1750 B.C.E.), the Athenian laws of Draco (c. 621 B.C.E.) and Solon (594 B.C.E.), and the Byzantine Roman Emperor Justinian's legal code (529-533 C.E.) were also forerunners of the constitutional principle. In fact, the Greek concept of the polis lies at the heart of the ethical ideal of constitutionalism. From the experience of ancient Athens in particular, Western culture had inherited the ethical value of the rule of law, the ideal of the polis, and the immanent legitimacy of the state that governs in the name and consent of the citizens.

**The Greeks.** The concept of the polis as a spiritual identification of the individual with the community was the hallmark of Greek civilization. Most important, in the evolution of Athenian democracy, the Greeks emphasized the superiority of the rule of law as opposed to the "rule of men" in the forms of monarchs and tyrants. Law and constitution create a sphere of political discourse, freedom, and dignity for the citizen that is absent in the rule of another human being, no matter how benevolent a despot. Freedom under the law became the highest moral principle for the Greek polis, and in the Greek mind it distinguished Greek civilization from barbarian civilizations. This idea was the point of departure between Aristotle's *Politics* (335-322 B.C.E.) and Plato's *Republic* (386-367 B.C.E.). Plato presented a constitution in the *Republic* that was based on the governance of picked individuals whose legitimacy was based on knowledge. Aristotle preferred constitutional rule founded on law, which preserved human dignity and participation. Only later in life did Plato rediscover the importance of this principle, as can be seen in *Laws* (360-347 B.C.E.). The connection of constitutional government to rule of law is the most significant political inheritance from the Greek experience.

**The Social Contract.** After the sixteenth century in Europe, through the age of Enlightenment, there emerged a movement for democracy and constitutionalism that was associated with the ideas of the social contract. This movement, which presaged the rise of the modern secular state, is descended from the ideas of Thomas Hobbes, John Locke, Jean-Jacques Rousseau, David Hume, and many others. Although there are many differences in the ideas of these authors, at their core was agreement about certain principles concerning constitutional government. In essence, they argued that a social contract preexists the contract of government. An original community must exist, and grounded upon established social relations, a contract of government may be created. This contract is the formal agreement of all within the community to accept laws and limitations on government, and hence government is legitimated by consent. Ultimately, no government is legitimate unless it governs in the name of the people.

**The Modern State.** Modern states rule in the name of the people. Most modern states do not rest their legitimacy on rule by a person, a dynastic family, or a theocracy. Even the most authoritarian regimes of the twentieth century claimed to rule in the name of the people. In this sense, modern states are constitutional governments. In fact, most modern states perceive themselves as "founded nations" and thus have required a founding document. Because most modern nation states are large and complex, and require participation by masses of citizens in their projects, constitutional government and consent evolved as the fundamental form of legitimization. The ideological basis of the secular state is supported by constitutionalism and law, and constitutions perform many functions.

**Functions.** Constitutions express the ideology of founded nations in their rules and structures. For example, the Constitution of the United States not only preserved private property and a free market but also reflected a desire for limited government in its separation of powers. Constitutions embody basic laws and rights of the people. These vary with the culture and experience of a people, and are influenced by the ideological origins of the state. Formally recognized rights and liberties are a major reason for establishing constitutional government. Constitutions define the organization of government and the distribution of powers. Herein lies the specific way in which governments submit to limitation. They must abide by the contract or be overthrown. Finally, constitutions hold the promise that people may change them as necessity requires. Because a constitution reflects the consent of the governed, the ability to amend a constitution may safeguard liberty and regime longevity.

Ultimately, these functions require qualification. This is how constitutions should function. Perhaps the greatest ethical problems in constitutional government are the importance of belief and the fact that it requires the participation of human beings, citizens and leaders, to make constitutions work on behalf of the people. Many authoritarian regimes have constitutions that espouse the values of consent, guarantees of rights, and rule of law. In fact, the rule of law is the ethical core of constitutional government. The essential promise of constitutional government is that no person, institution, or party may be above the law.

*—Anthony R. Brunello*

**See also** Jefferson, Thomas; Law; Locke, John; Rousseau, Jean-Jacques.

**Bibliography**

Duchacek, Ivo. *Power Maps: Comparative Politics of Constitutions*. Santa Barbara, Calif.: ABC-Clio Press, 1973.

Locke, John. *Two Treatises of Civil Government*. London: Dent, 1955.

Madison, James, Alexander Hamilton, and John Jay. *Selections from the Federalist*. New York: Appleton-Century-Crofts, 1949.

Plato. *The Republic*. Translated and edited by Raymond Larson. Arlington Heights, Ill.: AHM, 1979.

Rousseau, Jean-Jacques. *The Social Contract*. Translated by Maurice Cranston. Baltimore: Penguin Books, 1968.

## Consumerism

**Type of ethics:** Business and labor ethics

**Date:** Began late 1960's

**Associated with:** Ralph Nader

**Definition:** A movement aimed at improving the status and power of the consumer relative to the seller in the marketplace

**Significance:** Focuses attention on the proper use of marketplace power by manufacturers and their responsibilities to consumers in such areas as product safety, fair pricing, and honest advertising

The publication in 1965 of Ralph Nader's book *Unsafe at Any Speed*, which criticized the dangerous design features of the Chevrolet Corvair, is often viewed as the birth of modern-day consumerism. Since that time, Nader and others have founded such consumer organizations as the Center for Auto Safety, Public Citizen, the Health Research Group, and various buyers' cooperatives to promote safer products, lower prices, and full and honest disclosure in advertising. Two important trends have encouraged the growth of consumerism: the fact that sellers (manufacturers and retailers) increasingly tend to be giant corporations with whom individual buyers have little influence; and the growing complexity of many consumer products, which prevents buyers from making informed judgments. Consumerism has led to the passage of such legislation at the federal level as the Child Protection and Safety Act, the Hazardous Substances Act, and the Fair Credit Reporting Act, as well as the creation of the Consumer Product Safety Commission. The movement has been unsuccessful, however, in lobbying for the establishment of a federal cabinet-level Consumer Protection Agency.

> **Warning Label**
>
> Government warning: (1) According to the Surgeon General, women should not drink alcoholic beverages during pregnancy because of the risk of birth defects. (2) Consumption of alcoholic beverages impairs your ability to drive a car or operate machinery, and may cause health problems.

**See also** Business ethics; Nader, Ralph.

## Corporate responsibility

**Type of ethics:** Business and labor ethics

**Date:** Latter half of the nineteenth century to the present

**Associated with:** Collective responsibility, the theory of duty, and the inherent morality implicit in certain economic arrangements

**Definition:** That degree of moral duty that may be imputed to corporations beyond a simple obedience to conform to the laws of the state

**Significance:** Corporate responsibility raises important issues for ethics in regard to the nature of collective action and the division of personal and group morality; also, conflicts between economic efficiency and strict moral duty arise

Business corporations are collectivities of persons that are granted legal personhood and limited liability by the state for the purpose of carrying on commerce. The purposes for which a general corporation is created—primarily to make profit from commerce for its shareholders—raise questions about whether corporations ought to undertake supererogatory actions for the public good. This issue is further complicated by the issue of minority stockholders' rights, since there are few noncontroversial issues of public policy and the unanimous agreement of stockholders is scarcely to be anticipated in large, publicly traded corporations.

Milton Friedman has argued eloquently for restricting the moral obligation of corporations to obeying the laws of their respective nations. In this view, minority stockholders' rights are a prime consideration, but the economic efficiency of the market is another desired aim of this policy. The purely economic arrangement of the market, this theory argues, would be damaged by the noneconomic behavior of altruistic corporations. The lessening of the profitability of some enterprises, the potential for boycott, counter-boycott, and so forth, threaten the normal functioning of the capitalistic market economy, in this view.

The contrary view would hold that it is absurd to separate financial profitability from questions of the general quality of life: Would it make sense for a businessman to indulge in some as-yet legal form of polluting if that pollution would significantly shorten his life and/or that of his family? Would it be "profitable" for one to make money by legally selling weaponry to a potential enemy who might be expected to use those weapons to conquer or to destroy one's nation?

**See also** Affirmative action; Americans with Disabilities Act; Boycott; Business ethics; Conflict of interest; Consumerism; Employees, safety and treatment of; Equal pay for equal work; Exploitation; Fair Labor Standards Act; Fairness; Future generations; Hiring practices; Insider trading; Monopoly; Nader, Ralph; Nuclear energy; Pollution; Price fixing; Profit taking; Redlining; Sales, ethics of; Self-regulation; Wage discrimination; Whistleblowing.

## Corruption

**TYPE OF ETHICS:** Personal and social ethics
**DATE:** From antiquity
**DEFINITION:** Impairment of integrity, virtue, and moral principles; change from "good" to "bad" behavior
**SIGNIFICANCE:** Corruption completely destroys ethical systems; corrupt individuals, if numerous, will corrupt a society, which in turn may corrupt other societies, which in turn could lead to a decline of civilization

While a number of factors account for individual corruption, one important factor is contempt for humanity. A threshold of corruption has been crossed when a person comes to despise other people. Furthermore, most corrupt individuals share an overwhelming desire for power (control and domination) over others and a lust for wealth, and they will try to corrupt and/or ruin all those who stand in their way. Such a corrupt individual adapts easily. He or she can "move" and change stratagems quickly. Having an immoral or amoral approach to life (and ethics), such a person becomes a liar as needed, manipulates others as needed, uses the law as needed, and finds loopholes in laws and uses them to advantage as needed. Many corrupt people also exploit and hide behind religion.

Because of his or her contempt for others, a corrupt person becomes unscrupulous, "cold," and remote, in addition to being utterly ruthless, while also becoming consciously and deeply aware of his or her ruthlessness. Other traits include the individual's total absorption with his or her own affairs to the exclusion of all else, as well as secretiveness and extreme sensitivity to real or imagined insults. Such a person becomes a conspirator who is "positive" that others are conspiring against him or her. He or she then develops a rationale for his or her actions, actions that include "punishment" of others. The truly corrupted eventually become criminals (usually white-collar criminals). For example, the Watergate scandal and U.S. president Richard M. Nixon's White House tapes revealed that Nixon and many of his aides were totally corrupt and had committed criminal acts.

**Corrupt Societies.** Just as individuals become corrupt, so, too, do societies. They are usually ruled by a dictator or by a clique of lawless, ruthless people. Yet government under them is mediocre at best. The clique and the people it rules become intolerant and develop contempt for foreign peoples. The leader becomes something of a father-figure and near worship of him takes place. Rights—such as those found in the U.S. Constitution's Bill of Rights—are curtailed, and censorship becomes the order of the day. In the economy, extremes develop between fabulously wealthy people and the poverty stricken, with much of the wealth being amassed by the ruling clique. Furthermore, social mobility of any kind is restricted to certain elite groups.

Corrupt societies also exhibit decisiveness, instability, and senseless murders that devalue life, but turn cynical when such wrongs are committed. Furthermore, the state gives only minimal assistance to the needful young, old, and sick. Corrupt societies use religion as a type of "window-dressing," with most people who appear to be "saints" on their day of worship reverting to cold-blooded ruthlessness on the other days of the week. As a consequence, ethics go by the board, immorality replaces morality, sexual mores change for the worse, and families become weak to the point of almost ceasing to exist. Additionally, if the state has a heritage of "multiculturalism," the "in" groups eventually persecute and suppress the "out" groups, as was the case in Nazi Germany.

**The United States.** Unfortunately, many signs of corruption are evident in the United States, as the country moves into the twenty-first century. Everywhere, it seems, are signs that elites are expecting and demanding too much. In the savings and loan scandals, when bankers took billions of dollars, there was corruption. When many members of the House of Representatives practiced check-writing in their own "bank," in the 1990's, there was corruption. When defense contractors cheated on their government contracts from the 1940's to the present, again there was corruption.

When college football coaches or their "boosters" bribe the impressionable young, all parties become corrupted. When ministers commit immoral and perhaps illegal acts while continuing to beg for money, they become corrupt and may well corrupt all those around them, including their own congregations. When a college student cheats on examinations, that student becomes corrupt, and he or she may influence others to cheat, thereby corrupting them as well.

People who abuse relatives violently, sexually, or psychologically, become corrupt and may also "warp" the beliefs of the persons so abused. When the friendly neighborhood policeman takes his first bribe, the policeman becomes corrupt. When physicians treat the poor and charge them more than they can pay, the physicians become corrupt. Perhaps worst of all, corrupted individuals and societies have no sense of shame when such wrongs are committed.

Clearly, the United States—like many other countries—does not measure up to the standards set by the French Nobel Prize winner Albert Camus, a philosopher who held that the worth of an individual could be measured by observing what that individual would allow others to suffer and that a society's worth could be measured by observing how it treated its most unfortunate people. —*James Smallwood*

**See also** Cheating; Lying; Morality.

**Bibliography**


Benson, George C. S. *Political Corruption in America.* Lexington, Mass.: Lexington Books, 1978.

Enan, Mohammad Abdullah. *Ibn Khaldun: His Life and Work.* Lahore, India: Muhammad Ashraf, 1969.

Lacoste, Yves. *Ibn Khaldun.* London, England: Verso, 1984.

Payne, Robert. *The Corrupt Society: From Ancient Greece to Present-Day America.* New York: Praeger, 1975.

Schweitzer, Albert. *The Decay and Restoration of Civilization.* 2d ed. Translated by C. T. Campion. London, England: Adam and Charles Black, 1932.

Spengler, Oswald. *The Decline of the West.* Translated by Charles F. Atkinson. New York: Knopf, 1957.

Sykes, Charles J. *The Hollow Men: Politics and Corruption in Higher Education.* Washington, D.C.: Regnery Gateway, 1990.

Wise, David. *The Politics of Lying.* New York: Random House, 1973.


## Courage

**Type of ethics:** Personal and social ethics

**Associated with:** Virtue ethics

**Definition:** A state of character exhibited by persons who habitually stand firm in the face of danger, especially danger on the battlefield

**Significance:** The existence of human communities requires that some of their members be willing to give their lives, if necessary, to defend their communities against external aggressors

Courage, along with prudence, justice, and temperance, is one of the four cardinal virtues (states of character) of ancient Greek moral philosophy. Some authors and translators call it "fortitude" or "bravery."

In book 4 of his *Republic* (c. 390 b.c.e.), Plato describes what he believes would be the ideal city-state. It would include courageous soldiers who would go to war on its behalf. These soldiers would be taught what to fear and what not to fear. Furthermore, they would be trained to act in accordance with this knowledge when on the battlefield. Plato compares the courageous soldier to fabric that is dyed in such a manner that it retains its color when it is washed. The courageous soldier's "dye" must withstand the "lye" of pleasure, fear, and pain.

Plato's student Aristotle discusses the virtue of courage in book 3 of his *Nicomachean Ethics* (c. 330 b.c.e.). For Aristotle, many of the virtues are states of character that fall between opposing vices. Courage is a virtuous mean between the vicious extremes of cowardice on one side and rashness and excessive fearlessness on the other. The courageous person stands firm in the face of what is frightening. Although many things are frightening, courageous persons distinguish themselves most clearly from those who lack the virtue of courage by standing firm in the face of death, and it is in standing firm and fighting with confidence in the face of death on the battlefield that the virtue of courage is exercised to the fullest degree.

Aristotle's account of courage is more complicated than are his accounts of many other virtues, because it is a mean of two feelings: fear and confidence. Of the two, fear is the more important. The coward, who is both excessively fearful and deficiently confident, is distinguished most clearly by excessive fear of frightening things and fear of things that should not be frightening at all. There is no name (or was not in the Greek of Aristotle's day) for persons who have too little fear, because they are so rare. They are, he says, like madmen. Persons who are excessively confident about frightening things are rash, and they sometimes prove themselves to be cowards. Genuinely courageous persons do not seek danger. Rash persons, in attempting to imitate the courageous, wish for dangers but often retreat when they arrive.

While many of the Aristotelian virtues are means between extremes, they are not necessarily midpoints. Courage lies closer to excessive fearlessness and rashness than to cowardice. In other words, cowardice is the vice that is most directly opposed to the virtue of courage.

Aristotle identifies five states of character that are distinct from genuine courage but are often called "courage." The "courage" of the citizen-soldier is really desire for praise and honor, combined with fear of reproaches and legal penalties. Also included in this category are citizen-soldiers who stand firm and fight only because they are less afraid of their enemy than of their own officers. Experienced soldiers sometimes appear to be courageous when, in fact, they are standing firm only because their experience tells them they are not in great danger. When they learn that they actually are in great danger, they turn and run. Emotion is sometimes called "courage" but is not genuine courage. For Aristotle, persons act virtuously only when their rational faculties govern their emotions. Courageous soldiers fight with passion, but not all passionate soldiers are courageous. In addition, those soldiers who are optimistic only because they have been victorious many times in the past are not courageous. When they learn that their lives are in danger, they are no longer confident. Finally, soldiers who give the appearance of courage only because they are ignorant of their situation do not possess the virtue of courage.

Among the most significant developments in the history of courage between Aristotle's day and the twentieth century is that in the medieval synthesis of the classical and Christian traditions, while courage was still understood to be chiefly about death on the battlefield, martyrdom also came to be understood as an act of courage. Josef Pieper's *The Four Cardinal Virtues: Prudence, Justice, Fortitude, Temperance* (1965) provides a concise introduction to courage in the Christian tradition.

In twentieth century ethics, justice receives far more emphasis than do the other cardinal virtues. One area in which this imbalance of emphasis is most striking is that of the ethics of war and peace. Many writers address the questions of whether there can be just wars and, if so, what criteria should be used to distinguish just from unjust wars. Relatively little, however, is written about the courage of soldiers fighting in just wars. There is far more interest in the ethics of killing than in the ethics of dying. —*David Lutz*

**See also** Aristotelian ethics; Aristotle; Military ethics; National security; *Nicomachean Ethics*; Plato; Platonic ethics; *Republic*; Socrates; Virtue; Virtue ethics; War and peace.

**Bibliography**


Aristotle. *Nicomachean Ethics*. 2d ed. London: George Routledge, 1910.

Geach, Peter Thomas. *The Virtues*. Cambridge, England: Cambridge University Press, 1977.

Guardini, Romano. *The Virtues: On Forms of Moral Life*. Translated by Stella Lange. Chicago: Regnery, 1967.

Pieper, Josef. *The Four Cardinal Virtues: Prudence, Justice, Fortitude, Temperance*. Translated by Richard Winston, Clara Winston, et al. New York: Harcourt, Brace & World, 1965.

Plato. *Laches*. Hamburg, Germany: F. Meiner, 1970.

___________. *The Republic*. Translated by Benjamin Jowett. New York: Heritage Press, 1944.

Pybus, Elizabeth. *Human Goodness: Generosity and Courage*. London: Harvester Wheatsheaf, 1991.

Rachman, S. J. *Fear and Courage*. 2d ed. New York: W. H. Freeman, 1990.

Rittner, Carol, and Sondra Myers, eds. *The Courage to Care: Rescuers of Jews During the Holocaust*. New York: New York University Press, 1986.

Thomas Aquinas. *Summa Theologica*. Translated by Fathers of the English Dominican Province. Westminster, Md.: Christian Classics, 1981.

Tillich, Paul. *The Courage to Be*. New Haven, Conn.: Yale University Press, 1952.

Walton, Douglas N. *Courage: A Philosophical Investigation*. Berkeley: University of California Press, 1986.


## Covert action

**Type of ethics:** Politico-economic ethics

**Associated with:** Government, military, police, corporate, or industrial intelligence gathering or espionage

**Definition:** The gathering of proprietary information or the taking of physical action by clandestine means

**Significance:** Raises the question of what conditions justify the use of secretive means to achieve particular goals

In democratic, free, and open societies, the use of clandestine methods to achieve political, military, or industrial gains is the focus of argument. The argument is based on the question of whether it is moral and ethical to spy and engage in clandestine operations for the safety of the nation and its way of life or to obtain commercial advantage over a competitor. If it is decided to use secretive methods, what lengths and means are justified in pursuing particular goals? To what extent must the public be informed regarding the success or failure of the actions taken?

In totalitarian states, the morality of the governing power is the morality of the dictator or ruling group. In such states, the use of covert action is dictated by the goals and agenda of a single person or a small group of empowered individuals, without the consent or knowledge of the citizenry. In a democracy, a consensus is usually formed through elections, and national agendas reflect the morality and ethics of the majority of the population. As a result, government, military, and law-enforcement agencies must not violate the morality of the citizens, as understood by their elected representatives, in the pursuit of goals or information. This is an idealistic view. The perceived morality of a nation's people may vary greatly, depending on the extent of the governing mandate and the judgment of those who interpret the prevailing moral trends, and these trends may quickly shift direction depending on the public's views of and responses to perceived national threats, outrages, and insults, or to changes in elected officials. In the case of industrial covert actions, the morality and ethics of engaging in secretive methods in business are clearly linked to financial gain and competitive survivability, and as in totalitarian governments, the decision to use covert methods reflects the ethics and morality of corporate leaders. Most industrial covert action involves theft or sabotage. Government-sanctioned covert action is more complicated.

Societies of all types are most vulnerable to threats that are held in secret from them. For this reason, it is vital to be able to detect, identify, evaluate, and react to secret threats. To this end intelligence-gathering agencies exist. Collected intelligence data can be assessed to determine whether and how secret threats should be met, preferably by overt means if feasible, but when necessary and appropriate, by covert action. Covert actions are usually undertaken by one government to influence the affairs or policies of other nations by secret and unattributable means. The rationale for such actions is dictated by national interest, and national interest is defined by the moral and ethical values of totalitarian leaders or by a majority of a democratic nation's population. It is important to remember that when a democratic government takes covert action in the national interest, it does so under the umbrella of public consent. In either instance, covert actions are intended, at least in concept, to support broader national policy goals and to advance national interests. To this effect, covert actions are methods that support a nation's foreign policies and intent and that provide options located somewhere between diplomacy and military force. Whether in a totalitarian state or a free society, covert actions are ultimately "official" government-sponsored activities, despite being planned and conducted in a manner that hides or disguises their official sanctioning.

Covert actions are not a modern phenomenon. They have existed as long as groups of people have found points of disagreement and wish to influence the actions of others in a manner more favorable to themselves. As a result, the ethics of covert actions are reflective of the society that initiates them. If a nation can justify covert actions as a means to ensure its security or to further its national interests, or if a corporation can justify covert actions to ensure its commercial viability, then there is little posed in the way of a moral or ethical dilemma. When covert actions take place, they express the goals adopted by a nation and the values excepted, or tolerated, by its society. Covert actions reflect national behavior in the same manner as do other external actions, such as trade agreements, foreign aid, and military posturing. Because of their clandestine nature and their danger for those directly involved, covert actions are hidden from direct public knowledge and involvement. In many societies in which an open flow of information on government activities is available for public scrutiny, however, certain elements of society often express open disagreement over principles and beliefs that are related to both the ends and the means of their government's covert activities. Some democratic nations go so far as to define "covert actions" legislatively, in effect defining, or attempting to define, their national attitude toward the ethics of clandestine operations. In any case, the role and the extent of covert actions used as an instrument of a society's governmental or industrial policies reflect the ethics and morals of that society.

*—Randall L. Milstein*

**See also** Espionage.

**BIBLIOGRAPHY**

Ameringer, Charles D. *U.S. Foreign Intelligence: The Secret Side of American History.* Lexington, Mass.: Lexington Books, 1990.

Blackstock, Paul W. *The Strategy of Subversion: Manipulating the Politics of Other Nations.* Chicago: Quadrangle Books, 1964.

Dobson, Christopher, and Ronald Payne. *The Dictionary of Espionage.* London: Harrap, 1984.

Johnson, Loch K. *America's Secret Power: The CIA in a Democratic Society.* New York: Oxford University Press, 1989.

Kurland, Michael. *The Spymaster's Handbook.* New York: Facts on File, 1988.

Oseth, John M. *Regulating U.S. Intelligence Operations: A Study in Definition of the National Interest.* Lexington: University Press of Kentucky, 1985.

## Criminal punishment

**TYPE OF ETHICS:** Legal and judicial ethics

**DEFINITION:** An unpleasant consequence, such as a fine, imprisonment, or death, that a state imposes on an individual for violation of a legal rule

**SIGNIFICANCE:** Seeks to determine the moral justification for punishment and to determine which punishments are appropriate for particular crimes

Each society is ordered through various laws, which represent that society's understanding of what is important for the general welfare and what is right and wrong. When laws are violated, the society must take measures to minimize the violations in order to preserve itself and its values. This minimization is usually achieved by means of punishment.

Early human societies often viewed crimes as offenses against deities or ancestral spirits. They believed that the community would experience adversity if the violators were not punished. Death was a widely used form of punishment. One of the oldest codes of laws in existence, the Code of Hammurabi (Babylonia, c. 1700 B.C.E.), prescribed death for about thirty different offenses, including incest, swearing, casting a spell, burglary, and (for women) drinking in public.

Some people argue that punishment promotes social solidarity by reinforcing foundational social values, while others argue that punishment is usually imposed by the ruling economic and political class on the lower class to maintain the status quo. Still others reject punishment entirely, arguing that crime is a disease and should not be treated by inflicting pain upon criminals.

Attempts to address the issue of the moral justification of punishment have mainly fallen into two broadly opposed groups: utilitarian and retributive theories of punishment. The retributivist stresses guilt and desert, looking back to the crime to justify punishment. The basic characteristic of the utilitarian theory of punishment is that it is oriented toward the future, insisting that punishment can be justified only if it has beneficial consequences that outweigh the intrinsic evil of inflicting suffering. Retributivism holds that the justification for punishment is found in the fact that a rule has been broken—punishment is properly inflicted because, and only because, a person deserves it. The offender's desert, and not the beneficial consequences of punishment, is what justifies punishment. This is the "eye-for-an-eye" view, according to which a wrongdoer deserves to be punished in proportion to his or her crime.

The history of retributive punishment, which begins with biblical and Talmudic ethical and legal ideas, has been the most prevalent form of punishment. The most important and influential classical retributivist is Immanuel Kant (1724-1804). The classical form of retributivism holds not only that the guilty should be punished but also that there is a duty to punish the guilty. In knowingly breaking the law, the criminal declares, for example, that he or she has a license to steal, thus putting those who respect property rights at a disadvantage. The criminal weakens the fabric of justice and must be punished to vindicate justice. Failure to punish not only condones the wrongful act but also is unfair to those who practice self-restraint and respect the rights of others. Thus, punishment is imposed for the sake of justice.

Retributivists hold that wrongful acts and harms can be ranked in order of their moral gravity and that the proper amount of punishment is proportionate to the moral gravity of the offense. In its most complete form, the retributive theory of punishment contains the following tenets: (1) the moral right to punish is based solely on the offense committed; (2) the moral duty to punish is grounded solely on the offense committed; (3) punishment should be proportionate to the offense; (4) punishment annuls the offense; and (5) punishment is a right of the offender.

The utilitarian theory of punishment also has had a long history, beginning with Plato (c. 428-348 B.C.E.) The most comprehensive formulation of the theory is found in the writings of Jeremy Bentham (1748-1832). The utilitarian theory justifies punishment solely in terms of the good consequences that it produces. For a punishment to be justified, it should have at least some of the following good effects. First, the punishment should act as a deterrent to crime. It should sway the offender not to commit similar offenses in the future and serve as an example to potential offenders. Second, the punishment should be a means of reforming or rehabilitating the offender. The offender is reformed in the sense that the effect of the punishment is to change the offender's values so that he or she will not commit similar offenses in the future because he or she believes them to be wrong. A third good consequence should be the incapacitative effect of the punishment. When an offender is in prison, he or she is out of the general social circulation and thus does not have the opportunity to commit offenses. Finally, the punishment should act as a means of moral education in the community. It should demonstrate the moral wrongness and unacceptability of an offense and strengthen moral beliefs that curb criminal inclinations.

The utilitarian theory of punishment can be summarized in the following propositions: (1) social utility is a necessary condition for justified punishment; (2) social utility is a sufficient condition for justified punishment; and (3) the proper amount of punishment is that amount that will do the most good or the least harm to those who are affected by it.

Attempts have been made to mix the utilitarian and retributive theories in order to combine the positive elements of each. One such attempt maintains that the aim of punishment is to prevent or reduce crime, a utilitarian idea, but insists that only those who have voluntarily broken the law be punished and that the punishment be proportionate to the offense, which are retributive ideas. —*Cheri Vail Fisk*

**See also** Bentham, Jeremy; Consequentialism; Kant, Immanuel; Kantian ethics; Punishment; Utilitarianism.

**BIBLIOGRAPHY**

Baird, Robert M., and Stuart E. Rosenbaum, eds. *Philosophy of Punishment*. Buffalo, N.Y.: Prometheus Books, 1988.

Moberly, Walter. *The Ethics of Punishment*. Hamden, Conn.: Archon Books, 1968.

Murphy, Jeffrie G. *Punishment and Rehabilitation*. 2d ed. Belmont, Calif.: Wadsworth, 1985.

Primorac, Igor. *Justifying Legal Punishment*. Atlantic Highlands, N.J.: Humanities Press International, 1989.

Ten, C. L. *Crime, Guilt, and Punishment*. New York: Oxford University Press, 1987.

## Critical theory

**TYPE OF ETHICS:** Theory of ethics

**DATE:** Nineteenth and twentieth centuries

**ASSOCIATED WITH:** Karl Marx, the Frankfurt School, Jürgen Habermas, and Michel Foucault

**DEFINITION:** Hypothesis incorporating both social theory and political practice to oppose predominant disciplinary orthodoxies

**SIGNIFICANCE:** Holds that the oppressed must be provided with the insight and intellectual tools they need for empowerment and eventual emancipation

"Critical theory" is an umbrella term that is used to define a range of social theories that surfaced in the nineteenth century and continued through the latter part of the twentieth century. A critical theory is characterized by strong opposition to the traditions of all disciplines. These traditions have existed for the purpose of articulating and advancing "timeless" truths, "objective" facts, singular interpretations of texts, and so on. A critical theory posits that these universal truths, objective facts, and singular interpretations in all disciplines lack any sort of philosophical or theoretical grounding that could not be effectively challenged, and that to present them as if they arc objective is a politically destructive act.

Theories are usually removed from political practice, interpreting the world rather than prescribing a solution to whatever ills are discovered. Critical theory differentiates itself from other theories on this point; it has a very different view of the relationship between theory and practice. Striving to do more than define how society is unfair, critical theory attempts to turn the status quo upside down and offer a solution. This connection between social theory and political practice is critical theory's distinguishing characteristic.

Those who espouse critical theory believe that the traditional disciplines must attempt to change the world in a way that gives those who have been "marginalized," or placed on the fringes of society, the insights and intellectual understanding they need in order to empower and eventually free themselves. In his book *Critical Theory in Political Practice,* Stephen T. Leonard articulates three criteria that must be met if critical theory is to bring about self-emancipation. A critical theory must first of all provide a coherent explanation of how the self-conceptions of the marginalized are largely responsible for the reality of the situations of those people. Second, critical theory must provide a completely different perspective of social relations that the oppressed can adopt for their own vision. The third criterion is that the first two actions will be successful only if critical theory manifests a sufficiently deep understanding of itself that in the end, it can translate its theory into a language that is comprehensible to the very people it wants to empower.

Unlike other theories, critical theory is not judged simply by its ability to give an account of the world; instead, it is judged by its ability to show the oppressed how their institutionalized beliefs and conceptions of themselves help sustain their marginalization. Critical theory is successful when the oppressed act in their own interest to free themselves from their dependence upon the mainstream.

There have been several influential attempts at developing a critical theory, the first of which was the work of Karl Marx. Marx argued from a philosophical perspective that the point is to change the world, not simply to interpret it, and because of this view, Marx is considered by many to be the founding father of critical theory.

Marxism has presented many problems in the twentieth century, however, so even though Marx has had a tremendous influence upon defining critical theory, critical theory has not easily identified with Marx. His critique of nineteenth century capitalism has been difficult to apply to the capitalism of the twentieth century. Consequently, Marxist theorists have reinterpreted his theory, and those reinterpretations have been even more problematic. The most widely known of these interpretations has been orthodox Marxism, which has been used to support authoritarian regimes.

Other theorists have attempted to learn from the mistakes of the orthodox Marxists and have chosen to concentrate on the antiauthoritarian elements of Marx's theory. The most influential of these has been the Frankfurt School, which includes Max Horkheimer, Theodore Adorno, and Herbert Marcuse, as well as Jürgen Habermas. The Frankfurt School was interested in Marxism's insights but wanted to use them in a way that would be relevant to the twentieth century, without falling into a dogmatic theory of authoritarian social structures and political institutions.

"Western" Marxism, the Frankfurt School's theory, agrees with Marx that it is possible for modern society to overcome oppressive domination. It disagrees with both Marx and traditional Marxists, however, regarding the traditional Marxist theory that overcoming this domination can only be achieved through a revolution by the working class.

Marx, the Frankfurt School, and Jürgen Habermas are considered part of the modernist movement of critical theory, of which Western Marxism has been the most influential element thus far. Modernist theorists are characterized by their belief that the current forms of thought and action in society are neither critical nor reflective. They believe that critical theory is possible only if serious critical thought can be recaptured, which they believe is entirely possible.

Modernist critical theory has been followed by "postmodernist" critical theory. Most influential postmodernist thinkers have been French, and the historian Michel Foucault has been the most prominent postmodernist. Postmodernist critical theory shares with modernist critical theory a commitment to a social theory that is politically engaged and is opposed to domination as a political solution. Both schools of thought have been opposed to orthodox Marxism. What is distinctly different between the two is the postmodernist assertion that the recovery of critical reason in the modern world is not possible; therefore, emancipation cannot be achieved through the recovery of critical reason. Foucault argues that the recovery of reason is impossible because of the limitations of language.

Modernist and postmodernist theory have had an enormous influence in shaping critical theory. United on many fronts, these schools of thought have established good reasons for the necessity of a theory that incorporates both social and political theory. Much of the discourse between the two in the latter part of the twentieth century, however, has centered on their essential difference—the question of whether modern society holds the possibility of reason and critical thought—and little of it has concentrated upon articulating the theory to the oppressed for their empowerment.

*—Jill S. Marts*

**See also** Foucault, Michel; Marx, Karl; Marxism.

**BIBLIOGRAPHY**

Dewey, John. *Outlines of a Critical Theory of Ethics.* Westport, Conn.: Greenwood Press, 1969.

Eagleton, Terry. *Literary Theory: An Introduction.* Minneapolis: University of Minnesota Press, 1983.

Leonard, Stephen T. *Critical Theory in Political Practice.* Princeton, N.J.: Princeton University Press, 1990.

Merod, Jim. *The Political Responsibility of the Critic.* Ithaca, N.Y.: Cornell University Press, 1987.

Norris, Christopher. *Uncritical Theory: Postmodernism, Intellectuals, and the Gulf War.* London: Lawrence & Wishart, 1992.

## Cruelty

**TYPE OF ETHICS:** Personal and social ethics

**DATE:** From nineteenth century to present

**ASSOCIATED WITH:** Philip Hallie, Friedrich Nietzsche, Arthur Schopenhauer, Marquis de Sade, and Niccolò Machiavelli

**DEFINITION:** Intentional, malicious infliction of physical and/or psychological injury on another person or animal

**SIGNIFICANCE:** Illustrates the level of depravity to which humans can descend in their relationships with their fellow humans and other sentient beings

Although cruelty has existed at virtually all stages of civilization, philosophical interest in cruelty began in the nineteenth century. Earlier thinkers usually considered cruelty within the context of another concern. Niccolò Machiavelli (1469-1527), in *The Prince*, advocates the quick, expeditious use of cruelty by a prince to maintain unity, loyalty, and order in his state, since criminal behavior is encouraged when a ruler is too merciful to his subjects. Judicious cruelty creates fear, and if a prince cannot be both loved and feared, it is better to be feared than to be loved.

The French essayist Michel de Montaigne (1533-1592) condemns cruelty as being so repulsive that he approves of nothing harsher for criminals than quick execution, believing that anything "beyond plain death" is pointlessly wanton. He also condemns cruelty to animals, with whom humans share mutual obligations.

Although he is remembered more for his depravity than for his contribution to historiography and literature, the Marquis de Sade (1740-1814) is an important figure in the history and literature of cruelty. Sade provides, through his life and writing, extensive depictions of physical and mental cruelty as a prelude to sexual gratification. His justification of sexual cruelty is rooted in his belief that natural sexual pleasure is always preceded by an erotic desire to suffer and inflict pain, behavior that should not be censured, since it is the fulfillment of natural human instinct.

The earliest philosophical interest in cruelty is shown by Arthur Schopenhauer (1788-1860). Schopenhauer abhors cruelty, also censuring the insensitive treatment of animals, which stems from the erroneous belief that they cannot suffer. He sees in Christianity the root of this insensitivity because of the Christian emphasis on the unique and exclusive value of human life; in Asian culture, animals are better treated and more highly valued. Human cruelty springs from the suffering of the individual will in its struggle to satisfy its desires. A frustrated individual who believes that his own suffering is greater than that of others becomes envious. When envy and frustration become so great that the individual delights in the infliction of suffering, the individual has crossed the threshold from the moral frailty natural in everyone to a fiendish, diabolical cruelty. The only preventative for such deeply depraved acts is an equally deep compassion.

Friedrich Nietzsche (1844-1900) considers human cruelty from both a historical and a philosophical perspective. In *On the Genealogy of Morals*, he recognizes its powerful influence on human culture, attributing to cruelty a central role in the generation of historical memory: "Man could never do without blood, torture, and sacrifices when he felt the need to create a memory for himself; . . . all this has its origin in the instinct that realized that pain is the most powerful aid to mnemonics." Modern moral concepts are rooted in ancient legal obligations, in which justice was obtained through violent personal revenge as compensation for an injury, creditors having the right to "inflict every kind of torture and indignity upon the body of the debtor . . . as much as seemed commensurate with the debt." As communities become confident of their power, however, they become lenient toward those who injure them, there being a direct relationship between strength and humaneness, just as there is between vulnerability and the capacity for cruelty. In a strong, confident community, as in a strong, confident individual, cruelty evolves into mercy. The fact that cruelty provided pleasure for "more primitive men" explains the prevalence of violent atrocity, a feature of its past that modern humanity hypocritically denies. The tragedy of modern humanity, however, is that it has replaced primitive, blood-seeking cruelty toward transgressors with "psychical cruelty" against itself: it has abased itself before God, in whose eyes it deserves only punishment for its unworthiness.

The philosophical interest in cruelty that was initiated by Schopenhauer and Nietzsche has been maintained by American philosopher Philip Hallie, who gives it deliberate, intense philosophical attention. Hallie distinguishes "episodic cruelty" (unrelated, occasional acts of cruelty) from "institutionalized cruelty," which consists of using the fundamental institutions of society—government, education, and so forth—to execute and perpetuate both blatant and subtle acts of cruelty. He identifies the imbalance of power as a defining feature of cruelty and searches for its opposite, which he initially determines to be freedom. Freedom must be consummated by "hospitality," however, meaning the carrying out of a positive ethic of beneficence, often at significant risk to the benefactor, in addition to negative injunctions against doing harm. Hallie contrasts the Nazi Holocaust with the quiet, heroic goodness of the villagers of Le Chambon-sur-Lignon in southern France, whose goodness resulted in the saving of thousands of Jewish refugees during the Occupation, despite grave danger to themselves. Throughout Hallie's treatment of cruelty runs an exhortation against forgetting the presence and identity of the victim in every act of cruelty, an oversight that resulted in the systematic inhumanity of the Holocaust; it was the recognition of the victims that produced the "riskful, strenuous nobility" of the Chambonnais. *—Barbara Forrest*

**See also** Cruelty to animals; Hate; Machiavellian ethics; Pornography; Rape; Violence; Wickedness.

**BIBLIOGRAPHY**

Hallie, Philip. *Cruelty*. Middletown, Conn.: Wesleyan University Press, 1982.

___________. "From Cruelty to Goodness." In *Vice and Virtue in Everyday Life: Introductory Readings in Ethics*, edited by Christina Sommers and Fred Sommers. 3d ed. Fort Worth, Tex.: Harcourt Brace Jovanovich College Publishers, 1993.

Machiavelli, Niccolò. "*The Prince*." In *The Portable Machiavelli*, edited and translated by Peter Bondanella and Mark Musa. New York: Penguin Books, 1979.

Miller, James. "Carnivals of Atrocity: Foucault, Nietzsche, Cruelty." *Political Theory* 18 (August, 1990): 470-491.

Montaigne, Michel de. "Of Cruelty." Translated by Donald M. Frame. In *The Essays. Great Books of the Western World*. 2d ed. Chicago: Encyclopaedia Britannica, 1990.

Nietzsche, Friedrich. *On the Genealogy of Morals*. Edited and translated by Walter Kaufmann. New York: Vintage Books, 1967.

Schopenhauer, Arthur. *On the Basis of Morality*. Translated by E. F. J. Payne. Indianapolis: Bobbs-Merrill, 1965.

__________. *The World as Will and Representation*. Translated by E. F. J. Payne. New York: Dover, 1969.

Thomas, Donald. *The Marquis de Sade*. Boston: New York Graphic Society, 1976.

## Cruelty to animals

**Type of ethics:** Animal rights

**Date:** Eighteenth century to present

**Associated with:** Christian humane movements of the eighteenth and nineteenth centuries, and the twentieth century animal rights movement

**Definition:** Intentional or wanton infliction of suffering upon living creatures, or indifference to their suffering

**Significance:** To feel pleasure because of the suffering of animals is considered immoral according to the great world religions and ethical philosophies

The keenly perceptive twentieth century dramatist George Bernard Shaw observed that when a man kills a lion he is praised as being a sportsman, while when a lion kills a man he is condemned as vicious. Mohandas K. Gandhi, the charismatic moral and spiritual leader, once lamented that the terrible thing about the British was not only that they did terrible things to his people but also that they were not even aware of it. It is often the case that humans are cruel to animals without being aware they are. It has been widely accepted, as was maintained by British philosopher John Locke, that feeling pleasure in the suffering of others is the main ingredient in cruelty, but there are some who feel nothing. Thus, Tom Regan, animal rights philosopher, distinguishes between what he calls *sadistic cruelty,* which occurs when people *enjoy* causing suffering, and *brutal cruelty,* which involves *indifference* to suffering.

René Descartes, the father of modern philosophy, was so indifferent to cruelty to animals that he insisted that because animals do not reason, they cannot even feel pain. This meant that one could torture animals and still not be considered cruel. Indeed, only 150 years ago in Britain it was common for horses to be beaten to death. Cattle, sheep, and pigs were slowly bled to death, and there was no moral outcry against such cruelty.

The first time any legal effort was made to address the problem of cruelty to animals was 1800, when a bill was sponsored in England to outlaw bullfighting. Even so small an effort as that, however, was ridiculed by the London *Times.* Finally, after years of indifference, in 1822 Parliament passed an act outlawing cruel treatment to cattle.

Against a historical background of ethical indifference toward animals, in the eighteenth and nineteenth centuries some Christian leaders and free thinkers took a stand against cruelty to animals. The philosopher Lord Shaftesbury (Anthony Ashley Cooper) condemned the act of taking pleasure in the suffering of animals, calling it unnatural. A protest group known as the Clapham Sect denounced bullfighting as barbarous. Queen Victoria herself believed that there was something wrong with a civilization that would condone cruelty to animals or deny charity and mercy for them.

In 1824 in England, the Society for the Prevention of Cruelty to Animals (SPCA) was founded. In 1832, there appeared a Christian declaration that cruelty to animals was against the Christian faith. The drive to oppose cruelty to animals and to seek ethical treatment for them was gaining momentum. In answer to the charge that there should be no ethical concern for creatures who cannot reason, the nineteenth century British philosopher Jeremy Bentham declared that the question is not whether animals can reason or talk, but whether they can suffer.

As ethical concern for animals expanded, the very definition of cruelty to them also had to be expanded. Thus, Andrew Linzey, distinguished theologian and advocate of animal rights, enlarged the concept of cruelty to make it identical with wantonness, meaning any act that is not morally justifiable. In such terms, cruelty regardless of intention would include the use of animals for sport, recreation, pleasure, and entertainment, as well as negligence and lack of care toward them. Linzey ethically condemns as cruel "hunting," bull or cock fighting, and the use of performing animals in films, television, or the circus. For Linzey, both animals and humans are God's creations, and thus to be cruel to any of them is to offend God.

As philosophers came to believe that cruelty to animals was unethical, they also came to see that it was not possible to isolate cruelty to animals from cruelty to humans. The great eighteenth century Prussian philosopher Immanuel Kant observed that if people were indifferent to cruelty to animals, that would desensitize them, and they would become indifferent to cruelty to humans. The celebrated playwright George Bernard Shaw insisted that it would be impossible to be cruel to animals without damaging one's own character.

The famous medieval Catholic philosopher Saint Thomas Aquinas maintained that it is not that cruelty could dehumanize people but that it necessarily does. Thus, Andrew Linzey stated that cruelty to animals leads to moral meanness of life. C. S. Lewis, the celebrated twentieth century novelist and theologian, used the argument that if people can justify cruelty on the grounds of a difference in species, they can justify it on racial grounds, or on the grounds of advanced people against backward people, and the culmination of this kind of thinking is the behavior of the Nazis during World War II.

Following the lead of England in opposing cruelty to animals, in 1866 the American Society for the Prevention of Cruelty to Animals (ASPCA) was founded, and in the twentieth century many humane organizations have been formed that do not merely oppose cruelty to animals but also aggressively promote a general program of animal rights. In the space age, human beings have become interplanetary, and to meet the needs of such an age, people need a planetary ethics or a boundless morality encompassing all living

*Children who are taught to respect nonhuman forms of life are unlikely to be cruel to animals later in life.* (Cleo Freelance Photo)

creatures, such as that advocated by the twentieth century humanitarian Albert Schweitzer. —*T. E. Katen*

**See also** Animal research; Dominion over nature, human; Sentience; Singer, Peter; Vivisection.

**Bibliography**

Linzey, Andrew. *Christianity and the Rights of Animals.* N.Y.: Crossroad, 1987.

Regan, Tom, and Peter Singer, eds. *Animal Rights and Human Obligations.* 2d ed. Englewood Cliffs, N.J.: Prentice-Hall, 1989.

Ruesch, Hans. *Slaughter of the Innocent.* New York: Civitas, 1983.

Sharpe, Robert. *The Cruel Deception.* Wellingborough, England: Thorsons, 1988.

Spiegel, Marjorie. *The Dreaded Comparison.* Philadelphia: New Society, 1988.

## Cynicism

**Type of ethics:** Classical history

**Date:** Fourth century B.C.E. to sixth century C.E.

**Definition:** A movement that denounced all established conventions and emphasized asceticism, self-sufficiency, attention to natural values, and the practice of virtuous actions as the way to achieve happiness

**Significance:** Emphasized the importance of intellectual freedom, self-realization, and criticism of convention and inhibition; offered a practical example of imperturbability and happiness in times of political unrest

The movement that came to be known as Cynicism, the "dog philosophy," cannot be characterized by reference to a systematic philosophical doctrine or a rigorously organized school. Instead, it was formed by individual thinkers who embraced slightly varying sets of ethical tenets that were concerned primarily with practical ethics and who adopted ways of life that suited what they taught. Few members of the Cynic movement can be directly connected with their predecessors in terms of a master-pupil relationship. There is considerable chronological continuity of Cynics, however, who cover, in a fairly uninterrupted manner, a span of about ten centuries.

The origins of Cynic ideas can be traced to the end of the fifth or the beginning of the fourth century B.C.E., to the doctrine of Antisthenes, who was one of the closest companions of Socrates. The archetypical figure of the Cynic, however, is Diogenes of Sinope, a contemporary of Aristotle, Demosthenes, and Alexander the Great. Diogenes was an influential thinker whose death in 323 B.C.E. marked the beginning of a period of development and popularity for the Cynic movement. During the last decades of the fourth century and during the third century B.C.E., the Cynics Monimus of Syracuse, Onesicritus, Crates of Thebes and his wife Hipparchia, Metrocles of Maronea, Menippus of Gadara, Menedemus, Bion of Borysthenes, and Cercidas of Megalopolis extended the pure ethical core of the doctrine of Diogenes into domains such as literature and politics, making it known not only in Athens but also throughout the Hellenistic world. Cynicism lost its prominence during the next two centuries because of the growing influence of Epicureanism and Stoicism as well as the absence of charismatic Cynics. The movement revived in the mid-first century C.E. in the form of an almost anarchist reaction to Roman leaders such as Caligula, Nero, and Vespasian. The influence of the Cynics of the Roman period reached its peak in the late first century and early second century with Dio Chrysostom and Favorinus. Other well-known figures were Demonax of Cyprus and Oenomaus of Gadara. The reputation of Cynicism suffered, however, as a result of the activities of various charlatans who carried the staff and knapsack and wore the cloak of the Cynics without bearing any resemblance to the Cynics. The satirist Lucian (second century) and the emperor Julian (fourth century) spoke of a noisy crowd that imitated the mannerisms of Diogenes and Crates but was ignorant of Cynic philosophy and was socially worthless.

Although the various individual exponents of Cynicism adopted different tones in their teaching and stressed different things, there is a core of practical attitudes and ethical tenets that they all share.

A key notion of ancient Cynicism lies in the metaphor of devaluation—or, rather, defacing or falsifying—the currency of human standards. The Cynics set out to undermine and reverse all the values, practices, and institutions on which conventional society was based. This "falsifying of the coin" is necessitated by the fact that the pleasures, attachments, and obligations nurtured by conventional society are impediments to happiness. Society burdens humans with a set of artificial values and corrupts them by means of self-indulgence, ignorance, and confusion. It is an active source of unhappiness in that it gives rise to unsatisfied desires for physical goods and to irrational fears about the gods, the turns of fortune, malady, and death. The Cynic's aim is to free people from the fetters of passion and convention, to make them observe the demands of nature and to guide them toward a natural life. In order to obtain this result, humans must, first, eradicate the desire and quest for pleasure, and, second, acquire both the physical and the mental strength to arm themselves against the difficulties that fortune may bring. This strength (*ischys*) can be obtained only by means of constant training (*askesis*) involving significant toil (*ponos*) of both body and mind. The Cynics consider toil as an instrumental good, since it leads to the realization of a double ideal: the reduction of one's needs and desires to a bare minimum comparable to the minimal needs of animals, leading to self-sufficiency (*autarkeia*) and the achievement of spiritual freedom, independence, and impassibility (*apatheia*), which are truly godlike.

In line with the Socratic tradition, the Cynics believed that virtue was sufficient for happiness, and they partly analyzed it in intellectual terms. To them, virtue is based on "unlearning what is bad" and on developing a rational account of the distinction between natural and conventional values; it can be taught, and it probably depends heavily upon memory. The Cynic conception of virtue deviates from Socraticism, however, in that it has strong anti-intellectualist traits: Knowledge is not sufficient for virtue but must be complemented by training and strength. The two kinds of *askesis* (hardening of the body and exercising of the mind) are complementary, and the *askesis* of the body can establish virtue in the soul.

The reversal of values affects the Cynic attitude toward religion and politics, two particularly conspicuous domains of ordinary activity. In religion, the Cynics denounced superstition in all forms, criticized the providentialist conception of the gods as well as any notion of divine interference in human affairs, and contrasted the intentions and practices of traditional believers with the pious behavior of morally pure men. Although the most important Cynics were not acknowledged atheists but only professed ignorance about the nature of the divine, their "falsification of the coin" in religious matters extended to the very roots of traditional religion. Their agnosticism was a springboard for attacks on both the content and the practices of Greco-Roman religion, and it left little room for an active belief in the existence of divinities. Their criticisms of traditional mythology should also be seen in the light of this radical defacement of religious values.

In politics, the Cynics were among the first philosophers to defy citizenship and its obligations in a coherent and radical way. The Cynic has no attachment to the vestiges of the city-state and expresses no regret for the fall of the *polis*. Instead, the Cynic takes pride in being without a city (*apolis*) and professes to be a citizen of the world (*kosmopolites*). The Cynic's cosmopolitanism entails ignoring all civic rules and obeying the only law that ought to be obeyed; namely, the natural law. Its ideal implementation in Diogenes' utopian *Republic* embarrassed Cynic sympathizers: Incest, cannibalism, the abolition of coinage and arms, the dissolution of the family, and a limitless sexual freedom are some of the implications of substituting natural law for the laws of society.

Cynic ethics is both individualistic and philanthropic. The individualistic features of the movement are found primarily in the image of the self-sufficient, self-fulfilled, self-controlled sage, a solitary man detached from society and free from its bonds, a wandering, homeless (*aoikos*) beggar, a dog barking at those who approach him. The Cynic is also, however, "the watchdog of humankind," showing by example and through his own actions what people should do to liberate themselves from the illusions and fears that make them miserable and leave them defenseless in an unpredictably changing world. His sharp tongue and shameless behavior are pedagogic strategies rather than exhibitionistic devices: They convey the radicalism of the Cynic reform by stressing the extent to which the adherents of the movement must violate the conventional codes of society in order to function as "the heralds of God." —*Voula Tsouna McKirahan*

**See also** Asceticism; Autonomy; Cyrenaics; Hedonism; Socrates; Stoic ethics.

**BIBLIOGRAPHY**

Attridge, Harold W. *First-century Cynicism in the Epistles of Heraclitus*. Missoula, Mont.: Scholars Press for the Harvard Theological Review, 1976.

Downing, Francis Gerald. *Christ and the Cynics: Jesus and Other Radical Preachers in First-century Tradition*. Sheffield, England: JSOT, 1988.

Dudley, Donald Reynolds. *A History of Cynicism from Diogenes to the Sixth Century A.D.* 1937. Reprint. New York: Gordon Press, 1974.

Malherbe, Abraham J., ed. The Cynic Epistles: A Study Edition. Missoula, Mont.: Scholars Press for the Society of Biblical Literature, 1977.

Sloterdijk, Peter. Critique of Cynical Reason. Translated by Michael Eldred. New York: Verso, 1988.

## Cyrenaics

**TYPE OF ETHICS:** Classical history

**DATE:** Fourth and third centuries B.C.E.

**ASSOCIATED WITH:** Aristippus of Cyrene, in Libya, and later post-Socratics; hedonism; and Epicureanism

**DEFINITION:** Practitioners of a school of ancient Greek philosophy that taught that pleasure is the goal of life

**SIGNIFICANCE:** These pioneer hedonists deemphasized abstract studies and stressed practical ethics

Aristippus of Cyrene, founder of Cyrenaicism, was an associate of the philosopher Socrates (469-399 B.C.E.), and Cyrenaicism—along with Cynicism and Megarianism—was one of three diverging philosophical schools that soon sprang from Socrates' emphasis on rational control and ethical self-consciousness. Aristippus taught that, since humans can know only their own sensations, no universal standards of pleasure can be discovered, and all pleasures are thus equally valuable; in this view, any act has value only in its usefulness to the one who controls it. This notion, influenced by the Sophists' belief that knowledge comes only through direct experience, was amplified by Aristippus' grandson (also named Aristippus) and later modified by Hegesias, Annikeris, and Theodorus—thinkers whose names are associated with their own sects.

Socrates had taught that moral action should lead to happiness, so Aristippus concluded that life's meaning lay in pleasure. This attitude, called hedonism (from the Greek hedone, "pleasure"), explains one sense of the familiar Latin motto carpe diem, "seize the day."

**Cyrenaic Ethics.** In deducing their philosophy, Cyrenaics ignored physics and mathematics, concentrating instead on practical ethics under various headings: things to pursue and avoid, sensations, actions, causes, and proofs. They believed that all action should aim at pleasure; this meant not merely avoiding pain but also seeking palpable sensation. They devalued both memory and the anticipation of future happiness, and they emphasized physical pleasures over mental activities.

Cyrenaics aimed for rational control that would manipulate people and circumstances to their own pleasurable ends. They defined right and wrong in terms of personal pleasure and pain. Rather than abstinence, which contemporary Cynics urged, Aristippus favored the prudent "use" and control of pleasure.

**The Last Phase.** Early in the third century B.C.E., followers who tried to distinguish among higher and lower pleas-ures blurred the Cyrenaics' focus on self-interest, their central philosophical principle: Hegesias (the death-persuader) stressed avoiding pain (rather than pursuing pleasure) and actively encouraged suicide; Annikeris promoted social relationships, altruism, and patriotism; and Theodorus the Atheist urged a quest for enduring inner joy, not momentary physical pleasures. These disagreements seemed to splinter Cyrenaicism, which died out by 275, while another hedonistic school, Epicureanism, advanced. —*Roy Neil Graves*

**See also** Hedonism.

**BIBLIOGRAPHY**

Edwards, Paul, ed. The Encyclopedia of Philosophy. New York: Macmillan, 1967.

Hicks, Robert D. Stoic and Epicurean. New York, Russell & Russell, 1962.

Long, A. A. *Hellenistic Philosophy: Stoics, Epicureans, Sceptics.* 2d ed. Berkeley: University of California Press, 1986.

Owens, Joseph. *A History of Ancient Western Philosophy.* Englewood Cliffs, N.J.: Prentice-Hall, 1959.

Reese, William L. *Dictionary of Philosophy and Religion: Eastern and Western Thought.* Atlantic Highlands, N.J.: Humanities Press, 1980.

**Dalai Lama** (b. Tenzin Gyatso, June 6, 1935, Taktser, Amdo, Tibet): Religious leader

**TYPE OF ETHICS:** Religious ethics

**ACHIEVEMENTS:** The Dalai Lama, the spiritual and temporal head of the traditional Buddhist community of Tibet, is also the winner of the 1989 Nobel Peace Prize

**SIGNIFICANCE:** Since the 1950's, Tibet has been under Chinese occupation; Tenzin Gyatso's leadership of Tibet's government in exile has made him a symbol of religious and ethical opposition to oppression

Perhaps no other recent historical figure from Asia, except Mohandas K. Gandhi, has gained such world-wide recognition for his ethical teachings as has the fourteenth Dalai Lama. Like Gandhi's, Tenzin Gyatso's writings and actions reflect a concern for combining ancient religious traditions with a contemporary political cause. Also like Gandhi's, the Dalai Lama's cause is not limited to the political cause of his own country but extends to the arena of international politics and human relations generally. To understand how the fourteenth Dalai Lama came to represent the principles that won him the Nobel Peace Prize in 1989, one must investigate the traditional origins of the position that he holds in the Tibetan Buddhist world.

*The fourteenth Dalai Lama, Tenzin Gyatso* (Nobel Foundation)

**Gendun Drub: The First Dalai Lama and His Successors.** Properly speaking, the spiritual role of all Dalai Lamas since the life of the first (Gendun Drub, born in 1351, died in 1474) belongs within the broader religious framework of Buddhism, a religion that has various "schools." In somewhat narrower spiritual and temporal terms, the Dalai Lamas belong to the long national tradition of Tibet, a country nestled in the Himalayan mountain range between China and India.

It was Gendun Drub who, after studying both at the Padma Chöling Monastery, where his teacher called him "Omniscient One," and at the Evam Monastery, went on to found a monastery called Tashi Lhunpo in southern Tibet. There he compiled many spiritual works that have remained seminal Buddhist texts. Gendun Drub did not carry the formal title of Dalai Lama (a tradition initiated with the third in the lineage) but preferred a title given by his teacher: Tamche Khyenpa, "Omniscient One," a term still used by devout Tibetans when referring to the fourteenth Dalai Lama, Tenzin Gyatso.

Tashi Lhunpo remained the seat of the successors to Tamche Khyenpa until 1642 when the fifth Dalai Lama left the monastery under the keeping of his own tutor, Panchen Chökyi Gyaltsen. The latter was the first Panchen Lama, whose spiritual lineage is recognized in Tibet as second in importance only to the lineage of the Dalai Lamas.

Successors to the ultimate Tibetan spiritual and temporal post of Dalai Lama by the end of the twentieth century number thirteen. Each of these successors has been assumed to be an incarnation of his predecessor. The process of succession thus involves the discovery of the new Dalai Lama among the newborn of the Tibetan population in every generation. There is a rich tradition describing the importance of symbols that may serve to guide the devout Tibetan religious hierarchy in the search for a new Dalai Lama.

**Key Ethical Principles Represented by the Dalai Lama.** A number of key spiritual concepts appear in the writings and sermons of the Dalai Lamas over the centuries. One of these is associated with the tradition called *lo-jong*, which is reflected in the teachings of Tenzin Gyatso, the Dalai Lama during the second half of the twentieth century. Briefly stated, *lo-jong* involves spiritual discipline as a prerequisite for "training" the mind and imbuing it with the values of prior generations of Buddhist masters. Key to the *lo-jong* tradition (among other spiritual practices of Buddhism) is the importance of meditation based on the guidance of spiritual texts to help the individual escape the influences of the external world, which impede full spiritual realization. Such realization is believed to give rise to the fullest forms of love and kindness, which, ideally, should establish themselves in human interrelationships.

**The Dilemma of the Fourteenth Dalai Lama.** Two years after his birth in 1935 in the small farming village of Taktser in the Tibetan province of Amdo, Tenzin Gyatso was identified as the incarnation of the deceased thirteenth Dalai

Lama. Already during the period of the search for the new Dalai Lama, peculiarities of the traditional guiding signs that appeared, including curious cloud formations and the growth of a giant fungus in the northeast corner of the room in which the deceased Dalai Lama lay, were thought to be harbingers of change. The discovery of Tenzin Gyatso far to the northeast of Lhasa, not to the south (traditionally deemed the most auspicious direction) was taken to be confirmation of the significance of the celestial signs.

When he reached the age of four and one-half years, the child came to Lhasa and, upon mounting the Lion Throne, assumed his responsibilities as Tibet's highest leader. For more than a decade, the young Dalai Lama's educational progress, both in traditional religious and modern subjects, seemed to prepare him for normal passage to full responsibility for his people's spiritual and temporal welfare. The events of October, 1950, however, were destined to affect this passage. The Chinese Communist invasion of Tibet forced the Dalai Lama first to attempt to maintain the basic rights of his people even under occupation, and then—in the wake of violent uprisings (1956-1959) following unsuccessful attempts to negotiate Tibet's freedom—to flee to exile in neighboring India. Following Tenzin Gyatso's departure, the Chinese regime attempted to assign religious legitimacy to his immediate subordinate in the Tibetan Buddhist hierarchy, the Panchen Lama.

A particular role was thus cast for the fourteenth Dalai Lama, who assumed a much expanded symbolic function as a world-renowned spiritual and temporal leader during the troubled second half of the twentieth century. In a sense, Tibet's plight became part of the shared cause of those who defend justice wherever individual or group repression exists. This fateful calling not only affected the Dalai Lama's writings and actions but also brought recognition of the importance of his work in the form of the 1989 Nobel Peace Prize.

**Spiritual and Ethical Principles in Tenzin Gyatso's Life.** As a spiritual leader in exile, the fourteenth Dalai Lama found himself in a position to bring the troubled case of his country to the attention of the world as a whole. His writings and speeches tend to reflect his concern that Tibet's particular problem should serve to incite awareness of the human costs of oppression of body and spirit wherever they occur. Thus, his origins as a Buddhist leader in a particular area of the world provided a frame of reference for his focus on much wider considerations. Paramount among these is the importance of cooperation, not competition or hostility, among world religions. A secondary feature is recognition that all peoples living in the modern world need to find a path that can combine spiritual values with the possibilities presented by the application of reason and scientific knowledge. It was the Dalai Lama's emphasis on such principles and the importance of using them to develop happiness and kindness that built his reputation for supporting the cause of world peace.

**Award of the 1989 Nobel Peace Prize.** The Nobel Prize committee's selection of the Dalai Lama to receive its 1989 Peace Prize provided an additional framework for this extraordinary religious leader to try to emphasize the importance of combining ethical values and the development of humanitarian politics in the world. Although his Nobel lecture reflected specific political concerns in Tibetan-Chinese relations (including a compromise plan for resolution of the state of foreign occupation of his country), the Dalai Lama drew attention to a number of other "trouble spots" around the globe. Here, his diagnosis of the origins of political conflicts, as well as his prognosis of the best means of resolving them, mirrored the content of his spiritual writings: the idea that living with an attitude of love and kindness toward other individuals is the way to connect the inner sphere of existence with the external world of different peoples and nations.

*—Byron D. Cannon*

**See also** Bodhisattva ideal; Buddha; Buddhist ethics; Four noble truths.

**BIBLIOGRAPHY**

Avedon, John F. *An Interview with the Dalai Lama*. New York: Littlebird, 1980.

Hicks, Roger, and Ngakpa Chögyam. *Great Ocean: An Authorized Biography of the Buddhist Monk Tenzin Gyatso, His Holiness the Fourteenth Dalai Lama*. London: Penguin Books, 1990.

Gyatso, Tenzin [Fourteenth Dalai Lama]. *Freedom in Exile*. New York: HarperCollins, 1990.

Mullin, Glenn H., ed. *Selected Works of the Dalai Lama I*. 2 vols. Ithaca, N.Y.: Snow Lion, 1985.

Piburn, Sidney, ed. *The Dalai Lama: A Policy of Kindness*. Ithaca, N.Y.: Snow Lion, 1990.

## Darwin, Charles Robert

(Feb. 12, 1809, Shrewsbury, Shropshire, England—Apr. 19, 1882, Downe, Kent, England): Naturalist

**TYPE OF ETHICS:** Modern history

**ACHIEVEMENTS:** Author of *On the Origin of Species by Means of Natural Selection* (1859)

**SIGNIFICANCE:** Darwin's principle of natural selection was used by others as the basis for several ethical theories

Charles Darwin's lifelong concern was with the natural origins of animals and plants. He knew that animal and plant breeders had modified domestic species by selecting desired variants as breeding stock. Nature, he argued, was always doing the same thing, practicing natural selection by allowing certain individuals to leave more offspring than others. Each species constantly produces more eggs, seeds, or offspring than can possibly survive; most individuals face an early death. Any heritable traits that confer some advantage in this "struggle for existence" are passed on to future generations; injurious traits are destroyed.

In his writings, Darwin did not address the ethical implications of his theories, leaving such speculations to others. Herbert Spencer (1820-1903), who coined the phrase "survival of the fittest," founded an ethic of unbridled competition known as Social Darwinism. American Social Darwinists favored a ruthless competition in which only the strongest would survive; several industrialists used these ideas to justify cutthroat competition, the suppression of labor unions, and a lack of concern for the welfare of workers.

*Charles Robert Darwin* (Library of Congress)

Socialists and other political dissidents drew exactly the opposite conclusion from Darwin's works. They saw evolution as a theory of "progress," of merit triumphant over established privilege, and of science triumphant over religious superstition.

Natural selection is not necessarily a guide for human conduct: What is natural is not necessarily good. Natural selection has also been used to draw ethically opposite conclusions by those with different initial premises.

**See also** Eugenics; Evolution, theory of; Malthus, Thomas; Social Darwinism.

## Death and dying

**TYPE OF ETHICS:** Beliefs and practices

**DEFINITION:** The study of the cessation of human existence in its various dimensions: physiological, psychological, spiritual, and so forth

**SIGNIFICANCE:** A precise definition of death has become crucial to such medical and moral issues as euthanasia, living wills, quality of life, abortion, organ transplantation, and cryonics

The modern study of death and dying, thanatology (named for the Greek god of death, Thanatos), could be said to have begun in 1956, when the American Psychological Association held a symposium on death at its annual convention. This resulted in the publication in 1959 of an anthology of essays on death written by scholars from a wide range of disciplines. Popular attention focused on death and dying with the publication of Elisabeth Kübler-Ross's *On Death and Dying* (1969), a study of the stages of dying.

**Biological Definition.** Historically, the definition of death has undergone a number of revisions. The earliest medical determination of death was the cessation of heart activity, respiration, and all functions consequent thereon (now commonly referred to as "clinical death"). With the advancement of respirators and other sophisticated medical equipment, however, it became possible for a patient with no brain activity to be artificially kept "alive." In 1970, Kansas became the first state to adopt a brain-based criterion for determining death in addition to the cessation-of-vital-functions definition. A number of states followed this definition, while others eliminated the traditional definition altogether and focused solely on a "brain death" model. The term "brain death" in these legal documents referred to the total and irreversible cessation of the functions of the entire brain, including both the "higher brain," which is regarded as the seat of conscious mental processes, and the "brain stem," which controls cardiopulmonary activity. This usually takes place from three to five minutes after clinical death, although the process can take much longer in cases of death by freezing or barbiturate overdose.

In 1981, the President's Commission proposed a "Uniform Determination of Death Act," which defined death as either "irreversible cessation of circulatory and respiratory functions" or "irreversible cessation of all functions of the entire brain, including the brain stem." Such a determination, it added, must be made "in accordance with accepted medical standards." This legal definition was adopted by more than half the states within the first decade after its formulation. As is evident from this formulation, rather than viewing death as an "event," it is more accurate to define death as a process encompassing at least three different types of death: clinical death (the cessation of vital signs), biological death (including the cessation of brain activity), and cellular death (including the deterioration of all of the body's cells).

**Proposed Changes.** While state legislations have employed a "whole-brain" definition of death, there have been attempts made by some states to define death in terms of the cessation of cerebral activity in the upper portion of the brain. Proponents of this position argue that an individual's "personhood" relies upon the cognitive faculties of the "higher brain." According to this definition, an individual in a "persistent vegetative state" in which only the brain stem, controlling heartbeat and respiration, is functioning would not be considered a living "person." Since no consensus can be reached regarding the proper definition of "person," however, and since reliance on cognitive awareness would exclude severely senile, mentally deficient, and anencephalic individuals from the category of "persons," a "higher-brain" definition of death has been almost universally rejected by the medical community and general public.

**Autonomy over One's Death.** The American Medical Association's position that one need not use "extraordinary means" to keep a person alive is almost universally accepted. This is commonly referred to as "passive euthanasia." ("Euthanasia" comes from the Greek phrase meaning "good death.") This position has led to the development of a "living will," which states that the individual does not want life-sustaining devices and extraordinary medical procedures used to prolong his or her life. Although the "living will" is not a binding legal document in all states, it is considered by most courts of law to be a valid expression of the signer's wishes.

A more extreme example of belief in the authority of the individual to determine his or her death can be seen in the practice of "active euthanasia." Defined as the act of directly bringing about a person's death by a means unrelated to the illness itself (for example, injection, anesthesia without oxygen, and so forth), active euthanasia is illegal in virtually all parts of the world. The practice became widespread in the 1980's in Holland, however, where one out of every five deaths of elderly patients was caused by active euthanasia.

Although the usual argument for active euthanasia cites extreme physical suffering as an acceptable reason, other justifications, including psychological distress, old age, limited mental capacity, and an unacceptable "quality of life," also have been advanced. In fact, in the latter half of the 1980's, Holland extended the practice to include Down syndrome infants and anorexic young adults. Those ethicists opposed to active euthanasia point to the danger that more and more categories of candidates would become acceptable, were it to be allowed.

**Abortion.** For many people, the debate over abortion hinges on how the fetus is to be categorized. If the fetus can be considered a human being at a particular point in its prenatal development, abortion after that point would be regarded as the unlawful taking of a human life. A precise definition of both life and death is, therefore, crucial to the issue. Some people argue that the determination of where human life begins should employ the same criteria that are used to define the absence of life, or death.

**Organ Transplantation.** Even though the first organ transplant in the United States took place in 1954, early transplants did not meet with a great deal of success, because cadaveric organs were not widely available in the 1950's and 1960's as a result of the difficulty of defining death. With the establishment of brain-based criteria for determining death and with the discovery of the immunosuppresive drug cyclosporine, organ transplantation increased dramatically in the 1980's.

In order for organs from cadavers to remain viable for transplantation, heart and respiratory functions must be sustained artificially until the procedure can be performed. This necessitates a definition of death that would allow for the artificial maintenance of vital functions.

**Cryonics.** In the late 1960's, the procedure called "cryonic suspension" was first attempted. The procedure involves freezing the human body immediately after clinical death in the hope that it can be thawed and resuscitated at a later date when a cure for the illness causing the death is available. Since the procedure depends upon freezing the body before deterioration of the brain and other organs takes place, it is crucial that death be pronounced immediately so that the procedure can begin. An additional ethical issue arose when, in the 1980's, a prominent mathematician who had been diagnosed with brain cancer was denied permission from a U.S. court to have his head removed prior to his clinical death. He had requested that his head be placed in cryonic suspension in order to halt the deterioration of his cerebral functions. —*Mara Kelly Zukowski*

**See also** Abortion; Bioethics; Euthanasia; Kevorkian, Jack; Life and death; Quinlan, Karen Ann; Right to die; Suicide.

**Bibliography**

Choron, Jacques. *Death and Western Thought*. New York: Collier, 1973.

Kübler-Ross, Elisabeth. *On Death and Dying*. New York: Macmillan, 1969.

Ladd, John, ed. *Ethical Issues Relating to Life and Death*. New York: Oxford University Press, 1979.

President's Commission for the Study of Ethical Problems in Medicine and Biomedical and Behavioral Research. *Defining Death: A Report on the Medical, Legal and Ethical Issues in the Determination of Death*. Washington, D.C.: Government Printing Office, 1981.

Veatch, Robert M. *Death, Dying, and the Biological Revolution: Our Last Quest for Responsibility*. Rev. ed. New Haven, Conn.: Yale University Press, 1989.

## Deconstruction

**Type of ethics:** Modern history

**Date:** Late 1960's through the 1980's

**Associated with:** Poststructuralism, Jacques Derrida, and the "Yale School"

**Definition:** A strategy of interpretation that reduces a text to its fundamental elements, which, when unraveled, reveal that no single essence or meaning can be determined

**Significance:** A deconstructionist believes that ethics relies upon hierarchical opposites (good/evil, man/woman) to maintain order; the problem of ethics is moving from one element to its opposite while maintaining the equality of the two

The structuralism conference at The Johns Hopkins University in 1966 was intended to introduce into the United States structuralist theory, an approach to reading in which a poem or novel is viewed as a closed entity that has specific meanings. When Jacques Derrida read his paper, "Structure, Sign, and Play in the Discourse of the Human Sciences," the demise of structuralism and the arrival of a new theory, deconstruction, was unexpectedly announced.

Deconstruction has since become the main philosophical tenet of poststructuralism, an intellectual movement that is largely a reaction to structuralism. Poststructuralism includes not only the deconstructive analyses of Derrida, who has had an enormous influence on the development of literary theory, but also the work of other French intellectuals, including the historian Michel Foucault, the feminist philosopher and critic Julie Kristeva, and the psychoanalyst Jacques Lacan.

Ferdinand Saussure, the founder of modern structuralist linguistics, saw language as a closed, stable system of signs, and this view forms much of the foundation of structuralist thought. These signs helped structuralists to arrive at a better understanding of a text, because it was thought that they offered consistent, logical representations of the order of things, or what Foucault called "a principle of unity."

Rather than attempting to understand the logical structure of things, poststructuralism, and deconstruction in particular, attempts to do much more: It attempts to understand the limits of understanding. Deconstruction is an extraordinarily complex strategy of reading that is based primarily on two presuppositions.

The first presupposition relies heavily on Saussure's notion of signs; however, Derrida argues that rather than representing the order of things, signs represent disorder, because they can never be nailed down to a single meaning. He posits that because meaning is irreducibly plural, language can never be a closed and stable system.

The second presupposition involves Derrida's observation of Western modes of thought. He noticed that "universal truths" have gone unquestioned in terms of their "rightness," and that these concepts are defined by what they exclude, their binary opposites (for example, man is defined as the opposite of the identity that constitutes woman). Derrida's strategy is to reveal the hierarchy that is inherent in these binary oppositions and to show that by meticulously examining what are believed to be the distinctions between them, in each instance the pair is found not to be opposite after all.

Although some people see Derrida as a brilliant theorist who instigated a radical reassessment of the basic concepts of Western thought, critics have argued that deconstruction's main presupposition—that one must always be resigned to the impossibility of truth because meaning is irreducibly plural—makes Derrida's theory nihilistic at worst and an elitist, bourgeois game at best.

Derrida defends deconstruction against the charge of nihilism by positing that it is necessary to suspend ethics in order to arrive at ethical understanding. He claims that ethics has emerged as a defense against violence; however, the binary oppositions established by ethics to bring about order are also a form of violence because of their imposed hierarchy. He believes that the problem of ethics involves being able to move from one term in the pair to the other while maintaining the sameness of the two rather than their inequality.

While Derrida and other theorists were defending deconstruction, revelations surfaced that Paul de Man—a member of the "Yale School," a group of deconstructionists at Yale who helped to introduce Derrida to America—had written more than one hundred articles for an anti-Semitic, pro-Nazi newspaper in Belgium during World War II. After the discovery of de Man's collaboration, a great deal of comment was generated both against deconstruction and against de Man, who died in 1984, having successfully concealed his past from his colleagues and students.

In response, Derrida stated that de Man's acts were unforgivable; however, he believed that it must be realized that these acts were committed more than half a century earlier, when de Man was in his early twenties. That argument helped ameliorate to some extent the moral problems caused by de Man's wartime activities, but it did nothing to resolve the more serious problem that occurred after the war—his lifelong secrecy about the collaboration, a serious moral contradiction for a practitioner of a theory that has as its main goal the revelation of what is excluded, or kept secret, in a text. Thus, the idea that deconstruction is nihilistic was strengthened by the revelation of de Man's collaboration. Other theorists defended deconstruction by asserting that those who adopt deconstructionist positions have various agendas, including radical feminism and other progressive movements, so that any attempt to invalidate all deconstruction because of de Man's past is unfair.

Derrida has also had numerous well-publicized disagreements about deconstruction with Michel Foucault. Their conflict centered on Derrida's efforts to deconstruct texts in order to set free hidden possibilities and Foucault's attempts to experience history to reveal its latent structures. It is in these public disagreements that Foucault, whose writings centered on history and language and had nothing to do with deconstruction, has dramatically influenced poststructuralist theory. Much has been written about the disagreements, and most of these writings attempt either to reconcile or to choose between the writings of these two intellectuals.

Both opponents and proponents of deconstruction agree that while Derrida is radically subversive, his attack on Western notions of truth and reason does not lead to utter meaninglessness. Because of Derrida's influence, deconstruction has expanded the range of literary theory and has led to a much deeper questioning of the assumed naturalness of structure in systems of thought. Derrida's work shows that by unraveling key binary oppositions of the Western tradition, one may eventually uncover more important things that are just beyond the limits of ordinary understanding.

—*Jill S. Marts*

**See also** Derrida, Jacques; Foucault, Michel.

**BIBLIOGRAPHY**

Boyne, Roy. *Foucault and Derrida: The Other Side of Reason.* London: Unwin Hyman, 1990.

Con Davis, Robert, and Ronald Schleifer, eds. *Contemporary Literary Criticism.* 2d ed. N.Y.: Longman, 1989.

Darby, Tom, Bela Egyed, and Ben Jones, eds. *Nietzsche and the Rhetoric of Nihilism: Essays on Interpretation, Language and Politics.* Ottawa: Carleton University Press, 1989.

Eagleton, Terry. *Literary Theory: An Introduction.* Minneapolis: University of Minnesota Press, 1983.

Sallis, John, ed. *Deconstruction and Philosophy: The Texts of Jacques Derrida.* Chicago: University of Chicago Press, 1987.

Wiener, Jon. "Deconstructing de Man." *The Nation* 246 (January 9, 1988): 22-24.

## Deforestation

**TYPE OF ETHICS:** Environmental ethics

**DATE:** 1975

**ASSOCIATED WITH:** The United Nations, the Earth Summit, and the Green movement

**DEFINITION:** Deforestation is the destruction of timber and of forest ecosystems, either by direct exploitation or as an indirect result of human activities; as an issue in environmental ethics, it is usually considered on a national and international scale

**SIGNIFICANCE:** Humans are dependent on forests as a source of natural resources and have a deep, one might say archetypal, psychological and aesthetic link to the forest environment; forests are essential to the environmental health of the earth, and their rapid depletion is an ecological crisis of the first magnitude

Humankind's conquest of nature is an extremely dangerous victory. Until very recently, the "forest primeval" was regarded with awe, and the vast virgin forests of Siberia, northern and western North America, Southeast Asia, and the Amazon basin were considered to be inexhaustible, despite historical experience in Europe and the Mediterranean region.

Pressures from a logarithmically expanding population and simultaneously increasing per capita development rates fueled by new technologies led to explosive increases in deforestation in the years 1970 to 1990, leading to concern that the trend was irreversible and that global climatic changes would result. Massive deforestation increases the aridity of a region and contributes to the greenhouse effect by releasing stored carbon dioxide. When a forest is converted to agricultural land, supplies of fuel and lumber diminish, and biological diversity decreases. Of particular concern is degradation caused by improper management and general environmental deterioration; many cut areas seem destined neither to regenerate into healthy forests nor to provide quality agricultural land, but to become scrub and poor rangeland, subject to erosion and desertification.

The issue of deforestation was debated at length at the United Nations Earth Summit in Rio de Janeiro in 1992, but no binding protocols resulted because representatives of nations with extensive tropical forests, especially in Southeast Asia, wanted to preserve maximum exploitation rights. Third World nations understandably resent pressures to institute policies that hamper their own development and see themselves as being asked to sacrifice to compensate for past profligacy in the developed world. Aid from developed nations is critical to fostering ecologically sound forestry in the tropics. The rate of deforestation in the Amazon basin declined significantly between 1989 and 1992, but this may be the result of a poor global economy rather than of ecological policy.

**AVERAGE ANNUAL DEFORESTATION OF THE AMAZON RAINFOREST: 1850-1990**

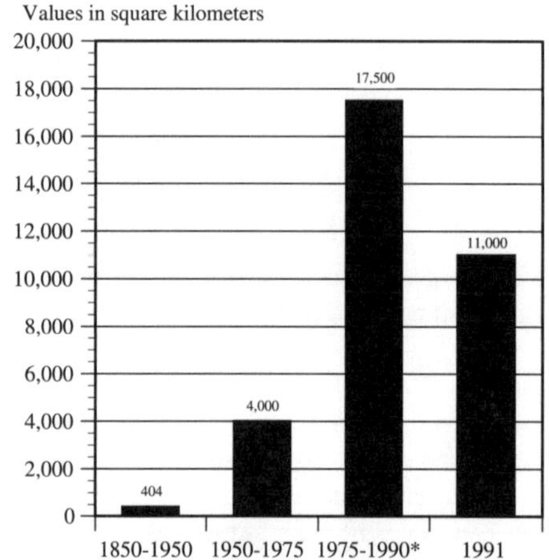


* The total area deforested in 1990 has been estimated at 404,000 square kilometers, or 10.9 percent of the Amazon region

**See also** Biodiversity; Conservation; Earth, human relations to; Greenhouse effect; Rain forests.

## Deism

**TYPE OF ETHICS:** Beliefs and practices

**DATE:** Coined sixteenth century

**ASSOCIATED WITH:** English philosopher and diplomat Herbert of Cherbury

**DEFINITION:** The belief that on the basis of reason and "natural religion," one can establish the existence of an intelligent and ethical supreme being, the creator and preserver of the universe

**SIGNIFICANCE:** Deism represents the deliberate attempt in the sixteenth, seventeenth, and eighteenth centuries to establish a nonsectarian basis for a theistic, rational morality

In the wake of the sectarian strife that swept Europe in the seventeenth century, there was a desire to find a rational and theistic basis for moral behavior that did not rest on the particular confession of any organized religious tradition, be it Protestant, Catholic, Orthodox, Jewish, Muslim, Buddhist, Hindu, Confucian, or Taoist. The father of deism was Lord Herbert of Cherbury (1583-1648), an English statesman and philosopher who had observed the horrors of religious war both in Britain and on the Continent. Because of the failure to arrive at a consensus regarding Christian ethics, he believed that a natural rather than a revealed religion could furnish the basis of civilized behavior. Taking the word "deism" (from *deus,* Latin for "god"), a term already in use, Lord Herbert taught, in such books as *On Truth* (1624), *On the Religion of Laymen* (1645), and *On the Religion of Gentiles* (1663), that such "self-evident truths" as the existence of a supreme being, who merits human worship and who is best served by moral action, should be sufficient religion for a modern person. In doing so, he forged a spiritual and theistic foundation for morality.

**See also** Enlightenment ethics; God; Humanism.

## Democracy

**TYPE OF ETHICS:** Politico-economic ethics

**DATE:** Emerging after c. 750 B.C.E.

**ASSOCIATED WITH:** The Greek polis (Athens), the Roman Republic, the democratic revolutions of the eighteenth century, and modern systems of self-government

**DEFINITION:** Rule by the people

**SIGNIFICANCE:** The idea of democracy is that people have the right and the ability to govern themselves; democracy recognizes the principle of intrinsic or basic human equality

The ideal of democracy is perhaps the most powerful force in politics since the seventeenth century. In fact, democracy can be traced all the way to the sixth century B.C.E., although the question of the efficiency and legitimacy of democracy has primarily been a modern issue. The irony of democracy has always been its elusiveness. Democracy means rule by the people, but that phrase has meant many different things and has been used as both a force for liberation and a cloak to legitimize tyranny. Ironically, few modern authoritarian regimes have neglected to claim that they rule in the name of the people.

**History.** The word "democracy" comes from the Greek word *d mokratia*, meaning "rule by the people." The Greek ideal, originating with the polis of Athens, was that only democracy and rule of law preserved human dignity. Athenians believed that citizens had both the responsibility and the ability to govern themselves. Self-governance preserved human agency and creativity in a way that was impossible for monarchy and dictatorship. Only when engaged in politics could a citizen be free from necessity and self-interest. Democracy and political action freed one to pursue the common good and immortal acts. As citizens within the polis, all were inherently equal. These core beliefs of responsibility, creativity, equality, and dignity are the foundation of democratic ethics.

Greek democracy is often criticized for being exclusive, yet after 500 B.C.E., citizenship in Athens was extended to all adult male citizens. Participation in the Assembly was open and membership in the Council of Five Hundred was chosen annually by lot, as were many positions in public service. Citizen participation was high, and the decision rules emphasized direct democracy. Wealth was no bar to citizen participation. In this environment, the values of democracy and of participation as the source of human dignity were established for the millennia.

**Modern Developments.** Much that had been taken from the Greeks was preserved in the Roman Republic. From the Romans, the world inherited a great legacy according to which law and human rights are inextricably linked by natural law. This idea was repeated in the American *Declaration of Independence* (1776) and in the French *Declaration of the Rights of Man* (1789). These documents demonstrated an evolving sense that citizen self-government is a right of all people that provides the greatest opportunity for human dignity. The source of this ideal is the belief in human equality.

Modern democracy is born of the democratic revolutions against European feudalism in the eighteenth century. The ideas of the social contract, found in the works of John Locke, Jean-Jacques Rousseau, and others, were lashed together with liberalism to ignite a democratic explosion in America and beyond. The consistent theme in these democratic revolutions was the belief in a natural human equality. This ideal did not originally include women and slaves or those without property, but the idea had a momentum that gradually expanded the rights and powers of citizen participation.

**Conflicts and Principles.** The ideas of liberal philosophy and the social contract theory of the Enlightenment imparted several themes. Social contract theory argued that the only legitimate government was one that was based on the consent of the governed. This denied the legitimacy of theocratic or personalist regimes. Liberalism, with its link to free-market capitalism, argued that all people were inherently equal and must have the opportunity to participate without regard to birthright. This attack on the prerogatives of feudalism hinged on the notion that freedom of choice and competition would make for social progress.

In liberal capitalism, equality is based on human value and requires only an equal opportunity to participate. Included herein were the ideas of inalienable rights, civil liberties, and freedoms espoused by modern democracies. It was not long before critics of the the liberal paradigm, in the wake of the pain of the Industrial Revolution, argued that this idea of equality was false. Competiton is not "equal" if those who are born poor and excluded do not enjoy either equality or the fruits of democracy. Associated with the ideas of socialism and Karl Marx, this critique of liberal capitalism argued that all societies in history are dominated by economic classes. According to this critique, capitalist democracy is only another form of class domination, and the liberal façade only masks the dictatorship of the capitalists.

Several streams of thought concerning democratic values and equality emerged. In the liberal capitalist idea, democracy was a direct outgrowth of the capitalist free market. For the socialist, democracy could be obtained only in a classless society that guaranteed not only equal opportunity but also material equality. All states rule in the name of a dominant class. Until social classes vanished, true democracy could not exist. To this may be added the anarchist vision that argued that all forms of government create hierarchies of power. For the anarchist, the only meaningful democracy is one founded in small communities based on direct democracy.

**General Outline**. Modern democracy has several key elements. In it, citizen participation in decision making always exists in some form. This usually includes a system of representation, which is necessary in large, complex nation-states. Representation must be the result of an open contest and pluralist setting. Democracies accept the rule of law, at least in the sense that the rule of a despot or a dictatorship is unacceptable. Governors and governed must submit to the same laws. An electoral system based on majority rule is usually present, and universal suffrage of all citizens is strongly featured. Some form of citizen equality must be present, and liberties and freedoms, recognized as rights and granted by the state, must exist to allow open participation, association, and expression. Significantly, there will be some kind of political education about democratic principles and responsibilities. Democratic polities must be educated polities if democracy is to be meaningful. To participate, citizens must understand rules, issues, and their own responsibility to the common good.

*Democracy in action: an early twentieth century political convention in the United States.* (Library of Congress)

The ethics of democracy go beyond the structure of governments. Equality, creativity, dignity, and the free space for political discourse that allows human beings to be free from self-interest and to make an immortal imprint on history—these are the immutable and elusive values of democracy.

*—Anthony R. Brunello*

**See also** Aristotle; *On Liberty*; Political liberty; Rousseau, Jean-Jacques.

**BIBLIOGRAPHY**

Almond, Gabriel A., and Sidney Verba. *The Civic Culture: Political Attitudes and Democracy in Five Nations*. Newbury Park, Calif.: Sage Publications, 1989.

Arendt, Hannah. *The Human Condition*. Chicago: The University of Chicago Press, 1958.

Aristotle. *The Politics of Aristotle*. Edited and translated by Ernest Barker. London: Oxford University Press, 1958.

Lincoln, Abraham. *The Gettysburg Address*. Los Angeles: G. Dawson, 1961.

Mill, John Stuart. *On Liberty*. New York: Macmillan, 1947.

## Deontological ethics

**TYPE OF ETHICS:** Theory of ethics

**DATE:** Eighteenth century to present

**ASSOCIATED WITH:** Philosophers such as Immanuel Kant, W. D. Ross, and John Rawls

**DEFINITION:** Considers actions to be intrinsically right or wrong, regardless of their consequences

**SIGNIFICANCE:** Represents one of the two major categories of modern ethical theory

Modern ethical theories can be divided into two broad categories: deontological and teleological, the ethics of duty and obligation versus the ethics of ends and consequences. In order to understand properly the nature of deontological theories, it is necessary to understand the essential features of teleological theories. A teleological theory gives the good priority over the right. The good is defined as the end or purpose of human actions; for example, "the greatest happiness for the greatest number." These theories evaluate moral actions in terms of whether they contribute to the good. For example, does one's action maximize happiness for the greatest number? If so, it is the right thing to do. In other words, the right is adjectival to the good and completely dependent upon it. Thus, according to teleological theories such as consequentialism, consequences or results determine the rightness or wrongness of moral actions.

Deontological theories, however, argue for the priority of the right over the good or the independence of the right from the good. Actions are *intrinsically* right or wrong, regardless of the consequences that they produce. The right or ethically appropriate action might be deduced from a duty or a basic human right, but it is never contingent upon the outcome or consequences of an action. In short, according to this perspective, actions do have intrinsic moral value.

The term "deontological" is derived from the Greek word *deon,* which means obligation or duty. Hence, deontological approaches to morality stress what is obligatory, what one ought to do, but with no reference at all to value or a conception of goodness.

An important distinction is generally made between act-deontological and rule-deontological theories. Act deontologists claim that moral judgments expressing obligations must be specific; for example, "In this situation I must not break my promise." They do not accept general obligations or rules such as "we must always keep promises." According to the act deontologist, one cannot generalize about obligations but must derive and formulate them in the context of particular circumstances. This view of ethics is expressed in the writings of the contemporary ethicist Edgar F. Carritt (1876-1964), such as his *Theory of Morals* (1928).

A more common approach is known as rule deontology. Rule deontologists maintain that morality consists of general rules that are usually expressed as duties or obligations. Such duties are fundamental and do not depend on the concrete circumstances of a particular situation. According to this viewpoint, one deduces one's particular obligation from a general rule or duty. The divine command theory, contractarianism or rights-based ethics, ethical intuitionism, and Kantianism represent some examples of rule deontology. The divine command theory, for example, argues that whatever God commands is right or obligatory. Thus, the rules of ethics might be the Ten Commandments or other divine commands revealed by God. Despite the appeal of this theory, it is considered problematic by ethicists for one basic reason: To interpret morality as something that depends on the will of another, including an infinite God, seems to undermine the autonomy of morality.

The most prominent deontological thinker is undoubtedly Immanuel Kant (1724-1804). According to Kant, an action's moral worth is not found in what it tries to accomplish but in the agent's intention and the summoning of one's energies to carry out that intention. Results, purposes, and consequences are excluded from Kant's moral philosophy, and this is obviously in direct contrast to consequentialism and teleological approaches to ethics. The moral person must perform actions for the sake of duty regardless of the consequences, but what is the duty of the rational moral agent? According to Kant, one's moral duty is simple and singular: to follow the moral law that is expressed in the categorical imperative—always act according to a maxim that is at the same time valid as a universal moral law. In other words, can the action in question (such as breaking a promise) pass the test of universalization? If not, the action is immoral and one has a duty to avoid it.

Ethical intuitionism is a related deontological theory developed by W. D. Ross (1877-1940). Ross claims that through reflection on ordinary moral beliefs, people can *intuit* the rules of morality. These rules are duties such as "one ought to keep promises and tell the truth." They are prima facie obligations, which means that they do allow for exceptions; however, one of these basic duties can be superseded only by a more important, higher obligation, usually only under very exceptional circumstances. Thus, a moral principle or prima facie duty can be sacrificed, but only for another moral principle. As with Kant, so with Ross; one is obliged to follow one's moral duty regardless of the consequences.

Finally, contractarianism (rights-based ethical theories) represents another species of deontological ethical reasoning. For example, in *A Theory of Justice* (1971), the contemporary philosopher John Rawls contends that the principle of justice as fairness is prior to the conception of goodness and must also limit that conception. According to Rawls's framework, a just society is one that requires "equality in the assignment of basic rights and duties." It is important to appreciate that in Rawls's view, it is the fairness of society's norms or rules, not their consequences, that gives those norms any genuine moral force.

Despite their differences, all these theories have in common the basic premise that the right is prior to the good and that beneficial results do not determine one's moral duty. They emphasize fidelity to principle and the independence of rightness, which is the main focus of the moral life.

—*Richard A. Spinello*

**See also** Divine command theory; Justice; Kant, Immanuel; Rawls, John; Teleological ethics.

**Bibliography**

Brandt, Richard B. *A Theory of the Good and the Right.* New York: Oxford University Press, 1979.

Frankena, William K. *Ethics.* 2d ed. Englewood Cliffs, N.J.: Prentice-Hall, 1973.

Kant, Immanuel. *Foundations of the Metaphysics of Morals* and *What Is Enlightenment.* Translated by Lewis W. Beck. London: Collier Macmillan, 1990.

Rawls, John. *A Theory of Justice.* Cambridge, Mass.: Harvard University Press, 1971.

Ross, W. D. *The Right and the Good.* Indianapolis: Hackett, 1988.

## Derrida, Jacques

(b. July 15, 1930, El Biar, Algeria): Philosopher

**Type of ethics:** Modern history

**Achievements:** Author of *L'Écriture et la différence* (1967; *Writing and Difference*, 1978) and *De la grammatologie* (1967; *Of Grammatology*, 1976)

**Significance:** Forced a reexamination of the nature of reality and absolute truths

Derrida, known for theories of literary criticism as well as for statements concerning the nature of reality, is one of the most prominent and controversial philosophers of the second half of the twentieth century. Much of Derrida's theory of philosophy and ethics is an attack on structuralism. Structuralism says that meaning is produced by applying systems of rules based on the relationships of things and concepts to one another. A 1966 conference at The Johns Hopkins University was intended to introduce structuralism to the United States; Derrida's paper instead announced the demise of structuralism and the advent of what he called "deconstruction."

Deconstruction suggests that words do not represent real things but instead are only references to other words. The interpretation of writing therefore can become an infinite process of tracing each reference to another, with texts having no single interpretation. Derrida's idea that there is no absolute truth presented in writing forced a reevaluation of ideas such as truth and consciousness. Derrida has argued that things cannot be perceived as their "true" selves because people have no direct sensory contact with them; things are always perceived as interpretations.

Derrida's ideas led to the reevaluation of legal studies and theology, among other areas. Critics attack his philosophy as abandoning traditional ideas without providing alternatives. He answers that metaphysics seeks final answers that cannot be found; therefore he does not have to provide an alternative.

**See also** Deconstruction; Metaethics; Transcendentalism; Universalizability.

## Descartes, René

(Mar. 31, 1596, La Haye, Touraine, France—Feb. 11, 1650, Stockholm, Sweden): Philosopher

**Type of ethics:** Renaissance and Restoration history

**Achievements:** One of the key founders of the modern scientific method; discovered coordinate geometry

**Significance:** Shifted the focus of philosophy from metaphysics toward the human self, preparing the way for the increased interest in ethics and human behavior that is typical of modern thought

Descartes was educated at the Jesuit College of La Flèche. In his influential works *Discours de la méthode* (1637; *Discourse on Method*, 1649) and *Meditationes de Prima Philosophia*

*René Descartes* (Library of Congress)

(1641; *Meditations on First Philosophy*, 1680), Descartes moved toward epistemology, questioning what a person can know. This move was accompanied by a particular method that proceeded by systematically doubting everything that could be doubted. Only an "unshakable foundation" that was absolutely impregnable to doubt could serve as a reliable basis for a system of knowledge.

Descartes believed that he had found this foundation in the formulation *cogito ergo sum*—"I think, therefore I am." Consciousness of one's own existence appeared to be a certainty that could not be doubted. The rest of his system proceeds from this initial certainty.

The Cartesian method, which aims to take nothing for granted and assumes that truth is to be defined in terms of certainty and mathematical clarity, presented ground rules of scientific inquiry that are still used.

Descartes' dualism, which divides reality into two categories of things—human consciousness, defined as "thinking things" (*res cogitans*), and all matter, defined as "place-filling things" (*res extensa*)—played a central role in founding the modern perception of human beings as "subjects" and things as "objects."

**See also** Christian ethics; Epistemological ethics; Stoic ethics.

## Desire

**TYPE OF ETHICS:** Personal and social ethics

**DATE:** Fourth century B.C.E. to present

**ASSOCIATED WITH:** Ancient Greek philosophers, especially Plato and Aristotle, and contemporary intentionalist action theory

**DEFINITION:** Wanting; positive psychological inclination toward possession of an object or achievement of a state of affairs; also (especially in the plural) particular desired objects or ends

**SIGNIFICANCE:** Motivates action; determines moral responsibility and the goal states for practical reasoning by specifying what an agent intends to do and why; particular desires can be morally praiseworthy or blameworthy

To desire something is to want it. Desire motivates action and directs an agent toward an intended object or state of affairs that the agent wishes to possess or bring about. It provides a reason to act and a structure by means of which connected series of actions can be ordered in means-ends relations to explain and sometimes justify why an agent behaves in a certain way. The desires that move persons to act are often essential to the moral evaluation of their actions.

**History.** The history of desire begins with prehuman animal wants and motivations. Desire features in the explanation of action from the time of the earliest Greek philosophy. Eros and Aphrodite (Venus), gods of love and desire, epitomize the inclination to possess or achieve desired objects. In ancient poetry and philosophy, Aphrodite in particular is frequently appealed to as the force that moves the cosmos.

In Plato's *Symposium*, Socrates presents the view that the search for knowledge and moral perfection begins with an attraction to and desire for physical beauty that leads to more intellectual desires. Philosophy itself is love of or desire for knowledge, from which Socrates concludes that the gods are not philosophers, since they already possess complete knowledge and cannot desire what they already have. In the *Nicomachean Ethics*, Aristotle maintains that all persons act out of the desire to achieve happiness, by which he means a good life in fulfillment of human purpose. This idea provides a foundational theory of moral action, according to which all actions are undertaken for the sake of accomplishing an end and all ends can be ordered in a hierarchy of ends, each of which contributes as a means to another end, terminating finally in the desire for happiness as the ultimate end.

Contemporary philosophy in the intentionalist tradition similarly emphasizes wants and desires in understanding what an agent intends to do, in order to explain and morally justify or condemn the agent's actions. Robert Audi, Roderick M. Chisholm, Donald Davidson, Joseph Margolis, and Richard Taylor are among recent philosophers who have developed theories of morally responsible action based on the intentional concepts of wanting or desire. They hold that desire is the intentional component of action in the same way that belief is the intentional component of knowledge.

**Explanation and Moral Evaluation.** An action is undertaken to satisfy a desire. Desires determine action goals, motivate, and give agents a reason to act. The agent wants to do something and may be aware of the desire that motivates the act. To explain a particular action according to this theory, it is necessary to identify the desire an agent tries to satisfy. Psychoanalysis presupposes that persons act out of subconscious as well as conscious desires, so that even seemingly meaningless actions for which the agent can give no explanation may also be driven by hidden desires or wants. Even if that assumption is not true, it is plausible to characterize all action as being motivated by desire. The simplest action of moving a finger for no other purpose is at least the result of a desire to move a finger. The fact that actions appear to be unexplained unless or until a desire is identified as an end for which action is the means of satisfaction supports the intentionalist theory that desire motivates action.

Desires can be good, bad, or indifferent, according to various moral outlooks and theories. Moral philosophies can often be distinguished and categorized on the basis of their attitudes toward desires and the kinds of desires they encourage, permit, or forbid. Ordinarily, it is regarded as wrong or morally blameworthy to desire that innocent persons suffer or that evil triumph over good, while it may be right or morally praiseworthy to desire the greatest possible happiness for all persons. Particular moral systems postulate that certain kinds of desires are intrinsically ethically right or wrong. Sometimes the desire for worldly things, especially when it involves the appetites, is considered wrong. The extreme form of this moral attitude is asceticism, in which ethical conduct is made synonymous with resisting temptations, exercising self-control, and renouncing bodily desires. More abstract or universal desires that are in accord with preferred moral principles, such as the desire for peace and mutual respect of persons, are usually judged to be intrinsically good.

**Conflicting Desires.** If Aristotle is right about the common hierarchy of purposes that has happiness as its ultimate end, then all other desires, even as proximate ends or purposes of other actions, are related as means to that single end. This idea implies that desires are in some sense mutually consistent and compatible. Yet there appear to be conflicts of desires that cannot be jointly satisfied, as is the case when a conscientious objector desires to obey both conscience and the law. Conflicts of this kind are often interpreted as moral dilemmas. Intentionalist action theory is divided over the question of whether Aristotle's foundational hierarchy of means and ends terminating in a single end is correct or whether the more appropriate model of desires involves many different shorter chains of actions as means to desires as ends that do not contribute to a single purpose but may either cohere or conflict with one another.

*—Dale Jacquette*

**See also** Aristotle; Asceticism; Dilemmas, moral; Intention; Intrinsic good; Means/ends distinction; Passions and emotions; Plato; Responsibility; Self-control; Temptation.

**Bibliography**

Audi, Robert. *Practical Reasoning*. London: Routledge, 1989.

Chisholm, Roderick M. *Person and Object: A Metaphysical Study*. London: Allen & Unwin, 1976.

Davidson, Donald. *Essays on Actions and Events*. Oxford, England: Clarendon Press, 1980.

Loar, Brian. *Mind and Meaning*. Cambridge, England: Cambridge University Press, 1981.

McGinn, Colin. *Mental Content*. Oxford, England: Basil Blackwell, 1989.

Margolis, Joseph. *Philosophy of Psychology*. Englewood Cliffs: N.J.: Prentice Hall, 1984.

Taylor, Richard. *Action and Purpose*. Englewood Cliffs: N.J.: Prentice Hall, 1966.

Thorndike, Edward Lee. *The Psychology of Wants, Interests, and Attitudes*. New York: Appleton-Century, 1935.

## Determinism and freedom

**Type of ethics:** Theory of ethics

**Dates:** Expressed in third millenium B.C.E. by Sumerians; question of possible conflict between being determined and being free explored in fifth century B.C.E. Greek tragedies such as *Oedipus Rex*

**Associated with:** Aristotle, Saint Augustine, Thomas Hobbes, John Locke, David Hume, Clarence Darrow, Paul Edwards, and C. A. Campbell

**Definition:** Determinism is the view that everything has a cause; a person is free when he or she decides how to act and acts on the basis of that decision

**Significance:** Some philosophers believe that determinism would rule out freedom and that without freedom people could not be morally responsible—that is, blameworthy or praiseworthy—for their actions

Compatibilism is the view that determinism is compatible with freedom and moral responsibility. Incompatibilism is the view that determinism is incompatible with freedom and moral responsibility. Libertarianism and hard determinism are the major varieties of incompatibilism. Libertarians claim that determinism is false and that people are free and morally responsible. In contrast, hard determinists claim that because determinism is true, people are neither free nor morally responsible.

A major argument for hard determinism goes as follows. "Everything one does is causally determined, and therefore no one can ever act otherwise than he or she does. That being the case, no one ever acts freely, and without freedom, no one is ever morally responsible for what he or she does."

It may be tempting to reject hard determinism because it is a socially dangerous view, providing as it does a wholesale excuse for any wrongdoing. This response, however, is irrelevant, since it is clear that a view can be socially dangerous and can still be true.

Agreeing that determinism would rule out freedom, libertarians reject the hard determinist argument by claiming that there is good introspective evidence for freedom and against determinism. They argue that the belief in freedom is justified by a feeling of freedom, a feeling of not being causally determined, when making moral decisions. While all people may have a feeling of some kind of freedom in these cases, for many it is not a feeling of libertarian "contracausal" freedom. Instead, one has a feeling of being able to choose as one wants, not a feeling of not being caused. Moreover, even if one does have a feeling of libertarian freedom, such feelings can be misleading. A person acting under posthypnotic suggestion may also have such a feeling. The feeling of being contracausally free does not seem to be a reliable basis for rejecting the hard determinist argument.

Even if libertarians can provide good evidence that people are contracausally free, they still need to explain why contracausal choices are not merely matters of pure chance. Libertarians try to account for contracausal choices by appealing to reasons that do not cause people to choose as they do. The view that reasons are not causes, however, seems less plausible than the view that reasons are causes. The latter view makes better sense of the relationship between reasons and actions and makes it clear how to distinguish one's real reason for acting from other reasons for acting. If neither noncausing reasons nor causes explain contracausal choices, such choices would seem to be pure matters of chance. If that is the case, it is difficult to see how people could be morally responsible for their choices.

Compatibilists maintain that the hard determinist argument is based on misunderstandings of key terms and phrases, such as "freely," "caused," and "could have done otherwise." Many compatibilists claim that acting freely is a matter of acting as one pleases, instead of acting without being caused to do so. They point out that acting as one pleases does not conflict with one's being causally determined to act as one does. Believing that freedom also requires the capacity to do otherwise, they attack the hard determinist argument by claiming that determinism would not rule out this capacity.

Many compatibilists claim that hard determinists are misled by a faulty theory of causality. Hard determinists think of causality in terms of necessitation, when in fact causality is nothing more than one type of event being regularly followed by another type of event. In this regularity view, causal laws do not prescribe what must happen; they describe only what does happen. Compatibilists maintain that since causes do not necessitate, being causally determined to act in a certain way does not rule out the capacity to act otherwise; therefore, the hard determinist argument fails.

The regularity theory is itself problematic. According to it, there are causal relations between types of events only because people live in a world in which these types of events happen to be constantly conjoined. Causal relations seem, however, to involve more than this. It seems incredible that arm wrestling is nothing more than one person's exertion that *simply is* followed by another person's arm going down. If one's arm goes down *because* of the force exerted against it, the regularity theory seems implausible.

Without relying on the regularity theory, other compatibilists still maintain that determinism would not rule out one's capacity to do otherwise. They analyze the phrase "He could have done otherwise" as "He would have done otherwise had he so chosen" and then point out that one's being causally determined to do something does not mean that one would not have done something else if one had so chosen.

This hypothetical sense of "could have," however, does not seem to be the one that is important for freedom. Consider a man who has no control over his choices, since he has been drugged and hypnotized. The reason that he does not act freely in this case is that he could not do anything else. He could have done otherwise, however, in the sense that he would have done otherwise if he had so chosen.

Compatibilist senses of "could have," such as "not having a dispositional property that rules out alternatives," may fare better. In any case, compatibilist accounts of freedom should take into account not only the ability to *do* otherwise but also the ability to *choose* otherwise. —*Gregory P. Rich*

**See also** Moral responsibility.

**BIBLIOGRAPHY**

Berofsky, Bernard, ed. *Free Will and Determinism*. New York: Harper & Row, 1966.

Hook, Sidney, ed. *Determinism and Freedom in the Age of Modern Science*. New York: Collier Book, 1961.

Morgenbesser, Sidney, and James Walsh, ed. *Free Will*. Englewood Cliffs, N.J.: Prentice-Hall, 1962.

Van Inwagen, Peter. *An Essay on Free Will*. New York: Oxford University Press, 1983.

Watson, Gary, ed. *Free Will*. New York: Oxford University Press, 1982.

## Deterrence

**TYPE OF ETHICS:** Military ethics

**DATE:** Coined 1950's

**ASSOCIATED WITH:** The Cold War

**DEFINITION:** A situation in which conflict is contained within a boundary of threats that are neither executed nor tested

**SIGNIFICANCE:** Raises the moral question of whether the means (the possibility of massive destruction) justifies the end (the maintenance of international peace)

Nuclear deterrence was conceived as preventing the use of nuclear weapons by others by assuring a second-strike capability that was capable of inflicting considerable damage on the aggressor. This concept replaced the traditional balance-of-power system of the conventional arms age, ushering in the balance-of-terror age of nuclear technology. While some will argue that it is instrumental in avoiding nuclear war and therefore helps to maintain international peace, others see it as a morally bankrupt policy. In a deterrence scenario, each party is constrained to see the other as a potential inflicter of harm, a scenario that encourages a mutual permanent state of distrust. Although there is a consensus regarding the moral importance of defending oneself against external aggression, where nuclear deterrence is concerned, there is more skepticism regarding the moral character of the means by which this is to be achieved. Perhaps what makes this concept so ethically controversial is the paradox it embodies: As one informed observer put it, people threaten evil in order not to do it, and the doing of it will be so terrible that the threat seems in comparison to be morally defensible.

**See also** Cold War; Mutually assured destruction (MAD); Research, weapons.

## Dewey, John (Oct. 20, 1859, Burlington, Vt.—June 1, 1952, New York, N.Y.): Philosopher

**TYPE OF ETHICS:** Modern history

**ACHIEVEMENTS:** Author of *Outlines of a Critical Theory of Ethics* (1891), *The Study of Ethics: A Syllabus* (1894), "Theory of the Moral Life" (1908, 1932), *Human Nature and Conduct* (1922), and *Theory of Valuation* (1939)

**SIGNIFICANCE:** The leading progressive ethicist of the twentieth century, Dewey used his studies of philosophy and psychology to develop a theory of ethics in which human moral development resulted from active engagement with a fluid environment

Dewey attacked traditional ethical theories. His objection to these theories (absolute idealism's categorical imperative and "will of the absolute," Herbert Spencer's Social Darwinism, and Jeremy Bentham's utilitarianism) was that they posited the existence of an absolute moral code independent from and knowable in advance of human interaction with an ever-changing environment. Dewey's ethical theory, "instrumentalism," was grounded in a progressivist prescription for participatory democratic decision making. His views on the normative and prescriptive requirements of ethical theory remain strongly influential.

**The Reflex Arc Concept.** Dewey came to believe that human experience was not shaped by the dualisms of traditional philosophy: mind and body, idea and sensation. Experience, Dewey wrote in "The Reflex Arc Concept in Psychology" (1896), was not "a patchwork of disjointed parts"; it was a "comprehensive, organic unity." The reflex arc concept, Dewey reasoned, required a model of stimulus and response in which both were "divisions of labor, functioning factors within the single concrete whole" rather than "disconnected existences." Humans functioned in this "unity of activity," or experience, unconsciously. Only with an interruption of coordinated, continuous experiencing, Dewey argued, did individuals need to become mindful of the reflex arc of stimulus, response, and intervening psychical event in order to resolve interrupted experiencing. Dewey's view of experience was to shape profoundly his theory of ethics.

*John Dewey* (Library of Congress)

For Dewey, components of the reflex arc, or circuit, did not consist of disassociated separate categories of stimulus and response in which sensory input (stimulus) is viewed as occurring chronologically prior to the event of muscular discharge (motor response), for example, with attention, awareness, or idea emerging as a central activity or intervening psychical event. Rather than being considered as distinctive partitions of experience, reminiscent of earlier formulations of body-mind dualism, the stimulus and response components of the reflex arc of human behavior required a conceptual shift in Dewey's view. He argued that stimulus and response are not distinctive entities, categories of human behavior used to describe sequential neural or physical events; they are integrative divisions of labor that are interrelated with the psychical component of the reflex arc to form an inclusive holism of human behavior. The psychical event, the attention given to maintenance or restoration of ongoing experiencing or human activity, Dewey described as mediation in *The Study of Ethics: A Syllabus* (1894), as intelligence in *Human Nature and Conduct* (1922), and as exploration for reasonable decision in the *Theory of Valuation* (1939).

**Theory of the Moral Life.** While Dewey noted his discontent with absolutist moral codes in *Outlines of a Critical Theory of Ethics* (1891) and utilized *The Study of Ethics: A Syllabus* (1894) to discuss "psychological ethics"—that is, the individual's conduct and its relation to moral experience—his theory of the moral life appeared originally with the publication of *Ethics* (1908), which included "Theory of the Moral Life." Stipulating that moral action was voluntary conduct, "activity called forth and directed by ideas of value or worth," Dewey argued that the moral life consisted of the individual's pursuit of self-realization through development of a democratic character. For Dewey, the challenge of moral life was, as he put it, "the formation, out of the body of original instinctive impulses which compose the natural self, of a voluntary self in which socialized desires and affections are dominant." For Dewey, humans were preeminently social beings; the moral person was one who transformed desires of the self into sympathetic regard for the common good. This view of a constructed rather than a received moral life permeates Dewey's later writing on ethical theory.

**Human Nature and Conduct.** *Human Nature and Conduct* (1922), subtitled *An Introduction to Social Psychology,* was Dewey's critique of behaviorist and psychoanalytic explanations of human behavior. Both explanations were reductionist, Dewey assumed: Freudian psychoanalysis restricted causation of human behavior to sexual impulses, a term Dewey preferred to "instincts"; behaviorists, to a simplistic map of stimulus and response. Defining "habit" as "special sensitiveness or accessibility to certain classes of stimuli, standing predilections and adversions," not mere recurring actions, Dewey reasoned that in a democratic society such as the United States ethical decisions should result only from the practice of habitual deliberation, not from "routine, unintelligent habit." This accent on deliberative intelligence, reflective thought, which assumed a special importance in Dewey's theory of ethics, given his claim of contingency and predictability as coexistent in the world, is manifest in Dewey's last major work on ethical theory, *Theory of Valuation* (1939).

**Theory of Valuation.** Written to contest British philosopher A. J. Ayer's assertion in *Language, Truth, and Logic* (1936) that ethical statements were merely emotive, irrational statements of preference and, as such, inexplicable by scientific canons of veracity, Dewey's *Theory of Valuation* highlights experiential contexts of value judgments. Given his conception of the importance to ethical theory of reflective thought responding to a "precarious and perilous" world, a view discussed in arguably his most philosophically comprehensive work of the 1920's, *Experience and Nature* (1925), Dewey eschewed any attempt to rank values hierarchically in *Theory of Valuation*.

Dewey believed that value judgments depended for their veracity on an experiential context and thus were subject to empirical testing. "Valuation," Dewey wrote, "involved desiring." Dewey insisted that desires be scrutinized carefully. Investigation, he averred, of the experiential conditions for human preferences and consideration of consequences resulting from acting on these desires would yield the efficacy of ethical judgments. Efficacy depended on the abolition of the experiential cause for desiring: "some 'trouble' in an existing situation."

**Implications for Ethical Conduct.** Dewey's philosophy challenges people to derive their morality from their everyday experiential world rather than from some predetermined cosmological order. In Dewey's view, the individual actively constructs morality through conscious and deliberate implementation of actions designed to achieve the most beneficial consequences. For Dewey, ethical conduct is a dimension of human behavior that the individual creates rather than passively receives from some external source of "goodness."

—*Malcolm B. Campbell*

**See also** *Human Nature and Conduct*; James, William; Peirce, Charles Sanders; Pragmatism; Progressivism.

**Bibliography**

Bernstein, Richard J. *John Dewey.* New York: Washington Square Press, 1966.

Boydston, Jo Ann, ed. *Guide to the Works of John Dewey.* Carbondale: Southern Illinois University Press, 1970.

Gouinlock, James. *John Dewey's Philosophy of Value.* New York: Humanities Press, 1972.

McDermott, John, ed. *Philosophy of John Dewey.* Chicago: University of Chicago Press, 1981.

Morgenbesser, Sidney, ed. *Dewey and His Critics.* New York: Journal of Philosophy, 1977.

Sleeper, R. W. *The Necessity of Pragmatism: John Dewey's Conception of Philosophy.* New Haven, Conn.: Yale University Press, 1986.

Sullivan, William. *Reconstructing Public Philosophy.* Berkeley: University of California Press, 1982.

Westbrook, Robert B. *John Dewey and American Democracy.* Ithaca, N.Y.: Cornell University Press, 1991.

## Diagnosis, ethics of

**Type of ethics:** Bioethics

**Date:** Fifth century B.C.E. to present

**Definition:** A body of rules used to govern the social behavior of physicians and issues of conscience in the primary events of human existence

**Significance:** Moral issues arise whenever human action or lack of action affects others; the medical diagnosis of a patient's condition and the decisions following that diagnosis necessarily introduce moral factors and issues of conscience into the equation

For many physicians, the principle of confidentiality tends to produce a kind of knee-jerk reflex. The popular belief is that confidentiality is essential to the physician-patient relationship and must be safeguarded at all costs. Contrary to popular belief, however, it is not an absolute principle. In many cases, health care is now a product of teamwork, so that the physician is forced to pool information to some degree. The advent of computers makes it far easier for the physician's duty of confidentiality to be abused. Thus, there is confusion among professionals and administrators about what should be and what should not be revealed. Attitudes among physicians have departed from absolute certainties to a confusion of views between those who would have no difficulty divulging information and those who feel that divulging information violates various ethical codes.

It is generally accepted that information gained by a professional in the course of a relationship with a client is the property of the client. Instances do occur, however, in which medical professionals must weigh their ethical duty against their secondary duty as citizens to prevent harm from befalling others. For example, physicians have a statutory obligation to disclose the existence of infectious diseases. In some way, however, disclosure should hinge around patient consent, whenever it is practicable.

There is a general consensus that physicians have an obligation to tell the truth. Some doctors assume that they also have a right, which they sometimes exercise, to withhold information from a patient about a condition. Many physicians find it difficult to tell their patients that they are terminally ill. Some believe that a failure to tell a patient the truth is a type of dishonesty. Various arguments for truthfulness apply in medical ethics in diagnosis. Medicine is practiced on the assumption that the patient consents to treatment, but consent becomes meaningless unless it is informed. Thus, truth-telling is vital to medical practice and medical diagnosis. The right to be adequately informed is based upon patients' freedom of choice, which becomes compromised if they are not given adequate data about their conditions. Reaction to the truth (of a terminal diagnosis, for example) is varied and unpredictable, and physicians are aware of this, as are pastors. In fact, "privileged communication" between patient and physician is one of the priestly aspects of the doctor's role that have been left over from ancient times.

A sensitive person can sympathize with one physician who showed, in a plaintive remark, the duty to tell the truth, yet his dislike of it. "Devotion to the truth does not always require the physician to voice his fears or tell the patient all he knows. But, after he has decided that the process of dying has begun, only in exceptional circumstances would a physician be justified in keeping the opinion to himself."

No one can better guard the ideal of absolute respect for the human person than the medical profession.

**See also** Confidentiality; Medical ethics; Physician-patient relationship.

## Dictatorship

**TYPE OF ETHICS:** Politico-economic ethics

**DATE:** Sixth century B.C.E. to present

**DEFINITION:** A system of government in which one individual has absolute authority and rules through force and terror

**SIGNIFICANCE:** Dictators create their own systems of law and order; their word becomes law and no opposition is allowed

**History.** Dictatorships have existed in all times and all places. In ancient Greece, "tyrants" were given temporary authority by the populace to rule during times of war and invasion. When the crisis passed, power was returned to the legitimate authorities and the tyrant stepped down. That custom continued in Roman society when absolute power was given to military rulers until order was restored. In ancient China, the emperor became a dictator during critical times and ruled with an iron hand. One of the bloodiest dictators in Chinese history, Ch'in Shih Huang Ti, killed thousands of his countrymen between 221 and 210 B.C.E. in an effort to put down peasant rebellions and opponents to his rule. According to the Chinese Legalists, proponents of a school of philosophy that stressed the wickedness of human nature, severe punishments and frequent use of the death penalty were necessary to keep order in society. Human beings only obeyed laws that were strictly and savagely enforced; without fear and terror, society would fall apart. Thus, Chinese Legalist philosophers presented the major ethical defense of absolute rule, a view echoed later by Thomas Hobbes, an English political theorist, in his book *Leviathan* (1561). Both the Chinese and Hobbes argued that most humans preferred order to freedom and that order became possible only with strict enforcement of laws. Only absolute authority could reduce criminal activity and create an orderly society.

In the twentieth century, dictatorships have been created principally to create a utopian vision of a perfect society. Whether in Joseph Stalin's Soviet Union, Adolf Hitler's Germany, or Mao Tse-tung's China, modern dictators have assumed absolute power, killed millions of people, and imposed horrifying levels of terror on their populations in the name of creating a better world.

Joseph Stalin, ruler of the Soviet Union from 1927 to 1953, achieved more absolute power than perhaps any other modern dictator. He summarized his ethical philosophy in a comment he made to Communist party leaders in 1932 when he was advised that Ukrainian farmers were causing problems by refusing to move to giant collective farms run by the Soviet government. In reply Stalin reportedly said, "No people, no problem." To carry out this policy, the Soviet dictator ordered all food to be taken out of Ukraine until his orders were obeyed.

**FAMOUS DICTATORS**

| Dictator | Nation | Years in Power |
|---|---|---|
| Ch'in Shih Huang Ti | China | 221-210 B.C.E. |
| Nero | Rome | 54-68 A.D. |
| Genghis Khan | Mongolia | 1241-1279 |
| Tamerlane | Central Asia | 1370-1405 |
| Ivan the Terrible | Russia | 1547-1584 |
| Napoleon Bonaparte | France | 1799-1815 |
| Benito Mussolini | Italy | 1923-1943 |
| Joseph Stalin | Soviet Union | 1927-1953 |
| Adolf Hitler | Germany | 1933-1945 |
| Kim Il Sung | North Korea | 1948-present |
| Mao Tse-tung | China | 1949-1975 |
| Fidel Castro | Cuba | 1959-present |
| Pol Pot | Cambodia | 1976-1978 |
| Saddam Hussein | Iraq | 1979-present |

Within two years more than 8 million Ukrainians had starved to death and the resistance to authority was crushed.

One rule of modern dictatorship is that the leader is the law. In the 1930's in the Soviet Union, Joseph Stalin came close to achieving this goal. Between 16 and 20 million Russians died in prisons and slave labor camps established to maintain order and control over the Soviet people. Stalin's secret police, a key ingredient in any successful dictatorship, had spies in every village, classroom, and office in the country. Spies informed on other spies and children were rewarded for turning in their parents for disloyal conduct. Disloyalty was defined as any questioning of Stalin's authority. Under such conditions a severe dictatorship emerged, though Stalin fell far short of his goal of turning the Soviet Union into a self-sufficient, economically successful worker's paradise.

Terror and death were defended, for as true communists believed, the killing of millions was necessary in order to create a class-free, perfect society. Would not the deaths of millions be justified if one could produce a perfect society on Earth? That Stalin and his supporters failed to come close to their goal makes his dictatorship even more horrifying.

Adolf Hitler, German dictator from 1933 to 1945, justified his mass murders with the phrase "life unfit for life." The German leader promoted biological warfare in his attempt to create a master race. Unlike most other modern dictators, Hitler did not seize power but took over the German government by constitutional means. Once in charge, however, *der Führer* ("the leader") followed the same methods as all the others, eliminating all opposition and imposing a violent reign of terror upon his nation. Soon there were no limits on Hitler's authority, and laws were passed that attempted to create a strict racial state. To build a master race, millions of "inferiors" were persecuted and eventually eliminated. Along with 6 million Jews, thousands of Gypsies, Slavs, homosexuals, and physically and mentally handicapped people were murdered on Hitler's command. Hitler used his immense power to benefit one group, the "pure-blooded Aryans," while all others were to be destroyed. Absolute power was used to perform absolute evil, and Hitler's empire was only brought to judgment by the bloodiest war in human history. "Life unfit for life" became the ethical standard for one of the most destructive régimes in human history.

The third example of modern dictators, Mao Tse-tung, who ruled China with total power from 1949 to 1975, also killed millions of people (the exact number is still subject to dispute) in his pursuit of a perfect society. Mao tried to destroy China's past totally and to create a new world order based on economic and political equality. He seized power in 1949 after a long civil war and declared a campaign of terror against his, and hence China's, enemies. He, like many dictators, saw himself as the voice of the people and someone who was supremely interested in their welfare and prosperity. If millions had to die, it was ethically correct because "the people" demanded it and because the deaths of traitors would help bring about a heaven on Earth. Executions of landlords, massacres of Buddhist monks and nuns, and rigid obedience to the teachings of the leader were all expected, encouraged, and accomplished during Mao's brutal reign of terror, which lasted for most of his tenure as Chinese ruler. Only his own death brought an end to his terrorist campaign against the people of China.

In recent years, relatively small-time dictators such as Kim Il Sung in North Korea (1948-present), Pol Pot in Cambodia (1976-1979), and Saddam Hussein in Iraq (1979-present), have continued the tradition of murdering opponents and creating secret police forces to terrorize their people. Dictatorships continue to exist, and dictators continue to impose suffering upon their people. This form of government has existed for thousands of years and is unlikely to disappear as long as dictators are able to command obedience through fear, terror, and promises of perfection.

*—Leslie V. Tischauser*

**See also** Hitler, Adolf; Hobbes, Thomas; Stalin, Joseph; Tyranny.

**BIBLIOGRAPHY**

Arendt, Hannah. *The Origins of Totalitarianism.* 2d ed. New York: Meridian, 1958.

Bullock, Alan. *Hitler and Stalin: Parallel Lives.* New York: Alfred A. Knopf, 1992.

Friedrich, Carl J., and Zbigniew K. Brzezinski. *Totalitarian Dictatorship and Autocracy.* 2nd ed. Cambridge, Mass.: Harvard University Press, 1965.

Talmon, Jacob L. *The Origins of Totalitarian Democracy.* New York: Praeger, 1968.

Wittfogel, Karl A. *Oriental Despotism: A Comparative Study of Total Power.* New Haven, Conn.: Yale University Press, 1963.

## Dignity

**TYPE OF ETHICS:** Religious ethics

**DEFINITION:** Refers to the nature of the inalienable rights of each person

**SIGNIFICANCE:** The concept of the dignity of humankind describes the evolving understanding of those basic individual rights that no government or person should ever be permitted to limit

The concept of the dignity of humankind was originally based on the theological belief that all men and women possess God-given rights because they are formed in the image of God. Foremost among these divine gifts are freedom and immortality. Unlike other animals, humans are not dominated purely by physical instincts. People can use their freedom to create works of great beauty and to improve the quality of life for themselves and others. Freedom may, of course, be abused if one chooses to limit the rights of others.

In his influential book *The City of God* (426), the Christian writer Saint Augustine argued persuasively that practices such as slavery, which demeaned individuals, were incompatible with Christian beliefs. Since God freely granted immortality to all men and women, it is absolutely essential that human beings respect the dignity and freedom of each individual. For Saint Augustine, Earth is a "city of God" in which all men and women enjoy the same basic rights and privileges. Saint Augustine, a North African bishop who lived on the outskirts of the Roman Empire, specifically rejected the belief that any government had the right to invade or dominate another country. Those who accept the basic tenet that all men and women possess freedom and immortality must ask themselves if certain forms of behavior are morally compatible with God's teachings on the dignity of all people. If there is a conflict between social practices and religious beliefs, a Christian is required to obey the higher divine law. Saint Augustine argued that a Christian is always responsible for his or her decisions. It is unacceptable to claim that one must simply obey all laws, since certain laws may be morally reprehensible if they fail to respect the dignity and rights of all men and women.

Saint Augustine's comments on the dignity of humankind had a profound influence on Christian ethics. In his 1580 essay "On the Cannibals," Michel de Montaigne stated that it was morally wrong for Europeans to colonize the New World. European political leaders had developed the specious argument that it was permissible for them to exploit Native Americans because they were superior to them. Montaigne denounced this position as racist. Like Saint Augustine, Montaigne recognized the dignity of each man and woman. Although Montaigne was both the mayor of Bordeaux and an adviser to French kings, his condemnation of the conquest of the New World was ignored by French government officials because an acceptance of his position would have put an end to French imperialism in the Americas.

Over the centuries, people have recognized that certain human rights are so important that they must be enumerated. A mere declaration of human rights is not sufficient. A mechanism must be created to protect these inalienable rights. In democracies, independent judges have the power to require even recalcitrant government officials to respect constitutionally protected rights. Famous declarations of human rights include the 1689 English Bill of Rights; the 1791 United States Bill of Rights; the Universal Declaration of Human Rights, which the United Nations approved in 1948; and the 1969 Human Rights American Convention of the Organization of American States. The founders of the American democracy felt that certain rights, such as freedom of religion, freedom of speech, and the right to a jury trial, were essential to the quality of life and that the American government should be permanently prevented from restricting these inalienable rights. Although it was admirable, the United States Bill of Rights was imperfect because it failed to recognize the rights of women and African Americans. The American Constitution may, however, be amended, and it was, in fact, amended in order to end slavery and to grant African Americans and women the right to vote.

The concept of the dignity of humankind has continued to evolve. In her famous 1949 book *The Second Sex,* Simone de Beauvoir argued persuasively that a failure to recognize the dignity and equality of women was morally unacceptable. Both the Universal Declaration of Human Rights and the Human Rights American Convention denounced torture and racism and also stressed the need to respect the rights of people from indigenous and minority cultures so that all citizens might enjoy the same rights and privileges. The right of citizens to use their native language has also been recognized as a basic human right. Canada, for example, is a bilingual country, and the Canadian Parliament has specifically declared that any Canadian may use either French or English in all public and private matters. Although the official languages of Canada are French and English, the Canadian Parliament also took specific action to recognize the linguistic rights of native peoples living in Canada. The ancient concept of the dignity of humankind is based on certain inalienable rights. Although numerous totalitarian governments have sought to limit personal freedoms, such efforts have consistently been resisted by those who respect the dignity and freedom of each man and woman.

*—Edmund J. Campion*

**See also** Civil rights; Freedom and liberty; Human nature; Human rights.

**Bibliography**

Augustine, Saint, Bishop of Hippo. *The City of God.* Translated by Marcus Dods. New York: Modern Library, 1983.

Baker, Herschel. *The Dignity of Man: Studies in the Persistence of an Idea.* Cambridge, Mass.: Harvard University Press, 1947.

Beauvoir, Simone de. *The Second Sex.* Edited and translated by H. M. Parshley. New York: Alfred A. Knopf, 1952.

Lawson, Edward, comp. *Encyclopedia of Human Rights.* New York: Taylor & Francis, 1991.

Montaigne, Michel de. *The Essays of Michel de Montaigne.* Edited and translated by Michael Screech. London: Allen Lane, 1991.

Osmanczyk, Edmund Jan. *Encyclopedia of the United Nations and International Relations.* New York: Taylor and Francis, 1990.

## Dilemmas, moral

**Type of ethics:** Theory of ethics

**Date:** From antiquity

**Definition:** Moral choices (usually forced) that, no matter how they are decided, have negative consequences

**Significance:** Moral dilemmas present tremendous difficulties for people who are striving to think and to behave rationally and ethically

Moral dilemmas represent some of the hardest choices that people must make in the course of their lifetimes. The core of a moral dilemma is the fact that, no matter what course is chosen by the person who is facing the dilemma, making the choice involves deciding on a course of action that will have negative moral consequences. The following are typical examples of situations that involve moral dilemmas: a sea captain on an overloaded life raft must select a small number of people to throw overboard if most of the people aboard the life raft are to be saved; a general who has been ordered to direct a suicide mission for the good of his country must decide which soldiers will be sent to a certain death; a German resistance leader can save only one of two Jewish families from death in a concentration camp at the hands of the Nazis. Such scenarios involve attempting to identify and choose the lesser of two evils.

**Baby Jane Doe.** In New York state in 1983, a moral dilemma arose regarding the fate of "Baby Jane Doe." She suffered from multiple difficulties, including a broken and protruding spine (spina bifida) and fluid on her brain (hydrocephaly). Worse, she had a brain that was abnormally small (microencephaly). She needed surgery immediately after her birth, but her parents refused to allow it. Without the surgery, Jane would live for two years at most, but the surgery would still leave her in a hopeless situation. A "right to life" group intervened and demanded that the surgery be done. The New York Supreme Court ruled in the group's favor, but a higher court immediately overturned the decision. Next, the Federal Justice Department intervened, launching an investigation to determine whether a "handicapped" person was being discriminated against, but a judge dismissed that suit also. Baby Jane did not receive the operations, went home with her parents, and soon died.

Were the parents right or wrong? A few more details might help the reader decide. If Jane had received the complicated surgeries, she would have had a 50 percent chance of living into her twenties, but her life never would have been anything approaching an existence that most people would want to experience. She would have been paralyzed, epileptic, and extremely vulnerable to various diseases, such as meningitis. She would never even have recognized her parents. It was these facts on which the parents based their decision.

**Facing the Dilemma.** The Baby Jane tragedy illustrates two typical elements of moral dilemmas. The first is the fact that human rights are involved. The second is that, as in Jane's case, two rights come into conflict: in that case, Jane's right to life and the parental right of choice. In a more ordinary case, most people would no doubt hold that Jane's right to life was paramount. The mitigating circumstances in Baby Jane's case, however, swayed various judges and many people in the general public to support the parents, who based their moral judgment on specific information and had good reasons for making that judgment. Most true moral dilemmas must be solved in the same way. Usually, two "wrongs" or two "rights" will be involved, and decision makers must weigh the facts of each case with impartiality (if that is possible) and then develop good reasons for their decisions. In other words, in a dilemma, one must weigh prima facie duties and good reasons for making a specific decision. If, for example, I have made a promise to you to meet for lunch tomorrow, I have a moral duty to keep that promise. If my father has a heart attack and is close to death, however, my duty to be at my father's side and help him far outweighs my promise to you. I will not keep the lunch date because I will have used my power of reason and will have decided that there is a good reason to follow the other course of action. Reason, self-examination, and internal argument pro and con—these factors help in solving moral dilemmas. People who are searching for moral answers to dilemmas must remember that moral "truth" is the truth of reason and logical thinking, and that dilemmas can be solved satisfactorily only if an individual's decision is based on the best reasons that are available. Conclusions backed by reason are the key element in solving moral dilemmas.

**Conclusions.** Certainly, people as members of society need all their powers of reason in facing the many moral dilemmas that arise in modern life. Is abortion absolutely right? Is it absolutely wrong? Can mitigating circumstances in individual abortion cases "tip" the answer one way or the other? Is euthanasia ever justified? Should society condone or oppose capital punishment? The list of contemporary moral dilemmas is endless, and it is the duty of reasonable people to try to resolve them. —*James Smallwood*

**See also** Prisoner's dilemma.

**BIBLIOGRAPHY**

Arthur, John, ed. *Morality and Moral Controversies*. Englewood Cliffs, N.J.: Prentice-Hall, 1981.

Cook, Fred J. *The Corrupted Land: The Social Morality of Modern America*. New York: Macmillan, 1966.

Dworkin, Ronald. *Taking Rights Seriously*. Cambridge, Mass.: Harvard University Press, 1977.

Gewirth, Alan. *Reason and Morality*. Chicago: University of Chicago Press, 1978.

Rachels, James. *The Elements of Moral Philosophy*. Philadelphia: Temple University Press, 1986.

__________. *Moral Problems: A Collection of Philosophical Essays*. 2d ed. New York: Harper & Row, 1978.

Ross, W. D. *The Right and the Good*. Oxford, England: Clarendon Press, 1930.

Singer, Peter. *Rich and Poor*. Cambridge, England: Cambridge University Press, 1979.

## Disability rights

**TYPE OF ETHICS:** Disability rights

**DATE:** 1960's to present

**ASSOCIATED WITH:** Rehabilitation Act of 1973, Americans with Disabilities Act, and the civil rights movement

**DEFINITION:** Aims to integrate the disabled into the mainstream of society through efforts to remove impediments to benefits and opportunities

**SIGNIFICANCE:** Represents a change in cultural values by guaranteeing to the disabled equal rights to mobility, dexterity, communication, and education formerly denied to them because of their limitations

Recognition of the special needs and requirements of the disabled and the emergence of legislation guaranteeing their civil rights have evolved slowly. Following other civil rights movements, disability rights laws were merely symbolic, and did not include strategies to guide policy implementation. With the enactment of the Rehabilitation Act of 1973 and the Americans with Disabilities Act of 1990, the rights of the disabled became legally enforceable.

**Historical Background and Societal Attitude.** A neglected minority constituting 20 to 25 percent of Americans differing in extent of impairment and range of ability, the disabled are not a homogenous group. The disabled historically have been stigmatized, viewed as "different" and therefore not equal to other members of society. Through prejudices and misunderstandings, personal fears and anxieties, reactions of pity, helplessness, uneasiness, and sometimes inaccurate media and literary representations, society has erected barriers that have kept the disabled from participating in various areas of American life. The needs of the disabled were ignored in the design of public buildings and facilities and the delivery of public services; educational programs and employment practices resulted in discrimination and exclusion of disabled persons.

Vocational rehabilitation programs following World War I were initiated in favor of veterans with combat injuries and later expanded first to all physically disabled persons and then to mental rehabilitation. Programs to provide income to persons whose disabilities prevented their employment—Social Security Disability Insurance and Supplemental Security Income—began in the mid-1950's and expanded in the 1970's. The Architectural Barriers Act of 1968 brought about such modifications as specially designated parking places for the disabled near commercial establishments and public buildings, special entrance ramps and doors, curb cuts, elevators with braille floor designations, and specially equipped restrooms.

**POLITICALLY INCORRECT LANGUAGE AND POLITICALLY CORRECT ALTERNATIVES**

| Incorrect | Correct |
|---|---|
| Handicapped, disabled person | Person with a disability |
| Impairment | Disablement |
| Deaf and dumb | Deaf and hearing impaired |
| Mute | Speech-impaired |
| Blind | Visually impaired |
| Insane, crazy | Emotionally impaired |
| Normal | Able-bodied person |
| Crippled, spastic | Mobility-impaired |
| Fit, spell | Seizure |
| Mongolism | Down syndrome |
| Harelip | Cleft lip |

**Rehabilitation Act of 1973.** Called a "bill of rights" for the disabled, the Rehabilitation Act of 1973 ensures that federally funded programs can be used by all disabled persons. It requires the institution of affirmative action programs to actively recruit, hire, train, accommodate, and promote "qualified disabled persons." The Act prohibits discrimination in the recruitment, testing, or hiring of the disabled, as well as special or different treatment that would tend to stigmatize or set apart handicapped people from the nonhandicapped. The Act also aims to grant to the disabled equal opportunity to participate or benefit in the services of federally funded government agency programs.

**Americans with Disabilities Act (1990).** Considered landmark civil rights legislation for all persons with disabilities, the Americans with Disabilities Act (ADA) provides for disabled persons legal protection in employment, access to state and local government, public transportation, public accommodation, and telecommunications. From July, 1992, until July 26, 1994, the ADA covers employers with twenty-five or more employees. After that date, it will encompass employers with fifteen or more employees. Agencies, unions, and joint labor/management committees are included; the U.S. government, Indian tribes, and tax-exempt private membership clubs are excluded.

Title I of the ADA and its Equal Employment Opportunity Commission (EEOC) regulations prohibit an employer from discriminating against a "qualified individual with a disability" in job application procedures, including recruitment and advertising, hiring, promotion, awarding tenure, demotion, transfer, layoff, termination, right of return from layoff, rehiring, compensation, job assignments, classifications, seniority, leaves of absence, sick leave, fringe benefits, training, employer-sponsored activities, and any other terms and conditions of employment.

Under the ADA, it is unlawful for an employer to use selection criteria or tests that tend to screen out persons with disabilities. Preemployment medical examinations are unlawful, but employment may be contingent on the results of a postemployment examination if required of all entering employees and if records remain confidential. The disabled have the same legal remedies that are available to other minorities under the Civil Rights Act of 1964, amended in 1991 to include compensatory and punitive damages for intentional discrimination.

Effective January 26, 1992, title II requires that all state and local government agencies, and public transportation agencies make all of their services accessible to the disabled. It also includes school systems, parks and recreation programs, jails, libraries, public hospitals and clinics, state and local courts and legislatures, and government activities carried out by private contractors.

Title III requires equal access to public accommodations in a variety of places, such as hotels, theaters, restaurants, parks, libraries, museums, and banks. Auxiliary aids and services to ensure effective communication with the hearing impaired and visually impaired must be provided.

Title IV requires that local and long distance telephone companies provide telecommunication relay services across the nation to permit persons using TDD's (telecommunication devices for the deaf) or text telephones to have conversations with persons using conventional telephones. All television public service announcements produced or funded by the federal government are required to include closed captioning.

**Other Rights.** Public school systems must provide a free, appropriate education to handicapped children. Federal money is available to states for special education. To the extent possible, handicapped children are to be educated with those who are not handicapped (a practice called "mainstreaming"). Disabled students at federally funded colleges must also be treated equally with nondisabled students. Health and social service agencies receiving federal assistance cannot discriminate against the disabled, and auxiliary aids must be provided. Discrimination in housing and access to air transportation is also prohibited. —*Marcia J. Weiss*

| PUBLIC ATTITUDES TOWARD PERSONS WITH DISABILITIES | |
|---|---|
| In 1991, Louis Harris and Associates conducted the first survey ever of American attitudes about persons with disabilities for the National Organization on Disability. The survey showed that Americans basically understand the many challenges persons with disabilities face in trying to earn a living and leading active lives as citizens, and that young Americans and those with a higher degree of education tend, more than others, to support persons with disabilities. | |
| Believe that persons with disabilities are not hired because of their disability | 59% |
| Believe that persons with disabilities are not fully using their potential. | 78% |
| Believe that employment of persons with disabilities would be a great "boost" to the United States. | 81% |
| Believe that more spending is needed to make schools, transportation, workplaces, and other public buildings accessible. | 89% |
| Persons with disabilities who believe that they have been discriminated against in their efforts to find jobs and to provide financially for themselves and their families. | 52% |
| Unemployed men with disabilities at the beginning of 1990 (according to the United States Attorney General). | 58% |
| Unemployed men with disabilities at the beginning of 1990 (according to the United States Attorney General). | 80% |

**See also** Americans with Disabilities Act; Discrimination; U.N. Declaration on the Rights of Disabled Persons.

**BIBLIOGRAPHY**

Albrecht, Gary L. *The Disability Business: Rehabilitation in America.* Newbury Park, Calif.: Sage, 1992.

DuBow, Sy. *Legal Rights: The Guide for Deaf and Hard of Hearing People.* 4th ed. Washington, D.C.: Gallaudet University Press, 1992.

Frierson, James G. *Employer's Guide to the Americans With Disabilities Act.* Washington, D.C.: BNA Books, 1992.

Percy, Stephen L. *Disability, Civil Rights, and Public Policy: The Politics of Implementation.* Tuscaloosa, Ala.: University of Alabama Press, 1989.

## Disappeared, The

**TYPE OF ETHICS:** Modern history
**DATE:** 1975-1980
**PLACE:** Argentina
**ASSOCIATED WITH:** Argentine military; Mothers of the Plaza de Mayo
**DEFINITION:** The Argentine military's reign of repression and terrorism, during which some 10,000 people "disappeared"
**SIGNIFICANCE:** Constituted the most serious mass violation of civil and human rights in Argentine history

After the fall of Argentine president Juan Perón in 1955, a struggle over political control and economic policy ensued between left-wing and right-wing civilian factions and between moderates and hard liners in the military. Except for the period from 1973 to 1976, the military controlled Argentina until 1983. In 1970, guerrilla war, waged by leftists, began and was countered by rightist groups. In 1975, the military intensified the war against subversion that it had begun in 1971. Between 1975 and 1980, the "dirty war" carried on by the Argentine military attempted to eliminate members of leftist organizations, the Peronista Party, and any group that was opposed to the military administration. This phase of guerrilla warfare was the most terrifying and bloody in Argentine history. Due process was ignored, systematic torture became routine, and at least 10,000 people "disappeared" and were assumed to have been tortured and killed. Repression was deliberately arbitrary, uncoordinated, and indiscriminate; military power was used to intimidate anyone who opposed it. By 1980, the repression declined, and it finally ended in 1982. One of the main groups that opposed the military terrorism was the Mothers of the Plaza de Mayo, who assembled weekly in silent protest in the Plaza de Mayo in front of the Casa Rosada, the Argentine White House. In 1985, the civilian government tried the top military leaders and sentenced them to life in prison for their crimes during the "dirty war."

**See also** Oppression.

## Discrimination

**TYPE OF ETHICS:** Civil rights
**DATE:** Twentieth century
**ASSOCIATED WITH:** The concept of equal rights
**DEFINITION:** Differential treatment based on physical and social affiliation
**SIGNIFICANCE:** Has a negative impact on just and moral behavior

Discrimination in one form or another appears to be endemic to all societies. In the United States, various groups have experienced various forms of discrimination, including racial discrimination, sexual discrimination (denial of certain rights to women), religious discrimination, discrimination against certain cultural groups (for example, Appalachians, the Amish, and so forth), discrimination against the disabled (both physically and mentally), discrimination against the aged, and discrimination against homosexuals. Many whites immigrating from Europe have at one time or another experienced discrimination.

Discrimination, according to Joan Ferrante in *Sociology: A Global Perspective* (1992), is the unequal treatment, whether intentional or unintentional, of individuals or groups on the basis of group membership that is unrelated to merit, ability, or past performance. Discrimination is not limited to individuals. In fact, the two most pervasive types of discrimination are legal discrimination and institutional discrimination. Legal discrimination is unequal treatment that is sustained by law. Institutional discrimination (or racism), according to Stokely Carmichael and Charles V. Hamilton's *Black Power* (1967), is a subtle form of unequal treatment based on race that is entrenched in social custom (that is, social institutions). Institutional discrimination may include segregated housing patterns, redlining by financial institutions, and the practice of minority group members being forced continually into low-paying jobs. Prejudice, which is often confused with discrimination, is the prejudgment of people, objects, or even situations on the basis of stereotypes or generalizations that persist even when facts demonstrate otherwise (for example, the majority of women on welfare are white, yet the stereotype of a female welfare recipient is that of a black woman with a brood of children).

The most pernicious acts of prejudice and discrimination in the United States have been directed against racial minorities. The history of race relations in the United States demonstrates that differential treatment has been accorded to all minority groups. A minority group, according to John E. Farley in *Sociology* (1990), is any group in a disadvantaged or subordinate position (in this sense, a minority may actually constitute a numerical majority; for example, blacks in South Africa). Minority populations have experienced the entire range of race relations, including assimilation, pluralism, legal protection, population transfer, continued subjugation, and extermination. While all minority populations have experienced some degree of discrimination, perhaps the most cruel and enduring discrimination has been experienced by those of African descent.

Africans were first brought to North America as slaves in 1619, one year after the *Mayflower* landed. They proved

*Because of discrimination in public education, segregated schools for African Americans in the American South had no funds even for textbooks.* (Library of Congress)

to be an excellent source of inexpensive labor for the developing European colonies. In its early development, slavery was not justified by attitudes of racial inferiority, but simply by the need for cheap labor. Racial justification for slavery came later as a strategy for maintaining the continued subjugation of blacks. Depicting blacks as subhuman, irresponsible, promiscuous, and lazy helped to stave off, for many years, groups (for example, abolitionists) bent upon ending slavery. The development of racist ideology during slavery has—over the years—continued to influence the relationship between blacks and whites in the United States.

According to Hernan S. Cruz in *Racial Discrimination* (1977), until the latter part of the eighteenth century, when the slave trade began to become a profitable business, there was very little prejudice based on race. Justification for slavery had to be found by the Christian slave traders who professed to believe in the brotherhood of all men and the ideals of democracy, which established the equality of all men before the law.

The end of slavery in the United States did not, and could not, bring an end to discrimination. Discrimination had become institutionalized—embedded in social custom and in the very institutions of society. Initially, the Thirteenth, Fourteenth, and Fifteenth Amendments to the Constitution, along with the Civil Rights Acts of 1866 and 1867, did much to eliminate legal discrimination against the newly freed slaves. Yet many of those gains were abrogated by state legislatures in the South following the abrupt end of Reconstruction in 1877. The states of the Old Confederacy were able to circumvent much of the legislation passed during the Reconstruction period. They were able to sanction discrimination and deny civil rights by means of a set of laws called the "black codes." The black codes virtually reintroduced many of conditions that existed during slavery. Although the Fourteenth and Fifteenth Amendments guaranteed citizenship and the right to vote, these rights were abridged through intimidation, the poll tax, the "grandfather" clause, and through literacy tests. Beginning in the 1880's, a more comprehensive set of laws—referred to as "Jim Crow"—gave rise to a system of legal segregation in South. This system of legal segregation was sanctioned by the "separate but equal" philosophy established in the *Plessy v. Ferguson* decision of 1896.

Substantial progress against Jim Crow did not occur until fifty-eight years later, with the *Brown v. Board of Education* decision (1954). In the *Brown* decision, the Supreme Court overturned *Plessy*, arguing that the concept of "separate but equal" was "inherently unequal" and had no place in a society that professes to treat all its citizens equally. The *Brown* decision helped to give rise to a determination on the part of African Americans to exercise the rights and privileges guaranteed to all citizens under the Constitution. Beginning in the 1960's, the underlying legal, political, and economic context of race relations changed in the United States. Demonstrations, sit-ins, and marches by African Americans and their supporters caused America to wake up and begin addressing the second-class citizenship of minority groups. As a consequence, epoch-making legislation was passed in the form of the 1964 Civil Rights Act, affirmative action (in employment and education) was introduced, and governmental agencies (for example, the Equal Employment Opportunities Commission, the U.S. Civil Rights Commission, the Office of Federal Contract Compliance Programs, and so forth) actively tried to stamp out much of the discrimination against minorities.

Yet riot after riot erupted across the nation in the 1960's. A combination of economic frustration, police brutality, resistance to desegregation (both in housing and schooling), and the assassination of the civil rights leader the Reverend Martin Luther King, Jr., contributed to the eruptions. The Kerner Commission, which was commissioned to study the conditions leading up to the riots, concluded that "white racism" and discrimination were responsible for the outbreak of violence. Joseph S. Hines suggests in *Politics of Race* (1975) that African Americans have operated in a caste-like racial structure in the United States that has relegated them to inferior status, relative powerlessness, material deprivation, and socio-psychic resentment. Segregation and discrimination have been used as mechanisms for maintaining the sociopolitical structure (status quo). Within this structure, African Americans are members of a racial category for life; they are generally consigned to marry within their group; they are often avoided, both as ritual and as custom; and they experience limited opportunities.

Although African Americans and other minorities have made substantial gains since 1954, they still have not experienced a society that judges them based upon merit and ability. They also have not experienced a society that does not prejudge them based upon physical characteristics and stereotypes. It could be said that discrimination continues to be embedded in the social, political, and economic fabric of the United States. Employment and promotional opportunities are still strongly influenced by race. Consequently, minorities typically earn only a fraction of what white males earn, they tend to hold political office far less often than their numbers in the general population should warrant, and they are still excluded from membership in certain elite clubs because of their race. —*Charles C. Jackson*

**See also** Bigotry; Civil rights movement; Racial prejudice.

**BIBLIOGRAPHY**

Cruz, Hernan S. *Racial Discrimination*. Rev. ed. New York: United Nations, 1977.

Feagin, Joe R., and Clairece B. Feagin. *Discrimination American Style*. Englewood Cliffs, N.J.: Prentice-Hall, 1978.

Kluger, Richard. *Simple Justice: The History of Brown v. Board of Education and Black America's Struggle for Equality*. New York: Alfred A. Knopf, 1976.

Van Dyke, Vernon. *Human Rights, Ethnicity, and Discrimination*. Westport, Conn.: Greenwood Press, 1985.

## Divine command theory

**TYPE OF ETHICS:** Religious ethics
**DATE:** Fourth century B.C.E. to present
**ASSOCIATED WITH:** William of Ockham (c. 1280-1347), René Descartes (1596-1650), and William Paley (1743-1805)
**DEFINITION:** Divine command moral theories maintain that the ethical values and principles binding upon human beings depend only on the commands of a god or gods
**SIGNIFICANCE:** One attempt to provide a foundation for morality

The attempt to evaluate human behavior in terms of moral laws often leads to questions concerning the origin and authority of such laws. Advocates of divine command theories of morality have attempted to answer these questions by maintaining that human ethical values and principles are as they are merely because a god has willed or commanded that they be so. According to this theory, the ultimate explanation for the rightness or wrongness of any action is that some divinity has willed that the action be either good or evil.

It is important to distinguish divine command theories of morality from other theistically oriented ethical theories that relate human morality to the will of some deity. Many philosophers and theologians maintain that God is connected to human morality insofar as God's freely bestowed grace is necessary for the possibility of human beings living lives of moral rectitude. It has also been maintained that God's will is necessary for the possibility of human morality insofar as God must somehow promulgate or make known those laws that humans are obliged to observe. In addition, the conviction that an individual's degree of happiness ought to correspond to his or her moral desert is sometimes reconciled with instances of good people suffering by appealing to God's commitment to see that the demands of justice are met in an afterlife. While all three of these points have accompanied divine command theories, none of them is a necessary component of a divine command theory. What is distinctive about divine command theories is their insistence on the following three points: the entire content of human moral principles is derived solely from the free choices of some god, the god in question is under no constraint to will a given set of moral principles, and the god could have willed the opposite of the set of moral principles that was, in fact, chosen.

The appeal of divine command theories is twofold. First, they offer an unqualified foundation for human morality. Second, they emphasize that God's freedom and power are unlimited by insisting that there are no moral principles that are independent of and binding upon the will of God. Despite these advantages, divine command theories have been attacked from a number of different directions. It has, for instance, been pointed out that divine command theories lead to the conclusion that God could have decided to make moral atrocities (such as child abuse, rape, murder, and genocide) morally praiseworthy. Insofar as it is well-nigh impossible to reconcile the possibility of a world in which child molestation would be truly good with one's deepest moral intuitions, the implication that a good god could bring about such a world is taken to show the absurdity of divine command theories. Though this is a troubling consequence of divine command theories, it is important to note that some divine command theorists have openly embraced this aspect of their theory. (See, for example, William of Ockham's *Super quattuor libros sententiarum subtilissimae quaestiones,* 1491.)

A somewhat different objection points out that if the divine command theory were true, then it would not make sense to wonder whether God's commands were morally good. Because the divine command theorist maintains that God's commanding an action is a necessary and sufficient condition for the action's moral goodness, it follows that it would be contradictory to suppose that a divine command was evil. This point is thought to be problematic because it implies that speculation concerning the moral status of divine commands is actually as pointless as speculation about the triangularity of a triangle. To see that speculation about the moral status of God's commands is meaningful, however, one may think of the moral uneasiness that most readers of the Old Testament experience upon encountering God's command that Abraham sacrifice Isaac, his son. (Indeed, it is comforting to read that an angel stays Abraham's hand at the last instant.) The moral qualms that naturally arise over God's command to Abraham show that people do, meaningfully, evaluate divine commands in moral terms, a practice that would be pointless if the divine command theory were true.

This objection, however, is not decisive, for most divine command theories are not, at bottom, theories purporting to describe human conventions of moral discourse; rather, they are theories concerning the origin of those moral laws that are truly binding upon human beings. It is thus open to the divine command theorist to argue that conventions of moral discourse have developed in the absence of a clear awareness of the connection between divine commands and moral laws, and thus explain the fact that linguistic conventions have led people to question, however inappropriately, the goodness of God's commands.

Perhaps the strongest objection of divine command theories points out that they undermine the possibility of upholding divine goodness. Since divine command theories take God's power to be primary and maintain that moral goodness is wholly consequent to this power, it follows that God transcends, and thus cannot be characterized by, moral goodness. For this reason, divine command theories are accused of reducing the worship of God to a mere power worship and of maximizing God's power only at the price of forfeiting God's goodness. —*James Petrik*

**See also** Descartes, René; God; Religion; Revelation.

**BIBLIOGRAPHY**

Burch, Robert. "Objective Values and the Divine Command Theory of Morality." *New Scholasticism* 54 (Summer, 1980): 279-304.

Chandler, J. H. "Is the Divine Command Theory Defensible?" *Religious Studies* 20 (September, 1984): 443-452.

Helm, Paul, ed. *Divine Commands and Morality.* New York: Oxford University Press, 1981.

Quinn, Philip L. *Divine Commands and Moral Requirements.* Oxford, England: Clarendon Press, 1978.

Wierenga, Edward. "A Defensible Divine Command Theory." *Nous* 17 (September, 1983): 387-408.

## Divorce

**TYPE OF ETHICS:** Beliefs and practices
**DATE:** From antiquity
**DEFINITION:** Dissolution of marriage
**SIGNIFICANCE:** Many social and religious groups believe that nonmarital sex is unethical. Divorce was traditionally justified as a punishment for unethical (often sexual) misconduct by a spouse and was also condemned as weakening the legitimacy of marriage

Divorce is related to two sets of ethical problems. The first has to do with the ethics of sexual behavior in societies in which the Judeo-Christian-Moslem tradition is dominant. Because only sex within a marriage is approved and marriage is supposed to last until one partner dies, divorce may both properly punish an adulterous partner and free the adulterer to form new sexual and marriage bonds. Freeing the adulterer has been viewed as encouraging immoral conduct in restrictive societies. As recently as the middle of the twentieth century, some Roman Catholic-influenced countries (Italy and Ireland) did not permit divorce.

The second set of ethical issues involves distributive justice issues having to do with the terms of division of marital assets and children upon divorce. Until the 1970's, more property was usually awarded to an innocent spouse at divorce; this unequal division was intended to punish the other spouse for engaging in unethical conduct. The dominant pattern near the end of the twentieth century was to place more emphasis on equal divisions of property, or divisions based on contributions, and less emphasis on division based on the immoral conduct of one spouse.

**History of Divorce.** In most ancient societies husbands treated wives and children as property. Some commentators have suggested that the golden ring of marriage is a relic of a slave collar used to restrain the wife, or perhaps of her chains, the literal "marriage bonds." In some primitive societies (for example, the Tiwi of Melville Island) husbands still purchase wives from fathers. In most of these societies divorce is mainly an economic affair; usually it involves returning the payments made at the time of the marriage. In traditional Eskimo society the family simply divided into two households.

Written rules about marriage and divorce in the Western world can be traced to ancient Hebrew and Roman laws and customs. The Old Testament of the Bible relates that a Jewish wife at that time did not have the right to divorce her husband, but she did have the right to remarry if her husband divorced her: "When a man takes a wife and marries her, if then she finds no favor in his eyes because he has found some indecency in her . . . he writes her a bill of divorce and puts it in her hand and sends her out of his house, and she departs out of his house, and if she goes and becomes another man's wife . . ." (Deuteronomy 24:1).

Roman law did not make marriage a legal formality, and religious ceremonies were not required. Parental consent was the main formal prerequisite. Both husband and wife could possess their own property and end the marriage by a sign, such as a formal letter, of a clear intent to divorce. This secular, economic, and amoral approach to marriage and divorce is common today in most cultures in which the Judeo-Christian-Moslem tradition was never dominant and is reappearing in Western cultures.

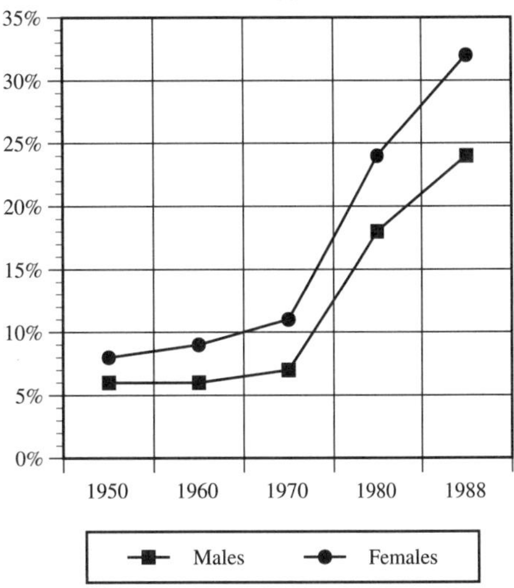


When the emperors of Rome became Christians, they worked to bring marriage and divorce under legal and religious authority. Justinian I, the lawgiver of the sixth century, sought to impose the church's view opposing divorce, but an outraged public successfully defended its traditional liberties. In the Christian church's view marriage was for life. The Roman Catholic canon law of the Middle Ages became the family law of most of Europe. Even after the Protestant Reformation, the Roman Catholic church continued to permit only a partial divorce from bed and board that did not permit remarriage in the case of sexual misconduct or if a spouse left the church. Priests could annul some marriages if a partner violated the marriage-related complex and arbitrary rules of canon law, providing a potential escape from at least some miserable marriages. Annulment meant that no marriage had existed, so it made remarriage possible.

The phrase from the marriage ceremony "What therefore God has joined together, let not man put asunder" (Matthew 19:6) states the canon law position on divorce. Martin Luther and other Protestants who successfully rebelled against the Roman Catholic church in the sixteenth century also rebelled against the theory that the ethical authority of the church permitted the religious regulation of marriage. Luther called marriage "an external worldly thing, subject to secular jurisdiction, just like dress and food, home and field." Most of the new Protestant religions sanctioned complete divorces for certain reasons, including unethical conduct such as adultery, cruelty, or abandonment.

In England, the Catholic church refused to allow Henry VIII to divorce a wife after she failed to provide him with a son. Arguing that the needs of England took precedence over church control of marriage, Henry VIII broke away from the Roman Catholic church and formed his own church. Regulation of divorce was transferred from church to Parliament. Parties had to lobby to obtain a special act of the House of Lords in Parliament to obtain a divorce. These legislative divorces were too expensive for most people. In 1857, Parliament established the Court for Divorce and Matrimonial Causes and initiated divorce by judge. The new civil courts had jurisdiction of divorces and made civil divorces available, but only when the party seeking the divorce was mainly blameless.

With the shift toward civil regulation of marriage came the adoption of many other civil law concepts into the relationship of marriage. Among these concepts were principles from the law of contracts, and marriage became a contractual relationship. The ethical basis of marriage and divorce shifted from religiously based concepts to concepts derived from the morality of contracts or commercial ethics.

In most places in the world where the courts regulated marriage, marriage was viewed as a status entered into by contract and the marriage vows as oral contracts. Therefore, viable grounds for divorce were those related to breaking the terms of the contract: fraud, breach of promise, inability to perform, and coercion. In divorce, fraud took the form of false representations prior to marriage. Adultery, desertion, and willful neglect were breaches of promise. An inability to perform took the form of impotence, homosexuality, habitual intemperance, conviction of a felony, and physical and mental cruelty. Only the injured party could initiate divorce, and courts considered the other party "at fault." This fault doctrine justified giving property and support payments to the injured party as a sort of fine against the wrongdoer. Under the fault rules, family law was much like tort or contract law, with plaintiffs suing defendants and courts deciding who was wrong and who was right. The "innocent" spouse received an award in the same way that a successful plaintiff received an award in a personal injury lawsuit.

The economic and social consequences of the fault doctrine were good and bad and depended largely upon fault. If a woman wanted to end a marriage and could not prove that her husband was at fault, she received no share of property acquired during the marriage and usually no alimony. If the husband wanted to leave or the wife could prove adultery or other grounds, however, then she could bargain. Property and alimony were the wages of sin and the price of freedom. The result was that economic necessity kept many people in failed marriages. There were few children living in single-parent households and few divorced adults.

**The Move to No-Fault Divorce.** "Where there's marriage without love, there will be love without marriage." (Benjamin Franklin)

Love without marriage for those in loveless marriages often took the form of adultery. Adultery was the primary cause of action for divorce suits under the fault doctrine rules. In the United States this doctrine was a casualty of social upheaval in the 1960's. The first change was to permit divorce if both parties gave evidence of their intentions by voluntarily separating and living apart for a specified time. In 1967, New York abandoned its rule that the only grounds for divorce were fault grounds such as adultery and allowed divorce for couples legally separated for two years. In 1969, the California legislature commissioned leading judges, family lawyers, law professors, and behavioral scientists to carry out extensive research on the fault system. Based on the research results, the California legislature passed, in January, 1970, the California Family Law Act, which abolished the fault doctrine requiring fault "grounds" for a divorce. The legislature replaced the traditional ethical-moral grounds for divorce (adultery, abuse, and so forth) with no-fault grounds of "irreconcilable differences leading to an irremediable breakup of the marriage." "Irreconcilable differences" means that one of the parties does not want to remain married. "Irremediable breakup" means that he or she is not going to change his or her mind. The significance of the California Family Law Act was that it was the first law in the Western world to abolish a showing of fault as a requirement of divorce and to permit divorce upon demand. Gradually, all other American jurisdictions followed California. Today, people can obtain no-fault divorces in all states, although twenty states also retain the traditional fault grounds. The modern trend is not to allow evidence of fault in court except for financial misconduct related to property and support awards.

Gone with the fault doctrine was the tort cause of action of "alienation of affection." This tort had allowed an innocent spouse to sue an adulterous spouse's lover for loss of affection and consortium—a legal remedy for moral outrage. Gone also in most states were all defenses against the divorce. The traditional defenses allowed a nonconsenting partner to block divorce proceedings by disproving the stated grounds for the divorce. Gone was the rule preventing the "at-fault" party from initiating the proceedings. Only a few jurisdictions retained the traditional defenses. Although the new laws abolished most of the traditional adversary trappings of divorce, fault was still important in custody disputes.

As no-fault divorces became the norm and the new rules reduced or eliminated the power of one partner to stop the divorce proceedings, the divorce rate increased. The graph below shows a sharp increase in the percentage of divorced persons in the adult population coinciding with the adoption of no-fault divorce.

**No-Fault Divorce and Ethical Issues.** Criticism of the no-fault doctrine also increased. Judge R. Michael Redman, in *Coming Down Hard on No-fault* (1987), comments that no-fault divorce has shifted the focus of marriage from a cornerstone of society, a moral statement, to a relationship of convenience, an "I'll love you until you get ugly" idea. He suggests that the legal system, with its adversary traditions, is best suited to determining fault and allocating property and support accordingly. He bemoans the trend away from viewing marriage as a protected relationship. Some family law experts object that no-fault is contrary to established ideas of morality, which hold that those who do wrong should suffer the consequences. Under a no-fault system, a marital partner who is blameless may still lose much property and may have to support an adulterous or brutal former spouse. Fault may protect an innocent spouse, and many no-fault states still apply fault considerations in some circumstances. Fault preserves the idea of individual accountability. Even when fault is no longer a legal issue, the fault of a partner may influence judges to be more generous to the innocent spouse. It is not coincidental that many of the sharpest critics of no-fault divorce have been women. Women are more likely to file for divorce because of alleged misconduct by their husbands, and alimony awards to women have decreased in the no-fault era.

Clients who want to have fault adjudicated in a divorce and be compensated will often abuse and manipulate the legal system to make a statement about the marriage. Couples denied expression of resentment in no-fault hearings dividing property may seek other avenues for their anger. It has been noted that in California, where fault is relevant only in custody disputes, couples tend to release their pent-up rage in those disputes, harming their children. Many divorcing people believe that ethical concerns and their view of justice should still dominate divorce.

Lawyers rarely see the long-term psychological damage done by a full-blown adversary process. Mental health professionals who do, however, have collected data showing long-term adjustment to be superior in parents who mediate rather than litigate their custody disputes. While advocates of a fault-based adversary system base the desirability of this system on moral grounds, the resulting harm to children violates other ethical values.

Many legal authors, trained to be advocates for a particular client, see the loss of fault grounds for divorce as promoting injustice. Rarely is either party in divorce completely innocent. The bitterness created by the adversary process usually causes harm outweighing the benefits arising out of the cathartic process of litigating disputes. The concept of justice in interpersonal relationships is more elusive than the legal-ethical concept of justice. It may be better for society and the involved parties to deal with the emotional issues of blame and anger with the help of therapists. Less adversarial divorce has made it easier to get divorced, however, and that development correlates with more frequent divorce.

Reducing the importance of fault does not eliminate the stress and pain of divorce. Data from the U.S. Bureau of the Census and the National Center for Health Statistics show that in 1988 the divorce rate was three times higher than the 1979 rate. The United States has the highest divorce rate in the world—twice that of England and Wales. The blended family is the new reality, and stepchildren are now 20 percent of all American children. Stepfamilies are created by loss and do not re-create nuclear families. The situation is not likely to improve soon. The U.S. Census Bureau estimates that close to two-thirds of children of married couples will experience their parents' divorce before they reach legal adulthood.

**Distributive Justice Issues and No-fault Divorce.** Legislatures based no-fault laws on the assumption that men and women are equals and should be treated equally. Judges assumed that spousal support for young healthy women, except on a short-term basis, was not needed, since women had equal opportunities to work. For numerous reasons, women are not usually the economic equals of men, and the equality assumption can lead to distributive injustices. One consequence of no-fault divorce has been a large increase in the number of women and children living in poverty, which violates ethical norms to protect children. This feminization of poverty has no simple solution. Working mothers tend to work fewer hours for lower wages than men in jobs that offer some flexibility in scheduling. Childcare expenses further reduce available funds. Child support payments, if collected at all, rarely fill the gap. Ethically, who is responsible for the harmful consequences of divorce on demand? Should divorced men without custody rights be impoverished to prevent the impoverishment of their former wives and children?

**Is State Control of Divorce and Marriage Legitimate?** Marriage is not only a religious or civil act; it is also a legal status entered into by means of a contract. Because marriage is a legal status, the state has clear and legitimate interests in it. Because lawmakers and judges consider it a matter of local state interest, state legislatures pass most marriage and divorce laws. Case law has established marriage and divorce as fundamental civil freedoms. Because the right to marry is a basic right, states can significantly interfere with this right only when the state interest is "compelling." The U.S. Supreme Court has made it clear that a father's failure to pay support to his former family after divorce is not cause for a state to prevent him from remarrying. Divorce is no longer seen as a pariah status created by moral failure, and the state creates no special disabilities for the divorced. By the 1990's, the change from conceptualizing divorce in religious-ethical terms to seeing it as a pragmatic, legal, and secular process seemed complete. —*Leland C. Swenson*

**See also** Adultery; Children's rights; Family values; Marriage.

**Bibliography**

Kitson, Gay C., and William M. Holmes. *Portrait of Divorce: Adjustment to Marital Breakdown.* New York: Guilford Press, 1992. An analysis of research into the reasons for, and the consequences of, divorce.

Macoby, Eleanor E., and Robert H. Mnookin. *Dividing the Child: Social and Legal Dilemmas of Custody.* Cambridge, Mass.: Harvard University Press, 1992. Discusses the effects of divorce and custody issues on children, paying special attention to the importance of workable relationships between divorced parents.

Schwitzgebel, Robert L., and R. Kirkland Schwitzgebel. *Law and Psychological Practice.* New York: Wiley, 1980. An excellent guide to the interaction of law and counseling. The chapter on divorce and family law contains interesting historical material.

Seichter, Marilyn P. "Alienation of Affection." *Family Advocate* 10, no. 2 (1987). A discussion of the use of the legal system to enforce social morality during the era of fault.

Swenson, Leland C. *Psychology and Law for the Helping Professions.* Pacific Grove, Calif.: Brooks/Cole, 1993. A guide intended to help those who are not attorneys understand the workings of the legal system. Approximately one-third of the book deals with family law, marriage, and divorce.

Tiemann, Adrian R., et al., eds. *Divorce Shock: Perspectives on Counseling and Therapy.* Philadelphia: Charles Press, 1992. This collection of articles addresses the issue of the effects of divorce on divorced spouses.

## Dōgen

**Dōgen** (1200, Kyōto, Japan—1253, Kyōto, Japan): Zen master

**Type of ethics:** Religious ethics

**Achievements:** Founder of the Sōtō school of Japanese Zen Buddhism; author of *Shōbōgenzō* (1244; Treasury of the Eye of the True Dharma); considered by many experts to be one of the finest prose stylists in the Japanese language

**Significance:** In the true spirit of Zen Buddhism, Dōgen taught no system of ethics as such; instead, he emphasized sitting meditation practice in the belief that truly ethical action arises out of the direct experience of reality in each moment

**Background.** Buddhism originated before 500 B.C.E. in India, where the historical Buddha Śākyamuni experienced an awakening, or enlightenment, and taught others that they too could experience such an awakening and be free from the suffering caused by ignorance of the true nature of reality. A thousand years later, Buddhism spread to China, where it combined with the native Taoist tradition and evolved into Ch'an Buddhism. Ch'an Buddhism then spread to Japan, where it became known as Zen Buddhism.

In 1227, Dōgen Kigen, a liberally educated Japanese Buddhist from an aristocratic family, traveled to China in search of an enlightened Ch'an master. Dōgen studied there for four years under T'ien-tung Ju-ching, who transmitted to him the seal of confirmation of the Ch'an lineage whose approach ultimately became that of the Sōtō school of Japanese Zen.

Dōgen brought the teachings to Japan, where much of Buddhism had come to rely too heavily on theory and ritual, neglecting the meditative practice that is the heart of Buddhism. Dōgen brought the focus of Japanese Zen back to *zazen*, or sitting meditation practice, revitalizing the Zen tradition in Japan.

There are two major schools of Zen: Rinzai and Sōtō. Both schools emphasize sitting meditation (*zazen*), but Rinzai Zen also utilizes *kōan* study, in which a practitioner examines an apparently paradoxical phrase (for example, "What was your original face before you were born?") that poses a problem that cannot be solved by means of logic, thus forcing the practitioner to bypass conceptual understanding. Dōgen's Sōtō Zen, however, emphasizes the practice of *shikan taza* ("simply sitting"), which involves cultivating awareness without striving for enlightenment.

**Ethical Implications**. Dōgen's fullest discussion of Zen ethics comes in "Shoakumakusa," part of his *Shōbōgenzō*. Dōgen denies any absolute distinction between good and evil—while still affirming traditional moral teachings—by interpreting an important classical Chinese scripture as a description of an ideal rather than a command. "The nonproduction of evil,/ The performance of good,/ The purification of one's own intentions:/ This is the teaching of all Buddhas." *Shōbōgenzō* also stresses experiencing the present moment and not wasting time. Dōgen's Sōtō Zen, like other schools of Buddhism, teaches the importance of compassion for all beings. In Buddhism, however, compassion is not a mode of behavior to which one strives to adhere; instead, compassion arises spontaneously when one experiences the true reality of each moment of existence.

—*Roy Neil Graves*

**See also** Bodhidharma; Bodhisattva ideal; Buddha; Buddhist ethics; Four noble truths; Hui-neng; Zen.

**Bibliography**

Dōgen. *Moon in a Dewdrop: Writings of Zen Master Dōgen.* Edited by Kazuaki Tanahashi. San Francisco: North Point Press, 1985.

Kasulis, T. P. *Zen Action/Zen Person.* Honolulu: University Press of Hawaii, 1981.

Kim, Hee-Jin. *Dōgen Kigen—Mystical Realist.* Tucson: University of Arizona Press, 1975.

Kodera, Takashi James. *Dōgen's Formative Years in China: An Historical Study and Annotated Translation of the Hōkyō-ki.* Boulder, Colo.: Prajñā Press, 1980.

Ross, Nancy Wilson. Three Ways of Asian Wisdom: Hinduism, Buddhism, Zen, and Their Significance for the West. New York: Simon & Schuster, 1966.

Yokoi, Yūhō, with Daizen Victoria. *Zen Master Dōgen: An Introduction with Selected Writings*. 4th ed. New York: Weatherhill, 1987.

## Dominion over nature, human

**TYPE OF ETHICS:** Theory of ethics
**DATE:** From antiquity
**ASSOCIATED WITH:** Many religious traditions, particularly Judaism and Christianity
**DEFINITION:** The idea that humanity has the right to use nature to further its own ends
**SIGNIFICANCE:** The range of human dominion over nature has increased to such an extent that many people think that humanity is endangering both human and nonhuman life on Earth

Human beings have always exploited natural resources for their own well-being. Early in human history, people learned how to domesticate plants and animals—to collect or capture them, to breed them selectively, and to harvest them for human use. People also learned how to "capture," "tame," and "harvest" many inanimate resources, such as fire, water, minerals, and fossil fuels.

In most societies, it was either assumed or explicitly taught that human dominion over nature was a natural, or even God-given, right, and as long as human populations were small, this philosophy posed no major problems. As the human population increased and technology made it increasingly easy to harvest natural resources, however, many natural resources began to disappear. Many people are now questioning the idea of the human right of dominion over nature, on both practical and ethical grounds.

**See also** Animal rights; Biodiversity; Conservation; Earth, human relations to; Ecology; Endangered species; Environmental ethics; Exploitation; Future generations; Nature, rights of; Profit economy.

## Dostoevski, Fyodor

(Nov. 11, 1821, Moscow, Russia—Feb. 9, 1881, St. Petersburg, Russia): Novelist

**TYPE OF ETHICS:** Modern history
**ACHIEVEMENTS:** Author of *Bednye lyudi* (1846; *Poor Folk*, 1887), *Dvoynik* (1846; *The Double*, 1917), Zapiski iz podpolya (1864; *Notes from the Underground*, 1918), *Prestuplenie i nakazaniye* (1866; *Crime and Punishment*, 1886), *Idiot* (1868; *The Idiot*, 1887), *Besy* (1871-1872; *The Possessed*, 1913), and *Bratya Karamazovy* (1879-1880; *The Brothers Karamazov*, 1912)
**SIGNIFICANCE:** Influenced by the political, economic, and social turmoil of mid-nineteenth century European culture and the horrors of life in czarist Russia, Dostoevski developed a radical philosophy based on individual freedom; his repudiation of the existing intellectual order resulted in the creation of a philosophic vacuum in which freedom is both the only good and the only evil

*Fyodor Dostoevsky* (Library of Congress)

Inherent in Dostoevski's literary canon is the primacy of the freedom of the individual. He argued in *The Double* and other works that the problems of society were caused by the absence of freedom; humankind had been "overcome" by the impact of human institutions—the church, the state, and economic structures—and by the assumed beliefs in God and in economic and social values. Dostoevski advanced a radical philosophy in which he condemned encumbrances to freedom. He maintained that the so-called "laws of nature" did not exist; sustaining a belief in these laws would inevitably result in the restriction of freedom. It was only through unbridled and anarchical freedom that the individual would be totally free and thus recognize his or her own identity. This condition would preclude all forms of ethics except for a hedonistic ethics based on the interests of the self. Dostoevski recognized the anarchical ramifications of his argument and attempted unsuccessfully to address them in *Crime and Punishment* and *The Brothers Karamazov*. If truth does not exist, there is no basis for ethical principles.

**See also** Anarchy; Freedom and liberty.

## Dresden, bombing of

**TYPE OF ETHICS:** Military ethics
**DATE:** February 13-15, 1945
**DEFINITION:** In February, 1945, the British Royal Air Force bombed the German city of Dresden, which was not an

important military target, killing thousands of civilians and leaving thousands of others homeless

**SIGNIFICANCE:** Raised questions about the need for and the morality of massive Allied bombings of German cities and civilian populations

On February 8, 1945, late in World War II, the Allied Combined Strategic Targets Committee reported to the Supreme Headquarters Allied Expeditionary Force (SHAEF), headed by American General Dwight D. Eisenhower, that the German city of Dresden had been made a target. Dresden reputedly was a center for German military movements toward the eastern front against the advancing Russians. Allied military officials conceded later, however, that one of their basic purposes in targeting Dresden was to demoralize the Germans in an attempt to shorten the war. The code name for such massive air operations against Germany, which had included thousand-plane raids on Berlin and Hamburg, was Clarion.

On the afternoon of February 13, British Royal Air Force (RAF) bombers struck Dresden in waves, exhausting anti-aircraft and fighter-plane resistance while smothering the city with incendiary bombs. These bombs drove 600,000 civilians and refugees out of shelters just as a more devastating attack began. The intensity of the fires caused a colossal "firestorm." Ultimately, losses were calculated at 18,375 dead, 2,212 seriously wounded, and 13,918 slightly wounded. Some 350,000 people were made homeless. Outrage at the raids was expressed in the British press and in the British Parliament. Critics of the raids charged that Dresden was an ancient, beautiful, culturally rich city that had little military value. In spite of the criticism, however, the Allied military leaders continued to conduct massive bombing raids against enemy cities. Dresden and the Japanese cities of Hiroshima and Nagasaki, which became targets of atomic-bomb attacks conducted by the U.S. military, became symbols of Allied brutality. The primary ethical issue involved was whether it is possible to justify morally the bombing of targets that consist primarily of civilians. Historians continue to debate the military value of the attacks on Dresden, Hiroshima, and Nagasaki.

**See also** *Art of War, The*; Hiroshima and Nagasaki, bombing of; Limited war; Military ethics; *On War*.

## Dronenburg v. Zech

**TYPE OF ETHICS:** Civil rights

**DATE:** 1984

**ASSOCIATED WITH:** U.S. Court of Appeals for the District of Columbia; Judge Robert Bork

**DEFINITION:** The Court held that a U.S. Navy regulation requiring mandatory discharge for homosexual conduct did not violate the constitutional right of privacy or the equal protection clause

**SIGNIFICANCE:** Judge Robert Bork's decision upheld the Navy's traditional condemnation of homosexual conduct and stated that it is "almost certain to be harmful to morale and discipline"

James Dronenburg, a twenty-seven-year-old U.S. Navy petty officer, was found to have engaged regularly in homosexual conduct. The Navy discharged him involuntarily, as its regulations required. Dronenburg admitted the allegations but appealed on the ground that there is a constitutional right of privacy that protects consensual homosexual conduct and that his discharge consequently deprived him of the equal protection of the laws. The Court of Appeals held against Dronenburg, 3-0. Judge Robert Bork's opinion argued that the constitutional right of privacy established by the Supreme Court is not as well delineated as are certain other constitutional rights. Moreover, it had never been held to cover homosexual conduct. Bork suggested that any change in these regulations should be determined by "moral choices of the people and the elected representatives" rather than by the courts.

**See also** *Griswold v. Connecticut*; Privacy.

## Drug abuse

**TYPE OF ETHICS:** Personal and social ethics

**DATE:** From antiquity

**DEFINITION:** The practice of using a substance, for non-medical reasons, that adversely affects the user's physical, mental, or emotional condition

**SIGNIFICANCE:** A person's choice to abuse drugs can lead to personal harm and have devastating social consequences

One of society's most challenging problems is drug abuse. The cost in terms of personal health problems, destabilizing families, crime, and accidents brought on by abusing drugs has been staggering. Drug abuse, often referred to as "substance abuse," includes any deliberate use of illegal or legal drugs that leads to physical, emotional, or mental problems.

**Extent of Drug Abuse.** The National Institute on Drug Abuse reports that in 1990, approximately 27 million people (13.3 percent of the population) in the United States used some form of illegal drug during the previous year. In addition, one must add to this number the roughly 14.5 million Americans who were believed to be problem drinkers or alcoholics. Alcohol, although a legal substance, has a long-standing record for being the most frequently abused drug. Marijuana, cocaine, hallucinogens, and stimulants were the most frequently used illegal substances.

**Potential Harm to Self or Society.** Ethical questions abound when an individual contemplates the decision to use an illegal drug. Is it wrong to take this drug? What will be the legal, emotional, or personal health consequences of taking this drug? Will the decision to take the drug have an impact on other people? Disregarding the fact that purchasing and using an illegal substance violates social norms and breaks the law, the morality of a particular behavior can be judged, in part, by its personal and social outcomes. Drug abuse involving a psychoactive drug (a drug that affects how a person thinks or feels) can lead to horrendous consequences. The National Highway Traffic Safety Administration reported in 1991 that there were nearly twenty thousand alcohol-related fatalities in the United States. This number represents only deaths, not the additional tens of thousands

**Total Fatalities in Motor Vehicle Accidents that Were Determined to Be Alcohol-Related.**

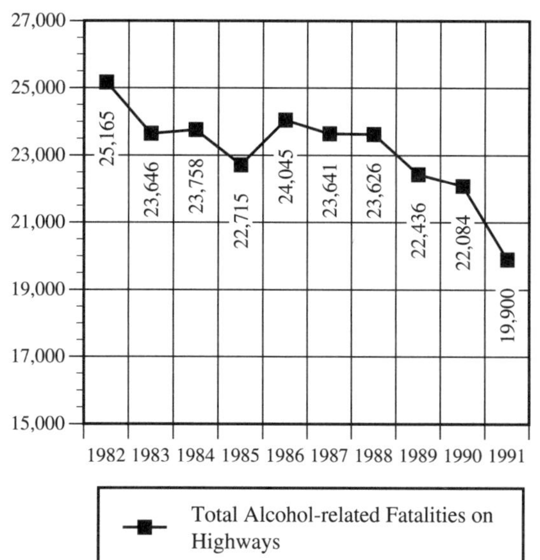


*Source:* National Highway Traffic Safety Administration (NHTSA), Washington, D. C.

of people who suffer severe head injuries in alcohol-related accidents.

Substance abuse can cut short the goals and aspirations of a person. It can lead to personal health problems and death (for example, cirrhosis of the liver, overdose). It can interfere with a person's desire to pursue an education or hold down a job.

What might have originally begun as a personal (free) decision to explore drugs and alcohol could eventually lead to both physiological and psychological dependency. This process of drug abuse turned drug addiction strips the individual of many of the personal freedoms he or she once enjoyed. The free choice to use or not to use drugs, when someone is addicted, is no longer present. Drug dependency leads to drug craving, which is difficult to overcome without intensive treatment. The control that a drug can exert on a person's life has profound ethical consequences for an individual's personal liberties.

Drug abuse can also do harm to society. People have a right to live in neighborhoods that are safe for raising families, working, and recreation. Social scientist Ronald Akers, in his book *Drugs, Alcohol, and Society* (1992), reports that substance abuse is significantly correlated with crime and juvenile delinquency. Society diverts billions of dollars each year that could go toward important social services in combating the violence and crime associated with drugs. Organized drug cartels and youth gangs pose formidable threats to community safety because of their involvement in drug trafficking.

Not only does society have to bear the cost of additional crime and law enforcement, but billions are spent each year for drug treatment and rehabilitation. The National Institute on Alcohol Abuse and Alcoholism estimates that the cost to society, for alcohol alone, is about $117 billion each year for treatment, reduced work productivity, prevention efforts, law enforcement, and so forth. Another social problem that is exacerbated by drug abuse involves the use of drugs that are administered parenterally which have contributed to the transmission of the AIDS virus. It could easily be argued that the harm caused by drug abuse for both individuals and society is not only unjust but also immoral.

**Legalization.** Efforts have been put forth to either decriminalize or legalize a number of psychoactive substances that are frequently abused. Decriminalization of marijuana by reducing the penalty of possession to less than a misdemeanor offense has come into law in a few states. The legalization of drugs such as marijuana has not, however, received state or national support. Advocates for the legalization of drugs argue that it is an individual right to be able to use drugs and that governments should stop interfering with them. In addition, advocates argue that many of the problems brought on by drug abuse (such as crime and violence) have been caused by the oppressive enforcement tactics of the government. They also state that monies that are used for drug interdiction and enforcement could be better spent on social programs.

Arguments against legalization include the prediction that the greater availability of drugs would increase the number of chemically dependent people—not decrease them as many advocates argue—thus posing even more of a threat to society. Furthermore, since the drugs influence the mind and behavior, the right-to-privacy principle does not apply because of the consequences incurred by those individuals in contact with the drug user.

*—Bryan C. Auday*

**See also** Lifestyles; Moral education; Permissible acts; Psychopharmacology; Public interest; Self-interest; Vice.

**Bibliography**

Akers, Ronald L. *Drugs, Alcohol, and Society: Social Structure, Process, and Policy.* Belmont, Calif.: Wadsworth, 1992.

Carroll, Charles R. *Drugs in Modern Society.* 2d ed. Dubuque, Iowa: W. C. Brown, 1989.

Doweiko, Harold E. *Concepts of Chemical Dependency.* Pacific Grove, Calif.: Brooks/Cole, 1990.

Goode, Erich. *Drugs in American Society.* 4th ed. New York: McGraw-Hill, 1993.

## Du Bois, William Edward Burghardt

(Feb. 23, 1868, Great Barrington, Mass.—August 27, 1963, Accra, Ghana): Writer, activist

**Type of ethics:** Modern history

**Achievements:** Author of *The Souls of Black Folk* (1903); editor of *The Crisis* (1910-1932)

**Significance:** Explored the ethical consequences of racial divisions

After a successful early career as a publishing scholar, W. E. B. Du Bois recognized that the resolution of American racial problems could not be accomplished solely by revealing the truth; therefore, he became an activist. His famous statement, "The problem of the twentieth century is the problem of the color line," demonstrates the focus of his ethical inquiries. Well-read in history, Du Bois argued that the premature end of Reconstruction left not only practical problems but also ethical ones. He believed that it was unethical for America to blame the freed slaves for the vices that had been instilled in them during generations of enslavement. Slavery, followed by a system of strict racial segregation, had left African Americans economically and psychologically vulnerable. Economically, slavery was replaced by peonage, a system in which indebted African American sharecroppers were forced to work in the fields or face starvation or imprisonment. Psychologically, black "double consciousness" caused a divided and vitiated purpose. The solutions to the problems were economic independence and the creation of an environment that would be free of racism and in which "true self-consciousness" could be attained. Du Bois is most famous for his disagreements with Booker T. Washington, the most prominent African American of the turn of the twentieth century. Du Bois believed that Washington, in his efforts to secure industrial training and a prosperous economic future for the masses of blacks, had depreciated the need for political rights, higher education, and acquaintance with the higher values of civilization. The promise of prosperity, Du Bois believed, could not substitute for civil rights and liberal learning.

*William Edward Burghardt Du Bois* (Library of Congress)

**See also** National Association for the Advancement of Colored People (NAACP); Washington, Booker T.

## Due process

**Type of ethics:** Legal and judicial ethics

**Date:** 1787

**Place:** Philadelphia, Pennsylvania

**Associated with:** The Constitution of the United States

**Definition:** Due process of law is the idea that there is a fair procedure of law to which a person is entitled should the government attempt to deprive him or her of life, liberty, or property

**Significance:** The due process clauses of the Fifth and Fourteenth Amendments to the federal Constitution and similar provisions in all state constitutions stand as barriers to arbitrary or tyrannical treatment of individuals by the government

The historical roots of due process go back at least as far as the Magna Carta (1215), by which King John of England was forced to eschew arbitrary power over the lives and estates of his barons. Although "due process" case law has become technically complex in the United States, its fundamental elements continue to be notice of the charges against one, an opportunity to defend oneself before a fair tribunal, and the benefit of general laws rather than any made for the particular case. The due process clause of the Fifth Amendment protects against the federal government, while a nearly identical clause of the Fourteenth Amendment protects against arbitrary state government action. These clauses promise that no person will "be deprived of life, liberty, or property without due process of law."

**See also** Bill of Rights, English; Bill of Rights, U.S.; Jury system; Law.

## Durkheim, Émile (Apr. 15, 1858, Épinal, France—Nov. 15, 1917, Paris, France): Social scientist

**Type of ethics:** Modern history

**Achievements:** Author of *De la division du travail social: Étude sur l'organization des sociétés supérieures* (1893; *The Division of Labor in Society*, 1933), *Les Formes élémentaires de la vie religieuse* (1912; *The Elementary Forms of the Religious Life*, 1915), and *Le Suicide: Étude de sociologie* (1897; *Suicide: A Study in Sociology*, 1951); founder of the French school of sociology

**Significance:** Durkheim suggested that the new industrial, urban order created a condition of "anomie" that undermined ethical and social structures; he maintained that reforms could be introduced through changes in education

Émile Durkheim expressed anxiety about the impact of modern society on the ethical basis of society. He argued that the advance of science and technology was not necessarily progressive; indeed, it resulted in creating a condition of "anomie" that was characterized by ethical and social isolation. Anomie resulted in a disconnected, rootless society in which ethical structures collapsed or were rendered meaningless. Durkheim's experiences as a youth during the Franco-Prussian War and the high expectations of his parents contributed to his naturally somber personality and his rather pessimistic sense of "reality." In *The Division of Labor in Society*, Durkheim identified the alienation of workers with the separation of work; in *Suicide*, he noted that suicides occur less frequently in societies that are ethically and culturally integrated. Durkheim maintained that a genuinely progressive, ethical, and enlightened society could be realized through education and religion.

**See also** Politics.

## Duty

**TYPE OF ETHICS:** Theory of ethics

**DATE:** From antiquity

**DEFINITION:** That part of morality that demands or requires the obedience of moral agents who are capable of obeying

**SIGNIFICANCE:** There is nothing in all of ethics that places greater demands upon human beings than does moral duty; thus, the highest priority in all of ethics is that one must know one's moral duty and attempt to fulfill it

The concept of duty is familiar to people from a very early age. Already in early childhood, there is an acute awareness that there are certain requirements regarding one's behavior. Usually, these are requirements to omit or refrain from certain types of forbidden behavior, and one quickly learns the types of behavior that one is expected to avoid.

Not all of one's duties are moral duties. Some duties are job related; for example, one has a duty to report for work at a certain time. Some duties arise because of one's role as a spouse or parent. Some duties are prescribed by the laws of the land. There are even duties that arise in the context of games, such as the duty of a pitcher to cover first base under certain circumstances. Some of these duties might also turn out to be moral duties, but in general they are not moral duties.

Moral duties are duties generated by morality itself; therefore, the failure to carry out these duties is a moral failure. In ethics, the failure to fulfill duty is referred to as action or inaction that is morally forbidden. More specifically, if one has a duty to perform a certain action, then it is forbidden to fail to perform the action. If one has a duty to refrain from a certain action, then it is forbidden to perform the action.

Ethicists are in perfect agreement that people must obey their duties, but there is a great deal of disagreement regarding what these duties are and how people can come to know what they are. Some philosophers have followed the lead of Plato by believing that there is a fixed, eternal, unchanging standard of what is good, holding that through serene contemplation of the Good or the Absolute Good one can come to know how to conduct one's life in accord with the requirements of morality. The contemplative tradition does not currently hold much appeal, however, at least in the moral tradition of Western culture, and contemporary moralists have looked elsewhere to find the sources or grounds of moral duty.

Many moralists have concluded that moral duty is grounded in religious truth. Here, the idea is that deities of one sort or another have decided or established how human moral agents ought to conduct their lives. The divine command theory, which states that moral duties are grounded in God's eternal decrees, is a version of this type of approach that is currently held by a relatively large number of philosophical and theological moralists.

The two dominant traditions in contemporary ethical thinking are the deontological and the consequentialist traditions, each of which provides an account of how moral duties are generated. The deontological tradition seeks to generate duty from a basic and fundamental principle that is seen as an unqualified good, dependent neither upon its results nor upon people's currently held ethical beliefs. Some people have proposed that principles of justice are fundamental to morality. Kantian ethics regards the categorical imperative as such a fundamental principle; roughly speaking, it asserts that people should act from a rule or maxim only if they are willing that this rule govern everyone's actions.

Consequentialist ethics seeks to ground duty in the good results that are produced by people's actions. For example, a simple version of act utilitarianism states that one has a duty to act in such a way as to bring about the greatest benefits for the greatest number of people. One's duty is not to obey some fundamental principle; it is to look to the future and do what is necessary to maximize utility.

Some moralists have shown a preference for returning to older ways of thinking about morality in which the concept of duty is assigned a less important role. There has been a resurgence of interest among contemporary philosophers in Aristotelian ethics, which places a greater emphasis upon the development of virtue and the avoidance of vice. Although it makes sense to talk about duty in the context of a virtue-based ethic, its role in such an ethic is much less significant than is the case in other systems currently in fashion.

There is also much disagreement about whether duties have an absolute standing. Some hold the view handed down from the tradition of Plato that duties rest upon standards that are absolute, eternal, and unchanging. In this view, there are moral standards that do not vary from culture to culture or from one period of history to another. Thus, one might argue that people have a duty to refrain from murder or from incest, and anyone who grows up in a culture that teaches otherwise and believes that these acts are permissible is simply mistaken. In this view, certain things are morally forbidden, regardless of what is believed by the people of one's culture or period of history.

Others, known as relativists, hold that there are no moral absolutes and that people's moral duties are generated by moral systems that are essentially human constructs. For example, a given culture might find that prohibitions against adultery or premarital sex lead to greater societal stability, and hence it becomes a moral duty to refrain from these activities in this culture. In this view, what counts as a person's duty is relative to the culture or time period in which one is reared. There are no duties that apply to everyone.

*—Gregory Mellema*

**See also** Permissible acts.

**BIBLIOGRAPHY**

Chisholm, Roderick. "The Ethics of Requirement." *American Philosophical Quarterly* 1 (April, 1964): 147-153.

Fishkin, James S. *The Limits of Obligation.* New Haven, Conn.: Yale University Press, 1982.

Gewirth, Alan. *Reason and Morality.* Chicago: University of Chicago Press, 1978.

Prichard, H. A. *Moral Obligation and Duty and Interest.* London: Oxford University Press, 1968.

Singer, Marcus. *Generalization in Ethics.* New York: Russell & Russell, 1971.

## Earth, human relations to

**TYPE OF ETHICS:** Environmental ethics
**DATE:** From antiquity
**DEFINITION:** Human beings' attitudes and behavior toward Earth and its ecosystems
**SIGNIFICANCE:** Relates to ways of understanding humankind's ethical relationship to Earth and its ecosystems

Human beings have a combination of qualities that are unique among other forms of life on Earth: the capacity for symbolic thought and communication, hands with opposable thumbs, and a predilection to accumulate goods. Their impact on Earth's ecosystems has been significant and distinctive.

**History.** Earth's origin is dated at 4,500 million years ago. Humankind's first known ancestors appeared approximately 5 million years ago. The span of human existence, then, has been limited to a mere one-tenth of one percent (0.1%) of the earth's existence.

Human evolution has not been strictly linear. There were both extinctions and overlappings among the variety of human species that existed between *Australopithecus,* the first ancestor, and the current species, *Homo sapiens.* The most anatomically modern human appeared 100,000 years ago.

Despite the seeming antiquity of the human presence on Earth, for most of that time, the species survived by gathering vegetation and scavenging meat until successful hunting methods were established; throughout all this time, the species had very little impact on Earth and its ecosystems. It was not until humankind began to domesticate animals and plants and had learned how to generate fire that the human species could begin making notable changes in the course of its future and in the future of the Earth's ecosystems. This power was acquired between nine thousand and twelve thousand years ago.

Humankind's psychosocial awareness—the basis for the development of an ethical system—emerged very gradually. In the earliest years, there was no recognition of being distinct as a species or as individuals. Life was a series of instinctive responses to the environment and to physical needs. Jean Gebser describes it as "a time of complete non-differentiation of man and the universe."

With humankind's growing awareness of its separateness from the rest of the ecosystem came a sense of insecurity about its relationship to the external world. As human societies began to experiment with their potential autonomy, they developed rituals to support their systems of magical beliefs in order to maintain an amicable relationship with the all-powerful outer world and to avoid any punishment for their "defection." Killing animals for food, for example, was no longer an instinctive behavior. It involved asking permission from some life-sustaining force. When disaster struck—or perhaps to forestall it—sacrificial rituals were offered to appease the force. Using rituals based on magical beliefs is evidence of perceiving an adversarial position between the human and outer worlds.

When humankind began to understand Earth's rhythms, some fears were resolved. The Earth-human relationship changed. Myth systems were developed to record and pass on the body of knowledge that humankind had been accumulating. It became possible to predict future occurrences based on past experiences and observations. This development, then, made it possible to begin taking advantage of predictable beneficial conditions and to try avoiding harmful ones. Agriculture made permanent settlements possible. The resultant increase in the size and density of human populations began overtaxing the environment. Cheryl Simon Silver reports that as early as eight thousand years ago, areas around the Mediterranean showed that wild animal populations were being replaced by domesticated ones. Plant communities there have been disrupted so badly and for so long that it is now difficult to determine what constituted the indigenous vegetation.

When humans turned their vision of the life-giving force from being Earth centered to being heaven centered, humankind assumed dominion over the rest of Earth's life forms and its nonliving "resources." Based on this concept, the most aggressive human societies have exercised their presumed right through activities such as strip mining, clear-cut logging, growing monocultures, using nuclear power, damming or channelizing rivers, forbidding human contraception, and in causing the deliberate extinction of other species.

**Discussion.** Because the ethical systems described above have evolved along with humanity's awareness of its uniqueness on Earth, it might seem that these paradigms exist along a continuum. In fact, they exist as diffuse elements within a mosaic design. They all still survive throughout the world and guide human behavior.

It does not seem likely or practical that individually any of these paradigms will or can solve the problems of environmental damage. The range of proposed solutions, however, is a reflection of each of them. Totally opposite conclusions, both of them based on faith, exist within the dominion-of-humankind paradigm. In humanistic ethical systems there is the belief that progress in technology will find solutions to overturn ecological damage. In religion-based systems, there is the belief that humanity should continue to take advantage of the provided resources and not be concerned about Earth's future, because a transcendent god will rescue at least a portion of humankind in times of mortal danger. Elements of the magical and mythical systems are expressed by groups such as the Nature Conservancy and Releaf, which advocate the preservation or rehabilitation of the environment. The first paradigm, in which there was no differentiation between humankind and its environment, is expressed in groups such as Earth First! or those that represent the deep ecology movement. They define their views as "ecoethics," because they hold that all other approaches to the environment are arrogantly egocentric, based entirely on human self-interest, and have little to do with the reality of humankind's minuscule time span in the total scheme of Earth's existence.

Since there has been evolution in ethical systems, however, there is reason to assume that humankind may evolve some other ethical system that might solve the problems that now threaten both Earth and human beings. Indeed, Daniel Kealey and Gebser believe that the new paradigm is emerging and that it is based on an integration of all the previous ethical systems. —*Marcella T. Joy*

**See also** Biodiversity; Conservation; Ecology; Environmental ethics; Environmental movement; Gaia; Nature, rights of; Sierra Club.

**BIBLIOGRAPHY**

Allsopp, Bruce. *Ecological Morality.* London: Frederick Muller, 1972.

Gebser, Jean. *The Ever-Present Origin.* Translated by Noel Barstad and Algis Mickunas. Athens: Ohio University Press, 1985.

Kealey, Daniel. *Revisioning Environmental Ethics.* Albany: State University of New York Press, 1990.

Maguire, Daniel. *The Moral Choice.* Garden City, N.Y.: Doubleday, 1978.

Miller, Alan. *Gaia Connections: an Introduction to Ecology, Ecoethics, and Economics.* Savage, Md.: Rowman & Littlefield, 1991.

Regan, Tom, ed. *Earthbound: New Introductory Essays in Environmental Ethics.* New York: Random House, 1984.

Silver, Cheryl Simon. *One Earth, One Future: Our Changing Global Environment.* Washington, D.C.: National Academy Press, 1990.

## Earth Day

**TYPE OF ETHICS:** Environmental ethics

**DATE:** April 22, 1970

**ASSOCIATED WITH:** Environmental Action, Senator Gaylord Nelson, and Denis Hayes

**DEFINITION:** Organized by Environmental Action through colleges, schools, and local organizations, Earth Day celebrated the earth and focused attention on the relationship of people to Earth

**SIGNIFICANCE:** Earth Day was the first nationwide event to focus on the environment; it emphasized individual and consumer responsibility for environmental quality

Earth Day was organized as an opportunity for "teach-ins" on the environment and on the effects of human actions on the environment. Many teach-ins focused on air and water pollution, the relationship between environmental quality and human health, and the individual consumer's responsibility for environmental quality. Grassroots activities included picking up litter along roads and streams. Colleges, universities, and public schools were the locales of many of the first Earth Day activities and continued to be the centers for organized Earth Days in subsequent years. In 1970, a reported twenty-five million Americans participated in Earth Day activities. Through intensive media coverage of Earth Day, information about the environment reached millions more. Following Earth Day, public opinion polls reflected increased awareness of environmental problems and increased support for maintaining environmental quality. Earth Day both reflected and increased public, media, and official interest in environmental quality and in individual responsibility for the environment. The media continue to present stories on environmental trends and issues on Earth Day each year.

**See also** Environmental movement; Pollution.

## Ecology

**TYPE OF ETHICS:** Environmental ethics

**DATE:** 1869

**DEFINITION:** The study of relationships among organisms and between organisms and the environment

**SIGNIFICANCE:** The scientific basis for the conservation and preservation ethic

Ecology is broadly divided into "autecology," pertaining to individual organisms or species, and "synecology," or the ecology of communities of organisms. Synecology places humankind in organic "communities," or ecosystems, thus positing a human ethical responsibility to the environment as broadly defined. Since World War II, an "ecological movement" has advocated programs designed to ensure that humankind will live within the limitations of the earth's resources. By means of these programs, communities modify their environments, thus causing successional replacement and moving toward stable, organic "climax communities" that are adapted to current environmental conditions. Short-term changes in community character, especially retreat from "climax," is a practical measure of humankind's effect on the ecosystem. Biogeography refers to community distribution, while paleobiogeography considers succession over geologic time. Ecology arose from Alexander von Humboldt's (1769-1859) approach to natural history and from Carolus Linnaeus' (1707-1778) studies of plant life histories. Plant ecology in America became well established in the early twentieth century in Nebraska, where Frederic Clements established the community concept and coined an overabundance of technical terms. Victor Shelford of the University of Chicago contemporaneously developed the fundamentals of animal ecology. Among subdivisions of ecology are limnology, oceanography, plant ecology, animal ecology, phenology, biogeography, and paleobiogeography.

**See also** Biodiversity; Deforestation; Environmental Protection Agency (EPA), U.S.; Gaia; Greenpeace; Sierra Club; *Walden*; Wilderness Act of 1964; Zero Population Growth (ZPG).

## Economic analysis

**TYPE OF ETHICS:** Politico-economic ethics

**DATE:** Eighteenth century to present

**DEFINITION:** A method of analyzing actions to determine their effects and of finding the least costly way to achieve a goal

**SIGNIFICANCE:** Provides a conceptual framework in which to analyze actions and policies

Economic analysis involves discovering how to meet desires at the lowest cost. Although most commonly applied to business and budgeting problems, economic analysis can be applied to virtually any decision involving expenditures of resources such as money, time, or even emotional energy.

**History.** The problems that economics addresses apply to all individuals and societies, even to the animal kingdom. Formal analysis of these problems began in earnest in the eighteenth century. Pioneers of what was called "political economy," including Adam Smith, David Ricardo, and Thomas Robert Malthus, wrote about such topics as division of labor, international trade, and population control. Economists quickly refined their tools of analysis and extended the range of topics under consideration. Gary Becker, winner of the 1992 Nobel Prize in Economics, has extended economic analysis to the study of marriage, the family, and discrimination, among many other topics.

**The Science of Economics.** Economics is designed to provide objective answers to questions. It is not intended to be a normative discipline (one that answers questions concerning values) and therefore is not itself a theory of ethics. The distinction often becomes blurred. Economics accepts value judgments and tells people how they can achieve what they want; it does not tell people what they should want. In practice, however, many economists promote their own values, trying to convince others that their goals are desirable.

One basic tool of economics is cost-benefit analysis, which weighs the costs of alternative actions against the benefits that will result from them. This tool allows identification of the least costly way of achieving a certain goal. The goal and the alternative actions are presented to the economic analyst, who is not supposed to pass judgment on the "correctness" of the goal. Economic analysis applies to any question involving a choice among alternatives but is most commonly used to address personal questions of budgeting and finance and societal questions of distribution and market behavior.

**Distribution.** Government policymakers face many issues of distribution of the various services. Many of the issues involve questions of perceived fairness. The most basic questions facing policymakers are what will be provided, how it will be distributed, and who will pay for it.

Economic analysis cannot answer any of these questions directly. It can, however, provide information that is helpful in making the decisions. For example, policymakers might consider spending money on education. Once policymakers have identified the different educational programs that could be provided, economists can determine the likely effects of each, giving some idea of the costs and benefits. They can also determine the benefits that would be derived by various individuals or groups, information that will help policymakers decide how to allocate the educational programs.

Economists also examine the ways of financing programs. Income taxes can be designed so that one income group pays a higher proportion of the cost than does another. Sales taxes do not affect everyone equally, because people spend and save different proportions of their income, thus paying the tax at different times in their lives. In addition, most sales taxes do not affect all products, so those buying more of the taxed products pay more in taxes. Typically, for example, taxes on gasoline, other forms of energy, liquor, and tobacco products place a heavier burden, proportional to income, on poor people. A fixed amount of tax on each person may appear to be fair, but it would represent a higher proportion of income for people who earn less. Issues of financing government programs thus become complicated. The normative questions of which programs should be provided, who should receive benefits, or how it would be fair to finance the programs can better be answered by policymakers once economists have provided their analysis.

**Markets.** Economic analysis applies to all types of behavior and all market systems. Costs and benefits are easier to identify in capitalist systems, in which virtually everything has a price that is determined by the market. Socialist systems also rely on economic analysis, however, with costs and benefits determined more abstractly by policymakers. Socialist policymakers sometimes have to make somewhat arbitrary decisions concerning the value or cost of a program, since there may not be prices to measure values. In societies in which medical care is provided free or at subsidized prices, for example, policymakers have a more difficult time deciding how to allocate that care, since no true price shows how much people value medical care. People tend to say that they value any service that is offered and to complain when any service is cut off. The question for economic analysis is to determine how much people would be willing to pay in an unsubsidized market.

Economic analysis can be used to help determine what types of markets will exist, even as broadly as analyzing the effects of establishing a communist versus a capitalist market. Branches of economics concern the behavior of various types of firms, such as monopolies, and how regulation affects them. It can provide information that is useful in determining government policy concerning such topics as population control, medical research, health insurance, education, the environment, use of nonrenewable resources, immigration, employment and unemployment, and foreign aid. Provision of benefits in any one of these areas may mean that money cannot be spent on benefits in another. Economic analysis can help in determining such tradeoffs among vastly different projects. It cannot determine which projects should be chosen but can help to identify the benefits of money spent on each one. *—A. J. Sobczak*

**See also** Antitrust legislation; Business ethics; Capitalism; Communism; Economics; Monopoly; Profit economy.

**BIBLIOGRAPHY**

Blinder, Alan S. *Hard Heads, Soft Hearts: Tough-Minded Economics for a Just Society*. Reading, Mass.: Addison-Wesley, 1987.

Brockway, George P. *Economics: What Went Wrong, and Why, and Some Things to Do About It*. New York: Harper & Row, 1985.

Gabor, Dennis. *The Mature Society*. New York: Praeger, 1972.

Rosenbaum, Robert A. *The Public Issues Handbook: A Guide for the Concerned Citizen*. Westport, Conn.: Greenwood Press, 1983.

Schumacher, Ernst Friedrich. *Small Is Beautiful*. New York: Harper & Row, 1973.

## Economics

**Type of ethics:** Politico-economic ethics

**Date:** From antiquity

**Associated with:** Adam Smith, John Locke, and Karl Marx

**Definition:** The study of the production, distribution, and consumption of goods and services

**Significance:** Many of the theoretical aspects and practical applications of economics are susceptible to ethical evaluation

The primary concern of economics is the production, distribution, and consumption of goods and services. One conventional view that has generated perennial debate is that economics is value-free or ethically neutral. This view rests primarily on what is called the "naturalistic fallacy" (identified, but not so named, by David Hume), according to which it is a mistake to attempt to deduce a conclusion concerning what ought to be the case from premises that state exclusively what is the case. In other words, it is impossible to derive an "ought" from an "is." Furthermore, precisely because economics is a social science, it is concerned only with descriptive statements and not at all with ethical considerations (including value judgments); descriptive statements, by definition, can imply nothing of an ethical nature whatsoever. Consequently, it does seem reasonable that, methodologically, economics can be said to be ethically neutral.

Even if a particular discipline, such as economics, is ethically neutral in its methodology, however, it is still an open question whether that same discipline is subject to ethical implications or associations either in its theoretical aspects or in its practical application. In fact, there is a vast array of ethical implications and associations in both the theoretical aspects and the practical applications of economics. Even on the theoretical level, the relationship between economics and ethics takes various forms. For example, an economist who specializes in economic systems—that is, the principles and technical methods by which both the ownership and the allocation of a society's resources are determined by that society—might engage in several different types of analysis, including the ethical evaluation of the diverse systems under consideration for comparison purposes. Such an evaluation would involve an intricate network of economic and ethical concepts.

Any attempt either to explicate this type of economic analysis or to survey some of its significant concepts is well beyond the scope of this article. Instead, the remainder of this article will consist of a sketch of some of the ethical implications of two theoretical concepts in economics, each of which is particularly relevant to Western societies: the profit motive and private property acquisition.

The premier argument for the profit motive is to be found in Adam Smith's *The Wealth of Nations* (1776). According to Smith, the development of a full-blown economy depends on the existence of various individuals in the society who possess a greater quantity of either raw materials or goods that have been produced than they themselves need. Such a phenomenon encourages the development of a system of bartering, which presents the opportunity for the various members of the society to devote their time, energy, and individual talents to a single economic endeavor. This "division of labor" benefits both the individual members of the society and the society as a whole. The individual members of the society derive benefit from this new opportunity to determine what particular economic activities they are, individually, suited for and interested in pursuing, and that can profit them the most. Important, too, is the expectation that to the extent that one is engaged in a particular economic activity, one should, over time, become quite adept at it. This skill should lead to an increase in both the quantity and the quality of individual production in such a way as to also increase the economic compensation of the individual worker. Moreover, such an improvement in the efficiency of production should result in higher-quality products at lower costs in the marketplace. Ultimately, the society as a whole is improved to the extent that this process represents an enhancement of the entire economy as well as an increase in the standard of living for all.

So it is, then, that, in the final analysis, the individual's pursuit of the profit motive is advantageous to the society as a whole. According to Smith, one neither does nor should pursue a particular economic activity in order to promote either the interests of others in the society or the interest of the society as a whole. Rather, one should pursue a chosen economic activity solely out of self-interest, because the economic relationship between the interests of the individual and the interest of the society as a whole is such that "an invisible hand" translates the former into the latter.

With the advent of the Industrial Revolution came harsh criticism of the type of competitive free-market economy that Smith had championed. The primary critic of the free-market type of economic system was Karl Marx. In various works, including *The Communist Manifesto* (1848; a collaborative effort with Friedrich Engels) and *Economic and Philosophic Manuscripts of 1844*, Marx argues at length against both the profit motive and private property acquisition.

The classical argument for private property acquisition and property rights is the fifth chapter of John Locke's *Second Treatise of Government* (1690), in which he maintains that even in a "state of nature"—that is, a social environment prior to the institution of any governmental authority—one is free and possesses oneself, which includes one's own body and, by extension, one's own labor. Furthermore, the earth's natural resources are owned by no one in particular but are held in common by all of humankind. The question becomes how one may legitimately appropriate to oneself some of the fruits of the earth in order to sustain one's own existence. Locke's answer is that upon "mixing one's labor" with some portion of the fruits of the earth in order to take it out of the state in which nature has left it and render it usable for human sustenance, one may, as a natural right, lay claim to it as one's own private property. Locke proceeds to add some practical limitations and to flesh out the details of this moral argument for private property acquisition and property rights.

Against both the profit motive and private property acquisition, Marx argues that, taken in conjunction, these two economic rights inevitably result in inordinate accumulation of wealth for the bourgeoisie (the owners of the means of production) and only subsistence wages for the proletariat (the working class). Workers in a capitalistic free-market economic system are actually selling their labor in order to sustain themselves, and thereby they become mere commodities to be bought by the bourgeoisie at the lowest possible wages. The profit motive is such that any profit that is realized from the sale of manufactured goods either is reinvested in the production process or merely becomes additional wealth for the bourgeoisie. The right to private property is such that the bourgeoisie, as the owners of literally all of the means of production, make the proletariat subservient not only to themselves but also to the means of production. All of this, together with numerous types of alienation that are experienced by the proletariat because of the menial and dehumanizing nature of their work, leads, by the nature of the case, to a class struggle in which the proletariat constantly fights to overcome its exploitation by the bourgeoisie.

It should be clear from only these two examples that even theoretical economic concepts and the arguments for their implementation engender an array of both ethical implications and moral disagreements. —*Stephen C. Taylor*

**See also** Class struggle; *Communist Manifesto*; Economic analysis; Locke, John; Marx, Karl; Smith, Adam.

**BIBLIOGRAPHY**

Locke, John. *Second Treatise of Government* (1690). Edited by C. B. Macpherson. Indianapolis: Hackett, 1980.

Myers, Milton L. *The Soul of Modern Economic Man: Ideas of Self-Interest, Thomas Hobbes to Adam Smith.* Chicago: University of Chicago Press, 1983.

Sen, Amartya. *On Ethics and Economics.* Oxford, England: Blackwell, 1987.

Smith, Adam. *The Wealth of Nations* (1776). New York: Knopf, 1991. See especially books 1 and 4.

Tucker, Robert C., ed. *The Marx-Engels Reader,* 2d ed. New York: W. W. Norton, 1978.

## Edwards, Jonathan (Oct. 5, 1703, East Windsor, Conn.—Mar. 22, 1758, Princeton, N.J.): Puritan clergyman, theologian, philosopher

**TYPE OF ETHICS:** Religious ethics

**ACHIEVEMENTS:** Author of *Freedom of Will* (1754) and "Sinners in the Hands of an Angry God" (1741)

**SIGNIFICANCE:** Edwards reiterated the strict Calvinistic doctrine of communion only for the elect—those predestined to salvation—while simultaneously stressing the individual emotional conversion experience

Arguably one of America's keenest intellectuals, Edwards was a commanding Puritan minister who emphasized traditional Calvinist doctrines of humanity's utter depravity and total dependence upon God. His *Great Christian Doctrine of Original Sin Defended* (1758) added a cornerstone to the debate regarding the fundamental depravity of human nature and provided a strenuous defense of Calvinism against the increasingly secularized Enlightenment. By combining Puritan intellectualism with a unique emotionalism, Edwards became a singularly dynamic preacher and theologian. Assuming leadership of the Northhampton, Massachusetts, parish in 1728 from his famous grandfather, Solomon Stoddard, Edwards became immediately controversial with his repudiation of Stoddard's Half-Way Covenant, the agency by which children of the predestined—themselves not necessarily of the elect—were entitled to receive communion. Edwards preached a peculiarly complex blend emphasizing the apparently antagonistic tenets of predestination and conversion experience. Although the development of evangelical religion was antithetical to traditional Calvinism, Edwards' emotionally charged yet intellectually compelling sermons inaugurated in New England the religious revival known as the Great Awakening. Amid controversy regarding his insistence on emotional conversion as proof of election, Edwards was dismissed from his Northhampton post in 1751; thereafter, he preached among Native Americans. Suggesting that the "great tribulations" of the Christian faith had passed, in his pioneer sermon "Humble Attempt to Promote Explicit Agreement and Visible Union of Gods People . . ." (1747), Edwards had earlier cleared his way by lessening theological inhibitions against missionizing.

**See also** Calvin, John.

## Egalitarianism

**TYPE OF ETHICS:** Theory of ethics

**DATE:** Sixth century B.C.E. to present

**DEFINITION:** The belief that human equality is a moral principle that should be upheld by society

**SIGNIFICANCE:** Egalitarianism is linked to the goal of justice through equality of treatment and rights

Egalitarian principles in Western thought originated in ancient Greece. Athenian citizens were chosen for political office by lot, since all were thought to be capable of fulfilling the functions of public office. All Spartan men served equally as soldiers. Christian thought has stressed egalitarian concepts, both in the notion that all human beings are equal in the sight of God, and that faith, not position or social status, determines one's worthiness for salvation. In a more secular approach, both Thomas Hobbes and John Locke, sixteenth century English thinkers, stressed that society was created by humans through mutual consent. Egalitarian ideas formed the basis for the American Declaration of Independence and the Rights of Man and the Citizen in the French Revolution, despite the persistence of slavery in America, and the fact that women were not accorded equal rights as citizens in France. The goal of equality was valued by the leaders of these revolutions and has profoundly influenced those societies in which they occurred. In the twentieth century, egalitarianism has influenced movements for civil rights, women's rights, and equal opportunities for the disabled, and has promoted the idea that equality is an important moral principle.

**See also** Americans with Disabilities Act; Civil rights; Natural rights; Social justice and responsibility.

## Egoism

**TYPE OF ETHICS:** Theory of ethics

**DATE:** Seventeenth century to present

**ASSOCIATED WITH:** British philosopher Thomas Hobbes; American novelist Ayn Rand; and twentieth century American philosophers Jesse Kalin, Tibor Machan, and Edward Regis, Jr.

**DEFINITION:** The doctrine that each person ought to maximize his or her own self-interest and that no one should ever sacrifice his or her self-interest

**SIGNIFICANCE:** Egoism is a challenge to every altruistic or other-regarding basis for ethics, since egoism maintains that one has no unconditional obligation to others; egoism thus implies that altruistic behavior is justified only as a means to self-interest and never for its own sake

Egoism is a normative guide to action and an outlook on life. It draws its inspiration from diverse traditions and sources, from the discussions of justice and advantage in Plato's *Republic* to the egocentric account of human nature in the writings of Thomas Hobbes. It both influences and is influenced by cost-benefit analysis in economics, the theory of practical reasoning, and libertarian political theory.

According to egoism, each person ought to do all and only those acts that maximize his or her self-interest. (The theory may also be formulated in terms of rules, or even virtues, but so-called "act" egoism is the most common variety.) Furthermore, according to egoism, one has no basic or unconditional obligations to others. Any obligations one might have to others are derived from one's interest in or use of them. Thus, egoism implies that one should be prepared to take advantage of others when this is in one's own interest.

Egoists maintain that maximizing self-interest is the most rational thing to do. Therefore, if rationality and moral rightness are equivalent, egoism will be a theory of moral rightness. If the two can conflict, however, egoism will be a nonmoral theory of rational action, and in cases of conflict between the rational and the right, egoism will give rise to the question "Why be moral?"

**Self-Interest.** Egoists have offered different accounts of self-interest. Some egoists have been hedonists, maintaining that only one's own pleasure is worth seeking for its own sake. Others have emphasized power, and still others have stressed wealth or honor. It has even been argued that virtue or good character is intrinsically good and is as much a part of a person's self-interest as pleasure, wealth, or power. Obviously, those who defend egoism must provide some specification of "self interest" in order to convey fully the content and practical implications of their theory. Many philosophers use "self-interest" in a generic sense to refer to "happiness" or "well-being." In this respect, defenders of egoism emphasize that one's obligations and decisions are grounded in one's long-term enlightened self-interest, not simply in the satisfaction of desire.

**Self and Others.** For egoism, self-interest is the criterion of overriding value. When one's interests come into irreconcilable conflict with others, egoism authorizes one to seek one's self-interest at their expense—not only when the other person is an enemy or stranger, but even when that person is a spouse, child, parent, or friend. This follows from the fact that one has no unconditional obligation to serve the interests of others. Of course, if helping others or refraining from harming them would help oneself, one ought to do so. Thus, according to egoism, one ought to keep promises, tell the truth, and give the appearance of being generally fair-minded and cooperative as long as these acts are in one's own self-interest. Yet egoists have no principled reasons to place constraints on self-interested behavior that might harm others.

**Criticisms.** Three distinct, if partially overlapping, criticisms have been raised against egoism. First, it has been argued that egoism is inconsistent, since in conflict-of-interest situations, egoism requires or authorizes that everyone come out on top. Defenders of egoism respond to this criticism by pointing out that egoism advocates that a certain state of affairs be brought about in which each person tries to maximize his or her self-interest. Moreover, conflicts can be resolved within a system of rules that it is in one's self-interest to adopt as long as others do so as well.

A second criticism is that since it would not be in one's self-interest for one's egoism to be widely known, egoists cannot participate in public activities and practices such as teaching, advocacy, and advising, which are characteristic of morality. Egoists argue that since acts of teaching, advocating, and advising are not, according to this criticism, to be justified in terms of self-interest, the criticism begs the question against egoism. In addition, egoists point out that where there are no conflicts, egoists can engage in sincere moral teaching, advocacy, and advising, and where conflicts do arise, egoists can keep their silence.

A third criticism is that egoism is simply an immoral doctrine. By maintaining that any act is justified if and only if it promotes self-interest, egoism is said to sanction acts of lying, theft, blackmail, and murder. Some defenders of egoism have responded to this criticism by denying that egoism, when properly formulated, would authorize acts of this kind. Others have conceded the theoretical possibility that such acts would be egoistically justified but have argued that it is very unlikely that immoral acts would in fact promote one's self-interest

Criticisms such as these have led defenders of egoism to numerous reformulations and refinements of the doctrine. Rule-based, rights-based, and virtue-based forms of egoism are developments in the project of making egoism a coherent, consistent, and morally defensible action-guide and outlook on life. —*Steven M. Sanders*

**See also** Altruism; Impartiality; Prisoner's dilemma; Self-interest.

**BIBLIOGRAPHY**

Baier, Kurt. *The Moral Point of View.* Ithaca, N.Y.: Cornell University Press, 1958.

Hospers, John. *Human Conduct.* 2d ed. New York. Harcourt Brace Jovanovich, 1982.

Kalin, Jesse. "In Defense of Egoism." In *Morality and Rational Self-Interest.* Edited by David P. Gauthier. Englewood Cliffs, N.J.: Prentice-Hall, 1970.

Machan, Tibor R. *Individuals and Their Rights.* La Salle, Ill.: Open Court, 1989.

Regis, Edward, Jr. "What Is Ethical Egoism?" *Ethics* 91 (October, 1980): 50-62.

Sanders, Steven M. "Is Egoism Morally Defensible?" *Philosophia* 18 (July, 1988): 191-209.

Williams, Bernard. "Egoism and Altruism." In *Problems of the Self.* Cambridge, England: Cambridge University Press, 1973.

## Egotist

**TYPE OF ETHICS:** Theory of ethics
**DATE:** Term first used in English in 1714
**DEFINITION:** An egotist is one who seeks to promote his or her own interests and goals in all or most of what he or she does
**SIGNIFICANCE:** Sometimes mistaken for the moral theory of egoism, egotism is widely regarded as a morally wrong attitude or policy of action

An egotist adopts the general policy of acting selfishly. In common parlance, the term "egotist" is used to label those people who have exaggerated opinions of themselves. Egotism, which is not a moral theory, must not be equated with egoism, which is the moral theory that one ought always to act to promote one's own interests. It might be thought that egotism is at least compatible with egoism. The two concepts are indeed compatible if acting selfishly is always in one's own best interests, but egoists have been known to argue that egotism is not in one's best interests. In any case, egotists do not usually have moral reasons for their policy of action. Also, to the extent that egotism reveals anything about the egotist's beliefs, it reveals that the egotist believes himself or herself to be superior to others in some general sense. The egoist is not necessarily committed to such a belief in personal superiority. Thus, while egoism is a moral theory whose merit must be investigated philosophically, egotism is a form of behavior whose causes and cure are a matter of psychological interest. Egotism certainly is incompatible with altruism, and thus is incompatible with most normative ethical theories.

**See also** Altruism; Self-interest; Selfishness.

## Either/Or: Book

**TYPE OF ETHICS:** Modern history
**DATE:** Published 1843 as *Enten-Eller: Et Livs Fragment*
**AUTHOR:** Søren Kierkegaard
**SIGNIFICANCE:** Presents two radically different forms of existence, the aesthetic and the ethical, in the writings of two fictional characters who typify those forms of existence, thereby challenging readers to choose between them

In the two volumes of *Either/Or*, Kierkegaard confronts readers with a sharp choice between two forms of existence, the aesthetic, which regards enjoyment and pleasure as the highest values, and the ethical, which views the world in terms of right and wrong. Rather than describing these two forms of existence, Kierkegaard brings them to life in the writings of two fictional characters. An unnamed sophisticated young man, designated "A," is credited with the widely varied essays and aphorisms that make up volume 1; Judge William, a family man and minor court official, writes the two long letters to "A" that make up volume 2. A third fictional character, Victor Eremita, claims to have found the papers of "A" and Judge William in an old desk and to have arranged for their publication.

**Volume 1.** After a preface in which Victor Eremita describes finding the papers that make up *Either/Or*, volume 1 is composed of the papers of "A." The first section is a group of aphorisms that "A" calls "Diapsalmata." These aphorisms set the tone for volume 1 by vividly conveying the cynical and world-weary but also sensitive and enthusiastic character of "A." These aphorisms further show "A's" strong interest in literary and musical art, an interest that is amply demonstrated in the five substantial essays on art and artistic themes that follow the Diapsalmata. The first and longest of these, "The Immediate Stages of the Erotic or the Musical Erotic," is an impassioned celebration of Mozart's opera *Don Giovanni*. Don Juan is significant to "A" because he represents a distinctive form of aesthetic existence: the immediate. An immediate aesthete, such as Don Juan, seeks pleasure in a wholly spontaneous, unself-conscious manner. His consciousness is confined to the here and now, and no thought of guilt for his many seductions ever clouds his enjoyments. While "A" enthuses over Don Juan, his self-consciousness, or reflectivity, separates his form of aesthetic existence decisively from the Don's. "A's" mode of aesthetic existence is best illustrated in the essay "The Rotation of

Crops," in which "A" humorously states his strategy for finding enjoyment and avoiding boredom. To seek pleasure directly, like Don Juan, eventually jades the self; overused enjoyments grow stale. So "A" constantly varies his amusements just as farmers rotate crops so as not to exhaust their fields.

Despite the witty, jesting tone of "The Rotation of Crops," this and other entries in volume 1 show "A" to be afflicted by a deep and dark melancholy. He even cultivates this melancholy as a source of enjoyment, calling sorrow his castle and naming hopelessness as the precondition of the aesthetic life. "A" is also profoundly interested in the sorrow of others. Many of his essays are analyses of tragic figures from literature that he presented to a ghoulish club, the Symparanekromenoi, "the society of the already dead."

The final section of volume 1, "Diary of a Seducer," is both the longest section of the volume and the most chilling picture of aesthetic existence. "A" claims to have copied a large section of the journal of an acquaintance named Johannes, which chronicles the devious seduction and callous abandonment of an innocent young girl. In his introductory remarks to the copied journal entries, "A" shudders at Johannes' calculating coldness and worries that Johannes reveals the demonic character of aesthetic existence by carrying it through to its logical extreme.

**Volume 2.** Kierkegaard brings the ethical form of existence to life in three letters, two very long and one short, from Judge William to "A." Judge William tries to convert "A" from aesthetic existence to ethical existence by (1) analyzing and criticizing aesthetic existence and (2) depicting ethical existence in a highly positive light. It is significant that Judge William writes letters rather than essays: he is not interested in a disinterested, impersonal, theoretical analysis of aesthetic and ethical existence. Rather, he speaks as a concrete, existing, concerned individual to another such individual.

Like "A," Judge William is especially concerned with the romantic dimension of human life. Whereas "A" focuses on brief and usually tragic romantic liaisons, Judge William is an enthusiastic advocate of marriage. Marriage represents for him the ideal example of ethical existence. It represents an open-ended, infinite commitment rather than a short-term, fulfillable task. Furthermore, Judge William uses the example of marriage to show that a life of duty is not less but more enjoyable than an aesthetic life, even though the aesthetic life makes enjoyment its highest end. The first of his letters to "A" is accordingly titled, "The Aesthetic Validity of Marriage." Here, Judge William argues at great length that duty, the obligation entered into with the wedding vows, preserves, nurtures, and strengthens spontaneous love rather than banishes it as "A" asserts. The second letter, "The Balance Between the Aesthetic and the Ethical in the Development of the Personality," makes the same essential point: the choice is not between a life of enjoyment and a life of duty; in living responsibly and ethically, the person can have a much better time and enjoy himself or herself much more thoroughly than if he or she is always focused on getting enjoyment. Volume 2 ends as did volume 1: with a copied text by someone else. Judge William sends to "A" a copy of a sermon written by an old university friend entitled "The Upbuilding That Lies in the Thought That in Relation to God We Are Always in the Wrong." The sermon emphasizes the infinity of the ethical demand and the impossibility of actually fulfilling it. Though Judge William writes that the sermon makes the same point he had been making in his two letters, it seems to call into question Judge William's whole project of existing as a morally righteous person. This ending of *Either/Or* points ahead to later works of Kierkegaard's in which religious modes of existence are contrasted with both the aesthetic and the ethical.

*—George Connell*

**See also** Kierkegaard, Søren.

**BIBLIOGRAPHY**

Kierkegaard, Søren. *Either/Or*. Translated by Edna Hong and Howard Hong. Princeton, N.J.: Princeton University Press, 1987.

Lowrie, Walter. *A Short Life of Kierkegaard*. Princeton, N.J.: Princeton University Press, 1942.

Mackey, Louis. *Kierkegaard: A Kind of Poet*. Philadelphia: University of Pennsylvania Press, 1971.

Malantschuk, Gregor. *Kierkegaard's Thought*. Translated by Edna Hong and Howard Hong. Princeton, N.J.: Princeton University Press, 1971.

Taylor, Mark. *Kierkegaard's Pseudonymous Authorship*. Princeton, N.J.: Princeton University Press, 1975.

## Electroshock therapy

**TYPE OF ETHICS:** Psychological ethics

**DATE:** 1938 to present

**DEFINITION:** The induction by electric current of convulsions in patients in order to alleviate severe depression and suicidal ideation

**SIGNIFICANCE:** Seeks preservation of life and relief from depression and distress; ethical issues involve the competency of patients to consent to or refuse treatment and the appropriate use of treatment

Depression is one of the most prevalent and most treatable life-threatening illnesses. As many as 5 percent of people are likely to experience an episode of clinical depression during their lifetimes. The most probable cause of death from depression is suicide: Approximately 15 percent of patients with major depression take their own lives.

Electroshock therapy, or, more properly, electroconvulsive therapy (ECT), is used to treat severe depression that does not respond to drug therapy or that occurs in patients who cannot tolerate antidepressant drugs.

**History.** ECT was introduced in 1938 by two psychiatrists, U. Cerletti and L. Bini, who devised a means of inducing a convulsion in a patient by using an electric current delivered via electrodes fastened to one or both of the patient's temples.

It had long been observed that some mental patients had temporary relief from their symptoms following a spontaneous seizure. Prior to Cerletti and Bini's work, seizures had been induced by the inhalation of various substances.

ECT enjoyed a peak of popular use during the 1950's and 1960's, when it was considered a virtual panacea for mental illness. It had the additional benefit of making otherwise "difficult" patients more manageable, causing it to be used in some cases for behavior control. Partly because of its misuse and its negative depiction in the popular media (such as in Ken Kesey's novel *One Flew Over the Cuckoo's Nest*), ECT has earned a reputation as a high-risk treatment with an enormous capacity for abuse and severe long-term side effects. This is not, in fact, the case.

**Indications and Effects.** ECT is extremely effective in the treatment of severe depression and the depressive phase of bipolar disorder. Patients with atypical depression, however, which includes features such as acute anxiety or vegetative symptoms, tend not to respond as well to ECT. The treatment is strongly indicated in cases in which suicide seems imminent. ECT is used primarily for patients who have not responded to, or who cannot tolerate, drug therapy. Studies have shown that between 50 percent and 80 percent of patients in this category respond positively to ECT.

There are no absolute contraindicators in the use of ECT. The treatment does raise blood and intracranial pressure, however, and therefore it must be used with caution in patients who already have high readings in these areas. ECT is often administered under anesthesia, and muscle relaxants are used to reduce the risk of bone fractures, so patients who have problems with these treatments need to be assessed carefully. Also, patients with cardiovascular problems are only rarely given ECT, because of reported complications. In studies to date, however, the highest mortality rate associated with ECT has been 0.8 percent.

The major side effect of ECT is memory loss. The loss is primarily short-term. Studies indicate that there is little, if any, observable difference six months after treatment between the memory abilities of patients who have had ECT and those who have not. Since memory impairment is associated with depression in general, it is difficult to assess what loss is attributable to ECT.

**Ethical Issues.** The ethical issues involved with the administration of ECT revolve around the determination of what constitutes informed consent and competency to give consent or refuse treatment. In all psychiatric treatments, the question of the competency of a patient who suffers from some form of mental illness to give consent is raised. Other issues include the use of ECT for behavior control and decision making for patients considered not competent.

**Informed Consent.** The ethical issue of informed consent may be divided into two areas: consent by a competent adult and consent for an incompetent patient.

The question of competency is raised in all cases of mental illness. Can a person in the depths of severe depression, with its accompanying hindrances of judgment, be considered competent under any circumstances? Legally, yes. Legal competency is judged on the basis of observable behavior rather than on the basis of the patient's mental status, which can only be inferred. If a patient can make what is considered to be a rational decision, shows no signs of delusions, and is able to understand the risks and benefits of a treatment, that person is considered competent. The common negative societal view of ECT, however, often causes legally competent patients to refuse the treatment. Can their biased view of ECT, which is based on fictional portrayals, be considered delusional? Furthermore, consistency of consent becomes an issue because of the indecisiveness inherent in depression.

If a patient is judged to be incompetent, determining who will make treatment decisions becomes an issue. Most commonly these decisions are made by a close relative. It must be ascertained that the best interests and values of the patient have primacy in the decision, rather than such issues as ease of management by caretakers or punitive measures by other parties.

In the case of the hospitalized patient, the aspect of voluntariness of consent must be considered. A patient does not automatically relinquish the right to refuse treatment upon hospitalization. If consent is sought, it must be clear that it is in no way coerced; for example, by telling a patient that release from the hospital will occur sooner if ECT is used.

**Risks and Benefits.** One of the important aspects of informed consent is the patient's ability to comprehend and evaluate the risks and benefits inherent in a given procedure. In the case of ECT, the risks of the procedure must be evaluated in the light of the continued risk of suicide in depressed individuals. A competent patient has the right to refuse ECT, however, if he or she considers that the risk of memory loss or other brain damage outweighs the possible benefits.

*—Margaret Hawthorne*

**See also** Mental illness; Psychology.

**BIBLIOGRAPHY**

"American Psychiatric Association Practice Guidelines for Major Depressive Disorder in Adults." *American Journal of Psychiatry,* supp. 150 (April, 1993): 4.

Bloch, Sidney, and Paul Chodoff, eds. *Psychiatric Ethics.* New York: Oxford University Press, 1981.

Childress, James F. *Who Should Decide?* New York: Oxford University Press, 1982.

Edwards, Rem B., ed. *Psychiatry and Ethics.* Buffalo, N.Y.: Prometheus Books, 1982.

Keller, Martin B. "The Difficult Depressed Patient in Perspective." *Journal of Clinical Psychiatry,* supp. 54 (February, 1993): 4-8.

Schoen, Robert E. "Is Electroconvulsive Therapy Safe?" *Postgraduate Medicine* 87 (May 1, 1990): 236-239.

## Elitism

**TYPE OF ETHICS:** Personal and social ethics; Beliefs and practices

**DATE:** Coined nineteenth century

**ASSOCIATED WITH:** Socrates, Plato, and Friedrich Nietzsche

**DEFINITION:** The doctrine that claims that some people are superior to others because of a special knowledge, ability, or characteristic that they possess

**SIGNIFICANCE:** Provides a basis for arguments against the ethics of equality as well as arguments in favor of some forms of ethical paternalism; it is sometimes associated with strongly individualist ethics such as existentialism

There have been many different types of elitism, such as those based on race, religion, sex, social class, or physical beauty. Racism, sexism, religious elitism, and so forth are generally condemned as unethical practices, if for no other reason than that the criteria used to sort out and rank people are seen as arbitrary. This view does not dismiss elitism completely, however, but only those forms that base it on irrelevant differences among people. More serious elitist arguments are a natural outgrowth of any doctrine that claims that human beings have a potential for excellence. Those who work toward realizing this essence will often view themselves as superior to those who do not. Two types of human potential stand out within elitist arguments—the potential to develop the intellect, and the potential to become unique individuals.

**Intellectual Elitism.** As early as 600 B.C.E., the Greeks spoke about the differences between human beings based on the development of a virtuous or unvirtuous character. For the Greeks, differences in character served as a natural basis for ranking people. The aristocracy saw this division as a sound justification for an unequal distribution of power and privilege as well as for the practice of slavery.

Socrates and Plato developed Greek elitism into a sophisticated philosophical doctrine. Socrates, after arguing for a strong dualism of soul and body, claimed that the soul constituted human essence and that the body was a mere vehicle, even a prison, for the soul. In the Socratic view, the perfectibility of the human soul and the avoidance of bodily temptations thus became the single most important task of life. Those who sacrificed their souls for the sake of their bodies became the objects of harsh criticism, as people who turned their backs on their own essential nature. The familiar image of Socrates testing the knowledge of others through his questioning can be understood as his effort to determine the true elite of Greek society.

Plato took the Socratic teaching and developed it further with complex metaphysical and epistemological theories. Plato argued that the soul was positioned between a world of shadows generated by the opinions of mass society and a world of absolute truth accessible only to the trained human intellect. Plato took it as obvious that the person who disciplined his mind to seek truth was better than the person who gave himself over to the world of opinion. He argued that justice could be obtained only if all political power was handed over to the wise elite of society, holding that the ignorant masses should not be allowed to participate in the political process. Intellectual elitism of this sort has been prevalent throughout the history of philosophy and is still easy to find.

**Individualist Elitism.** In the nineteenth century, Friedrich Nietzsche argued for a different type of elitism based on a human being's capacity for development as a singular, unique, and powerful individual. In works such as *Thus Spoke Zarathustra* and *Beyond Good and Evil*, Nietzsche argued that all reality consists fundamentally of assertions of power. Thus, he asserted that humans could be divided up into two basic groups: those who embrace and assert their power, and those who fear and repress their power. Nietzsche's elitism considers the powerful ones to be masters and the repressed ones to be slaves. The master is the true individualist, a free spirit, a creator and a warrior. He or she is "beyond" the social conventions, taboos, morés, and moral imperatives that slaves create to hold themselves and others back. The slaves, however, try to subordinate individuality and uniqueness to generalized rules for appropriate thought and behavior. While the master creates rules by means of an individual act of will, the slaves subordinate themselves to the community will and follow the orders of others.

**Ethical Principles.** Despite their obvious differences, both these forms of elitism share important similarities: Both advocate that it is an ethical duty for humans to develop that potential which will make them superior people—the intellect or the will. Both advocate the duty to avoid that which will corrupt—the world of shadows or the commonplace. Each offers a definition of the highest good in terms of that which will perfect a human being—truth or power.

Both forms of elitism are faced also with the ethical problem of what attitude and/or behavior the elite few should take toward the nonelite majority. While intellectual elitists will have a tendency to avoid the ignorant masses, they do not shun community life itself. Rather, they seek associations within an elite community founded on the books, music, plays, films, and so forth that serve to improve the mind and provide rational insight into truth. Moreover, the intellectual elitist often feels a certain duty to protect the ignorant from their own degradation and to persuade them to partake in their own self-improvement. This attitude, however, creates a moral dilemma. Socrates was tried and executed as a "corrupter" of the youth by the people he claimed he was trying to help. Today, as well, the well-intentioned social reformer is often accused of both elitism and paternalism by those persons whom the reformer seeks to help.

Nietzschean individualists draw a different lesson from the trial and death of Socrates. They feel no moral duty to help the nonelite to do better and will try to avoid them entirely. The master does not desire a community of masters but is instead driven more toward a reclusive and solitary life. The Nietzschean hero Zarathrustra lives alone like a god, high in the mountains, with only powerful animals such as lions and snakes as his companions. —*Daniel Baker*

**See also** *Beyond Good and Evil*; Nietzsche, Friedrich; Plato; Socrates.

**BIBLIOGRAPHY**

Arendt, Hannah. *The Human Condition*. Garden City, N.Y.: Doubleday, 1959.

Nietzsche, Friedrich. *Beyond Good and Evil*. Translated by Helen Zimmern. Buffalo, N.Y.: Prometheus Books, 1989.

__________. *Thus Spoke Zarathustra: A Book for All and None*. Translated by Walter Kaufman. New York: Penguin Books, 1983.

Pareto, Vilfredo. *The Rise and Fall of the Elites*. Totowa, N.J.: Bedminster Press, 1968.

## Emancipation Proclamation

**TYPE OF ETHICS:** Civil rights

**DATE:** January 1, 1863

**ASSOCIATED WITH:** American Civil War

**DEFINITION:** Abraham Lincoln ordered the United States military forces to free slaves in the Confederacy during the Civil War

**SIGNIFICANCE:** The Emancipation Proclamation extended the legal state of freedom to most American slaves

Although the American Civil War was the result of sectional conflict regarding the issue of slavery, both the Union and the Confederate governments initially denied that slavery was a war issue. The Confederate government claimed that it was fighting only to defend the principle of states' rights. The Union government claimed that it was fighting to preserve the Union of states against Confederate efforts to destroy it.

**Lincoln's Cautious Approach to Emancipation.** From the very beginning of the war, abolitionists, radical Republicans, and black activists urged President Abraham Lincoln to use the war as an opportunity to strike down slavery. Lincoln, though, acted in a cautious manner in the early months of the war. Until September, 1862, Lincoln refused to include the abolition of slavery as one of the Union's war aims. Furthermore, when radical commanders in the Union Army ordered the emancipation of slaves in parts of the occupied South in 1861-1862, Lincoln countermanded the orders.

These actions caused reformers to question the depth of Lincoln's own commitment to antislavery. In Lincoln's defense, it must be noted that Lincoln both publicly and privately often expressed a heartfelt abhorrence of slavery. Yet Lincoln knew that a premature effort to turn the war into a crusade for emancipation would be counterproductive to the cause of freedom. An early act of emancipation would prompt loyal slave states such as Kentucky, Maryland, and Missouri to join the Confederacy and probably cause the defeat of the Union. From a practical point of view, the Union government could not abolish slavery in the South if it lost the war.

**The Origins of Lincoln's Emancipation Policy.** Lincoln was finally encouraged to seek emancipation because of the actions of the slaves themselves. During the war, some 600,000 slaves—about 15 percent of the total—escaped from their masters. Slaves understood that the advance of the Union Army through the South presented them with an unprecedented opportunity for escape. Most escaped slaves sought shelter with the Union Army.

The presence of large numbers of slaves within Union Army lines presented Union commanders with the question of whether the slaves should be returned to their rebellious masters or allowed to stay with the Army and use up its scarce resources. Most Union commanders allowed the slaves to remain with the army, justifying this decision out of military necessity. Pointing to the right of armies under international law to seize or destroy enemy property being used to sustain the war effort, Union commanders claimed the right to seize the Confederacy's slave laborers as contraband of war.

The actions of Union commanders shifted the focus of emancipation from human rights to military necessity, thereby encouraging Lincoln to adopt a general policy of emancipation and giving Lincoln an argument with which to win public support for this policy.

**The Proclamation and Its Limits.** Lincoln's Emancipation Proclamation, which was issued January 1, 1863, declared that slaves in areas in rebellion against the United States were free. Slaves in the loyal slave states and slaves in areas of the Confederacy already under Union control were not freed by the Proclamation. Because of this fact, some commentators have criticized the Proclamation, claiming that the Proclamation had little impact because it sought to free the Confederate slaves who were beyond Lincoln's control and neglected to free the slaves within his control. This criticism ignores several facts regarding Lincoln's action. The Emancipation Proclamation amounted to an announcement that henceforward, the Union Army would become an army of liberation. Whenever the Union Army captured an area of the Confederacy, it would automatically free the slaves in that region.

Additionally, the limited scope of Lincoln's Proclamation was prompted by the limited powers of the President under the Constitution. Lincoln pointed out that, as president, his only constitutional power to emancipate slaves was derived from his power as commander-in-chief to order the military destruction of property that supported the enemy's war effort. Slaves belonging to masters in states loyal to the Union and slaves belonging to masters in areas of the Confederacy previously captured were not currently being used to support the enemy's war effort. In making this argument, Lincoln was not being evasive or cautious in seeking the emancipation of all American slaves. One month before he issued the Emancipation Proclamation, Lincoln proposed to Congress the passage of a constitutional amendment that would have freed all slaves living in the loyal border states and in currently occupied portions of the Confederacy.

**The Effects of the Proclamation.** In the end, perhaps two-thirds of American slaves were freed by the Emancipation

# The Emancipation Proclamation

## January 1, 1863

## By the President of the United States of America

A Proclamation Whereas, on the twenty-second day of September, in the year of our Lord one thousand eight hundred and sixty-two, a proclamation was issued by the President of the United States, containing, among other things, the following, to wit:

That on the first day of January, in the year of our Lord one thousand eight hundred and sixty-three, all persons held as slaves within any State or designated part of a State, the people whereof shall then be in rebellion against the United States, shall be then, thenceforward, and forever free; and the Executive Government of the United States, including the military and naval authority thereof, will recognize and maintain the freedom of such persons, and will do no act or acts to repress such persons, or any of them, in any efforts they may make for their actual freedom.

That the Executive will, on the first day of January aforesaid, by proclamation, designate the States and parts of States, if any, in which the people thereof, respectively, shall then be in rebellion against the United States; and the fact that any State or the people thereof, shall on that day be, in good faith, represented in the Congress of the United States by members chosen thereto at elections wherein a majority of the qualified voters of such States shall have participated, shall, in the absence of strong countervailing testimony, be deemed conclusive evidence that such State, and the people thereof, are not then in rebellion against the United States.

Now, therefore, I, Abraham Lincoln, President of the United States, by virtue of the power in me vested as Commander-in-Chief, of the Army and Navy of the United States in time of actual armed rebellion against the authority and government of the United States, and as a fit and necessary war measure for suppressing said rebellion, do, on this first day of January, in the year of our Lord one thousand eight hundred and sixty-three, and in accordance with my purpose so to do, publicly proclaimed for the full period of one hundred days, from the day first above mentioned, order and designate as the States and parts of States wherein the people thereof, respectively, are this day in rebellion against the United States, the following, to wit:

Arkansas, Texas, Louisiana (except the parishes of St. Bernard, Plaquemines, Jefferson, St. John, St. Charles, St. James, Ascension, Assumption, Terrebonne, Lafourche, St. Mary, St. Martin, and Orleans, including the City of New Orleans), Mississippi, Alabama, Florida, Georgia, South Carolina, North Carolina, and Virginia (except the forty-eight counties designated as West Virginia, and also the counties of Berkeley, Accomac, Northampton, Elizabeth City, York, Princess Ann, and Norfolk, including the cities of Norfolk and Portsmouth); and which excepted parts are, for the present, left precisely as if this proclamation were not issued.

And by virtue of the power, and for the purpose aforesaid, I do order and declare that all persons held as slaves within said designated States, and parts of States, are, and henceforward shall be, free; and that the Executive government of the United States, including the military and naval authorities thereof, will recognize and maintain the freedom of said persons.

And I hereby enjoin upon the people so declared to be free to abstain from all violence, unless in necessary self-defense; and I recommend to them that, in all cases when allowed, they labor faithfully for reasonable wages.

And I further declare and make known, that such persons of suitable condition, will be received into the armed service of the United States to garrison forts, positions, stations, and other places, and to man vessels of all sorts in said service. And upon this act, sincerely believed to be an act of justice, warranted by the Constitution, upon military necessity, I invoke the considerate judgment of mankind, and the gracious favor of Almighty God.

In witness thereof, I have hereunto set my hand and caused the seal of the United States to be affixed.

Done at the City of Washington, this first day of January, in the year of our Lord one thousand eight hundred and sixty-three, and of the Independence of the United States of America the eighty-seventh.

**ABRAHAM LINCOLN,** **By the President**

**WILLIAM H. SEWARD,** **Secretary of State**

Proclamation. The remainder of American slaves were freed by the laws of state governments in loyal slave states and by the Thirteenth Amendment (1865), which abolished slavery in the United States. —*Harold D. Tallant*

**See also** Abolition; Civil rights; Slavery.

**BIBLIOGRAPHY**

Berlin, Ira, et al. *Slaves No More: Three Essays on Emancipation and the Civil War*. Cambridge, England: Cambridge University Press, 1992.

Cox, LaWanda. *Lincoln and Black Freedom: A Study in Presidential Leadership*. Columbia: University of South Carolina Press, 1981.

Foner, Eric. *Nothing But Freedom: Emancipation and Its Legacy*. Baton Rouge: Louisiana State University Press, 1983.

Franklin, John Hope. *The Emancipation Proclamation*. Garden City, N.Y.: Doubleday, 1963.

McPherson, James M. *Ordeal by Fire: The Civil War and Reconstruction*. 2d ed. New York: McGraw-Hill, 1992.

## Emerson, Ralph Waldo (May 25, 1803, Boston, Mass.—Apr. 27, 1882, Concord, Mass.): Theologian, essayist, poet

**TYPE OF ETHICS:** Modern history

**ACHIEVEMENTS:** Author of *Nature* (1836), "The American Scholar" (1837), "Divinity School Address" (1838), and "Self-Reliance" (1841)

**SIGNIFICANCE:** The leading proponent of New England Transcendentalism, Emerson inspired individuals to develop their spiritual selves

The catalyst for most of Emerson's finest writings was his search for a liberating personal philosophy.

Ordained a minister, Emerson resigned his pastorate at a Boston Unitarian church because he believed that conventional religions told their parishioners what to think and how to act rather than instructing them how to use their own divinely inspired "moral sentiments." He believed that only through this innate moral sense could one adequately meet one's most important ethical responsibility: self-reliance.

Failure to follow one's conscience was to live in a mind-numbing conformity that was, at bottom, spiritually suicidal. In a controversial address, he urged a graduating class of Harvard divinity students to "cast behind you all conformity, and acquaint men at firsthand with Deity." He attributed Americans' overreliance on material things to a lack of self-reliance: Citizens "measure their esteem of each other, by what each has and not by what each is." His solution was for each person to find in the expansive American natural setting an "original relationship to the universe."

Emerson believed that nature itself embodied ethical principles; thus, it could be used as a kind of holy sanctuary in which the individual, without the aid of irrelevant intermediaries such as dogmas, rituals, and ministers, could "transcend" material considerations and achieve a spiritual union with the deity. Despite the affirmative tone of his essays, Emerson, like Thoreau, sometimes despaired of finding a vocation. In a materialistic society, Transcendentalists were neither allotted a place of respect nor afforded the kind of meaningful work they were eager to perform. Not considered "good citizens," they believed that most of the ordinary work of humanity, even that devoted to the best causes, required conformity rather than originality and therefore precluded the original use of one's own spirit.

**See also** Thoreau, Henry David; Transcendentalism.

*Ralph Waldo Emerson* (Library of Congress)

## Emotivist ethics

**TYPE OF ETHICS:** Theory of ethics

**DATE:** Twentieth century

**ASSOCIATED WITH:** American philosopher Charles L. Stevenson and British philosopher A. J. Ayer

**DEFINITION:** The notion that the purpose of ethical language is to prescribe behavior by stirring one's emotions and influencing one's attitude

**SIGNIFICANCE:** Emotivist ethics is an important development in the evolution of ethical theory because it represents a departure from cognitive ethical theory; in its extreme form, it denies that ethical judgments can be rationally justified

To a certain extent, emotivist ethics has its roots in the philosophy of David Hume (1711-1776). In the second book of the *Treatise of Human Nature* (1739), Hume argues that reason is subordinate to the emotions and that moral judgments are "sentiments." These sentiments are feelings of approval or disapproval toward an action. The bottom line for Hume is that morality is derived from and based on feeling. As he observes in the *Treatise,* "Morality is more properly felt than judged of."

The real impetus for this well-known movement in ethics came from logical positivism, which could not accept intuition as a means of verifying propositions. Since moral judgments cannot be verified, they could not be meaningful or significant propositions. Positivism stresses that propositions must be verifiable, and since this is not possible with ethical propositions, they must be treated very differently. Thus, according to A. J. Ayer, echoing David Hume, moral judgments serve only to express the feelings or sentiments of the speaker.

Emotivism as a full-fledged ethical theory was developed primarily by the American philosopher Charles L. Stevenson (1908-1979). Stevenson wrote *Ethics and Language* (1944), which has become one of the most significant and influential ethical works of the twentieth century.

The fundamental premise of emotivist ethics is that language has different functions. One function or purpose of language is to state facts or to describe some aspect of reality. For example, "It's quite cold outside—the temperature is 23 degrees Fahrenheit." This statement can be easily verified. When language is used in this fashion it is considered to be descriptive. According to the emotivist theory of ethics, however, moral discourse is definitely not descriptive, since it does not convey any such factual information. What, then is the purpose and import of moral language? According to Stevenson, moral discourse has two key features. In order to explain the first feature, Stevenson drew a sharp distinction between beliefs and attitudes. In making a moral judgment, it is possible to distinguish between the facts that are the subject of judgment and the positive or negative evaluation of those facts. Hence, if someone makes the judgment that "euthanasia is wrong," euthanasia is the state of affairs under scrutiny and a negative evaluation is being advanced. This negative evaluation represents one's attitude about euthanasia. In moral disputes, there is a divergence or disagreement in attitude. For example, someone may disagree with opponents of euthanasia: They may believe that euthanasia is permissible, which means that they have a different attitude toward euthanasia.

The second feature of moral discourse is its dynamic character, or magnetic power. Hence, according to Stevenson, besides expressing an attitude, moral judgments "create an influence," since they seek to provoke a response in those to whom the judgment is addressed. With regard to this second feature of moral discourse, Ayer and Stevenson would agree that ethical terms such as "good," "right," and so forth are emotionally provocative. In his seminal work *Language, Truth, and Logic* (1936), Ayer points out that ethical terms such as "good" and "evil" are similar to aesthetic words such as "beautiful." Such words do not describe or state facts; instead, they express feelings and seek to evoke a response.

In short, then, ethical language and judgment has a dual function. Its first purpose is to express the belief as well as the attitude of the speaker, and its second purpose is to change the attitude of those to whom this language is addressed. Hence, when someone utters the moral judgment that euthanasia is a grave moral error, that person is expressing a feeling and an attitude about this controversial topic. The speaker is also trying to persuade others to adopt this same attitude if they have not already done so. Thus, moral discourse is clearly influential: It seeks to influence others and change attitudes.

In its extreme form, emotivism does not recognize the validity of rational arguments that might support one's ethical attitude or feelings. This appears to be A. J. Ayer's position. Stevenson, however, does not go so far; he admits the possibility of such rational justification. Thus, Stevenson concedes that the attitudes that are expressed in ethical judgments are based on beliefs, and people can offer reasons and justifications for those beliefs. For Stevenson, however, it is unclear whether the most fundamental ethical attitudes are grounded in any rational beliefs; if this is so, these attitudes would be irrational, since they could not be swayed by reason.

Philosophers recognize that there is considerable merit to the line of reasoning put forward by emotivists such as Stevenson, but they also point out some problems. To begin with, it is not clear that the purpose of influencing attitudes is distinctive of moral discourse. Also, there is nothing necessarily emotional about rendering a moral judgment—after all, is it not possible to articulate a judgment in an unemotional and dispassionate way? Finally, emotivism stresses that moral discourse is used primarily to produce an effect—to change the attitude of others. If one evaluates moral judgments in terms of their effectiveness, however, one looks away from the reasons and arguments underlying that judgment, and this is somewhat problematic. Simply because a moral judgment is effective does not mean that it is valid.

*—Richard A. Spinello*

**See also** Ayer, Alfred Jules.

**BIBLIOGRAPHY**

Ayer, A. J. *Language, Truth, and Logic.* Harmondsworth, England: Penguin Books, 1971.

Stevenson, Charles L. *Ethics and Language.* New Haven, Conn.: Yale University Press, 1960.

Urmson, J. O. *The Emotive Theory of Ethics.* New York: Oxford University Press, 1969.

Werkmeister, W. H. *Theories of Ethics: A Study in Moral Obligation.* Lincoln, Nebr.: Johnsen, 1961.

## Employees, safety and treatment of

**TYPE OF ETHICS:** Business and labor ethics

**DATE:** Since the Industrial Revolution

**DEFINITION:** Means of promoting worker efficiency and societal order by protecting the lives and promoting the well-being of workers

**SIGNIFICANCE:** When the safety of workers is ensured and workers are fairly treated by their employers and their governments, society becomes more efficient and orderly

Worker treatment generally falls into two basic categories: the physical safety of employees in the workplace; and the rights of workers to fairness and dignity with respect to hiring, compensation, promotions, job security, and discrimination.

**Physical Safety.** Since approximately 10,000 workers are killed each year and 2.8 million workers are injured (these numbers do not include workers who suffer from occupational diseases, which can take decades to develop), safety is a critical issue in business. Ensuring physical safety requires the elimination of workplace hazards and the implementation of safety standards. Although many hazards have been eliminated or controlled, many dangerous conditions still exist. Among these dangers are textile fibers that can cause brown lung disease, paint vapors that can lead to emphysema, and excessive noise that can result in hearing loss.

To improve worker safety and to establish a forum where employees could seek remuneration, individual states in the United States began enacting legislation to guarantee payment for workplace injuries as early as 1920. This legislation, however, only compensated workers for existing injuries and did not address eliminating the dangerous conditions that can lead to injuries. Because it is always better to prevent injuries, the federal government enacted the Occupational Safety and Health Act (OSHA) in 1970.

As a result of OSHA, employers now have a legal duty to design a safe working environment, maintain it, provide proper supervision, and educate their employees about their products and their workplace. OSHA requires all employers to conform to certain minimum safety standards, and it seeks to reduce hazards in the workplace by establishing corporate responsibilities for improving worker safety and health. OSHA sometimes plays hardball with employers who think that paying off injured workers is cheaper than implementing costly safety standards. OSHA will impose criminal penalties upon individuals within the corporate structure—rather than only upon the corporation itself—if it believes that corporate managers understood the risks to workers and ignored them.

One famous example of how disastrous it can be for a company to fail to provide for employee safety is Johns Manville, formerly the leading manufacturer of asbestos products. Johns Manville discovered in the 1930's that exposure to asbestos could result in serious, even fatal, disabilities. Manville kept this information private and did not inform thousands of workers about the hazards of asbestos exposure. When the dangers became known to the public in the early 1980's, thousands of lawsuits were filed by former employees of Manville and other companies that used asbestos supplied by Manville. As a result, Manville declared bankruptcy, established a fund to help pay for injuries, and became widely vilified for its failure to warn workers. The result of Manville's negligence was catastrophe—for the injured workers and their families, and for the company, which was nearly destroyed.

Today, safety in the workplace is of paramount importance to all ethical employers, and ideas about what constitutes safety are constantly evolving as new knowledge becomes available. A classic example of how opinions can change regarding what constitutes a safe workplace is the issue of second-hand smoke. Should employers protect employees from the second-hand smoke of their coworkers? Fifteen years ago,

**NUMBER OF U.S. WORKERS KILLED OR DISABLED ON THE JOB, 1960-1989**

| Year | Deaths[a] | Disabling Injuries[b,c] |
|---|---|---|
| 1960 | 13,800 | 1,950,000 |
| 1965 | 14,100 | 2,100,000 |
| 1970 | 13,800 | 2,200,000 |
| 1975 | 13,000 | 2,200,000 |
| 1980 | 13,200 | 2,200,000 |
| 1984 | 11,500 | 1,900,000 |
| 1985 | 11,500 | 2,000,000 |
| 1986 | 11,100 | 1,800,000 |
| 1987 | 11,300 | 1,800,000 |
| 1988 | 10,800 | 1,800,000 |
| 1989 | 10,400 | 1,700,000 |

Notes:

[a] Rounded to the nearest hundred.

[b] Rounded to the nearest thousand.

[c] Includes injuries that resulted in death or that caused physical impairment for a full day or more.

*Source:* Data are from Statistical Abstract of the United States, 1991

the answer would have been no. Today, the answer is a resounding yes.

Occupational safety will continue to be an important element of employee treatment. Although there is no doubt that the workplace has become safer and that employers' concern for the safety of workers has increased, the issue of safety merits continued close attention.

**Workers' Rights: The Issue Is Fairness.** All workers have the right to expect fairness from their employer and to be treated with respect and dignity. Fairness is especially important in the areas of hiring practices, compensation, promotions, privacy, discrimination, job security, and sexual harassment.

The federal government has enacted legislation to protect employees from discrimination in the workplace based on race, religion, sex, color, and national origin. Title VII of the Civil Rights Act of 1964 specifically protects women, African Americans, Hispanics, Native Americans, and Asian-Pacific Islanders. In addition, some states and local communities have added more protections—such as those that relate to marital status, veteran status, and sexual orientation—to the list. The Pregnancy Discrimination Act of 1978 protects pregnant women from discrimination, and the Age Discrimination in Employment Act extends protection to persons forty years of age or older. The 1990 Americans with Disabilities Act requires all companies with more than fifteen employees to make reasonable accommodations in order to employ workers with disabilities. The objective of all of this legislation is to incorporate fairness into the workplace so that ability will be the primary criterion in decisions that involve hiring, promotions, compensation, discipline, and firing.

Another key issue in the workplace is sexual harassment, which is a form of discrimination. Sexual harassment occurs when sexual favors are a requirement (or appear to be a requirement) for advancement in the workplace. Sexual harassment can also exist when a worker has been made to feel uncomfortable because of unwelcome actions or comments relating to sexuality. Since sexual harassment is murky—what constitutes sexual harassment for one person may not to another—the determination of whether it exists is based on the reaction of the victim, not the intentions of the harasser. It is also determined from the point of view of a "reasonable" person. Harassment is an ethical issue because it unfairly focuses job advancement or retention on a factor other than the ability to do a job. As a result of legislation and well-publicized lawsuits, many companies have adopted guidelines for dealing with sexual harassment as well as training programs to educate employees about the dangers of harassment and discrimination.

This article has dealt with only a few of the ethical issues that involve worker treatment and safety. Because workers are any company's most important and valuable asset, the ethical issues inherent in employee treatment are among the most important in business. —*Jonathan Mann*

**See also** Ageism; Business ethics; Civil Rights Act of 1964; Fairness; Racial prejudice; Sexual abuse and harassment.

**Bibliography**

Benson, George C. S. *Business Ethics in America*. Lexington, Mass.: Lexington Books, 1982.

Cederblom, Jerry, and Charles L. Dougherty. *Ethics at Work*. Belmont, Calif.: Wadsworth, 1990.

De George, Richard T. *Business Ethics*. New York: Macmillan, 1982.

De George, Richard T., and Joseph A. Pichler, eds. *Ethics, Free Enterprise, and Public Policy: Original Essays on Moral Issues in Business*. New York: Oxford University Press, 1978.

Des Jardins, Joseph R., and John J. McCall, eds. *Contemporary Issues in Business Ethics*. 2d ed. Belmont, Calif.: Wadsworth, 1990.

Shaw, William H., and Vincent Barry. *Moral Issues in Business*. 4th ed. Belmont, Calif.: Wadsworth, 1989.

## Endangered species

**Type of ethics:** Environmental ethics

**Date:** 1900 to present

**Definition:** Endangered species are those species that are threatened with extinction in all or part of their geographical range

**Significance:** Seeks to identify and preserve species of plants and animals for future use and study

An endangered species is one that has so few individual survivors that it could soon become extinct in all or part of its range. Examples include animals such as the California condor and plants such as orchids and cacti. Those species classified as threatened are presently abundant in their range but likely to become endangered within the near future because of a decline in numbers. Examples include the grizzly bear and the bald eagle.

**Wildlife Protection.** There are three general methods to prevent wildlife from becoming endangered. These methods are to establish treaties and laws to protect a particular species from being killed and to preserve their habitat; to use gene banks, zoos, botanical gardens, and research centers to preserve species and possibly breed individuals of a critically endangered species to reintroduce them to the wild; and to preserve a variety of unique and representative ecosystems, which tends to save a variety of species rather than an individual species.

The U.S. Congress has passed a variety of legislation for the protection of endangered species. Legislation to prohibit the illegal collection of species began in 1900 with the Lacey Act. In 1966, the Endangered Species Preservation Act made an official list of endangered species and authorized the expenditure of funds to acquire their habitats. The Endangered Species Conservation Act of 1969 banned the importation and sale of wildlife threatened with worldwide extinction. These legislative acts applied only to vertebrate animals; they did not protect species that were threatened,

| SELECTED ENDANGERED SPECIES | | | |
|---|---|---|---|
| **Species** | **Locales inhabited** | **Approximate numbers left** | **Reason for being endangered** |
| Barbary leopard | Morocco | 100 | Trophy hunting |
| Square-lipped rhino | Zaire, Africa | 20 | Poaching, war |
| European bison | Białowieza, Poland | 1064 | Wars |
| Eskimo curlew | Texas to Atlantic Coast | may be extinct | Hunting |
| Wood bison | Alberta, Canada | more than 100 | Hunting |
| Leseur's rat kangaroo | West Australian Islands | unknown | Habitat loss |
| Spectacled bear | Andes Mountains, South America | 2000 | Persecution by humans |
| Korean leopard | Siberia, North Korea | 15 | Persecution by humans |
| Siberian tiger | Siberia, North China | 300 | Persecution by humans |

and they provided no absolute protection against major federal projects that could exterminate a species.

The 1973 Endangered Species Act protected endangered and threatened species and provided a program for the recovery of those species. The 1973 act included all plants and animals except a few that had been determined to be pests. The act recognized the relationship between a species and its environment by requiring the Department of the Interior to determine the critical habitat of endangered and threatened species. The act authorizes the National Marine Fisheries Service of the Department of Commerce to identify and list marine species, and the Department of the Interior's Fish and Wildlife Service to identify all other plant and animal species threatened in the United States or abroad. Any decision by either agency to add or remove a species from the list must be based solely on biological grounds without economic consideration.

The 1973 Endangered Species Act also prohibits interstate and international commercial trade involving endangered plant or animal species. Section 7 directs federal agencies not to carry out, fund, or authorize projects that would jeopardize endangered species or destroy habitats critical to their survival. This section was challenged in 1975 when conservationists filed suit against the Tennessee Valley Authority to stop construction on the $137 million Tellico Dam on the Little Tennessee River because the river would flood the only known breeding ground of the tiny snail darter, an endangered species. Courts stopped construction on the dam, though the dam was 90 percent complete. In 1979, Congress passed special legislation exempting the project from the Endangered Species Act. The case of the Tellico Dam raises the ethical problem that if one interprets the 1973 act as favoring species over development in all cases, then the value of the species would be so high that it could not be exceeded by the benefits of development. The ethical principle of saving endangered species is a high one, but it is not absolute. In some cases, there are higher values that must take precedence over endangered species preservation. Though environmentalists understand this principle, they have argued that the Endangered Species Act is not being carried out as directed by Congress because of budget cuts and administrative rules.

**Ethical Principles.** The ethical principle of preserving all plant and animal species often entails practical costs that are extremely high. There will continue to be situations in which a development project that is truly necessary for human well-being will come into conflict with the existence of one or more species. With only limited resources, a priority system must be devised so that the maximum number of species is saved. The ecological value of a species is the value of the species in question to its native habitat or what the impact of its extinction will be on the ecosystem. The uniqueness of a species places greater value on a species if it is the only existing member of a family rather than one of many members of a given family. Those species with a current or promising biological, medical, or chemical utility have a high preservation effort. Those species with a commercial value should not be allowed to be harvested to extinction.

In some cases, extinctions may be ethically justifiable. The following reasons may apply in such cases: benefits accrue to large numbers of people and not merely a chosen few; the beneficial action is related to genuine human needs, not luxuries; the preservation costs are too great to be borne by society; the species is not unique and has no known medical value; alternate habitats are not available. Justifiable extinctions include those of the smallpox virus and of some nonharmful animals in East Africa.

By saving endangered species and preserving Earth's genetic pool, options are kept open for nature and science to maintain a healthy environment in the future. There is a growing understanding that all life forms are part of one interdependent ecosystem and that the declining health of one species signals danger for all species, including humans.

*—David R. Teske*

**See also** Biodiversity; Environmental ethics; Moral status of animals; Nature, rights of; Rain forests.

**BIBLIOGRAPHY**

Allen, Thomas B. *Vanishing Wildlife of North America.* Washington, D.C.: National Geographic Society, 1974.

Fritsch, Albert J., et al. *Environmental Ethics: Choices for Concerned Citizens.* Garden City, N.Y.: Anchor Press, 1980.

Kohm, Kathryn, ed. *Balancing on the Brink of Extinction: The Endangered Species Act and Lessons for the Future.* Washington, D.C.: Island Press, 1991.

Korn, Peter. "The Case for Preservation." *The Nation* 254 (March 30, 1992): 414-417.

Miller, G. Tyler, Jr. *Environmental Science: An Introduction.* Belmont, Calif.: Wadsworth, 1986.

## Enlightenment ethics

**TYPE OF ETHICS:** Enlightenment history

**DATE:** 1688-1789

**DEFINITION:** A mode of thought based on the concepts of secular humanism, rationalism, and democracy, which developed principally in Europe and the United States

**SIGNIFICANCE:** Established as influential principles the natural civil rights of all people, the concept of government as a contract between the governed and the governing, the concept of the innate goodness of the natural world, and the idea that happiness and goodness can be achieved through reason

During the Enlightenment, the hundred-year period from 1688 to 1789, a diffuse group of political and philosophical leaders shared dynamic key ideas that reshaped the political and religious institutions of European culture, culminating in the establishment of the United States of America and the French Revolution. These ideas were in open conflict with the established beliefs of Christian churches and of the monarchical governments of that time.

**History.** The ideas of Enlightenment writers developed from two primary sources: the ancient classics of Greece and Rome and the Protestant movement within Christian Europe. Beginning with the Renaissance, when many "lost" works of ancient Greek and Roman writers were reintroduced into Europe, European students and scholars mastered Latin and Greek in order to know and appreciate these classics. Students studied, along with traditional religious works, many pre-Christian Latin and Greek texts, such as Plato's *Republic*. These pagan texts reintroduced ancient philosophical ideas to Europeans and sanctioned ethical views that contradicted Christian teachings, such as the idea that the power of reason, instead of faith, could lead humans to perform good actions.

The ancient Greek spirit of scientific inquiry also inspired this period. From the Renaissance on, well-educated men such as Francis Bacon and Isaac Newton applied principles of rational inquiry to the study of the natural world, and in doing so they established the scientific method of investigation as a powerful means of gaining new knowledge of the physical world. This mode of inquiry turned away from pious Christian thinking and toward empirical experience in the search for objective universal law. The practitioners of scientific investigation were tough-minded, worldly, and philosophical.

As a result of the Protestant religious movements of the previous centuries, education had become more widely available in northern European countries. This occurred because literacy was a necessary prerequisite for reading and interpreting the Bible as part of religious worship. This practice developed close critical reading and thinking skills, confidence in working with written texts, and tolerance for diverse views of religious topics. The tragic psychological and economic effects of religious persecution of Europe also had brought about a greater appreciation of religious tolerance.

In 1688, a change in England from absolute monarchy to constitutional government signaled the opening of the new age of the Enlightenment. This glorious revolution, which banished an autocratic Catholic king and substituted a Protestant king with legally curtailed royal powers, was accomplished without war. This revolution successfully applied the idea that legitimate government was established by a legal contract between the people and their monarch, instead of by a divine right given to the monarch by God. This transformation of England's government and the surge of economic prosperity that followed it marked the beginning of radical social changes that culminated in the French Revolution in 1789.

**Ethical Principles.** Tolerance for new ideas and confidence in the human power of reason as a means to achieve the good life characterize the core ethical views of Enlightenment thinkers. The human mind rather than sacred teachings and values became the focus of intellectual life as humankind's quest for life, liberty, and the pursuit of happiness on Earth gradually overshadowed a lifestyle of Christian values lived for rewards that would be received in a spiritual life after death. Although the vast majority of Europeans remained Christian, the leading thinkers, such as John Locke, Voltaire, David Hume, Immanuel Kant, and Jean-Jacques Rousseau, were often atheists, agnostics, or deists. They regarded God's place in the world as remote or even nonexistent.

**Natural Morality.** The secular morality developed during the period conceives of humans using reason, not faith, to find the good life. Their well-developed faculty of reasoning and common sense, together with their natural desire for pleasure, can lead people to shun evil and pursue good. This process makes it possible for people to enjoy happiness, the goal and reward of living well, on Earth.

Concerning the basic nature of human beings, some leading thinkers claimed that people are inherently good and that their desire for pleasure, if guided by reason, can lead them to the good life. Other Enlightenment thinkers, however, asserted that humans are inherently neither good nor evil but are made good or evil by the environment in which they live.

Natural morality recognizes that an egoistic desire for pleasure and aesthetic enjoyment motivates human action and thought; thus, according to this idea, virtue is defined as creating the greatest happiness and pleasure for the greatest number of people. Therefore, a virtuous person expresses self-interest and self-love in a way that not only avoids causing pain in others, since all people have an equal right to experience pleasure and happiness, but also increases happiness for others.

**Humanism.** The natural morality of the Enlightenment emphasizes the fraternity of humankind in the shared innate faculty of reason, the shared innate desire for pleasure, and the universal power of education to bring happiness to all people. In theory, all people may pursue and find happiness by cultivating their reasoning powers, so fraternity may minimize political, economic, racial, and religious inequities. In fact, however, the political and social institutions of the time did not create equal opportunities for all to become educated and pursue the good life. Enlightenment ideas did promote a cosmopolitan spirit in Europe, since those accepting the idea of humanism acknowledged a bond of commonality stronger than those of nationalism and patriotism. The philosopher Rousseau declared, "There are no longer Frenchmen or Germans . . . there are only Europeans."

**Scientific Inquiry.** Scientific thinking developed and gained enormous credibility during the Enlightenment for several reasons. Science serves as an excellent means of exercising and developing the ability to reason, a faculty necessary to achieving happiness. It also promotes discussion and criticism and thus furthers more general education in society. Publications of experimental studies and meetings of scientific societies play an essential role in the growth of scientific thinking and are key components of scientific inquiry. During the Enlightenment, leading philosophers envisioned scientific inquiry and its fruits of inventions and discoveries about the natural world as the sure path to an ideal future life. Thus, the idea of progress through science to a perfect life sparked the imaginations of Enlightenment thinkers.

**Manners.** The qualities of reasonableness came to be regarded as those of good manners during the Enlightenment; showing in one's behavior rationality, tolerance, self-control, cordiality, partiality, and modesty became fashionable. Good manners were not only an expression of humanity but also a humanizing way of behavior. Women also became more influential in public life, in part because of new ideas about manners and in part because women came to be regarded as reasonable beings instead of only as caretakers of the home, or as property.

**Issues of Enlightenment Ethics.** The role of religion in natural morality was a key issue during this period. Other significant issues were the roles of laws, education, and government in leading humankind to live the happy life.

With respect to religion, a powerful group of atheist thinkers, including David Hume and Denis Diderot, envisioned society totally without religion, with reason alone being able to guide people to a good life. Another group, including the brilliant and influential Voltaire, called themselves deists and argued that humankind should recognize the role of the higher power of God in forming and sustaining the world.

All members of these groups agreed that European Christianity had failed to prepare humankind for a happy life and had instead destroyed its happiness. These groups allied themselves in passionate rejection of all Christian doctrines and rituals. Some asserted that Christianity was a disease that made society sick and therefore should be destroyed. "Crush the infamy!" (*Écrasez l'infame!*) became the slogan of Enlightenment philosophers as they endeavored to annihilate both the doctrines and the customs of the Catholic and Protestant churches.

These philosophers wanted to replace religion with education and the development of reason to guide people to the good life. To accomplish their objective, a group of French Enlightenment thinkers prepared and published, in 1751, an impressive thirty-seven volume *Encylopédie*, a collection of all knowledge in a great scheme of education through reading. They also argued for separating schools, universities, and libraries from the control and influence of churches, the traditional custodians and guardians of educational institutions of Europe. Even though they, the enlightened ones, were the products of church-influenced education, they advocated a sharp break with tradition.

Supporters of Enlightenment ideas also expanded the scope of education to include decreasing crime through the education of criminals and delinquents; they assumed that wrong ideas and antisocial behavior could be changed by education. Enlightenment thinkers rejected the traditional basis of government, the divine right of kings as God's representatives on Earth to carry out a divine plan. Instead, they claimed, governments should be negotiated contracts between the governed subjects and the representatives of government. The role and responsibility of such governments should be to assist the people by promoting their happiness. Only those governments constituted by legal contract were believed to serve the best interests of the people they ruled. Thus, the Enlightenment thinkers dismissed traditional forms of government and the wisdom gained through centuries of trial and error. One issue related to the role of government and the governed is the right of people to reject a government that does not serve them well. Enlightenment philosophers defended this right and therefore supported the American Revolution and the French Revolution.

**The Influence of Enlightenment Ethics.** The ideas and ideals of the Enlightenment have had profound and lasting effects on government, education, and religion. Other social institutions, such as the family and marriage, have also been shaped by Enlightenment ideas.

The primary influence of the Enlightenment has been increased tolerance of diverse ideas and opinions, together with a shift away from orthodoxy. The modern ideals of open-mindedness and acceptance of diversity stem from the Enlightenment. The traditions of a free press with clearly limited government censorship and of a literate population that participates in a free exchange of ideas also are legacies of the period.

In the realm of government, one famous creation derived directly from Enlightenment ideas is the government of the United States. Established during the Enlightenment (1776-1792) partly as a philosophical experiment, the U.S. government has remained a successful democracy for two hundred years. The Declaration of Independence, the first policy statement made in formulating that government, is regarded as a preeminent Enlightenment document of civil liberty. The United States government's humanistic ideals and policies have been relevant and flexible enough to have adapted to changing social and economic conditions for two centuries; also, it has served as a model for incorporating democratic elements into government institutions.

Regarding education, the tradition of humanistic learning as a means to becoming a well-rounded person continues to be valued today. In many colleges and universities, certain courses are labeled humanities or liberal arts subjects, in accordance with the Enlightenment concept of reason leading the individual to become a humane and liberal person.

Another related Enlightenment notion that survives in education today is the separation of church and school. The goals of education are perceived as distinct from, although related to, the goals of religion; as a result, the path of inquiry and knowledge need not conform to church doctrines, a key factor in the development of scientific thought.

The position of Christianity with reference to science was influenced dramatically by Enlightenment ideas. Before the Enlightenment, scientists had been imprisoned as heretics or agents of Satan, sometimes to be tortured and executed for holding forbidden ideas that had been censored by religious authorities; after this period, however, scientists were relatively free to pursue their investigations and experiments. In fact, the doctrines of Christian churches were attacked virulently by Enlightenment philosophers, and church leaders were forced into defensive positions on scientific issues such as the accuracy of biblical accounts of historical events.

*—Patricia H. Fulbright*

**See also** Hume, David; Kant, Immanuel; Locke, John; Rousseau, Jean-Jacques; Voltaire.

**Bibliography**

Durant, Will, and Ariel Durant. *The Age of Voltaire: A History of Civilization in Western Europe from 1715 to 1756, with Special Emphasis on the Conflict Between Religion and Philosophy*. New York: Simon & Schuster, 1965. An excellent historical discussion of the period that refers to writings of key philosophers and philosophical works. This is a fine first text for a student of this topic, since it is readable and well organized.

Gay, Peter. *The Rise of Modern Paganism*. Vol. 1 in *The Enlightenment: An Interpretation*. New York: Alfred Knopf, 1967. A detailed scholarly discussion of ancient Greek and Roman texts and thinkers that influenced Enlightenment philosophers. This work traces the legacy of the classics and the conflict between pagan and Christian ideas.

__________. *The Science of Freedom*. Vol. 2 in *The Enlightenment: An Interpretation*. New York: Alfred Knopf, 1969. An excellent scholarly presentation of political issues related to Enlightenment philosophy. Includes a comprehensive bibliography and extensive notes.

Hazard, Paul. *European Thought in the Eighteenth Century from Montesquieu to Lessing*. Translated by J. Lewis May. Cleveland, Ohio: World Publishing, 1963. A criticism of major Enlightenment philosophers that focuses on their major ideas and works.

## Enquiry Concerning the Principles of Morals, An: Book

**Type of ethics:** Enlightenment history
**Date:** Published 1751
**Author:** David Hume
**Significance:** The classic statement of British skeptical empiricism concerning moral and ethical issues

David Hume, perhaps Great Britain's greatest philosopher, considered *An Enquiry Concerning the Principles of Morals* to be his finest work, a judgment shared by many of his contemporaries and later readers who admire the clarity and objectivity of his examination of a complex and complicated subject.

The *Enquiry* is in large part a revision and extension of book 3 of Hume's masterpiece *A Treatise of Human Nature,* in which he surveyed the full range of human psychology, but it is a much more concentrated review of the topic. In the *Enquiry*, Hume has two basic purposes. The first is to establish a method of writing about human ethical behavior; the second, to describe that behavior and explain its workings. In neither case, however, does Hume explicitly prescribe specific moral or ethical activities or values as "good," "bad," or even "indifferent." Instead, he objectively describes what actions and beliefs human beings have characteristically labeled "good" and "evil" and explains why those judgments have been rendered. In this sense, the *Enquiry* is a study of how human ethics operate rather than an argument for or against any particular ethical theory or system.

**Benevolence and Justice.** Seeking to build in the realm of philosophy upon the scientific achievements of Sir Isaac Newton (1642-1727), Hume attempted to discover the ultimate principles of human morality and ethics. In the *Enquiry*, Hume first examined what he considered the two most fundamental human and social virtues, benevolence and justice, which he viewed as the basis of both individual and communal happiness and progress.

In Hume's view, actions are accounted ethical or good by human beings for one or both of two reasons: either because they appeal to human sympathy or because they serve the purpose of social utility. In other words, actions appear to be good or worthwhile either in themselves or because they make human intercourse not only possible but also enjoyable and profitable.

Benevolence is valued because it appeals instinctively to human sympathy, in large part because almost every individual can appreciate how personally beneficial benevolence can be. In addition, Hume notes, human beings connect benevolence with social good. When a benevolent person is praised, there is always mention, and therefore recognition, of the good or satisfaction that he or she brings to the general community, because the inherent appeal to human sympathy is reinforced by the call of social utility.

Justice, however, is viewed by Hume as having a purely utilitarian function, primarily because he has defined the word in rather narrow terms and is concerned with property relationships rather than human or social affairs. These Hume discusses under the heading of impartiality as an aspect of fully moral judgment. In the usual run of human experience, Hume states, justice is a matter of what best serves the individual or society in terms of the overall situation. For example, nations habitually suspend traditional rules of international law during warfare because to adhere to them would impose obvious and, in Hume's and humanity's view, unwarranted disadvantages. In the largest sense, then, human law and justice are nothing more than agreed-upon conventions that advance the common good of all human beings.

Hume provides a variety of examples to demonstrate that justice is valued for its utility to human society and that it is defined by that utility. For example, respect for property is universally acknowledged as an element of justice, but if an honest man is captured by outlaws, he acts in accordance with justice if he seizes his captors' weapons and uses them against them. Practical utility, rather than abstract idealism, is the determining factor of human considerations of justice.

**Utility Is the Basis of Virtues.** Hume's intellectual background made him the successor of philosophers John Locke (1632-1704) and Bishop George Berkeley (1685-1753). Locke had rejected the concept of innate ideas in his famous concept of the mind as a *tabula rasa*, or blank slate, upon which outside impressions were engraved, while Berkeley argued that abstract ideas did not exist and that only sense perception confirmed, and perhaps even established, the reality of objects outside the mind. Building upon these precepts, Hume established a rigorous skepticism that sought to replace abstruse metaphysical reasoning with practical logic.

Hume argued that the real basis of all human virtues was utility, or how well these particular beliefs and actions served to advance and preserve human society. He rejected the view proposed by Thomas Hobbes (1588-1679) that all human beings acted primarily out of selfish interests; instead, he stated that there was a natural sympathy among human beings that recognized and appreciated virtues such as humanity, friendship, truthfulness, and courage. Hume further proposed that these virtues were judged according to a universal standard of utility, which in the moral sphere corresponded to the physical laws discovered and enunciated by Newton.

**Moral Judgment Comes from Sentiment, Not Reason.** Finally, Hume made a distinction between judgments based on reason and those based on sentiment. The first kind of decision plays but a relatively small part in moral life. Rationality is primarily used in determining objective truths, such as those of mathematics, which are independent of human beings. Situations calling for a moral or ethical response, however, incite a response that is emotional rather than strictly rational. Reason may be necessary to determine the complexities of a certain situation, but once the essence has been established, sentiment determines how one will act. As Hume puts it, the moral response "cannot be the work of the judgment, but of the heart."

In Hume's view, then, human morals are subjective in that they depend upon the internal, emotional response of the individual. Since there is a universal bond among human beings that creates a single standard for moral actions, however, this subjectivity is tempered by a common unity that can be discovered by empirical study. —*Michael Witkoski*

**See also** Hobbes, Thomas; Hume, David; Locke, John; Utilitarianism.

**BIBLIOGRAPHY**

Ayer, A. J. *Hume*. New York: Oxford University Press, 1980.

Flew, Antony. *David Hume: Philosopher of Moral Science*. New York: Basil Blackwell, 1986.

Hume, David. *Enquiries Concerning Human Understanding and Concerning the Principles of Morals*. 3d ed. Oxford, England: Clarendon Press, 1975.

Mackie, John Leslie. *Hume's Moral Theory*. Boston: Routledge & Kegan Paul, 1980.

MacNabb, D. G. C. "David Hume." In *The Encyclopedia of Philosophy*, edited by Paul Edwards. Vol. 4. New York: Macmillan, 1967.

Morice, G. P., ed. *David Hume: Bicentenary Papers*. Austin: University of Texas Press, 1977.

## Entrapment

**TYPE OF ETHICS:** Media ethics

**DATE:** Mid-1970's to present

**ASSOCIATED WITH:** Investigative journalism

**DEFINITION:** The use of an undercover investigation to lure subjects into a compromising statement or act

**SIGNIFICANCE:** The zealous pursuit of a story based upon a presupposition that wrongdoing exists, requiring reporters to use deceptive information-gathering strategies, may promote wrongdoing that otherwise would not occur

Investigative journalism was propelled into prominence during the 1970's as a result of the Watergate scandal uncovered by

*The Washington Post*, the leaking of the Pentagon Papers to *The New York Times*, and the general adversarial tone that characterized the relationship between government and the media throughout the Vietnam War. In subsequent years, technological advancements and the proliferation of broadcast shows that relied on videotape footage to document undercover findings swelled both the number and the scope of such investigations. Issues subject to such treatments have included home and commercial lending practices, nursing home care, governmental corruption, abortion practices, and military information confirmation.

The Federal Bureau of Investigation (FBI) and other law enforcement agencies frequently use undercover operations to expose criminal wrongdoing. Their activities, unlike those in journalism, are subject to explicit guidelines and legal restrictions that help to establish the line between legitimate investigative work and coercing or abetting in the commission of a crime. For journalists, however, that line is largely one of interpretation because of the broad latitude and significant freedoms offered by the First Amendment. It is incumbent upon journalists, therefore, to wrestle with a number of ethical considerations, such as the morality of devising an enticement for illegal activity and the awareness that reporters themselves may become, if even indirectly, agents of wrongdoing.

Industry misgivings about the practice exist, as revealed in the Pulitzer Prize committee's reluctance to recognize stories that rely on undercover investigations because of their deceptive nature. The usage continues, however, because of the journalistic belief that news organizations have an overriding obligation to distribute information to a democratic society and a moral responsibility to consider society's needs, thereby providing the greatest good for the greatest number of people. This approach, with its emphasis on consequences, accepts the belief that the end justifies the means. Therefore, the media's "watchdog role" in preserving and protecting the public interest—a good and moral end—is justified in its aggressive pursuit of certain undercover investigations. Because the journalism profession also professes a strong commitment to accuracy and truthfulness, however, any use of deception must be carefully weighed.

Recognizing that integrity is its greatest asset, the press is especially vigilant in upholding standards that do not erode or detract from its credibility, including the use of deception. Because codes of ethics among the media are more advisory than mandatory, however, much of the decision is left to interpretation by individual journalists who adjudge the specifics of individual situations. The longstanding reliance on consequential reasoning has typically emphasized the social benefit derived from an undercover investigation. For example, a series entitled "Abortion Profiteers" by the *Chicago Sun-Times* in November, 1978, relied on information obtained by reporters who, obscuring their identity as journalists, went to work for several outpatient abortion clinics where gross negligence as well as medical misconduct had been reported. The articles resulted in a number of new state laws regulating outpatient abortion clinics, the closing of two of the four clinics under investigation (one of them permanently), and the imprisonment of one doctor. Several other doctors left the state. It was agreed by the editors and reporters involved that the overwhelming benefit to the community of such an investigation outweighed the price of the deception. Another case involving a different publication, however, reveals that a positive outcome is not the only measure in weighing the ethical considerations of going undercover. In 1988, *Newsday* conceived and planned—but did not execute—an undercover investigation designed to confirm the suspected practice of real estate "steering," a method of maintaining racially segregated neighborhoods by directing potential buyers only to those areas already populated by people of the same race. After a year of preliminary work, management decided that the operation was logistically untenable and that the same information could be obtained through other methods, such as interviews with buyers and real estate records. Anthony Marro, the editor at the time, also questioned the existence of probable cause, wondering if the appropriate level of presumed bad conduct merited the use of entrapment techniques.

The Society of Professional Journalists, whose code of ethics is widely invoked by individual journalists and news organizations, in 1993 introduced a new approach to ethical decision making that combined the long-used consequential reasoning with an effort to examine a number of other factors, such as the characteristics of the situation, as well as journalistic values, loyalties, and professional principles. In addition, the new code set forth a number of conditions, all of which must be met to justify deceptive information-gathering strategies:

1. The information sought must be of profound importance.
2. Other alternatives have been exhausted.
3. The reporter is willing to make public the deception.
4. Excellence has been pursued through full allocation of the news organization's resources.
5. The harm prevented by the deception outweighs the harm of the deception.
6. Conscious, thoughtful, moral, ethical, and professional deliberations have been made.

In addition, the revised code outlined specific rationalizations that do not meet ethical standards and may not be used to justify the use of deception. These include:

1. Winning a prize.
2. Beating the competition.
3. Saving costs or time.
4. Others have "already done it."
5. The subjects, themselves, are unethical.

Out of concern for their role as protectors of the public interest, journalists avoid concrete rules regarding the use of deception and undercover operations. They maintain the right to use such tactics ethically and morally on a situational basis when a greater good is served and when other methods have been exhausted. *—Regina Howard Yaroch*

**See also** Journalistic ethics.

**BIBLIOGRAPHY**

Black, Jay, Bob Steele, and Ralph Barney. *Doing Ethics in Journalism: A Handbook with Case Studies.* Greencastle, Ind.: Sigma Delta Chi Foundation and the Society of Professional Journalists, 1993.

Bovee, Warren G. "The End Can Justify the Means—But Rarely." *Journal of Mass Media Ethics* 6, no. 3 (1991): 135-145.

"Cases and Commentaries: The Norfolk Abortion Case." *Journal of Mass Media Ethics* 5, no 2. (1990): 136-145.

Christians, Clifford G., Kim B. Rotzell, and Mark Fackler. *Media Ethics: Cases and Moral Reasoning.* 3d ed. New York: Longman, 1991.

Dufresne, Marcel. "To Sting or Not To Sting?" *Columbia Journalism Review* 30 (May/June 1991): 49-51.

## Environmental ethics

**TYPE OF ETHICS:** Environmental ethics

**DATE:** Begun in the early 1960's, with major work done in the late 1980's

**ASSOCIATED WITH:** Early influence came from Henry David Thoreau and John Muir

**DEFINITION:** A standard of conduct based on moral principles that supports a holistic, biocentric view of the relationship of humans with the environment

**SIGNIFICANCE:** Applies ethical principles to resolve problems and challenges related to the relationship of humans with the environment

Humans have always exploited nature in the belief that the biosphere was so vast and enduring that people could never inflict devastating harm. Events since the 1980's have called this perception into question. Half the biospheric change caused by humans has taken place since World War II. Humans have transformed or manipulated half the ice-free ecosystems on the planet and have made a significant impact on most of the rest. People have steadily reduced the number of other species in the world through pollution, hunting, and the destruction of natural habitat.

Projections vary. A book called *Beyond the Limits* (1992) argues that if human activity continues at the present rate, within a few decades humans will "overshoot" the carrying capacity of the biosphere and precipitate a collapse. Other scientists say that the earth itself is in no danger at the hands of humans. Still others acknowledge harm to the biosphere but justify it because of the benefits received from growth, development, and technology. They assert that some degree of harm to the biosphere is a cost of the Western lifestyle. Increasingly, complex problems are reduced to a "jobs or owls" choice.

Is it possible to prevent broad damage to the biosphere while accommodating the economic needs of a growing population? The answer is no unless the world adopts a new paradigm for environmental ethics—one based on common values. Once people agree at a values level, they can begin to communicate and develop solutions to perhaps the greatest challenge faced by humanity.

**Do No Harm—Unless . . .** Much of the debate about business and the environment has involved harm versus benefits. Industrial accidents happen, factories shut down, the stock market takes a plunge, pollutants are released into the atmosphere; in all cases, some people suffer harm. The benefits of economic activity are weighed against the harm they cause. In this model of environmental ethics, decisions are based on whether the harm is offset to a significant extent by a corresponding benefit. For example, clear-cutting tropical rain forests causes long-term ecological harm. That harm may outweigh any immediate economic concerns, but the argument is that stopping the activity would deprive many people of their only means of livelihood and further impoverish Third World countries. If one can prove that its benefits outweigh its harmful effects, then a destructive activity is permitted. Few people disagree with this trade-off, provided it protects existing human beings. The controversy occurs when people consider the harm done to future generations of humans, animals, plants, or the planet itself.

Costs and profits guide corporate behavior in this ethical model. If an incident's long-term damage is small, it pays to adopt a strategy of reaction or defense. If the long-term damage is perceived to be high, the strategy should be one of proaction or accommodation.

Introduced in the 1960's, this management model, called the mechanistic school, entails an anthropocentric view in which humanity perceives itself to be the center and ultimate goal of the universe, viewing the environment as existing for its convenience. Nature is viewed as a mere storehouse of raw materials for human use. The environment is seen as relatively stable, unlimited, and well understood. Although many businesses now embrace newer models of environmental decision making, many large, hierarchical, rigid corporations are stuck at this level.

In the 1970's came the organic school. In this more adaptive model of decision making, the goal is the exploitation of rapid changes through innovations and the exploration of new opportunities. It views the environment as highly unpredictable, turbulent, dangerous, and presenting unlimited new market opportunities.

Organizations embracing this model look for opportunities in the environmental movement. Consumers and investors are voting with their dollars and businesses see the opportunities. Sacha Millstone and Ferris Baker Watts, in *The Greening of American Business* (1992), cite surveys indicating that 77 percent of Americans say that a company's environmental reputation affects what they buy. Too often, however, businesses operating in this management model exploit the trend rather than integrate and fully embrace environmental responsibility.

One example of this type of thinking is explored in David Chittick's writings in *The Greening of American Business.*

Chittick makes a strong financial case for proactive environmental programs. By being environmentally responsible, a corporation can save millions of dollars by avoiding costs of waste disposal, costs of penalties and fines for noncompliance, costs of handling hazardous materials (insurance, protective equipment), costs of negative publicity, and costs of decreased employee morale and community confidence. The emphasis, however, is on taking advantage of the opportunity presented by environmental programs.

**Shift to Biocentrism.** By the late 1980's, more and more individuals and businesses began shifting to a model of environmental ethics that embraces biocentrism, viewing the planet Earth as a living system of interdependent species. This approach's "do no harm" principle provides an adaptive model of decision making. It takes a holistic view in which ethical and environmental considerations enter into all decisions. A balance is sought between organizational goals and environmentally based values. The environment is viewed as fragile, limited in resources, and vulnerable to organizational actions. It sees the planet as a community of life-forms in which each contributes to and depends upon all the others. Every act of pollution and resource depletion is viewed not as an isolated event, but as a contributing factor to a collective impact of increasingly accelerating global proportions. As Brian Edwards Brown, an attorney and professor at Iona College, explains: "Nature is not merely an object of anthropocentric concern, an environment that, if contaminated or otherwise damaged, interferes with human use and enjoyment. . . . Nature is a subject in its own right, a totality of diverse, unique, interdependent life-forms, of which the human is but one and without which the human would not be possible."

**A Difference of Values.** The difference in values prohibits the development of workable solutions. The anthropocentric view is the older one. The biocentric view reflects strides that the science of ecology has made in discovering and understanding the intricate interdependence of species, as well as the interconnectedness of their habitats. It reflects an increased understanding of the environment and its problems. It is an ethically based view. These value differences contribute to difficulties in communication between holders of the two views. They lead to mistrust and misinterpretation of the other's arguments and proposals.

Both groups have an obligation to seek to understand the other's views and arguments. Candid, honest, and respectful communication can lead to the creation of shared values. Communication should include education. The anthropocentrics should undertake to know and understand the workings and interdependencies of the biosphere. The biocentrics should seek to understand the concerns of business. A holistic view considers all the parts of the problem. It is not realistic to attempt to eliminate all business, to retreat to a lifestyle of a prior century, or to prevent growth in developing countries. People must, however, evaluate the ways in which they live and make appropriate changes. People must consider ethics and the environment in all of their decision making.

**We Are All Responsible.** If, for example, one asks who is responsible for the pollution caused by automobiles, the answer is the auto manufacturers, the gasoline manufacturers, the auto users, and perhaps even the members of the community that do not provide mass transportation. Everyone shares the responsibility, and everyone must work together for solutions.

Environmental problems are ethical dilemmas. People begin to solve any ethical dilemma with an acknowledgment of facts and perceptions. Next, with a new paradigm, people change their perception of the biosphere and their relationship to it. Then, as in solving all ethical dilemmas, it is necessary to begin with an analysis of the alternatives and their various effects on each stakeholder. A new paradigm of environmental ethics broadens the stakeholder concept. The old paradigm did not include all components of the biosphere, or future generations, as stakeholders. It is not surprising that the solutions put forth have been less than adequate. With the stakeholder analysis complete, it is possible to proceed to synthesis, choice, action, and communication.

This new paradigm creates a permanent shift in the way business operates. With an environmental ethics view, the mission of a corporation is to "manage in an ethical and effective manner in order to maximize shareholder value," replacing the less restrictive, "maximize shareholder value."

**Examples.** In 1989, the Coalition for Environmentally Responsible Economies (CERES) adopted the Valdez Principles, which define guidelines for responsible corporate behavior regarding the environment. Briefly, these principles are:

*Protection of the biosphere.* "Minimize and strive to eliminate the release of any pollutant that may cause environmental damage to the air, water, or earth or its inhabitants."

*Sustainable use of natural resources.* "Make sustainable use of renewable natural resources, such as water, soils and forests . . . conserve nonrenewable resources through efficient use and careful planning . . . protect wildlife habitat, open spaces, and wilderness, while preserving biodiversity."

*Reduction and disposal of waste.* "Minimize the creation of waste, especially hazardous waste, and wherever possible recycle materials . . . dispose of all waste through safe and responsible methods."

*Wise use of energy.* "Make every effort to use environmentally safe and sustainable energy sources . . . invest in improved energy efficiency and conservation . . . maximize the energy efficiency of products" produced or sold.

*Risk reduction.* "Minimize the environmental, health and safety risks to . . . employees and the communities . . . by employing safe technologies and operating procedures and by being constantly prepared for emergencies."

*Marketing of safe products and services.* "Sell products or services that minimize adverse environmental impacts and that are safe as consumers commonly use them. Inform consumers of the environmental impacts" of products and services.

*Damage compensation.* "Take responsibility for any harm . . . caused to the environment by making every effort to fully restore the environment and to compensate those persons who are adversely affected."

*Disclosure.* Disclose to employees and to the public incidents or potential harm caused by the operation relating to environmental harm or that pose health or safety hazards. Take no action "against employees who report any condition that creates a danger to the environment or poses health and safety hazards."

*Environmental directors and managers.* Put on the board of directors at least one member "qualified to represent environmental interests." Demonstrate the commitment to these principles by funding an "office of vice president for environmental affairs or an equivalent position, reporting directly to the CEO, to monitor and report" the implementation efforts.

*Assessment and annual audit.* Conduct and make public an annual self-evaluation of progress in implementing these principles and complying with all applicable laws and regulations throughout worldwide operations.

Although the Valdez Principles are a good start, they are noticeably general. They do not identify specific standards of conduct. There are also loopholes, in that these principles are expressed in terms of "take every effort" or "minimize." Still, they set the stage for a new look at environmental ethics.

Collaboration is a key word in successful environmental programs. For example, a joint effort of the Environmental Defense Fund and McDonald's Corporation has been seeking solutions to McDonald's environmental problems. The organizations jointly commissioned four scientists to examine ways in which McDonald's could reduce and recycle waste. The result was a set of sound proposals, including the phasing out of bleached paper; the testing of reusable cups, coffee filters, and shipping containers; the use of recycled materials; and continuing experimentation.

More and more companies are looking at what consultant Joel S. Hirschhorn calls taking a total approach to environmental ethics. In this approach, the company culture is permanently changed to include environmental values. Since culture can be broadly defined as the collection of the individual values of the people in the organization, a total approach must begin with individuals. It recognizes the importance of having every person in the organization passionately interested in environmental responsibility.

In this new paradigm, a company does not look at regulatory compliance, which concentrates on better management of wastes and control of pollutants. It looks instead at the beginning of the process—at what the company produces, how it produces it, and how it markets its products and services.

An example of this new type of company is The Body Shop, which not only uses posters, pamphlets, and window displays in the shop to promote environmental messages but also starts with the product. The Body Shop manufactures and markets naturally based skin and hair products. It actively seeks out suppliers in remote parts of the world, including many Third World countries. It has an ambitious recycling program and does not test cosmetics on animals. Its marketing programs do not promote idealized notions of beauty or claim that the company's products will perform cosmetic miracles. Practicing what it preaches, The Body Shop encourages its employees to devote time and energy to volunteer projects in their communities.

**First Steps.** Hirschhorn calls for setting three priorities in redefining the corporate culture: First, to focus on people and the corporate culture to develop and deepen the commitment to corporate environmental responsibility. Second, to focus on technology, manufacturing facilities, and products to improve environmental performance. Third, to focus on products and customers to incorporate effective "green marketing" into the strategic planning of the firm.

A significant first step was taken in June, 1992, when most of the world's top political, spiritual, and business leaders gathered with leading environmentalists in Rio de Janeiro for the historic United Nations Conference on Environment and Development—the Earth Summit. The purpose of the Summit was to reconcile the conflicting demands of the environment and development into global strategies that will ensure a viable future. Among the Summit's accomplishments were the following:

- Establishing the environment as an international issue—a point of transition on how to deal with global issues.
- An agreement on the concept that human development and protection of the earth's environment are inextricably intertwined.
- A legally binding treaty that recommends curbing emissions of carbon dioxide, methane, and other "greenhouse" gases thought to warm the climate by trapping the sun's heat close to Earth.
- A legally binding treaty that requires making inventories of plants and wildlife and planning to protect endangered species.
- A realization of the difficulties of negotiating worldwide solutions to worldwide problems.
- Gathering together the greatest number of world leaders ever assembled with a single aim.
- The creation of a Sustainable Development Commission to monitor compliance with the promises made at Rio. The commission will rely on evidence gathered by private environmental groups and will use peer pressure and public opinion to shame countries into following the policies agreed to at the Summit.

• The realization that there is no common paradigm for environmental ethics. There is a gap between those who say that humans are at the center of concerns and those who say that by putting humans at the center of things, with the implied right to dominate and exploit the rest of nature, humans perpetuate existing problems and create new ones.

The Earth Summit, by its very purpose, was a major step toward adopting a new paradigm for environmental ethics. The human species now ranks with grand natural forces such as volcanoes as a transformer of the earth's life-support system. The model that people will embrace to solve environment and development conflicts will determine not only the very survival of the human race, but also the quality of life for future generations. —*Kathleen D. Purdy*

**See also** Business ethics.

**Bibliography**

Gore, Albert. *Earth in the Balance—Ecology and the Human Spirit.* Boston: Houghton Mifflin, 1992. Embracing the new paradigm in environmental ethics, Gore argues that only a radical rethinking of the human/Earth relationship can save Earth's ecology for future generations. The book presents a comprehensive plan for action.

Hargrove, Eugene. *Foundations of Environmental Ethics.* Englewood Cliffs, N.J.: Prentice-Hall, 1989. Presents a justification for protecting nature using an argument called "ecocentric holism."

National Conference on Business Ethics. *Business, Ethics, and the Environment—the Public Policy Debate.* Edited by W. Michael Hoffman, Robert Frederick, and Edward S. Petry, Jr. New York: Quorum Books, 1990. A collection of essays addressing the public policy question of how to regulate corporations or how corporations should regulate themselves to deal with important environmental issues.

__________. *The Corporation, Ethics, and the Environment.* Edited by W. Michael Hoffman, Robert Frederick, and Edward S. Petry, Jr. New York: Quorum Books, 1990. A companion book to *Business, Ethics, and the Environment.* This collection addresses the role of business in protecting the environment. Presents a series of cases and analyses, corporate strategies, and suggestions.

Scherer, Donald, and Thomas Attig, eds. *Ethics and the Environment.* Englewood Cliffs, N.J.: Prentice-Hall, 1983. A basic book that puts forth a range of ecocentric approaches to environmental issues.

Sullivan, Thomas F. P., ed. *The Greening of American Business.* Rockville, Md.: Government Institute, 1992. Readings on the impact of the green movement on business. Topics include labeling, liability, market opportunities, and investing.

## Environmental movement

**Type of ethics:** Environmental ethics

**Date:** 1960 to present

**Definition:** The involvement of individuals, organizations, and governments to make others aware of environmental issues and attempt to solve environmental problems

**Significance:** Seeks appropriate measures to enrich the environment for the good of all without harming the economic or social interests of others

**Historical Background.** The environmental movement is a movement of organizations that are concerned about various types of environmental degradation. The environmental movement began in the early 1960's, prompted by the publication of Rachel Carson's book *Silent Spring* (1962), by growing concern over nuclear war and weapons testing, and by widespread awareness of the damage brought about by postwar growth and technology.

*Silent Spring* was a widely read account of the ways in which pesticides damaged the environment. The book led to an increased awareness of environmental issues on the part of the public. In 1963, the Life Sciences Panel of U.S. president John F. Kennedy reviewed pesticide use and issued a call for legislative measures to safeguard the health of the land and its people against pesticides and industrial toxins. Carson's poetics were thus transformed into a public policy.

In the 1960's, various environmental organizations were founded as a result of increased environmental awareness. In 1967, the Environmental Defense Fund was founded to build a body of case law to establish a citizen's right to a clean environment. In 1970, the U.S. government established the Environmental Protection Agency. Since its founding, the Environmental Protection Agency has grown to thirty times its original personnel. Environmentalism has continued to grow in the U.S. government. In the Executive Branch, twenty-four or more government agencies, bureaus, or services deal with the environment.

On the world scene, the United Nations Environment Programme has been called upon to coordinate numerous United Nations bodies together with diverse international and regional organizations, both governmental and commercial, to monitor, assess, advise, and in some cases to take action on environmental problems.

**Religious Concerns.** Environmental movements have taken root in the religious community. Christian concern over environmental issues began in 1961, when at the World Council of Churches' New Delhi Assembly, Lutheran theologian Joseph Sittler pointed out the declining health of the world's environment. In 1967, *Science* magazine published an address entitled "Historic Roots of Our Ecologic Crisis." It claimed that through such ideas as human dominion, the desacralizing of nature, and the belief that ultimate human destiny is with God and not with Earth, Christendom has encouraged a destructive use of creation. Early evangelical thinking suggested that the chief value of creation was to fuel human industry. Against this anthropocentrism, environmentalists have often viewed human life as merely one node in a cosmic web. More recently, Christian missions and relief organizations have come to recognize that environmental and developmental needs are not only compatible but also inseparable.

One of the environmental problems facing religious groups is the fact that no environmental problem is greater than that of the growing human population. Even if couples today agreed to limit their families to two children, the world's population would continue to grow, because much of the population is below childbearing age.

**Nuclear Accidents.** Another concern of the environmental movement, spanning international boundaries, is that of nuclear weapons and energy production. Accidents have taken place that have harmed vast areas of land. In the early days of the Cold War, the Chelyabinsk complex, which developed plutonium for Soviet nuclear weapons, dumped 76 million cubic meters of high-level radioactive waste into the Techa River. Sickness and death along the river caused the government to evacuate 8,000 people from twenty settlements. Those not evacuated were not allowed to use the river. In 1951, the high-level waste was stored in large steel tanks. In 1957, one of these tanks exploded in an event called the Kyshtym Disaster, after which twenty-three villages were taken off the map. Because of these incidents, people of the Chelyabinsk region have become more assertive about their environment. In 1991, a nonbinding referendum was held in Russia on the building of new reactors; in it, people voted against new breeder reactors. The environmental movement, though young, is growing in Russia.

In the United States, the environmental groups that once were on the political fringes of 1960's activism have become an integral part of the American political process in the 1990's. Some groups have as much economic clout as do large industrial concerns. Greenpeace revenues were $157 million in 1990. If the annual revenues of all the conservation groups in the United States were taken into account, the sum would approach $1 billion.

**Environmental Groups.** In the United States, there are a few basic types of environmental groups that contribute to the environmental movement. The "eco-philosophers" are usually not well known outside of the environmental community. These are individuals who articulate the philosophical basis of the environmental movement. They sometimes call for fundamental changes in the economic and social structure. The conservationist organizations constitute the largest category. These organizations are generally moderate in their positions. The legalist organizations are full-time organizations that encompass those formed by the activism of the late 1960's, which eventually brought about much environmental legislation. These groups have a strong legal focus. Other groups have a very strong grass roots presence because they profess to believe firmly in the concept of citizen empowerment—that is, getting ordinary people involved in local environmental problems. Organizations of local citizens may form in response to local environmental issues. Though these groups may not have significant technical expertise, they are experts on local conditions.

*—David R. Teske*

**See also** Conservation; Earth, human relations to; Greenpeace; Greens; Sierra Club; *Silent Spring*.

**List of Major Environmental Concerns**

1. Air Pollution
2. Food Resources
3. Fossil Fuels
4. Hazardous Waste
5. Human Population
6. Nonrenewable Mineral Resources
7. Nuclear Energy
8. Pesticides
9. Pest Control
10. Soil Resources
11. Solid Waste
12. Water Pollution
13. Water Resources
14. Wildlife Resources
15. World Hunger

**Bibliography**

Del Tredici, Robert. "First Puzzlement; Then Action." *The Bulletin of the Atomic Scientists* 49, no. 2 (March, 1993): 24-29.

Goodpaster, K. E., and K. M. Sayre. *Ethics and Problems of the Twenty-First Century.* Notre Dame, Ind.: University of Notre Dame Press, 1979.

Miller, G. Tyler, Jr. *Environmental Science: An Introduction.* Belmont, Calif.: Wadsworth, 1986.

Perry, John. *Our Polluted World: Can Man Survive?* Rev. ed. New York: Franklin Watts, 1972.

Williams, Terry Temptest. "The Spirit of Rachel Carson." *Audubon* 94 (July/August 1992): 104-107.

## Environmental Protection Agency (EPA), U.S.

**Type of ethics:** Environmental ethics

**Date:** Established December 2, 1970

**Associated with:** Richard Nixon, Environmental movement, and U.S. Congress

**Definition:** The EPA was established to bring all of the U.S. federal government's environmental programs under the control of one independent federal agency that would be responsible for the development and implementation of environmental management programs

**Significance:** The goals of the EPA were the protection of the environment from degradation and harm as a result of human industrial endeavors, and the protection of human health from dangers arising from those endeavors

President Richard M. Nixon created the EPA by Executive Order, as Reorganization Plan 3 of 1970 (dated July 9, 1970) to be effective December 2, 1970. The Reorganization Plan brought fifteen separate components of five executive departments and agencies with programs related to the environment under one independent executive agency that reported directly to the President. The EPA took responsibility for the control of pollution in seven environmental areas: air, water, solid and hazardous waste, pesticides, toxic substances, radiation, and noise. The EPA was created in response to rising public concerns about the increasing degradation of the environment in those areas. The job given to the EPA was to set and enforce standards that would adequately protect the environment, which constituted an acknowledgment of the seriousness of the problems of pollution and a recognition of the interrelated nature of environmental problems. The role of the EPA grew over time as the U.S. Congress passed more environmental protection legislation, although the issues upon which the EPA focuses shift from public health to the ecological depending on political and social concerns of the times.

**See also** Clean Air Act; Clean Water Act.

## Envy

**Type of ethics:** Personal and social ethics

**Associated with:** Moral psychology, the seven deadly sins, and theories of social motivation

**Definition:** Envy is a species of ill-will brought on by regarding the possession of some good by another as turning one's own lack of that good into an evil

**Significance:** Envy is second only to pride in the measure of its viciousness; it is destructive both of its sufferer and of relationships between and among people

Envy is precipitated by occasions in which another person enjoys something that, though valued greatly, is lacked by the person who is subject to the envy. The other's enjoyment and the person's lack are not by themselves sufficient to result in the experience of envy; the lack of the good thing must be regarded by the individual as evil, and must be so regarded simply because the other person possesses that good. A salient feature of this vice is that the envious individual's actual deprivation of the good at issue need not be caused by the envied person's possession of that good (as if there was "not enough to go around").

The envious response in such circumstances is felt as a gnawing, resentful anguish over the other person's possession or achievement of a good. Less frequently, joy may be felt when evils befall the envied person. Several types of desires typically arise in the envious person. First is the impulse to deny (to oneself and others) that one lacks the good at issue. Second is the urge to deny (to oneself and others) that the person who is envied really does possess the good for which he or she is envied. Third is the urge to deny that the envied one really does enjoy the good possessed or achieved. Finally, and most common, is the drive to disparage and denigrate the good that the other is acknowledged to possess and enjoy. The actions that all these desires prompt the envious person to choose may be manifested either in thought or in word and deed. If the envy is strong enough, the person may be prompted actually to destroy the good possessed by the one who is envied ("If I can't have it, no one can!"). This result of extreme envy is one reason why the vice is especially deadly; the other reason concerns the effect of the vice on the one who is envious.

Most vices appear to bring good at least to their practitioners; for example, a glutton derives pleasure from overindulgence, a slothful person enjoys chronic relaxation, and so forth. Envy, however, essentially involves a painful experience of deficiency or privation and accordingly is both agonizing to experience and difficult to acknowledge to oneself. Furthermore, the vice wreaks havoc with the envier's own system of values. As noted above, envy naturally leads to the urge to denigrate a good thing enjoyed by someone else. If this urge is acted upon, then the pain caused by the experience of deficiency (in the light of the other's enjoyment) is assuaged, since the object of envy no longer appears to be so good. The envious desire has prompted one to act, however, in a way that negates (at least in thought) precisely what one values.

This most deadly vice has manifestations at the level of society; the object of envy can be the types of goods enjoyed by a whole class of people, in addition to a specific good enjoyed by a specific person. The "have-nots" may envy the "haves" for the great goods they enjoy. Because of this possibility, the haves may accuse the have-nots of merely acting out of envy when they (the have-nots) demand, in the name of justice, changes in society. This correlates with the accusation against the haves by the have-nots of merely acting out of avarice when they (the haves) demand, in the name of justice, maintenance of the status quo. The desire to *be* envied and the counter-tending *fear* of being envied must also be considered among the social aspects of this vice. A desire to be the object of others' envy leads some people to engage in conspicuous displays of good fortune. The fear of being envied (based on anticipated efforts by enviers to deprive one of goods enjoyed) leads other people to engage in the reclusive and protected enjoyment of good fortune. An awareness of and commitment to what is truly good and just appears to be the only way to avoid these social manifestations of envy.

Envy is, however, an extremely difficult vice to overcome (in part, because it is so difficult to become aware of in oneself). The most rational response to an occasion of envy is to attempt to possess or achieve the good at issue for oneself. If this is not possible, one must try to admire or appreciate the fact that *someone is* enjoying something highly valued. Such a response, though very difficult, is consonant with one's values. If this effort is too demanding, then simply trying to be content with the goods one does enjoy is the only reasonable remaining response. The difficulty arising in each of these rational reactions to what precipitates envy stems from the general principle operative in the vice; the primary cause of one's lack of a good, being evil, is regarded as the mere fact that someone else enjoys that good. Thus, the surest remedy for envy is to rid oneself of this idea. —*Mark Stephen Pestana*

**See also** Evil, problem of; Impartiality; Jealousy; Pride; Self-respect; Sin; Vice.

**BIBLIOGRAPHY**

Kant, Immanuel. "Jealousy and Its Offspring—Envy and Grudge." In *Lectures on Ethics*, translated by Louis Infield. New York: Harper & Row, 1963.

Nozick, Robert. *Anarchy, State, and Utopia*. New York: Basic Books, 1974.

Rawls, John. *A Theory of Justice*. Cambridge, Mass.: Harvard University Press, 1971.

Taylor, Gabriele. "Envy and Jealousy: Emotions and Vices." *Midwest Studies in Philosophy* 13 (1988): 233-249.

## Epictetus (c. 55, Hierapolis, Phrygia—c. 135, Nicopolis, Epirus): Stoic philosopher

**TYPE OF ETHICS:** Classical history

**ACHIEVEMENTS:** Founder of a Stoic school; his sayings were preserved in the *Enchiridion* (c. 140) and *Discourses* (c. 140)

**SIGNIFICANCE:** Epictetus' emphasis on a disciplined life conforming to natural law affected later religious and philosophical movements

Epictetus' ethical system identified areas where personal freedom and individual responsibility coexisted with a deterministic universe. His approach resembled that of earlier Stoics: The purpose of life is happiness, which is reached through conformity with a pantheistic natural order. Reason makes the good life possible by disclosing those things that are beyond human power and those that are not. Environmental forces such as health and status belong to Providence; freedom and responsibility operate in matters of opinion, aim, and desire. Attempts to dominate outside forces produce frustration and unhappiness. Disciplined impulses directed toward proper ends bring liberation, establish a proper relationship between the self and the cosmos, allow the exercise of responsibility toward others, and benefit society. Much of Epictetus' work consisted of practical advice on controlling and directing impulses. His school at Nicopolis, in Epirus, presented Stoicism as a way of life as well as a set of general principles. Epictetus' austere, subjectivist ethics inspired later Roman stoics and reinforced stoic elements in Christianity. His approach to the problems of freedom and dependence also influenced later systems of natural religion and rationalistic philosophical movements such as Kantian idealism.

**See also** *Foundations of the Metaphysics of Morals*; Marcus Aurelius; Self-control; Stoic ethics.

## Epicurus (341 B.C.E., Samos—270 B.C.E., Athens, Greece): Philosopher

**TYPE OF ETHICS:** Classical history

**ACHIEVEMENTS:** Developed the ethical theory that the highest good is pleasure for the self

**SIGNIFICANCE:** Epicurus developed a theory of ethics that was also a way of life; he founded the Garden, a prototype of an Epicurean community

The only writings of Epicurus that have survived are various fragments and three letters presented in Diogenes Laertius' *Life of Epicurus*. From these writings and from the writings of his disciples, however, one may obtain a reliable description of Epicurus' ethical theory. In an uncertain world, the immediate experiences of the senses are the most certain knowledge available. The senses respond to pleasure and pain. Thus, Epicurus equates pleasure with good and pain with evil. Practical wisdom is necessary if one is to weigh pleasures and pains. According to Epicurus, the duration of pleasure is more important than its intensity; thus, mental pleasures are preferred to physical ones. It is better to strive for the absence of pain than for the high peaks of pleasure. His theory of atomism, that everything is composed of material atoms, allows Epicurus to banish the two fears that bring so much pain to human beings: the fear of God and the fear of death. Epicurus sees philosophy as the medicine of the soul. If one desires little and is able to distinguish natural and necessary desires from those that are artificial, then one will be able to attain *ataraxia*, or serenity. This state involves peace of mind and bodily health. The best life is that lived with friends, engaged in moderation of the passions.

**See also** Egoism; Friendship; Hedonism.

## Epistemological ethics

**TYPE OF ETHICS:** Theory of ethics

**DATE:** From antiquity

**DEFINITION:** The relationships among how one knows what one knows, what is good and right, and whether one has become good and/or has done the right thing

**SIGNIFICANCE:** The determination of what is real (epistemology) and what is good (ethics) are intertwined; if one has no awareness of what is real, then one cannot know if one's actions achieve their objective, if they are based on knowledge of the real world, and if all of life is a dream

When one makes a specific ethical claim, one presupposes that one knows what one is talking about. Epistemology deals with how one knows, what one knows, and the source of one's knowledge. If, for epistemological reasons, one must be skeptical about one's knowledge, then one must be skeptical about one's ethical claims. Thus, one might claim, "Not paying a worker a living wage is wrong." Someone might ask "How do you know that is true?" A complete answer to the question would involve an analysis of the terms used in the statement itself. Ethics is involved in making the claim of right and wrong, good or bad. Epistemology is involved in assuring that the claim in this case is in contact with reality, that it is true or false.

When one moves from individual ethical and epistemological analysis to examine in general the relationship of ethical claims and reality, one is involved in metaethics and metaepistemology. One is also involved in a possible discussion of the relativity, subjectivity, and objectivity of ethics. The reason is that one is discussing whether what one ought to do is or is not reflected in the world outside one's conscience and in one's consciousness. Is ethics a mind game that has no contact with reality?

**Is Ethics in Contact with All Reality?** Many people believe that what one ought to do or ought not do is not made up by one's imagination or desires. Some people believe that the way one thinks and what one thinks about puts one in contact with the world outside one—reality. That is why, they suggest, the human development of mathematics and the hard sciences has made it possible, through technology, to change the world. Ethical decisions are the same as scientific decisions. When one sees what a situation is and decides what is the right way to act in the situation, one is dealing with reality both in analyzing the situation and in deciding how to act. Ethical values are like scientific facts: They hold true no matter what the circumstances, everywhere in the world. There is an ethical order beyond human wishes, knowledge, and desires. One can know that order, and when one disagrees with it, one acts at one's own peril.

Those who obtain their ethical order from the revelation of a God also believe in the human ability to know what God reveals and, with God's help, to follow God's commands. God created an ordered world. God reveals how humans fit into that order, and humans must follow God's will or suffer the consequences.

**Is Ethics Primarily in Contact with Human Reality?** Many contemporary ethicists have difficulties with the seemingly naive realism of the previous position. Empirically, they observe the variety of ethical systems throughout the world. There is no single system in today's world. Human values are, from this perspective, more like opinions than like facts. Facts can be proved by the scientific method. Values cannot be proved; they exist only within human beings and are expressed in their actions. Psychological, sociological, and cultural circumstances do make a difference in what is held to be right and wrong. To say that there is some objective norm that can be known with certainty is to make a claim that is contrary to experience and also to claim that ethics can never change because of circumstances.

**Ethics Is in Contact with Humans Within a Real World.** If one stops thinking of humanity and reality as separate and begins to realize that one's thoughts both express and influence reality, one can begin to see that the ethical as well as the epistemological endeavor is an involvement with an ever-changing reality, which means that when one does the good that one claims one must do, one has already changed the reality that motivated that claim. When one swims in the ocean, one can do so only because of the water (reality), and every stroke (doing good) places one in a different part of the ocean, providing one with courage to continue to swim to shore and the necessity to swim differently in order to get there. The waves one makes change the ocean in which one swims. One's thoughts as well as one's ethical actions happen only because one is part of the reality in which one wishes to become better. Each person swims in the reality of an ever-changing ethical sea.

While the sea changes, however, one must realize that there are constants—one is in the sea, one is swimming, and there is a shore toward which to strive. Most contemporary ethicists agree that ethical statements are action guiding. If one says that it is immoral to lie, one's actions will be guided by this principle. Most would also agree that when one uses words such as "right," "wrong," "good," and "bad," one is, at the very least, saying that actions that coincide with these judgments should be judged accordingly. Thus, when someone tells a lie in a situation that is nearly identical to one in which it is judged wrong to tell a lie, that person has not acted ethically.

Although there are many ethical theories and systems of lived ethics, as the world becomes more homogeneous and its languages similar, the desire for universal moral judgments will increase. The fact of language and the fact of the human ability to communicate with those of vastly different cultures and languages suggest that a common sense of right and wrong will grow as the ability to communicate in this ever-shrinking world increases. If people cannot communicate about general principles of right and wrong, there is little hope of any significant communication taking place.

*—Nathan R. Kollar*

**See also** Ethics; Metaethics; Truth.

**BIBLIOGRAPHY**

Audi, Robert. *Belief, Justification, and Knowledge*. Belmont, Calif.: Wadsworth, 1988.

Brandt, Richard B. "Epistemology and Ethics, Parallel Between." In *The Encyclopedia of Philosophy*, edited by Paul Edwards. New York: Macmillan, 1967.

Chisholm, Roderick. *Theory of Knowledge*. 3d ed. Englewood Cliffs, N.J.: Prentice-Hall, 1989.

McCloskey, Henry John. *Meta-ethics and Normative Ethics*. The Hague: Martinus Nijhoff, 1969.

## Equal pay for equal work

**TYPE OF ETHICS:** Sex and gender issues

**DATE:** 1964

**ASSOCIATED WITH:** Civil Rights Act of 1964

**DEFINITION:** The principle that persons who perform the same tasks in the workplace must be paid the same regardless of racial, ethnic, or gender differences

**SIGNIFICANCE:** Equal pay for equal work, which is formally established in federal law by the Civil Rights Act of 1964, expresses the principle that people should be compensated for work actually performed; in this view, the race, gender, or ethnic background of the individual is irrelevant; people who perform the same services for an employer should be compensated identically

Equal pay for equal work is a principle long contended for by the labor, civil rights, and feminist movements in the United States. Throughout most of the twentieth century, there was great workplace discrimination against women and nonwhites. At the time of the passage of the Civil Rights Act of 1964, women who were doing the same jobs as men were being paid salaries that were about two-thirds the amounts of those that were being paid to men. People of color were similarly disadvantaged. The Civil Rights Act of 1964 makes these practices unlawful, though it does not address the greater problem of the relegation of minorities to inferior jobs.

**See also** Americans with Disabilities Act; Civil Rights Act of 1964; Equality.

## Equal Rights Amendment (ERA)

**Type of ethics:** Sex and gender issues

**Date:** First proposed in 1923

**Definition:** A proposed constitutional amendment that mandates that both sexes be treated equally under the law

**Significance:** If passed, the amendment would abrogate legal distinctions between the sexes

In 1921, the National Woman's Party, fresh from its battles for woman suffrage, decided to push for passage of an Equal Rights Amendment. The Party thought that the Equal Protection Clause of the Fourteenth Amendment did little to address those areas of discrimination against women that still remained. Under the leadership of Alice Paul, the ERA was first introduced to Congress in 1923.

Resolutions proposing the ERA were introduced in every succeeding Congress until 1971. Several times the ERA almost passed the Houses, but with riders attached that effectively nullified the resolution. In 1971, Representative Martha Griffiths introduced it again. This time, the ERA passed both Houses and was sent out to the states for ratification. Originally, the time limit for ratification was seven years. President Jimmy Carter extended the deadline for an additional thirty-nine months. At the end of this time, the ERA failed to achieve ratification by a margin of three states. Seventeen months later, in 1983, when it was introduced in Congress again, it failed to pass. Since then, interest in the ERA has been minimal.

The success and failure in passage of the ERA in both the Congress and the states have had much to do with changing conditions and circumstances in the country. For example, opponents have always feared that legislation that protected women's rights in the workplace would be negated by passage of the ERA. This fear was undercut when Title 7 of the Civil Rights Act of 1964 included women as a protected class. Opponents have also feared that if the ERA passed, women would be drafted into the military. The ERA passed Congress when the Vietnam War was coming to an end and the fear of women being drafted was diminished; it did not command enough of the states' votes when the war in Afghanistan was starting and the fear had returned. When the ERA passed Congress, there had been no gender discrimination cases that the Supreme Court had decided in favor of women. After the ERA passed Congress, the Supreme Court decided and has continued to decide several cases under the Equal Protection Clause of the Fourteenth Amendment favorably to women, thus diminishing the need for an ERA. Finally, when the ERA passed Congress, abortion was illegal. Passage of the ERA by the

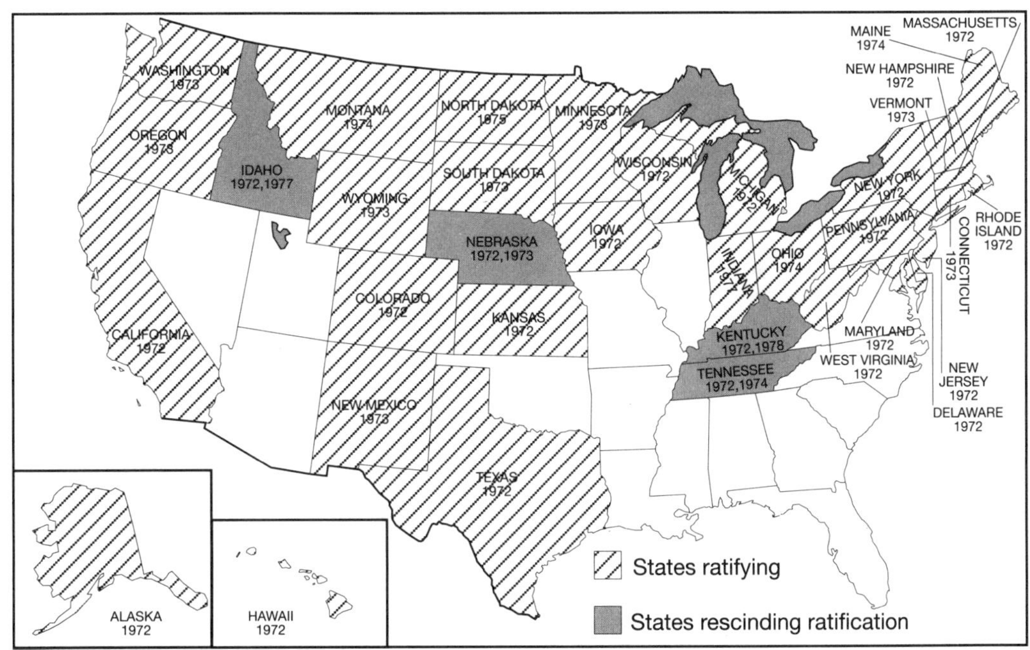


*States Ratifying and Rescinding the ERA: 1972-1982*

*Source:* Data are from Janet K. Boles, *The Politics of the Equal Rights Amendment.* Pp. 2-3. New York: Longman, 1979.

states might have meant and may still mean today that those who oppose abortion and wish to see it regulated would be silenced. As long as it is tied so intimately to the changing and conflicting conditions and needs of the populace, enactment of the ERA into a constitutional amendment mandating the equality of the sexes before the law will remain problematic. Until it is enacted, however, inequalities between the sexes, even if subtle, will continue to exist.

**See also** Civil Rights Act of 1964; Equal pay for equal work; Feminism; Sexual stereotypes; Wage discrimination; Women's liberation movement.

Most analyses of human life find that individuals are unequal in many respects—in intelligence, talents, wealth, lifestyles, and so forth. Further, equality is difficult to define precisely and is, indeed, ambiguous, unless qualifiers are added. Equality can be expressed as an equation. What is on the right side must be exactly equal to what is on the left side; for example; 4 + 4 = 7 + 1. To express this equation in relation to equality, one must specify which entities are under consideration and in what dimension those entities exist.

Although opinions vary as to the exact nature of equality, most people would agree that human beings share many characteristics. All are members of one species and are the same "class" of objects (*Homo sapiens*). All have basic needs to sustain their lives (food, for example), all can feel pleasure and pain, and all are thinking creatures and have some capacity for reason and "common sense" logic. It follows, then, that all should be of equal dignity and worth. It follows, next, that all people are entitled to be treated equally because they all have the same moral and natural rights to life. Likewise, in a just society, all people deserve legal

*An equal rights demonstration.* (Library of Congress)

## Equality

**TYPE OF ETHICS:** Theory of ethics

**DATE:** From antiquity

**DEFINITION:** The belief that all humans innately have the same value, status, or class and that all should have the same legal, civil, economic, and social rights

**SIGNIFICANCE:** Since ethics is most concerned with theories of moral principles or moral values, with moral duties and responsibilities, and with right and wrong, the question of equality versus inequality is central to ethics

equality. In this view, equality simply seems to be the norm and inequality a deviation. Equality should never be abandoned unless there are strong reasons to do so—as when equality as a basic value collides with another value, in the case, for example, of wartime hoarders of food who leave others to starve. The hoarders demand equal treatment in terms of property rights, but because the starving have a right to live, the hoarders' excess food might be confiscated.

Perhaps the "idea" of basic equality could be expressed thus: If I have a pizza party with four friends and I split the pizza into five equal parts, I will have no critics and need make no justification. Alternatively, if I give one-half of the pizza to one friend and split the other half into four very small but equal pieces, I will be expected to give an explanation for my action.

Given the general belief that in many ways humans are equal, it is not surprising that almost all literature that depicts humankind's societal dreams depicts an egalitarian society. Many fictional paradises may not be democratic and may be ruled by a benevolent despot, but virtually all stress equality of people.

**Equality and Religion.** Modern religious thinkers usually assert that all people are equal but then talk and act as if all are unequal. Martin Luther believed that all people were equal in possessing capacity for spiritual understanding, but John Calvin turned that notion on its head, arguing that, yes, people were equal—equally depraved and sinful.

Jacob Viner argued that it was an error to see egalitarianism in religion, for the rich do not usually voluntarily share with their poor brothers—except to put a little money in the weekly collection plate. Further, he maintained that such equality as did exist in churches was equality in the next world—"pie in the sky when you die"—not in this world. Viner added that in "heaven" egalitarianism may be practiced, but only in that all must accept common subordination to God's authority.

**History.** Plato believed in the political equality of men and women, and Aristotle thought that all free citizens were equal, but the ancient Greek Stoics were the first philosophers to assert that all humans were rational beings who had an equal capacity for virtue. The religious expression of a similar idea is found in the New Testament, which recognizes the equality of all souls.

Although the Lollards and Hussites of the late Middle Ages also espoused a doctrine of equality, they were not influential, because they were trapped in a world where hierarchy and antiegalitarianism ruled. The modern concept of egalitarianism arose in the seventeenth century. In a limited way, Calvinists advanced the cause by stressing the equality of the "elect." Some of the Parliamentarians in the English civil war gave secular expression to the same idea when they spoke of natural rights and the social contract. Such ideas became so popular during Thomas Hobbes's times that he took it for granted that humans were equal in the state of nature.

Some later philosophers supported Hobbes's assumption. They agreed with critics who still scorned egalitarianism and who still pointed to the obvious inequalities they saw all about them; they argued that among humans differences of intelligence and talents did indeed exist, but that they existed because people lived in different environments and had different life experiences. At birth, they believed, all people have similar, virtually unlimited, potentialities. Even Rousseau granted this argument, while holding that the world's "sophisticated" societies bred social inequalities. Indeed, Rousseau tried to square natural equality with the political authority of the one or the few who ruled the many.

The doctrine of equality saw its greatest manifestation near the close of the eighteenth century in both the American and the French revolutions, revolutions wherein leaders made explicit the freedoms that human beings should have. The revolutionaries focused on political and social rights, however, while ignoring economics and the great chasm between the rich and the poor. Nineteenth and twentieth century socialists emerged to champion the cause of economic equality, but they found followers in only a few areas. Indeed, the collapse of the Soviet Union in the 1990's probably ended the last hope of those who favored worldwide socialism. The world might, however, one day evolve into a moderate socialist society such as Sweden's. Still, it is ironic that the world appeared to be "captured" by the capitalistic system, which revels in human avarice and which allows the exploitation of many humans by the few who control the means of production. Workers actually produce the profit that the rich reap, but the workers receive few rewards. Unequal capitalistic exploitation is also unconcerned about "means and ends." Whatever makes money counts, and profits remain the measure of all things. The fate of human beings in the capitalistic systems matters not, as long as they are consumers who put money on the table.

Yet even within the capitalistic system, reformers still try to ensure some elements of equality. Various welfare programs in the United States, for example, provide aid to the poor, programs including outright monetary payments, food stamps, free or partially subsidized medical aid, and so forth. Mothers with dependent children also receive assistance, as do the physically or mentally disabled. Likewise, the unemployed at any age qualify for temporary assistance. In addition, the poorest students qualify for aid and receive a subsidized education. All the above examples work to "level the playing field" in that they all relate to equal opportunity and are intended to allow industrious people to "work" their way out of dangerous poverty.

**Characteristics of Egalitarianism.** The traditional definition of the term "egalitarianism" included impartiality, a view that required equal responsibilities and equal rewards for all who performed similar jobs. Other related values include equal justice instead of justice according to rank, wealth, other personal consideration, and so on; and equal economic opportunity rather than discrimination based on race, ethnic group, gender, age, sexual preference, and so forth. Further, humans are thought to deserve the equal satisfaction of basic needs such as food, housing, and personal freedoms.

In many cases, cries for equality have been directed at specific inequalities. Patrician misrule of the Roman Empire led Plebeians to revolt on many occasions, demanding a greater voice in the empire's affairs (political equality). The American civil rights movement of the 1950's and 1960's attacked racial inequality. The women's movement, from the 1960's to the present, demanded that gender inequality cease. The modern senior citizen movement sought to end discrimination based on age. Even the modern environmental movement embraces the concept of equality by holding that small minorities (big business, for example) should not be allowed to forever foul the environment that all people need to share for their ultimate survival. Reformers who advocated change such as that mentioned above are pursuing a secular version of a religious doctrine that held that God created the world and wanted it to be a vast treasure trove that all people would share equally.

**Equality and Problematic Issues.** Typical dictionary definitions of equality, while leaving much to be desired, nevertheless include: (1) the condition of having equal dignity and rank as others; (2) the condition of being equal in power; and (3) society operating with fairness and equity. Applying these definitions has sometimes led to contradictions. Critics of the equality doctrine pointed out that if humans (in the real world) are unequal in talents, skills, and excellence, then adherence to definition 3 will violate definition 1. Likewise, adherence to definition 1 will violate definition 3.

After observing the above contradictions, some thinkers have held that, because humans operating in the real world are not all equal in terms of ability and excellence, elevating those people who have inferior ability and intelligence would be an injustice to the former group. A degree of inequality, therefore, seemed to be the natural result of equity and fairness. To continue arguing for maximum equality in an unequal world, some thinkers developed the concept of "equal shares to equals"—equal pay for equal work in an economic world in which differing levels of talent and skills supposedly justify some inequalities.

In reference to economic issues, critics of the equality doctrine threw yet one more dart: Equality of opportunity, through time, usually produces inequalities of wealth, given people's differing intelligence, motivation, and career choices. Further, some critics question the equality doctrine by referring to the concept of justice, which demands that each person be given his or her due but that only equal people receive equal rewards, given differences in intelligence and drive—in other words, to each according to personal merit. Additionally, some philosophers pointed out that if all work rewards were equal, rational people would probably minimize their work as much as possible, a pattern that would lead to gross inefficiency. Thus, equality, critics contended, would work only in a perfect world in which work was not necessary or in which work was a pleasure.

Some philosophers asserted further that, at times, egalitarian rules sometimes conflict not only with each other (equal opportunity and welfare, for example) but also with important social goals. Critics contended that tension will always exist between equal welfare and equal freedom. In pursuing equal welfare, government necessarily imposed more restrictions on economically dominant groups. Yet it was freedom of opportunity that created the unequal situation in the first place. Likewise, political freedom for all citizens might lead to a situation wherein the dominant majority suppresses a certain minority (slavery is the best example). Worse, critics argued that egalitarianism could lead to a decline of civilization, for it might bring a downward leveling of society, wherein cultural excellence, great diversity, and individuality would be stifled.

**Specific Examples of Reforms Leading to Greater Egalitarianism.** In modern America, President Franklin D. Roosevelt in 1941 signed Executive Order 8802, which banned racial discrimination in the defense industry. By 1945, at least two million African Americans were working in that industry. In 1948, President Harry Truman, campaigning for another term, advocated national health insurance. Although Truman did not have enough congressional support to accomplish the goal, he made the effort. On that issue, he proved to be a progressive egalitarian who was more than half a century ahead of his time.

Truman also campaigned against racism and later set up the Civil Rights Commission; its investigations led to a well-researched report condemning racial segregation and discrimination. Success in resolving the civil rights question would have to wait more than fifteen years: Nevertheless, President Lyndon B. Johnson signed the historic Civil Rights Act of 1964, and that act, enforced over time, changed the social and political face of the United States. Johnson also shared Truman's concern for health insurance and the elderly. When he signed his Medicare legislation, Johnson flew to Truman's home in Independence, Missouri, to allow the ex-president to witness the signing.

The Medicare act was only one of a host of reforms that Johnson advocated in his "Great Society" program. Although his program affected many different groups in society (notably the poor), to show the egalitarian intent, one need mention only the massive financial aid that the federal government poured into education—education being one avenue that could provide equal opportunity for millions of people and allow them to rise both economically and socially.

**Equality and Today's America.** From the 1970's to the present, there seemed to be a retreat from equality. American society became more inegalitarian. In American economic life, the rich added much to their coffers at the expense of the poor. When President Johnson began his "Great Society" in the mid-1960's, approximately 25 percent of all Americans fell below the government's definition of the "poverty line." When Johnson left office, that definition fit only 11 percent of the people. As the country approaches the twenty-first century, the figure is soaring above 25 percent again.

Economic gloom aside, the inegalitarian trend was also seen in social life. Now, more than ever, the "underclass" (people who live in soul-crushing poverty) is further away from the middle and upper classes. Likewise, the gap is growing between the middle and upper classes, with the latter engaging in vulgar conspicuous consumption and the former trying desperately to keep up. In many other aspects of life, inequality can be seen. In the health care field, for example, despite some modern reforms, the rich continue to get the best care, while the poor do without care because they cannot pay the price. In law, modern America said that all were equal, for justice was blind and knew no prejudice. In fact, however, the wealthy hire the best lawyers while the poor settle for public defenders or abandon their rights and stay out of court altogether.

Although there have been more inegalitarian setbacks, such as the failure to ratify the Equal Rights Amendment and the institution of unfair taxation policies (regressive taxes that unfairly hurt the poor and the aged), general trends suggest that the country is still moving slowly in the direction of greater egalitarianism. In the 1990's, reformers began gaining more support and therefore exercised more power to bring change.

**Conclusions.** The simplest ethical or moral argument in favor of continuing to extend the doctrine of equality is an appeal to reason. A person should grant equalities to others that he or she would demand for himself or herself; one should grant equalities that no rational human would be willing to voluntarily give up. No human should be so morally deficient as to withhold from others in similar circumstances benefits that he or she has demanded for himself or herself. In other words, one's equality may well be conditional; for a person to maintain and protect his or her own equality, it may be necessary to grant equality to all.

There are remedies for inequalities in American life, but a new "Great Society" program or another "New Deal" likely will be necessary. Further, the elite (economic and social) must stop taking more than its share and must remember that others must live, too. —*James Smallwood*

**See also** Egalitarianism; Fairness; Human rights; Natural rights.

**BIBLIOGRAPHY**

Cecil, Andrew R. *Equality, Tolerance, and Loyalty: Virtues Serving the Common Purpose of Democracy*. Dallas: University of Texas at Dallas Press, 1990. Cecil makes a strong case for the virtues he names in the hope that Americans will turn away from intolerance and selfishness; otherwise, the country will likely not survive.

Cook, Fred J. *The Corrupted Land: The Social Morality of Modern America*. New York: Macmillan, 1966. Although he wrote more than two decades before the country's savings and loan fiasco and the major Wall Street scandals, Cook exposed the corruption of everyday "ethics" in the business world and found that those ethics were, indeed, unethical.

Kaus, Mickey. *The End of Equality*. New York: Basic Books, 1992. Kaus examines the modern United States as it approaches the twenty-first century. He focuses on liberalism and social classes, and, true to his title, he finds much inequality among different racial, ethnic, and income classes.

Rousseau, Jean-Jacques. *Discourse on the Origin of Inequality*. Translated by Donald A. Cress. Indianapolis: Hackett, 1992. Rousseau is a good starting point on the subject of equality, for he argued that equality was most "unnatural." His ideas must be addressed.

Ryan, William. *Equality*. New York: Pantheon Books, 1981. With his focus on the modern United States, Ryan discusses in depth the following topics: equal pay for equal work, sexual discrimination in employment, equality before the law, and American social policy. Like other researchers, he finds much inequality.

Slote, Michael A. *From Morality to Virtue*. New York: Oxford University Press, 1992. Reexamining the philosophy of Immanuel Kant, Slote surveys many topics, including ethics, virtue, "common sense," and utilitarianism.

## Espionage

**TYPE OF ETHICS:** Politico-economic ethics

**DEFINITION:** The effort to discover by clandestine means the secrets of others

**SIGNIFICANCE:** Espionage involves the secret gathering of information in order to influence relationships between two entities; prevailing cultural attitudes often view the clandestine nature of spying as immoral

Secrecy exists, and is maintained, for the advantage of one entity over another. Keeping information secret has always been recognized as a highly effective means of ensuring success in military operations, diplomatic negotiations, private enterprise, and even many personal interactions. The fact that secrets exist and are maintained for one entity's advantage over another makes it imperative that the opposition acquire the secrets of rivals. The acquisition of secrets is the fundamental task of espionage.

The element of secrecy is responsible for the distinction between standard intelligence gathering and espionage. Most electronic and human intelligence gathering, despite its elaborate secrecy, is carried out overtly. Espionage, however, is carried out entirely in a covert manner: Espionage is the effort to discover by clandestine methods the secrets of others. It must be made clear that espionage is the secret act of information gathering and should not be confused with other covert activities such as sabotage, misinformation campaigns, the placement of agents of influence or agents provocateurs, and assassination.

In all forms of espionage, the act of secretly gathering vital information is carried out by espionage agents—spies. Spies, who are usually highly trained and motivated individuals dedicated to their information-gathering mission, are sent from one entity to secretly gather information about another entity. People from one entity who sell information or inform to another entity are not spies, but traitors. This is an important and often overlooked distinction. A spy is required to conceal his or her true identity by assuming a false one; to hide the nature of his or her mission and lines of communication, operate under a cloak of secrecy, and if captured deny organizational affiliation. Because the ultimate goal of any spy is to steal secrets, spies must often employ tactics that are perceived as immoral to fulfill their information-gathering missions; for example, blackmail, bribery, coercion, deception, burglary, and subterfuge. As a result, no matter how noble the cause, spies are commonly regarded as criminals and outcasts even by their own organizations. Historically, the portrayal of the spy as a criminal has been reinforced by propaganda and popular entertainment venues. Because of the spy's cultural image and the amoral or even immoral aspects of espionage operations, the organizations initiating them camouflage or deny their existence. Most governments and businesses publicly disavow use of espionage agents and, when a spy is captured, deny any association with that person. Those who employ spies to gather information, however, do so believing that their spies are noble, self-sacrificing individuals, while the opposition's spies are evil interlopers.

Despite many negative societal attitudes regarding the secret nature of espionage, it is a legitimate and essential function of every government and many large corporations that are aware of their responsibilities to either citizens or shareholders. The practice of espionage is justified by the knowledge that all nations, and most competitive businesses, conceal important phases of their activities from rivals. With this understanding, it then becomes a necessity to acquire knowledge about the disposition of concealed information that may influence or threaten a nation's peace and security or a corporation's competitive standing in the marketplace. Espionage gathers this important information and places it in the hands of authorities who use it to build a database of intelligence from which they can plan future decisions and actions. By this definition, espionage is an important activity that is separate from any moral view of the act of spying. Because of the clandestine nature of espionage and the fact that its ultimate goal is to steal secrets, it is perceived as the most unethical and lawless activity in which a government or corporation may engage, short of unwarranted hostilities. Using clandestine means to obtain secret information is ethically justifiable, however, if the end use of the gathered intelligence meets the goals and objectives of the society or organization that initiates the espionage activity. The setting of goals and objectives for espionage operations is reflective of the culture initiating the espionage activity. In totalitarian states and many private corporations, espionage operations are initiated by individuals or small groups whose objectives and actions are not answerable to the remainder of society.

In open societies, representative governments and publicly owned corporations who use espionage are often obliged to defend their decisions before the public if the activities are disclosed. —*Randall L. Milstein*

**See also** Covert action.

**Bibliography**

Bergier, Jacques. *Secret Armies: The Growth of Corporate and Industrial Espionage.* Translated by Harold J. Salemson. Indianapolis: Bobbs-Merrill, 1975.

Dobson, Christopher, and Ronald Payne. *The Dictionary of Espionage.* London: Harrap, 1984.

Farago, Ladislas. *War of Wits: The Anatomy of Espionage and Intelligence.* New York: Funk & Wagnalls, 1954.

Kurland, Michael. *The Spymaster's Handbook.* New York: Facts on File, 1988.

Turner, Stansfield. *Secrecy and Democracy: The CIA in Transition.* Boston: Houghton Mifflin, 1985.

## Ethical monotheism

**Type of ethics:** Religious ethics

**Date:** Term coined nineteenth century

**Associated with:** Christianity, Judaism, and Islam

**Definition:** A belief in one personal transcendent God who requires strict moral conduct and metes out rewards or punishments

**Significance:** This belief has determined the way in which practitioners of the world's three great monotheistic religions—Christianity, Islam, and Judaism—have conducted their lives and viewed others

The major monotheistic religions generally suppose that ethical monotheism was the original religion revealed to the first human parents (Adam and Eve) but was quickly corrupted through error and transgression. Judaism maintains that ethical monotheism was reconfirmed to the patriarch Abraham, who battled against the widespread belief in the many, often capricious and amoral, gods of the ancient Near East. He taught that God is ethical and demands the same from all adherents to true religions. Islam validates the role of Abraham while claiming him as their progenitor and proclaiming Muḥammad to be the last and greatest of a long line of prophets to teach ethical monotheism. It has sometimes been asserted that Christianity does not profess pure monotheism because of its dogma of the Holy Trinity. Critical, scholarly, nineteenth century theories saw monotheism as an evolutionary step emerging from polytheism. More modern views have argued that ethical monotheism developed as a response in opposition to polytheism. Scholars see ethical monotheism as a remarkable achievement of Hebrew history, though they disagree about the period in which the explicit worship of "the one true God" began. There is no question, however, that ethical monotheism has been a major world force in determining the behavior of nations and civilizations, and that it formed the foundation for such codes as the Ten Commandments.

**See also** Christian ethics; God; Islamic ethics; Jewish ethics; Muḥammad al-Muṣṭafâ; Pantheism; Ten Commandments.

## Ethical Principles of Psychologists: Professional publication

**TYPE OF ETHICS:** Psychological ethics

**DATE:** December, 1992

**ASSOCIATED WITH:** American Psychological Association

**DEFINITION:** A professional ethical code required of psychologists and enforceable through sanctions from various bodies

**SIGNIFICANCE:** The application to the varied roles of psychologists of fundamental ethical priorities such as promoting happiness, human rights and independence, self-fulfillment, and the good of society

The Ethical Principles are primarily based on the potential for harming others through incompetence, improper emotional coercion, or misinformation that curtails free and informed thought and behavior. Freedom of inquiry and expression is central to psychology, but discriminating against others or allowing the misuse of research is unethical. Psychologists have a particular responsibility to be self-aware, honest, and to use the methods of science, scientific explanation, and critique, rather than expressing mere personal opinion and authority. They must be aware of the basic and unique needs of other people and groups. Supervision, instruction, advisement, and treatment have considerable intellectual and emotional power.

Psychologists must avoid potential harm or exploitation by being candid about their services and fees, qualifications, confidentiality, allegiances, the requests they make of research volunteers (informed consent specifying risks and benefits, providing feedback, and minimizing deception), and avoiding potentially harmful multiple relationships. Psychologists do not engage in sexual relationships with students, supervisees, and patients because of the potential for biased judgment or exploitation through lack of interpersonal reciprocity. Tests, diagnoses, evaluations, and interventions must be based on scientific competence and avoidance of harm.

**See also** Animal research; Bioethics; Medical research; Professional ethics; Therapist-patient relationship.

## Ethics

**TYPE OF ETHICS:** Theory of ethics

**DATE:** Ethics as a philosophical discipline dates from the fifth century B.C.E.

**ASSOCIATED WITH:** Moral philosophy

**DEFINITION:** The term "ethics," from the Greek word *ethos* (character), refers to the philosophical science that deals with the rightness and wrongness of human actions

**SIGNIFICANCE:** The conception of ethics is the basis of all less-general ethical concepts

Ethics has been in many ways the most general study of human behavior, since every other form of analysis of human action, whether economic, psychological, sociological, anthropological, or historical, can be subjected to an ethical analysis.

In Plato, the subordination of ethics to ontology and epistemology was manifest, and it was not until Aristotle that ethics achieved full status as an independent branch of the philosophical sciences. In the *Nicomachean Ethics* especially, Aristotle was at pains to distinguish ethical knowledge from other forms of human knowledge—as when he contrasted the exactitude to be anticipated in mathematics from that attainable in ethical reasoning.

Today, ethics is the name given to that most general study of the rightness and wrongness of human actions, including not only the determination of whether particular acts are morally permissible but also the derivation of those theories by which such a determination may be made, as well as an analysis of the meaning of the language that is peculiar to such determinations and derivations. Today, ethics is divided into normative ethics, on the one hand, which involves both standard ethical theory and its application to particular actions and classes of actions, and metaethics, on the other hand, which examines the meaning of ethical language. From its beginnings, ethics—the more general term—has concerned itself with the human "mechanism" of morality: the faculties of the human soul and the needs, passions, and desires of the human mind and body.

Plato and Aristotle did not neglect the theoretical side of ethics, and Aristotle especially presented a rather systematic theoretical framework throughout his exposition of natural eudaimonism. In Plato, much of the emphasis on human character and motivations does not remain restricted to the words of the philosophical disputations but is embedded in the action/drama of the dialogues themselves. In the *Republic*, one sees Thrasymachus storm away from the discussion, driven by the angry passion that drove his lawless philosophy of unrestrained power. In the *Euthyphro*, the eponymous character fled from Socrates, motivated by the senseless pride that had imprisoned him in the darkness of ignorance. In the *Philebus*, Protarchus had to bear the burden of the argument for hedonism, because Philebus, the archvoluptuary, could not be bothered to defend his ethical position or to leave his pleasures to indulge in philosophical disputations.

Instead of considering the virtuous man in the abstract, Plato related incidents from the life of Socrates. Socrates remained sober and articulate into the dawn in the *Symposium*, in which dialogue he is also shown resisting the sexual blandishments of Alcibiades. At his trial, Socrates (in the *Apologia*) was unmoved by the danger he faced and displayed compassion toward his accusers, whom he did not blame for their machinations. In the *Phaedo*, awaiting execution, Socrates calmly speaks with friends on the immortality of the soul, and in the *Crito*, he refuses to contemplate flight or any other stratagem to save his life. Thus, Socrates served as a kind of *spoudaios*—the wise, virtuous man whom Aristotle counsels the young to observe and imitate.

In the Middle Ages, patristic and scholastic writers continued to explore the boundaries of ethics, but with a heavy concern for theological ethics. Saint Thomas Aquinas' ethics, for example, which are directly descended from Aristotle's natural eudaimonism, are designated supernatural, or theological, eudaimonism on account of the regard that his ethical system gives to the attainment of beatitude in the afterlife. This concentration upon theological concerns led to an emphasis upon free will for theodic purposes—making evil the product of the human will and the human will the necessary source of virtue, as well as the cause of evil.

From the coming of the Renaissance well into the latter half of the eighteenth century, ethical philosophy returned to its classical roots and once again emphasized the passions and sentiments in humanity that conflict and that drive those behaviors that support the institutions of society, from friendship and the family to cooperative activities and the nation-state.

In the latter half of the eighteenth century, Immanuel Kant returned ethics to a theoretical orientation with his development of the categorical imperative. Kant's deontology—or science of duty, as he called it—contained many complex aspects, such as the autonomous and heteronomous wills and the hypothetical and categorical imperatives, thus giving priority again to abstract, theoretical models of ethical thought. Indeed, Kantian formalism temporarily eclipsed the firm concretization that necessarily accompanies consequentialistic analysis.

Although the nineteenth century saw a step back from the degree of formalistic abstraction inherent in Kantian ethics, Hegelian and other forms of idealist ethics, utilitarianism (of both the Benthamite and Millian variety), and the variegated Darwinistic ethical systems failed to return to the classical model of virtue analysis.

In the twentieth century, the proliferation of academic publications and university-based scholars has been instrumental in the resurrection, if not the reinvigoration, of virtually every philosophical tradition in ethics. Nevertheless, virtue- and sentiment-based ethical theories have enjoyed a rather desiccated existence, except in somewhat altered form under the various phenomenological approaches.

In general, metaethical investigations have predominated throughout the discipline in recent years, undoubtedly stimulated by G. E. Moore's discovery of the naturalistic fallacy and the renewed interest in the Humean is/ought dilemma that Moore caused. Contributing to the same effect has been the dominance of logical positivism and its offshoots, which have insisted upon the analysis of language as the key methodological operation in philosophy.

Finally, the central role of commerce and the professions in modern life has led to a significant compartmentalization of normative ethics: Legal ethics, business ethics, biomedical ethics, ethics of engineering, and so forth, each with its specialized vocabulary and subject matter, have threatened to replace the general overview of the duties of person and citizen (the classical model) as the primary focus of normative ethical inquiry. —*Patrick M. O'Neil*

**See also** Ethics/morality distinction; Morality; *Nicomachean Ethics*.

**BIBLIOGRAPHY**

Aristotle. *Nicomachean Ethics*. Indianapolis: Hackett, 1985.

Kant, Immanuel. *Foundations of the Metaphysics of Morals and What Is Enlightenment*. Translated by Lewis White Beck. 2d ed. New York: Macmillan, 1990.

Mill, John Stuart. *Utilitarianism and Other Essays*. Edited by Alan Ryan. New York: Penguin Books, 1987.

Plato. *The Republic*. Translated by A. D. Lindsay. New York: Knopf, 1992.

## Ethics: Book

**TYPE OF ETHICS:** Renaissance and Restoration history
**DATE:** Published in 1677 as *Ethica*
**AUTHOR:** Baruch Spinoza
**SIGNIFICANCE:** Spinoza believed that the knowledge of the systematic unity of all things, and of God as their source and essence, is humankind's greatest good and blessedness

**The Geometric Method.** In Baruch Spinoza's chief work, the *Ethics*, he attempted to deduce his results from certain fundamental conceptions by using the geometric method. He even adopted the external form of Euclidean geometry, beginning each of the five parts into which the work is divided with definitions, axioms, and postulates, and advancing by formally demonstrating a series of definite propositions. Spinoza, like René Descartes before him, believed that mathematics furnished the universal type of true science, and he assumed that absolute certainty, which was then generally regarded as essential to science, could be attained only by following the same method. It has been pointed out that what is most valuable in Spinoza's system is not the result of his formal deductions, however, but the genius evident in his speculative intuition and keen psychological analysis.

**Freedom.** In the *Ethics*, Spinoza is most directly concerned with the problem of humanity's place in nature—its relation to God or the total system of things—and the possibility of freedom. He demonstrates the possibility that human freedom depends upon first recognizing that one is part of nature and that one's mind, like everything else, is subject to uniform natural laws. It is not contingency or some peculiar power of free will that governs mental experiences; here as well as elsewhere, all takes place according to law and necessity. Nature's laws, he argues, are always and everywhere the same. Thus, there should be one method of understanding the nature of all things: through nature's universal laws and rules.

**The Emotions.** Spinoza goes on to consider human actions and desires in the same way that he considers lines, planes, and solids. From this standpoint, he gives a scientific account of the origin and nature of the emotions, showing how they necessarily arise from certain assignable causes and how their intensity depends on definite natural conditions. The emotions are all found to be variations of the primary states: desire, pleasure, or joy, which is the passage of the organism to a higher state of perfection; and pain, or sorrow, which is the passage to a lower state. To pass to a higher or lower state is not to become better or worse in the moral sense, but to become more or less active. The man of inadequate ideas is passive in that what he does depends on what happens to him rather than what he does or who he is.

This reduction of the emotions to law, however, is only a preliminary step in Spinoza's treatment. To attain freedom, it is first necessary to recognize the bondage of humanity, the fixed determination of the emotions through natural laws. Just as knowledge is power with regard to external nature, however, so one can free oneself from the emotions by understanding their laws. In Spinoza's view, the mind is something more than a series of passive states. Its essence consists in an effort to preserve its own being to promote its own good. In carrying out this purpose, it finds that nothing is so helpful as knowledge.

**Knowledge and Intuition.** Through knowledge, it is possible to free humanity from the bondage of emotions. An emotion, when understood, becomes transformed and ceases to be a mere state of passivity. Moreover, when the conditions of an emotion are understood, it is possible to arrange and associate the various emotions in such a way as to strengthen and promote the occurrence of those that are desirable and to weaken and repress those that are harmful. The highest kind of knowledge for Spinoza is not scientific reason, but intuition, the direct insight that all things follow necessarily from the nature of God and hence form one system. To see all things not as a series of events in time but in their necessary logical relation to God is what Spinoza calls viewing the world under the form of eternity. Spinoza's conception of God is very different from the ordinary theological one. For Spinoza, God is not transcendent, existing apart from nature, but nature itself as an active self-determining process.

**Humanity's Highest Good.** This highest knowledge gives rise to the intellectual love of God, which is the highest good, or blessedness, for humanity. It is through the strength of this emotion, which is not a passion but the highest activity of mind, that the other emotions are most successfully governed and transformed. This intellectual love of God enables the mind to renounce entirely all finite or personal desires, as well as all envy and jealousy. Spinoza argues that he who loves God does not demand that God should love him in return. He demands nothing for himself; instead, he acquiesces completely in the order of the universe. Moreover, Spinoza maintains that since this knowledge and the intellectual love to which it gives rise are eternal, the mind that experiences these must have something in it that is eternal and that cannot be destroyed with the body. An interesting feature of Spinoza's philosophy is the close relationship between the individual and society. It is not merely the individual good that he sought but one that as many as possible would share. In many passages in the *Ethics*, Spinoza approaches the modern conception of the individual as standing in an organic relation to society. —*Genevieve Slomski*

**See also** Freedom and liberty; Intuitionist ethics.

**BIBLIOGRAPHY**

Bennett, Jonathan. *A Study of Spinoza's Ethics*. Indianapolis: Hackett, 1984.

Grene, Marjorie, ed. *Spinoza: A Collection of Critical Essays*. Notre Dame, Ind.: University of Notre Dame Press, 1979.

Hampshire, Stuart. *Spinoza*. New York: Penguin Books, 1987.

Joachim, Harold H. *A Study of Ethics of Spinoza*. New York: Russell & Russell, 1964.

Strauss, Leo. *Spinoza's Critique of Religion*. Translated by E. M. Sinclair. New York: Schocken Books, 1965.

## Ethics/morality distinction

**TYPE OF ETHICS:** Theory of ethics

**DATE:** Eighteenth century to present

**ASSOCIATED WITH:** Moral relativism

**DEFINITION:** Moral philosophers define ethics as the study of moral judgments and choices, whereas morality refers to the rules by which such choices are made

**SIGNIFICANCE:** In pluralist societies, ethical principles are easier to define as generalities than are the more specific rules (morality) by which ethical principles should be implemented

Ethics refers to the most important values and beliefs of an individual or a society. These beliefs help shape the character of the people in that society, teaching them what is good and bad. Ethics implies knowledge of these basic principles and the responsibility to make the appropriate choice when necessary. The strong bond between ethics and a society's customs raises the issue of relativism. Moral philosophers argue that ethics implies values that are universal and are not tied to one society or time period.

The particular rules implementing ethical beliefs in a specific society may change, but not the fundamental principles. In a society composed of subcultures, the specific laws or customs of each may be expressed differently. The distinction between ethics and morality becomes important when the rules used by different groups are not understood or accepted. Unacceptable behavior may be assumed to mean unacceptable values. In that case, the ethos, or unifying characteristics, of a society is weakened and individuals within that society must justify their actions, because morality cannot be assumed.

**See also** Moral education; Morality; Multiculturalism; Pluralism.

## Ethnic cleansing

**TYPE OF ETHICS:** Race and ethnicity

**DATE:** First documented between 745 and 727 B.C.E.

**DEFINITION:** The forced expulsion of a specific population from a territory

**SIGNIFICANCE:** Because ethnic cleansing is predicated on the idea that a particular group of people is undesirable, it brings into focus many ethical issues in the areas of bigotry, prejudice, and human rights, to name only a few "Ethnic cleansing" is a euphemism for murder and land theft that is sanctioned by a state government. It usually refers to the expulsion of an "undesirable" population from a given territory for political, strategic, or ideological reasons, or because of religious or ethnic discrimination. Forced emigration and population exchange are elements of ethnic cleansing. Forced population removal or transfers have occurred repeatedly throughout history, most often to create or secure an ethnically homogeneous homeland or state.

The Assyrian king Tiglath-Pileser III (745-727 B.C.E.) carried out the first recorded case of ethnic cleansing. One-half of the population of any land that he conquered was forcefully removed and replaced by settlers from other regions who were loyal to him. Many centuries later, European settlers in North America slowly "cleansed" the land of most Native Americans with the tacit consent of the state. By expelling the entire East Indian community from Uganda in the early 1970's, Idi Amin of Uganda "cleansed" that country of East Indians so that indigenous Africans could take over their land and businesses. Most recently, Serbians in the former Yugoslavia have tried to "cleanse" territory that they are claiming for Serbian Christians by driving out Muslim citizens. They have used murder, rape, starvation, and a variety of other deplorable techniques to achieve their goal.

There is no moral justification for ethnic cleansing. It is carried out by those who hope that if they occupy the land long enough, their right to it will not be challenged. Yet history has shown that time neither heals every wound nor justifies every action. Ethnic cleansing is and has always been criminal. It should not be sanctioned by any self-respecting government, because it is ethically unjust.

**See also** Bigotry; Racial prejudice; Racism.

## Ethnocentrism

**TYPE OF ETHICS:** Race and ethnicity

**DATE:** Coined c. 1906

**DEFINITION:** The attitude according to which one's own race or society is the central criterion for evaluating other groups or cultures

**SIGNIFICANCE:** Promotes loyalty to the group, sacrifice for it, and hatred and contempt for those outside it

Ethnocentrism is the emotional attitude that places a high value on one's own customs and traditions and belittles all others, rating as least valuable those who differ most. One's own group is the center of everything, and all others are scaled with reference to it. Each group nourishes its own pride and vanity, believes itself to be superior, exalts its own divinities, and looks with contempt on outsiders. Sociologists and anthropologists have found that people everywhere seem to believe that the groups to which they belong are the best and that their ways and morals are superior. Others outside their group are something else—perhaps not defined—but not real people: the Jews divided all mankind into themselves and the Gentiles, the Greeks and Romans called outsiders "barbarians," the Arabs referred to others as "infidels," and the whites in South Africa called the blacks "kaffirs." Although ethnocentrism serves a useful purpose in that it performs the function of discipline and social control within the group, it can be very irritating and disruptive, and when it gets out of hand, it may be dangerous and even fatal.

**See also** Bigotry; Racism.

## Etiquette

**TYPE OF ETHICS:** Personal and social ethics

**DATE:** 2500 B.C.E., when the first known account of polite behavior was written

**ASSOCIATED WITH:** Baldassare Castiglione, Lord Chesterfield, Emily Post, and Miss Manners, who have been leading arbiters of etiquette in different eras

**DEFINITION:** Etiquette offers a code of well-mannered behavior that applies to social interactions; it depends on custom and hence varies in forms with time and place

**SIGNIFICANCE:** Whether etiquette is a branch of ethics or has no connection with it is a controversial issue; how this issue is resolved will affect both ethical theory and conduct

Normative ethics and etiquette are alike in that each offers prescriptions concerning how people ought to behave. Ethics tells people to avoid certain forms of conduct because they are morally reprehensible and recommends that they engage in others because they are morally admirable. Etiquette, in contrast, prohibits certain forms of conduct because they are discourteous or vulgar and recommends others as polite or elegant. Ethics and etiquette are separate at least to the extent that ethical violations can be committed without violating etiquette, and to violate at least some aspects of etiquette, it is not necessary to violate ethics.

Etiquette, unlike ethics, is much concerned with characterizing the social meanings of forms of behavior, determining what behavior expresses respect, contempt, gratitude, aggression, and so forth. Different societies have very different conventions about these matters. For example, in Turkey, the normal way in which men greet one another with respect is by kissing, while in English-speaking lands, kissing is deemed improper and a handshake is preferred. Since these conventions vary so widely, the prescriptions of etiquette are far more socially relative than are those of ethics. The maxim "When in Rome do as the Romans do" generally applies to etiquette, though it is less sound as a maxim of ethics.

The *Instructions of Ptah Hotep*, an Egyptian text dating from about 2500 B.C.E., provides the earliest known account of polite behavior. Later Western notions of etiquette are rooted in medieval chivalry, according to which the knight should be not only a powerful warrior but also honorable and well mannered. In particular, he is to display gentle, sincere devotion toward ladies, and they, in turn, are to be delicately refined and of absolute purity. The Renaissance writer Baldassare Castiglione expresses these ideals in *The Courtier* (1528). Later, the term "etiquette" entered English with the publication of Lord Chesterfield's *Letters to His Son* (1774), in which the author expounded gentlemanly deportment.

These codes of manners were aristocratic. Persons of lower-class birth did not understand or conform to them and therefore were marked off from the upper class. In the nineteenth and twentieth centuries, however, class divisions weakened and an expanding circle of people sought to advance themselves socially by cultivating good manners. Books on etiquette multiplied. In the United States, the writings of arbiters such as Emily Post, Amy Vanderbilt, and Miss Manners (Judith Martin) have enjoyed wide circulation. These authors have sought to present etiquette not class-consciously but democratically, offering guidance in civility for everyone. They consider not only everyday personal etiquette but also special areas of etiquette; for example, in business, in the professions, in diplomacy, and so on.

| ETIQUETTE | |
|---|---|
| **Areas Addressed** | **Types of Prescriptions** |
| Eating | Style and self-restraint in table manners, table settings, service. |
| Dressing | Modesty and elegance according to sex, age, and occasion, formal or informal. |
| Communicating | Tact and skill in handling introductions, polite conversation, writing letters, telephoning, use of calling cards. |
| Socializing | Graciousness in giving and attending parties and other entertainments, having and being house guests, making and receiving social visits. |
| Celebrating | Appropriate degrees of ostentatious formality in private celebrating of weddings, engagements, births, graduations, anniversaries. |
| Rituals | Propriety in observing formalities of official diplomatic, religious, military, or governmental ceremonies. |

Iconoclastic persons often view etiquette with contempt, because they condemn class-conscious snobbishness and artificial conventions and because they suppose that the ethical virtues of sincerity and truthfulness are all that are needed in life. They are right, of course, that arbiters of etiquette sometimes have defended frivolous rules and sometimes have done so for blameworthy reasons. They are wrong, however, to suppose that egalitarian society has no need of etiquette and that social interactions could successfully proceed were manners guided by sincerity and truthfulness alone. The point that they miss is that human beings in their everyday contacts readily generate antagonisms that can become destructive unless they are covered by the cloak of tactfulness and smoothed by the oil of polite formalities. A society that is polite, at least to a judicious degree, can function more efficiently and more happily than can a sincerely truthful but uncivil society.

Do ethics and etiquette sometimes conflict? It might seem so, since ethics is thought to prescribe that people not engage in lying or deception, while etiquette encourages the use of white lies. ("I'm so sorry, but I'm busy that night," one is supposed to say, instead of the more truthful "I don't like you and don't want to come.") This supposed conflict between ethics and etiquette is not deep-seated, however, since the white lies of etiquette can be justified in terms of the ethical principle of nonmaleficence (avoiding hurting the feelings of others). Moreover, the saying of something not literally true is scarcely a lie when everyone knows that it is prescribed by social custom.

Etiquette enjoins people always to be polite. In rare cases, of course, when there are strongly countervailing ethical considerations, one ought to abandon politeness in order to do what is morally right (for example, a firefighter, in order to extinguish a fire, may have to intrude violently on someone's privacy). Usually, however, etiquette conflicts very little with ethics, and violations of etiquette commonly are violations of ethics also, because they tend to injure others, at least mildly.

A controversial question that philosophers have not discussed extensively is whether politeness itself should be classified as a moral virtue, along with honesty, fidelity, modesty, and the like. If by "moral virtues" are meant those admirable human qualities that enhance a person's capacity for contributing to the well-being of society, then politeness can be a virtue in this sense. Notice, however, that being polite is not the same thing as being favorably disposed toward everyone else. Someone possessing the virtue of politeness knows ways of politely expressing negative reactions toward others, and especially toward those who are out of line. —*Stephen F. Barker*

**See also** Chivalry.

**BIBLIOGRAPHY**

Castiglione, Baldassarre. *The Book of the Courtier*. Translated by George Bull. Harmondsworth, England: Penguin Books, 1976.

Chesterfield, Philip, Earl of. *Lord Chesterfield's Letters to His Son and Others*. London: Dent, 1963.

Post, Emily. *Emily Post's Etiquette*. 15th ed. New York: HarperCollins, 1992.

Singer, Peter, ed. *A Companion to Ethics*. Cambridge, Mass.: Blackwell Reference, 1991.

Vanderbilt, Amy. *The Amy Vanderbilt Complete Book of Etiquette*. Rev. ed. exp. by Letitia Baldrige. Garden City, N.Y.: Doubleday, 1978.

## Eugenics

**TYPE OF ETHICS:** Bioethics
**DATE:** Founded 1869
**ASSOCIATED WITH:** Sir Francis Galton (1822-1911)
**DEFINITION:** The attempt to alter human evolution through selection
**SIGNIFICANCE:** Raises serious ethical questions, including those related to racism and genocide

Eugenics is the attempt to alter human evolution through selection. Two main strategies are possible: increasing the gene contributions of those who have desirable traits (positive eugenics) and decreasing the gene contributions of those who have undesired traits (negative eugenics). Genetic testing must first determine what traits people have and to what extent each trait is heritable. Supporters of eugenics claim that intelligence is genetically determined, but most data concerning this claim are suspect, and the true heritability of intelligence is still hotly debated.

Positive eugenics encourages people with desirable traits to leave more offspring. Encouragement could include monetary rewards, educational expenses for children, and so forth. Sperm of desirable men could be collected and stored for the future artificial insemination of selected women, but this suggestion has rarely been followed because of the expense of the procedure.

Negative eugenics means that individuals carrying undesired traits could be killed or sterilized. Advocates of eugenics say that this cruelty is for the greater good of humanity, but opponents strongly object. Beyond this issue, other ethical questions arise: Which traits are desired? Who will make the decisions? Since many traits vary by race, negative eugenics raises questions of racism and brings humanity close to the dangers of genocide. (The only nationwide eugenics laws in history were used in Nazi Germany to exterminate Jews and other non-"Aryans.") Geneticists have also determined that negative eugenics is very limited in its ability to change gene frequencies. Most genetic defects are rare, and selection against rare traits is very ineffective. Selection is especially ineffective if a trait is influenced by environment or education, as intelligence scores are. Also, if negative eugenics could succeed, it would reduce the genetic variability of the population, and variability may itself be desirable, especially if future environments change.

**See also** Genetic counseling; Genetic engineering.

## Euthanasia

**TYPE OF ETHICS:** Bioethics
**DATE:** Fourth century B.C.E. to present
**DEFINITION:** The act of actively or passively bringing about the death of a person in order to prevent suffering
**SIGNIFICANCE:** Poses a philosophical, theological problem: Is it ever ethical to cause the death of a person either by intervening directly to cause death or by withholding treatment?

The term "euthanasia" is derived from the Greek phrase that means a pleasant or easy death. Relieving suffering was part of the Hippocratic oath, dating from the fourth century B.C.E., when Greek physicians were sworn to preserve life and never willingly to take it. This sanctity-of-life principle was not, however, honored always and in all places. The Greeks and Romans, for example, ruled that slaves and "barbarians" had no right to life. In Sparta, the law required the death of deformed infants. The philosophers Plato and Aristotle regarded infanticide and abortion as acceptable, and Plato himself was a victim of compulsory suicide.

Before and during World War II, Nazi Germany practiced euthanasia on those viewed as socially unproductive: Jews, the elderly, the deformed, the chronically ill. Memories of these compulsory deaths have caused many people to resist the idea and practice of euthanasia, even by what would be considered humane methods. In 1969, however, England's House of Lords debated and passed—by a vote of 60 to 40—a Voluntary Euthanasia Bill. Earlier such bills had been proposed and defeated in 1938 and 1950. The main purpose of the bill was to authorize physicians to give euthanasia to a patient thought to be suffering from an incurable physical condition and who has made a declaration requesting euthanasia. A clause provides that a declaration may be revoked at any time. Passive euthanasia had been generally accepted, but Parliament by this act legalized active euthanasia.

Euthanasia is divided into two types: active and passive. Active euthanasia is direct intervention to bring about the death of one suffering from a terminal illness, while passive euthanasia is letting nature take its course. The intent to bring about death requires ethical analysis to find a moral consensus, since the rights of an individual and those of society come into play.

Well into the twentieth century, Western churches—the Catholic church in particular—took a strong stand against both types of euthanasia. In the medieval era, Saint Augustine of Hippo and Saint Thomas Aquinas affirmed that only God is the arbiter of life and death. They taught that pain and suffering have purpose in God's sight. In 1940, the Catholic church officially condemned the administration of euthanasia for any reason as contrary to natural and divine law. In late 1957, however, Pope Pius XII, speaking to an International Congress of Anaesthesiologists, stated that "morally one is held to use only ordinary means" to sustain life and that in cases of terminal illness, there is no obligation to continue lifesaving measures. Differences exist, however, regarding what constitutes ordinary versus extraordinary means and who should decide when death is preferable to treatment.

Ordinary means of treating a sick or dying person are means that are in common use, while extraordinary means involve nonstandard treatment, the new and the rare. Scientific and technological advances have transformed the extraordinary into the ordinary. This development complicates the issue, since such factors as scarce funds and facilities also come into play, introducing another ethical problem: the acceptability of utilitarianism.

The sanctity-of-life principle holds that it is absolutely prohibited either intentionally to kill a patient or intentionally to let a patient die and to base decisions for the prolongation or shortening of human life on considerations of the quality of that life. Under no circumstances is there a "right to die." This is true irrespective of the competency or noncompetency of a person to decide for himself or herself whether to choose euthanasia.

The patient, the doctor, and the patient's family are generally the decision makers in cases of possible euthanasia, whether active or passive. Some states—thirty-eight, as of 1988—accept living wills whereby competent adults give directions for the health care they want if they become terminally ill and cannot direct their own care. Those who believe in the sanctity of life fear that these living wills are a wedge that will allow nonvoluntary euthanasia to become acceptable.

While staunchly opposed to euthanasia, some churches and courts accept the "double-effect" principle. This principle holds that an action whose primary effect is to relieve suffering may be ethically justified, although a secondary effect may be death. Physicians, they argue, have a duty to relieve pain as well as to preserve life—although doing so may shorten the person's life.

Much debate centers on the quality-of-life ethic. Some argue that if there is little hope that a given treatment prolonging a person's life will allow that person to live a beneficial, satisfactory life, then euthanasia is justified. In such cases, the sanctity-of-life principle is set against the quality-of-life approach. How can a proper quality of life be guaranteed to all citizens and an equitable distribution of medical care be ensured? Using utilitarianism as a guideline, providing high-quality life for a majority takes priority over prolonging the lives of a few. Cost-effectiveness becomes a major factor in the decision to choose or not to choose euthanasia. This is unacceptable to many persons, since it places an economic value on people.

The counterargument is made that while every person is equal to all others, not every life is of equal value. The case of Karen Ann Quinlan (1954-1985) is cited as an example of the quality-of-life and sanctity-of-life dilemma. The victim of a car accident, Quinlan went into a coma in 1975 and was kept on a respirator for several years. After repeated requests from her guardian, a court decision allowed discontinuance of the respirator. Quinlan's life was not benefitting her and was burdening her parents unduly. The quality-of-life judgment prevailed in that case.

In 1990, the U.S. Supreme Court ruled that patients have a constitutional right to discontinue life-sustaining medical treatment. In 1992, The Netherlands Parliament approved liberal rules on euthanasia and doctor-assisted suicide. The guidelines require, however, that the patient must be mentally competent; must be suffering unbearable pain and request euthanasia repeatedly; and the doctor must consult a second physician before proceeding.

The right to die with dignity, free of terminal agony, is a concept that enjoys strong public support. Most of this support, however, is for passive euthanasia; support for active euthanasia is more moderate. The notion of a right to die is still very controversial, making moral standards of judgment ever more imperative. Whether supporting the sanctity-of-life doctrine or the quality-of-life argument, there is general agreement among those most engaged with this issue that not every patient's life ought to be prolonged. The moral debate is over how this life should be ended. Individuals, families, courts, and ethics committees struggle over euthanasia, striving for justice for both patient and society.

*—S. Carol Berg*

**See also** Bill of rights, medical; Health care allocation; Hippocrates; Right to die.

**Bibliography**


Bernards, Neal, ed. *Euthanasia: Opposing Viewpoints.* San Diego, Calif.: Greenhaven Press, 1989.

Churchill, Larry R. *Rationing Health Care in America: Perspectives and Principles of Justice.* Notre Dame, Ind.: University of Notre Dame Press, 1987.

Kluge, Eike-Henner W. *The Ethics of Deliberative Death.* Port Washington, N.Y.: Kennikat Press, 1981.

Lammers, Stephen E., and Allen Verhey, eds. *On Moral Medicine: Theological Perspectives in Medical Ethics.* Grand Rapids, Mich.: William B. Eerdmans, 1987.

Weir, Robert F., ed. *Ethical Issues in Death and Dying.* 2d ed. New York: Columbia University Press, 1986.


## Evers, Medgar (July 2, 1925, Decatur, Miss.—June 12, 1963, Jackson, Miss.): Civil rights activist

**Type of ethics:** Race and ethnicity

**Achievements:** In 1954, Evers became the National Association for the Advancement of Colored People's (NAACP) first field secretary in Mississippi and helped organize many local chapters in the state

**Significance:** Evers became one of many civil rights activists to lose his life in the crusade for racial equality, a crusade ultimately won (in part) because such leaders were willing to risk their lives for freedom and first-class citizenship for minorities

After growing up and attending segregated high schools in Decatur and Newton, Mississippi, Evers served in the army, seeing action in the European theater of World War II. Afterward, he attended the all-black Alcorn Agricultural and Mechanical College, graduating in 1950. He became an insurance salesman but devoted much spare time to his work for the NAACP. Trying to organize local affiliates for the NAACP, he visited most areas of the state and began building a wide-ranging base of support. By 1954, he had moved to Jackson to become field secretary for the entire state.

In relocating to Jackson, Evers had moved to a city that had rigid segregation. To bring change, in 1963 Evers organized a massive nonviolent protest movement. Day in, day out, Evers challenged segregation and discrimination by personally leading the protests. The protests and Evers' life were cut short when, on June 12, 1963, Evers was assassinated. No one was ever convicted of the crime.

In the twelve weeks after Evers' death, 758 racial demonstrations occurred in the United States. Such pressures convinced President John F. Kennedy to send a civil rights bill to Congress, a bill that eventually became the Civil Rights Act of 1964, a law that gave minorities more justice than they had ever had before.

**See also** Civil Rights Act of 1964; Civil rights movement; King, Martin Luther, Jr.; National Association for the Advancement of Colored People (NAACP); Racism.

## Evil, problem of

**TYPE OF ETHICS:** Religious ethics

**DATE:** Problem formulated c. 300 B.C.E.

**ASSOCIATED WITH:** Theistic religious traditions

**DEFINITION:** A philosophical and theological problem that arises from three propositions: God is almighty; God is perfectly good; boundless evil exists in this world

**SIGNIFICANCE:** Philosophically and theologically, the problem of evil threatens to destroy an individual's or a society's belief in God, thereby sweeping away one origin of ethics, one origin of right and wrong—a development that could lead some individuals to stress humanistic values but could lead others to take an "all is allowed" amoral approach to life

The contradiction within the problem can be solved logically only by denying any one of the three propositions. One must hold that God is not all powerful or that God is not all good. Alternately, theists such as Saint Augustine denied that evil exists; instead, there is only privation caused by humankind's distance from God. Modern Christian Scientists and Stoics generally follow the thought of Augustine. Some philosophers, however, such as William James, tried to solve the contradiction by denying the omnipotence of God, arguing instead that God had much, but limited, power.

All monotheistic religions that stress the omnipotence and goodness of God develop a system of ethics that defines what is right, what is wrong, what is good, and what is bad. The presence of evil in the world, however, threatened to destroy belief in God and thereby destroy absolute ethical values. In God's defense, theodicy developed. Theodicy, in its classical form, is the philosophical and/or theological attempt to justify the righteousness of God.

The Greek philosopher Epicurus (341-270 B.C.E.) was apparently the first to formulate the dilemma that the "question of evil" raises. The ancient Hebrews also grappled with the problem, as did early Christian theorists such as Saint Irenaeus, Saint Augustine, and Saint Thomas Aquinas. In the modern era, scholars who have examined the problem are Immanuel Kant, David Hume, John Stuart Mill, and Albert Camus.

**Definitions.** Several kinds of evil exist. The first is moral "radical" evil that occurs when an intelligent person knowingly and willingly inflicts suffering upon and harms another being, human or animal. The second type is natural evil, which is self-explanatory and which includes all manner of natural calamities such as earthquakes, tornadoes, tidal waves, cancer, heart disease, and so forth. The third is metaphysical evil, an abstract concept that "wonders" why a perfect, all-powerful God did not create a perfect universe.

Within the definitions above, the magnitude of evil varies. Some evil is personal, as is the case when an individual beats, robs, or murders another person. Evil can be "transpersonal," as is the case when one group (German Nazis, for example) tries to murder millions of other people. Evil can be "transgeneric"; that is, if imperfect beings exist on other planets, evil goes beyond humanity as we know it; and finally, evil can be cosmic, as is the case when nuclear powers threaten to blow up the world or when greed-driven corporations foul the world's environment beyond repair.

Genocide, terrorism, threats of nuclear war, individual callousness, and cruelty—all are evil. In a Texas town in the early 1990's, eight adults were charged with multiple counts of sexual assault on children who were related to the perpetrators—this is radical evil. In another state, four teenagers were found guilty of the murder of a twelve-year-old girl who was beaten, whipped, sodomized with a tire iron, raped and—finally—doused with gasoline and burned alive; this is radical evil. The prosecutor in the case said that the girl would have lived despite the torture if she had not been set on fire. Until the mid-1980's, the West German police abetted the Joseph Mengele family, who managed to thwart the attempts to bring Auschwitz's "angel of death" to the bar of justice; this is another example of evil. During one of his trips to Germany, President Ronald Reagan made a visit to an S.S. war cemetery, no doubt much to the glee of modern neo-Nazis in both the United States and Germany. Such evils, multiplied thousands of times are, according to nonbelievers, what the "silent" God must explain.

**The Problem's Complexity.** Within the framework of monotheism, the existence of evil suggests that God does not exist. If God does exist amid flourishing evil, then He is either not all powerful or is not all good. To paraphrase philosopher David Hume: Is God willing but not able to stop evil? Then He is impotent. Can He stop evil but is not willing to do so? Then He is not all good, and is probably malevolent. If He is willing and able, how does evil survive?

Looking at the problem another way, one might formulate the following set of ideas: Individuals are aware of the world around them; they see the world's evil, which causes death and suffering; they then have *prima facie* evidence that either there is no God or God is not all-benevolent; if God is not all-benevolent, if He allows innocents to suffer, He is capricious and cannot be trusted. Some critics say that it would be better to have no God than to have one who is capricious enough to allow evil.

Philosophically and theologically, the problem can be solved only through "belief" in the unknown, only with some rapid mental "footwork," with a mental "leap" of logic. For example, various scholars, including Saint Augustine, the historic defender of the faith, advance the "free will" concept, which blames humankind for most evils, beginning with the original "sin" of Adam and Eve (either literally or symbolically). Critics reply, however, that a good God would have made the pair incapable of sin, would have given them such basic values that they would always choose not to do wrong.

One nineteenth century German critic, Friedrich Schleiermacher, argued that God, being perfectly good, could only have created a perfectly good Adam and Eve. They would have been free to sin, but they would never have to do so. To cite them as the authors of a willful evil crime is to assert a major contradiction—it is, in effect, to assert that evil has created itself *ex nihilo* (out of nothing).

Another rationalization hinges on the process of "soul-making," which incorporates ideas that imperfect humans who created evil must, with God's help, evolve into better beings and that evil and suffering are a part of the evolutionary process. Critics charge, again, that a perfect God could have created better beings in the first place. Furthermore, they point out that part of the "soul-making" has to do with developing virtues, but why should this be necessary if everything is perfect in heaven?

Another aspect of the debate is the Augustinian and Calvinist doctrine of predestination. Indeed, predestination sets up another dilemma. If God wants to "save" all humans but cannot do so, He has limited power. If, on the other hand, He chooses to "save" some and eternally damn all others to eons of torture, then He is not perfectly good and, indeed, has a streak of sadism. Sadism, of course, is a form of evil. Therefore, is God Himself evil?

The concept of "hell" also raises problems. Hell as laypeople understand it is a place of torment where "bad" people go to be punished forever through eternity. How could a good God create such a place or allow it to exist? Why would a good God create such a place or allow it to exist? Is God, then, not good? Is He again playing the role of a sadist who enjoys watching people suffer? Many fundamentalist televangelists would gleefully tell one so.

Associated with "hell" is Satan, or the "Devil," a supposed fallen angel that, many Christians, Jews, and Moslems believe, causes moral and natural evil. The concept of Satan probably had its origins in "extreme" religious dualism, one way that some people tried to rationalize about the existence of evil in a good world. One such dualistic religion was founded by Zarathushtra (Zoroaster) about 1200 B.C.E. Zoroastrianism (or Mazdaism) taught that God—called Ohrmazd—was perfectly good but not all-powerful. Ohrmazd had a powerful antagonist, Ahriman, the personification of evil, destruction, and death.

Zoroastrianism also had its Adam and Eve, whose names were Mashye and Mashyane. Ahriman tempted them with lies, and they believed him—thus committing their first "sin." Then they offered an ox as a sacrifice—their second "sin." Zoroastrianism has various concepts in common with Christianity; for example, the fighting between God and the Devil (Ahriman) generally follows the Christian pattern.

Another example of dualism—a good being fighting a bad being, with the two having almost equal power—is found in Manichaeanism, a movement that was contemporary with early Christianity; indeed, Manichaeanism attracted Saint Augustine for a time.

Other philosophers turn to natural evils and explain them on the basis of the natural scientific laws of the universe. God, they argue, will never change those laws, because humankind needs their stability; without them, each new day would bring chaos to the natural world. Detractors again point out that an all-powerful God could intervene when necessary to modify natural laws (in the interest of saving human lives, for example).

As if they have taken a "lesson" from Zoroastrianism and Manichaeanism, some lay Christians have "promoted" Satan to the post of junior god; they believe that this world is ruled by Satan and has been since he was cast down from heaven. True, demonology does not have the following that it did in the medieval era, but even so, many laypersons, especially fundamentalist Protestants, still believe that the Devil exists and has power over this world. Even if the Devil is directly responsible for evil, a philosophical problem still exists, because God is responsible for everything in the universe, including Satan. If Satan is responsible for evil, why does a perfectly good all-powerful God allow "him" to exist?

Just as some modern theists and believers deny that real radical evil exists, many also deny that Satan exists. Again, such a view is problematic; it contradicts what is found in the Bible. Specifically, belief in the Devil permeates the New Testament. The gospels show that Jesus knew that Satan and demons really existed, because he was forever speaking of them and trying to cast them out of people. It appears that, dogma aside, Christianity has developed a type of dualism within monotheism. The dualism is represented by the struggle between the good God and the Devil; hence, evil results.

Some philosophers (Friedrich Nietzsche, for example) did not grapple with the above questions, but instead rejected God on other grounds. Nietzsche argued that the very definitions of the words "good" and "evil" had become corrupted. Christian good led to meekness, humility, and cowardliness. Conversely, Christians labeled as evil such traits as creativity, passion, self-assertion, and the willingness to fight for ideals. Nietzsche then proclaimed that "God is dead" and said that people should go beyond "good and evil"; Nietzsche stressed moral relativism rather than moral absolutism. Christianity had only mired people in guilt and made them escapists who would settle for rewards in heaven because, surely, they would get no rewards in this world. Nietzsche argued that the strong, with a "will to power," were the right people to lead a civilization; they could lead without guilt or regret.

Twentieth century horrors such as the death and destruction of two world wars—the last of which witnessed the genocide of approximately six million Jews and at least that many Slavs—convinced many intellectuals that God did not exist, since He would have stopped such evil. The optimistic progressivism that characterized philosophical theism before 1914 gave way when mass destruction and death forced many thinkers to confront evil directly.

After living to see such evil, the existentialist Jean-Paul Sartre stressed the apparent powerlessness of God and went on to present a unique criticism. Sartre held that of the many people who try to believe in one God, a good number suffer overwhelming anxiety and puzzlement; they try to believe but are torn by doubt. After referring to the anxiety, the puzzlement, the doubt, Sartre added simply that an all-powerful and all-good God would never allow his "children" to have such negative and perhaps destructive thoughts and feelings. Sartre's contemporary and countryman Albert Camus developed the concept of the absurd—that is, the nonexistence of God, the meaningless of human life, and the existence of evil all around. Camus believed that the appropriate response was to face the meaninglessness, to create personal meaning by making a commitment to something larger than oneself, and to work to make life as meaningful as possible.

Other writers have attacked theodicy in more specific ways. For example, some scholars have studied the testimony given at the Nuremberg War Crimes trials after World War II. One particularly unsettling type of murder at Auschwitz was committed by Nazi guards who isolated children who were too young or too sick to work. Those children would then be thrown directly into crematorium furnaces or into blazing pits. Some witnesses noted that the children were thrown in while still alive and that their screams could be heard all over the camp. Of course, no witnesses knew just how many children were viciously murdered in this way.

After he had studied the appropriate trial transcripts and had learned of the burning children, Irving Greenberg attacked theists with a vengeance. In making their defense of theodicy, Greenberg demanded that they should propose no argument, theological or otherwise, that would not be credible in the presence of the burning children. Greenberg submitted that no attempted justification of God was possible, that anyone who attempted it—with the burning children in mind—was guilty of something even worse than blasphemy.

Elie Wiesel, a victim who managed to stay alive in a Nazi death camp, added his own testimony about the problem of evil. He saw babies burned alive, yet the death by hanging of a small fifteen-year-old boy seemed to trouble him the most—perhaps because the boy was so slight that the hanging did not immediately kill him. Instead, hanging by the rope, the boy struggled in the air, and twisted and turned; he suffered for at least an hour before he died. Just then, someone asked Wiesel "Where is God now?" Wiesel pointed at the boy on the gallows and spit out the word: "There!"

Animal pain is another aspect of evil. In the animal "kingdom," one species preys on and devours another. Still-conscious animals are literally eaten alive by their predators. Painful accidents and diseases are also common. Indeed, nature is "red in tooth and claw." How can nature's struggle of survival be reconciled with an omnipotent and perfectly good Creator? Scholarly attempts to answer such a question fall short of the mark. Some argue that animals live totally in the present and lack the human abilities of memory and anticipation that give rise to suffering; even though an animal's life may be violently terminated, the animal's life is most likely active and pleasurable up to the point of death. Such arguments about animal suffering are morally bankrupt, and such rationalizations may well be part of the evil world that no one can adequately explain.

Another answer to nature's brutal ways was advanced by such philosophers as C. S. Lewis, who, in *The Problem of Pain*, argued that Satan's premundane fall has had cosmic consequences, one of which was the perversion of the entire evolutionary process to create a savage world. Again, however, such statements can be criticized because the all-powerful God allows Satan to exist. —*James Smallwood*

**See also** *Beyond Good and Evil*; Goodness; Moral principles, rules, and imperatives; Morality; Right and wrong.

**BIBLIOGRAPHY**

Hick, John. *Evil and the God of Love*. London: Collins, 1970.

__________. *Philosophy of Religion*. Englewood Cliffs, N.J.: Prentice-Hall, 1963. Two volumes that advance the "soul-making" theodicy that holds that humans are finite and fallible beings who, in this world, need to be "schooled" in the ways of perfection, and that evil plays an important role in building the "character" of humans, who will eventually grow into the "likeness" of their Creator.

Midgley, Mary. *Wickedness: A Philosophical Essay*. London: Routledge & Kegan Paul, 1984. Midgley takes on all philosophers, past and present, who have ever investigated God's supposed role in the problem of evil. Blaming God, Midgley holds, is an intellectual exercise that is beside the point; instead, she looks at the human role in the creation of the problems of the world.

Parkin, David, ed. *The Anthropology of Evil*. New York: Basil Blackwell, 1985. A collection of fourteen essays written by outstanding anthropologists. Parkin's introduction is especially noteworthy because it helps readers understand the problem of evil.

Peterson, Michael L., ed. *The Problem of Evil: Selected Readings*. Notre Dame, Ind.: University of Notre Dame Press, 1992. A book that covers its topic from many viewpoints, including classical statements on the problem, modern statements, logic and the issues, existentialism and the problem, theodicy and the issues, and the nature of the perfectly good God.

Plantinga, Alvin. *God, Freedom, and Evil*. New York:

Harper & Row, 1974. A classic statement of the free-will defense and the minimalist defense in answering how a good God and evil can exist side by side.

Russell, Jeffrey Burton. *The Prince of Darkness: Radical Evil and the Power of Good in History*. Ithaca, N.Y.: Cornell University Press, 1988. An outstanding volume that "follows" the Devil through a many-sided philosophical maze. Among the chapters are "The Good Lord and the Devil," "Dualism in the Desert," "The Classical Christian View," "Auschwitz and Hiroshima," and "The Meaning of Evil."

Surin, Kenneth. *Theology and the Problem of Evil*. New York: Basil Blackwell, 1986. A well-written volume that analyzes theodicy, the philosophical and/or theological method that tries to justify the righteousness of God—an exercise that must also attempt to reconcile the existence of evil with a morally perfect deity.

Zweig, Connie, and Jeremiah Abrams, eds. *Meeting the Shadow: The Hidden Power of the Dark Side of Human Nature*. Los Angles: J. P. Tarcher, 1991. A reader that includes work by Carl Jung. Unlike many philosophical treatises, this volume delves into the "common" life of ordinary people and shows what harm radical evil can do; topics are covered from many points of view—religious, psychological, and sociological; even political scientists had a place in the volume.

## Evolution, theory of

**TYPE OF ETHICS:** Modern history
**DATE:** 1859
**PLACE:** Great Britain
**ASSOCIATED WITH:** Charles Darwin
**DEFINITION:** Offered an explanation for the appearance and extinction of species; identified mechanisms that rendered organisms more or less fit for survival and propagation
**SIGNIFICANCE:** Darwin's theory challenged the authority of revealed religion, strengthened biologically deterministic arguments, and encouraged an ethical outlook based on processes at work in the natural world

In his seminal work *On the Origin of Species* (1859), Charles Darwin advanced a convincing explanation for the changes that occurred in life forms throughout geological time. His conclusions, based partly on insights gleaned from prevailing economic theory and new geological discoveries and largely on his own extensive investigations, contradicted the biblical view of creation. It also challenged the previously dominant eighteenth century deistic view of a benign, carefully designed cosmos. In place of a master watchmaker harmonizing creation, Darwin posited a violent, indifferent natural order in which advances occurred as the more fit vanquished the less fit. In the Darwinian universe, values were placed at the service of natural selection.

**History.** The idea of evolution gradually gained momentum throughout the eighteenth and nineteenth centuries. This was largely the result of significant advances in several specific areas: classification, which placed living beings in logical relationships with one another; comparative anatomy and embryology, which allowed comparisons between simpler and more complicated organisms; and paleontology, which increasingly revealed a progressive fossil record. Pre-Darwinian evolutionary theories were, however, overspeculative, lacked sufficient evidence, and had weak theoretical underpinnings. Darwin's work profited from Sir George Lyell's geological analyses, which greatly extended the known age of the earth, and the economic writings of David Ricardo and Thomas Malthus, which introduced the allied concepts of population pressure on scarce resources and the struggle for existence. Darwin's theory of evolution through natural selection intertwined a massive volume of evidence with those leading ideas. The result was a methodologically convincing tour de force; criticism of Darwinian evolutionism was generally based on its religious and ethical implications rather than on any pronounced scientific deficiencies.

**Ethical Implications.** The theory of evolution advanced the view of an amoral universe in which change occurred blindly and was perpetuated through impersonal mechanistic processes. Random mutations made a given organism more or less able to cope with its environment and more or less able to propagate itself. Its relative success in the struggle for existence defined its value. In the intense interspecies and intraspecies competition for scarce resources, the rule was survival of the fittest. Individuals and species were naturally selected; that is, harsh environmental factors determined survivability. Favorable changes accumulating through time produced more fit, and therefore more highly evolved, individuals and species. Darwin did not always present the selection process as a direct function of an unforgiving environment, since he discussed the possible impact of variables such as accidents and sexual selection. In a later work, *The Descent of Man* (1871), he also praised the value of cooperation, altruism, and self-sacrifice. Even then, however, perpetual strife remained the motor of evolutionary change. Sexual selection was competitive, accidents were chance outcomes issuing from a violent context, and the value of traits such as cooperation and altruism lay in their contribution to the survival of one group that was engaged in competition with others. Darwin's dour deterministic theory impartially challenged beliefs in a benign universe, a personal savior, the biblical view of special creation, and ethical systems derived from revealed religion.

**Social Darwinism.** Darwin noted that humans were less subject to evolutionary pressure than lower organisms were because societies modified their environments. Social theorists such as Herbert Spencer, Benjamin Kidd, and Lewis H. Morgan, however, were less exacting; known as Social Darwinists, they applied Darwin's ideas to human behavior in a wholesale fashion. Adopting concepts such as variation and natural selection, they placed social and cultural differences in an evolutionary context and justified existing power relationships as examples of survival of the fittest. In the late nineteenth century and early twentieth century, Social Darwinists promoted unrestricted competition, laissez-faire economics, and neocolonialism in the belief that survival of the fittest invariably produced advances in civilization. The movement declined as it became apparent that human societies could not easily be classified as more or less primitive, that evolutionary change did not automatically mean progress, and that the notion of survival of the fittest provided cover for the unequal treatment of individuals and groups.

**Nature Versus Nurture.** The theory of evolution perpetuated, in secularized form, traditional disputes regarding free will and predestination. That issue was exacerbated in the second half of the twentieth century by two important developments: breakthroughs in genetics that further underscored the characteristic biological determinism of Darwinism; and advances in the study of animal behavior (ethology), which had immediate sociological implications. The activities of ethologists such as Nikolaas Tinbergen, Konrad Lorenz, and E. O. Wilson were particularly significant because they related human behavior to the wider context of ethology. By rigorously examining evolutionary antecedents, parallels, and alternatives to human behavior, they reopened the nature/nurture controversy in the sharpest possible way. In one way or another, their investigations touched upon numerous ethical issues. Was aggression learned or biologically dictated? What was the evolutionary value of aggression? Were gender roles social constructs or did they reflect natural, necessary biological relationships? By placing such issues into an evolutionary context, they revisited an investigative path followed cautiously by Darwin and much less carefully by the Social Darwinists—that is, the attempt to align human behavior with the physical laws of nature. —*Michael J. Fontenot*

**See also** Aggression; Social Darwinism; Sociobiology.

**BIBLIOGRAPHY**

Archer, John. *The Behavioural Biology of Aggression*. Cambridge, England: Cambridge University Press, 1988.

Darwin, Charles. *On the Origin of Species By Means of Natural Selection*. New York: Avenel Books, 1979.

Dawkins, Richard. *The Blind Watchmaker: Why the Evidence of Evolution Reveals a Universe Without Design*. New York: W. W. Norton, 1987.

Ruse, Michael. *The Darwinian Revolution: Science Red in Tooth and Claw*. Chicago: University of Chicago Press, 1979.

Wilson, E. O. *Sociobiology: The New Synthesis*. Cambridge, Mass.: Harvard University Press, 1975.

## Excellence

**TYPE OF ETHICS:** Theory of ethics

**DATE:** Eighth century B.C.E. to present

**ASSOCIATED WITH:** Homer, Plato, and Aristotle

**DEFINITION:** The highest intellectual and moral functioning of a human being; for ancient Greeks, synonymous with "virtue" (aretê), meaning the effective performance of a thing's proper function

**SIGNIFICANCE:** Excellence is the ideal toward which humans should strive in order to fulfill their unique capacities of moral deliberation and reasoned action

Although "excellence" is prominently associated with the ethical thought of Plato and Aristotle, the concept dates back to Homeric Greece (eighth century B.C.E.), when it designated not strictly the virtues of personal character but the uniquely Greek "aretê," the skillful performance of any function, be it running, fighting, or even thinking. It applied also to certain masculine and feminine virtues necessary for the protection of countrymen and family.

The masculine and feminine excellences may be viewed as "competitive" and "cooperative" excellences, respectively, denoting the proper fulfillment by men and women of the obligations entailed by their social and cultural roles. The competitive excellences of men were indispensable to the defense of countrymen, family, guests, and friends. To be virtuous, a man had to be well-armed, strong, swift on his feet, and skilled in the strategy and techniques of warfare, qualities that explain why courage was a centrally important virtue in Homeric Greece. He also had to possess wealth, which implied high social status. A man in whom all these conditions were met was the epitome of Homeric excellence. Women, who had no need for the competitive excellences and were not permitted to demonstrate them, were designated as excellent by virtue of the cooperative or "quiet" excellences—beauty, skillful weaving, housekeeping, chastity, and fidelity, the latter being the central feminine virtue. Hence, whereas men protected society and family by acquiring largely military virtues, women offered protection of a different sort to home and family by cultivating the domestic virtues.

Homeric excellence was modified by fifth-century Athenians to include additional virtues. "Sôphrosunê," self-control, had greater importance as a virtue for both men and women, indicating that men were judged in the fifth century according to a "quiet" virtue that had once been considered a criterion of feminine excellence. In addition, social status was less a determinant of excellence than it had been during the Homeric period. This evolution of the understanding of "aretê" culminated in the sense that the term ultimately acquired in the moral theory of Plato and Aristotle, although it was Aristotle who, in his *Nicomachean Ethics*, conferred upon this concept its most prominent philosophical status.

In the classical view epitomized by the thinkers of fifth and fourth century Athens, excellence was determined by one's generic role as a human being in addition to one's particular societal role. There were now as many excellences as there were functions for an individual to perform. One could be an excellent father, physician, and citizen, and therefore an excellent human being. The latter excellence, however, denoting the quality of intellect as well as character, both encompassed and eclipsed in importance the virtues derived from more specialized (and therefore secondary) roles. The cooperative virtues played a more prominent role in classical excellence. In addition to the competitive Homeric virtue of courage, there were the virtues of friendship, self-control, wisdom, and justice, all contributing to the civic virtue of citizenship, without which one could not be good. There was general agreement that these virtues were proper to humanity even while there was disagreement about their definition, as in Plato's *Republic*, in which the point of contention was the nature of justice.

The *Republic* was the culmination of Plato's earlier dialogues in which the nature of virtue was a common theme. Plato depicted virtue as highly personalized, attainable by the individual who controlled his passions and made constructive use of his ambition through the exercise of disciplined intelligence. Platonic excellence, therefore, consisted of the harmonious interaction of the virtues of self-control, courage, and wisdom, which together constituted the civic virtue of justice. It was achieved only by the most intellectually gifted—Plato's "philosopher-kings"—who, after an educational process marked by rigorous intellectual discipline, were endowed with intuitive insight into genuine moral goodness. In a larger context, the excellence of the state was an extension of this personal excellence, constituted by the wise, disciplined governance by the philosopher-kings of their fellow citizens, whose natural capabilities relegated them to the more mundane activities of society.

Whereas for Plato true excellence was confined to the philosopher-kings, Aristotle believed that excellence was achievable in various degrees by anyone with sufficient experience and rational judgment. While Aristotelian excellence was to some extent compatible with the common wisdom of ordinary men, it was, however, refined and most prominently exemplified in the intellectually accomplished. This reflected Aristotle's division of excellence into intellectual and moral excellence, intellectual excellence being attained through education, and moral excellence through virtuous habits. Genuine human excellence, therefore, consisted of being intelligent enough to judge correctly how to do the right thing at the right time in the right place and in the right manner, and to do so consistently and deliberately, thus fulfilling the proper function of a human being.

Although for Aristotle excellence was essentially a "mean"—a point of equilibrium between extremes—it was, paradoxically, an extreme as well: it was the mean, or perfect moderation, between two vices, while also the extreme, or highest degree of what is right and good, with respect to feeling and action. Successfully ascertaining the mean and avoiding extremes of feeling and action required the keenest exercise of the powers of rational judgment. For Aristotle, as for Plato, excellence was highly personalized but also inextricably linked to citizenship; the exercise of personal virtue could not be comprehended apart from the political context.

The idea of excellence as virtue is found in the ethical theory of modern thinkers. Alasdair MacIntyre, in *After Virtue: A Study in Moral Theory*, retains the understanding of excellence as virtue in essentially its original Aristotelian form. John Rawls, in *A Theory of Justice*, regards the "excellences" as natural talents and assets such as wit and beauty, as well as personal virtues such as courage and self-control. For both thinkers, excellence as the rational exercise of the virtues acquires significance only within a social and political context. —*Barbara Forrest*

**See also** Aristotelian ethics; Golden mean; Justice; MacIntyre, Alasdair; *Nicomachean Ethics*; Platonic ethics; Rawls, John; *Republic*; Virtue.

**BIBLIOGRAPHY**

Adkins, Arthur W. H. *Merit and Responsibility: A Study in Greek Values*. Chicago: University of Chicago Press, 1975.

Aristotle. "Nicomachean Ethics." In *Introduction to Aristotle*. 2d ed. Chicago: University of Chicago Press, 1973.

Homer. *The Iliad*. Translated by Robert Fitzgerald. Garden City, N.Y.: Anchor Press, 1975.

MacIntyre, Alasdair. *After Virtue: A Study in Moral Theory*. 2d ed. Notre Dame, Ind.: University of Notre Dame Press, 1984.

Plato. *The Dialogues of Plato*. Translated by R. E. Allen. New Haven, Conn.: Yale University Press, 1984.

Rawls, John. *A Theory of Justice*. Cambridge, Mass.: Belknap Press, 1971.

## Executive Order 10988

**TYPE OF ETHICS:** Human rights

**DATE:** Signed 1962

**ASSOCIATED WITH:** Federal-sector labor relations

**DEFINITION:** Federal Executive Order 10988 gave federal employees the right to form unions and to bargain collectively through them

**SIGNIFICANCE:** This new order made the labor policies of the federal government consistent throughout the country, and influenced the labor policies of state and local agencies

Before the 1960's, federal agencies dealt with organized labor unions individually; some agencies recognized unions, and some refused to negotiate with them. The administration of President John F. Kennedy took a more favorable attitude toward unions. On January 17, 1962, Kennedy signed Federal Executive Order (EO) 10988, giving federal employees the right to form unions and to bargain collectively through them. Under the terms of the order, employees had the right to form a union but could not be forced to join one. Federal agencies were required to bargain with properly elected unions. These unions were forbidden to strike. Once the order was signed, there was a tremendous increase in the number of federal employees represented by unions, especially among white-collar workers. Some groups, including postal workers, are represented by unions for all of their contract negotiations. The rights of federal employees were amended several times during the late 1960's and the 1970's. In 1978, the Civil Service Reform Act became the first unified code of federal sector labor relations, formalizing the bargaining rights first endorsed by EO 10988.

**See also** Labor Management Relations Act.

## Existentialism

**TYPE OF ETHICS:** Theory of ethics

**DATE:** Nineteenth century to present

**ASSOCIATED WITH:** Søren Kierkegaard, Friedrich Wilhelm Nietzsche, Nikolai Berdyaev, Jean-Paul Sartre, and Martin Heidegger

**DEFINITION:** An approach to ethics that emphasizes individual subjectivity, freedom and responsibility, and the irrational as primary features of the human condition

**SIGNIFICANCE:** In contrast to most Western thought, which recognizes the rational as the supreme guide to conduct, existentialism emphasizes the existing individual as the starting point for ethics

**Background.** The history of systematic ethics started with the ancient Greek philosopher Socrates' (469-399 B.C.E.) question "Is the unexamined life worth living?" Socrates, like most Western philosophers since, believed that the intellect was the key to answering this question. Moreover, prior to existentialism, most ethicists had assumed that humankind's essential nature was rational. Consistent with these views, Western ethical tradition has generally assumed that the rational individual pursuing the rational life is the essence of "the good life."

In contrast, existentialism—a broad movement in philosophy and literature—boldly challenges these basic assumptions of the Western tradition. Existential ethics refuses to understand the good as a norm or a law. Existentialists contend that Western thought has been obsessed by the idea of regulating the life of the world by reason. Hence, unlike previous ethics, existentialism emphasizes the tragic and absurd facets of life rather than the empirical and rational facets.

**The Term "Existentialism."** It is impossible to discuss an existential theory of ethics without briefly considering the existential movement as such. The term "existentialism" may be properly used in at least two senses. The first is a narrow one referring to a movement in philosophy and literature that emerged in the nineteenth and twentieth centuries. The second and broader sense refers to a much earlier trend in Western thought dating back to the Old Testament book of Ecclesiastes (300 B.C.E.) and including such diverse works as *The Confessions* (c. 400) of Saint Augustine, the *Pensées* (1670) of Blaise Pascal, and the works of William Shakespeare (1564-1616) and Fyodor Dostoevsky (1821-1881). In the broader sense, the existential movement is seen in the tendency of some Western religious and literary writers to dwell upon the sense of paradox and tragedy in the human condition. Even within the narrow sense of the term, however, there is little substantive agreement among existentialists on specific ethical precepts; thus, easy generalizations about existential ethics cannot be drawn.

A partial list of existentialists will help the reader appreciate the diversity of ideas and viewpoints that constitute this "school." Kierkegaard, an early nineteenth century Danish existentialist, was a fanatical Christian. Nietzsche, another nineteenth century existentialist, was a militant atheist. In twentieth century existentialism, there is an equal degree of heterogeneity. Martin Heidegger was a Nazi, Martin Buber (1878-1965) a Jew, Albert Camus (1913-1960) a humanist, Jean-Paul Sartre a communist, and Gabriel Marcel (1889-1973) a Roman Catholic. The list could go on with further diversifications. It is sufficient to note, however, that there is no common denominator of substantive agreement within the existential movement. Existentialism does not predefine any substantive moral program. Many philosophers have described existentialism as more of a "mood" or "attitude" than a doctrine of thought.

**Some Common Existential Themes.** In spite of the above-noted diversity, there do appear to be several elements upon which most existentialists agree. For example, existentialists generally regard freedom, responsibility, suffering, and commitment as the highest of human values. They tend to have a pessimistic or despairing view of the human condition. The religious existentialists, however, balance this with a great hope. Although existentialists generally reject such a thing as human nature, they agree that it is meaningful to speak of the human condition. The existential approach to ethics emphasizes the freedom and responsibility of the existing individual as the wellspring of all ethical considerations. Several other common themes appear to run through most, if not all, existentialist ethics: people are free to choose how they will live, no system can guide them; the highest good is in the struggle to be one's authentic self. Existentialists endlessly contrast the "authentic" with the "inauthentic" and agree that any philosophy that is not actually lived is worthless. Any appeal to a transcendent rule or utilitarian principle would constitute "bad faith"—that is, self-deception.

By looking at the historical situation in which existentialism arose and the systems against which existential thought protested, one may see some of the common core of existential thought. Historically, existentialism arose as a reaction against idealism, materialism, and empirical science. The existentialists have staunchly protested any "ism" that would encapsulate humanity. A review of several historical examples may sift out several of the unique qualities that are associated with existential ethics.

**Some Historical Examples.** Søren Kierkegaard's writings were an attack upon the work of G. W. Hegel (1770-1831), who was an idealistic philosopher of the metaphysical system-building variety. Hegel proposed that the individual was a subordinate cell in the organic whole of the cosmos. Kierkegaard rebelled fiercely against what he believed was the excess rationalism and collectivism of

Hegel. In this sense, Kierkegaard was antirational and opposed to any system that made society greater than any existing individual member.

In existential ethics, the question "What ought I do?" can never be answered by appeals to logic or society's norms. For Kierkegaard, the ethical act is unique and unrepeatable—in other words, existential. Only the existing individual in the crucible of his or her own inner life can answer the question. Here no elder, no rule book, no formula can apply. Consequently, authentic ethical behavior has no ultimate court of appeal except the individual. There is only the existing individual, with his or her freedom and responsibility. Sartre puts it unequivocally: "Man is the undisputed author of his own behavior."

Nietzsche, the militant atheistic existentialist, proclaimed that "God is dead!" The God who was the basis for all ethical and moral values underpinning the old rules for guiding conduct has become obsolete. Nietzsche notes that this strange and awful event of God's death, which at first seemed so terrible, is actually a great gift. For now humankind is truly free to create its own values. The only criterion for ethical conduct becomes the quality of life. Is the quality of life enhanced or ennobled by this action? Nietzsche does not refer to the maximum quantity of life; the quality of life that he hoped would guide people's actions has more to do with human nobility and the individual overcoming his or her all-too-human weaknesses.

**Ethical Knowledge.** Existential ethical knowledge attempts to give a concrete presentation of human life—its meaning, aims, and values. The basis of existential ethics is concrete moral experience. A dialectic that does not rest upon any moral experience is only an intellectual game. Ethics cannot be a merely theoretical discipline; it is also a moral and existential activity. Existential ethics attempts to turn to reality itself, to actual life, and to overcome the duality that undermines the value of academic or traditional philosophy. According to Berdyaev, a Russian Christian existentialist, the dilemma of ethical knowledge is that existence is irrational and individual, but people can know only the general and universal. Consequently, existential ethics moves from the epistemological subject of traditional philosophy to the concrete individual. Existential writers believe that what is essential about ethics is not that people should have ideas about what authenticity is, but that they should live authentically. Ethical knowledge is communion with truth and existence. Ethical objects cannot be described in a formal scientific way at all. They are revealed only to the person who performs creative acts of valuation and commitment.

Abstract a priori systems of ethics have minimal value. Sartre's often quoted existential dictum "Existence precedes essence" points to the irrelevance of any a priori system. One's identity and values emerge from one's choices, not from some essence of human nature that was given to one at birth. The individual, in struggle and anguish, must wrest his or her essence from existence by means of concrete moral choices. Humankind cannot rely on animal instinct, and people do not have some prepackaged morality that will serve to guide their choices. Nothing is authoritative. Thus, Sartre notes that people are "condemned to freedom." Moral life presupposes freedom in evil as well as good. Yet for Sartre it is unclear how it is possible to escape the no-win scenario of "bad faith" that he depicted. Sartre appeared to believe that it was impossible for humans to escape one form or another of "self-deception," no matter how hard or what they tried.

**Existentialism and Pleasure.** Hedonistic ethics, whether it be heavenly or earthly, ultimately rests on fear. A hedonistic individual is bound to fear for his or her happiness and the happiness of others. Happiness is threatened with danger on all sides and bought at the cost of opportunism in actions and judgments. Berdyaev notes, "If I make happiness my aim I am doomed to fear all the time." Thus, the existentialists univocally renounce pleasure or happiness as a criterion of action. This renunciation takes resolve and courage. For Heidegger, the resolve of the authentic life alone liberates one from fear. For Paul Tillich (1886-1965), a Christian existentialist, the "courage to be" triumphs over fear.

**Existential View of Humankind.** Existentialists often recognize a dual nature of human beings and an ensuing inherent tension between these contradictory natures. Although humans are endowed with reason, they are irrational beings. The human being is a wounded creature. For the Christian existentialist, human beings aspire to the loftiest values and divine reality. Kierkegaard, discovering in human nature fathomless darkness, conflict, and pain, also recognized that the human being is a creator of values in the image and likeness of God. For Christian existentialists, human beings do not exist apart from the divine element in them. Thus, the authentic person is a bearer of the divine image. The soul is afraid of emptiness: Without *commitment*, it has no positive creative content and becomes filled with false illusions and fictions. At the same time, each person is a sick being, divided within and influenced by a dark subconscious. Sartre, taking a consistently atheistic position, defines each individual as a "useless passion."

The cognitive and optimistic psychology of either humanism or behaviorism, according to which people seek bliss and positive reinforcement, is erroneous. Humans are irrational beings who may long for suffering rather than happiness. "Happiness" is a meaningless and empty human word. Existential ethics, far from seeking happiness, may call people to the line of greatest resistance to the world, demanding heroic efforts.

**Suffering as the Criterion of Authenticity.** Kierkegaard notes there are two kinds of suffering: the redeeming suffering that leads to life and the dark suffering that leads to death. Suffering may raise and purify people or crush and humiliate them. An individual may go through life suffering serenely and graciously and be born into a new life as a result of it. All the suffering sent to humankind—the death of nearest and dearest, illness, poverty, humiliation, and disappointments—may serve to purify and regenerate an individual depending on the attitude that the individual takes toward them.

Victor Frankl (b. 1905), an existential psychiatrist, points out that the individual can go through tremendous suffering if he or she sees meaning in it. Attempts to avoid suffering only create more suffering; such an escape is one of the greatest delusions of life. Paradoxically, suffering is tied to alienation and despair, but it is also the way to light and renewal.

**Existentialism and Eastern Views.** Existential ethics may be contrasted with Eastern thought. Unlike Hinduism, for example, existentialism stresses the individual's separateness from the world as a positive value. There is no *tat twam asi* (That art thou) in existentialism. The "other" is seen as truly "other," which serves to enrich the individual self through communion rather than merger. For the existentialist, the highest expression of selfhood does not entail the drop of water returning to the ocean; instead, it is an affirmation of the individual self and its higher destiny, which is, in some inescapable sense, separate from the world and from others.

**The Primacy of the Individual.** The history of ethics is complicated by the opposing rights of the individual and those of society. As early as the time of Socrates, Greek thought tried to free itself from the power of law and society and penetrate to the individual authentic conscience. The moral conscience of Socrates came into conflict with the Athenian democracy. As a consequence, Socrates was martyred by the mob. Socrates proclaimed the principle that "God ought to be obeyed more than men." This means that God, conscience, truth, the inner light ought to be obeyed more than society or any formal law. Radical reliance on truth alone provides authenticity. Thus, Socrates made a tremendous advance toward the liberation of personality and the discovery of the individual conscience. Existentialists go further than Socrates, saying, "You must always act individually, and everyone must act differently." Authentic existential behavior is truly original, not determined by social influences.

**Society and the Individual.** Existentialists have been outspoken in declaring the tyranny of the social unit. The power of society over the individual has been found everywhere in history. Because of Western society's conditioning, the individual is not aware of living in a madness that is only superficially concealed. R. D. Laing, an existential psychiatrist, argues that the "fleet" is off course; hence, the individual "deviating" ship may represent the true course. Thus, society's norms are useless. The task of existential ethics is to distinguish between the authentic and the social in moral life and to reveal the pure conscience. In its essence, the authentic moral life is independent of social life. Christian existentialists urge people to remember the eternal principle in the human soul that is independent of historical changes, which in this sense is not social. Existential ethics places the individual above the law. A person *is* a value. A living human being is of higher value than any abstract idea—even the idea of the good.

In the work of Nietzsche, ethics cannot depend upon the herd morality, since it represents a slavish image of humankind, an image based upon resentment and cowardice. Nietzsche's noble individual, who is a yea-sayer to life, embodies the highest good and the supreme value. Everything that increases life is good, and everything that decreases life, leading to death and nonbeing, is evil. Such an ethic rejects any form of hedonism. A rich, full life is good and valuable even if it brings with it suffering rather than happiness. Thus, Nietzsche's championing of the noble life led to his being a bitter enemy of hedonism and utilitarianism. The supreme value and good is not life as such, but the authenticity with which it is lived.

**Death and Existential Ethics.** Existentialists, whether atheistic or religious, agree that one's attitude will be more authentic if one regards all people as though they were dying and determines one's relationships with them in the light of death—both their death and one's own. Berdyaev writes, "Every man is dying, I too am dying, I must never forget about death."

For Frankl, death is a message of hope, not doom. The imminence of death provides the impetus that is needed to live life authentically, above the petty cares that would otherwise fetter human fulfillment. The ever-present possibility of death, while terrifying, gives a sense of preciousness to the "now" that would otherwise be missing.

**Existentialism: An Ethics of Freedom.** Ethics would be meaningless without freedom, since "ought" implies "can." Humans are free, creative beings who prefer freedom to happiness. Existential analysis details the insidious assaults upon human freedom. The mass media pose a number of false images of happiness as supreme values. These misrepresentations of "happiness" as the supreme good and final end have been instilled in people to keep them in slavery. Human freedom and dignity forbid the individual to regard popular images of happiness and satisfaction as the primary goals of existence.

Any person—even a slave—can be inwardly free. Frankl's experience in a Nazi concentration camp proved that acceptance of circumstances that have fallen to one's lot can be interpreted as mastery over the external world. It is an existential victory. This does not mean that one must not try to improve one's circumstances or strive for social reform. One must, however, remain spiritually free even in prison.

The point of fundamental importance for existential ethics is that one must strive first and foremost to free oneself from slavery. Because every state that is incompatible with existential freedom is evil, the inner conquest of slavery is the fundamental task of moral life. Every kind of slavery is meant here: slavery to the pull of the past and the future, slavery to the external world and one's self, and slavery to one's lower self. One's existential task in life is to radiate creative energy that brings with it light, strength, and transfiguration. —*Paul August Rentz*

**See also** Berdyaev, Nikolai; Buber, Martin; Kierkegaard, Søren; Nietzsche, Friedrich; Sartre, Jean-Paul; Tillich, Paul.

**BIBLIOGRAPHY**

Barnes, Hazel. *An Existentialist Ethics*. New York: Alfred A. Knopf, 1967. An exciting book dealing with an existential approach to liberating the individual that is based on the groundwork of Jean-Paul Sartre. Hazel Barnes, unlike Sartre, finds viable alternatives to bad faith. Especially useful for those interested in how existentialism relates to Eastern philosophy; seventy pages of the text explicitly compare the two. A good reference for those already familiar with the basics of existential ethics.

Barrett, William. *Irrational Man: A Study in Existential Philosophy*. Garden City, N.Y.: Doubleday, 1962. A superb introductory reference to existential philosophy. This work is widely recognized as the finest definition of existentialism written by an American. This book addresses the literary and religious approaches to existentialism as well as the rigorously philosophical approach. Strongly recommended.

Berdyaev, Nikolai. *The Destiny of Man*. Translated by Natalie Duddington. New York: Harper & Row, 1960. A somewhat advanced work in existential ethics written by a former Russian communist who converted to Christianity after the Russian Revolution. In "Concrete Problems of Ethics," Berdyaev deals with sex, love, family, technical progress, and other topics from a rigorously existential viewpoint. An excellent reference for the serious student.

Frankl, Viktor. *Man's Search for Meaning*. 3d ed. New York: Simon & Schuster, 1984. Millions of copies of this book have been sold to both laypersons and mental health professionals who wish to understand how existential ethics were lived in a Nazi concentration camp. The original title of this work was *From Death Camp to Existentialism*. An excellent reference for those interested in psychology, ethics, and existentialism.

Kaufmann, Walter. *Existentialism from Dostoevsky to Sartre*. Rev. ed. New York: New American Library, 1975. An extremely rich anthology of readings from ten leading representatives of the existential movement. Kaufmann's introduction tells the reader how to approach the specific texts. An excellent collection of primary sources in existentialism for the beginning student who would like to read what the existentialists actually said. Accessible and widely available.

## Experimentation, ethics of

**TYPE OF ETHICS:** Scientific ethics

**DATE:** Nineteenth century to present

**ASSOCIATED WITH:** Claude Bernard, World Medical Association, and the U.S. Department of Health and Human Services

**DEFINITION:** The subdiscipline concerned with the analysis of moral principles involved in the conduct of research, especially with human subjects; the inhumanity of the Nazi experiments called attention to the moral issues in human research

**SIGNIFICANCE:** Seeks to protect the rights and welfare of human subjects used in scientific research

What are the moral principles to be considered in evaluating the rightness or wrongness of using humans as research subjects?

In *The Patient as Partner* (1987), Robert M. Veatch has summarized the ethical principles and issues involved in research: The principle of *beneficence*, which has its roots in the ethics of medical treatment, states that research with humans is justified only when some good can come from it; this is the minimum justification for human research.

Research may do good (therefore meeting the criterion of beneficence) but may also cause harm. Research that causes harm is morally wrong; that is, it does not meet the principle of *nonmaleficence.* When research causes both good and harm, which principle, beneficence or nonmaleficence, takes priority? If avoiding harm takes priority, then a vast amount of research with human subjects with the potential for doing much good would be considered unethical. Therefore, the ratio of benefit to harm is a more reasonable criterion for justifying human experimentation.

If benefit/harm is adopted as the moral principle, a new problem emerges, because this principle would justify inhumane experimental procedures such as those employed by the Nazis as long as it could be shown that severe harm or death to a few human subjects was of benefit to large numbers of people.

Benefit/harm, a form of beneficence, is therefore a necessary but insufficient justification for research with human subjects. Additional principles are required.

The principle of *autonomy* recognizes that among the inalienable rights of persons is the right to liberty. The principle of autonomy implies a right to self-determination, including the right, when informed of the benefits and harms, to consent to participate in research that may entail certain risks to the subject. Therefore, autonomy is the basis for the use of informed consent in research with human subjects; informed consent helps to mitigate some of the problems posed by sole reliance on beneficence as a moral criterion.

Still another principle involves considerations of *justice* (fairness) in the conduct of human research. According to one theory of justice, distributive justice, fairness involves attempting to equalize the benefits and harms among the members of society. This principle has implications for the selection of subjects for research in the sense that disadvantaged subjects—for example, members of minority groups—should not be chosen as subjects, since this would add another burden to an already unduly burdened group. This principle would not apply when minority status was a variable under study in the research.

The three principles adumbrated above—namely, beneficence, autonomy, and justice—form the basis for some of the criteria set by the U.S. Department of Health and Human Services (DHHS) and used by institutional review boards (IRBs) for judging whether proposed research involving human subjects is ethically sound. These criteria are: (1) risks to subjects are minimized, (2) risks are reasonable relative to anticipated benefits, (3) prior informed consent will be obtained from subjects or their legal representative, (4) informed consent will be documented, and (5) selection of subjects will be equitable. Two additional criteria are that (6) subjects' privacy and confidentiality will be maintained and that (7) the research plan involves monitoring the data, when applicable, so as to ensure subject safety.

The application of ethical principles to particular instances of research with human subjects highlights the complexities involved in the use of these principles. One question that arises concerns the obligations of a scientist when the nature of the research precludes informed consent, as in psychological research that involves the use of deception. While many people believe that deception is permissible under certain limited conditions—for example, when there is little or no risk to subjects and there are no alternative ways of gathering the data—others feel that deception is intrinsically harmful to subjects and is never justified.

Another question has to do with the issue of informed consent with subjects who may not be competent to give informed consent; for example, in cases involving children or individuals who were formerly competent but are no longer so (such as individuals who have some form of dementia). When risks are minimal, informed consent by parents of children and informed consent by guardians of the formerly competent have been employed as criteria.

In circumstances in which the subject is competent but informed consent may be obtained under potentially coercive conditions, as in the case of prisoners or clinic patients, complex ethical questions are raised.

The ethics of experimentation also extend into such other areas as issues of animal care and rights, and the ethical obligations of scientists with regard to the integrity of the research process. —*Sanford Golin*

**See also** Animal rights; Bioethics; Medical research; Milgram experiment; Nazi science; Science, ethics of.

**BIBLIOGRAPHY**

Caplan, A. L. *When Medicine Went Mad: Bioethics and the Holocaust.* Totowa, N.J.: Humana Press, 1992.

Garattini, Silvio, and D. W. van Bekkum, eds. *The Importance of Animal Experimentation for Safety and Biomedical Research.* Boston: Kluwer Academic, 1990.

Group for the Advancement of Psychiatry. *A Casebook in Psychiatric Ethics.* New York: Brunner/Mazel, 1990.

Sieber, J. E., ed. *Fieldwork, Regulation, and Publication.* Vol. 2 in *The Ethics of Social Research.* New York: Springer-Verlag, 1982.

Veatch, R. M. *The Patient as Partner: A Theory of Human-Experimentation Ethics.* Bloomington: Indiana University Press, 1987.

## Exploitation

**TYPE OF ETHICS:** Beliefs and practices

**DEFINITIONS:** The indecent or illegitimate use of others for one's own advantage or profit

**SIGNIFICANCE:** Seeks to establish what constitutes exploitation as well as to determine that which can be exploited

**Discussion.** Many ethicists find that the definition of what exploitation is and what can be effected by it are inextricably linked. By examining the categories of existence that are understood to be capable of being exploited, however, a clearer, broader view of the definition can be seen.

What is considered as decent or legitimate must be sorted out in the context of what is merely socially acceptable and what is ethical, correct conduct. According to Peter Singer, "Ethics takes a universal point of view. This does not mean that a particular ethical judgment must be universally applicable. . . .What it does mean is that in making ethical judgments we go beyond our own likes and dislikes."

The area in which exploitation has been studied most is the ethical treatment of human beings. Even so, there are many unanswered questions, and new ones arise as technology advances. Yet human behavior has still not even caught up with ethical standards that are already well established in nearly every society. For example, slavery is no longer deemed acceptable in most cultures, but near-slavery conditions continue to exist in many of these cultures. To provide for the wealthy minority in the technologically developed industrialized world, millions of people live in desperate poverty. These people earn lower than subsistence wages by performing hazardous and strenuous jobs, live in unsanitary and unsafe housing, eat a diet that does not provide adequate nutrition, receive insufficient medical care, and are unable to obtain enough education to be informed citizens. Surely these pitiable people are being exploited.

How can such an unethical situation exist? There are at least three possible explanations. First, perhaps not many people are aware of the situation. Second, perhaps there are not sufficient numbers of aware people with both enough political power and enough ethical strength to stop the situation. Third, perhaps humanity has ceased to care. As Elizabeth Pybus states, "If it is possible to turn a blind eye to suffering, it may also be possible to direct a steady seeing eye towards it."

The situation of near slavery, however, is an old problem. Other human problems that have arisen in more recent times have to do with dilemmas such as the mass marketing of untested medical devices, double-blind drug tests, the whole range of uses of the information obtained from the human genome study, the use of prison labor for commercial enterprises, and informed consent in medical testing and treatments.

Exploitation does not always involve humans as its objects. Various people are working on the problems of animal rights and the humane treatment of animals. One of the first philosophers to formalize a system of proposals for the ethical treatment of animals was Jeremy Bentham. He believed that the basis for human behavior toward animals is in exploitation's definition of "other." He maintained that the point is not whether animals can reason or speak, but whether they can suffer. Their capacity to feel is called sentience. Peter Singer believes that what will determine ethical treatment of animals is for humans to give them "equal consideration" of their interests. Ethicists such as Singer believe that people will come to realize that the use of animals for food, to test cosmetics and drugs, or as pets constitutes animal exploitation and that understanding this concept will guide people to treat animals more humanely.

Most philosophers have maintained that only sentient, living creatures can be exploited, because those that are not in this category have no interests that need to be considered. Yet the concept that even plant species can be exploited has crept into the human consciousness and vocabulary. Consider trees in an old-growth forest that are exploited for their timber or patches of tasty wild mushrooms that are harvested to extinction. Are these truly cases of exploitation? The answer lies in the definition of the concept. Are these human uses indecent or illegitimate? Yes, because people have planned poorly in using forest products and have wasted vast amounts of forest "resources." Yes, because the mushrooms are not essential for human sustenance.

In these examples concerning plants, two conditions in the definition of exploitation—indecent or illegitimate use for advantage or profit—have been met. The problem lies with the third condition: that in these situations, a nonsentient "other" has been so used. Singer asks that humans do not practice "speciesism" in their treatment of animals, yet even he maintains that only sentient creatures need be given this consideration. It is when ethicists push past animal rights into the area of ecoethics that equal consideration for plants comes into question.

Ecoethics has existed throughout the ages, manifesting itself in such systems as Jainism and Native American belief systems. Since the nineteenth century, there has been a growing formalized understanding of what ecoethics involves. The study has become much more intense since about 1950, with Aldo Leopold's discussions of a "land ethic," and the early 1960's, with Rachel Carson's revelations in *Silent Spring* about pesticides accumulating in the environment.

The concept of ecoethics allows that it is possible for humankind to exploit any of the environment's manifestations, capacities, or systems. Each of these elements has been recognized as one of the "others" from the definition of exploitation. Therefore, it is possible to exploit not only plants but also mineral deposits or other geologic formations. It is possible to exploit a water table or an oil deposit. Wetlands and whole forests are potential victims of exploitation. So are the oceans and the atmosphere.

Terms that have been used with increasing frequency in discussing the environment are the biosphere and the Gaia concept. Using this expanded vocabulary, humankind is beginning to understand its potential for damaging, through exploitation, all that sustains human life.

As human technology progresses, people are beginning to discuss whether it will be necessary to apply ethical standards to any potential "rights" of artificial intelligence systems and robots.

**Conclusion.** Since organized human behavior seems to lag far behind the establishment of ethical injunctions, it might seem unlikely that humankind will ever stop its practice of exploiting all that it encounters. Yet it is in an increasing awareness of these universal views and in self-examination that the possibility of the human practice of exploitation coming to an end exists. —*Marcella T. Joy*

**See also** Abuse; Animal rights; Child labor legislation; Gaia; Human rights; Ideal observer; Medical research; Nature, rights of; Therapist-patient relationship; Wage discrimination.

**BIBLIOGRAPHY**

Allsopp, Bruce. *Ecological Morality.* London: Frederick Muller, 1972.

Attfield, Robin. *A Theory of Value and Obligation.* New York: Croom, 1987.

Maguire, Daniel. *The Moral Choice.* Garden City, N.Y.: Doubleday, 1978.

Miller, Alan. *Gaia Connections: an Introduction to Ecology, Ecoethics, and Economics.* Savage, Md.: Rowman & Littlefield, 1991.

Pybus, Elizabeth. *Human Goodness.* London: Harvester Wheatsheaf, 1991.

Singer, Peter. *Practical Ethics.* New York: Cambridge University Press, 1979.

## Fact/value distinction

**TYPE OF ETHICS:** Theory of ethics
**DATE:** Seventeenth century
**ASSOCIATED WITH:** Emotivist ethics
**DEFINITION:** A distinction between that which is either true or false and that which can be neither true nor false
**SIGNIFICANCE:** If the domains of fact and value are mutually exclusive, with normative ethics within the latter, then the language of normative ethics can be neither true nor false

The fact/value distinction is based upon the intuition that there is an important difference between sentences whose truth-value can and sentences whose truth-value cannot be determined empirically (with one or more of the five senses) or mathematically (by thinking about logical, numerical, or spatial relationships). Among the sentences whose truth-value cannot be determined empirically or mathematically are those of normative ethics: sentences about what is ethically obligatory, permissible, and forbidden, good and evil, right and wrong. Few would deny that there is such a difference and that it is important, but there is profound disagreement concerning the nature of the difference. In one camp are those who maintain that even though it is not possible to determine the truth-value of normative-ethical language by empirical observation or mathematical reflection, it is just as true, or just as false, as the language of physics and biology, geometry and logic.

Just as there is a real, material world and a real world of mathematics, so there is moral reality. Normative ethical statements are true when they conform to that moral reality and false when they do not. In the opposing camp are those who say that since the truth-value of normative ethical sentences cannot be determined by empirical or mathematical means, they are neither true nor false. (This is an oversimplification, because there is disagreement within each camp, and some ethical theorists attempt to stake out intermediate positions, but seeing the disagreement between the extremes is the best way to understand the importance of determining whether the domains of fact and value are mutually exclusive.)

Like most concepts in ethical theory, the fact/value distinction has a long history. While its roots can be found in ancient ethical theory, its rapid growth began with the Enlightenment. In English-language ethical theory, "fact" was contrasted with "right" before being opposed to "value." In *Leviathan* (1651), Thomas Hobbes distinguishes "matters of fact" and "matters of right," and the third Earl of Shaftesbury draws a distinction between a "mistake of fact" and a "mistake of right" in his *Inquiry Concerning Virtue, or Merit* (1711). The meaning of the English word "value," as used in phrases such as "fact/value distinction" and "value judgment," owes its origin in part to the influence of nineteenth century German writers, especially theologian Albrecht Ritschl and philosopher Friedrich Nietzsche.

Perhaps the clearest explicit distinction between statements of fact and judgments of value is found in British philosopher A. J. Ayer's *Language, Truth, and Logic* (1936; 1946). Many philosophers observe a distinction between sentences and propositions, in order to account for both the fact that different sentences, in different languages or different contexts, for example, can have the same meaning, and the fact that a single sentence can have different meanings, for example, when written by or about different persons. Given this distinction, propositions are either true or false; it is possible, however, for a sentence to be neither true nor false, because not all sentences express propositions. With this distinction in mind, Ayer writes: "Since the expression of a value judgement is not a proposition, the question of truth or falsehood does not here arise." At another point he adds: "In saying that a certain type of action is right or wrong, I am not making any factual statement."

Ayer did not claim that to say that a certain type of action is right or wrong is to do nothing. He argued that sentences of normative ethics express emotions rather than propositions and are sometimes calculated to change other persons' behavior by arousing their emotions. Thus, the metaethical theory that normative ethical language does not express propositions is called "emotivism."

While ethical subjectivism, relativism, and emotivism are clearly distinct from one another at the level of metaethical theorizing, they frequently have the same cash value for those whose life's work is not the study of ethical theory. According to both subjectivism and emotivism, the meaning of normative ethical language is to be understood in terms of emotions. The difference is that according to subjectivism such language states propositions about the speaker's emotions, while emotivism says that such language expresses the speaker's emotions. According to both relativism and emotivism, there is no absolute truth in normative ethics. The difference is that according to relativism there is only relative truth in normative ethics, while emotivism says there is no truth at all. For someone wondering whether, for example, abortion is immoral, these distinctions have little relevance and often tend to blur.

Although the question of whether the domains of fact and value are mutually exclusive cannot be answered by empirical observation or mathematical reflection, simple logic does reveal the magnitude of the bullet one must bite in order to maintain that they are. If only one sentence about the immorality of child abuse, torture, rape, murder, cannibalism, or genocide both makes a value judgment and states a fact, then no line can be drawn between facts and values.

*—David Lutz*

**See also** Absolutes and absolutism; Ayer, A. J.; Cognitivism and noncognitivism; Emotivist ethics; Enlightenment ethics; Epistemological ethics; Is/ought distinction; Language; Metaethics; Moral realism; Moral-sense theories; Naturalistic fallacy; Normative vs. descriptive ethics; Objectivism; Ought/can implication; Passions and emotions; Post-Enlightenment ethics; Relativism; Subjectivism; Values; Values clarification.

**BIBLIOGRAPHY**

Arkes, Hadley. *First Things: An Inquiry into the First Principles of Morals and Justice*. Princeton, N.J.: Princeton University Press, 1986.

Ayer, A. J. *Language, Truth, and Logic*. London: V. Gollancz, 1936.

Nietzsche, Friedrich. *On the Genealogy of Morals*. Translated by Walter Kaufmann. New York: Vintage Books, 1967.

Ritschl, Albrecht. *The Christian Doctrine of Justification and Reconciliation*. Edinburgh, Scotland: T & T Clark, 1902.

Stevenson, Charles L. *Facts and Values*. New Haven, Conn.: Yale University Press, 1963.

## Fair Labor Standards Act

**TYPE OF ETHICS:** Business and labor ethics

**DATE:** June 25, 1938

**ASSOCIATED WITH:** U.S. Congress

**DEFINITION:** Labor legislation regulating child labor, wages, and hours of labor

**SIGNIFICANCE:** This Act recognized the progressive ideal of governmental responsibility to provide for the economic and social welfare of laboring people by regulating business

The Supreme Court ruled unconstitutional attempts such as the National Industrial Recovery Act of 1933 by the Roosevelt Administration to regulate prices, wages, hours, and other labor conditions. In 1938, however, Congress passed wages and hours legislation as an omnibus bill, and the Supreme Court upheld it in 1941. The Fair Labor Standards Act regulated minimum wages, overtime pay, child labor, and the production of goods for interstate commerce. Beginning with the third year after its effective date, the Act raised the minimum wage to forty cents per hour, made it subject thereafter to review by a congressional committee, and required overtime pay of one and one-half times the employees' regular pay above forty hours work per week. The Act eliminated child labor (by children under age sixteen) with certain exceptions. One of the most significant amendments to the Act, which came in 1963, required equal pay for equal work without regard to sex. Although more than forty exemptions to the Act exist, including the regulation of professional employees and outside salespersons, the Act is a milestone for labor, since in it Congress and the president recognized their responsibility to be the guardians of economic and social justice for labor.

**See also** National Labor Relations Act.

## Fairness

**TYPE OF ETHICS:** Beliefs and practices

**DATE:** Fourth century B.C.E. to present

**ASSOCIATED WITH:** Theories of social justice, especially those in the social contract tradition, such as that of John Rawls

**DEFINITION:** A moral principle used to judge procedures for distributing benefits and burdens among parties

**SIGNIFICANCE:** An important standard for the moral evaluation of decisions and practices that considers processes in addition to outcomes and weighs the relevant differences among people

Fairness is one of several ethical concepts, along with justice and equity, that are concerned with the distribution of benefits and burdens among individuals and groups. It is sometimes used in a broad sense, connoting attitudes and features characteristic of much wrongdoing, including putting one's own interests ahead of others and favoring oneself or one's own at the expense of others. In this broad sense, fairness is a central component of the moral point of view, in contrast to a purely egoistic or self-interested standpoint. The individual adopting the moral point of view is fair-minded, looking at claims in a balanced, impartial, and reasonable way.

The ancient Greek philosopher Aristotle, in his classic discussion of justice in book 5 of the *Nicomachean Ethics,* observed that justice is used in a narrow sense as well as a broad sense. Fairness, like justice, seems to have a narrower sense as well. In fact, it might be more accurate to say several narrower senses or uses. One of these senses is exemplified in cases of the differential treatment of individuals on arbitrary or irrelevant grounds. The awarding of a job on the basis of political favoritism or nepotism is usually condemned as unfair. Another related sense is that used in connection with procedures; for example, when people speak of a fair trial or a fair contest. In these cases, fairness is a matter of there being rules or guidelines that are closely followed. Additionally, the rules or guidelines shaping the procedure should not give an undue advantage to certain parties. Sometimes these notions are referred to as "procedural fairness" and "background fairness."

A third sense involves profiting at another's expense; if such advantage-taking is not allowed by the rules of some competition, it is deemed unfair. Oddly, however, allowing another to gain at one's own expense is not regarded as unfair. A fourth sense of fairness and unfairness is found in situations of blame and punishment: Punishing an innocent person ("scapegoating") and blaming or punishing an individual more than is deserved are seen as unfair. While several elements of unfairness are present in such cases, the main offense to fairness seems to be the singling out of the individual for disfavor, the sacrificing of that individual even if he or she is not totally innocent and even if some greater good will come of it.

While the concepts of justice and fairness are closely related and are used interchangeably in some contexts, they are not identical. The terms "just" and "unjust" often carry a stronger tone of condemnation than do "fair" and "unfair." At times, there is a readiness to admit that something is unfair but to tolerate it nevertheless, perhaps with an observation that "life is not fair." By contrast, the idea of tolerable or justifiable injustices is not countenanced. John Stuart Mill, in his discussion of justice in *Utilitarianism* (1861), made note of the avoidance of the idea that there can be "laudable injustice" by accommodating language so that "we usually say, not that justice must give way to some other moral principle, but that what is just in the ordinary case is, by reason of that other principle, not just in the particular case." Furthermore, fairness seems more appropriately applied to procedures and processes, while justice is often used for outcomes. Familiar examples of this are references to fair trials and just verdicts.

In *A Theory of Justice* (1972), philosopher John Rawls develops a theory of social justice that he calls "justice as fairness." He makes use of this association of the idea of fairness with procedures to extract principles of a just society as ones that would be the outcome of a bargaining process among parties under conditions marked by background fairness. One notion of fairness discussed by Rawls is identified with pure procedural justice. Pure procedural justice is characterized by the existence of a correct or fair procedure without an independent criterion of a correct or right result. In such a situation, provided the procedure has been followed, the result is correct or fair, whatever it happens to be. The fairness of the procedure transfers to the result. In *A Theory of Justice*, Rawls attempts to develop a theory of a just society by treating social justice as a type of fairness or pure procedural justice. Pure procedural justice is contrasted with perfect procedural justice, in which there is an independent criterion of a correct result and the possibility of devising a procedure to arrive at that result, and imperfect procedural justice, in which there is an independent criterion of a correct outcome but no possibility of devising a procedure to consistently achieve that outcome.

Rawls also provides an extensive discussion of the principle of fairness or fair play. This is a principle of duty or right action, which relates to the sense of fairness in not taking advantage of others. If people enjoy the benefits of cooperative activities, benefits made possible by the contributions of others, then they have a duty to contribute their share or to do their part. Otherwise they are "free-riding." The tax evader who benefits from tax-supported programs is an example of a person unfairly benefiting from the efforts of others. —*Mario F. Morelli*

**See also** Free-riding; Justice; Mill, John Stuart; Rawls, John; Utilitarianism.

**Bibliography**

Aristotle. *The Ethics of Aristotle: The Nicomachean Ethics*. New York: Penguin, 1974.

Barry, Brian. *Political Argument*. London, England: Routledge & Kegan Paul, 1965.

Mill, John Stuart. *Utilitarianism*. Indianapolis: Hackett, 1979.

Rawls, John. *A Theory of Justice*. Cambridge, Mass.: Belknap Press of Harvard University Press, 1971.

Shklar, Judith N. *The Faces of Injustice*. New Haven, Conn.: Yale University Press, 1990.

## Fairness and Accuracy in Reporting (FAIR)

**Type of ethics:** Media ethics

**Date:** Founded 1986

**Associated with:** Liberal and populist movements

**Definition:** FAIR encourages the news media to report the diverse concerns and opinions of the American public

**Significance:** FAIR was one of the first national media watchdog groups working to correct conservative and centrist bias in news reporting

FAIR believes that the national and local news media are increasingly influenced by political and economic powers—that instead of independently challenging and criticizing government and big business, the news media tend to accept and pass along official versions of events. For example, FAIR examined news coverage of the 1991 Gulf War and found that most news stories and editorials echoed official government press releases and statements, and reflected little or no attempt to confirm or refine government versions of events. When some official statements turned out to be exaggerated or false, corrections were given minimal attention. FAIR also found that on talk shows and other analysis programs, only a small range of views was presented, and the views of those opposed to the war were seldom heard. In 1989, FAIR published an important report showing that the guest analysts on two of the most widely watched television news programs were overwhelmingly white males from large institutions. Representatives of labor, social movements, minority groups, and local civic groups were very rarely featured on these programs. FAIR maintains contact with the public through a magazine that is published eight times a year and through a weekly radio program.

**See also** Accuracy in Media (AIM); Sources of information.

## Family

**Type of ethics:** Personal and social ethics

**Date:** From antiquity

**Definition:** A fundamental social group, often consisting of a man and a woman and their offspring

**Significance:** The family is the basic social unit that makes up larger societies; a society's concept of family determines, in large part, the nature of that society

All known societies value the family. In American society, the family is customarily defined as a social group based on a heterosexual partnership of procreation that creates a community of parents and children. This article will focus on the changing nature of the family in the United States and the ethical issues related to the family.

**Family Types.** The concepts of household and family should not be confused. A household is a group of people who live together and share cooking and toilet facilities. Households may include unrelated boarders who rent rooms from a family, as is the case with many college students. "Household" is a descriptive term, whereas the term "family" is prescriptive. A family consists of people who are related to one another by blood or marriage and who thus ought to care for one another and share life's joys and sorrows. Duty and obligation bind family members as much as rights and privileges do. Family and household often overlap but do not necessarily do so. Members of a family may live in scattered households.

There are many types of family, each of which has evolved in response to different circumstances. In the United States, the term "family" commonly refers to the "nuclear family": a husband, a wife, and their children, all of whom share a home, often cook and eat together, and offer one another support. The word "family" also refers to a person's ancestors and other relatives, such as aunts, uncles, and cousins. Most families are based on kinship, which simply means that the family members are related to one another by blood, marriage, or recognized forms of adoption. "Foster families" are an exception, because the children are neither adopted nor related to their foster parents by blood or marriage. Despite this fact, the members of such families live together and treat one another as family members.

Anthropologists, sociologists, and psychologists believe that nuclear families were well adapted to the demands of industrial America. Their small size made it easy for industrial workers to relocate when employment demanded that they move. From the 1840's until the 1940's, the nuclear family was considered the norm in the United States and in the industrialized sections of Europe.

*A Mexican American family celebrates a wedding.* (James L. Shaffer)

In the post-industrial United States, many other types of families are emerging. Skyrocketing housing costs have forced many parents with children to move in with grandparents, forming three- or even four-generational "extended families" made up of two or more nuclear families. Like the nuclear family, such a family is a "conjugal family," because some of its members are related by blood and others are related by marriage. Because many husbands and wives work, grandparents often provide no-cost child care for young couples. An extended family might also include aunts, uncles, and cousins. Many immigrant families form "joint extended families" composed of several related families that live together, pool their earnings, and share most expenses. Many of these families are headed by an elderly patriarch and his wife. Usually, married sons and their wives and children, as well as unmarried children, attach themselves to a grandfather's household to form a joint family. Such families are more common among families that own property or businesses than they are among the working class. Family type represents adaptation to circumstances, not moral imperatives. Ethics develop to justify and reinforce family structures.

Extended families can accumulate capital rapidly, which encourages early entry into small businesses. Family members often work in these businesses without pay in return for total support for themselves and their children. Since family members feel obligated to work for relatives, even without pay, some sociologists are critical of these families. They believe that this arrangement amounts to little more than slavery and exploitation. Sometimes, children are forced to work and, as a result, miss school to help maintain the family business.

These families raise many moral issues. Do obligations to extended family members limit an individual's freedom and stifle personal growth? If so, is a person justified in ignoring these demands? What duty do people owe their grandparents and relatives who are not within their immediate families? If one inherits financial benefits from distant relatives, especially as a result of heinous institutions, such as slavery, does one also inherit a moral obligation to right those persons' wrongs? Should those who prosper under a system work to change that system if they know that it is morally wrong? History has often provided examples of families that chose practicality and personal gain over morality; for example, slave-owning families.

Chinese immigrants provide an example of a type of extended family that is known as the "stem family." Betty Lee Sung's book *The Story of the Chinese in America* notes that filial piety and a display of absolute loyalty to and respect for parents obligate one married son to live with his aging parents and become their caretaker. Other sons and daughters are free to marry and leave the family unit without being condemned for abandoning or neglecting the parents. This social obligation would make it both unethical and unthinkable for first-generation Chinese Americans to place their aging parents in homes for the elderly or allow them to struggle to maintain a household alone. Although caring for aging parents is a burden and may create economic hardships, moral imperatives take precedence in this situation. This tradition often changes in the second and third generation.

**Decline of the Nuclear Family?** Some social scientists argue that the American family is doomed because "single-parent families" are a growing phenomenon. Rising levels of education make it possible for many women to support children without help from a father. Welfare creates similar options for less-well-educated poor women.

The conservative view of female-headed households implies that they are not ethical. Bearing children out of wedlock is considered immoral. Also important to conservatives is the fact that children born out of wedlock cost the government billions of dollars annually. Conservatives often assert that women who develop what conservatives like to think of as irresponsible sex lives contribute to the growing feminization of poverty. People who think in this way believe that character flaws, bad values, and personal weakness on the part of such women create "matrifocal families." These are "consanguineal families" in which the members are related by blood ties only. This view ignores the possibility that the man may have abandoned the woman or that a woman may be widowed or divorced. Conservatives also believe that matrifocal families unfairly condemn millions of children to live as welfare wards and dependents of the state, plagued by persistent poverty.

Most families on welfare are matrifocal. Some observers believe that welfare is debilitating because it undermines the work ethic, which values work rather than leisure. To many Americans, work is a moral duty and an obligation to the family, the community, and the state. As early as 1898, Jacob Riis's book *How the Other Half Lives* (1898) argued that poor families should be given jobs, not charity. Riis believed that work restored a moral environment, which was the key to reducing poverty, strengthening nuclear families, and restoring people's self-respect and dignity. Conservative supporters of welfare reform echo Riis's views. They want to tie welfare eligibility to moral norms. Workfare programs are built on this assumption, and some of them allow nuclear families to receive aid if parents assume responsibility for the family and seek work or self-improvement through education in preparation for future jobs.

When investigating how female-headed families form, a different picture emerges. In slum neighborhoods, many single mothers have that status thrust upon them by high levels of male unemployment. *The Truly Disadvantaged* (1990), by sociologist William Julius Wilson, notes that in 1950, 80 of every 100 ghetto males were gainfully employed; by 1980, however, the number had dropped to 17 of every 100. The result is that few ghetto males are able to support a wife and children. Wilson believes that economics is largely responsible for this disaster. These fathers without families feel guilty because they accept society's dictate that they should care for their children. Such shame is dysfunctional, and many males seek to escape from it by means of alcohol, drug abuse, or crime. Consequently, 25 percent of African American males between the ages of 17 and 35 are caught up in the criminal justice system, and many others are in the armed forces. In either case, they are not in their communities.

The absence of these endangered males from slum communities creates a void. Many men contract AIDS while they are in prison because they engage in homosexual affairs or become intravenous drug users and share dirty needles. Once the infected person is released from prison, the disease is transmitted to his female lovers. For this reason, epidemics and drug abuse threaten to destroy urban low-income families.

As medical science increases longevity, society strives to offer all its members that benefit, but often only wealthy families benefit. This problem is most evident in figures calculating life expectancy in terms of race. Whites can expect to live ten years longer than African Americans may expect to live, because many whites can afford better diets, health clubs, and medical care for their families. This fact creates an ethical dilemma. Are rich families entitled to live longer than poor families? Is access to adequate health care a privilege or a right?

Another cause of matrifocal families is the falling infant mortality rate, which is reflected in the increased number of adolescent girls who give birth. In *When Children Want Children* (1989), Leon Dash points out that, although the overall rate of adolescent births has declined since 1970, the number of infants born to unwed mothers has increased threefold, from 91,700 in 1960 to 270,076 in 1983. Add to this the fact that 23 percent of these mothers said that they intentionally became pregnant and the moral crisis becomes clear. Early unmarried parenthood is closely tied to reduced education, marginal income-earning capacity, and welfare dependence. Teenage mothers also tend to have larger-than-average families, and married teenage couples have the highest divorce rate in the United States. Children of teenage mothers have lower-than-average health, lower-than-average IQ scores, low cognitive scores, and a better-than-average chance of living in a disruptive home during their high school years, and these children are more likely to become sexually active before marriage and repeat this tragic cycle than are other teenagers. The ethical crisis is clear, but the remedy is far from clear, despite the fact that Peter Laslett's book *Family Life and Illicit Love in Past Times* argues that this dilemma has faced Americans since the frontier era. In the past, high infant mortality rates and forced marriages covered up moral lapses. Decreasing infant death rates and greater freedom in mate selection are bringing old dilemmas into sharp focus, according to Laslett. Is technology revealing a conflict between family ideals and reality?

**Power Relationships Within Families.** Practical matters dictate that there are vast differences in power within families. Traditionally, American men were expected to be monarchs within the family and to wield great power. The father's word was final. Recently, it has become clear that, in an alarming number of cases, the intimacy of the family conceals abuses of this power involving incest and beatings of wives, children, and older relatives. Family members may engage in denial and hide such abuse even from themselves. The rights of women, children, and the elderly within families need to be made clear and public in order to protect these people. The abuse of power becomes institutionalized when fathers are also the sole judges of injustice and their victims are delegated roles as custodians of patience, forgiveness, and forbearance. Lord Acton noted that power corrupts and that absolute power corrupts absolutely. This seems to be true within families; relations should be democratized by distributing power within the family to minimize abuses of all kinds.

**Familial Favoritism and Power.** Plato (430-437 B.C.E.) charged that families were bad because they made people acquisitive and thus subverted devotion to the good of the community. In his ideal republic, the guardian class would live and reproduce in communal groups, thus creating one huge extended family based on group marriage. This would reduce psychological and material divisions. The practice was tried in Israel and Russia, with little success. Thomas Jefferson wanted to allow private households and nuclear families but limit inheritance as a method of reducing the advantages that family wealth would give one American over another. Inheritance is an element of the issues of family favoritism and nepotism, which are banned for those who hold public office because they give family members unfair opportunities to secure jobs, political office, income, and other benefits.

**Divorce.** In 1930, an American schoolchild would have been shocked if one of his or her peers admitted to having divorced parents. Today, such information is commonplace. Although this fact gives rise to fear that the family is breaking down, such fear is unrealistic. The highest divorce rate of the twentieth century occurred in 1945, following World War II. This occurred because many couples married hurriedly, without knowing each other. The men went off to war, and the stress of separation caused both men and women to develop other relationships, leading to divorce after the war. The divorce rate dropped sharply after 1945 but began to rise steadily again between 1950 and 1980. Although the current rate is high, it is not nearly as high as the 1945 rate.

Divorce alone is not responsible for the increase in single-parent families, as some people have suggested. Drastic reductions in death rates mean that fewer parents are widowed and fewer children are orphans than was the case earlier in the century. These statistics offset the increase in single-parent households caused by divorce. Moreover, record numbers of parents remarry shortly after a divorce and form "blended families." Although stepparents assume responsibility for the children of their new spouses, remarriage raises questions. What are the best interests of the children? Who should have custody? Children who have been given up for adoption can now use their rights to divorce their biological parents if there is an attempt to reunite them. Children who have done so have argued that they do not know their biological parents and are happy with their adopted social parents. Adopted parents choose these children out of love. In such cases, the genitor, or social parent, supersedes the biological parent. The courts have upheld the right of children to remain with adopted parents despite the wishes of the biological parents who put them up for adoption earlier in life. Is it ethical for the state to uphold individual rights at the expense of group rights?

**Conclusions.** Although some people have predicted the demise of the American family, the evidence suggests that this is not a likely scenario. The family is undoubtedly changing in response to new social environments and new challenges, but it remains basically healthy. In fact, families may be stronger than ever. Lesbian and gay couples, for example, do not wish to destroy the family; instead, they view it as an institution that is so desirable that they want its definition expanded to include same-sex couples who wish to make lifelong commitments. In the years ahead, society will be challenged to redefine the family, its mission, and the ethics of relationships within it as it becomes possible to reproduce asexually through cloning and as other developments take place. Future families are likely to be more democratic and to avoid abusive sexism. Families may even drift away from privatism and favoritism toward close relatives, but changes in this area should be expected to occur slowly. Since families play pivotal roles in shaping the morality of the nation, business is likely to become more involved in family issues in order to ensure a steady supply of trustworthy and reliable workers. The declining roles of churches and schools as shapers of values may force business to play such a role. Finally, as families become more democratic, children will acquire more power within them, and those children must be taught how to use that power appropriately. The future of the family holds many problems and many ethical challenges. *—Dallas Browne*

**See also** Abuse; Child abuse; Children; Children's rights; Divorce; Duty; Family values; Marriage; Sexual stereotypes; Values.

**Bibliography**

Aiken, William, and Hugh LaFollette, eds. *Whose Child? Children's Rights, Parental Authority, and State Power*. Totowa, N.J.: Rowman & Littlefield, 1980.

Blustein, Jeffrey. *Parents and Children: The Ethics of the Family*. New York: Oxford University Press, 1982.

Dash, Leon. *When Children Want Children: The Urban Crisis of Teenage Childbearing*. New York: William Morrow, 1989.

Ditzion, Sidney. *Marriage, Morals, and Sex in America: A History of Ideas*. New York: Bookman Associates, 1953.

Dreikurs, Rudolf, and Vicki Soltz. *Children: The Challenge*. New York: Duell, Sloan & Pearce, 1964.

Laslett, Peter. *Household and Family in Past Times*. Cambridge, England: Cambridge University Press, 1972.

Okin, Susan Moller. *Justice, Gender, and the Family*. New York: Basic Books, 1989.

Scarre, Geoffrey, ed. *Children, Parents, and Politics*. New York: Cambridge University Press, 1989.

Teichman, Jenny. *Illegitimacy: An Examination of Bastardy*. Ithaca, N.Y.: Cornell University Press, 1982.

Wilson, William J. *The Truly Disadvantaged: The Inner City, the Underclass, and Public Policy*. Chicago: University of Chicago Press, 1990.

## Family therapy

**Type of ethics:** Psychological ethics

**Date:** 1960's to present

**Associated with:** Systems theory, Virginia Satir, Gregory Bateson, structured theory, and the American Association of Marriage and Family Therapists

**Definition:** A type of psychotherapy that views an individual's problems as originating in that individual's current environment and family system

**Significance:** Raises important questions about the role of the therapist vis-à-vis each family member and the dynamics between family members as influenced by the therapist

Family therapy is guided by systems theory, which believes that psychological problems of the individual must be approached as a dysfunction of life within the family. Rather than attempting to promote behavioral and cognitive changes in the dysfunctional individual alone, the family therapist views the family unit as the agent or system for achieving change. It is through the family that understanding of individual behavior is achieved. Actions by any single family member have an effect on all other family members. Family therapists may work with individuals, couples, parents and children, siblings, the nuclear family, the family of origin, and social networks in order to understand their clients' problems and to formulate a strategy for change.

**Ethical Standards in Family Therapy.** Gayla Margolin (1982) observed that the ethical questions facing the family therapist are even more different, numerous, and complicated than those faced by therapists who do individual therapy. In an attempt to provide guidance on how to deal with these ethical issues, the American Association of Marriage and Family Therapists published a Code of Ethics in 1991. The code addresses eight areas: (1) responsibility to clients; (2) confidentiality; (3) professional competence and integrity; (4) responsibility to students, employees, and supervisees; (5) responsibility to research participants; (6) responsibility to the profession; (7) fees; (8) advertising.

Most of these areas (areas 3 through 8) are essentially the same for individual and family therapists because they focus on only the therapist: his or her qualifications and training, behavior, and income. It is in the first two areas of responsibility to clients and confidentiality that unique ethical issues confront the family therapist. These unique ethical concerns have been summarized by Gerald Corey, Marianne Schneider Corey, and Patrick Callanan (1993) in four general areas:

*1. Treating the entire family.* Most family therapists believe that it is crucial for all members of the family to participate. Ethical questions arise when a family member or members refuse to participate. Coercing militant members to participate is unethical. Some therapists may withhold therapy until all members participate, but this strategy is controversial. Besides resembling coercion, it can be argued that this tactic denies therapy to the willing participants.

Conversely, Rachel T. Hare-Mustin (1981) contends that involving the whole family may not always be in the best interests of a particular member. Giving priority to the good of the entire family may jeopardize the legitimate goals or desires of that member. Ethical considerations require the therapist to minimize risks for any family member.

*2. Value system of the therapist.* The therapist's value system crucially influences the course of family therapy in two ways: first, when the therapist has values that are different from those of a member or members of the family, problems can arise; second, value systems influence the formulation and definition of the problems that are presented, the goals and plans for therapy, and the course the therapy takes. For example, Irene Goldenberg and Herbert Goldenberg (1991) contend that family therapists generally believe in maintaining the family way of life. Such a belief could, however, be harmful or inappropriate under some circumstances.

Ethical considerations demand that the therapist make known his or her attitudes and commitments to each family member. Gerald Corey et al. (1993) further state that it is not the function of the therapist to make decisions for clients or dictate how they should change. The therapist's role is to provide insight into family dynamics and to help and encourage the family to make necessary changes. The therapist must be aware of how his or her values can influence the course of therapy.

*3. The ethics of consulting.* This issue arises if one of the family members terminates joint sessions and begins therapy with another therapist. To complicate the situation further, Corey et al. (1993) pose a situation in which a person might persuade other family members to also consult with his or her therapist while still seeing their original therapist. Is this new therapist ethically obligated to consult with the original therapist? Are the two therapists ethically obligated to receive permission of their clients before talking with each other? Would it be ethical for the two therapists to ignore each other? These are difficult questions to answer.

*4. The issue of confidentiality.* In the course of family therapy, the therapist will see the family as a group and also individually. During individual sessions, of course, the client may divulge information that is not known to other family members. What is the ethically correct approach regarding the confidentiality of information revealed during these one-to-one sessions? Some therapists will not reveal such information. Other therapists believe that it is appropriate to reveal such information under appropriate circumstances that would benefit the rest of the family. Again, this is a difficult issue to resolve. The implications of revealing confidences can be serious. Revealing confidences may, however, facilitate resolution of the family's problems. Corey et al. (1993) suggest a middle position. The therapist is ethically obligated to inform the family that information revealed during private sessions may be divulged, if in the therapist's opinion that shared information would benefit the family. This position allows the therapist maximum flexibility and options to act in the family's best interests.

In conclusion, the increasing popularity and usefulness of family therapy requires sensitivity to and understanding of the unique ethical issues it can present to the family therapist.

—*Laurence Miller*

**See also** *Ethical Principles of Psychologists*; Group therapy; Therapist-patient relationship.

**BIBLIOGRAPHY**

Corey, Gerald, Marianne Schneider Corey, and Patrick Callanan. *Issues and Ethics in the Helping Professions.* Pacific Grove, Calif.: Brooks-Cole, 1993.

Goldenberg, Irene, and Herbert Goldenberg. *Family Therapy: An Overview.* Pacific Grove, Calif.: Brooks-Cole, 1991.

Margolin, Gayla. "Ethical and Legal Considerations in Marital and Family Therapy." *American Psychologist* 37 (July, 1982): 788-801.

Nichols, Michael P., and Richard C. Schwartz. *Family Therapy: Concepts and Methods.* 2d ed. Boston: Allyn & Bacon, 1991.

Patten, Christi, Therese Barnett, and Daniel Houlihan. "Ethics in Marital and Family Therapy: A Review of the Literature." *Professional Psychology: Research and Practice* 22 (April, 1991): 171-175.

## Family values

**TYPE OF ETHICS:** Personal and social ethics

**DATE:** 1980's to present

**DEFINITION:** Qualities of life that are necessary for the preservation of the social institution known as the "family," especially the nuclear family

**SIGNIFICANCE:** Variety in family types, individualism, the rights of children, and similar issues challenge traditional values and the traditional family unit itself

"Family values" is a complex concept, and such terms as "family," "family life," and "moral development" appear as frequently as does the term "family values." No one word or idea adequately expresses all that is involved; however, the two words in the phrase suggest two vital elements: a family unit and values that hold the family unit together so that both social and personal needs are met.

**Background.** "Family values" means, first of all, the existence of a family. In biblical thought (Gen. 1-2), the idea of family was integral to the creative activity of God. The beginning of humankind was cast in the form of family; namely, Adam and Eve and their children. Thus, values associated with the family are religious values or have religious connotations.

This religious idea of family carries through to the New Testament. When presenting a family code of behavior (Eph. 5-6), the Apostle Paul specifically drew on Old Testament concepts. Ephesians 5.31 refers to Genesis 2.24, and Ephesians 6.2-3 refers to the Ten Commandments. Paul gave the family code as an example of walking (living) the Christian life (Eph. 4.1, 17; 5.1, 8, 15). Then he placed the code within the context of mutual submission of family members to one another (Eph. 5.21). The code itself (5.22-6.9) further emphasized these mutually beneficial relationships with a literary framework that may have roots in Aristotle (*Politics*, book 1, chapters 3, 12, 13). Thus, Paul Christianized the code and raised the status of every family member by emphasizing genuine care and concern of the members for one another—care based on Christian principles. Finally, the passage on walking the Christian life concluded with a call for Christians to overcome evil, not only in the home but everywhere, by means of all the defensive and offensive armor provided by God (Eph. 6.10-20).

With this as its background, the Christian concept of family takes on an aura of religious commitment. A man leaves his father and mother and cleaves to his wife. A woman leaves her father and mother and cleaves to her husband.

**Love.** This commitment and the mutual care and concern of the members provides enough glue to hold the family together for its own sake and against all assaults from outside. Without the glue, the unit dissolves. Whatever the reasons for joining together in the first place, there is a sense of mutual responsibility and commitment. At the heart of the idea of "values" in "family values" is love.

For this reason, child abuse, for instance, is regarded as a heinous crime, not only because an individual is hurt but also because the whole concept of a caring family unit is endangered. Similarly, divorce is also regarded as the antithesis of family because it dissolves the unit. Because of these views, many religious groups reach out to embrace and care for these splintered families. The individuals are valued for themselves, and this caring also helps to preserve the picture of the ideal family by showing that splintering is not the ideal.

**Ideal Family.** In "family values," the ideal family is one with at least two essential poles: mother and father. Children are usually included in the ideal. This traditional concept is generally consistent with both philosophical commentary on the family and Christian views. In Christian thought, however, the ideal family is considered to be an instrument of God and the best means of fulfilling human needs and development.

Alternative family concepts challenge this ideal. Some of these alternatives result from necessity. Others exist because of choices people have made. For example, there are single-parent families with female or male parents, couples without children, and families with divorced or separated parents. The list can go on and on. According to traditional ideals of family values, however, these alternatives are not the ideal and are therefore deficient to some degree.

**Family Values, Not Business Values.** "Family values" are about the family, not about business or religion or politics, even though "family values" intersect other sets of values. For example, one set of "family values" may include belief in God as integral to the family itself. Obviously, this value intersects specifically religious values. Beliefs that prohibit family members from lying and stealing and cheating also affect other values. Economic, educational, and other social values interact with "family values." A family does not live in an ivory tower. Nevertheless, "family values" are usually given preference.

**Responsibility.** In order to have a family and "family values," someone must take responsibility for choosing and enforcing values. Someone must say, "We do this. We do not do that." Enforcing values usually has two aspects. On the one hand, someone must exercise discipline to enforce the values. On the other hand, someone must say, "I love you" and hold out a comforting embrace when the values are not met. Choosing and enforcing values in autonomous families is traditionally the task of parents, not that of state or social agencies.

*—S. M. Mayo*

**See also** Christian ethics; Family; Individualism; Love; Marriage.

**Bibliography**

Blustein, Jeffrey. *Parents and Children: The Ethics of the Family*. New York: Oxford University Press, 1982.

D'Antonio, William V., and Joan Aldous, eds. *Families and Religions: Conflict and Change in Modern Society*. Beverly Hills, Calif.: Sage Publications, 1983.

Herlihy, David. "Family." *American Historical Review* 96 (February, 1991): 1-16.

Scudder, C. W. *The Family in Christian Perspective*. Nashville: Broadman, 1962.

Stacey, Judith. *Brave New Families: Stories of Domestic Upheaval in Late Twentieth Century America*. New York: Basic Books, 1990.

Trueblood, Elton, and Pauline Trueblood. *The Recovery of Family Life*. New York: Harper, 1953.

## al-Fârâbî, Muḥammad ibn Muḥammad ibn Ṭarkhân

(870, Farab, north of Tashkent in Kazakhstan—950, Aleppo, Syria): Philosopher

**Type of ethics:** Religious ethics

**Achievements:** Author of *The Opinions of the Inhabitants of the Virtuous City* and *The Agreement of Plato and Aristotle*

**Significance:** Influential in Islamicate ethics and in medieval Europe, al-Fârâbî attempted a reconciliation of Plato, Aristotle, and Neoplatonic thought, along with providing original insights

Al-Fârâbî's ethical thought is intimately intertwined with his Neoplatonic emanation scheme, in which the One generates a hierarchy of concentric spheres. The Intellect of the lunar sphere (the Active Intellect) emanates pure intelligibles to the human realm. In *The Opinions of the Inhabitants of the Virtuous City*, al-Fârâbî argued that the immortality of the soul was dependent on its actualization in apprehension of that Intellect. The virtuous city is well-led, so that its citizens are reminded of a life beyond this one. Its citizens achieve moral virtue, which allows reason to govern appetites and passions, *and* they turn their attention to the gifts of the Active Intellect. Such souls find bliss in the afterlife. Less-actualized souls simply cease to exist (if they were ignorant of the Active Intellect) or, if they were excessively attached to bodily pleasures, endure a limited series of transmigrations or torment caused by separation from the body after death. Al-Fârâbî had an important place in the philosophy of Avicenna, Albertus Magnus, and, through them, Saint Thomas Aquinas.

**See also** Avicenna; Islamic ethics.

*Italian fascist dictator Benito Mussolini* (National Archives)

## Fascism

**TYPE OF ETHICS:** Politico-economic ethics

**DATE:** Coined 1919

**ASSOCIATED WITH:** The dictatorships of Adolf Hitler and Benito Mussolini

**DEFINITION:** The word "fascism," which derives from ancient Roman symbols of authority called *fasces*, denotes a governmental system or political belief advocating total control over the citizenry

**SIGNIFICANCE:** Fascism severely restricts or eliminates personal liberty; punishes opponents by imprisonment, torture, or death; and regards all peoples not of the officially decreed nationality as inferior

Like communism, fascism is a type of totalitarian system that attempts to control every aspect of life (political, economic, and personal), usually through a secret police force. Unlike communism, however, fascism allows private ownership of industry as long as the government or its authorities are served. Fascism also promotes extreme patriotism ("state over self"), militarism, and the organized persecution of minorities. A fascist government controls newspapers, radio, and other means of communication in order to issue propaganda supporting its policies and to silence all opposing views. Some historians trace the origins of modern fascism to the dictatorship of Napoleon Bonaparte I of France, who controlled his country through some fascist means. Later dictators adopted many of his methods, as well as harsher ones. Benito Mussolini, who first used the term "fascism," controlled Italy from 1922 to 1943. In Germany (where fascism reached its zenith) Adolf Hitler and his fascist party (Nazis) began in 1933 to wipe out all opposition and systematically destroy the Jewish race, Slavs, gypsies, the mentally ill, and other "inferior" groups. In the 1930's, fascist parties gained much support in Hungary, Japan, Romania, and Spain. Fascists usually come to power after some national disaster by promising to revive the economy and to restore national pride.

**See also** Hitler, Adolf; Natural rights; Nazism; Oppression; Tyranny.

## Fatalism

**TYPE OF ETHICS:** Beliefs and practices

**DATE:** From antiquity

**DEFINITION:** The belief that all events are predetermined by forces beyond human intentionality and activity, and hence that one's destiny cannot be altered

**SIGNIFICANCE:** Fatalism inclines one toward resignation or acceptance of the role of factors in life that are larger and stronger than personal moral initiative; submission to one's destiny is the ultimate ethical wisdom

Fatalism is a concept as ancient as civilization and as widespread as the human race. The English word "fate" is from the Latin root *fatum*, meaning "oracle" or "prophecy." Both the Greeks and Romans were persuaded that three goddesses, the

Fates—Atropos, Clotho, and Lachesis—determined one's destiny. Similar beliefs, however, were evidenced in Celtic, Germanic, and other mythologies, in which "norms" or "powers" overruled human desires and initiative. Fatalism is apparent in the Hindu concept of *karma* (the factor that binds one to cycles of rebirth), the Muslim teaching of *kismet* ("one's allotted role"), and certain types of Christian predestinationism. Modern philosophies and psychologies have offered "fatalism" in "secular garb," viewing history or personality as being controlled by impersonal and amoral forces.

**See also** Accountability; Determinism and freedom.

## Fâṭima

(c. 606, Mecca, Arabia—632, Medina, Arabia): Daughter of Muḥammad

**Type of ethics:** Religious ethics

**Achievements:** An exemplar of piety, spiritual purity, and spiritual power in Islam

**Significance:** Revered throughout the Islamic world as an exemplary woman and as the matriarch of the house of ʿAlî.

The daughter of Khadîja and the Prophet Muḥammad, Fâṭima was married (in August, 623, or June, 624) to the Prophet's cousin, ʿAlî ibn Abî Ṭâlib, and was the mother of Ḥusayn and Ḥasan. She and Khadîja were the women most beloved by the Prophet, and the tragedies that befell her husband and sons contribute to the pathos of her story. Reverence for Fâṭima, whose father is the Prophet, is so deep that she is often referred to as *umm abîhâ* ("her father's mother"). The Qur'*ân* refers to God's wish "to remove uncleanness far from" the "Folk of the Household" of the Prophet (*sûra* 33:33). Fâṭima is often included in that Household, which has contributed to her popular image as a paradigm of purity (much as Mary the mother of Jesus is revered in Islam). Such spiritual purity brings with it spiritual power (*barakat)*, and Fâṭima is often asked to intercede on behalf of the faithful. Fâṭima, ʿAlî, and their descendants are still specially honored as *sâdât* (singular, *sayyid*) or *ashrâf* (singular, *sharîf*), and widely believed to participate still in the residual *barakat* of Muḥammad.

**See also** ʿAlî ibn Abî Ṭâlib; Ḥusayn ibn ʿAlî; Islamic ethics; Muḥammad al-Muṣṭafâ.

## Fear

**Type of ethics:** Business and labor ethics

**Date:** 1960's

**Definition:** An emotion experienced in the face of threats or danger that a person feels unable to control

**Significance:** Fear is both a cause of and a result of unethical behavior

Fear is fuel for unethical behavior, and unethical actions are fuel for fear. Fear is therefore both a cause of, and a result of, unethical behavior. When people manage ethically, they do not operate in an environment of fear. Fear is an emotion experienced in the face of threats or danger that one feels unable to control. It has two components: the presence or perception of a danger or threat and a lack of control over the danger or threat. Kathleen Ryan and Daniel Oestreich, in their book *Driving Fear Out of the Workplace* (1991), observe, "We see fear as a background phenomenon that undermines the commitment, motivation, and confidence of people at work. It is most easily observed as a reluctance to speak up about needed changes, improvements, or other important work issues."

**Effects Of Fear.** Managers often do not see the impact of fear because it is hidden in the process of how the work gets done. The cost of having fear in the workplace can be figured out by examining the influence of negative emotions on people's work. Ryan and Oestreich's research indicates that the two greatest impacts fear has on an organization are negative feelings about the organization and decreased quality and productivity. Fear translates into a loss of trust and pride, and employees often react to fear by increasing self-protective behavior. Negative feelings about the organization also result in sabotage (theft, fraud, and the destruction of company property). Fear translates into a lasting resentment, the making and hiding of mistakes, or failure to meet deadlines and budgets. W. Edwards Deming has said that quality is impossible to achieve when people are afraid to tell the truth. They fear being ethical. Scrap and breakage are hidden, numbers and schedules are misrepresented, and bad products are shipped to customers because someone is afraid to stop the production line.

Fear shows up in "falsifying" reports and overpromising customers. Employees may not ask for personal time off for fear that their supervisors will not understand and their requests will be denied, so they lie and call in sick. Falsifying reports, overpromising customers, and calling in sick when one is not soon become the norm. Employees become used to behaving unethically. There is an old saying, "It is easy to tell a lie, but difficult to tell only one." Negative feelings about the organization make unethical behavior easier to live with.

Fear is often at the center of "whistleblowing." The employee fears the results of the improper activity (harm to employees, customers, or the community) and also management's reaction. He or she feels pushed to go outside to have the injustice resolved. The employee does not trust management to handle the problem.

**What Creates Fear?** The employee's relationship with his or her immediate supervisor has the most impact on creating fear. Ambiguous or abusive behavior destroys trust. Other behaviors contributing to fear are blaming, insulting, and ignoring. A manager who is not fair, who plays favorites, or takes credit for an employee's idea invites mistrust from subordinates and executives. Unethical actions such as asking employees to mislead and lie to customers send a signal that perhaps the employees are being misled and lied to as well. Ethical management is at the center of efforts to create an atmosphere in which fear cannot survive. A good relationship with one's manager is a start.

The systems, procedures, and culture of the organization also contribute to fear. Will the company support the employee or not? The employee asks, "My manager is okay, but if I complain to the human resources department about a sexual harassment incident, will I be labeled a trouble-maker and laid off in the next round of cutbacks? Is top management really concerned about people, customers, and employees? Is the leadership honest and does it convey a sense of integrity? Is management honestly communicating to employees about the health of the company?" The prevalence of rumors signals a culture of fear.

In an atmosphere of fear, managers and employees do not trust one another. Managers believe that employees are manipulative and operate only on the basis of self-interest. Employees worry that their managers will put their own self-interest ahead of the needs of employees and customers. Each group fears the other and reacts out of fear. It becomes a self-propagating behavior. If I fear that you will act first in your self-interest, I will interpret all your actions in the light of that fear, and react accordingly with self-preserving behavior and retaliation. It is not difficult to imagine the unethical actions that permeate such an environment.

**Fear and Unethical Behavior.** Laura Nash says, in *Good Intentions Aside* (1990), "I cannot think of a single ethical problem in business that does not rest on a . . . betrayal of trust." Which comes first, lack of trust and fear or unethical behavior? Fear is not the only cause of unethical behavior. Another cause is the lack of awareness of the ethical implications of decision making. Unethical behavior is not fear's only result. Good employees often leave a company in which there is an environment of fear. Fear is both a cause of and a result of unethical behavior. It is a red flag, a signal that the health of the organization needs attention. If company employees and managers look for the effects of fear and take action to develop an atmosphere of trust, the ethical pulse of the organization will improve accordingly.

Howard Putnam, in *The Winds Of Turbulence* (1991), summarizes fear's effect: "Fear is the most imposing barrier to transformation. Fear flows from the feelings of instability caused by dealing with the unknown, and it can strangle creative thinking."

*—Kathleen D. Purdy*

**See also** Trust.

**BIBLIOGRAPHY**

Covey, Stephen R. *Principle-Centered Leadership.* New York: Simon & Schuster, 1992.

DeGeorge, Richard T. "Whistle-Blowing." In *Business Ethics*. 3rd ed. New York: MacMillan, 1990.

Nash, Laura L. *Good Intentions Aside.* Boston: Har vard Business School Press, 1990.

Putnam, Howard D. *The Winds of Turbulence.* New York: Harper Business, 1991.

Ryan, Kathleen D., and Oestreich, Daniel K. *Driving Fear Out of the Workplace.* San Francisco: Jossey-Bass, 1991.

## Feminine Mystique, The: Book

**TYPE OF ETHICS:** Sex and gender issues

**DATE:** Published 1963

**AUTHOR:** Betty Friedan

**SIGNIFICANCE:** Challenged the view (that prevailed in the 1950's and 1960's) that women should be completely (and only) fulfilled by their roles as wives, mothers, and homemakers

*Betty Friedan, author of The Feminine Mystique*

Friedan defined the feminine mystique as the myth of female fulfillment based on domestic labor and proposed that the myth is based on a vision of woman not as a whole person but only in terms of her sexual role. This limiting view of woman, which further suggested that a woman's value could only be expressed through her potential as wife and mother, discouraged women from pursuing educations or professions, thus effectively trapping them within the myth. According to Friedan, post-World War II economic and social factors combined to force American women to confine their interests and energies solely to serving their husbands and children through their roles as housewives, a situation that led women to devalue themselves and their contributions to society. She based this assessment in part on extensive interviews with women, many of whom were highly educated and were plagued with feelings of frustration, guilt, and inadequacy because they were not completely satisfied by the rewards of homemaking. These women felt isolated from one another and alienated from society by their failure to conform to the myth. Friedan asserted that women must look outside the narrow role assigned to them by the feminine mystique in order to discover identity and fulfillment.

**See also** Women's ethics; Women's liberation movement.

## Feminism

**TYPE OF ETHICS:** Sex and gender issues

**DATE:** Coined 1895; American feminist movement began in 1848

**ASSOCIATED WITH:** The women's rights movement

**DEFINITION:** The view that inequality between women and men exists, is unjust, and must be corrected

**SIGNIFICANCE:** Feminism raises questions about the meaning of equality, the nature of the family, and the ethical obligations of women and men

American society claims to offer "liberty and justice for all" in a context in which "all men are created equal." Feminists allege that this second statement is taken literally in the United States, which grants liberty, justice, and equality to men but has failed to extend it to women. Feminists emphasize that some of the negative aspects of women's lives provide evidence of women's subordinate status. They have pointed out that although women constitute half of the work force outside the home, they earn only two-thirds of what men earn and are overwhelmingly concentrated in low-wage jobs. Feminists see this as a lack of equality for women. Feminists have brought to public consciousness statistics showing that women are the targets of violence and harassment by men both inside and outside the home and that they are often subjected to further harassment when they report the initial abuse. Feminists see this as a lack of justice for women. Feminists see women as having minimal control over their reproductive capacities, since the availability of birth control is decided by legislators and pregnancy, and labor and birth are managed largely by male physicians. Feminists see this as a lack of liberty for women. Furthermore, feminists believe that media portrayals of women as mindless bodies available for sexual use by men perpetuate the view that women need not be regarded as persons. From the feminist perspective, women should be regarded as persons in and of themselves. Therefore, women deserve the same rights as men both within the family and in the larger society. The feminist agenda for change is to bring about liberty, justice, and equality for women through a variety of strategies.

**Varieties of Feminism.** In the popular media, "feminists" are portrayed as a unified group, with a single set of goals or values. Actually, "feminism" is the name for a variety of views about what constitutes a just society, what is inequitable and unjust in the relationships between women and men in society, and what are the ethical methods for achieving justice and equality. The different feminist views inform the various agendas for change pursued by feminists in the United States and other countries. The views have been articulated clearly by feminist scholars in philosophy, sociology, and political science. The three views that inform most feminist thought and action are called "liberal feminism," "socialist feminism," and "radical feminism."

According to liberal feminists, in a just society, women and men would have equal opportunities to compete in the educational, economic, and political marketplaces. Given this opportunity, women would reach high levels of achievement. According to liberal feminists, women have been denied opportunities for achievement because practices that discriminate against them, such as unequal pay, sexual harassment on the job, inadequate family leave policies, and different career tracks for women and men, are not illegal. Just laws would promote the equality of women by prohibiting practices that impede women's climb to success.

According to socialist feminists, in a just society, the relationships between women and men would be regulated by respect and love rather than by their reactions to economic forces. Because the capitalist economic system concentrates wealth in the hands of a few large business owners, the vast majority of women and men are low-wage workers in factory or service jobs. Men who are at the bottom of a hierarchy in the workplace compensate by asserting their dominance over women at home. Women are forced to marry and, sometimes, to remain in abusive marriages in order to support themselves and their children financially. Because the inequality of women is caused by an unjust economic system, the way to bring about equality, according to socialist feminists, is to reform the economic system. Reforms proposed by socialist feminists include educating employers in business ethics, expanding government programs that aid the poor, passing legislation that limits the power of large businesses to grow, and promoting the growth of worker-owned businesses in which all owners share profits equally.

Radical feminists believe that the men who hold power in society abuse that power by consciously and deliberately blocking women's access to it. One way to do this is to portray women as unsuitable for the exercise of power. Radical feminists believe that in a just society, individuals and groups would have both the power to define themselves and the freedom not to arrange their lives in conformity with culturally accepted stereotypes. Women as well as men are constrained in thought and action by mainstream beliefs about what it means to be female and male, feminine and masculine. For example, men may feel that they must be aggressive to be masculine and women may feel that they must be passive to be feminine, beliefs that perpetuate problems of domestic violence. Women must take the lead in reforming thinking about sex and gender by forming exclusively female organizations with the power to define their own values and goals. Radical feminists distrust reforms that come through established social institutions such as the law or the economy. Such reforms, they believe, can easily be co-opted by selfish individuals or groups so that changes that appear to serve women may in the long run oppress them further. (An example of such reform is protective labor legislation, which was initially designed to make factory work conditions safe for women but which finally made employers decide that compliance with these laws made it too expensive to hire women at the same wages as men.)

Many women who consider themselves feminists have challenged the three mainstream feminist views on the grounds that they do not aim adequately at the goal of liberty, justice, and equality for *all* women. Some feminists who are lesbians argue that mainstream feminism is so focused on reforming the relationships between women and men that the interests of women who live with women are not considered. Poor women, women of color, and Third World women argue that mainstream feminism has been too focused on issues of concern to upper-middle-class white women, whose access to professional advancement often has been bought by paying low wages to poor women to take over childcare and housecleaning responsibilities. Cultural feminists claim that mainstream feminists are so focused on women's equality in the professional, economic, and political arenas that they devalue the significant cultural accomplishments of traditional women through the ages and across cultures in such areas as folk art, folk dance, and religion.

**Family Values.** All varieties of feminists say that if women are to have the freedom to achieve professionally or to define new sex roles, they must first have the freedom to make choices about reproduction and childcare. Therefore, the fundamental family-values issue raised by feminism is whether biology is destiny. In other words, if women's bodies are designed to produce babies after sexual intercourse, then is it the responsibility of sexually active women to devote their lives to rearing children? The traditional nonfeminist answer is yes, on the grounds that women must recognize and respect the fact that God created them with the ability to bear children. In response, feminist author Shulamith Firestone asserted in 1971 that human beings are distinguished from animals by their ability to control their environment through technology. As human beings, women have the privilege of using the technology of birth control and, in the foreseeable future, artificial reproduction to have children when and how they desire. Therefore, feminists advocate the free use of birth control and, when birth control fails, the easy availability of safe and legal abortions. Even if destroying a fetus is destroying a future human being, feminists argue that the quality of life of the mother, a fully developed human being with goals and plans, is of primary importance.

After women give birth, someone must care for the children. The traditional American family structure is one in which the man works outside the home to provide financial support for a woman and children at home. Traditionalists view this arrangement as natural, saying that men are better suited for the aggressive world of work and women are better suited for the caring communal life of the family. For a traditionalist, it is unethical to go against the order of nature. Philosopher John Locke, however, pointed out in 1690 that people have no way of knowing what women's and men's natural roles are, since they have never seen women or men raised outside of a particular society with its norms for gendered behavior. In 1869, philosophers John Stuart Mill and Harriet Taylor extended Locke's point, arguing that it is irresponsible to praise the status quo without looking to see which alternative arrangements of the relations between women and men might be better.

Following Mill and Taylor's suggestion, contemporary feminists have proposed a number of alternative arrangements for the care of children. Some liberal feminists have argued that because women's participation in the work force benefits employers, employers ought to make it easier for women to participate by offering childcare programs, family leave, and job sharing. Liberal feminists lobby legislatures to pass laws requiring employers to offer these benefits. Some socialist feminists have argued that the responsibility for providing adequate childcare falls upon the government, whose job it is to provide basic necessities for its citizens. These feminists believe that free public education should begin at birth in the form of safe, professionally staffed childcare centers. Some radical feminists believe that gender roles within the family should be restructured. Men should take responsibility for the care of their children just as women do. Each parent or set of parents needs to decide who will be responsible for which family maintenance tasks, including childcare, housecleaning, cooking, shopping, and earning money.

Feminist journalist Susan Faludi has pointed out that some antifeminists interpret many women's frustration with the dual life of career and family to mean that women are realizing that caring for a family is the natural vocation of women. Faludi has responded to the antifeminists by pointing out that the support necessary for women with families to succeed in the workplace has not been provided by employers, husbands, or the government. According to Faludi, employers, husbands, and the government have failed to fulfill their responsibilities to women and hide their guilt by blaming women for their own failures.

**Feminist Ethics.** Feminist ethics provide an alternative to traditional women's ethics. In keeping with the traditionalist view that women are well-suited to caring for home and family, traditionalists say that women should display those virtues that preserve a traditionally structured family. For example, philosopher and theologian Saint Augustine asserted (c. 400) that since the natural order is for a man to lead a household and a woman to follow her husband, an intelligent woman is one who has the ability to follow orders, while an intelligent man is one who has the ability to give orders. Philosopher David Hume argued that women must display the virtues of chastity and modesty, because if a wife is unfaithful, her husband can never be certain that the children who are inheriting his property are really his. Since no such problem arises when a husband is unfaithful, chastity and modesty should not be required of men. Philosopher Jean-Jacques Rousseau, who wrote on the education of women (1762), believed that women should avoid cultivating any special talents and instead learn to be obedient, attractive, and cunning, since it is only by periodically withholding sex that a woman can keep a man interested in her and so preserve her marriage and her family. In contrast, Rousseau thought that men should learn to be self-sufficient, strong, and honorable.

Liberal feminists respond to the traditionalist view by saying that in fact women and men have the same virtues and that both sexes should be held to the same ethical standards. For example, liberal feminist Mary Wollstonecraft responded to the traditionalists (1792) by saying that because women and men are both human beings, they have the same ethical obligations. Human beings are distinguished from animals by their ability to shape their emotions and morals through reason. Therefore, the cultivation of reason, which leads to self-control, independence, and orderly thinking, is the basic responsibility of every human being. Rational people can respect one another, and, in fact, a happy and stable marriage can be achieved only if the partners respect each other. Liberal feminists do recognize, however, that society is a long way from their ideal and that women are often evaluated negatively when they display virtues that are traditionally thought of as men's virtues. For example, feminist studies of workplace behaviors show that women are often viewed as poor managers if they display decisiveness, aggressiveness, and competitiveness, while men who display these same behaviors are perceived as effective managers.

Radical feminists argue that women must define their own ethics as they redefine their social role. They must not merely seek to follow standards of behavior set for men. Radical feminist Mary Daly believes that women should reject traditional Christian accounts of men's and women's virtues. Those virtues are merely a smoke screen behind which power-hungry bishops hide their true natures, while calling on others to be "humble," "meek," and "loving" so that they will not also seek power. Daly can say what the new feminist ethics will not be—they will not be based on hierarchy and deception—but she cannot say what they will be, for women must engage in the process of unmasking deception before they can construct their own ethics.

Some women psychologists, sociologists, and philosophers have allied themselves with cultural feminism by defining a distinctively feminine approach to ethics. The approach developed as a response to the work of Harvard psychologist Lawrence Kohlberg (1981), who studied boys in order to discover the stages of moral development. Kohlberg found that the most mature level of ethical decision making was the application of abstract rules of justice without regard to the individuals involved in particular situations. In later studies, Kohlberg found that women rarely reach this highest level of development. Instead, they always seem to be concerned with particular individuals and about how other people will evaluate their decisions. Kohlberg's feminist colleague, Harvard psychologist Carol Gilligan (1982), studied girls as well as boys and found that many women who make mature ethical decisions follow principles that they consider higher than abstract rules of justice. These women apply an "ethic of care," in which every ethical decision aims at preserving relationships with others. Within an ethic of care, it is important to consider the needs of the individuals involved and to be concerned about what others think, since enhancing the emotional and physical well-being of others is a factor in every ethical decision.

Many feminist thinkers have adopted the ethic of care and used it to argue that women have a special responsibility to work toward peace, racial harmony, and concern for the environment. For example, Sara Ruddick writes that the virtues women learn through mothering—the ability to preserve, nurture, and train others—should be used in the political sphere to work toward peace. Ecofeminists such as Susan Griffin and Karen Warren believe that women's ability to care for others who are different from them gives women a special affinity with animals and plants. Women have the responsibility to articulate that affinity as they work toward the ethical treatment of animals and nondestructive farming practices. Philosopher Maria Lugones draws on women's ability to empathize when she suggests that racial understanding can best be achieved by giving up arrogant perceptions and seeing the lives of others from their points of view.

An equal number of feminist thinkers, however, have questioned the ethic of care. To some, the ethic of care appears to be a simple restatement of the traditional feminine virtues that pointed women toward a narrow devotion to home and family. To others (such as Sandra Lee Bartky), the ethic of care, if misapplied, can lead to moral evil. For example, women have nurtured their war criminal husbands, later confessing that they wanted to leave them because they disapproved of the moral atrocities their husbands were committing. To still other feminist thinkers, the ethic of care is a simplistic description of women's moral reasoning.

Women apply the ethic of care when it is appropriate, and apply other types of ethical thinking, including the ethics of justice, when they are appropriate.

—*Laura Duhan Kaplan*

**See also** Abortion; Equal pay for equal work; Equal Rights Amendment (ERA); *The Feminine Mystique*; National Organization for Women (NOW); Pornography; Rape; *The Second Sex*; Sexism; Sexual abuse and harassment; Sexual stereotypes; Suffrage; Wage discrimination; Women's ethics; Women's liberation movement.

**Bibliography**


Faludi, Susan. *Backlash: The Undeclared War Against American Women*. New York: Crown, 1991. A meticulously researched refutation of the view that feminism is destructive to society and harmful to women.

Gilligan, Carol. *In a Different Voice: Psychological Theory and Women's Development*. Cambridge, Mass.: Harvard University Press, 1982. An articulation of the ethic of care, supported with interviews and case studies of women's ethical decision making.

Jaggar, Alison M., and Paula S. Rothenberg, eds. *Feminist Frameworks: Alternative Theoretical Accounts of the Relations Between Women and Men*. 3d ed. New York: McGraw Hill, 1992. An anthology of popular articles laying out the basic social and ethical issues raised by the different varieties of feminism.

Kourany, Janet A., James P. Sterba, and Rosemarie Tong, eds. *Feminist Philosophies*. Englewood Cliffs, N.J.: Prentice-Hall, 1991. An anthology of scholarly articles. Part 1 presents feminist perspectives on socialization, sex, work, violence, and the family. Part 2 presents the different feminist views about what constitutes a just society and how it can be achieved.

Rossi, Alice S., ed. *The Feminist Papers*. 1973. Reprint. Boston: Northeastern University Press, 1988. Excerpts from the writings of leading feminist activists and thinkers from 1771 to 1949. Includes excellent biographical and thematic introductions to each excerpt, laying out the major issues with which feminists grapple.

Ruddick, Sara. *Maternal Thinking: Toward a Politics of Peace*. New York: Ballantine Books, 1990. A literary-philosophical defense of the thesis that women learn a special ethical perspective through the practice of mothering.

Schneir, Miriam, ed. *Feminism: The Essential Historical Writings*. New York: Random House, 1971. A collection of brief excerpts from the writings of famous feminist activists and thinkers from 1776 through 1929, designed to present an easy-to-read introduction to the history of feminist thought.

Tong, Rosemarie. Feminist Thought: A Comprehensive Introduction. Boulder, Colo.: Westview Press, 1989. A textbook-like summary of the conflicting views of different varieties of feminists on such philosophical topics as ethics, politics, knowledge, and education.


## First Amendment

**Type of ethics:** Civil rights

**Date:** 1791

**Associated with:** Constitution of the United States

**Definition:** The First Amendment to the Constitution of the United States provides that the federal government may not establish a religion, interfere with an individual's

**First Amendment Controversies**

| Issue | Reasons to Limit | Reasons Not to Limit |
|---|---|---|
| Does the First Amendment protect the right of members of the Native American Church to smoke peyote as part of their religious rituals? | Peyote is a controlled substance. To permit its use might endanger the lives of the user and others. | The free exercise of religion by the Native American Church requires the use of peyote. Freedom of religion should not be infringed. |
| Does the First Amendment protect the right of art galleries to display publicly artworks that may be considered obscene or offensive? | The First Amendment does not protect pornography or obscenity. If a work is considered offensive by people in the community, it should not be displayed. | Freedom of speech and freedom of the press imply free expression. Art is in the eye of the beholder. |
| Does the First Amendment protect those who burn the American flag in violation of state laws? | The flag is the country's most important symbol. State governments ought to be allowed to protect it. | Burning the flag is as legitimate an act of protest as speaking out against a government policy. Preventing flag-burning would be banning a form of political expression. |
| Should schools and public libraries ban books that contain racially offensive terms? | Use of some racial terms is offensive and may lower the self-esteem of minority students. | Censorship restricts the flow of ideas. Students would be prevented from reading literature that was written in a time when such terms were considered more acceptable. |
| Should the press be allowed to print any government documents? | The press's freedom should be restricted to ensure national security. | Government decisions should be exposed to the will of the people. |
| Should newspapers and the media be allowed access to participants in a trial before a verdict has been delivered? | Unlimited discussion of trial-related matters in a public forum may infringe upon Fifth Amendment rights to due process. | Matters of public concern should be open for discussion. |

religious liberty, or abridge freedom of speech, press, or assembly or the right to petition the government for a redress of grievances

**SIGNIFICANCE:** The freedoms of religion and speech are the central guarantees that neither the government nor its officials may interfere with an individual's conscience; where these liberties exist, people are free to believe what they wish, pursue any inquiries they may wish to make, and freely criticize the government and its policies

For the framers of the Bill of Rights, the freedoms of religion and speech were the most important substantive liberties. Years of struggle, often violent, between Protestants and Catholics in England persuaded Americans that the government should have no role in promoting religion or in controlling religious observances. Three additional themes provide the most common justifications for considering these the "first" liberties: The first stresses the value of liberty of conscience in promoting individual self-realization and self-expression, the second emphasizes the importance of free communication and discussion for informing the citizenry in a representative democracy, and the last emphasizes the value of free discussion in establishing truth in the "marketplace of ideas."

First Amendment questions often arise in the United States, and many Supreme Court cases have been devoted to settling such issues as subversive advocacy, obscenity, school pr, and flag burning.

**See also** Bill of Rights, U.S.; Mill, John Stuart; *Sedition Act of 1798.*

## Five precepts

**TYPE OF ETHICS:** Religious ethics

**DATE:** c. Sixth century

**ASSOCIATED WITH:** Buddhism

**DEFINITION:** The Buddhist vows to abstain from taking life, stealing, sexual misconduct, lying, and using intoxicants

**SIGNIFICANCE:** The five precepts, which are incumbent upon all Buddhists, both laity and priests, are the basic ethical tenets of Buddhism

Traditionally associated with the Buddha (Siddhārtha Gautama, c. 563-c. 483 B.C.E.) but generally taught in older Hinduism as well, the five precepts are roughly equivalent to the ethical rules in the Ten Commandments. (1) The precept to abstain from taking life includes any intention to use either direct or indirect means to cause death. It refers not only to human but also to other animal life. As a consequence, most Buddhists are vegetarians. (2) The precept to abstain from taking what is not given includes trickery and gambling as well as outright stealing. The blameworthiness of an offense depends partly on the value of whatever is stolen and partly on the worth of its owner. (3) The precept to abstain from sexual misconduct precludes homosexual sexual relations as well as heterosexual relations with family members, married persons, concubines, slaves, and others. For monks, the precept requires celibacy. (4) The precept to abstain from false speech refers to words and actions that are intended to deceive others. It also prohibits deliberately concealing the truth. (5) The precept to abstain from intoxicants includes both alcohol and other drugs that dull the mind. These precepts are supplemented by as many as five more for monks or serious lay practitioners.

**See also** Ahiṁsā; Buddhist ethics.

## Forgiveness

**TYPE OF ETHICS:** Personal and social ethics

**DATE:** Appears in the oldest traditions of the Old Testament, approximately tenth century B.C.E.

**ASSOCIATED WITH:** Christianity, Jesus, Judaism, and virtue ethics

**DEFINITION:** The act of intentionally ending hatred or other negative emotions one has toward a person who has morally wronged or seriously disappointed one

**SIGNIFICANCE:** Forgiveness is a defining characteristic of God in the Judeo-Christian tradition and a central human virtue in Christian ethics, but it is a questionable virtue in modern secular ethics

The concept of forgiveness occurred first as a revealed characteristic of God: God announced to Moses that God forgives creatures' sin (Exodus 34:6-7). Early Judaism (c. 250 B.C.E. to 200 c.e.) taught that forgiveness was a personal virtue for humans. The New Testament commands people always to forgive one another, because they all have enjoyed God's forgiveness (Matthew 5:7, 6:12, 14-15, 18:21-35; Ephesians 4:32; Colossians 3:13; and the book of Philemon).

Outside this Judeo-Christian context, a forgiving spirit has been called a vice rather than a virtue. Moral philosophers since the 1970's have examined in the context of secular ethics both the definition of forgiveness and the ethics of forgiveness (Is a readiness to forgive always a virtue for humans? Is forgiveness a duty?). Here are some highlights of this rich debate.

What is forgiveness? (1) The occasion for forgiveness entails one (or someone one identifies with—as a parent identifies with her child, for example) being mistreated by someone. This offense may be moral wrongdoing, but it is also possible to forgive close friends when they do nothing morally wrong but deeply disappoint one. (2) Forgiveness is not an emotion itself, but it involves letting go of negative emotions such as hatred, contempt, or deep disappointment toward the offender. Forgiveness may be a decision, but often it is a difficult process of construing in a new way the mistreatment and the offender, and this process is only partially under one's control. (3) Either way, forgiveness must be deliberate and directed toward mistreatment. Simply forgetting about it, and coming to see it as not mistreatment after all, and engaging a therapist to focus one's attention away from it are ways of curbing negative emotions caused by the injury, but they do not count as forgiving the offender. Also (4), the reason for forgiving must be concern for the offender's welfare or some other concern for others. Letting go of negative emotions only because one is tired of dealing with them might be advisable sometimes, but it is not forgiveness, because it is self-absorbed.

A forgiving spirit has seemed to many to be a virtue because forgiveness appears to be a morally acceptable, healthy way of dealing with negative emotions. Hatred or disappointment, when harbored, begin to distort one's moral sensitivity and sense of fairness toward others. Releasing these emotions helps one to see and to act morally. In the context of a personal relationship, forgiveness enables us to reestablish the intimacy and caring we enjoyed.

Is forgiveness always morally acceptable? Consider a tough case. Suppose a person motivated by cruelty hurts one in a serious way. Self-respect and respect for the moral law (which includes condemnation of all malicious wrongdoing) causes one to be angry at this cruel offense. Why should one ever give up one's righteous indignation and forgive the offender? If one forgives, will one not either ignore wrongdoing or cease to condemn it? Either way (by willful ignorance of or lack of concern for moral offense) one will endorse cruel treatment of others and fail to respect oneself as a person valued by the moral community. In this case, is not forgiveness morally wrong?

Granted, if one's ultimate loyalty is to an abstract moral order, forgiveness in this and other such cases would be unacceptable. The order must be preserved, and one must do one's part to preserve it by harboring righteous hatred for serious moral offenders. We cannot afford to "hate the sin but love the sinner." In the context of a secular ethic, a generous, forgiving spirit would be a vice.

Yet in the Judeo-Christian worldview from which the concept of personal forgiveness originated, one's ultimate loyalty is to a generous God who desires the moral growth and flourishing of each created person. The moral order is important in this perspective, but human loyalty to it is part of one's fundamental commitment to God. When one is cruelly treated, one naturally responds with anger first. Yet one prays to see the situation from God's point of view. As one deeply enters God's perspective, one continues to see the offense honestly, in all of its cruelty, and the offender as malicious. One also sees the offender in a more complex way, however, as a person with problems, hurting herself and others, and yet a person deeply loved by a God who can reform and correct her. A Christian must leave to God the role of judge and executioner, and accept a role as a coworker with God in caring for the offender. This perspective enables one to love the offender, while maintaining self-respect and respect for the moral order.

The recent debate on forgiveness highlights key differences between secular and Judeo-Christian ethics. These differing moral evaluations of forgiveness remind one that ethical theories cannot be fully understood or evaluated apart from the worldviews that they presuppose.

*—Robert B. Kruschwitz*

**See also** Christian ethics; Jesus; Jewish ethics; Mercy; Revenge; Secular ethics; Sin; Virtue.

**BIBLIOGRAPHY**

Adams, Marilyn McCord. "Forgiveness: A Christian Model." *Faith and Philosophy* 8, no. 3 (July, 1991): 277-304.

Haber, Joram Graf. *Forgiveness.* Savage, Md.: Rowman & Littlefield, 1991.

Kselman, John, James H. Charlesworth, and Gary S. Shogren. "Forgiveness." In *The Anchor Bible Dictionary, Volume II*, edited by David N. Freedman. New York: Doubleday, 1992.

Murphy, Jeffrie G., and Jean Hampton. *Forgiveness and Mercy.* Cambridge, England: Cambridge University Press, 1988.

Richards, Norvin. "Forgiveness." *Ethics* 99, No. 1 (October, 1988): 77-97.

## Foucault, Michel (Oct. 15, 1926, Poitiers, France—June 25, 1984, Paris, France): Philosopher

**TYPE OF ETHICS:** Modern history

**ACHIEVEMENTS:** Author of *Folie et déraison: Histoire de la folie à l'âge classique* (1961; *Madness and Civilization: A History of Insanity in the Age of Reason*, 1965), *Surveiller et punir: Naissance de la prison* (1975; *Discipline and Punish: The Birth of the Prison*, 1977), *Les mots et les choses: Une archéologie des sciences humaines* (1966; *The Order of Things: An Archaeology of the Human Sciences*, 1970), and *Histoire de la sexualité* (1976-1984; *The History of Sexuality*, 1978-1987), among many other works

**SIGNIFICANCE:** Foucault believed that societal norms and morality are revealed in studies of those individuals who are excluded from society and the ways in which they are contained by institutionalization

Michel Foucault was a twentieth century French philosopher who studied the concept of "principles of exclusion." The career of this professor at the University of Paris-Vincennes and the College de France expressed two broad themes. The first, which was represented in his 1961 book *Madness and Civilization*, focused on mental illness and society's response through the institution of the insane asylum.

Later, Foucault began to expand the concept of exclusion to include the penal system and prisons, and in 1975 he published *Discipline and Punish: The Birth of the Prison.* In this book, Foucault described the societal changes that led to the move from castigating the body by means of torture to imprisoning both the body and the spirit. Capitalist society, said Foucault, is a carceral society of control and domination. Later in his life, Foucault focused on the evolution of human self-mastery. In *The Order of Things: An Archaeology of Human Sciences*, he surveyed the history of ideas and categories of thought in order to understand societies' self-definitions. His *History of Sexuality* was an attempt to determine the relationships of individual and social attitudes with human sexuality.

**See also** Criminal punishment; Institutionalization of patients.

## Foundations of the Metaphysics of Morals: Book

**Type of ethics:** Enlightenment history

**Date:** Published 1785 as *Grundlegung zur Metaphysik der Sitten*

**Author:** Immanuel Kant

**Significance:** The book is the clearest and most concise statement by Kant of his basic approach to ethics, an approach that is now regarded as the paradigm of rationalist, deontological ethics

*Foundations of the Metaphysics of Morals* is a preliminary sketch of the fundamental metaphysical laws governing moral experience. These laws are metaphysical in that they can be discerned a priori—that is, by the exercise of pure reason and without reference to psychology. Kant's goal is to set forth the supreme principle of morality. The attempt is organized into three sections. In the first section, he argues that only a will may be good in any unqualified sense. For Kant, a good will is one that acts not only in accordance with duty but also from a sense of duty. The standard of a morally good action, then, is that it is performed simply because it is right. This conception of duty (as the condition of a will that is good in itself) leads Kant to formulate the principle that governs the good will. He calls this principle the categorical imperative: Act only according to that maxim that you can at the same time will that it should become a universal law. In section 2, Kant offers a closer analysis of the nature of the categorical imperative and of derivative (and thus, he thinks, equivalent) formulations of it. Finally, he defends the autonomy or freedom of the will in section 3.

**See also** Deontological ethics; Goodness; Kant, Immanuel; Means/ends distinction; Motivation; Reason and rationality; Will.

## Four noble truths

**Type of ethics:** Religious ethics

**Date:** Formulated sixth century B.C.E.

**Associated with:** Buddhism

**Definition:** The four noble truths state that existence is marked by suffering, that suffering is caused by desire, that desire can be overcome, and that there is a specific way to overcome desire

**Significance:** The doctrine of the four noble truths, which is perhaps the most basic tenet of Buddhism, provides the foundation of Buddhist ethics

The first of the four noble truths states that life entails suffering. There is no way to escape this facet of existence. The fact that existence is characterized by suffering should not, however, be taken to mean that suffering is all that is experienced in life. It is also possible to feel happiness, joy, comfort, and many other positive and neutral emotions and sensations. The problem is that no sensation lasts. When an individual experiences joy, it is inevitable that that joy will end. It is also true that negative emotions and sensations do not last, but that is not where the problem lies. It is the transitory nature of happiness and satisfaction that causes problems for people.

The second noble truth states that the cause of suffering is desire. People typically seek experiences that they believe will make them happy and shun experiences that they think will make them unhappy. This process is, however, extremely problematical. Often, the process of striving for happiness does not give rise to happiness. People's positive expectations about their lives may remain unrealized. Unexpected problems may arise or things simply may not happen in the way that was intended. In such cases, it is all too easy for people to attempt to block out negative experiences and continue to strive for happiness. This attempt is easy to understand, but it can lead to an unwillingness to accept the unpleasant experiences that are an inescapable part of human existence, and when people attempt to reject the unpleasant parts of their lives, they can begin to live in a world of fantasy, divorcing themselves from their own experiences and creating further suffering for themselves by refusing to see things as they are. When people do not face up to the truth of their situations, they are hampered in their attempts to put things right.

**The Four Noble Truths**

1. All existence is characterized by suffering.
2. Suffering is caused by desire.
3. Desire, and therefore suffering, can be overcome.
4. The way to overcome desire and suffering is to follow the eightfold noble path.

The third noble truth states that there is a solution to the problem of suffering. It is not necessary to live in a world of wishes that will never be fulfilled. There is a definite method by which the problems of suffering can be overcome. This does not mean, however, that following this path will mean that one experiences no more suffering in life. What it does mean is that it is possible to accept all situations as they are, without magnifying or minimizing them. The real problem is not so much one's experiences as it is the way in which one reacts to one's experiences.

The fourth noble truth states that the solution to the problem of suffering is to follow the comprehensive method set forth in the eightfold noble path. The eight aspects of the path are (1) *samyag-dṛṣṭi*, right understanding; (2) *samyak-saṁkalpa*, right aspiration; (3) *samyag-vācā*, right speech; (4) *samyak-karmanta*, right action; (5) *samyag-ājīva*, right livelihood; (6) *samyag-vyāyāma*, right effort; (7) *samyak-smṛti*, right mindfulness; and (8) *samyak-samādhi*, right concentration.

Right understanding involves, first, knowing and understanding the basic concepts of Buddhism. After one understands them rationally, one must work to test those concepts and, if one finds that they are sound, one comes to understand them on an experiential level.

Right aspiration means not only aspiring to understand and to practice Buddhism but also aspiring to do so for the right reasons. Basically, this means that one should not be practicing to benefit oneself. Right aspiration means working toward living in a more selfless way.

In order to practice right speech, one must refrain from lying or deceiving in any way. In addition, one should not indulge in harsh language toward others or engage in slander or backbiting. Instead, one's speech should serve to promote harmony among people.

Right action involves refraining from killing sentient beings, from stealing (or taking what is not given in any way), and from engaging in unlawful sexual intercourse, such as adultery or incest.

Right livelihood means not earning one's living by means of deception or trickery, not trading in arms, not trading in living beings of any kind, not selling flesh of any kind, not selling intoxicants or poisons, and not engaging in any kind of livelihood that involves killing beings, such as being a soldier, a hunter, or a fisherman.

Right effort means preventing evil thoughts, suppressing those evil thoughts that have arisen, cultivating good thoughts, and maintaining good thoughts after they have arisen.

**THE EIGHTFOLD NOBLE PATH**

| | English | Sanskrit |
|---|---|---|
| 1. | Right understanding | *samyag-dṛṣṭi* |
| 2. | Right aspiration | *samyak-saṁkalpa* |
| 3. | Right speech | *samyag-vācā* |
| 4. | Right action | *samyak-karmanta* |
| 5. | Right livelihood | *samyag-ājīva* |
| 6. | Right effort | *samyag-vyāyāma* |
| 7. | Right mindfulness | *samyak-smṛti* |
| 8. | Right concentration | *samyak-samādhi* |

Right mindfulness and right concentration refer to the practice of meditation, which can take many forms. It particularly involves the cultivation of awareness and the direct perception of reality as it is, including particularly the truth that all things that apparently exist are in fact empty. There is no self, although people cling to the idea that the individual self exists.

By exerting oneself in these eight areas, according to Buddhist doctrine, it is possible to rid oneself of the desire that causes suffering, thereby solving the primary problem of existence by cutting it off at the root.

—*Shawn Woodyard*

**See also** Bodhisattva ideal; Buddha; Buddhist ethics; Five precepts; Mādhyamaka; Nirvana.

**BIBLIOGRAPHY**

Conze, Edward. *Buddhism: Its Essence and Development.* 3d ed. Oxford, England: B. Cassirer, 1957.

___________. *Buddhist Thought in India.* London: Allen & Unwin, 1962.

Dharmasiri, Gunapala. *Fundamentals of Buddhist Ethics.* Antioch, Calif.: Golden Leaves, 1989.

Sangharakshita. *A Survey of Buddhism: Its Doctrines and Methods Through the Ages.* 6th rev. ed. London: Tharpa, 1987.

Snelling, John. *The Buddhist Handbook: A Complete Guide to Buddhist Schools, Teaching, Practice, and History.* Rochester, Vt.: Inner Traditions, 1991.

## Fraud

**TYPE OF ETHICS:** Legal and judicial ethics

**DATE:** Coined 1330

**DEFINITION:** Intentional deception intended to give one some advantage in a transaction

**SIGNIFICANCE:** Ethicists believe that fraud is one of the fundamental kinds of unethical acts

The long history of ethical condemnation of deception helps to show fraud's significance to ethics; in the Judeo-Christian tradition, for example, one of the Ten Commandments is "Thou shalt not bear false witness." This commandment is broad enough to cover fraud.

The famous English Statute of Frauds, which was passed in 1677 and has now been adopted in one form or another in almost every part of the United States, requires that one must "get it in writing" before one can sue to recover more than a specific monetary amount (for example, $500) or to enforce a contract that extends beyond a certain period of time (for example, one year). The statute's point was to reduce the number of claims regarding purported fraud. Leaving important matters to memories of oral statements resulted too often in cases that pitted one person's word against another's.

Good faith precludes fraud even when honest mistakes are made. The classic slogan defining good faith is "white heart and empty head," which refers to having good intentions but being stupid. Stupid mistakes are not fraud.

Deceptive advertising is a matter of degree, but at some point, exaggeration becomes fraud. This is especially true of intentionally false quantitative claims. Qualitative claims are difficult to classify as fraud, since quality is characteristically a matter of opinion rather than fact. Therefore, U.S. law recognizes "puffing" as nonfraudulent falsehood. Puffing is, essentially, an overstatement of the quality of something that is being sold. An example of puffing is a cologne maker's claim that Cologne X makes one as "mysterious as the wind." Furthermore, if the falsehood is so obvious that no reasonable person would be deceived by it, then stating that falsehood does not constitute fraud. (For example, one brand of toothpaste was sold with the claim that it would straighten teeth!)

Fraud can be committed by either commission or omission. A fraud of commission involves lying or making some other type of material misrepresentation. A fraud of omission involves the failure to disclose some significant fact that the law requires to be disclosed. Libertarianism, an ethical principle that has been politically influential, endorses the idea of *caveat emptor* ("Let the buyer beware") rather than the idea that some bureaucracy should interfere with the free market by legally requiring disclosures. Libertarianism supports laissez-faire capitalism with only minimal government and opposes the welfare state that began with President Franklin Delano Roosevelt's New Deal. Libertarianism condemns fraud but defines it narrowly, requiring that a lie be committed for fraud to exist.

Egalitarianism, by contrast, is an ethical principle that allows the mere withholding of information to be considered fraud. Egalitarians condemn exploitation, which involves taking advantage of an innocent person's predicament. Therefore, egalitarians support laws defining fraud so as to include the failure to disclose key facts. Libertarians do not recognize the applicability of the concept of exploitation in its ethically pejorative sense. They view charging whatever the market will bear, for example, not as exploitation but as entrepreneurship, which they see as a virtue. The two approaches of libertarianism and egalitarianism correspond at least roughly to actual fraud and constructive fraud, respectively. Actual fraud involves some active deception or lie. Constructive fraud includes any act of commission or omission that is contrary to law or fair play.

As Richard Whately has said, "All frauds, like the wall daubed with untempered mortar . . . always tend to the decay of what they are devised to support." The law tries to enhance this ethical tendency by punishing fraud.

*—Sterling Harwood*

**See also** Cheating; Lying.

**Bibliography**


Beringer, Johann Bartholomans. *The Lying Stones of Dr. Johan Bartholomans Adam Beringer*. Berkeley, Calif.: University of California Press, 1963.

Bok, Sissela. *Lying: Moral Choice in Public and Private Life*. New York: Pantheon Books, 1978.

____________. *Secrets*. New York: Pantheon Books, 1982.

Broad, William, and Nicholas Wade. *Betrs Of The Truth*. New York: Simon & Schuster, 1982.

Cahn, Steven M. *Saints and Scamps: Ethics in Academia*. Totowa, N.J.: Rowman & Littlefield, 1986.

Gould, Stephen Jay. *The Mismeasure of Man*. New York: W. W. Norton, 1981.

Kant, Immanuel. *Critique of Practical Reason and Other Writings in Moral Philosophy*. Edited and translated by Lewis White Beck. Chicago: University of Chicago Press, 1949.

Magnuson, Warren G., and Jean Carper. *The Dark Side of the Marketplace: The Plight of the American Consumer*. Englewood Cliffs, N.J.: Prentice-Hall, 1968.

Newman, John Henry Cardinal. *Apologia Pro Vita Sua: Being a History of His Religious Opinions*. New York: Modern Library, 1950.

Plato. *Republic*. 2d rev. ed. Harmondsworth, England: Penguin Books, 1986.

Rawlins, Dennis. *Peary at the North Pole: Fact or Fiction?* Washington, D.C.: Robert B. Luce, 1973.

Weiner, J. S. *The Piltdown Forgery*. London: Oxford University Press, 1955.


## Free enterprise

**Type of ethics:** Politico-economic ethics

**Date:** Eighteenth century to present

**Associated with:** Individualism, egoism, capitalism, and Adam Smith

**Definition:** An economic system based on the principles that individuals are responsible for their own welfare and have the right to be free from coercion in order to pursue it

**Significance:** Applies the ethical principle of individualism to politics and economics

Free enterprise is an economic system characterized by private property and private investment decisions, the profit motive, supply and demand as the regulator of prices, and limited government involvement. The economic systems of most western European nations, the United States, Canada, Australia, and Japan are to varying degrees free enterprise systems.

Advocates of free enterprise fall into two categories. Members of the first category hold that free enterprise is morally neutral and that it is justified on practical grounds as the most efficient system known for producing wealth. Members of the second category agree that free enterprise is practical, but they argue that it is justified primarily on moral grounds.

**Moral Justification.** Free enterprise is advocated as the only system that is, in principle, compatible with the requirements of human survival. To survive, individuals need values such as food and shelter. These values must be created by individual initiative and effort. (Cooperative ventures depend for their success on individual initiative and effort.) Therefore, human survival depends on individual initiative and effort.

In a social context, however, individuals run the risk of coercion by other individuals. Coercion is a danger to human life because it undermines individual initiative and effort: Coercion can end an individual's life (murder) or remove to some degree an individual's control over his or her life (slavery, assault, or theft). Coercion, accordingly, is wrong in principle, and all social arrangements should be based on the principle that only voluntary interactions are moral.

The rejection of coercion is spelled out in terms of rights. If murder, slavery, and theft are, broadly speaking, the fundamental social *wrongs,* then life, liberty, and property are the fundamental social *rights.*

**Role of Government.** Since some individuals will resort to coercion in order to benefit from the productive efforts of other individuals, and since the primary social need of individuals is *freedom* from such coercion, it follows that there is a need for an institution with the power to protect individuals' rights: government.

The moral task of government is to ensure that individuals are at liberty to use their property as they see fit to sustain and enhance their lives. Governments thus are given the power to use coercion in defense of individuals' rights.

A government can use coercion against individuals, however, so individuals also need protection from their government. In a free enterprise system, this protection is provided by a constitution that limits the coercive power of government to *defensive* purposes. Since the political power of government is a coercive power and free enterprise requires that all economic transactions be voluntary, the constitution of a free enterprise system will require a separation of economics and politics. Governments will not be able to use political power to subsidize one business at the expense of another or, more generally, to redistribute wealth from one individual or group of individuals to another.

**Practicality.** If individuals thus have a reasonable guarantee of freedom from both other individuals and the government, they will invest, produce, and reap as much profit as their skills, dedication, and ingenuity allow them. They will be free to reinvest or consume their profits. They will be free to form voluntary associations (such as partnerships, corporations, and stock markets) to enhance their production and hence their profits. They will be free to pursue specializations, since specialization generally yields higher production, and to exchange their products in a market in which rates of exchange (prices) are governed by the forces of supply and demand.

The practicality of free enterprise is a consequence of individual effort. The freedom to pursue profit releases enormous amounts of human productive energy, and this explains the historical success of free enterprise systems.

**Criticisms.** Free enterprise is sometimes criticized for being harsh, since it provides no guarantee of success for all individuals. Since some individuals will fail, the critics continue, the government should use its coercive power to redistribute some wealth from the successful to the needy. Advocates of free enterprise respond that using coercive means to redistribute wealth is not only impractical—since coercion undermines the conditions of wealth production in the first place—but also immoral, since it involves coercively using individuals as a means to the ends of others. There is nothing to prevent the establishment of voluntary charitable associations to assist those in need, and in a free enterprise system the only moral way to solve problems is through voluntary associations.

Free enterprise is also criticized for encouraging the profit motive. Advocates of free enterprise respond that the profit motive is moral. It is moral that individuals take charge of their lives, and profit is necessary for life. To stay alive, an individual must consume at least as much energy as he or she expended in producing the value to be consumed, and to grow, an individual must consume more energy than he or she expended in producing the value. In economic terms, this means he or she must achieve a net return on the investment—that is, profit.

Finally, free enterprise is sometimes criticized for leading to inequalities in wealth. Advocates of free enterprise respond that the only relevant sense of equality in this context is equality before the law. As long as the government ensures that everyone plays by the same rules, the fact that individuals of differing natural endowments, acquired skills, and moral characters will acquire different amounts of wealth is perfectly just. —*Stephen R. C. Hicks*

**See also** Capitalism; Economics; Marxism; Socialism.

**BIBLIOGRAPHY**

Hayek, Friedrich. *The Road to Serfdom.* Chicago: University of Chicago Press, 1944.

Hazlitt, Henry. *Economics in One Lesson.* New Rochelle, N.Y.: Arlington House, 1979.

Rand, Ayn. *Capitalism: The Unknown Ideal.* New York: New American Library, 1966.

Reisman, George. *The Government Against the Economy.* Ottawa, Ill.: Caroline House, 1979.

Von Mises, Ludwig. *Liberalism.* Translated by Ralph Raico. Edited by Arthur Goddard. Mission, Kan.: Sheed Andrews and McMeel, 1978.

## Free-riding

**TYPE OF ETHICS:** Beliefs and practices

**DATE:** Mid-seventeenth century to present

**ASSOCIATED WITH:** Rational choice theories in ethics and other fields, such as economics and game theory

**DEFINITION:** Enjoying a benefit produced by the efforts of others without contributing one's fair share

**SIGNIFICANCE:** Free-riding is unfair behavior that threatens the success of cooperative endeavors among people

Free-riding, as the expression suggests, involves gaining a benefit, such as a ride, at no cost to the one enjoying the benefit. Such free-riding activity is seen as unfair, at least where the provision of the benefit involves costs borne by some and there is an expectation that those enjoying the benefit share in the cost.

One of the more common uses of the idea in ordinary contexts is in connection with union membership. Typically, in labor relations in the United States, one union or agent is authorized to serve as the exclusive representative of workers in a bargaining unit. Under such exclusivity, the union can speak for all the employees, but all the employees in turn have a right to be fairly represented by the union as their agent. Each employee is thought to have a duty to pay a fair or proportionate share of the cost of such representation; those not paying their share are accused of free-riding. Samuel Gompers, an early leader in the American labor movement, stated the point as follows: "Non-unionists who reap the rewards of union efforts, without contributing a dollar or risking the loss of a day, are parasites. They are reaping the benefits from the union spirit, while they themselves are debasing genuine manhood." Two points are illustrated in the labor example. The first is the moral condemnation of free-riding as unfair. The other is the more general issue about the provision of certain types of benefits or goods from cooperative activities: Benefits made possible by the cooperative efforts of some are available to all. Some goods or benefits are not easily divisible; therefore, it is not feasible to exclude noncontributors from enjoying them. In the case of such goods, it may seem rational in a sense to free-ride, since one can obtain the benefits at no cost to oneself. Cooperative ventures producing goods available to all need to provide some way of discouraging such free-riding. In the organized labor arena, unions have sought closed-shop or union-shop arrangements to prevent free- riding of the sort decried by Gompers. Under these arrangements, employers either must hire only union members or may hire anyone, with the proviso that all employees hired and retained must join and remain in the union.

Thomas Hobbes's classic work *Leviathan* (1651) is seen as the earliest treatment of the free-rider issue, posing it in the context of self-interested individuals in a state of nature using reason to find a way out of the miserable condition of life stemming from the absence of a sovereign power "to keep men in awe." While mutual restraint is the reasonable way out, it is not a sound choice for an individual who has no assurance that others will restrain themselves. The famous Hobbesian solution is the creation of an enforcement mechanism, the sovereign or "great Leviathan," who will lay down rules of conduct to secure peace and order and will enforce the rules against any law-breakers or free-riders.

One of the points about free-riding behavior that is illustrated in Hobbes's discussion is the problematic connection with rational choice. From the narrow view of the individual intent on maximizing personal satisfaction, free-riding seems like the reasonable course of action, so long as enough others are willing to cooperate and contribute to a sufficient extent to make the cooperative venture a success. From a more general standpoint, however, when cooperation with others offers substantial mutual benefits, then it seems reasonable for each individual to cooperate and thus not free-ride. The free-rider seems to threaten the establishment of a cooperative endeavor or the stability of an endeavor that is already underway.

Of course, many cooperative ventures can get started and remain going concerns even when there are some free-riders, since the benefits of cooperation are great enough that many persons are willing to contribute regardless of free-riding. In welfare economics and public finance, the often-used example of a public or collective good susceptible to free-riding is that of the lighthouse. Some shipowners may find it worth their while to build and maintain a lighthouse for use by their vessels, even though other ships will be able to use the lighthouse for navigation. The owners of these other ships will be free-riding—that is, benefiting without paying any share of the cost—if they make no contribution to the building or maintenance of the lighthouse. The free-riding owners are not, however, adding to the costs of those supporting the lighthouse. Despite the free-riders, building the lighthouse may be a rational choice for the contributing shipowners because the benefits of the lighthouse outweigh the cost of construction and maintenance.

In ethics, the unfairness of much free-riding poses a difficulty for utilitarian theories that seek to equate wrongdoing with doing harm, since free-riding often does not harm contributors to a cooperative scheme. It does not always harm them in the sense of adding to their costs, although it may engender feelings of resentment toward the free-riders and lessen the morale of contributors, who believe that they are being made "suckers." Other ethical theories emphasizing the role of consent and contract also find it difficult to account for the wrongness of free-riding, since free-riders are typically not breaking any contract. The unfairness of such conduct, the act of taking advantage of others, seems to provide the most plausible and direct explanation for its wrongness. —*Mario F. Morelli*

**See also** Cheating; Fairness; Hobbes, Thomas; *Leviathan*; Responsibility; Selfishness.

**Bibliography**

De Jasay, Anthony. Social Contract, Free Ride. New York: Oxford University Press, 1989.

Gauthier, David P. *Morals by Agreement.* New York: Oxford University Press, 1986.

Hobbes, Thomas. *Leviathan.* New York: Cambridge University Press, 1991.

Klosko, George. *The Principle of Fairness and Political Obligation.* Lanham, Md.: Rowman & Littlefield, 1992.

Olson, Mancur. *The Logic of Collective Action.* Cambridge, Mass.: Harvard University Press, 1965.

## Freedom and liberty

**Type of ethics:** Personal and social ethics

**Date:** c. 2300 B.C.E. to present

**Associated with:** Individualism, egoism, free enterprise, and libertarianism

**Definition:** Psychologically, the capacity to choose; socially, the ability to act without interference from others

**Significance:** The degree of freedom possessed by individuals determines the extent to which they control their own lives

Freedom of the will, sometimes referred to as "free will" or "volition," makes ethics possible and necessary. Free will is the capacity to control the direction one's thoughts and actions take, and even whether one thinks or acts at all. Because humans do not think or act automatically, their thinking and acting can go in a variety of directions, some of which are beneficial and some of which are not. Since whether a beneficial or a harmful direction is taken is within one's control, one is responsible for the direction taken. Accordingly, moral praise is warranted for using one's volitional capacity to select beneficial thoughts and actions, while moral blame is warranted either for not exercising one's volitional capacity or for using it to select harmful thoughts and actions.

"Freedom" and "liberty," then, designate fundamentally a capacity of human nature. Freedom of the will is the capacity to choose between alternatives; by extension, social freedom is the ability to act upon one's choices without interference from others. In parallel, the term "libertarianism" is sometimes used to name the position that holds that freedom of the will exists, as well as the social philosophy that holds that respect for individual freedom is the fundamental social principle.

In this essay, it will be taken for granted that humans have the psychological capacity of free will, and the essay will focus on freedom in its moral and social dimensions.

**History.** Freedom is a fragile thing. Throughout most of human history, it has existed only in brief, isolated instances. The city-states of classical Greece experimented successfully with democratic social institutions, and classical Rome derived much of its strength from its republican social institutions. Yet Rome's decline marked the West's return for a thousand years to the historical norm of human social arrangements: tribal and feudal versions of authoritarian social arrangements. Not until the end of the Middle Ages did freedom begin to become an increasingly normal part of some humans' existence.

During the Renaissance and the Enlightenment, a number of major, related institutional changes brought about a gradual decentralization of intellectual, economic, and political power, and a corresponding increase in the powers and freedoms enjoyed by individuals. Intellectually, the rapid growth of science contributed to the increasing secularization of society and gave rise to a greater diversity of opinions; and in Northern Europe, the impact of the Reformation and Protestantism's emphasis upon each individual's being able to read and interpret the Bible was partly responsible for the rapid increase in the number of literate individuals. Politically, the decline of the European monarchies gave rise to a variety of democratic and republican forms of government. Economically, the rapid increase in wealth made possible by increasing international trade and new forms of finance and production, culminating in the Industrial Revolution, gave increasing numbers of individuals unprecedented economic control over their lives.

The rise of liberal social arrangements in economics, politics, and the quest for knowledge often occurred prior to an explicit, theoretical understanding of their political, economic, and intellectual value. While the practical value of liberty became obvious to many, it was also obvious that liberty conflicted with many traditional theories of morality. Accordingly, an explicit theoretical understanding of freedom's moral standing became crucial. Indeed, most opposition to individual economic and political freedom stems fundamentally from moral disagreements with freedom's individualist ethical foundations.

**The Morality of Freedom.** The morality of freedom is based on its being a requirement of human survival. To survive, individuals need values such as food and shelter. These values must be produced by individual initiative and effort. Production, however, depends upon the individual's having acquired the requisite knowledge, and the acquisition of knowledge in turn depends upon the individual's exercise of free will to control his or her mind's operations. Human survival, therefore, depends ultimately upon freely directed individual initiative and effort. Individuals need to choose to think, in order to acquire knowledge, in order to put their knowledge into practice, and in order to produce the values they need to consume in order to survive and flourish. At each step of the process—thinking, production, and consumption—the individual's freely chosen initiatives determine the degree of his or her self-determination.

Humans live in social groups. Although social arrangements can yield great benefits to individuals, social living also raises the risk of the use of coercion by some individuals against other individuals. Coercion, which can take many forms—killing, slavery, kidnapping, assault, theft—is a danger to human life because it removes to some degree an individual's control over his or her life. Coercion, accordingly, is wrong in principle, and all social arrangements should be based on the principle that only freely chosen interactions are moral; that is, respect for individual freedom is the fundamental social principle.

The rejection of coercion and the protection of freedom are often spelled out in terms of rights. Rights specify spheres of autonomy that leave individuals free to think and act as they deem necessary to sustain their lives. An individual's right to control his or her own life is the fundamental social principle in terms of which all other rights are defined. Since the process of life involves three subprocesses—thinking, producing, and consuming—the right to life is specified in greater detail to make explicit the protection individuals need in each subprocess. Individuals need to think independently in order to acquire knowledge; therefore, people recognize the right to freedom of conscience. Individuals need to act upon their beliefs, so people recognize the right to liberty; and since the actions that individuals believe are necessary often involve communicating and acting cooperatively with other individuals, people recognize the rights to freedom of speech and freedom of association. Since individuals need to consume the values they have produced, they need to be able to control the fruits of their production; therefore, people recognize the right to property. Overriding an individual's rights in any area means undermining that individual's freedom, which in turn means undermining that person's self-control.

**The Role of Government.** Since some individuals will resort to coercion in order to benefit from the productive efforts of other individuals, and since the primary social need of individuals is freedom from such coercion, government is established as the institution charged with protecting individuals' rights. The moral task of government, then, is to ensure that individuals are at liberty to use their property as they see fit to sustain and enhance their lives. A government thus is given the power to use coercion defensively, in protecting individuals' rights.

Since a government too can use coercion against individuals, however, individuals also need protection from government. In liberal social systems, this protection is usually provided by a constitution that explicitly limits the coercive power of a government to defensive purposes in the service of individuals' rights. As a further safeguard, the power given to a government to do its job is broken up and spread among the various branches of government so that each branch can serve as a check upon possible abuses by the others.

**Economics and Liberty.** Such liberal political arrangements have economic consequences. If individuals have a reasonable political guarantee of freedom from both other individuals and government, they will invest, produce, and reap as much profit as their skills, dedication, and ingenuity allow them. They will be free to reinvest or consume their profits. They will be free to form voluntary associations (such as partnerships, corporations, and stock markets) to enhance their production and hence their profits. They will be free to specialize, since specialization generally yields higher production, and to exchange their products in a market in which rates of exchange (prices) are governed by the forces of supply and demand.

The practicality of free enterprise is a consequence: The freedom to pursue profit releases enormous amounts of human productive energy, and this explains the historical success of liberal social systems.

**Criticisms of Liberty.** Neither such moral justifications of individual liberty nor the historical success of liberal social institutions has won over the advocates of the many doctrines that are opposed to freedom. Opposition to and attacks upon individual freedom generally stem from opposing fundamental premises about morality. In most such attacks, the common theme is that the individual's life and freedoms have less moral significance than does the individual's duty to sacrifice himself or herself for the benefit of some higher being. Opponents of freedom disagree among themselves about what or who that higher being is, although religion, monarchism, and collectivism have been the three historically dominant sources of candidates for beings for whom individuals should be willing to sacrifice their lives and liberties.

**Religion and Liberty.** The history of the relationship between religion and liberty has been long and varied. Some religious theorists conclude that secular liberty and independence are compatible with religious obedience and subservience to a higher being—God—by arguing, first, that God created humankind to be His stewards of the natural world and charging them with the task of using the world's resources efficiently and fruitfully, and, second, that politically and economically free social systems are more efficient and fruitful than are authoritarian systems. The central thrust of most religions, however, has been to exalt God's power and, correspondingly, to diminish humans' power. Instead of individuals volitionally selecting their lives' goals and the methods to achieve them, the ends and means of human life are held to be established by God. The range of valid options open to individuals is thus limited severely by God's decrees; and moral virtue, it follows, consists not in liberty in thought and action, but rather in strict obedience to God's commands. Although many religions grant that one has the volitional capacity to think independently and freely, such self-indulgence is held to be immoral; to be moral, one must choose to recognize one's dependence and be obedient. To the extent that religion is translated into political doctrine, theocracy is the result: God's agents on Earth are charged with the authority to enforce God's commands, so they should have the political power to enforce obedience on the part of the rest of society.

**Monarchy and Secular Authoritarianism.** Structurally, monarchy is a secular form of theocracy. Individuals are held to exist to serve and glorify a higher being—in this case, the king or queen, rather than God. The ends and means of individuals' lives are established by the monarch, and the monarch's decrees serve to limit the range of options open to individuals. Moral virtue again does not consist fundamentally in independence in thought and liberty in action, but rather in obedience to the monarch's commands. Individual liberties exist only by default; that is, to the extent that the monarch fails to prescribe the course of his or her subjects' lives or is politically unable to enforce his or her decrees.

Historically, some advocates of secular monarchies have used religious appeals to justify the concentration of political power in the hands of a monarch who is not also a duly constituted religious authority. According to the doctrine of the divine right of kings, the monarch's possession of great power is justified not merely by the fact that he or she has succeeded in acquiring it or by the fact that he or she is the biological descendant of the previous monarch, or by the claim that the concentration of political power in the monarch's hands is the most efficient means of realizing political aims in the best interests of the subjects, but rather by his or her selection by God to carry out part of God's plan on Earth.

Another general form of secular authoritarianism is based on collectivist ethical principles. According to collectivism, individual human beings are of less moral value than is some larger group to which they belong; therefore, individuals are expected to devote their lives to serving the larger group. Different versions of collectivism define the larger group differently; some hold that the appropriate group is the nation, while others hold that it is the race, the culture, one's economic class, or, more vaguely, society as a whole. Collectivists argue that individuals are not morally free to pursue their own ends, but rather that they have a duty to sacrifice and to serve the ends of the collective, as determined by the collective's leaders.

The twentieth century saw the rise of several versions of collectivism, with a corresponding diminution of individual freedoms to the extent that collectivist doctrines were practiced.

Marxism, for example, holds that the dictatorship of the proletariat (the working class) is a necessary step in the transition between capitalism and international socialism. During the dictatorship of the proletariat, the leaders of the Communist Party will hold absolute power and will determine what is necessary, while individuals will sacrifice themselves, voluntarily or not, to bring about a new collective entity—the international socialist state.

Fascism, to take another prominent example, holds that dictatorship is a necessary step toward realizing a national or racial version of socialism. Again, the leaders of the party will hold absolute power and will determine what is necessary, while individuals will sacrifice themselves, voluntarily or not, to bring about a new collective entity—the national socialist state.

Some versions of radical environmentalism, to take a final example, hold that the ecosystem is the collective entity that is the unit of value, and that humans exist to serve the ecosystem as a whole. While humans have a duty to serve the ecosystem, however, most of them seem short-sighted and have abused their freedoms (by causing pollution and overpopulation). Accordingly, the freedoms of individuals to produce and reproduce should be overridden by enlightened leaders who have the best interests of the ecosystem as a whole at heart.

**Pessimism Versus Freedom.** In addition to religious, monarchic, and collectivist attacks on individual freedom, certain positions on the status of human nature have also led directly to attacks on freedom. To the extent that a pessimistic evaluation of human nature is accepted, there is a tendency to reject political and economic freedom in favor of some version of paternalism. Paternalists typically hold that humans are too evil or too incompetent to be left free to determine their own affairs. Accordingly, rather than conceiving of the state as a servant whose job it is to protect individuals' freedoms while they pursue their lives; paternalists urge the state to take control of individuals' lives, either as a strong and stern authority suppressing the natural tendencies of humans to do evil, or as a wise and benevolent leader organizing individuals' lives so as to protect them from their own incompetencies.

**The Scope of Freedom.** Individual freedom is at stake in scores of major practical moral controversies. People continue to debate, for example, abortion, censorship, free trade, taxation, the use of alcohol and drugs, the military draft, and homosexuality. Each practical issue focuses on whether individuals should be free to act as they judge best or should be forced to act as some other individual or group judges best. In each debate, the acceptance or denial of the legitimacy of individual freedom is a conclusion derived from more fundamental premises about metaphysics, human nature, and ethics. If, for example, God has all the power, then humans have none; therefore, freedom is not an issue. If humans are not intellectually competent enough to run their own lives, then intellectual control should be given to someone who is, so censorship is a viable option. If humans are basically evil, then freedom is folly, and so is allowing humans access to alcohol and drugs. If individual humans are merely servants of a larger collective, then freedom is unnecessary; therefore, a draft is justifiable. A full defense of freedom and liberal social institutions, then, depends on a full philosophical system of premises demonstrating that human beings are by nature none of the above—that, instead, they are competent individuals who are morally ends in themselves.

*—Stephen R. C. Hicks*

**See also** Egoism; Freedom of expression; Libertarianism; Locke, John; Mill, John Stuart; *On Liberty*; Platonic ethics; Self-control.

**BIBLIOGRAPHY**


Hayek, Friedrich A. *The Road to Serfdom.* Chicago: University of Chicago Press, 1944. A critical analysis of some of the twentieth century's major collectivist attacks on freedom.

Locke, John. *Two Treatises of Government.* Edited by Peter Laslett. New York: Cambridge University Press, 1988. Locke's second treatise defends individual freedom from a natural rights perspective.

Mill, John Stuart. *On Liberty* (1859). Reprint. *On Liberty and other Essays.* Edited by John Gray. New York: Oxford University Press, 1991. Particularly influential in its defense of freedom of speech, Mill's work gives a utilitarian defense of liberty.

Novak, Michael. *Free Persons and the Common Good.* Lanham, Md.: Madison Books, 1989. Argues that Catholicism, a traditionally hierarchical religion, is compatible with the capitalist system of economic liberty.

Plato. *The Republic.* New York: Vintage Books, 1991. A classic argument against liberty and in favor of communal authoritarianism, based explicitly upon argued metaphysical, epistemological, and ethical premises.

Rand, Ayn. *Atlas Shrugged.* New York: Random House, 1957. A twentieth century classic of fiction and a philosophical defense of intellectual independence and laissez-faire capitalism.

Rosenberg, Nathan, and L. E. Birdzell, Jr. *How the West Grew Rich.* New York: Basic Books, 1986. An economic history of the role of liberalism and pluralism in making possible the West's great increases in wealth.

RR ETHICS

# LIST OF ENTRIES BY CATEGORY

HISTORY, RENAISSANCE AND RESTORATION



HUMAN RIGHTS



INTERNATIONAL RELATIONS



LEGAL AND JUDICIAL ETHICS



MEDIA ETHICS



MILITARY ETHICS

RELIGIOUS ETHICS



SCIENTIFIC ETHICS



SEX AND GENDER ISSUES

THEORY OF ETHICS